INTRODUCTION

The Virgin Encyclopedia Of Dance Music is one in the major series of books taken from the multi-volume *Encyclopedia Of Popular Music*. Other titles already available are:

The Virgin Encyclopedia Of Fifties Music
The Virgin Encyclopedia Of Sixties Music
The Virgin Encyclopedia Of Seventies Music
The Virgin Encyclopedia Of Eighties Music
The Virgin Encyclopedia Of Popular Music (Concise)
The Virgin Encyclopedia Of Indie & New Wave
The Virgin Encyclopedia Of The Blues
The Virgin Encyclopedia Of R&B And Soul
The Virgin Encyclopedia Of Reggae
The Virgin Encyclopedia Of Country Music
The Virgin All Time Top 1000 Albums

ENTRY STYLE

Albums, EPs (extended play 45s), newspapers, magazines, television programmes, films and stage musicals are referred to in italics. All song titles appear in single quotes. We spell rock 'n' roll like this. There are two main reasons for spelling rock 'n' roll with 'n' as opposed to 'n'. First, historical precedent: when the term was first coined in the 50s, the popular spelling was 'n'. Second, the 'n' is not simply an abbreviation of 'and' (in which case 'n' would apply) but a phonetic representation of n as a sound. The ' ', therefore, serve as inverted commas rather than as apostrophes. The further reading section at the end of each entry has been expanded to give the reader a much wider choice of available books. These are not necessarily recommended titles but we have attempted to leave out any publication that has little or no merit.

We have also started to add videos at the ends of the entries. Again, this is an area that is expanding faster than we can easily cope with, but there are many items in the videography and further items in the filmography, which is another new section we have decided to include. Release dates in keeping with albums attempt to show the release date in the country of origin. We have also tried to include both US and UK titles where applicable.

ALBUM RATING

Due to many requests from our readers we have now decided to rate all albums. All new releases are reviewed either by myself or by our team of contributors. We also take into consideration the review ratings of the leading music journals and critics' opinions.

Our system is slightly different to most 5 Star ratings in that we rate according to the artist in question's work. Therefore, a 4 Star album from Prodigy may have the overall edge over a 4 Star album by Jive Bunny.

Our ratings are carefully made, and consequently you will find we are very sparing with 5 Star and 1 Star albums.

Outstanding in every way. A classic and therefore strongly recommended. No comprehensive record collection should be without this album.

Excellent. A high standard album from this artist and therefore highly recommended.

Good. By the artist's usual standards and therefore recommended.

Disappointing. Flawed or lacking in some way.

Poor. An album to avoid unless you are a completist.

PLAGIARISM

In maintaining the largest text database of popular music in the world we are naturally protective of its content. We license to approved licensees only. It is both flattering and irritating to see our work reproduced without credit. Time and time again over the past few years I have read an obituary, when suddenly: hang on, I wrote that line. Secondly, it has come to our notice that other companies attempting to produce their own rock or pop encyclopedias use our material as a core. Flattering this might also be, but highly illegal. We have therefore dropped a few more textual 'depth charges' in addition to the original ones. Be warned.

ACKNOWLEDGEMENTS

Our in-house editorial team is lean and efficient. Our EPM Database is now a fully grown child and needs only regular food, attention and love. Thanks to the MUZE UK team and their efficiency while the cat's away: Susan Pipe, Nic Oliver and Sarah Lavelle and the drum and bass of Roger Kohn's parrot, Acu. Our outside contributors are further reduced in number, as we now write and amend all our existing text. However, we could not function without the continuing efforts and dedication of Big John Martland and Alex Ogg. Much of the initial preparation and many of the newer entries were researched and written by Charlie Furniss.

Other past contributors' work may appear in this volume and I acknowledge once again; Simon Adams, Mike Atherton, Gavin Badderley, Alan Balfour, Michael Barnett, Steve Barrow, Lol Bell-Brown, Johnny Black, Chris Blackford, Pamela Boniface, Keith Briggs, Michael Ian Burgess, Paul M. Brown, Tony Burke, John Child, Linton Chiswick, Rick Christian, Alan Clayson, Tom Collier, Paul Cross, Bill Dahl, Norman Darwen, Roy Davenport, Peter Doggett, Kevin Eden, John Eley, Lars Fahlin, John Fordham, Per Gardin, Ian Garlinge, Mike Gavin, Andy Hamilton, Harry Hawk, Mark Hodkinson, Mike Hughes, Arthur Jackson, Mark Jones, Simon Jones, Dave Laing, Steve Lake, Paul Lewis, Graham Lock, John Masouri, Bernd Matheja, Chris May, Dave McAleer, Ian McCann, David McDonald, York Membery, Toru Mitsui, Greg Moffitt, Nick Morgan, Michael Newman, Pete Nickols, Lyndon Noon, Zbigniew Nowara, James Nye, Ken Orton, Ian Peel, Dave Penny, Alan Plater, Barry Ralph, John Reed, Emma Rees, Lionel Robinson, Johnny Rogan, Alan Rowett, Jean Scrivener, Roy Sheridan, Dave Sissons, Steve Smith, Mitch Solomons, Jon Staines, Mike Stephenson, Sam Sutherland, Jeff Tamarkin, Ray Templeton, Gerard Tierney, Adrian T'Vell, Pete Wadeson, Ben Watson, Pete Watson, Simon Williams, Dave Wilson and Barry Witherden.

Record company press offices are often bombarded with my requests for biogs and review copies. Theirs is a thankless task, but thanks anyway to them all. Thanks for the enthusiasm and co-operation of all our new colleagues at Virgin Publishing under the guidance of Rob Shreeve, in particular to the elegant and diplomatic Roz Scott.

To the quite splendid Pete Bassett, not to forget the delicious Bassettes; Emily Williams and Emma Morris. To our owners at Muze Inc., who continue to feed the smooth running of the UK operation and are the business partners I always knew I wanted but never knew where to find. To all colleagues at the office on 304 Hudson Street in New York. In particular to the completely settled Tony Laudico, the crisply attired Paul Zullo, Steve 'Figures' Figard, Marc 'Substitute' Miller, Gary 'the Timid Shrew' Geller, Mike Nevins, Raisa Howe, Chris Bugbee, Jim Allen, David Gil de Rubio (down by the schoolyard), Kim Osorio, Ric Hollander, Stephen Parker, Terry Vinyard, Deborah Freedman, Scott 'nice beard' Lehr, Amanda Denhoff, Jannett Diaz, Tracey Brandon, Ed 'gentleman' Moore and Solomon Sabel. And welcome to some new Muze chums; Phil Fletcher, Matt 'dodgy geezer' Puccini, Bill Schmitt, Thom Pappalardo, Duncan Ledwith, Gail 'on the button' Niovitch, Silvia Kessel and all the other Klugettes.

And to the monumental Trev Huxley, the gossamer Cathy Huxley and the five Turkeys. Finally to my musically literate tin lids; remember, the cymbal bit always comes before the boomf boomf boomf bit.

Colin Larkin, October 1998

THE *Virgin* ENCYCLOPEDIA OF

DANCE MUSIC

COLIN LARKIN

Virgin

IN ASSOCIATION WITH MUZE UK LTD.

Dedicated To Sally Larkin

First published in Great Britain in 1998 by
VIRGIN BOOKS
an imprint of Virgin Publishing Ltd
Thames Wharf Studios, Rainville Road
London W6 9HT

A catalogue record for this book is available from the British Library

ISBN 0 7535 0252 6

Written, edited and produced by
MUZE UK Ltd
to whom all editorial enquiries should be sent
Iron Bridge House, 3 Bridge Approach, Chalk Farm, London NW1 8BD
e-mail: colin@muze.co.uk. http://www.muze.com
Editor In Chief: Colin Larkin
Production Editor: Susan Pipe
Research Assistant: Nic Oliver
Editorial Assistant: Sarah Lavelle
Typographic Design Consultants: Roger Kohn & Acu
Special thanks to Trev Huxley, Tony Laudico, Paul Zullo
and all the Klugettes at Muze Inc.,
and to Rob Shreeve of Virgin Publishing.
Typeset by Boomf Boomf Boomf Studios
Printed and bound in Great Britain by Butler & Tanner Ltd, Frome and London

A GUY CALLED GERALD

Heavily influenced by Chicago house and acid, Gerald Simpson's solo career has thus far failed to ignite as many predicted. Simpson, who once sold copies of the *Socialist Worker* on the streets of Manchester, left 808 State after complaining in the press about unpaid royalties. His most notable contribution to the dance scene was 'Voodoo Ray', which reached number 55 in April 1989 before re-entering at number 12 two months later. Those statistics barely reflect the reverence with which it came to be regarded on the club scene. He was still working at McDonald's at the beginning of the 90s when he was offered the chance to remix for Cabaret Voltaire and Turntable Orchestra. CBS Records allowed him to create his own Subscape label, but it proved impossible to recreate former glories. Simpson did, however, put together a tape to accompany a book by Trevor Miller entitled *Trip City*, and 1992's 'Juicebox' featured old 808 sparring partner MC Tunes on its rap section.
● ALBUMS: *Hot Lemonade* (Rham 1988)★★★, *Trip City* cassette only (Avernus 1989)★★★, *Automanikk* (Columbia 1990)★★★, *Black Secret Technology* (Juice Box 1995)★★★.
● COMPILATIONS: various artists *Juice Box Concentrate* (Juice Box 1998)★★★.

A HOMEBOY, A HIPPIE AND A FUNKI DREDD

This UK dance team made their name with the club hit 'Total Confusion', for Tam Tam in 1989, which led to a contract with Polydor Records. Original 'hippie' Casper Pound (b. *c*.1970) soon departed, to find wider fame as The Hypnotist, head of Rising High Records, and various other projects. HHFD member Marc Williams continued to work with Pound's new label under the title Project One. It was with their November 1993 single, 'Here We Go', that the group became firmly etched into the record-buying public's minds. This came through the unprecedented coverage of a television advert for British Knights sportswear, using the single as its theme tune. On MTV alone it was shown 277 times in the two months following release, but it was to be their final effort.

A MAN CALLED ADAM

This mellow house group, formed in the late 80s in north London, England, first began life as a 10-piece jazz band. Clubgoers, however, came to know them through the distinctive vocals of Sally Rodgers, and the layered Chicago house sounds promulgated by musician Steve Jones. Paul Daley, later half of Leftfield, was also an early collaborator, alongside future members of the Sandals. Their debut releases were 'A.P.B.' and 'Earthly Powers' for Acid Jazz Records, but after a short spell with Ritmo Records (for whom they released 'Musica De Amor') they moved on to a major contract with Big Life Records. The group's spatial and rhythmic experiments were immediately successful, despite an apparent awkwardness with lyrical construction. Easily the best representation of the band was their minor chart success, 'Barefoot In The Head', which remained a highly respected club song well into the 90s. It was followed by 'I Want To Know', which was remixed by Steve Anderson of Brothers In Rhythm and Graeme Park, and became a major club hit. However, by 1993 the group's relationship with Big Life had soured and, following a spate of unsuccessful big budget remixes of their work, they were unceremoniously dropped from the label. The duo eventually responded with the formation of the Other Records label, which began in 1994 with the jazz-tinged disco of 'I Am The Way'. Subsequent releases, including 'Love Comes Down' and 'Easter Song', and tracks by their dub alter ego, Beachflea, have returned the group to the forefront of British house music in the 90s

A TRIBE CALLED QUEST

This US male rap group originally consisted of Q-Tip (b. Jonathan Davis, 20 November 1970, New York, USA), DJ Ali Shaheed Muhammed (b. 11 August 1970, Brooklyn, New York, USA), Jarobi and Phife Dog (b. Malik Taylor, 10 April 1970, Brooklyn, New York, USA). They formed at school in Manhattan, New York, where they started out as part of the Native Tongues Posse, with Queen Latifah and the Jungle Brothers, and were given their name by Afrika Baby Bambaataa of the Jungle Brothers. Following their August 1989 debut, 'Description Of A Fool', they had a hit with 'Bonita Applebum' a year later, which was apparently based on a real person from their school. Their biggest success came the following year with the laid-back 'Can I Kick It?', typical of their refined jazz/hip-hop cross-match. It was later used extensively in television advertisements. Q-Tip also appeared on Deee-Lite's 1990 hit, 'Groove Is In The Heart'. As members of the Native Tongues Posse they were promoters of the Afrocentricity movement, which set out to make US Africans aware of their heritage, a theme emphasized in their music, and that of De La Soul (Q-Tip guested on 'Me, Myself And I'). While their debut, *People's Instinctive Travels And The Paths Of Rhythm*, was more eclectic, and even self-consciously jokey, *The Low End Theory* (recorded as a trio following the departure of Jarobi) saw them return to their roots with a more bracing, harder funk sound. They were helped considerably by jazz bassist Ron Carter (who had worked with Miles Davis and John Coltrane), whose contribution rather dominated proceedings. Tracks such as 'The Infamous Date Rape' stoked controversy, while samples from Lou Reed, Stevie Wonder and Earth, Wind And Fire were used in a frugal and intelligent manner. By *Midnight Marauders* there were allusions to the rise of gangsta rap, although they maintained the optimism predominant on their debut. Q-Tip appeared in the 1992 film *Poetic Justice* opposite Janet Jackson, and helped to produce Tony! Toni! Tone! (whose Raphael Wiggins made an appearance on *Midnight Marauders*), Nas, Shyheim and labelmate Shaquille O'Neal. They were rewarded with the Group Of The Year category at the inaugural *Source Magazine* Hip Hop Award Show in 1994, before being pulled off the stage by the arrival of 2Pac and his Thug Life crew, attempting to steal some publicity. Two years elapsed before *Beats, Rhymes And Life* was released and it debuted at number 1 on the *Billboard* album chart. Their lyrics on this album were highly evolved, addressing issues with greater philosophy than the crude banter of their past recordings. Q-Tip's conversion to the Islamic faith may have had some bearing on this style.

● ALBUMS: *People's Instinctive Travels And The Paths Of Rhythm* (Jive 1990)★★★, *The Low End Theory* (Jive 1991)★★★, *Revised Quest For The Seasoned Traveller* remixes (Jive 1992)★★, *Midnight Marauders* (Jive 1993)★★★, *Beats, Rhymes And Life* (Jive 1996)★★★★.

A13 PRODUCTIONS

The key to record label A13's swift rise to prominence in UK dance circles was A&R head/managing director Chris Massey, who was 22 years old when he founded the label in October 1993. He had formerly worked as head of promotions for General Production Recordings for two years until 1992. A13 Productions, its name taken from the label's base off the A13 road in Benfleet, Essex, was established after Massey attended a free music industry course for the unemployed, and was aided by money from the Prince's Trust. The first release arrived in November 1993 with the *Gapar* EP, from former GPR act Repeat (aka Mark Broom, with Ed Handley and Andy Turner from Black Dog). A second release came from highly respected techno/trance producer Simon Berry (Art Of Trance), and the *Northern Lights* EP. A flurry of demo tapes led to a release from Connective Zone with the *The Holistic Worlds* EP, before a second Mark Broom/Repeat four-track, *Acrux*. With further material issues, including the techno of Red Union and a compilation album, A13 had quickly established itself in the hearts of dance fans.

ABOVE THE LAW

Gangsta rappers from Pomona, California, USA, whose ultra-violent lyrics betray a keen nose for breezy rhythm tracks, largely sampled from 70s soul. They also utilize live keyboards, bass and guitar to back the rhymes of the self-styled 'hustlers' - Cold 187um (b. Gregory Hutchinson), K.M.G. The Illustrator (b. Kevin Dulley), Total K-oss (b. Anthony Stewart) and Go Mack (b. Arthur Goodman). Their debut album consisted of two quite separate themes on the Mega and Ranchin' sides. The first dealt with graphic, unpleasant street violence narratives, while the second observed leering sexual scenarios. It was an unappetizing mix, despite the presence of label boss Eazy-E on 'The Last Song' (both he and Dr. Dre chaired production while they were still on speaking terms), and some otherwise attractive instrumental work. The follow-up mini-album, *Vocally Pimpin'*, at least boasted improved studio technique, but their second long-playing set did not do well. Cold 187 (as he is now known) went on to produce Kokane's *Funk Upon A Rhyme* debut album for Ruthless/Relativity. *Uncle Sam's Curse* attempted greater lyrical depth with little success, although the grooves were still imaginative. They were still plugging away with the same formula on 1997's *Legends*, which included a reworking of Luther Vandross's 'Promise Me'.

● ALBUMS: *Livin' Like Hustlers* (Ruthless 1990)★★★, *Vocally Pimpin'* mini-album (Ruthless 1991)★★, *Black Mafia Life* (Ruthless 1992)★★★, *Uncle Sam's Curse* (Ruthless 1994)★★, *Time Will Reveal* (Tommy Boy 1996)★★★, *Legends* (Tommy Boy 1997)★★★.

ACID HOUSE

DJ Pierre was the man, alongside his partner Spanky, who was largely heralded as the figurehead of this musical movement. The sound was developed in a basement in Chicago, Illinois, USA, in 1986, where the duo had just purchased and installed a bass machine, the Roland TB 303: 'We'd got the 303 and we were trying to figure out what knobs do what. The machine already had acid in it. At first I thought it was some kind of shit we gotta erase out of it before we programme it. Spanky had a 15-minute beat track he'd programmed a couple of days earlier . . . and I kept turning the knobs to see what kind of effect they had on the bassline.' That session was recorded and passed to DJ Ron Hardy, who mixed it into his sets at Chicago's Warehouse club. Soon this new sound was being much discussed and became known as Hardy's *Acid Tracks* (an alternative theory has been advanced that Marshall Jefferson developed the 'sound' of acid, but Pierre's version has generally been given more credence). Ironically, the 303 was a budget bass synthesizer that was designed for use with the 606 drum machine, but flopped commercially. The 'acid' element came about due to the five hand-tuned filters that could manipulate and 'squelch' or stress the bass notes, as they were being played back. Originally the 'acid' prefix was bereft of drug connotations. While Pierre released the influential *Acid Trax* series on Phuture, the sound gripped the UK club scene in 1988, and bands such as D-Mob took up the mantle with a bastardized version. Records such as 'Acid Man' by Jolly Roger (actually Eddie Richards, later DJ to the Shamen) started to feature in the charts. Ably represented by the 'Smiley' logo and the warehouse party culture, the acid phenomenon of 1988 rivalled the punk scene of the previous decade for its notoriety within the establishment and British press. This time, the connection between Ecstasy, the scene's drug of choice, and the music was made more explicit. Eventually, the style went underground once more as it was superseded by techno and other dance forms. Notable archivists such as Richie Hawtin and Ege Bam Yasi have done much to revive the style, or 'the 303 sound', in the 90s, as have Hardfloor, Laurent Garnier and Cosmic Baby in Europe.

ACID JESUS

Acid Jesus are based in Darmstadt, Germany, and consist of Roman Flugal and Jorn Elling-Wuttke who also record as Rebel Youth, Holy Garage, Playhouse and Primitive Painter. Elling-Wuttke is jointly responsible for running the highly regarded Delerium record store, and helps in-house labels such as Ongaku, Klangeltronik and Playhouse: 'We're against the whole movement that has developed. In Delerium, we try to show the kids in Frankfurt real techno. Every musician who comes into our shop is offered the chance to come into our studio and be shown how to work the equipment.' Flugal is a classically trained pianist who occasionally drums for a jazz band. His partner once played in a rock band entitled the Sheets, who toured with the Wedding Present. Among their alter egos are, strangely enough, Alter Ego, who recorded an album of psychedelia-tinged material, promoted by the 'Nude Restaurant' single, which was remixed by David Holmes and Black Dog Productions, both of whom also remixed Acid Jesus's 'Move My Body', along with Derrick May. As Primitive Painter, meanwhile, they generally build songs around the 808 drum machine, and produce material influenced by Robert Owens, Fingers Inc and Felix Da Housecat.

● ALBUMS: as Alter Ego *Alter Ego* (Harthouse 1994)★★★, as Primitive Painter *Primitive Painter* (R&S 1994)★★★.

ADAMSKI

b. Adam Tinley, *c.*1968. Adamski's first recordings were cut at the age of 11 as a member of the Stupid Babies, a pre-teen punk duo (with his brother) immortalized on the Fast Products *Earcom 3* sampler. He was also a member of Diskord Kaskord in 1987, who released one single - a cover version of X-Ray Spex's 'Identity' (his brother subsequently formed Garden Of Eden). Adamski went on to record as a keyboard player on instrumental dance records. His solo breakthrough came with the release of 'N-R-G', which reached number 12 in the UK charts. Unfortunately, legal action from Lucozade, who claimed the single plagiarized their advertising slogan, forced him to donate £5,000 of his royalties to charity. He replied with the massive dancefloor hit and UK number 1, 'Killer'. This tautly orchestrated electronic piece was enhanced by the emotive vocals of guest vocalist Seal. A follow-up, 'The Space Jungle', which derived from 'All Shook Up', was hammered by the critics. While his former vocalist went on to national adoration, Adamski slipped from view, although he did enjoy a minor hit with 'Flashback Jack' at the end of 1990. An epitaph, of sorts, was offered on the *Naughty* track, 'Take The Money And Run': 'I've been chewed up and spat out by the restrictions of dance'. Many critics judged such petulance as sour grapes following his commercial decline. The same year he joined with Elton John to remix 'Medicine Man' for charity, but was not sighted for some time afterwards. He now forms part of the remix team the Jet Slags with Mr Monday, working on projects including Bump's 'I'm Rushin''. He returned in July 1998 with a new single, 'One Of The People'.

● ALBUMS: *Live And Direct* (MCA 1990)★★, *Doctor Adamski's Musical Pharmacy* (MCA 1990)★★, *Naughty* (MCA 1992)★★.
● VIDEOS: *Live And Direct* (MCA 1990).

ADEVA

b. Patricia Daniels, 1960, Patterson, New Jersey, USA. The youngest of six children, Adeva joined a church choir at the age of 12 where she remained for 10 years, eventually becoming its director and vocal coach. Her mother was a missionary and her father a deacon, and her parents had once instructed, 'You sing gospel or nothing at all.' Between stints of teaching (for emotionally disturbed children), she found time to take part regularly in talent contests. She was eventually banned from entering several competitions because she won so often, and turned professional by starting out on the local club scene in the mid-80s. She teamed up with Mike Cameron of the Smack Productions team to record 'In And Out Of My Life' for New York label Easy Street, before signing to Cooltempo in 1988. Her success in the singles chart, initially more considerable in the UK than the USA (where, strangely, her first three solo releases all went to number 17), included 'Respect', 'Treat Me Right', 'Warning', 'Beautiful Love', and the collaboration with New York producer and recording artist Paul Simpson, 'Musical Freedom (Moving On Up)'. However,

Adeva never quite made the commercial transition that was expected, and she was dropped by Cooltempo in August 1992.

● ALBUMS: *Adeva* (Cooltempo 1989)★★★, *Love Or Lust* (Cooltempo 1991)★★.
● COMPILATIONS: *Hits* (Cooltempo 1992)★★★.
● VIDEOS: *Live At The Town And Country Club* (Chrysalis Music Video 1991).

AFRIKA BAMBAATAA

b. Afrika Bambaataa Aasim, 4 October 1960, New York, USA. His name deriving from that of a nineteenth-century Zulu chief, translating as 'Chief Affection', Bambaataa was the founding father of New York's Zulu Nation. The name was inspired by the film *Zulu*, starring Michael Caine, and the code of honour and bravery of its black participants. A loose community of mainly black street youths, Zulu Nation and its leader, more than any other element, helped to transform the gangs of the late 70s into the hip-hop crews of the early 80s. Bambaataa himself had been a member of the notorious Black Spades, among other sects, and from 1977-85 he had a social importance to match his towering MC and DJ profiles, organizing breakdance competitions and musical events promoting the ethos of peace and racial tolerance. By 1980 he was the pre-eminent hip-hop DJ in New York, commanding massive followings and eclipsing even Grandmaster Flash in popularity. He made his recording debut the same year, producing two versions of 'Zulu Nation Throwdown' for two rap groups associated with the Zulu Nation - Cosmic Force and Soul Sonic Force. Signing to the independent label Tommy Boy Records, he made his first own-name release in 1982, as Afrika Bambaataa And The Jazzy Five, with 'Jazzy Sensation' (based on Gwen Guthrie's 'Funky Sensation'). It was followed by his seminal 'Planet Rock', a wholly synthesized record, this time based on Kraftwerk's 'Trans-Europe Express'. In one leap it took hip-hop music far beyond its existing street rhyme and percussion break format. The contribution of Arthur Baker and John Robie in programming its beats was also highly significant, for in turn they gave birth to the 'electro' rap movement that dominated the mid-80s and paved the way for the popularization of dance/house music. 'Planet Rock' also gave its name to the record label Bambaataa established in the Bronx. 'Looking For The Perfect Beat' continued the marriage of raw lyrics and synthesized electro-boogie, and was another major milestone for the genre. The follow-up album, *Beware (The Funk Is Everywhere)*, even included a take on the MC5's 'Kick Out The Jams' (produced by Bill Laswell). Bambaataa also recorded an album as part of Shango, backed by Material members Laswell and Michael Beinhorn, in a party dance vein that accommodated a cover version of Sly Stone's 'Thank You'. Never one to stay in one place for long, he went on to record two vastly different and unexpected singles - 'World Destruction' with ex-Sex Pistols vocalist John Lydon, and 'Unity' with the funk godfather, James Brown. He fell out of the limelight in the latter half of the 80s, as new generations of disc jockeys and rappers stepped forward with their own innovations and fresh beats. However, *The Light* included an enterprising cast (UB40, Nona Hendryx, Boy George, Bootsy Collins, Yellowman and George Clinton - the latter a huge early musical and visual influence on Bambaataa). *The Decade Of Darkness (1990-2000)* also went some way towards redressing the balance, including an update of James Brown's 'Say It Loud (I'm Black And I'm Proud)'. In March 1994, he appeared on Run DMC's Profile label with the disappointing 'What's The Name'. However, Bambaataa's influence on rap's development is pivotal, and is felt in many more subtle ways than, for example, the direct sampling of his work on 90s crossover hits such as 95 South's 'Whoot! There It Is' or Duice's 'Dazey Duks'.

● ALBUMS: with Zulu Nation *Zulu Nation* (1983)★★★, with Shango *Funk Theology* (Celluloid 1984)★★★, with Soul Sonic Force *Planet Rock - The Album* (Tommy Boy 1986)★★★★, *Beware (The Funk Is Everywhere)* (Tommy Boy 1986)★★★ *Death Mix Throwdown* (Blatant 1987)★★★, *The Light* (Capitol 1988)★★★, *The Decade Of Darkness (1990-2000)* (EMI 1991)★★★, *Don't Stop - Planet Rock Remix* (ZTT 1992)★★★.

AFRO-CELT SOUND SYSTEM

A bold attempt to fuse modern dance music styles with ethnic rhythms from the African and Celtic traditions, Afro-Celt Sound System is the brainchild of Grammy-nominated producer Simon Emmerson. He brought together a diverse team of musicians, including members of Baaba Maal's band, Jo Bruce (son of Jack Bruce), James McNally (of the Pogues), Irish traditional singer Iarla O'Lionaird, Breton harpist Myrdhin, Davy Spillane and Ronan Browne (who toured with the phenomenally successful *Riverdance* show), to record together over a week in July 1995. With artwork from Jamie Reid (famed for his Sex Pistols graphics), the album, *Volume One Sound Magic*, embraced many disparate sounds, from jungle to trip-hop and ambient trance, underpinned by the performers' Celtic and African heritage. Before its release in 1996 the same group appeared at the 1995 WOMAD Festival, followed by a repeat performance the following year. Bruce tragically died in 1997.

● ALBUMS: *Volume One Sound Magic* (Real World 1996)★★★★.

AFRO-PLANES

Based in Atlanta, Georgia, USA, these four rappers mix Jimi Hendrix with Funkadelic samples, infused with an Afrocentric consciousness and a taste for the comic. Their debut album convincingly berated Ice Cube for endorsing sales of malt liquor, among other effective skits and parodies about the rap arena and their place within it.

● ALBUMS: *Afro-Planes* (BMG 1994)★★★.

AFROS

Taking as their theme crazy 70s fashions in general, and blaxploitation movies in particular, the New York rappers Afros were led by the clean-shaven Hurricane and Koot Tee, while DJ Kippy-O arrived sporting the 70s haircut from which they took their name. Hurricane was formerly a DJ for the Beastie Boys, recording for their Grand Royal label. The album was co-written and co-produced by DJ 'Jam Master Jay' (aka Jason Mizell) from Run DMC, and was released on his own JMJ label. Sight gags aside, the Afros' raps considered political viewpoints alongside wry looks at black culture. The repartee was old school, with call-and-response rhymes over a churning, funky backbeat.

● ALBUMS: *Kickin' Afrolistics* (JMJ/Columbia 1990)★★.

AHMAD

b. *c.*1975. From South Central Los Angeles, Ahmad utilized the half-sung, half-rapped approach invoked by Snoop Doggy Dogg and Domino. He was signed to Giant after rapping freestyle in front of president Cassandra Mills, who signed him on the spot. The rhythm tracks on his debut were built with the help of his high-school friend Kendal Gordy, son of Motown's Berry Gordy. Old soul loops and R&B dominated, and he often revealed the lyrical incisiveness to match. Carefully avoiding the excesses of gangsta rap clichés, Ahmad was instead more articulate: 'There's millions of ordinary, average, real people there (the South Central ghetto), who are trying to do the right thing and get out of the situation. But a lot of rappers don't touch on that - they just talk about the gangbanging, like it's so great and hunky-dory and glamorous. It's not at all, because I've been to many funerals and I realise that the time has come to stop all this bullshit.' His first single, 'Back In The Day', emphasized this view, with a discussion on the merits of old-school hip-hop culture.

● ALBUMS: *Ahmad* (Giant 1994)★★★.

AIR LIQUIDE

This ambient techno trio comprises Walker (b. Ingmar Koch, Germany), Jammin' Unit and Mary S. Applegate. Koch is a half-German, half-Hungarian music graduate from the University of Cologne, where he specialized in electronic composition. The strangely named Jammin' Unit is a half-Turkish, half-Finnish musician who had recorded *avant garde* and experimental music for over a decade before the group formed in 1992. He is also a professional sound engineer who runs Air Liquide's Ocean Blue studios, alongside Koch. Applegate, an expatriate American, is the group's lyricist, having previously composed over 20 chart hits including Jennifer Rush's 'The Power Of Love'. This unlikely collaboration was informed by mutual tastes in underground exotica and electronica, which was wonderfully captured by the release of 'If There Was No Gravity'. This combined the wide-eyed wonder of Applegate's delivery with an unsettling ambient production from her partners. The subsequent album, again licensed to Rising High Records in the UK, was similarly fêted, and preceded a collaboration with that label's Caspar Pound on The New London School Of Electronics project. Koch also provided a set for the unrelated but phonetically similar New Electronica series, and records solo as Walker (the best example of which is 'Don't Fuck With Cologne' for DJ.Ungle Fever). Jammin' Unit's solo excursions, meanwhile, include 'Flower Swing' for the same label, which is one of some 14 labels that Koch operates (under the Structure Records umbrella). In 1996 EMI Records resurrected their Harvest label to release a series of Air Liquide-related albums.

● ALBUMS: *Nephology* (Blue/Rising High 1994)★★★★, *Liquid Air* (Harvest 1997)★★★.

AKINYELE

b. *c.*1970, Queens, New York, USA. Akinyele first started rhyming after hearing 'Rapper's Delight' for the first time. He went to the same high school as Nas, Kool G Rap and Large Professor, working together as part of a team and also individually. Together with Nas, he rapped on Main Source's 'Live At The BBQ' cut from *Breaking Atoms*. When Akinyele signed to Interscope, he enlisted the production services of Large Professor. The first single from the set, 'Ak Ha Ha! Ak Hoo Hoo?', introduced his trademark blend of sprightly braggadocio, often punctuated by a 'drop', wherein his voice lowered in pitch to emphasize a key word. The title of his debut album may have raised a few eyebrows, but he is in fact a no-drink, no-drugs rapper: 'The name of the album is *Vagina Diner*, only because I'm a cunning linguist, not a cunnilinguist.'

● ALBUMS: *Vagina Diner* (Interscope 1993)★★★, *Put It In Your Mouth* mini-album (Zoo 1996)★★.

ALCATRAZ

A duo of Jean Phillippe Aviance and Victor Imbres from Washington, DC, USA, Alcatraz's debut single, 'Give Me Luv', was released on Deep Dish's Yoshitoshi label at the beginning of 1995. It was the duo's first collaboration, but slowly built journalistic and club support until at the end of 1995 a major dance label bidding war erupted. A&M Records eventually secured the rights to release the single at the beginning of 1996. A minimal, hard house track, it followed neatly in the tradition established by artists such as Josh Wink. The duo had first met when Imbres was engineering a remix of Deep Dish's 'Satori' by Aviance. Though it was not envisaged as a permanent collaboration, the resultant exposure gained by 'Give Me Luv' on the London club scene encouraged them to work together on new material for A&M. They also remixed BT's 'Loving You More' UK hit.

ALI DEE

This rap production star formerly worked alongside the Bomb Squad and learned much of his craft from them. He has his own Manhattan recording studio, Gabrielle Productions, and his credits include work on 7669's debut album, and the Collision/Warner Brothers rapper, L-Boogie.

● ALBUMS: *Bring It On* (EMI 1993)★★★.

ALKAHOLICS, THA

This rapping outfit specialized in fun, funky tunes, and consisted of J-Ro (b. James Robinson, c.1970, Los Angeles, California, USA), Tash (b. Rico Smith, Ohio, USA) and DJ E-Swift (b. Eric Brooks, Ohio, USA). Despite raised eyebrows over their name and gaudy stage performances, Tha Alkaholics have become popular proponents of 'party rap'. J-Ro had intended to become a rapper since the age of 13, spending countless hours in his bedroom making tape recordings when he should have been at school, or later, work. His two accomplices had already formed a partnership for house parties, with E-Swift switching to the turntable. The trio came to the attention of King Tee, who was searching for a back-up band, and they joined him in time for his Tha Triflin' Album, and its attendant single, 'I Got It Bad Y'All'. It was the latter that kick-started Tha Alkoholics' career, having adopted their name from a suggestion made by King Tee. They progressed to support slots with Ice Cube, KRS-1 and Too Short, allowing them the opportunity to hone their skills in front of a live audience. On their return, a major label contract awaited them, the first results of which were the high-profile singles 'Make Room' and 'Likwit'. The follow-up album revealed a more mature lyrical outlook.

● ALBUMS: *21 & Over* (RCA/Loud 1993)★★★, *Coast To Coast* (RCA/Loud 1995)★★★.

ALLEN, MARK

Like many involved with the psychedelic trance scene, Allen was switched on to the sound while in Goa in 1991. On returning to the UK he trained as a solicitor and began to DJ as part of the legendary Pagan sound system, which also featured the DJs Yazz, Chrisbo and Loll and whose parties graduated from a squat in Brixton to Linford Studios. Following another trip to India in the early 90s, Allen decided to pursue a career in music and, with Phil Ross and Janice Duncan, began Return To The Source at the Rocket in London. It has since become the most successful trance club in the UK, often featuring Tsuyoshi Suzuki. (During the mid- to late 90s, Return To The Source put on events throughout Europe and further afield, including New York, Sydney and Mount Fuji in Japan. In October 1997 Return To The Source helped to organize Earthdance, which featured such artists as Banco De Gaia, Hallucinogen, Medicine Drum and System 7, and

was part of a global event organized to raise money in support of the Tibetan issue.) In 1995 Allen began to record with Chrisbo, Simon Maine and John Ford as Minefield. While working at Return To The Source, Allen met Tim Healey (DJ Squid) and in 1996 the pair formed Quirk. Their album *Machina Electrica & Fornax Chemica* was released on Matsuri Productions in 1997 to an enthusiastic response. Allen has also collaborated on various projects with the Green Nuns Of The Revolution, Andy Guthrie and Nick Taylor (Snake Thing) and compiled a number of mix CDs, including the first *Deck Wizards* album (Psychic Deli 1995) and Return To The Source's *Shamanic Trance Vol. 2* (Positiva 1998). He has continued to co-promote and DJ at Return To The Source around the world.

ALOOF

One of the few dance acts capable and willing to transfer their music to a live arena, the Aloof were formed in London, England, in 1990. Their prime mover is DJ Dean Thatcher, who has been a member of many recording outfits, particularly through his activities at Cowboy Records, and co-runs Flaw Records with Richard Thair. Thair is also a member of Red Snapper, and an *ad hoc* percussionist for Sabres Of Paradise. Singer Ricky Barrow adds another unusual facet in that he gives the band a recognizable lead vocal presence where so many other dance groups utilize guest performers. The rest of the band comprises Jagz Kooner and Gary Burns, both sound engineers who have also worked with Sabres Of Paradise. From their inception (originally just as a duo of Kooner and Thatcher), they set out to use a broad palate of musics to inform and expand electronic dance music, with Jamaican dub the most easily detectable. After recruiting the other members, their debut single was picked up for wider distribution by ffrr Records, but they passed on any further options. By 1993 the group had reached something of an impasse, leading to Thair and Thatcher setting up Flaw Records in 1993. The original intention was to release Aloof records, but the label also became a home for Thair's Red Snapper, whose three EPs were later repackaged as an album for Warp Records. The Aloof also made the most of their new outlet, releasing three singles in 1994, followed by their debut album, *Cover The Crime*. Via the recommendation of *Melody Maker Muzik* journalist Ben Turner, this was picked up for distribution by East West

Records in 1995. Buoyed by a new major label contract, the band embarked on a nationwide tour that culminated in an appearance at the Glastonbury Festival in June 1995. *Sinking* was assured and hypnotic although the negativity of the lyrics belies the rich overall sound.
● ALBUMS: *Cover The Crime* (Flaw 1994)★★★, *Sinking* (East West 1996)★★★.

ALT

b. Al Trivette, Rosemonte, California, USA. As well as being the intitals of his name, ALT also stands for 'Another Latin Timebomb'. Having been raised in Rosemonte, four miles east of Los Angeles, he witnessed at first hand the problems that drugs and violence had caused the Latin community. He was quickly picked up by a major label, keen to capitalize on hardcore street rap, but unwilling to allow it free reign. His debut album was hampered by instructions not to use foul language, and a parting of the ways followed soon after. Linking instead with the Inner City independent, he previewed his second set with 'Riding' High', a diary of a day in the Latin neighbourhood.
● ALBUMS: *ALT* (East West/Atlantic 1991)★★, *Stone Cold World* (Inner City/Par 1993)★★★, *Altitude* (Alt 1995)★★★.

ALTERN 8

Hardcore ravers from Stafford, England, Altern 8 consisted of Mark Archer and Chris Peat, and were an offshoot of their Nexus 21 pure techno act. Of the two, Archer was the house music aficionado, while Peat was a former music technology student with an interest in computers. They crashed the chart with 'Infiltrate 202' and 'Activ8', two chaotic slices of overground techno. They were aided in their chart aspirations by the circulation of fictitious press stories concerning their alleged activities, which included promoting the decongestant Vicks Vapo Rub, which, it was claimed, heightened the effects of the Ecstasy drug; playing shows in a hot-air balloon and dispensing to the crowd Christmas cake laced with Ecstasy; and standing as candidates for the 1993 General Election. Their live 'events' were also designed as eye-catching performances, where the band donned RAF chemical warfare suits and dust-masks: 'Dance music is there to be danced to, not to be looked at like rock music is. But, unfortunately, dance acts have to perform live on occasion, and, when we do, we want to provide something visual.' They were aided by their resident dancers Crez and John Parkes, and, in the case of their gig at Stafford Bingley Hall, an actual shaman. His job was to cleanse the venue of its 'rock 'n' roll' past', prior to performance. Their vinyl outings, in addition to the hits, consisted of the *Overload* EP (1990), 'E Vapor 8' (1991) and 'Frequency', 10,000 copies of which were on sale for a single day only. The protagonists long maintained that this was a temporary diversion from their main project, Nexus 21, and confirmed this by releasing a 'final' Altern 8 single, 'Everybody', in June 1993. Mark Archer has gone on to form Slo-Moshun, a duo of Archer and Danny Taurus from Stoke-on-Trent. They released 'Bells Of New York', one of the biggest dance hits of early 1994, breaking the Top 30 on the back of its house/hip-hop undulations. However, some of the Altern 8 methodology remained - this time the scam was to trick everyone into thinking it was a US import. Their second single was 'Help My Friends'.
● ALBUMS: *Full On ... Mask Hysteria* (Network 1992)★★★.

AMADIN

A duo formed by disc jockeys John Amatiello and Kristian Lundin in Sweden in 1992, Amadin additionally feature the rapping skills of 'Swing' (b. USA). Their debut single, 'Alrabaiye Take Me Up', was based on the Arabic phraseology for 'Come, follow', and incorporated an Eastern-influenced musical platform with prominent dance beats. The idea for Amadin was fermented when the two principal songwriters met as disc jockeys and agreed to work together writing jingles for a radio station they intended to start. They were immediately noticed by Euro-dance star Dr. Alban, who signed them to his own Dr. Records label (through Cherion Records).

AMBER

b. Netherlands. One of the first Euro-dance vocalists to make an impact in the USA in the mid-90s, Amber rose to prominence when her single, 'This Is Your Night', became a Top 40 hit for Tommy Boy Records. Unlike most Euro crossover hits, the artist had been signed directly to the label rather than being the subject of an opportunistic licensing arrangement. Indeed, this success came despite the fact that the single had yet to be released in Amber's native homeland. The follow-up single was 'Colour Of Love', also the title track of the artist's 1997 debut album. Again, this was produced by Amber's writing/production team,

Christian and Frank Bermann. Extensive US and European touring followed, leading the artist to conclude that: 'When I was a little girl, I always dreamed of being a big star - little did I know it would be so exhausting, too.' She had grown up in a musical family, her mother teaching piano, while her father was a professional opera singer. She first met the Bermann brothers in 1992, a full two years before they achieved their first international successes with Real McCoy. Although the two parties began working on material together in 1994, it was two years before these sessions were aired, first in the form of 'This Is Your Night', and then on her debut album.
● ALBUMS: *Colour Of Love* (Tommy Boy 1997)★★★.

AMBERSUNSHOWER

b. New York, USA. Ambersunshower - which is her real name - made a big impact in 1996 with the release of her debut album for Gee Street Records. Marketed by her label as 'alternative soul', the record's judicious combination of R&B, swing, pop and hip-hop endeared her to a wide-ranging audience. The title *Walter T. Smith* came from the artist's grandfather, who was also a musician. 'Walter T.' was also the first single to be taken from the album, which was produced by PM Dawn and Tikk Takk, among others. Her first performance experiences had come when combining soul music with poetry and spoken-word work, ensuring that when she toured with a full band to promote her debut, she was well versed with stage etiquette and had the confidence to animate her eclectic songwriting.
● ALBUMS: *Walter T. Smith* (Gee Street 1996)★★★.

AMG

b. Jason Lewis, 29 September 1970, Brooklyn, New York, USA. This male US rapper's lyrics were unfortunately highly misogynistic. Typical titles on his debut album, which unaccountably made number 63 in the *Billboard* charts, included the ominous title track, 'Lick 'Em Low Lover' and 'Mai Sista Izza Bitch'. His justification was equally skewered: 'OK, so my record's nasty. But come on. I'm surrounded by negativity. If I go make a positive record, it might flop. So here's what I do: I use me something negative to make enough money to do something positive.'
● ALBUMS: *Bitch Betta Have My Money* (Select 1991)★★.

ANCIENT BEATBOX

In their spare time, two members of Blowzabella, Paul James (b. 4 April 1957, Southampton, Hampshire, England) and Nigel Eaton (b. 3 January 1966, Lyndhurst, Hampshire, England), applied electronics and mixers to French dance tunes, and produced a turntable dance hit with 'My Eyes Are Filled With Clouds', which featured a vocal by ex-Monsoon singer Sheila Chandra.
● ALBUMS: *Ancient Beatbox* (Cooking Vinyl 1989)★★.

ANDERSON, CARLEEN

b. May 1957. Anderson started her professional life as a clerical worker, with very few ambitions to enter the world of showbusiness. Her parents, conversely, had been stalwarts of James Brown's touring revue in the 60s and 70s. Her mother, Vicki Anderson, was also a backing vocalist, and her stepfather was Bobby Byrd of the Famous Flames. By her mid-20s Anderson had married, given birth to a son, and started a college scholarship in Los Angeles to train to be a music teacher. However, times were tough, and she eagerly accepted an offer from her parents to travel to London to investigate the emerging soul scene. There she linked with the duo Young Disciples. Though never an official member of the band, she wrote and sang on most of their best songs, notably 'Apparently Nothin'', written about the Gulf War. However, her tenure with the Young Disciples ended, amicably, with the release of *Dusky Sappho*, a limited edition EP. Its title referred to Phyllis Wheatley, an American poet and slave who had come to Britain and was a prime mover in the lesbian movement. Speculations about Anderson's sexuality followed with predictable speed, although she advocated celibacy.

Anderson's debut solo single came with 'Nervous Breakdown' on Circa Records, a seven-minute soul/dance track, and *True Spirit* went on to become a silver album. Newly signed to Virgin Records, Anderson broke a three-year silence when her soulful cover version of Paul McCartney's 'Maybe I'm Amazed' reached number 24 in the UK charts.
● ALBUMS: *True Spirit* (Circa 1994)★★★, *Blessed Burden* (Virgin 1998)★★★.

ANDERSON, JHELISA

b. Jackson, Mississippi, USA. British-based soul-dance vocalist, and cousin of Carleen Anderson, whose fame initially revolved around her work for the Shamen ('Ebeneezer Goode') and Soul Family Sensation ('I Don't Even Know If I Should Call You Baby'), having left her media course and session singing duties in Los Angeles for London in 1988. After guesting on Björk's debut album, she earned herself a solo contract with Dorado Records. The first single to emerge was the self-written 'Sally's Knockin'', followed by 'All I Need', a jazzy hip-hop workout that saw her united with Lee Hamblin (famed for his production with Christy Moore, PM Dawn, Sindecut, Maxi Priest, etc.).

ANGEL

b. Brooklyn, New York, USA. A singer, writer, remixer and producer, Angel's talents had largely been honed in her adopted second home of London, before she returned to the west coast of America in 1994. Her lively cocktail of funk and jazz dance won her a contract with Delicious Vinyl subsidiary Brass ('I recycle the things I love and give it that 90s edge,' she has said of her music). She rose to prominence with her first single for Brass, 'Spirit Of Love', before embarking on a debut album. She is also a prominent remixer, working with the Pharcyde, Brand New Heavies and Soul Sonics.
● ALBUMS: *Message From The Angel* (Brass 1994)★★★.

ANGEL, DAVE

b. 13 May 1966, London, England. Based in Clapham, south London, techno DJ and recording artist Dave Angel's father was a professional jazz musician. As a result, he grew up listening to Charlie Parker and Miles Davis, and became a jazz session drummer by the age of 14. However, his background was also one of stifling poverty, his father buying him his first drum-kit the day the electricity was cut off. He released his debut single in 1989, shortly after returning from a nine-month prison term for possession of cannabis. He had recorded a bassline on a standard tape deck, and in a moment of inspiration, mixed it against a nearby copy of the Eurythmics' 'Sweet Dreams'. Once approval had been given from RCA Records, who licensed the record, it was released as a white label, before Angel moved to Dave Dorrell's

Love label for 'Never Leave'. He began his career in earnest with two strong EPs, *Royal Techno* and *Of The Highest Order*. The critically acclaimed *Family* followed in 1993, before *Third Voyage* (originally released in April 1991). He has maintained his broad musical vision: 'People always use the word techno to describe what I do, but I prefer to call it "future jazz"'. His debut album was released in association with Island Records in 1995. He continues to DJ at the Orbit club and to remix for various clients, including Sun Electric's 'En-Trance', Katana for Eastern Bloc and the *Seas Of Tranquillity* EP for his own label, Rotation Records.
● ALBUMS: *X-MIX-4 - Beyond The Heavens* (Studio 1995)★★★, *Tales Of The Unexpected* (Island 1995)★★★, *Globetrotting* (Island 1997)★★★.
● COMPILATIONS: *Classics* (R&S 1996)★★★.

ANOTHA LEVEL

Freestyling old school-fixated rap newcomers from Los Angeles, California, USA, Anotha Level featured a four-man MC crew - Ced Twice, Stenge, Imani and Bambino. They are protégés of producer Laylaw, ex-manager of Above The Law, who had previously produced cuts for Ice Cube (who executive-produced the album) and Yo Yo. Preoccupations on their debut album included girls and Super Nintendo, while Cube guested with them on one cut, 'Level-N-Service', and the Pharcyde joined the party for 'Phat-T'. Sexism permeated tracks such as 'Don't Stimulate', but it stopped short of obnoxiousness. Arguably the best cut was 'Let Me Tell Ya', the opening track, which featured dancehall DJ Don Jagwarr.
● ALBUMS: *On Anotha Level* (Priority 1994)★★★.

ANTOINETTE

b. Queens, New York, USA. Hurby 'Lovebug' Azor introduced Antoinette on his compilation album, *Hurby's Machine*. Described as a tough-talking rap mama, there was more to Antoinette than merely that. Although fresh and natural, her debut was largely straightforward gangster-talk, but the follow-up established her as a much more flexible talent, as her raps moved through sexually explicit narratives to defiant snippets of feminist tract, over waves of music that encompassed funk, go-go and house.
● ALBUMS: *Who's The Boss* (Next Plateau 1989)★★★, *Burnin' At 20 Below* (Next Plateau 1990)★★★.

APHEX TWIN

b. Richard D. James, 1972, Truro, Cornwall, England. During the 90s James, under a variety of names, has become one of the leading exponents of 'intelligent techno', 'ambient techno' and other terms invented to describe his brand of electronic music. As a child he was not interested in music, but instead amused himself 'making noises and banging on things'; later, he began recording his efforts on tape and began building and customizing his own synthesizers. While DJing at parties and raves, he sometimes included in his sets the occasional original tune, such as 'Didgeridoo': 'I wanted to have some tracks to finish the raves I used to play in Cornwall, to really kill everybody off so they couldn't dance any more'. 'Didgeridoo' was a dark, pulsating dance track, with analogue sounds bubbling over a splashy breakbeat. He eventually released the *Aphex Twin* EP and 'Analogue Bubblebath' on the Exeter-based Mighty Force label in 1991. His breakthrough came the following year when he released 'Didgeridoo' on R&S Records. Much of his work from around this time, such as 'Phloam' and 'Isopropanol', was built from incredibly abrasive sounds, but a different style, by which he became more widely known, emerged on the album *Selected Ambient Works '85 - '92* (1992). In the same year, Warp Records included his 'Polygon Window', credited to the Diceman, on their *Artificial Intelligence* compilation. This track opened the album *Surfing On Sine Waves*, which James released the following year. Much of the music sounded quite unique and followed few of the dancefloor trends of the time; nevertheless, the press quickly invented the term 'ambient techno'. However, some of the tracks are anything but ambient and 'Quoth' (which was also released as a single in 1993), with its coarse kick-drum sound, has more in common with much hard acid techno. Even so, there are a number of more introspective tunes, notably 'If It Really Is Me', with its forlorn melodies, and 'Quino - phec', in which James creates a barren, Eno-like texture. The *On* EP in November 1993 followed his signing to Warp on a permanent basis and the next year he released the eagerly awaited *Selected Ambient Works Vol. 2*, which was not as well received as its predecessor. In 1995 Aphex Twin released the album *I Care Because You Do* and the EPs *Ventolin* and *Donkey Rhubarb*, and, as AFX, two *Hangable Auto Bulb* EPs. These were followed the next year

by *Richard D James Album*, on which his usual combination of caustic noises and forlorn textures was set beside more varied rhythms, showing the influence of drum 'n' bass. In the early 90s he set up his own Rephlex Records with Grant Wilson-Claridge. He has also become associated with deliberately obscure DJ sets in which he has been known to put sandpaper on the turntable. James is one of the few dance artists to have managed to establish an individual sound. Often hailed as electronic music's most experimental individual, it seems, after a number of albums, that much of his work tends to revolve around the same ideas. Hysteria in the press may have also obscured his tendency towards self-indulgence. Other names under which he has released material include Caustic Window, GAK, Blue Calx and PCP.
● ALBUMS: *Selected Ambient Works '85 - '92* (R&S 1992)★★★★, as Polygon Window *Surfing On Sine Waves* (Warp 1993)★★★, *Selected Ambient Works Vol. 2* (Warp 1994)★★, *I Care Because You Do* (Warp 1995)★★★, *Richard D. James LP* (Warp 1996)★★★.

APOLLO 440

This UK trance-techno group, featuring Trevor Gray (keyboards, vocals), Howard Gray (backing vocals) and Noko (vocals, guitar, keyboards), initially recorded for their own Stealth label. Following the release of early singles 'Blackout', 'Destiny' and club favourite 'Lolita', Apollo 440 soon became more widely known for their remix work, numbering U2, Liz Francis ('Rhythm Of Life'), EMF and Pop Will Eat Itself among their clients. Further notoriety came with their sample of Emerson Lake & Palmer on their 1993 single, 'Astral America'. They have also recorded as Fast ('Fast' - Stealth 1992, a pure adrenalin rush at 155 bpm) and made the UK Top 10 in February 1997 with 'Ain't Talkin' About Dub'. They returned to the Top 10 in July 1998 with the title song to the film *Lost In Space*, a reinterpretation of the theme to the original television series.
● ALBUMS: *Electro Glide In Blue* (Stealth Sonic/Epic 1997)★★★.

ARIWA SOUNDS

One of only two studio-owning reggae labels to survive in the UK for any length of time (the other is Fashion Records), the success of Ariwa Sounds can be attributed to the determination of one man, Neil Fraser. Guyana-born Fraser started Ariwa as a four-track operation in his living room in Thornton Heath, south London, in 1979, prompted by a lifelong love of electronics and reggae, plus an interest in Philly soul and the related sweet sounds of lovers rock. Those first recordings, including the debut of the late lovers legend Deborahe Glasgow, can be found on *The Early Sessions* album. By 1982 Fraser had moved premises to Peckham, working on, at first, eight-track, and subsequently, 16-track equipment. Styling himself as the Mad Professor, and calling his band the Sane Inmates, Fraser rapidly acquired a reputation for eccentric, attention-grabbing records. Though his influences could clearly be discerned, his mixes soon revealed a highly unique quality, to the point where an Ariwa recording could be easily differentiated from all others. His 'Dub Me Crazy' series, eventually running into double figures, won him a reputation on the alternative rock scene, and disc jockey John Peel was an early champion. Early albums with Tony Benjamin, Sergeant Pepper and Ranking Ann did not sell especially well in the reggae market, but were always distinctive or noteworthy. By 1984 Fraser had teamed up with Sandra Cross, a lovers rock singer and sister of Victor Cross, an early Ariwa sessioneer. The siblings had worked together as the Wild Bunch, an Ariwa album act, before Sandra, a sweet-voiced, confident singer, proved capable of providing Ariwa with the hits it was seeking. Her *Country Life* (1985), built around a string of hits including a cover version of the Stylistics' 'Country Living' (previously covered in the reggae idiom by the Diamonds), was something of a commercial breakthrough. Other albums from Jamaican singer Johnny Clarke and DJs Peter Culture and Pato Banton brought further acclaim, and the open-minded Fraser began to work with acts as diverse as UK indie bands and sound system legend Jah Shaka. Wolverhampton-based DJ Macka B's debut album, *Sign Of the Times* (1986), was the strongest Ariwa release yet, and remains perhaps the most effective roots statement ever recorded in the UK. A move to West Norwood found Fraser the boss of the largest black-owned studio complex in the UK, with two consoles, one a powerful, outboard-littered 24-track. It was here that he fashioned some of his most wonderful lovers rock records, including John Mclean's 'If I Give My Heart To You' (actually produced by Captain Sinbad at Ariwa in 1988), Sandra Cross's 'My Best Friend's Man' and Kofi's revival of her own earlier hit, 'I'm In Love With A Dreadlocks'

(both 1989). Fraser also attracted some heavyweight Jamaican names to his premises, including Bob Andy, Lee Perry and Faybiene Miranda. He did not neglect his eccentric side, however, cutting strange tunes such as Professor Doppler's 'Doppler Effect', and 'Echoes Of Deaf Journalists', an attack on the writers at *Echoes* newspaper. Although recent times have seen less frequent appearances from the Mad Professor in the UK reggae charts (Fraser has always shied away from the guns'n'sex sound of ragga), he retains huge respect and a loyal following worldwide. Regular Ariwa jaunts from New York to Holland, Australia to Poland, and elsewhere, have ensured strong export sales for his unique talents.
● ALBUMS: *Dub Me Crazy* (Ariwa 1982)★★★★, *Mad Professor: The African Connection* (Ariwa 1984)★★★, with Jah Shaka *Jah Shaka Meets Mad Professor At Ariwa Sounds* (Ariwa 1984)★★★, *Negus Roots Meets The Mad Professor* (Negus Roots 1984)★★★★, *Dub Me Crazy Part 5* (Ariwa 1985)★★★, with Pato Banton *Mad Professor Captures Pato Banton* (Ariwa 1985)★★★★, *Schizophrenic Dub* (Ariwa 1986)★★★, *Stepping In Dub Wise Country* (Ariwa 1987)★★★, *The Adventures Of A Dub Sampler* (Ariwa 1987)★★★★, *Dub Me Crazy Party* (Ariwa 1987)★★★, *Roots Daughters* (Ariwa 1988)★★★, with Lee Perry *Lee Scratch Perry Meets The Mad Professor, Volumes 1 & 2* (Ariwa 1990)★★★, with Perry *Lee 'Scratch' Perry Meets The Mad Professor In Dub, Volumes 1 & 2* (Angella 1991)★★★, *Dub Tek The Voodoo* (Ariwa 1996)★★★★, with Jah Shaka *A New Decade Of Dub* (RAS 1996)★★★.
● COMPILATIONS: Various Artists *Roots Daughters* (Ariwa 1988)★★★, *Ariwa Hits '89* (Ariwa 1989)★★★.

ARKARNA

Formed in England in the mid-90s, 'future-dance trio' Arkarna comprises Ollie Jacobs (b. *c*.1975, England), James Barnett (b. *c*.1974, England) and Lalo Creme (b. *c*.1974, England). Jacobs, the group's programmer and vocalist, was by this time already an established studio hand, having worked as an engineer and producer in his father's London studios, Rollover, from the age of 14. As a result, by the time he started the group, he had already mixed for artists ranging from Dread Zone and Leftfield to Deep Forest. However, Jacobs was not the only member of the band with 'connections'. Acoustic guitarist and backing vocalist Barnett was formerly a member of Lunarci, who recorded for Big Life Records and regularly appeared on the Megadog club scene. Lalo Creme, meanwhile, the final member to join the group, is the son of Lol Creme, of Godley And Creme fame. After playing guitar for a series of Trevor Horn sessions, he was directed to Rollover Studios where Jacobs and Barnett were in the process of crystallizing their musical ideas. The trio were signed to WEA Records by Clive Black and Raz Gold in June 1995, but had to wait over a year and a half before the release of their debut single, 'House On Fire', and *Fresh Meat*.

● ALBUMS: *Fresh Meat* (WEA 1997)★★★.

ARRESTED DEVELOPMENT

This rap collective came from Atlanta, Georgia, USA, and were headed by Speech (b. Todd Thomas, 1968, Milwaukee, Wisconsin, USA; lead vocals). He originally met DJ Headliner (b. Timothy Barnwell, 1967) while they were studying at the Art Institute Of Atlanta. Speech, then known as DJ Peech, had already formed Disciples Of Lyrical Rebellion, a proto-gangsta outfit that evolved into Secret Society. They soon switched musical tack to a more community-conscious act, changing the name to Arrested Development and gradually picking up new members. These included Aerle Taree (b. Taree Jones, 1972; vocals, clothes design), Montsho Eshe (b. Temelca Garther, 1974; dancer), and Rasa Don (b. Donald Jones, 1968; drums). They developed an Afrocentric outlook, and all moved into the same house while maintaining their own daytime jobs. Afterwards, spritualist Baba Oje (b. 1933), whom Speech had known as a child, was added as the group's symbolic head man. Influenced heavily by Sly And The Family Stone, when Arrested Development arrived on 1992's music scene they brought an intriguing blend of charisma and wisdom. While most modern rap uses urban dystopia as its platform, this band drew on a black country narrative as well as more universal themes. Speech penned a regular column for the *20th Century African* newspaper and took his views on race issues on lecture tours. Cited by many critics as the most significant breakthrough of 1992, singles 'Tennessee', 'People Everyday' and 'Mr Wendal' confirmed their commercial status by enjoying lengthy stays in the US and (for the latter two) UK Top 10. Their debut album (titled after the length of time it took them to gain a record contract after formation) also embraced a number of issue-based narratives, in particular 'Mama's Always On The Stage', a feminist treatise, and 'Children Play With Earth', an exhortation for children to get back in touch with the natural world that surrounds them. They released the live album, *Unplugged*, early in 1993, taken from their set at New York's Ed Sullivan Theatre the previous December, featuring an expanded 17-person line-up. The same year also brought two Grammy awards for Best New Artist and Best Rap Duo Or Group. Speech's first production project, with fellow southern funk-rappers Gumbo, also met with critical approval. A second album, *Zingalamaduni*, Swahili for 'beehive of culture', emerged in 1994, once again extending their audience beyond the hip-hop cognoscenti. As well as introducing new vocalist Nadirah, plus DJ Kwesi Asuo and dancer Ajile, it saw the departure of Taree, who had gone back to college. The album was a commercial failure, and the members of the band went their separate ways at the end of 1995. Speech released a disappointing solo album in 1996.

● ALBUMS: *3 Years, 5 Months, And 2 Days In The Life Of ...* (Chrysalis 1992)★★★★, *Unplugged* (Chrysalis 1993)★★★, *Zingalamaduni* (Chrysalis 1994)★★★.

● COMPILATIONS: *The Best Of Arrested Development* (Chrysalis 1998)★★★.

ASIAN DUB FOUNDATION

Asian Dub Foundation were formed in 1993 at the Community Music centre in London, which had been established by jazz drummer John Stevens. The Dub Foundation line-up features Das, Chandrasonic, Deedar, Pandit G and Sun J, who perform a combination of ragga, garage punk and traditional Indian ragas. The fusion of the sounds has proved especially popular on the festival circuit, where the band have built a huge following. They have performed twice at the Essential Roots day festivals, sharing the same stage as Bunny Wailer, Buju Banton, Augustus Pablo and Lee Perry. By 1995 the group released their debut, *Facts & Fictions*, which clearly demonstrated the influence of Jamaican dub on their sound. They continued touring, proving especially popular in Europe where the band's follow-up, *Real Areas For Investigation*, was released in France. This album dealt with issues relating to the Indian diaspora, including miscarriages of justice and a chance to redress items of historical interest ignored by the historians. The group enjoyed media interest when pop group Primal Scream acknowledged them as the best live group in England, and a major label contract soon followed. The Foundation's credibility with the indie genre was further enhanced when Primal Scream were involved in producing tracks from their album. A variety of television appearances followed to promote the single, 'Change'. The group's second album was then remixed and re-released as *Rafi's Revenge*, paying lip service to the Pakistani-born Bollywood singer Mohamed Rafi.

● ALBUMS: *Facts & Fictions* (Nation 1995)★★★, *Rafi's Revenge* (London 1998)★★★.

ASTRAL PROJECTION

The roots of this pioneering Israeli trance outfit lie in the group SFX, formed in 1989 by Lior Perlmutter and Avi Nissim, who had already made a name for himself as an acid house DJ. After two years of recording and playing in Israel's underground clubs, they had their first release, 'Monster Mania', on the Belgian label Music Man Records. During the early 90s Perlmutter spent some time in the USA working as an engineer, and SFX consequently brought out four singles on X-Rave Records. Later, Yaniv Haviv, whom Perlmutter had known since childhood, and Guy Sabbag joined SFX back in Israel and in 1994 all four formed Trust In Trance Records. Their debut album, *Trust In Trance Vol. 1*, was released on that label through Phonokol Records later that year, after which Sabbag left the group to pursue his own interests. At this point Perlmutter, Nissim and Haviv opened their Dance City studio, where they began recording their second album as Astral Projection. *Trust In Trance Vol. 2* (1995) entered the Israeli album chart at number 2 and became popular with a number of European DJs; two tracks in particular, 'Mahadeva' (released as a single on Transient Records in 1996) and 'Power Gen', were favourites of Danny Rampling and Paul Oakenfold. Released in the UK through TIP Records, *Trust In Trance* was their most successful album yet and helped them to break into the European market. It was supported by the singles 'Enlightened Evolution' and 'People Can Fly' and by over 30 live shows throughout Israel and Europe. The following year the group switched to Transient Records for *The Astral Files*, which contained some new material as well as a number of remixes from the previous album. After its release, Haviv left the group to work on his own material. *Dancing Galaxies* presented a collection of new material in the same

vein as before, but was perhaps the most focused and consistent of all their albums to date. Astral Projection are known as the original and best exponents of the Israeli style of psychedelic trance, which they have distilled to its finest point while others have moved on to a new approach. Rather than the sparsely arranged abstract noises employed by many of their contemporaries, the group's sound relies on layered riffs based around Eastern-sounding scales, thick synth pads and heavy reverbs, while the solid, four-on-the-floor drum patterns reflect none of the tendencies towards more varied, funky breakbeats. Towards the end of the 90s, this style came under criticism from some areas as being formulaic and clumsy, as a large number of artists attempted to recreate the sound. However, few managed to match Astral Projection's economy, remarkably consistent production and logical, organic arrangements, which together created one of the most unique and identifiable sounds in their field.

● ALBUMS: *Trust In Trance Vol. 1* (Smart 1994), *Trust In Trance Vol. 2* (Smart 1995), *Trust In Trance* (TIP 1996)★★★, *The Astral Files* (Transient 1997)★★★, *Dancing Galaxies* (Transient 1997)★★★★.

ASTRALASIA

Astralasia rejoice in mystical techno/ambience, with song titles such as 'Genesis The Spark Of Life' and 'Astral Navigation', while their personnel are known as Swordfish, Nosmo, King Os and Moonboot. One ex-member was Jason Relf, whose father was the late Keith Relf - singer with the original Yardbirds. Jason in turn had enjoyed a brief stint as keyboardist in the Magic Mushroom Band before joining Astralasia. When Jason left the band he formed Booma with Scott James (ex-Shave Yer Tongue), who released an eponymous debut single on Leftfield's Hard Hands label. The duo had previously released a 12-inch, 'Pleasure', as SYT on Andy Weatherall's Sabres Of Paradise label. Relf has also released solo records as Solar Plexus and Tangled Feet.

● ALBUMS: *Astralasia* (Fungus 1990)★★★, *The Politics Of Ecstasy* (Magick Eye 1992)★★★, *Pitched Up At The Edge Of Reality* (Magick Eye 1993)★★★, *Whatever Happened To Utopia?* (Magick Eye 1994)★★★, *Axis Mundi* (Magick Eye 1995)★★★, *Astralogy* (Magick Eye 1995)★★★, *Seven Pointed Star* (Magick Eye 1996)★★★★, *White Bird* (Magick Eye 1998)★★★.

ATARI TEENAGE RIOT

This caustic punk/house collective makes music that rails against the rise of the fascist right in Germany. From Berlin, frontman Alec Empire grew up interested in the punk scene and was in bands from the age of 12, but later became involved with acid house. He began DJing in the late 80s and released politically minded techno tunes for the Force Inc label. Bored with the pulpit life of the DJ, he joined Carl Crack (b. Switzerland) and Hanin Elias (b. Spain) to play live again. Together they signed to Phonogram as Atari Teenage Riot; although heavily hyped, their records failed to sell in the anticipated quantities, despite an unlikely techno cover version of Sham 69's 'If The Kids Are United', and they were dropped after two singles. Empire founded the Digital Hardcore label to release extreme music from bands such as Shizuo, Ec8or and Christoph De Babalon. He continued to release material with Atari Teenage Riot and as a solo artist, under his own name and a multitude of pseudonyms (including The Jaguar, PJP, The Destroyer, Deathfunk, Safety Pin Sex).

● ALBUMS: *Delete Yourself* (DHR 1995)★★★, *Burn, Berlin, Burn!* (DHR 1997)★★, *The Future Of War* (DHR 1997)★★.

ATKINS, JUAN

b. 1962, Detroit, Michigan, USA. Atkins attended Belleville High until 1980, where he met Derrick May and Kevin Saunderson, his future techno compatriots. He acquired his love of dance music listening to the various mix shows on the radio, and in particular those of the Detroit DJ The Electrifying Mojo. Inspired by the emergence of synthesizer technology, Atkins first came to prominence in the early 80s with Cybotron, a techno-electro outfit he formed with Rick Davis, achieving some success, most notably with 'Clear'. From 1985 Atkins started working solo as Model 500, releasing polished, minimalist, hi-tech dance music gems such as 'No UFO's', 'The Chase' and 'Night Drive' on his own Metroplex label (home to the first releases by many of the Detroit stars), which were pivotal in the development of techno (most of these were later reissued on R&S Records' *Classics*). Atkins' reputation took off in the late 80s, when the new Detroit dance movement reached the shores of Europe, and was frequently invited to remix tracks for artists as diverse as Inner City, Coldcut, Fine Young Cannibals, Seal and the Style Council. During the exploitative early 90s Atkins remained justifiably aloof, with his own artistic output somewhat limited, although during this period he continued to work in conjunction with Mike Banks and Underground Resistance, helping to produce such classics as Underground Resistance's *Galaxy 2 Galaxy* and the excellent Red Planet series of releases.

In 1992 he reopened his Metroplex label, and when Model 500 signed to R&S, releases such as the *Classics* compilation and the brilliant EP *Sonic Sunset* received the attention they deserved. With the album *Deep Space*, Atkins treated a new generation of dance enthusiasts to his typically highly crafted compositions. More recently, a second compilation of his earlier, Metroplex-based work under the name Infiniti has been released by Tresor Records. Although at times sounding formulaic, the compilation does include 'Game One' (produced with Orlando Voorn), one of Atkins' most memorable records, capturing his classically minimal yet warm style.

● ALBUMS: as Model 500 *Deep Space* (R&S 1995)★★★.

● COMPILATIONS: as Model 500 *Classics* (R&S 1993)★★★★, as Infiniti *The Infiniti Collection* (Tresor 1996)★★★.

ATLAS, NATASHA

(see Transglobal Underground)

ATOM HEART

Atom Heart is the latest in a prestigious list of 'name' producers from Frankfurt, Germany that includes Sven Vath, Peter Namlock and Jam El Mar of Jam And Spoon. He started making music in 1991 and within three years had released over 60 different records on a variety of labels: Pod, Rising High, Delirium, After 6am, US Instinct and Fax. Among his biggest tunes were 'I'm A Secretary' on Fax, 'Mihon' by Ongaku, and 'Elektronikkaa' by Pink Elm and Atom Heart on Rising High. He also works as Atmo Shinzu, Cover Atomique, Datacide, Millennium, I, Lisa Carbon and Resistance D. The name Atom Heart was chosen because he was, and remains, interested in the combination of the emotional and the mechanical/technical.

● ALBUMS: *Softcore* (Fax 1994)★★★.

AUDIO TWO

The sons of First Priority label boss Nat Robinson, and brothers of USA rappers MC Lyte, Mike and DJ Gizmo Dee certainly began their careers with a pedigree. Though occasionally they have fallen foul of the political correctness lobby, there is much to admire in their descriptions of Brooklyn inner-city life, with a good eye for detail, particularly on breakthrough singles 'Top Billing' and 'Hickeys On My Neck'. Their second album contained a career high and low, the elegiac, distressing 'Get Your Mother Off The Crack', soured by the openly anti-gay 'Whatcha' Lookin' At?'.
● ALBUMS: *What More Can I Say?* (First Priority/Atlantic 1988)★★, *I Don't Care - The Album* (First Priority/Atlantic 1990)★★.

AURAL ASSAULT

An important component of the UK techno label Rising High's roster is Mike Ash, whose home studio recordings have gradually established his reputation on the hardcore techno scene. However, his interest in dance music grew out of the late 80s' acid movement, a heavy nod to which occurs on Aural Assault's *Planet 303* EP. His work under this title is characterized by disconcertingly hard rhythms, broken by samples, often taken from film dialogue. As such he has released some of Rising High's most successful tracks ('Pink And Purple Experience', 'Total Techno'). He also records for RH sister label Sappho, under the title Space Cadet (*Don't You Want My Love* and *Third Wave* EPs). He has formed his own record label, Dancing In Complete Apathy, and maintains links with Rising High.

AUTECHRE

Sean Booth (b. 1972, Rochdale, Lancashire, England) and Rob Brown (b. 1970, Torquay, England) met in Rochdale in 1987 when they discovered a mutual interest in the hip-hop scene. Over the next few years, first acid house and later more industrial sounds, notably Meat Beat Manifesto and Renegade Soundwave, came to their attention and they were consequently inspired to begin making their own electronic music. In 1991 they released the single 'Cavity Job' under the name MYSLB Productions but unfortunately they fell foul of cowboy record companies. Spurred on by the success of LFO (from Leeds), Booth and Brown sent a demo to Warp Records who released 'Crystel' and 'The Egg' on their acclaimed *Artificial Intelligence* compilation in 1992. Refusing to follow the fashions and formulae of much contemporary house and techno, these two tracks featured more subtle melodies and electronic sounds, and more diverse, hip-hop-related beats. They continued this approach on the album *Incunabula*, which entered the UK indie charts at number 1 and was the last in the Warp's Artificial Intelligence series of artist albums. Following the successful 10-inch box-set of 'Basscadet' remixes, in 1994 they released the *Anti* EP which was written in response to the government's Criminal Justice Bill. The b-side, 'Flutter', was written with non-repetitive beats, 'to show how stupid the whole thing is . . . You should be able to play this all night long without the party being stopped.' The proceeds were donated to the civil rights organization Liberty. After the release of their harder-edged second album, *Amber*, Autechre made a tour of small venues around the UK in 1995 and the following year ventured further afield to Europe and America. Unlike many electronic acts, the group perform entirely live, improvising their manipulations of sound and textures. *Tri Repetae*, their toughest-sounding work to date, was described as 'a random journey around the extreme edges of electronica' and 'hardly human', and was generally well received. In 1997 they released *Chiastic Slide*. The duo have remixed a number of artists including Beaumont Hannant and Saint Etienne. Autechre have, on the whole, ignored the phases that quickly come and go as much of their music is not aimed at the dancefloor. While this has led many to congratulate Autechre for their experimental approach, some might feel that, having found their own formula, they have since been complacent in remaining within its boundaries.
● ALBUMS: *Incunabula* (Warp 1993)★★★, *Amber* (Warp 1994)★★★★, *Tri Repetae* (Warp 1995)★★★, *Chiastic Slide* (Warp 1997)★★★.

AZ

b. Brooklyn, New York, US rapper AZ made his debut on Nas's acclaimed *Illmatic* debut, guesting on that album's 'Life's A Bitch'. Raised in the same Queensbridge housing complex that spawned Mobb Deep, Mic Geronimo and Nas, he made his solo bow in 1995 with 'Sugar Hill', which instantly made headway in the *Billboard* R&B, rap and pop charts. Like Nas before him, AZ's concerns were firmly rooted in the ghetto life that produced him,

and his attempts to break free from it - as the single intimated, 'No more cuttin' grams or wrapping grands up in rubber bands'. The title, 'Sugar Hill', referred to the suburban district so beloved of the black middle class, which had given its name to rap's first proper record label. It prefaced AZ's debut album, released in October, one of the strongest hip-hop debuts of the 90s. In 1997 AZ collaborated with Foxy Brown, Nas and Dr. Dre as part of the hugely successful rap 'supergroup', the Firm. *Pieces Of A Man* was a strong second album, with funky production from Dr. Dre and Trackmasterz adding commercial appeal to excellent tracks such as the single 'What's The Deal'.
● ALBUMS: *Doe Or Die* (EMI 1995)★★★★, *Pieces Of A Man* (Noo Trybe 1998)★★★★.

AZULI

This record label is run by Dave Piccioni through the Black Market dance shop, and specializes in high-quality garage material. Azuli's output began with Chocolate Fudge's 'In A Fantasy' (1991), a collaboration between Miles Morgan, 'Baby' Sean Casey and Larry Dundas, and the *Disco Elements* and *Sensory Elements* EPs. The first two of these were released bedecked with New York telephone numbers and shrinkwrapped to give the impression of being imports. The following year saw Underground Mass featuring Lisa White's 'Music (Takes Control)' and 'Didn't I'. The label continued to expand, bringing other catalogues such as Paramodo from the USA and their own Gyroscope under the Black Market/Azuli umbrella. Their 1994 roster included Andrea Mendez's 'Real Love', while they enjoyed a major hit with label stalwart Romanthony's 'In The Mix', a disco/house groover released as a tribute to Tony Humphries, with his name used repeatedly as its hookline. Romanthony had been discovered by Piccioni on one of his frequent trips to the USA.

B

B-BOY RECORDS

B-Boy was formed in 1987 in the Bronx's East 132nd Street, by Jack Allen and Bill Kamarra. The label, one of the first specialist independent rap concerns, came to prominence with the advent of Boogie Down Productions' *Criminal Minded*. It would go on to release no less than three related items following the death of Scott La Rock - *Man And His Music*, *Hot Club Version* and then the 'remix' selection, *A Memory Of A Man And His Music*. The label's most notable other signings were the Cold Crush Brothers and J.V.C.F.O.R.C.E., alongside KG The All, Michael G, Levi 167, Spyder D and Sparkey D. However, just as it was gaining a foothold in rap circles, Bill Kamarra was imprisoned and the momentum was lost.
● COMPILATIONS: Various Artists *B-Boy Sampler* (B-Boy 1988)★★★.

B., DEREK

b. Derek Bowland, 1966, Bow, East London, England. Derek grew up a fan of the Who as well as the more conventional black sounds of Aretha Franklin, Al Green and Bob Marley. He started out as a DJ when he was 15 as part of a mobile unit touring London clubs. He then moved into radio, working for pirate stations such as Kiss FM and LWR before beginning his own WBLS station. In 1987 he became bored with the disc jockey role and took a job at the Music Of Life label as an A&R man. Alongside Simon Harris (world yo-yo champion, it has been alleged) he signed several of the most notable early UK hip-hop groups, including Overlord X, MC Duke, Hijack, the She Rockers and Demon Boyz. He subsequently started to record his own material for the label. While in New York (visiting his family who had moved there), Derek met the DJ Mr Magic, who played his record to Profile Records, granting him a licensing contract in the USA. His debut single, 'Rock The Beat', and its follow up, 'Get Down' (which featured the rapping of EZQ - Derek B under another pseudonym), both made an early impact. His hip-hop sounded a little ham-fisted in comparison to New York's more natural feel, which made the self-congratulatory raps sound increasingly hysterical: 'We kept on goin' for hours and hours/Straight after to the bathroom for a shower/Just before leaving she held me close and said/I think you're the greatest thing in bed' ('Get Down'). He hit the UK charts in 1988 with 'Goodgroove' and was the only rapper on the Free Mandela bill at Wembley Stadium. Further minor hits came with 'Bad Young Brother' and 'We've Got The Juice', after he set up his own Tuff Audio label through Phonogram. However, that relationship declined when he attempted to push for a harder sound. Further one-off contracts with a variety of labels failed to offer anything of significance, though while at SBK he did ghost-write tracks for Vanilla Ice. He then became a member of PoW.

● ALBUMS: *Bullet From A Gun* (Tuff Audio 1988)★★★.

B., HOWIE

b. Howard Bernstein, England. Glasgow-based producer Howie B shot to fame in 1994 as one of the most favoured exponents of trip-hop, even though he himself remained suspicious of the term. Renowned for his productions of the scene's leading artists, Tricky and the Mo Wax roster, he had previously worked with acts as diverse as Soul II Soul, Massive Attack, Goldie and Siouxsie And The Banshees. In 1994 he founded Pussyfoot Records and was engaged in a number of projects, including the *One Hell Of A Storm* set, which saw poets and musicians such as Lemn Sissay, Malika B and Haji-Mike join together for a dubbed-up funk session. Bernstein's impressive contribution was a collaboration with the poet Patience Agbabi on 'There's Gonna Be One Hell Of A Storm'. He then joined Mat Ducasse for an album, *No 1.*, credited to Skylab. This exhibited the influence of spaghetti westerns and classical and ambient music, and in interviews, Bernstein readily admitted the influence that Brian Eno's *My Life In The Bush Of Ghosts* had had on the album. After this he worked simultaneously on several projects, including work with the Stereo MC's singer Cath Coffey and Japan's Major Force West, and also on Björk's *Post*. In 1995 he worked on U2's *Passengers* project, produced remixes for Annie Lennox, Simply Red and New Order and added samples to the 1996 U2 album.

● ALBUMS: *Music For Babies* (Polydor 1996)★★★, *Turn The Dark Off* (Polydor 1997)★★★★.

B., LISA

b. Lisa Barbuscia, c.1971, USA. A corporate-groomed garage house diva, Barbuscia attended the New York School of Music and the Performing Arts (as featured in the popular *Fame* television series) before being taken on by a modelling agency at the age of 17. In turn she won a recording contract with London dance subsidiary ffrr, who teamed her with producers of the calibre of Mike McEvoy (Soul II Soul), Paul Oakenfold and Gianfranco Bortolotti (of Italy's Media team). The resulting material, typified by singles such as 1993's 'Fascinated', was very pop-orientated and, it was suggested, none too authentic. Her record company had trouble convincing the dance world of the former model's credentials, and perhaps her relationship with the Marquess Of Cholmondeley (30th in line to the throne) also hampered her musical credibility.

B., STEVIE

Miami, Florida-based Latin hip-hop artist, whose records were bedecked with vocals for which the term crooning was not too strong. As well as dance numbers and rap excursions, he was equally adept at balladeering. In fact, the latter style gave him his first crossover hit, 'Because I Love You (The Postman Song)'. However, long before he entered the mainstream, Stevie B was selling huge quantities of his product, going platinum and gold on several records in ethnic markets. As his career progressed, the mood swung from rap to slick dance or swingbeat. It was all carried off with a lack of subtlety and a pre-teen image.

● ALBUMS: *Party Your Body* (LMR 1988)★★★, *In My Eyes* (LMR 1989)★★, *Love & Emotion* (LMR 1991)★★.

B12

Based in Ilford, Essex, England, B12 consist of Michael Golding (a computer expert) and Steven Rutter (a bank employee). Single releases prior to their album for Warp were credited to alter egos Red Cell and Musicology and released on their own B12 label. Another pseudonym is C-Metric. When *Electro Soma* arrived as the fourth instalment in Warp's *Artificial Intelligence* series, it made a good impression. The intention was to try to create the feel of pure, timeless techno: 'Derrick May, Juan Atkins and the rest of the guys started something that I suppose we feel obliged to continue.' However, as they were keen to point out, this was hardly conventional dance music: 'I don't believe anyone's ever played it in a club.'

● ALBUMS: *Electro Soma* (Warp 1993)★★★, *Time Tourist* (Warp 1996)★★★.

BABBLE

UK pop/dance band Babble are a duo of Tom Bailey (b. 18 June 1957, Halifax, Yorkshire, England) and Alannah Currie (b. 20 September 1959, Auckland, New Zealand; percussion, saxophone) - formerly members of the hugely successful 80s group the Thompson Twins. Babble was inaugurated in order to allow them to tread a more experimental path, particularly in the use of keyboard textures and electronica without their previous reliance on pop choruses. *The Stone* revealed how deeply Bailey and Currie had immersed themselves in club culture, featuring dub basslines set against house and techno rhythms. *Ether*, released in 1996, continued this refinement. It was promoted by the single 'Love Has No Name', remixed by Todd Terry, with hip-hop/R&B singer Teremoana Rapley on vocals.

● ALBUMS: *The Stone* (Eternal/WEA 1993)★★★, *Ether* (Eternal/WEA 1996)★★★.

BABY D

After playing with a variety of bands and working as session musicians, Baby D were formed in 1990 in north-west London, England. Featuring Baby D (b. *c*.1969; vocals), MC Nino (b. *c*.1972; keyboards, vocals), Claudio Galdez (b. *c*.1970; keyboards, vocals) and Dice (b. *c*.1970; writer and producer), they released their first single, 'Daydreaming', in January 1991. Though it failed to reach the national charts, it rose to number 27 in the dance charts. Their first major success came in December 1993 when 'Destiny' reached number 69 in the UK charts. 'Casanova', released in July 1994, was a similar minor success, but the group's fortunes changed substantially with the release of 'Let Me Be Your Fantasy' in November 1994. This rose to number 1 in the UK charts, and sold just short of half a million copies. It had originally topped dance charts two years prior to its mainstream breakthrough. The follow-up single was a cover version of the Korgis' 'Everybody's Gotta Learn Sometime'. By this time, original member Dice had left the band, though he still helped out

in a production capacity. Before the release of 'Everybody's Gotta Learn Sometime', it emerged that another band, NRG, intended to record it, leading to a struggle for the publishing rights. Baby D's version eventually climbed to number 3 in the UK charts in June 1995. 'So Pure' reached the same position in January 1996, and was followed by the band's debut album.

● ALBUMS: *Deliverance* (London 1996)★★★.

BABY FORD

b. Peter Ford, Bolton, Lancashire, England, though he moved to New Zealand at the age of 10. Ford, based in Wigan, is a prolific recording artist whose studio sounds can be heard on dozens of recordings, including 'Oochy Koochy (FU Baby Yeh Yeh)', a classic acid house track, which was a hit in 1987, and 'Chikki Chikki Ahh Ahh', both of which were released on the vibrant *Ford Trax* EP. They were co-produced with Eon. 'It's not hardcore,' he said, 'I'm about moods and feelings.' Various remix projects followed, and he played stylophone at venues such as the Hacienda in Manchester during his tours. The limited edition 'Change' was released in 1990, then 'In Your Blood' the following year, both of which unveiled a more pure techno approach. He moved further away from pop accessibility with the *B Ford 9* album, exploring a minimal analogue sound. He has also recorded for Brute Records as Doucen ('White Sands'), and on his own Ifach, Trelik and PAL-SL labels as Perbec, Baird Remo, El Mal, Casino Classix, Solcyc, Eco Tourist and Minimal Man (with Eon). Several of these tracks were reinterpreted on the minimalistic *Headphoneasy Rider*, which appeared on the Black Market label.

● ALBUMS: *Ford Trax* mini-album (Rhythm King 1990)★★★★, *Ooo The World Of Baby Ford* (Rhythm King 1990)★★★, *B Ford 9* (Rhythm King 1992)★★★★, *Headphoneasy Rider* (Black Market 1997)★★★.

BABYFACE

b. Kenneth Edmonds, 10 April 1959, Indianapolis, Indiana, USA. Babyface's achievements as a songwriter and producer throughout the late 80s and 90s, especially with L.A. Reid, sometimes overshadowed his own efforts as a performer, which go back to the mid-70s with the funk outfit Manchild. His early solo efforts showed a sophisticated, adult-orientated strain of urban soul, going against the current grain of rap-influenced explicitness and raunchy swingbeat; wisely, perhaps, as his light, pleasant voice could not really compare to earthier singers such as R. Kelly. It was not until 1995, when the single 'When Can I See You' won a Grammy, that he could claim the commercial success that had been heaped on his own protégés such as Boyz II Men, Bobby Brown and Toni Braxton. In fact, since the split with Reid, Babyface's main success has been as a producer and writer of film soundtracks, with *The Bodyguard* and *Waiting To Exhale* both going multi-platinum. Expectations were high for his 1996 solo album, which should have sealed his claim to be taken seriously as a contemporary soul performer. Unfortunately, *The Day* turned out to be something of a back-slappers' showcase; guest spots by the likes of Stevie Wonder, Eric Clapton, LL Cool J, Mariah Carey and even Shalamar could not obscure the fact that the songs Babyface kept for himself were simply not as strong as those he provided for other members of the R&B royalty.

● ALBUMS: *Lovers* (Solar 1987)★★, *Tender Lover* (Solar 1989)★★, *A Closer Look* (Solar 1991)★★, *For The Cool In You* (Epic 1993)★★★, *The Day* (Epic 1996)★★, *MTV Unplugged NYC 1997* (Epic 1997)★★.

BADMARSH

b. Yemen. This DJ and producer grew up in east London, England, and consequently absorbed a range of musical styles from various cultures as a child (his name is Urdu for scoundrel or trickster). While he was working for a reggae label that hired sound systems and PAs to clubs, he came into contact with dance music and began to DJ. With his brother, he ran a pirate radio station in Walthamstow called Ali FM and later played house at Labyrinth. It was a natural progression to begin making his own music, and as Easy Mo he released a number of house tracks on his own label, Pure Vibes. In the mid-90s he turned towards drum 'n' bass and signed to Outcaste Records, where he worked on various projects that reflected his multicultural background. After the promo 'I Am That Type Of Badmarsh', he contributed to Nitin Sawhney's second album, *Displacing The Priest* (1996), and as Badmarsh And Shri he worked with the multi-instrumentalist Shrikanth Sriram for the album *Dancing Drums* (1998). Here the pair blended funky, busy breakbeats and dubby grooves with traditional Indian instruments and Shri's nimble bass guitar playing. Some tracks, such as the excellent reworkings of Shankar's 'Dancing Drums', employ Indian-

sounding melodic ideas, while others, notably 'Gharana' and '130 Steps', focus more on rhythm and percussion. The album also contains an excellent version of the Dave Pyke Set's late 60s sitar-led track 'Mathar', while the title track was featured on Outcaste's *Untouchable Outcaste Beats* compilation in 1997. At the same time, Shri continued to work as a solo artist and released some material with Ubiquity Records and a second promo on Outcaste, 'I Am That Type Of Badmarsh II'. He has DJed and performed in various countries around the world, including the USA and France.

● ALBUMS: as Badmarsh And Shri *Dancing Drums* (Outcaste 1997)★★★★.

BAHMADIA

b. Philadelphia, USA. Considered by many as a natural descendant of Queen Latifah, US rapper Bahmadia had already 'paid her dues' to hip-hop by the time she made her career breakthrough in 1996 - by which time she was already a 28-year-old mother of two. She had begun by break-dancing in Philadelphia at the age of 10, before she became a DJ and MC at 'block parties' from 1983 onwards. It took the release of 'Ska Rock' by the Funky Four (Plus One More) to inspire her to make records. Years of demo recordings failed to secure a professional career, however, despite guest appearances on recordings by others. Her 1993 independent single, 'Funk Vibe', finally convinced others of her abilities, including Gang Starr's Guru who offered his help and encouragement. This eventually led to a contract with Guru's UK record label, Cooltempo Records. *Kollage*, released in 1996, comprised a series of thoughtful, lyrically complex raps rooted in her 18 years at the heart of the hip-hop experience.

● ALBUMS: *Kollage* (Cooltempo 1996)★★★.

BAKER, ARTHUR

b. 22 April 1955, Boston, Massachusetts, USA. Arthur Baker began in music as a club DJ in Boston, Massachusetts, playing soul and R&B for the clubgoers. He moved into production for Emergency Records shortly thereafter, including work on Northend and Michelle Wallace's 'Happy Days' (his first record, only released in Canada, was Hearts Of Stone's 'Losing You'). This preceded a move to New York where he became intrigued by the rap scene of 1979. He entered the studios once more, this time in tandem with Joe Bataan, to record a pseudo rap record, 'Rap-O-

Clap-O', but the projected record company, London, went under before its release. The proceeds of the session did emerge later, although Baker went uncredited, after he returned to Boston. His next project was 'Can You Guess What Groove This Is?' by Glory, a medley that hoped to find a novelty market. From there, back in New York, he joined Tom Silverman's Tommy Boy Records operation to record 'Jazzy Sensation' with Afrika Bambaataa and Shep Pettibone. Afterwards, he partnered Bambaataa on his seminal 1982 'Planet Rock' single, before starting Streetwise Records. Though interwoven with the development of hip-hop, Baker's later releases were inspired by the club scene (Wally Jump Jnr's 'Tighten Up', Jack E Makossa's 'The Opera House' and Criminal Orchestra Element's 'Put The Needle On The Record'). He went on to become an internationally renowned producer, working with legends such as Bob Dylan and Bruce Springsteen, and performing important remixing work for artists including New Order. In 1989 he collaborated with the Force MD's, ABC and OMD, among others, on a showcase album that saw Baker working through various dance styles under his own auspices. A year was spent working on a biography of Quincy Jones's life before returning in 1991 with rapper Wendell Williams for club-orientated material such as 'Everybody', and a commercially unsuccessful follow-up to the Merge album.

● ALBUMS: with the Backbeat Disciples Merge (A&M 1989)★★★, Give In To The Rhythm (Arista 1991)★★★.

BALEARIC

The most difficult of the dance and techno genres to describe, at least in terms of musical content. Balearic is a term that documents the sets played in the Balearic islands (notably Ibiza) in the mid-80s. This 'feel good' vibe was imported back to England from venues such as Amnesia, Koo and Pacha by Danny Rampling, Paul Oakenfold and Nicky Holloway in the late 80s. Oakenfold even held a 'Ibiza Reunion' party in London, although the music's impact rapidly faded as house progressed into the 90s. Experienced clubbers still go misty-eyed at the mention of the original Ibiza party scene, which the UK partially emulated. As a music, Balearic also accounted for records outside of the conventional dance format as long as the atmosphere, one of uplifting, happy, commercial music, was maintained.

BALL, DAVE

b. 3 May 1959, Blackpool, Lancashire, England. Ball came to notice as the keyboard player in the duo Soft Cell with Marc Almond. His early interest in electronics crystallized at Leeds Polytechnic where he joined a band that utilized three vacuum cleaners. This led to his composing music to accompany Almond's theatrical shows and the formation of Soft Cell in October 1979. Although contributing much to their sound, Ball maintained a low profile. In June 1983, he scored the music for a revival of Tennessee Williams' play Suddenly Last Summer. Later that year Ball released the solo instrumental In Strict Tempo, before the break-up of Soft Cell in December. The following year he wrote the score for the German film Decoder and produced the Virgin Prunes. The soundtrack to Derek Jarman's Imagining Oktober followed in 1985, and in 1987 he produced Jack The Tab.

By the end of 1988 Ball had produced a single for train-robber Ronnie Biggs in Brazil and had started working with Jack The Tab's acid-house singer Richard Norris. This evolved into psychedelic dance outfit the Grid, which quickly found acceptance in ambient/new age/dance clubs by exploring the interface between Kraftwerk, Brian Eno and Pink Floyd. Other current activities include composing music for television commercials (Shell, TSB, etc.), film soundtracks, remix/production work for Art Of Noise, Bhundu Boys and Marc Almond, plus one-off collaborations with LSD guru Dr. Timothy Leary and Rolf Harris.

● ALBUMS: In Strict Tempo (Some Bizzare 1983)★★★.

BANCO DE GAIA

With a background in classical music, heavy metal, folk, jazz and bhangra, Toby Marks formed Banco De Gaia in Leamington Spa in 1989 after absorbing sounds he heard while travelling around the world. For the first six years he worked closely with the producer and sound engineer Andy Guthrie. Along with groups such as Transglobal Underground and Loop Guru, Banco De Gaia began performing live at Megadog and Whirl-Y-Gig events, which benefited from a more broad-minded and eclectic feel than most clubs, often featuring 'world dance'. He first released material on tapes and Freeform Flutes And Fading Tibetans on his own World Bank label. Following tracks on a number of compilations, including Planet Dog Records' *Feed Your Head*, Marks released 'Desert Wind' in November 1993, which was followed by the albums *Maya* and *Last Train To Lhasa*. While some dance music is often criticized as formulaic and lacking individuality, Banco De Gaia's varied melodies, rhythms and textures make a refreshing change, blending techno, hip-hop, ambience, dub and rock with samples of traditional music from around the world, particularly the Middle East and Asia. Tracks such as 'Last Train To Lhasa' and 'Amber' encapsulate Banco's moderate-paced, melodic sound, while 'Kuos' and 'Data Inadequate' present a more percussive, four-on-the-floor side; 'China', complete with storyteller, provides some moments of blissful ambience. *Live At Glastonbury* is more upbeat than the studio albums, with less ambient tracks, different mixes and an enthusiastic festival audience. The 1997 release *Big Men Cry* is perhaps the weakest of all, at times sounding rather like Pink Floyd, but still features some memorable moments, particularly 'Drippy' and 'Drunk As A Monk'. In live performances since *Big Men Cry*, Marks has worked with a live band that includes percussion, drums, bass guitar, saxophone and flute, sometimes edging towards a rock sound.

● ALBUMS: *Maya* (Planet Dog 1994)★★★, *Last Train To Lhasa* (Planet Dog 1995)★★★★, *Live At Glastonbury* (Planet Dog 1996)★★★★, *Big Men Cry* (Planet Dog 1997)★★★.

BAND OF GYPSIES

Band Of Gypsies are alternatively known as 3 Man Island, and consist of the production, writing and recording team of Nigel Swanston and Tim Cox, not to be confused with the Jimi Hendrix trio of the same name. Swanston and Cox met when the latter auditioned as a guitarist for Swanston's band (eventually gaining a job as their keyboard player). They have been working with the Pulse 8 label since their present manager, Steve Long, found a record they had produced and traced them through their publishing house. As 3 Man Island they had already enjoyed a US Top 10 hit with a 'joke' record, while the original 'Band Of Gypsies' project was actually a track developed over a longer period of time that eventually emerged as a first single (eponymously credited). They continued to use the name for their productions for Pulse 8 with Sue Chaloner and Rozalla. Their own singles include 'Take Me Higher' and 'Stand Up', recorded with ex-September vocalist Juiliette Jaimes.

BANDULU

Formerly members of the Infonet Records network, which they helped establish alongside founder Chris Abbott, Bandulu are John O'Connell (b. *c*.1970, England) and former graffiti artists/breakdancers Jamie Bissmire (b. *c*.1969, England) and Lucien Thompson (b. *c*.1970, England). In the early 90s they established their headquarters at Bissmire's parents' home in Muswell Hill, north London. Influenced by Detroit techno, New York electro and Chicago house, Bandulu additionally added tribal percussion, sampling and 'real' instruments (guitars, drums, etc.) to their potential musical sources. Retrospectively, the group have claimed their primary influence on forming in 1990 to be the creative decline of dance music at that time. 'It was all Kylie Minogue, all pop music. So we just decided to each put £50 in a pot and go into a studio', claimed O'Connell. Bandulu's early singles, such as 'Phaze-In-Version', were widely categorized within the fledgling 'trance' house movement, though the execution was more intricate and more flexible than that of many of their peers who relied more on simple repetition. Their debut release was 'Better Nation', followed by 'Internal Ocean' at the end of 1992. They also record under aliases such as ECC (Earth Coincidence Control), Sons Of The Subway, Koh Tao, Escobar, Shy Man and Thunderground. As the latter they include 'fourth member' Lewis Keogh, the Orb's resident DJ. With Bandulu he remixed the Orb's 'UFOrb'. Thunderground is also the name of the club night they host at London's Bass Clef venue. With a discernible debt to the experimental electronic music of Philip Glass and Laurie Anderson, Bandulu have nevertheless forged their own identity in the dance world. In the summer of 1994 they released another widely admired single, 'Presence', followed by a second studio album. In 1995 they signed to Warner Brothers Records' subsidiary Blanco Y Negro, for whom their debut release was the promotional-only EP *Running Time*. This was accompanied by live appearances at the Orbit Club's 5th Birthday party, the Omen in Germany and the Ministry Of Sound's celebratory night at Wembley Stadium. In March 1996 they released a further EP, *Troubleshooter*, which prefaced their major label debut album, *Cornerstone*. This included nods to

prevailing dance trends, such as jungle in 'Selah' and hard house in 'Jester'. It was promoted with a series of live appearances, although critics judged these shows to be inferior to the efforts of peers such as Orbital and the Prodigy in translating techno to a performance art medium.
● ALBUMS: *Guidance* (Infonet 1992)★★★, *Antimatters* (Infonet 1994)★★★, *Cornerstone* (Blanco Y Negro 1996)★★★.

BANG THE PARTY

This London-based techno/dance duo were responsible for putting kinky sex on the agenda of the deep house scene. A forerunner of the cybersex, virtual-reality revolution, Bang The Party, comprising DJ Kid Batchelor (Keith Franklyn) and Bullet, broke through with their 1990 hit, 'Bang Bang You're Dead', which introduced its approach with the line: 'It's basically using music as an everyday stimulant to your heart.' The single was typical of their craft - syncopated, almost hypnotic, rhythms aimed firmly at producing a sensual atmosphere. Franklyn went on to join Azuli artists KCC.
● ALBUMS: *Back To Prison* (Warriors Dance 1990)★★.

BANTU

Formed in Liverpool, Merseyside, England, this hip-hop trio made their debut with a promotional single, 'Urbanglo', its meaning translating as Urban Anglo or Black British, in the autumn of 1991. It earned them a reputation as 'the 90s version of the Last Poets' among some critics. As spokesman Ibrahim pointed out: 'White people have had their time in Liverpool, like the Beatles, but that basically came off the back of what black people had done'. Their track revisited black British musical achievements, from Soul II Soul to Loose Ends. Bantu themselves had something of a pedigree. They had originally formed in 1984, leaving for New York the next year to work with Jalal Nuridin of the Last Poets and producer Davey D. Unfortunately, they proved unable to follow up their excellent debut.

BASEHEAD

aka dcBasehead, from Maryland, Washington, USA. Playing a cut-and-paste combination of rap, R&B, reggae and funk, Basehead comprises frontman Michael Ivey (vocals, guitar, writer, producer), backed by his DJ, Paul 'Unique' Howard, guitarist Keith Lofton, drummer Brian Hendrix and bass player Bill Conway. Their sound has been loosely categorized as alternative dance music or intelligent hip-hop. A debut album was recorded, intially for small independent concern Emigre, in 1991, on a tiny budget. 'There are hip-hop elements in there, but if a hardcore hip-hop fan bought it, they might be disappointed', was Ivey's frank description in 1992. *Play With Toys* gained strong reviews and extensive airplay, with Ivey fêted as one of hip-hop's most imaginative talents. *Not In Kansas Anymore* was equally enthralling, and featured Ivey's full touring band on several tracks. In 1994, Ivey put together the B.Y.O.B collective, with shared songwriting and vocal contributions. He reassembled Basehead in 1996, releasing the spiritually inclined *Faith*.
● ALBUMS: *Play With Toys* (Emigre/Imago 1991)★★★★, *Not In Kansas Anymore* (Imago 1993)★★★, as B.Y.O.B (13/Rykodisc 1994)★★★, *Faith* (Imago 1996)★★★.

BASEMENT BOYS

The Basement Boys are a Baltimore dance/techno production team consisting of Tommy Davies (b. c.1958), Jay Steinhour (b. c.1948) and Teddy Douglas (b. c.1963). They first came to notice by taking the Crystal Waters track 'Gypsy Woman (La De Dee)' into the clubs with their 'Stripped To The Bone' remix. It eventually reached number 2 on the mainstream charts. Their first credit arrived in 1986 with a remix of Rose Royce's 'Love Don't Live Here Anymore' for Jump Street. They also produced a track for Profile entitled 'Don't Blame Me', credited to Sublevel featuring Andrea Holdclaw. The big break came with Ultra Nate's 'It's Over Now', which was heavily supported by Tony Humphries. The trio went on to produce an EP for Nu Groove as 33 1/3, and then 'Tonite' as Those Guys for MCA. Other successes included the succulent Mass Order tune, 'Lift Every Voice (Take Me Away)'. They have continued to remix widely, counting among their core clients Cut N Move ('Get Serious') and Paula Abdul (*Vibeology* EP).
● ALBUMS: *Blue Notes In The Basement* (Warners 1991)★★★.

BASS BUMPERS

This Germany-based dance/techno act consists of Henning Reith, Caba Kroll (from Bochum's Tarm Center) and vocalist Nana, and they signed to the Dusseldorf-based Dance Street label in 1990. The resultant 'Can't Stop Dancing' became a huge underground hit throughout Europe and the USA that summer, even making the *Billboard* charts. When the group returned a year later with a new single, 'Get The Big Bass', rapper E-Mello (b. Ian Freeman, England) had stepped in for Nana. However, it was early 1994 before they began to make their presence felt again with 'The Music's Got Me', primarily through the commercial success of its Paul Gotel remix.

● ALBUMS: *Bass Bumpers* (ZYX 1992)★★★.
● COMPILATIONS: *Best Of Bass Bumpers* (Dance Street 1995)★★★.

BASS IS BASE

Formed in Toronto, Canada, Bass Is Base is a multi-ethnic group comprising Chin Injeti (b. India; bass, vocals), rapper MC Mystic (b. Roger Mooking, Trinidad) and Ivana Santilli (keyboards, vocals; of Italian extraction). Influenced by Philly soul, Seattle rock, calypso and soca, the group's sound reflects the ethnic melting pot that is modern Toronto. Injeti had formerly studied music at the University of Toronto, while Santilli is also a classically trained pianist who previously performed with her father's Latin American band. Both were originally members of the group Syndicate 305 when they met Mooking at the 1993 Music West conference in Vancouver, where he was performing with Maximum Definitive. When that group won a Muchmusic video award, Mooking invited his new acquaintances to back him during his spot at the television presentation. Within a few months the trio had coalesced in a new group, Bass Is Base. After supporting artists including Jamiroquai, Galliano and the Pharcyde on their Canadian tours, they recorded their first album in two weeks in Injeti's brother's bedroom. Self-distributed and promoted, it sold a respectable 20,000 copies after a single and video taken from it, 'Funkmobile', received substantial airplay. The album won them a Juno Award for Best R&B/Soul Recording and touring engagements with Barenaked Ladies and Crash Test Dummies. They eventually signed a new contract with A&M Records subsidiary Loose Cannon after deflecting nearly a dozen other offers. Loose Cannon president Lisa Cortez evidently won their blessing after she had travelled to see them and became so excited she ended the evening dancing on the stage.

Their debut major label album was produced with Digable Planets, De La Soul and Marxman collaborators Shane Faber and Mike Mangini. It included six songs reworked from their debut album.

● ALBUMS: *First Impressions For The Bottom Jigglers* (SoulShack 1994)★★★, *Memories Of The SoulShack Survivors* (Loose Cannon 1995)★★★.

BASS-O-MATIC

Bass-O-Matic is a pseudonym for England-born William Orbit (b. William Wainwright), a leading mixer, writer and composer who came to prominence in 1990 with the techno anthem 'Fascinating Rhythm'. This was included on a debut set that also featured the services of Sharon Musgrave, percussionist Fergus and MC Inna One Step, the title of which was a reference to Pink Floyd's 'Set The Controls For The Heart Of The Sun'. In the process, Bass-O-Matic spearheaded a movement in the dance scene that rediscovered elements of music from yesteryear, finding much in sympathy with the trancelike state of 90s house. The album actually included a cover version of the Floyd standard, as well as the band's debut single, 'In The Realm Of The Senses'. A year later Orbit unveiled a follow-up, this time utilizing vocalist Sindy (ex-Well Red) and rappers Glory and Divine. It proved another competent and intoxicating collection, with Orbit's keen sense of rhythm carrying the album through from deep house to more pop-orientated cuts.

● ALBUMS: *Set The Controls For The Heart Of The Bass* (Virgin 1990)★★★, *Science And Melody* (Virgin 1991)★★★.

BASSHEADS

This Birkenhead, Merseyside, England-based duo consists of Desa and Nick Murphy and originally came to prominence in 1991 with the release of 'Is There Anybody Out There?'. Although they reached the UK Top 10, they found themselves being sued by Afrika Bambaataa, the Osmonds, Pink Floyd and even Talking Heads' representatives for the samples they had employed. Subsequent singles 'Back To The Old School' and 'Who Can Make You Feel Good' refused to compromise on their pulsating house/sample work. However, by the time of their debut long-player in 1993, the Bassheads had begun to embrace the ambient house movement spearheaded by the Orb and Aphex Twin. At the core of the album was a 24-minute track, 'C.O.D.E.', which owed a debt to Brian Eno and Talking Heads.

● ALBUMS: *C.O.D.E.S.* (1993)★★★.

BATU

Brighton, England-based six-piece band who mingle ethnic drumming with house music, with vocals by Sharon Scott (who previously worked with Soul II Soul). Formed in 1992, they attracted the powerful advocacy of Kiss-FM disc jockey Patrick Forge after they handed over a tape at a Talkin' Loud club night in London. He was excited by the authentic Brazilian sounds the band created. Batu's guitarist Chris Franck, after playing samba while studying for a degree in France, was tutored by two expatriate Brazilians, Pedro (guitar) and Beberto de Souza (octopusine percussion). Their debut single, 'Seasons Of My Mind'/'Hold It Now', prefaced a samba/house contribution to Island Records' *Rebirth Of Cool* series. Their feel for Latin music was profound: 'What Batu are doing is taking an authentic approach to Brazilian music, but we're 90s people, we come from a club culture. You can't carry on making music now without being aware of hip-hop production.'

BAXTER, BLAKE

From Detroit, Michigan, USA, Baxter is a first-generation Detroit hero of 'Ride 'Em Boy' and 'Forever And A Day' fame, whose early recordings (with their edgy experimentation) provided a guiding light for the Aphex Twin and others. Closely involved with the *Techno Sound Of Detroit* compilation, he subsequently severed his links with the city's 'Big Three' (Juan Atkins, Derrick May and Kevin Saunderson) and moved on to the Detroit independent Incognito. He released 'Sexuality' and the *Crimes Of The Heart* EP for the latter, which prefaced a debut album in early 1990. He also provided Jeff Mills/Mad 'Mike Banks' Underground Resistance with a rare outside production in 1991 with 'Prince Of Techno'. Skilled as both a drummer and DJ, he recorded for several European labels in the 90s after relocating to Berlin, including 1992's 'One More Time' and 'Brothers Gonna Work It Out' for Logic.
● ALBUMS: *The Underground Lives* (Incognito 1990)★★★, *The Vault* (Mix/Disko B 1995)★★★.

BEASTIE BOYS

Former hardcore trio who went on to find international fame as the first crossover white rap act of the 80s. After forming at New York University, original members John Berry and Kate Shellenbach departed after the release of

'Pollywog Stew', leaving Adam 'MCA' Yauch (b. 15 August 1967, Brooklyn, New York, USA), Mike 'D' Diamond (b. 20 November 1965, New York, USA) and the recently recruited guitarist Adam 'Ad Rock' Horowitz (b. 31 October 1966, New York City, New York, USA) to hold the banner. The group was originally convened to play at MCA's 15th birthday party, adding Horowitz to their ranks from The Young And The Useless (one single, 'Real Men Don't Use Floss'). Horowitz, it transpired, was the son of dramatist Israel Horowitz, indicating that far from being the spawn of inner-city dystopia, the Beasties all came from privileged middle-class backgrounds. They continued in similar vein to their debut with the *Cookie Puss* EP, which offered the first evidence of them picking up on the underground rap phenomenon. The record, later sampled for a British Airways commercial, earned them $40,000 in royalties. Friend and sometime band member Rick Rubin quickly signed them to his fledgling Def Jam label. They did not prove hard to market. Their debut album revealed a collision of bad attitudes, spearheaded by the raucous single 'Fight For Your Right To Party', and samples of everything from Led Zeppelin to the theme to *Mister Ed*. There was nothing self-conscious or sophisticated about the lyrics, Mike D and MCA reeling off complaints about their parents confiscating their pornography or telling them to turn down the stereo. Somehow, however, it became an anthem for pseudo-rebellious youth everywhere, becoming a number 11 hit in the UK. In the wake of its success *Licensed To Ill* became the first rap album to top the US charts. By the time follow-up singles 'No Sleep Till Brooklyn' and 'She's On It' charted, the band had become a media *cause célèbre*. Their stage shows regularly featured caged, half-naked females, while their Volkswagen pendants resulted in a crimewave, with fans stealing said items from vehicles throughout the UK. A reflective Horowitz recalled that this never happened in the USA, where they merely stole the car itself. More disturbing, it was alleged that the band derided terminally ill children on a foreign jaunt. This false accusation was roundly denied, but other stories of excess leaked out of the Beastie Boys camp with grim regularity. There was also friction between the group and Def Jam, the former accusing the latter of withholding royalties, the latter accusing the former of withholding a follow-up album. By the time the band reassembled after a number of solo projects in 1989, the public, for the most part, had forgotten about them. Rap's ante had been significantly raised by the arrival of Public Enemy and NWA, yet *Paul's Boutique* remains one of the genre's most overlooked pieces, a complex reflection of pop culture that is infinitely more subtle than their debut. Leaving their adolescent fixations behind, the rhymes plundered cult fiction (Anthony Burgess's *A Clockwork Orange*) through to the Old Testament. It was co-produced by the Dust Brothers, who subsequently became a hot production item. Moving to California, *Check Your Head* saw them returning, partially, to their thrash roots, reverting to a guitar, bass and drums format. In the meantime, the Beasties had invested wisely, setting up their own magazine, studio and label, Grand Royal. This has boasted releases by Luscious Jackson, plus The Young And The Useless (Adam Horowitz's first band) and DFL (his hardcore punk project). Other signings included DJ Hurricane (also of the Afros), Noise Addict and Moistboyz. However, in 1993 Horowitz pleaded guility to a charge of battery on a television cameraman during a memorial service for River Phoenix. He was put on two years' probation, ordered to undertake 200 hours' community service and pay restitution costs. His connections with the Phoenix family came through his actress wife Ione Sky. He himself had undertaken film roles in *The Santa Anna Project*, *Roadside Prophets* and *Lost Angels*, also appearing in a television cameo for *The Equalizer*. By this time, both he and Diamond had become Californian citizens, while Yauch had become a Buddhist, speaking out in the press against US trade links with China because of the latter's annexation of Tibet. In 1994 Yauch set up the Milarepa Fund to raise funds and public awareness of the situation in Tibet, and organized the Tibetan Freedom Concerts from 1996-98. *Ill Communication* was another succesful voyage into inspired Beastie thuggism, featuring A Tribe Called Quest's Q Tip, and a second appearance from Biz Markie, following his debut on *Check Your Head*. *The In Sound From Way Out* was a space-filler of b-sides and instrumental takes. The long-awaited *Hello Nasty* (a title inspired by their agent's telephone greeting), their first full studio album in four years, was a return to a more sparse, hip-hop-dominated sound after the funky feel of *Ill Communication*. The album was preceded by the single release of 'Intergalactic', which reached the UK Top 10 in June 1998.

● ALBUMS: *Licensed To Ill* (Def Jam/Columbia 1986)★★★, *Paul's Boutique* (Capitol 1989)★★★★, *Check Your Head* (Grand Royal/Capitol 1992)★★★★, *Ill Communication* (Grand Royal/Capitol 1994)★★★★, *The Root Down EP* (Grand Royal/Capitol 1995)★★, *Aglio & Olio* mini-album (Grand Royal/Capitol 1996)★★★, *The In Sound From Way Out* (Grand Royal/Capitol 1995)★★, *Hello Nasty* (Grand Royal 1998)★★★★.
● COMPILATIONS: *Some Old Bullshit* (Capitol 1994)★★★.
● VIDEOS: *Sabotage* (1994), *The Skills To Pay The Bills* (1994).

BEAT PUBLIQUE

This UK trio featured former Soul II Soul vocalist Do'Reen (b. Doreen Parker), plus Lunarci (b. Jim Barnet, *c*.1973) and Gary Masters. Do'Reen had provided vocals for Soul II Soul's 'Feel Free' and 'Happiness', and also worked on sessions for MC Tunes, the Moody Boyz and Don-E. It was while working for the latter that she met Lunarci (famed for 'Communion' and collaborations with PM Dawn) and Masters (behind Praise's 'Only You'). Together they released 'Realise' for Beat Fantastique in July 1992. Do'Reen went on to work on sessions as a solo artist with Peter Harder and also sued Jazzie B for underpayment on her Soul II Soul recordings.

BEATMASTERS

This UK writing and production team consisted of Richard Walmsley (b. 28 September 1962), Amanda Glanfield and Paul Carter, and were initially most famous for their work with Betty Boo on tracks such as 'Hey DJ, I Can't Dance (To The Music You're Playing)'. Among their other UK chart coups were the Cookie Crew's breakthrough hit, 'Rok Da House' (number 5), Yazz's 'Stand Up For Your Love Rights' (number 2), and MC Merlin's 'Who's In The House' (number 8). They also worked on the P.P. Arnold comeback hit, 'Burn It Down'. This production line of pop hits won them few critical admirers, but their methodology had been honed when Glanfield and Carter spent time working on television commercial jingles for a production house (Brook Street's 'Get A Job', among them). Although they fell short of the commercial knack of Stock, Aitken And Waterman, they did manage notable hits under their own steam, such as 1988's 'Burn It Up'. A second album for Rhythm King saw guest appearances from JC001 and MC Precious. The group enjoyed something of a creative renaissance with 'Boulevard Of Broken Dreams' in 1991, built on Young-Holt Unlimited's 'Light My Fire', but lack-lustre efforts including 'I Dunno What It Is'.

● ALBUMS: *Anywayawanna* (Rhythm King 1989)★★, *Life And Soul* (Rhythm King 1991)★★.

BEATNUTS

This American hip-hop trio established their name with remix credits for Prime Minister Pete Nice, Naughty By Nature, Da Lench Mob and Cypress Hill, and also produced Chi-Ali, Da Youngstas and Fat Joe. The trio comprises Psycho Les (b. Lester Fernandez), Ju Ju (b. Jerry Tineo) and Fashion (b. Berntony Smalls). Their own material, which kicked off with 1993's *Intoxicated Demons* EP, features a light touch and plenty of humour. This should not mask the level of innovation and insight they bring to their recordings, however, with samples drawn from their direct environment (i.e., children talking) rather than movie themes and old funk records. The release of their debut EP had been delayed when Fashion was arrested on a drug-related charge and imprisoned for six months. Before joining the other two, he had recorded 'Let The Horns Blow' with members of De La Soul and Chi-Ali in 1991. The trio's two studio albums offer healthy doses of their twisted world view.

● ALBUMS: *The Beatnuts* (Violator/Relativity 1994)★★★, *Stone Crazy* (Relativity 1997)★★★.

BEATS INTERNATIONAL

This studio team of musicians was formed by Norman Cook (b. Quentin Cook, 31 July 1963, Brighton, Sussex, England; ex-Housemartins) following the break-up of his former employers. Its basic composition was Cook (bass), Linda Layton (b. Belinda Kimberley Layton, 7 December 1970, Chiswick, London, England; vocals), Lester Noel (b. Lester John Noel, 3 September 1962, Paddington, London, England; vocals, ex-Grab Grab The Haddock; North Of Cornwallis), Andy Boucher (keyboards) and MC Wildski (rap). However, to these personnel could be added a range of occasional members ranging from Billy Bragg to Definition Of Sound to Captain Sensible. The first Beats International single, 'For Spacious Lies', gathered numerous rave reviews, and was much closer to traditional pop fare than subsequent releases. It included a contribution from Noel, who had met Cook when North Of

Cornwallis supported the Housemartins on tour. Beats International shot to prominence in the UK when 'Dub Be Good To Me' hit number 1 in the UK charts in 1990. Controversy followed it shortly afterwards, as the audience placed the bassline as a note-for-note lift from the Clash's 'Guns Of Brixton'. In truth, the song also borrowed heavily from the SOS Band's 'Just Be Good To Me'. This 'creative theft' may have diminished royalty cheques, but the interpretation of various styles and even passages of music proved a deliberate strategy in Beats International's armoury. Although the subsequent 'Burundi Blues' single, a delicate mix of soul, jazz and African music, failed to repeat the success, Cook was heavily in demand as a remixer for a variety of projects, ranging from Aztec Camera to the Jungle Brothers. The impossibly diverse debut album charted at number 17, while the follow-up concentrated heavily on ska and reggae rhythms and included a disastrous version of 'In The Ghetto'. Cook disbanded Beats International in order to put together his new band, the acid jazz-styled Freak Power, and concentrate on further production work. He has also recorded as Pizzaman, and has recently enjoyed major chart success as Fatboy Slim.

● ALBUMS: *Let Them Eat Bingo* (Go! Discs 1990)★★★, *Excursion On The Version* (Go! Discs 1991)★★★.

BEDOUIN ASCENT

Essentially an outlet for the work of Kingsuk Biswas, or 'Bis' for short, Bedouin Ascent are one of Rising High's UK techno/experimental dance projects. Based in Harrow, Biswas's output reflects his interest not only in techno but also in improvised jazz and ambient soundscapes. Indeed, he spoke confidently in interviews of merging the boundaries between diverse forms of house, dance and electronic music, rather than reinforcing differences. This is not surprising as Biswas had previously spent time in punk, industrial funk, glam rock and space rock bands. His debut album was recorded in autumn 1993, but was not released until January 1995 when the artist, a quiet perfectionist, was fully satisfied with it. This followed two Rising High EPs and a collaboration with writer and performer David Toop.

● ALBUMS: *Science, Art And Ritual* (Rising High 1995)★★★.

BEKKER, HENNIE

b. c.1932, Nkana, Zambia. Multi-instrumentalist and songwriter Hennie Bekker pursued a long and varied musical career before eventually realizing his potential in his mid-60s. By that time he had been based in Toronto, Canada, for over a decade. Bekker was raised in the small town of Mufulira, 10 miles south of the Congo/Zaire border. At the age of 15 he began playing piano in the Bulawayo, Zimbabwe-based Youth Marvels. His own jazz band, the Hennie Bekker Band, was formed in 1959. His apprenticeship as a session musician and arranger began in Johannesburg, South Africa, where he was forced to flee after his group's engagement at a Zairean nightclub was curtailed by the Katanga revolution. In Johannesburg he became a staff music director and producer for Gallo Records, and also worked periodically in England. He returned to South Africa to work as a highly successful composer of television and radio commercials, subsequently becoming a respected film composer. He then settled in Canada in 1987, forced there by racial tensions in Johannesburg. He worked for a time composing stock music for the John Parry library, before collaborating with Dan Gibson on combined wildlife/new age recordings. *Harmony* was the first in a series of 13 such albums recorded by the pair up to 1996. In the 90s Bekker began to release his own, new age-themed records. He quickly made up for lost time, issuing numerous records in two thematic series - the 'Kaleidoscope' cycle (*Summer Breeze, Spring Rain, Winter Reflections, Lullabies, Autumn Magic*) and the 'Tapestry' cycle (*Silk & Satin, Vivaldi, Temba*). In addition there has been a Christmas album, plus a television-marketed ambient music series of albums for Quality Music. Bekker is also part of a trio including Greg Kavanagh and DJ Chris Sheppard who record contemporary techno as BKS. Their albums, *For Those About To Rave ... We Salute You* (1992), *Dreamcatcher* (1993) and *Astroplane* (1996), have sold a combined 100,000 copies in Canada. Bekker continues to take great pleasure in shocking adolescent fans when they discover one of Canada's most successful techno groups is spearheaded by a man in his mid-60s. However, it is as one of the most successful and prolific new age composers on the North American continent that Bekker is best known.
● ALBUMS: with Dan Gibson *Harmony* (Holborne 1989)★★★, *Summer Breeze* (Holborne 1993)★★★, *Spring Rain* (Holborne 1993)★★★, *Winter Reflections* (Holborne 1994)★★★, *Tranquillity Volume 1* (Quality Music 1994)★★★, *Awakenings* (Quality Music 1994)★★★, *Silk & Satin* (Holborne 1995)★★★, *Vivaldi* (Holborne 1995)★★★, *Temba* (Holborne 1995)★★★, *Classic Moods And Nature* (Quality Music 1995)★★★, *Christmas Spirit* (Holborne 1996)★★★, *Christmas Noel* (Quality Music 1996)★★★, *Transitions* (Quality Music 1996)★★★, *Classics By The Sea* (Holborne 1996)★★★, *Lullabies* (Holborne 1997)★★★, *Autumn Magic* (Holborne 1997)★★★, *Mirage* (Avalon 1997)★★★.

BELOVED

Initially known in 1983 as the Journey Through and comprising Jon Marsh (b. c.1964), Guy Gousden and Tim Havard, UK band the Beloved fell into place a year later when Cambridge University student and ex-postman Steve Waddington (b. c.1959) joined on guitar. It was no straightforward initiation ceremony. Marsh had placed an advert in the music press that ran thus: 'I am Jon Marsh, founder member of the Beloved. Should you too wish to do something gorgeous, meet me in exactly three years' time at exactly 11am in Diana's Diner, or site thereof, Covent Garden, London, WC2'. Tentative stabs at heavy psychedelia evolved into a more pop-orientated formula by the mid-80s, with the Beloved's dark, danceable sounds often being compared to New Order and garnering attention throughout Europe. Marsh became a contestant on television quiz show *Countdown* in 1987, featuring on nine programmes before being knocked out in the semi-finals. It was not until 1988, however, that the Beloved started living up to their name; Waddington and Marsh, heavily influenced by the nascent 'rave' scene in London at that time, split from Gousden and Harvard and started forging their own path. Unshackled from the confines of a four-cornered set-up, the revitalized duo dived into the deep end of the exploding dance movement, subsequently breaking into commercial waters with the ambient textures of 'Sun Rising'. The *Happiness* album, backed by Marsh and Waddington's enthusiastic chatter concerning the virtues of flotation tanks and hallucinogenic substances, perfectly embodied the tripped-out vibe of the times and sealed the Beloved's fashionable success in worldwide territories. By 1993's *Conscience*, Marsh had left his former partner Waddington (who joined Steve Hillage's System

7), using his wife Helena as his new creative foil. The resultant album was more whimsical and understated than previous affairs, with a pop rather than club feel. Their third album relied too heavily on electronic gimmickry, detracting attention from individual songs. Returning in 1996 with *X*, the group's sound showed no signs of progression.

● ALBUMS: *Happiness* (Atlantic 1990)★★★, *Blissed Out* remix of *Happiness* (East West 1990)★★★, *Conscience* (East West 1993)★★★, *X* (East West 1996)★★.

BELTRAM, JOEY

b. *c*.1971. Widely considered to be one of the gurus of New York hardcore, Beltram's 1991 release 'Energy Flash' (R&S Records) was a milestone of the genre, providing a bassline that has re-emerged countless times (not least on Beltram's own recordings). By the age of 16 he was recording as Code 6 and Lost Entity for New York labels such as Nu Groove: 'Initially producing records was my way of getting better DJ jobs.' At school he had saved his dinner money in order to buy records at the end of the week to make mix tapes. He certainly boasts eclectic tastes in dance music, at the last count owning over 60,000 records. The follow-up single, 'Mentasm', was credited to Second Phase, a collaboration with Mundo Muzique, and was one of several *noms de plume* that include Final Exposure ('Vortex', on Plus 8), Disorder ('Panic'/'Groove Attack', on Rhythmatic Rage) and Program 2 ('The Omen', on R&S). He has also recorded in a less frenetic house vein. His work on the Cutting Records label (Vice Tribe's 'Something Unreal') is a good example of this, while under his own name he has also provided a three-track EP (Beltram Presents...Odyssey Nine - 'Drums Of Orbit') for Visible, which dabbled in trance. However, his best recent work is undoubtedly the *Caliber* EP for Warp, which saw many critics drawing comparisons to the mighty 'Energy Flash'; Beltram himself commented, 'I'm not one of those people that gets too moody and wants to change my style totally all the time. I'm always trying to keep a link between my old records and new records.' His remixes include Orbital's 'Oolaa' and the Smarte's 'Sesame's Treet', for US consumption.

● ALBUMS: *The Re-Releases* (Trax 1994)★★★, *Places* (R&S 1995)★★★, *Close Grind* (Novamute 1996)★★★.

● COMPILATIONS: *Classics* (R&S 1996)★★★.

BENTLEY RHYTHM ACE

Richard March (who had previously played bass with Pop Will Eat Itself) and Mike Stokes began recording together in the mid-90s. In 1996 the pair sent a four-track demo of their work to Skint Records and consequently signed to that label as Bentley Rhythm Ace, taking the name from an old drum machine. Later that year the band gained widespread attention when they released a demo, which included the track 'Bentley's Gonna Sort You Out!', as the EP *This Is Carbootechnodisco*. This was followed by the *Last Train To Bentley On C* EP (1996) and the single 'Midlander' (1997), which prompted attention from the major labels. They eventually signed to Parlophone Records and released the album *Bentley Rhythm Ace* in 1997. During the same period the pair toured around the UK, played at various festivals around Europe, and visited the USA at the end of the year. Their sound combines a variety of prominent sampled beats with bass guitar, synth patterns and riffs. However, unlike much of the big beat movement, with which they have often been associated, Bentley Rhythm Ace have a unique style on account of the range of influences that can be heard in the music, and the notoriously bizarre samples that highlight the band's eccentric sense of humour.

● ALBUMS: *Bentley Rhythm Ace* (Skint/Parlophone 1997)★★★.

BENZ, SPRAGGA

b. Carlton Errington Grant, 30 May 1969, Kingston, Jamaica, West Indies. Among the fast-rising stars of 1993 were Chuckleberry, General Pecus, Bounty Killer and Spragga Benz. His title was inspired by the prevailing trend for a fusion of hip-hop and ragga, and the fact that Spragga frequently appeared with a Mercedes Benz insignia dangling from his gold chain. Early hits included the Sly And Robbie-produced 'No Cater' and, with Steely And Clevie, 'Girls Hooray'. By 1994 he was recording with many of Jamaica's top producers, including Bobby Digital on 'The Wuk' and 'Sweet Sugar Pie', while King Jammy's son John John produced 'Bad Man No Beg No Friend', along with 'Born Good Looking'. In 1995 his prolific output encompassed the renowned 'W', a combination tune with Tamma Hawk, 'Flex Insane', as well as 'Car Crash', 'She Wrong' and 'Plan B', which were all dancehall favourites. His reputation grew when, in combination with Bounty Killer and

General Degree, 'More Gal Book Book' appeared on the UK reggae Top 10. Many reggae performers have set up their own labels and Benz was no exception, releasing 'A1 Lover' on his Spragga Speculous imprint. The single featured vocals from Chevelle Franklin, who enjoyed an international hit when she accompanied Shabba Ranks on his Sony remake of 'Mr Loverman'. Conceivably induced by reggae's flourishing acceptance, Capitol Records signed Benz, releasing the single that featured on *Uncommonly Smooth*. The outcome of previous major label reggae releases had often been disappointing, but with this release, Benz was able to maintain artistic control and a fine collection of his work ensued.

● ALBUMS: *Jack It Up* (VP 1995)★★, *Uncommonly Smooth* (Capitol 1995)★★★★.

BERNARD, JAMES

A native New Yorker who programmes synthesizers for Korg as a day job, but releases a gamut of techno odes, under a variety of names, in his spare time. Under his own name he recorded a debut album for Rising High that was a gruelling, slightly moribund, ambient affair. However, as Influx he provided the Sappho label (a subsidiary of Rising High) with their first full-length album release on a set that reflected Influx's familiar, old school use of electro-drums. It followed three 12-inch releases, 'Influx', 'OD' and 'Disrupticon', for the same stable. Among his other guises is the *nom de plume* Cybertrax, whose notable credits on the main Rising High label included 'Songs For A Rainy Day' and 'Flexor'.

● ALBUMS: *Atmospherics* (Rising High 1994)★★★; as Influx: *Unique* (Sappho 1994)★★★, *The TB Rage* (Sappho 1994)★★★.

BETTER DAYS

Steve Proctor from Liverpool, England, began DJing in 1979, before moving to London in the mid-80s, guesting at Shoom and Sunrise. He subsequently played at the Promised Land at the London Fitness Centre and Love at the Wag. His 'balearic' reputation revolved around him playing all sorts of tracks at the latter club that had 'love' in the title (including Fleetwood Mac). Better Days was the title Proctor chose as his recording vehicle. Two singles were completed for Virgin before departing for Music For Nations. A club night also titled Better Days came into being at London's Villa Stefano, as did a label of the same

title. Releases such as Museka's 'Beautiful In Red', Marshall Hains' 'Dancing In The CIty' and John DaSilva's Disco Universe Orchestra's 'Soul On Ice' and 'Sing It' followed. Other artists included the Better Days Project and Santa Esmerelda.

BEYOND RECORDS

This record label from Birmingham, England, produces ambient dub compilations. The head of the company, Mike Barnet, has said, 'Beyond was originally set up as an outlet for intelligent dance.' They also run the Oscillate club and work with the Original Rockers and Higher Intelligence Agency. Many of the acts to be found on the ambient series also play live at Oscillate.

BEYOND RELIGION

Beyond Religion is both a group and record label headed by joint-songwriters Karen Mercer (vocals) and Pete Spence (instrumentalist), based in Enfield, London, England. The group made their debut with the *Two Worlds* EP in 1993, which comprised four tracks of synthesized dub and ambient house. The group, previously known as Chromatic, was formed following problems with that outfit's attempts to secure a major label record contract. Beyond Religion staked their claim (and an Enterprise Allowance grant) with songs that were generally fully formed compositions rather than merely rhythmic tracks. Subsequent releases included 'Planet Of Our Own' (a promotional only release), 'Magic', 'Rescue Me' (remixed by Marc Wilkinson from Flying Records) and 'Bring On The Goodtimes'.

BG THE PRINCE OF RAP

b. Washington, DC, Maryland, USA. One of rap's woefully inadequate types, BG, the self-proclaimed Prince Of Rap, specializes in empty rhetoric. He is an ex-GI, now based in Germany, whom one reviewer unkindly renamed the 'Prince Of Wack'. Conversely, Columbia introduced him as the 'most exciting dance/rap act to emerge from Germany since Snap!', which gave some indication of his style and of the record company's marketing gambit. BG was involved in Washington's go-go movement until he was introduced, via an army colleague, into the world of hip-hop. When his regiment moved to Germany he took part in local rapping competitions there, until he came to the attention of producer Jam El Mar, of Jam And Spoon fame. The resulting 'Rap To The World' single was a major hit in German clubs, and its follow-up, 'This Beat Is Hot', made it into that country's Top 20.

● ALBUMS: *The Power Of Rhythm* (Columbia 1992)★★.

BIF NAKED

b. 1971, New Delhi, India. Confrontational, tattooed, hard rock singer-songwriter Bif Naked was born to two private-school teachers who quickly gave her up for adoption. She was adopted by two American missionaries, and her childhood was spent in locations including Lexington, Kentucky, USA, and Winnipeg and Manitoba in Canada. Her first group was Jungle Milk, who specialized in rap cover versions of Doris Day songs backed by 10 conga players. She then worked with two of Canada's premier underground bands - Gorilla Gorilla and Chrome Dog. She made her debut with her own band in 1994 with the EP *Fours Songs And A Poem*. It won her instant attention, and heralded a talent that was more fully realized on a full-length album released later that year. With the rest of her band - Randy Black (drums), Rich Priske (bass) and X-Factor (guitar) - the major theme of the lyrics was the politics of sex and love. However, it was her skill in articulating different perspectives on gender issues that really distinguished her - from the male lust expressed in 'Everything' to an account of her own rape ordeal ('Tell On You'). The musical backgrounds ranged from conventional, grinding hard-rock to the seductive hip-hop beats of 'Daddy's Getting Married', a song concerning the remarriage of her father, which became the first single released from the album. She and her band then travelled to the UK for their first British tour, in support of Life Of Agony early in 1996.

● ALBUMS: *Bif Naked* (Plum/A&M 1994)★★★.

BIG DADDY KANE

b. Antonio M. Hardy, 10 September 1969, Brooklyn, New York, USA. Self-styled 'black gentleman vampire', whose KANE moniker is an acronym for King Asiatic Nobody's Equal. Kane followed his cousin into hip-hop by rapping in front of a beatbox for his first shows on Long Island, New York. Aided by his DJ Mr Cee, he has released several albums of laconic, fully realized songs pitched halfway between soul and rap. His tough but sensual work is best sampled on the hit singles 'Ain't No Stoppin' Us Now' and 'Smooth Operator'. The production skills of Marley Marl and the deep groove worked up by Mr Cee play no

small part in the refined ambience of his better work. Despite being an obvious ladies' man, his appeal is enhanced by his ability to handle tough street raps, of the nature of the debut album's 'Raw', his contribution to Public Enemy's 'Burn Hollywood Burn', or his own Afrocentric, Muslim tracts. He also joined with Ice-T on a speaking tour of black high schools in Detroit in the late 80s. A huge fan of soul, obvious similarities to Barry White are given further credence by the duet he shares with that artist on *Taste Of Chocolate*. On the same set he also produced a comedic duet with Rudy Ray Moore. He can, however, be guilty of the rap genre's unfortunate propensity for insulting women, the fantasy world of songs such as 'Pimpin' Ain't Easy' being an immediate example. He straddled the rap and mainstream R&B markets with several decidedly mellow albums, and also worked widely as a freelance lyricist for Cold Chillin', writing with Roxanne Shante and Biz Markie, among others. Kane also moved into acting, appearing in *Posse* and *Gunmen*, and appeared in Madonna's erotic photo book *Sex*. *Looks Like A Job For Big Daddy* and *Daddy's Home* toughened his sound, but struggled to make a commercial impact.

● ALBUMS: *Long Live The Kane* (Cold Chillin' 1988)★★★★, *It's A Big Daddy Thing* (Cold Chillin' 1989)★★★★, *Taste Of Chocolate* (Cold Chillin' 1990)★★★, *Prince Of Darkness* (Cold Chillin' 1991)★★, *Looks Like A Job For Big Daddy* (Cold Chillin' 1993)★★★, *Daddy's Home* (MCA 1994)★★, *Veteranz Day* (Blackheart 1998)★★★.

BIG LIFE RECORDS

The company was established in 1987 by Jazz Summers and Tim Parry (b. 21 June 1956, Reading, Berkshire, England), which saw its third release, 'Doctorin' The House', by Coldcut and Yazz, reach number 6 in the UK charts the same year. They had been introduced to the Coldcut production team via Dave Lee (aka Joey Negro): 'We began life as a management company. Our first act was the Soup Dragons . . . But out of frustration with major record companies, we decided to start doing stuff ourselves'. Summers had formerly managed Parry in the Crooks and Blue Zoo. They also worked together on the Danse Society, Summers managing and Parry producing. Summers then took over the Wham! reins for three years, while Parry looked after the slightly less prosperous March Violets. After they decided to collude on Big Life the rewards were instantaneous. Their fourth release, Yazz's solo effort 'The Only Way Is Up', reached the top of the UK charts, remaining there for five weeks and becoming 1988's biggest-selling single. Subsequent hits arrived from Blue Pearl, the Orb and rappers De La Soul and Naughty By Nature (the latter two via a strong link with US rap base Tommy Boy). They had already released one of the earliest UK rap singles in London Posse's eponymous debut. There was even room for distinctly non-dance acts such as Mega City Four, though their biggest successes came with the Orb, until they departed, acrimoniously, in 1993. Big Life also managed Youth as a producer, housing his own label, Butterfly Recordings. Other licensees, at various times, have included WAU! Mr Modo, Black Market and Kool Kat (later Network).

BIOSPHERE

Biosphere was the creation of former Bleep mainman Geir Jenssen (b. Norway). Jenssen had originally played in Bel Canto, with friends Anneli Decker and Nils Johansen. Bleep's tally amounted to four 12-inch singles and a solitary album between 1989 and 1990. Three of those singles, 'Sure Be Glad When You're Dead', 'In Your System' and 'A Bite Of AMC' (the video for which was directed by Norwegian film-maker Casper Evenson, who subsequently became responsible for Biosphere's visuals), were included on Bleep's debut set, *The North Pole By Submarine*, released in 1990. The album was recorded after spending endless nights shivering in a tent, listening to short-wave radio, while taking part in an archaeological expedition to the Arctic Circle. It was followed by 'The Launchpad', bringing Bleep a UK club hit with their final release. The 90s saw Jenssen inaugurate the Biosphere name, releasing the widely acclaimed *Patashnik* set. However, he also found time to score a soundtrack to the Norwegian film *Evige Stjerner*, produced sounds and images for an exhibition at the Norwegian Ministry of Arts, and collaborated with ambient maestro Peter Namlook on an album, *The Fires Of Ork*. As if that were not enough, he also undertook another expedition in 1994, this time as part of an eight-man team scaling mountains in Nepal. Jenssen gained a measure of commercial success when the track 'Novelty Waves' was used as a soundtrack to a Levi's advert. In 1996 he collaborated with Higher Intelligence Agency on the improvisational 'Polar Sequences'. As part of a productive 1997, he released *Substrata*

and the soundtrack to Erik Skjoldbjaerg's *Insomnia*, moving ever further from the rhythmic innovations of *Patashnik*.

● ALBUMS: as Bleep *The North Pole By Submarine* (SSR 1990)★★★, as Biosphere *Microgravity* (Origo Sound/Apollo 1991)★★★, *Patashnik* (Apollo 1993)★★★★, with Peter Namlook *The Fire Of Ork* (Fax 1993)★★★, *Substrata* (All Saints 1997)★★★, *Insomnia* film soundtrack (Origo Sound 1997)★★★.

BITE IT! RECORDS

Bite It! Records is Trevor Jackson's (aka Underdog) hip-hop label, based in London, England. The business was founded first as a graphic design concern, providing sleeve designs for records such as the Stereo MC's' *33, 45, 78*. The high-quality packaging was continued when Bite It! became an autonomous record label. Its first release was the Brotherhood's 'Descendants Of The Holocaust', released in 1990. After one more release from the Mighty Ethnics the label lay dormant until 1992, at which time it began to re-emerge with further material from the Brotherhood ('Wayz Of The Wize') and Scientists Of Sound (*Scientists Of Sound* EP). By this time the Underdog had become a celebrated remixer to artists including U2, House Of Pain and Shara Nelson, and the Bite It! label expanded its roster accordingly. The Brotherhood, widely regarded as potential 'saviours' of British hip-hop, remained with the label when they signed a contract with Virgin Records in 1994, ensuring that Bite It!'s high-quality threshold (in terms of both design and production) was continued with the release of *Elementalz*.

BIZ MARKIE

b. Marcel Hall, 8 April 1964, Harlem, New York, USA. This member of Marley Marl's posse delivered his tales of bogey-picking, bad breath and other niceties in a jerky manner that came close to self-parody, but found a niche market in adolescent circles. His progress was aided by an unlikely hit single, 'Just A Friend', in 1989. Resolutely old school, he nevertheless brought a sense of humour and undoubted rhyming talents to hip-hop. His 1993 album featured 'Let Me Turn You On' over a sample of 'Ain't No Stoppin' Us Now', on which he actually sang. The set's title, *All Samples Cleared!*, was more than an unjustified whinge at copyright laws. Each and every sample was cleared by the relevant artist's representatives, after Markie had previously come under threat of imprisonment. This stemmed from his sampling of Gilbert O'Sullivan's 1972 ballad 'Alone Again' on his *I Need A Haircut* album. Judge Kevin Thomas Duff awarded punitive damages, ruling that 'sampling is theft under criminal law', giving all rap artists cause for concern and changing the way hip-hop albums were prepared for release. Markie appeared as a guest vocalist for the Beastie Boys, who were early supporters of his style.

● ALBUMS: *Goin' Off* (Cold Chillin' 1988)★★, *The Biz Never Sleeps* (Cold Chillin' 1989)★★★, *I Need A Haircut* (Cold Chillin' 1991)★★★, *All Samples Cleared!* (Cold Chillin' 1993)★★★.

● COMPILATIONS: *Biz's Baddest Beats* (Cold Chillin' 1994)★★★.

BIZARRE INC.

Hardcore disco/fusion activists from Stafford, whose 1991 hit 'Playing With Knives' was a popular staple of many dancefloors (ending up, through a circuitous route, as '(Can You) Feel The Passion' by Blue Pearl). Other singles, such as 'X-Static', 'Plutonic' and 'Raise Me', followed. The members included Andrew Meecham (b. *c.*1968), Dean Meredith (b. *c.*1969) and Carl Turner (b. *c.*1969), plus singers Angie Brown and Yvonne Yanni. Mark Archer, of Altern 8 fame, had also been a founding member. Their debut album was primarily deep house, with the reliable remixing input of Todd Terry on 'I'm Gonna Get You' (featuring Angie Brown), which was only available as part of a limited edition CD version. When released as a single in 1992, it became another hit. Subsequent singles, included 1996's 'Suprise' and 'Get Up Sunshine Street'.

● ALBUMS: *Energique* (Vinyl Solution 1992)★★★, *Surprise* (Mercury 1996)★★.

BJÖRK

b. Björk Gudmundsdóttir, 21 November 1965, Reykjavik, Iceland. The former Sugarcubes vocalist, armed with a remarkable, keening vocal presence, has crossed over to huge success via her club-orientated material. The success of *Debut* culminated in awards for Best International Newcomer and Best International Artist at the 1994 BRIT Awards. However, she had made her 'debut' proper as far back as 1977, with an album recorded in her native territory as an 11-year old prodigy (including cover versions of pop standards by the Beatles and others). It was only the start of a prodigious musical legacy. Her next

recording outfit was Tappi Takarrass (which apparently translates as 'Cork that bitch's arse'), who recorded two albums between 1981 and 1983. A more high-profile role was afforded via work with KUKL, who introduced her to future Sugarcubes Einar Örn and Siggi. The group's two albums were issued in the UK on the Crass label. Björk returned to Iceland after the Sugarcubes' six-year career, partially to pay off debts, recording a first solo album in 1990 backed by a local be-bop group. She re-emerged in 1993 with *Debut* and a welter of more house-orientated material, including four hit singles. These chiefly came to prominence in the dance charts (Björk having first dipped a toe in those waters with 808 State on *Ex:El*) via their big-name remixers. The most important of these were Underworld and Bassheads ('Human Behaviour'), Black Dog ('Venus As A Boy'), Tim Simenon of Bomb The Bass ('Play Dead', which was also used on the soundtrack to *The Young Americans* film and featured a distinctive Jah Wobble bass hook) and David Morales, Justin Robertson and Fluke ('Big Time Sensuality'). Björk appeared at the 1993 BRIT Awards duetting with PJ Harvey, while in 1994 she co-wrote the title track to Madonna's album *Bedtime Stories*. Released in 1995, *Post* was an impressive and even more eclectic album, ranging from the hard techno beats of 'Army Of Me' to the shimmering 'Hyperballad'. Now an unwilling media star, Björk made the headlines following her attack on an intrusive reporter, and through her liaison with jungle artist Goldie. Following a desultory remix album, Björk released her third solo set, the self-produced *Homogenic*. Though she received critical plaudits for her seemingly tireless musical invention, the album was also notable for lyrics revealing a more personal side to the singer, reflecting on her troubled year.

● ALBUMS: *Björk* (Fàlkinn 1977)★★★, with Trió Gudmundar *Gling-Gló* (Smekkylesa 1990)★★★, *Debut* (One Little Indian 1993)★★★★, *Post* (One Little Indian 1995)★★★★, *Telegram* (One Little Indian 1996)★★★, *Homogenic* (One Little Indian 1997)★★★★.

● COMPILATIONS: *The Best Remixes Of The Album, Debut, For All The People Who Don't Buy White Labels* (One Little Indian 1994)★★.

● VIDEOS: *Björk* (Propaganda 1994), *Vessel* (PolyGram Music Video 1994).

● FURTHER READING: *Post: The Official Björk Book*, Penny Phillips.

BLACK BOX

One of the leading exponents of a wave of Italian House music that flourished on the dancefloors of the late 80s, Black Box were made up of three Italian studio musicians (Daniele Davoli, Mirko Limoni and Valerio Simplici), collectively known as Groove Groove Melody. They were based in the Regio D'Emillia area of Northern Italy, and made frequent use of singer Katrine (b. Catherine Quinol, Paris, France, of Guadelope descent). Simplici was a clarinet teacher and played in the La Scala Classical Music Orchestra in Milan. Davoli was a well-known Italian club DJ (known as DJ Lelewel), largely at the Marabu Starlight Club, while Limoni was the computer and keyboard whizz kid of the trio and had previously engineered for Italian pop act Spagna. The Groove Groove Melody team were established as one of the top two production outfits in Italian dance music, churning out more than a dozen singles a year in their native country. Katrine was spotted by Spagna's guitarist at a club, and, after introductions, featured as vocalist on 'Ride On Time'. The single became the first of a series of Italian House records to cross over to the UK charts, staying at number 1 for six weeks in 1989. Controversy reigned when it was realized that the single had sampled the voice of singer Loleatta Holloway from the 'Love Sensation' single she made with Dan Hartman in the late 70s. An agreement was eventually worked out with Salsoul (who owned the rights) as both companies benefited from 800,000 UK sales. The Groove Groove Melody team were also behind the production of Starlight's 'Numero Uno' and Mixmaster's 'Grand Piano', another prime example of 'Italo-house', and another crossover hit. Under seven or more pseudonyms, they turned out numerous further records. However, as Black Box, their hits included 'I Don't Know Anybody Else', 'Everybody Everybody' (the last of the 'Ride On Time' trilogy), and 'Fantasy', a revamp of the Earth, Wind And Fire hit. They were also responsible for, among other remixes, ABC's 1991 comeback single, 'Say It'. In 1995 they released the single 'Not Anyone'.
● ALBUMS: *Dreamland* (RCA 1990)★★★, *Remixed Reboxed Black Box/Mixed Up* (RCA 1991)★★★.
● COMPILATIONS: *Hits & Mixes* (Camden 1998)★★★.
● VIDEOS: *Video Dreams* (BMG Video 1990).

BLACK DOG PRODUCTIONS

Ken Downie joined up with Ed Handley and Andy Turner, who themselves formed Plaid, in 1988 to form Black Dog Productions, a secretive east London techno crew, communicating with the outside world from the infamous Black Dog Towers, and determinedly obscuring their identities. After attempting to persuade Larry Heard to remix their first tracks (he turned them down on the grounds that the music was 'too weird'), Black Dog released their first record, the *Virtual* EP, on Black Dog Records a year later. With the subsequent *Age Of Slack* and *Black Dog* EPs, despite their limited distribution (in part, the result of the distributor melting down half of the 1,000 copies of *Black Dog*), Black Dog had attracted a strong and loyal fanbase. With the inspirational use of breakbeats (at the time being hijacked by the 'happy hardcore' brigade) and melodies, in these early recordings Black Dog created some of their finest work, and indeed some of the finest abstract techno to emerge from the UK. They continued in style with the *Parallel Squelch* EP, released on the newly formed GPR label, attracting the interests of Warp and R&S Records. In 1993 Black Dog released their debut album, *Bytes*, as part of Warp's Artificial Intelligence series. Certainly one of the highlights of the series, the album highlighted their subtle sense of songwriting propriety, and attracted the attention of numerous artists, resulting in remix and production work for artists such as Nicolette and Björk. *Temple Of Transparent Balls*, on GPR, followed a year later, although much of the work had been produced prior to *Bytes*, and had been spilt between Ken Downie on the one hand, and the pairing of Ed Handley and Andy Turner on the other. *Spanners*, the last album featuring the original band line-up, was released in 1995. Sounding more accomplished, the album occasionally lacks the raw feel of some of their earlier cuts, although the sheer inventiveness of the synthetic sounds and percussion still manages to entrance the listener. Following *Spanners*, Handly and Turner departed, leaving Downie to continue working alone under the Black Dog name. The first 'solo' Black Dog album was released on Warp in 1996.
● ALBUMS: *Temple Of Transparent Balls* (GPR 1993)★★★, *Bytes* (Warp 1993)★★★★, *Spanners* (Warp 1995)★★★★, *Music For Adverts (And Short Films)* (Warp 1996)★★★.
● COMPILATIONS: *Parallel* (GPR 1995)★★★★.

BLACK MOON

Brooklyn-based rappers, whose entrance on the New York scene was rewarded with sales of over 200,000 of their debut cut, 'Who Gots The Props'. Black Moon, who comprise 5ft Excelerator, DJ Evil Dee and Buckshot (later joined by T.R.E.V.), signed with Nervous Records' offshoot, Wreck, despite stern competition, in 1991. There were certainly offers on the table from major companies: 'It seems to me that whenever anyone signs with a major company here in the US, and I'm specifically talking about rappers, they begin to lose control of their careers, their destiny.' Black Moon (signifying Brothers Lyrically Acting Combining Kickin' Music Out On Nations) have also revealed similar enlightenment in the way they handle their own affairs. They have set up their own production and management companies, Beat Minerz (Evil Dee and his brother Mr. Walt) and Duck Down (Buckshot and Big Dru Ha). The latter also looks after the affairs of Wreck's second signing, Smif And Wessun. Musically, Black Moon are a throwback to rap's old school - bleak bass and beatbox underpinning their considered raps for minimalist impact. Their debut album was afforded a strong critical reaction, no less than KRS-1 himself noting it to be '...the phattest shit I've heard in a long time'. It included their second single, 'How Many MC's (Must Get Dissed)', before they embarked on a national tour with Das EFX. Buckshot also worked with Special Ed and Master Ace, as the Crooklyn Dodgers, on the title track to Spike Lee's film, *Crooklyn*.

● ALBUMS: *Enta Da Stage* (Wreck 1993)★★★, *Diggin' In Dah Vaults* (Wreck/Nervous 1996)★★★.

BLACK RADICAL MK II

b. Felix Joseph, London, England. Joseph grew up listening to Jamaican reggae from Peter Tosh and Bob Marley, as well as by Steel Pulse. However, when he picked up on Public Enemy and Boogie Down Productions for the first time, he was an instant convert to the rap phenomenon. Although Joseph's convictions and ideas were clear, he sometimes lacked the dexterity to express them, as the *This Is War* EP's 'Hard Timez' revealed: 'They fuck us up just like we're vaginas / They even fucked up the miners / They gave them a disease that was called Heseltinisis.' Cuts like 'Sumarli' were more impressive, demonstrating his commitment to women's rights. A graduate of economics, Black Radical Mk II spent much of 1993 on an all-black film project, *Welcome To The Terrordome*.

● ALBUMS: *The Undiluted Truth* (Mango/Island 1991)★★★.

BLACK SHEEP

Rap duo comprising Andre 'Dres' Titus (b. *c*.1967, Sanford, North Carolina, USA) and William 'Mista Lawnge' McLean (b. 11 December 1970, Sanford, North Carolina, USA), who are based in the Bronx, New York, though they actually met in North Carolina in 1983. Titus's father, an army officer, was stationed there, while McLean's mother had relocated to the state while he was in school. He was sharing the bill with Sparkie Dee at a gig when her DJ, Red Alert, advised him that if he ever moved back to the capital, he should contact him. He did just that in 1985, linking up with the Jungle Brothers and A Tribe Called Quest, before telephoning Titus to invite him to join a band. Finally together, they arrived from a similar angle to the Native Tongues Posse, of which they were members, but doused their Afrocentricity in humour. Their self-produced debut album made the *Billboard* Top 30, mainly on the back of the excellent single, 'The Choice Is Yours', the video for which brought the band an *MTV* award. The album that housed it was filled with spoken interludes, heightened accents and ramshackle comedy. By the advent of their second longplaying set, the duo had toughened up slightly, but kept their musical stance sprightly. The album was prefaced by a single, 'No Way, No How'. They had also set up their own label operation, One Love Records, the first signing to which was a crew entitled Legion.

● ALBUMS: *A Wolf In Sheep's Clothing* (Mercury 1991)★★★, *Non Fiction* (Mercury 1994)★★★.

BLADE

b. Armenia, but settled in New Cross, London, England. One of the most forceful presences in UK rap in the 90s, Blade is widely regarded for his ability to tear up audiences live (though indie Carter USM fans bottled him offstage when he acted as the latter's support). More impressive still is his commitment to his art. After starting rapping at age 12, he financed his career by literally hand-selling his records as they emerged, slowly building up a network of fans. His debut album on his own label included contributions from Sista Nubia, MC Mell 'O' and Afriqsoul on 'As

Salaamo'. Blade's ferocious, Chuck D-styled delivery has marked him out as practically the only UK rapper to carry off a hardcore stance with conviction. However, he was still fiercely independent. He opened a subscription service to raise £25,000 for the recording of his second album, and received it from his enthusiastic fanbase. The resultant set celebrated Blade's victory over the music industry. It included an answerphone message from someone in the business who had originally turned Blade down, and was pleading to be in on the action.

● ALBUMS: *Survival Of The Hardest Workin'* mini-album (691 Influential 1992)★★★, *The Lion Goes From Strength To Strength* (691 Influential 1993)★★★.

BLANDO, DEBORAH

b. Brazil. After moving to America, dance/pop singer Deborah Blando achieved a degree of commercial success with the release of 'Boy', an affecting song included on her non-charting Epic Records debut album. After this commercial disappointment she returned to Brazil and set about re-establishing her career. She did so to impressive success, achieving four number 1s in the Brazilian charts, including 'Innocence', which stayed at the top for 13 weeks. Back in New York in the mid-90s, she chanced upon the music of flamenco band B-Tribe. Purchasing their 1994 album *Fiesta Fatal!*, she mentioned it to Jason Flom, president of Lava Records with whom she had recently signed. Flom said that he had been involved in the project, and agreed to fly Blando to B-Tribe's base in Germany. She contributed to three songs on B-Tribe's resultant *Suave Suave* album, including the single 'Nanita'. On her return, she set about recording tracks for her own Lava Records debut, with the assistance of producers Patrick Leonard and David Foster.

● ALBUMS: *Deborah Blando* (Epic 1990)★★.

BLISSED

(see Prana)

BLOOD OF ABRAHAM

This Los Angeles rap outfit consists of Jewish MCs Benyad and Mazik, plus DJs JJ and Lott Loose, and the group's origins can be traced to high school when the members first started writing poetry, which evolved into rap. Their early shows saw them discovered by NWA's Eazy-E; this was newsworthy because of Eazy-E's former employers' on-record comments about the nation of Israel. Accordingly, Blood Of Abraham were somewhat suspicious of his motives, not wishing to be perceived as 'gangsta rappers'. They did, however, sign to Ruthless with his endorsement. Their debut utilized comic spoken-word samples and looping bass-heavy rhythmic structures. However, their efforts to cakewalk racial territory, notably on cuts such as 'Niggaz And Jewz (Some Say Kikes)', was clumsy. Their response was most effective when tackling black racism towards Jews: 'Pull out the butt and let the smoke get deep / Cuz the Jews are the brothers that the niggas shouldn't fuck with'. The set, which ended with sampled dialogue from Martin Scorsese's film *Taxi Driver*, was produced by Bret 'Epic' Mazur, who had introduced them to Easy-E, alongside Lott Loose. A single, 'Stabbed By The Steeple', attacking organized religion, was also released from the album, but failed to achieve anything more than the gimmick coverage with which the band have become so irritated.

● ALBUMS: *Future Profits* (Ruthless/Relativity 1993)★★★.

BLOW

Blow are essentially Gordon Matthewman, who came to prominence in 1988 with the club hit, 'Go'. Several follow-ups failed to ignite, and it was not until 'Cutter' that he had another hit. Its popularity followed the mailing of 12 acetates to selected DJs, with the stock copy eventually emerging on Ten. The track's unusual use of trumpet and synthesizer endeared it to many, and it was also remixed by Altern 8. He continued to record into the mid-90s, and by 1994 had moved on to Nutbush/Parlophone for 'You'.

BLOW, KURTIS

b. Kurt Walker, 9 August 1959, Harlem, New York, USA. A producer and rap pioneer who had one of the genre's earliest hits with 'Christmas Rappin' in 1979, written for him by J.B. Ford and *Billboard* journalist Robert Ford Jnr. Blow had previously studied vocal performance at the High School Of Music and Art at the City College of New York. Afterwards, he began working as a DJ in Harlem where he added his first tentative raps to liven up proceedings. By this time he had made the acquaintance of fellow City College student Russel Simmons (see Run DMC), who convinced him to change his name from Kool DJ Kurt to Kurtis Blow. Playing in small clubs alongside other early innovators such as Grandmaster Flash, he signed to Mercury Records just as the Sugarhill Gang achieved the first rap chart success with 'Rapper's Delight'. Blow in turn became the first rap artist to cut albums for a major label. His 1979 hit, 'The Breaks', for which his partner Davy D (b. David Reeves Jnr.; originally titled Davey DMX, and best known for recording 'One For The Table (Fresh)') provided the first of his backing tracks, was a massive influence on the whole hip-hop movement. The early 80s were quiet in terms of chart success, before he re-emerged in 1983 with the *Party Time* EP and an appearance in the movie *Krush Groove*. *Ego Trip* was an impressive selection, bolstered by the presence of Run DMC on the minor hit '8 Million Stories'. He rapped on Rene And Angela's hit 'Save Your Love (For Number One)', doubtless an experience of which he would not wish to be reminded. He has also produced for the Fearless Four and Dr. Jeckyll And Mr Hyde, among others. His yearly album cycle continued with the patriotic *America*, whose earnest, sensitive moments (particularly, 'If I Ruled The World', which appeared on the soundtack to *Krush Groove* and as a single) were rather undermined by the presence of 'Super Sperm'. The following year he organized the all-star King Dream Chorus and Holiday Crew who recorded the Martin Luther King tribute, 'King Holiday', which campaigned for King's birthday to be enshrined as a national holiday. *Kingdom Blow* featured guest appearances from the likes of Bob Dylan, and George Clinton on an amazing interpretation of 'Zip-A-Dee-Doo-Dah'. However, Blow was largely overtaken by the young guns of the genre (notably Run DMC, ironically) that he helped to create, a fact underlined by the miserable reception offered the misnomered *Back By Popular Demand*, and he has not enjoyed a chart hit since 'I'm Chillin'' in 1986.

● ALBUMS: *Kurtis Blow* (Mercury 1980)★★★, *Deuce* (Mercury 1981)★★, *Tough* (Mercury 1982)★★, *Ego Trip* (Mercury 1984)★★★, *America* (Mercury 1985)★★★, *Kingdom Blow* (Mercury 1986)★★, *Back By Popular Demand* (Mercury 1988)★★.

● COMPILATIONS: *Best Of* (Mercury 1994)★★★.

BLOWZABELLA

Essentially a UK folk dance band, formed in 1978, which achieved a deal of success both on the live music circuit and on record. The group were almost as well known for the frequent changes of personnel as for their music. In 1987, sole remaining founder-member John Swayne (b. Jonathan Rock Phipps Swayne, 26 June 1940, Hereford, England; alto and soprano saxophones, bagpipes) left, and Jo Fraser (b. Jo-Anne Rachel Newmarch Fraser, 4 December 1960, St. Albans, Hertfordshire, England; saxophone, vocals, whistles) joined. In 1989, Fraser changed her name to Freya, as there was an Equity member with the same name. The rest of the group were Paul James (b. 4 April 1957, Southampton, Hampshire, England; bagpipes, soprano saxophone, percussion), Nigel Eaton (b. 3 January 1966, Lyndhurst, Hampshire, England; hurdy gurdy), Ian Luff (b. 4 January 1956, Brighton, Sussex, England; cittern, bass guitar), Dave Roberts (d. 23 February 1996; melodeon, darabuka) and Dave Shepherd (fiddle). Shepherd had joined the group in 1982, having previously played with folk rock band Dr. Cosgill's Delight, alongside James. Luff joined in 1985. Blowzabella toured Brazil for the British Council in 1987, playing a large number of concerts, and *Pingha Frenzy* emerged from over 50 hours of taped sessions. *A Richer Dust* came from the music the band had written for the 500th Anniversary of the Battle of Stoke Field. A concert featuring the piece was performed on 18 June 1987. James and Eaton formed Ancient Beatbox as a part-time project. Freya, by 1989, was also pursuing a career outside Blowzabella, notably touring with Kathryn Locke (b. 30 May 1961, Upminster, Essex, England; 'cello). Shepherd left to get married and moved to live in Germany, and Andy Cutting (b. 18 March 1969, West Harrow, Middlesex, England; melodeon) joined in 1989. Cutting had previously filled in on occasional dates when Shepherd was unavailable. Later that same year, Swayne rejoined the band. The group's repertoire included a wealth of dance material from northern Europe and France. Although considered a dance band, Blowzabella gave many concerts in such places as Ghana, Nigeria, Sierra Leone, Europe and Brazil. They played a 'farewell tour' in 1990 as it had become uneconomical to stay together and tour. The various members have become involved in their own projects and continue to perform.

● ALBUMS: *Blowzabella* (Plant Life 1982)★★★, *Blowzabella In Colour* (Plant Life 1983)★★, *Bobbityshooty* (Plant Life 1984)★★★, with Frankie Armstrong, Brian Pearson *Tam Lin* (Plant Life 1985)★★★, *The Blowzabella Wall Of Sound* (Plant Life 1986)★★★, *The B To A Of*

Blowzabella (1987)★★★, *Pingha Frenzy* (Some Bizzare 1988)★★★, *Vanilla* (Topic 1990)★★.
● COMPILATIONS: *** (Osmosys 1995)★★★.

BLUE PEARL

UK band Blue Pearl enjoyed some success in the 90s with their 'Naked In The Rain' hit. Its incisive pop instincts were matched by an album, which featured cameos from Pink Floyd members Dave Gilmour and Rick Wright, alongside Youth of Killing Joke and Brilliant, who wrote, played and produced. Just as the single had been, the set was notable for the attractive voice of Durga McBroom, not least on a version of Kate Bush's 'Running Up That Hill'. Other singles such as '(Can You) Feel The Passion' followed, but the latter prompted a legal battle because it was based around a Youth remix of Bizarre Inc's 'Playing With Knives', which that group had rejected. In 1993 McBroom ceased to record exclusively with Blue Pearl, teaming up with German producer Johann Bley and British remixer Ben Watkins. Her debut single was 'Fire Of Love' on Logic, based on the Psychick Warriors Ov Gaia standard, 'Jungle High'. On her trial separation, McBroom commented: 'Being in a group is like a marriage. If you're married to the same person for a long time and you divorce you start dating again. So I've had a lot of good dates recently'.
● ALBUMS: *Blue Pearl* (WAU! Mr Modo 1991)★★★.

BLUE ROOM RELEASED

Trance-techno label Blue Room has always maintained a distinctive character within this field, with boss Simon Ghahary taking an alternative approach with his acts to that taken by many other dance labels: 'The label is here to promote the up and coming talent, the freeform and the psychedelic, not just trance'. The music and presentation have tended to avoid the fashion for the eastern-spiritual vibe favoured by the trance scene, choosing instead a more spartan electronic feel for the compilations *Signs of Life* and *Made on Earth*. However, the label's diversity is its strength, with the Saafi Brothers' dubby, chilled-out album *Mystic Cigarettes* sitting comfortably beside Kox Box's complex electronics on *Dragon Tales*; Ghahary 'won't be put off by breakbeats or vocals', refusing to succumb to the kind of snobbery prevalent in much dance music. Many bands, such as Juno Reactor, place an emphasis on live performance as well as studio work and Ghahary is also eager to promote the careers of his artists rather than release a string of anonymous singles and albums.

BOLLAND, C.J.

b. Christian Jay Bolland, Tyneside, England. Techno maestro Bolland moved with his family to Antwerp, Belgium at an early age, and began making his own music as a three-year-old. Widely respected on the Euro techno circuit, Bolland works principally at the R&S label, specializing in hard-edged rave tunes. He has recorded as Sonic Solution ('Music') and has released the *Ravesignals 1, 2* and *3* EPs. However, *The 4th Sign* in 1993 saw him dispense with his other former *noms de plume* (Pulse, the Project, Space Opera). It included the new dancefloor techno anthem 'Carmague'. His remixes include Human Resource's 'Dominator' and Baby Ford's 'In Your Blood'.
● ALBUMS: *The 4th Sign* (R&S 1993)★★★, *Electronic Highway* (R&S 1995)★★★, *The Analogue Theatre* (Internal 1996)★★★.

BOMB SQUAD

Public Enemy's production arm, made up of four cornerstones: Chuck D (b. Carl Ridenhour), Eric 'Vietnam' Sadler, Hank Schocklee and Keith Schocklee. As well as spearheading Public Enemy's dense, embittered records, they were soon in demand for work on all manner of projects. Arguably the most successful was Ice Cube's *Amerikkka's Most Wanted* opus, but other clients included Ali Dee, Doug E. Fresh, Run DMC, Leaders Of The New School, Son Of Bazerk and many more. They also introduced outsiders to their technique by allowing younger producers such as Gary G-Wiz to work alongside them. In 1990 Hank Schocklee launched the SOUL (Sound Of Urban Listeners) label with former Def Jam Promotion Vice President Bill Stephney. The first signings were Young Black Teenagers. By the advent of Public Enemy's fifth album proper, *Muse Sick N Our Mess Age*, in 1994, the Bomb Squad had been enlarged to include the aforementioned G-Wiz, Kerwin 'Sleek' Young (who played a large role in shaping Professor Griff's *Pawns In The Game*), EZ Moe Bee (featured on Big Daddy Kane's *Looks Like A Job For...*) and Larry 'Panic' Watford.

BOMB THE BASS

Techno dance outfit who are a collective front for Tim Simenon (b. 1968, Brixton, London, England; of Malay Chinese and Scottish parents). After attending a course in studio engineering he shot to prominence in 1988 with 'Beat Dis', which reached the Top 5, where the subsequent album followed. Both 'Megablast' and 'Say A Little Prayer' were also Top 10 hits, the latter featuring Maureen Walsh, who went on to her own solo career, beginning with a cover version of Sister Sledge's 'Thinking Of You' for Urban. Simenon then worked with Neneh Cherry (producing her hits 'Buffalo Stance' and 'Manchild'). After completing work on his new studio he took up production duties for an album by Prince sidekick Cat. Co-production on Adamski's 'Killer' and the Seal single 'Crazy' followed. However, feeling aggrieved at the lack of credit and financial recompense he gained from these ventures, he returned to Bomb The Bass. His timing was less than apt, as the 1991 Gulf War made continued use of the name indelicate. He reverted to his own name for the single 'Love So True', co-written with bass player Doug Wimbush (Sugarhill Gang, Tackhead) and vocalist Loretta Heywood. By this time he was also working extensively with guitarist Kenji Suzuki, in addition to a myriad of guest vocalists. Bomb The Bass returned in 1995 with a new album, *Clear*, their finest and most eclectic collection to date, which featured vocal contributions from maverick English writer Will Self. Simenon also unveiled his own label, Stoned Heights, distributed through Island.
● ALBUMS: *Into The Dragon* (Rhythm King 1988)★★★, *Unknown Territory* (Rhythm King 1991)★★★, *Clear* (Stoned Heights 1995)★★★★.
● VIDEOS: *Don't Make Me Wait* (Weinerworld 1988).

BON ROCK AND THE RHYTHEM REBELLION

This early 80s group, comprising lead rapper Bon Rock and his Rhythem (sic) Rebellion backing vocalists, Tania Battiste and Diane Hawkins, were formed by Bon after pestering the owners of the Now Music record store in New York City, New York, USA. The proprietors (Ed Pavia and Anthony Giammanco) had decided to set up a record label, Reelin' And Rockin', which housed Rhythm Rebellion's debut single, 'Searchin' Rap'. This was built over the framework of a sample of Unlimited Touch's 'Searchin' To Find The One'. However, the band was short-lived and had expired by the early 80s. Battiste and Hawkins later played live sets at the Audubon Ballroom in New York and released 'Junior Wants To Play' for Tommy Boy Records, a reworking of soul star Junior Giscombe's 'Mama Used To Say'.

BONE THUGS-N-HARMONY

Based in Cleveland, Ohio, USA, Bone Thugs-N-Harmony were one of the most successful rap groups to break into the mainstream in 1995. Formed in 1993, they consist of Layzie Bone, Bizzy Bone, Krayzie Bone, Wish Bone and Flesh-N-Bone, and were 'discovered and nurtured' by the founder of Ruthless Records, the late Eazy E. Their initial impact was astounding, even within a musical genre associated with a fast turnover of star acts. Their 1994 debut EP, *Creeping On Ah Come Up*, had spent over 70 weeks in *Billboard*'s Top 200 album chart by 1996, with sales of over four million. *E. 1999 Eternal* went to number 1 in the same album chart, selling over 330,000 copies in its first week of release. The group's popularity is due to their appealing combination of R&B harmonies and rapping, as featured on the single '1st Of Tha Month'. In Bone Thugs-N-Harmony, melody had arrived to a previously hard and often musically devoid genre. Much of Stevie Wonder's smooth harmony style was brilliantly mixed with techno rap, and even if their gangsta rapping became tiresome, their debut somehow managed to put it into the background. The group returned with the overindulgent double-disc *The Art Of War* in 1997, which stretched the group's lyrical and musical ideas far too thinly over its 70-minute length.
● ALBUMS: *E.1999 Eternal* (Ruthless/Relativity 1995)★★★★, *The Art Of War* (Ruthless 1997)★★.

BONES, FRANKIE

This popular New York DJ has completed a number of remix and production projects. As a solo artist he has enjoyed hits such as 'Just As Long As I Got You' (1988) and has also worked as Liquid Oxygen, Break Boys ('And The Break Goes On'), Looney Tunes ('Just As Long As I've Got You' and 'Another Place Another Time') and Lake Errie ('Sex 4 Daze'). While he has recorded for a number of labels including Nu Groove Records, Bones ran Pyramix Records, which housed Mister C's 'Don't Stop', among others. In 1990 he released the album *Dance Madness And The Brooklyn*

Groove on RCA Records. With Tommy Musto he had success with such tracks as 'Dangerous On The Dance Floor' and 'All I Want Is To Get Away' and released an album *The Future Is Ours* in 1990. Bones has continued to DJ around the world, with regular visits to the UK.

● ALBUMS: *Dance Madness And The Brooklyn Groove* (RCA 1990), with Tommy Musto *The Future Is Ours* (Citybeat 1990).

BOO-YAA T.R.I.B.E.

Of Samoan descent, Boo-Yaa T.R.I.B.E. were born and bred in the Los Angeles neighbourhood of Carson, where their father was a Baptist minister. Life was tough, evidence of which exists in their choice of name (slang for a shotgun being discharged). Running with the Bloods gang, every member of the clan had endured a stretch in prison, and one of their brothers, Robert 'Youngman' Devoux, was shot dead before the family turned musical. The brothers freely admit to having had involvement with drug production and brokering, as well as gun running. Ultimately the group took the death of their kin as a sign from God, and headed for Japan to escape the gang warfare, staying with their Sumo wrestler cousin. There they subsisted by working as a rap/dance outfit in Tokyo, which convinced them their success could be imported back to LA. Island Records were the first to see a potential market for a sound that fused gangster imagery with hardcore hip-hop, and obtained their signatures. They appeared in Michael Jackson's Walt Disney film *Captain EO* as breakdancers, as well as television shows *Fame* and *The A-Team*. The line-up boasts lead rapper Ganxsta Ridd (aka Paul Devoux), EKA, Rosco, Ganxsta OMB, The Godfather (aka Ted Devoux), and Don-L. Some members of the Los Angeles Police Department still harbour suspicions that the Tribe is merely a front for their continued illicit activities, but powerful singles such as 'Psyko Funk' represented a genuine, bullying rap presence. Their second album, featured further gangland narratives such as 'Kreepin' Through Your Hood' and 'Gangstas Of The Industry' - a put-down of rank commercialism and fake posturing for profit.

● ALBUMS: *New Funky Nation* (4th & Broadway 1990)★★★, *Doomsday* (Bulletproof 1994)★★★, *Angry Samoans* (Bulletproof 1997)★★★.

BOOGIE BEAT RECORDS

This UK dance music record label has become one of the most popular homes to hardcore/jungle since its inception in February 1992. 'Kid' Andy, a former pirate radio disc jockey, was joined by George Power, administrative director, and engineer/co-producer Ben Wilson as the nucleus of the team. The label's first release was Order 2 Move's 'Rizla Bass', followed by further releases from Audio Illusion, Intellect, Dance On Arrival, Ministers Of Dance, Technicians Flingdown, D-Code, Mixmaster Max, Trance 4 Mist, Charl E, Agent 24K, Weekend Rush, Sonic The Dreadlocks and several others. Many of these were faintly ridiculous *noms de plume* for the label personnel themselves, but most of the singles were also highly respected in the expanding jungle market, where the anonymity of those involved is virtually a prerequisite.

BOOGIE DOWN PRODUCTIONS

This Bronx, New York-based rap duo comprised DJ Scott La Rock (b. Scott Sterling, c.1962, d. 27 August 1987, South Bronx, New York, USA) and rapper KRS-1 (b. Lawrence 'Kris' Parker, 1966, USA). KRS-1 (aka K.R.S.-One) is an acronym for Knowledge Reigns Sumpreme Over Nearly Everyone, and 'edutainment' remained a central theme in the work of Boogie Down Productions. Similar to most New York rap crews, their lyrics highlighted the problems of blacks living in a modern urban environment, compounded by the increasing drug problems, gang wars and use of weaponry on the streets. Indeed, La Rock and KRS-1, who had formerly worked with 'joke' rap act 12:41 ('Success Is The Word'), met at a homeless people's shelter in the Bronx, where La Rock was a counsellor and KRS-1 a client. Following their first release, 'Crack Attack', their debut album, *Criminal Minded*, was produced in conjunction with fellow Bronx crew, the Ultramagnetic MC's. It was a set that actively suggested that young blacks were entitled to use 'any means necessary' in order to overcome years of prejudice and discrimination. It sold over 500,000 copies and was instrumental in kick-starting the gangsta rap movement. After Scott La Rock became the victim of an unknown assassin while sitting in a parked car in the South Bronx, KRS-1's lyrics enforced an even stronger need for a change in attitude, demanding an end to violence and the need for blacks to educate themselves.

Criminal Minded had, of course, depicted the duo wielding guns on its sleeve. The follow-up sets, *By All Means Necessary* and *Ghetto Music: The Blueprint Of Hip-Hop*, are arguably just as convincing; tracks such as 'The Style You Haven't Done Yet' taking pot shots at KRS-1's would-be successors. There was certainly much to admire in KRS-1's style, his method becoming the most frequently copied in aspiring new rappers. He was also setting out on lecture tours of American universities, even writing columns for the *New York Times*. Like contemporaries Public Enemy, KRS-1/Boogie Down Productions retained the hardcore edge necessary to put over their message, and in doing so, brought a more politically aware and mature conscience to the rap scene. However, 1990's *Edutainment* possibly took the 'message' angle too far, featuring only lacklustre musical accompaniment to buoy KRS-1's momentous tracts. The live set that followed it was not the first such hip-hop album (2 Live Crew beating KRS-1 to the punch), but it was certainly the best so far, with a virulent, tangible energy. Since the release of *Sex & Violence*, KRS-1 has elected to release new material under his own name and abandoned the Boogie Down Productions moniker.

● ALBUMS: *Criminal Minded* (Sugarhill/B-boy 1987)★★★★, *By All Means Necessary* (Jive 1988)★★★★, *Ghetto Music: The Blueprint Of Hip Hop* (Jive 1989)★★★★, *Edutainment* (Jive 1990)★★★, *Live Hardcore Worldwide: Paris, London & NYC* (Jive 1991)★★★★, *Sex And Violence* (Jive 1992)★★★.

BORTOLOTTI, GIANFRANCO

One of dance music's most colourful ambassadors, Bortolotti is the name behind many 'Italo-house' classics as manager of Media Records. Bortolotti had originally found himself in the DJ world to supplement his university days. He was initially influenced by DJ Pierre (not the US version), learning his craft from him, and when the latter's career began, actually helped in distributing records. His involvement grew until he too recouped the rewards of a couple of minor hit singles, reinvesting the money in a home studio and founding the Media label. Since then he has never looked back - and now owns no less than 10 studios. His main complex in Brescia, North Italy, is built on the Motown/SAW principle, churning out hits at a rate other factories ship beans. Capella's breakthrough hit, 'Heylom Halib', introduced the

insistent rhythms, zany samples, tinkling piano and memorable choruses and catchphrases. This in turn predicted the wave of Italo-house hits (Black Box's 'Ride On Time', Starlight's 'Numero Uno', Mixmaster's 'Grand Piano') that dominated the 1989 dance scene. It has continued unabated ever since. Whatever the names employed - 49ers ('Touch Me'), Fargetta ('The Music Is Movin''), East Side Beat, Clubhouse, Clock, DJ Professor, RAF - the hits have continued to flow. Just as Berry Gordy might have envisioned had he enjoyed access to the technology, the Media set-up is strictly businesslike, with three main producers (DJ Pierre, DJ Professor or RAF) working on their own floor. Each record is mixed between 15 and 20 times to suit individual territories. It is an astoundingly efficient and economic approach to making music.

● COMPILATIONS: Various Artists *Power Of The Media* (Media 1994)★★★.

BOSS

b. Detroit, Michigan, USA. A self-avowed 'Born Gangsta' pushing hardcore rap feminism into new territories, Boss announced her intentions with the inviting debut single, 'I Don't Give A Fuck', a phrase regularly repeated on her debut album. Originally operating alongside partner MC Dee, the album detailed their experiences on the streets of South Central, Los Angeles, and New York. The overriding factor was to encourage women to take control of their own lives, rather than expecting the benevolence of a male figure to help them out. In turn she has set up her own production company, Boss Productions, to help other aspiring hip-hop stars in Detroit. She also completed soundtrack work, recording 'Run, Catch, And Kill' for the *Mi Vida Loca* movie.

● ALBUMS: *Born Gangstaz* (DJ West 1993)★★★.

BOTANY 5

UK band Botany 500 were formed by ex-Juggernauts (one single, 'Throw Yourself Under The Monstrous Wheels Of The Rock 'n' Roll Industry As It Approaches Destruction') vocalist Gordon Kerr (b. Sterling, Scotland) and David Galbraith. Their early use of ambient textures along with funk and jazz interludes was persuasive and pleasant. A debut single for Supreme, 'Bully Beef', even featured live string accompaniment. Kerr split from Galbraith in 1989, winning a Tennent's Live! talent competition run by Glasgow's Ca Va studio. He signed to Virgin, replacing his partner with Jason Robertson (guitar) and Stevie Christie (keyboards). The name was shortened to Botany 5 when a lawsuit was threatened from the American company Botany 500, responsible for wardrobe on television fare such as *Kojak*. A single, 'Love Bomb', preceded Botany 5's debut album, which was significantly ahead of its time, predicting the chilled house tones of the Orb, Aphex Twin, etc. It was created as a deliberate antidote to the excesses of the Summer Of Love: 'Our album's for when kids come home from raves. No crazy, out of hand stuff. More artistic; slow, mellow, subdued . . . quiet'. The trio were joined for live extravaganzas by former Orange Juice drummer Zeke Manyika and Paul Weller associate Carmel, in order to provide more organic backing.

● ALBUMS: *Into The Night* (Virgin 1991)★★★.

BOTTOM LINE RECORDS

Brooklyn, New York label, established in November 1991 with the release of Devastating's 'Givin' It 2 U'. From its base in Coney Island, the label is run by expatriate Moscow legend Ed 'The Red' Goltsmann, with his wife Nancy Kay (additional help is often provided by Nelson Roman). Together they are responsible for producing all the tracks on the varied and much admired Bottom Line catalogue. The duo had originally worked as live musicians at parties, clubs and wedding receptions, and first recorded for New Jersey's Vista Sounds (Intro's 'Under Your Spell' and two releases from Red Follies). Even though neither was particularly familiar with the New York club scene, they have gone on to produce a succession of releases that remain highly sought after on the dance scene. Their biggest successes have included Tammy Banks' 'My Life' and Flow's 'Another Time'. They also record as the aforementioned Devastating ('Givin' It 2 U' and 'Wherever You Are Right Now'), Hearsay ('Move Yo Body, Work Yo Body'), Sample Minded ('Eternity', 'The Sounds Of Redness'), ODC ('My Mind Is Going'), Fast Wheels ('I Never Dreamed It Could Be Like This'), Passion Is Fashion ('You Make Me Want To Love You') and Secret Lovers ('Do Me Right'). They also continued to record as Red Follies ('We Will Survive', 'Sweet Love'), using the vocals of MJ White. More recent productions have been distinguished by material such as 'Tonite', a simple jazzy tune credited to Jerzey Boy, or Nelson's 'Paradise'.

BOUNCER, PETER

So named because of his previous employment in nightclub security, UK-born Peter Bouncer first had a hit with Shut Up And Dance's UK number 2 hit, 'Ravin' I'm Ravin'', in May 1992. He was formerly a devotee of reggae, and a popular dancehall DJ with Unity Sounds. He made his solo debut in a very different vein, that of unrelenting hardcore, on 'So Here I Come'. His forbidding reputation preceded him, but his soulful voice was stretched too thinly over the throbbing grooves. Described in the music press as the 'Sinatra of hardcore', he has yet to establish a significant audience in this field or any other.

BOY'S OWN RECORDS

This label was founded in 1990 by a loose collective of DJs that included the influential acid house figures Terry Farley and Andrew Weatherall. Since 1986 the pair had, with Steven Hall, produced a fanzine called *Boy's Own* that chronicled football, fashion, music and other elements of youth culture, and, towards the end of the decade, documented the rise of acid house. At the same time they were playing at such clubs as Danny Rampling's Shoom and Paul Oakenfold's Future, and as the scene expanded they began working on various remixes: Farley's work included the Happy Mondays' 'Wrote For Luck' and the Farm's 'Stepping Stone', while Weatherall reworked Primal Scream's 'Loaded'. The trio consequently set up Boy's Own Records, in association with London Records, to release material written by themselves and their friends. The first release was 'Raise (63 Steps To Heaven)' by Bocca Juniors (Farley, Pete Heller, Hugh Nicholson and Weatherall) and was followed over the next few years by a series of Balearic singles that became club hits, including Less Stress's cover version of Crowded House's 'Don't Dream It's Over' and DSK's 'What Would We Do', and a number of diverse albums from One Dove, Denim and other artists. After a few years, Weatherall left to start Sabres Of Paradise, shortly before Farley and Hall severed their ties with London to start an independently distributed label under the name Junior Boy's Own Records.

● COMPILATIONS: Various: *The Junior Boy's Own Collection* (Junior Boy's Own 1994)★★★, *The Junior Boy's Own Collection 2* (Junior Boy's Own 1997)★★★, *Junior Boy's Own: A Perspective 1988-1998* (Heavenly 1998)★★★★.

BOYMERANG

Boymerang is the alter ego of Bark Psychosis's Graham Sutton. Sutton, based in London, England, is among a new generation of UK artists attracted to the possibilities of jungle in the mid-90s - hardcore and techno having hit a creative *cul de sac* and 'become the new puritans of the dance scene'. Fascinated by this nascent movement, Sutton started to patronize north London's Lucky Spin hardcore shop, buying many of the anonymous white label 12-inches, eventually deciding to experiment himself. Having previously programmed tracks for Bark Psychosis, he applied that knowledge to produce the *Boymerang* EP in early 1995. Released on Leaf Records, his input into the jungle scene, rather than creating suspicion, was widely welcomed, and engendered a sizeable genre hit. Sutton also contributes to an ambient 'chill out' show on the Kiss FM radio station and plays sets at some of the UK capital's more adventurous clubs.
● ALBUMS: *Balance Of The Force* (Regal 1997)★★★.

BRAND NUBIAN

From the Bronx, New York, and led by Grand Puba (b. Maxwell Dixon; ex-Masters Of Ceremony), Brand Nubian's work is as cool, classy and unaffected as hip-hop comes. Joined by Lord Jamar (b. Lorenzo Dechelaus, 17 September 1968, New Rochelle, New York, USA), Sadat X (b. Derrick Murphy, 29 December 1968, New Rochelle, New York, USA) and DJ Alamo (the latter two cousins), Puba sings Muslim-influenced lyrics, backed by steals from some of soul music's greatest moments. Samples of James Brown and Roy Ayers ensured the backing was never less than interesting. In 1991 Grand Puba left to go solo, taking DJ Alamo with him, but Brand Nubian elected to continue as a three-piece unit with the addition of DJ Sincere. Their first album following his defection was *In God We Trust*, focused more on their intensely held beliefs with tracks such as 'The Meaning Of The 5%', 'Allah And Justice' and 'Ain't No Mystery'. The album title referred to a significant element of Five Percent doctrine. 'We represent ourselves as god', said Lord Jamar, 'and we're not trusting any mystery in the sky to help us with what we have to do. When a religion teaches you to depend on something else instead of being self-sufficient, then that becomes the downfall of people.' *Everything Is Everything* was a disappointing album, with laboured beats failing to raise the interest level.
● ALBUMS: *One For All* (Elektra 1990)★★★★, *In God We Trust* (Elektra 1993)★★★, *Everything Is Everything* (Elektra 1994)★★.

BROADWAY

b. Dion Barnes, Bronx, New York, USA. Broadway originally rose to prominence as part of the hip-hop group Strictly Roots in the early 90s, who recorded for his own label Friends Connection. That group achieved its breakthrough in 1993 with the release of the single 'Begs No Friends', which featured guest appearances from Fat Joe Da Gangsta and Grand Puba. Barnes had grown up in the active hip-hop streets of the Bronx when Grandmaster Flash and DJ Kool Herc were still in their prime. The connection with Herc, the first to combine hip-hop with Jamaican styles, is instructive - as Broadway is the son of reggae great Sugar Minott. His easy, laconic delivery embraces both the Jamaican and Bronx traditions, and often sees him adopt patois lyrics. He also idolizes KRS-1, who rewarded him with membership of his Boogie Down Productions collective. His first solo single, 'Must Get Paid', was produced by KRS-1 and released as part of the expanding Nervous Records hip-hop roster.

BROTHER D

From the Bronx, New York, USA, and one of the earliest 'reality' rappers, Brother D. (b. Daryl Aamaa Nubyahn) was a maths teacher, and recorded the mighty 'How We Gonna Make The Black Nation Rise', on Clappers (a label set up by expatriate Jamaican Lister Hewan Lowe). Based on the popular Cheryl Lynn 'Got To Be Real' break, it acted as a soundtrack to the political organization National Black Science.

BROTHERHOOD

Formed in Edgware, north London, England, in the mid-80s, rap collective the Brotherhood took a long time to coalesce into the streamlined trio who released 1996's groundbreaking *Elementalz* collection. Shyloc, Spice and DJ Mr Dexter were the survivors from the original eight-piece who had tasted underground success with three singles and an EP, including the popular 'I Might Smoke A Spliff But I Don't Sniff. In 1994 the group were signed to Virgin Records via their producer Trevor Jackson's (the Underdog) subsidiary imprint, Bite It! Records. Bite It! had earned strong plaudits for its packaging and style, a quality that was continued on *Elementalz* with the aid of *avant garde* photographer David McKean. Jackson remained in charge of production (he has previously worked with U2, Shara Nelson and Massive Attack), though the album's release was delayed for six months following the death of Jackson and the Brotherhood's manager, Marts Andrups. Two singles were drawn from *Elementalz*, 'Alphabetic Response' and 'One Shot', while the album itself included contributions from Brian Auger and samples from UK acts such as King Crimson and Soft Machine. Even before its release, *Elementalz* was widely championed in both the mainstream and hip-hop media as representing UK rap's coming of age, a claim that songs such as 'Going Underground' (not the Jam song) and the agenda-setting 'British Accent Pride' fully justified.

● ALBUMS: *Elementalz* (Bite It!/Virgin 1996)★★★★.

BROTHERS IN RHYTHM

London, UK-based producer Steve Anderson and Leeds, UK-based DJ David Seaman, who met through the DMC organization in 1988, established themselves as one of the UK house scene's most adventurous and popular remixing teams. They initially came to public prominence with startling revisions of yesteryear such as Heaven 17's 'Temptation' and Frankie Goes To Hollywood's 'Welcome To The Pleasuredome'. Other work included engagements with Sabrina Johnson ('Peace'), Pet Shop Boys ('We All Feel Better In The Dark', 'DJ Culture', 'Was It Worth It?', 'Seriously'), Kylie Minogue ('Finer Feelings'), Ce Ce Peniston ('We Got A Love Thang'), Lulu ('Independence') and Judy Cheeks ('Reach'). They also earned the honour of being the first British team to remix Michael Jackson ('Who Is It?' - and they would also work on a track for sister Janet Jackson). Their own work as Brothers In Rhythm included the singles 'Such A Good Feeling' (remixed by Sasha) and 'Peace And Harmony', though they left 4th & Broadway in 1992, delaying the release of a third, 'Forever And A Day'. They have also recorded under the alias Brothers Love Dub ('Ming's Incredible Disco Machine') and Creative Thieves ('Nasty Rhythm'). Seaman was also a leading light behind the DMC/Stress empire, and also signed a publishing contract with MCA.

BT

b. Brian Transeau, Maryland, USA. Arguably the most accomplished and recognizable of the largely anonymous trance-house set, Transeau made a huge mid-90s impact with releases such as 'Loving You More' and 'Embracing The Future' for Perfecto Records. As well as being staples of European dancefloors, they also reached the UK charts. Both songs were segued together in a 40-minute blockbuster by Sasha to form the centrepiece of BT's similarly successful debut album, *Ima*. Afterwards, his 'dream house' style became widely impersonated (but rarely equalled), to the evident frustration of the artist: 'So many people were ripping off things I was emotionally attached to without putting any of their own emotion into them. They were turning it into a formula and it was never intended to be like that. It was very emotional, altruistic, heartfelt music.' As a consequence he jettisoned an album's worth of material for a projected follow-up effort, and concentrated on remixing duties (including Grace's UK Top 20 hit, 'Not Over Yet', and Tori Amos's US chart-topper, 'Blue Skies'). His own solo output suffered as a result. Laborious sessions for the 25-minute single 'Hand In Hand', which paired him with 'Loving You More' singer Vincent Covello, were highly stressful: 'I was going nuts trying to finish it', he told *Music Week*. In the event he elected to go back to basics for the follow-up single, 'Flaming June'/'Orbitus Terranium', and his second album, *ESCM*. Again, this featured a bizarre array of sounds, ranging from the mating calls of tree frogs and wild turkeys to the vocals of Manchester folk-singer Jan Johnston and sufi vocalist T.H. Culhane.

● ALBUMS: *Ima* (Perfecto 1995)★★★, *ESCM* (Perfecto 1997)★★★.

BUCKETHEADS

The creation of revered DJ and producer Kenny 'Dope' Gonzalez, the Bucketheads project arose out of a 'burst of inspiration' in 1994. From his home in Brooklyn, New York, USA, Gonzalez crafted the US and UK Top 40 hit 'The Bomb! (These Sounds Fall Into My Mind)'. Released on Henry Street/Big Beat Records in America and on Positiva Records in the UK, the single included an unlikely sample of Chicago's 'Street Player'. The resultant album, *All In The Mind*, a collection of largely instrumental hip-hop and house tunes, confirmed the promise. It was a major departure from Gonzalez's established sound as half of the Masters At Work production team. A third single, 'Got Myself Together', provided another world-wide club and chart hit.

● ALBUMS: *All In The Mind* (Henry Street/Positiva 1995)★★★.

BUMP

Bump is an umbrella name for the activities of UK DJ Mark Auerbach and studio engineer Steve Travell. The two initially met at the 1991 New Music Seminar, where they were overheard congratulating each other on their work. They swapped addresses before returning to their 'day' jobs - Mark DJing with the Slam boys and working with Adamski, while Steve launched his group, the Orange. When that venture ground to a halt he got back in touch with Mark. Under their joint auspices they recorded 'I'm Rushin''. Convinced they had found the perfect meter, they sent out promo copies to prominent DJs, pressed on their own Good Boy Records. Sampling a vocal line from Sir James' 'Special', it saw a stock release on the Strictly Rhythm imprint. In the wake of its success they were invited to provide remixes, notably of David D'or's 'Yad Anougah', also working with Sue Chaloner, Supereal, Soundsource and the Reese Project. In 1992 they noted: 'We're reaching the threshold where we can be remixers for the rest of our lives if we want to.' However, as Auerbach added, there were drawbacks: 'There's a lot of pressure to turn shit into gems.' Their style has been described as progressive house, though this is not a bracket with which they themselves are happy.

BUSH RECORDS

This UK record label is co-owned by Eric Powell and Eric Gooden (aka Sweet Mercy and Temper Temper, respectively). They were responsible for discovering Melanie Williams, who sang with Sub Sub before going solo. Bush began life as a 'trance-house' label whose style predated the progressive boom. Releases included Trinity's self-titled debut, and a remix of T-Coy's 'Carino'. The team later collaborated with Felix Da Housecat for 'Thee Lite'. Felix had actually tracked down the duo after hearing their earlier releases, such as Reason featuring Alicka's 'Heartache' and the Sandman's 'Psychosis' (the b-side to which featured Jean Michel Jarre). 1994 brought fresh material from Dave Clarke ('Red 2').

BUSHWICK BILL

b. Richard Shaw, Jamaica, West Indies. A founder-member of the Geto Boys, from Texas, USA, Bushwick Bill aka Dr Wolfgang Von Bushwick began his solo career in 1992 with a successful solo album. He had lost his right eye in a shooting in May 1991, and some critics, appalled by his graphic descriptions of violence and sex, pointed out that he suffered from myopia both literally and figuratively. It was one of the first records, however, to predict the rise of the horror film-fixated raps ('horror core') subsequently taken up by the Wu-Tang Clan and others. *Phantom Of The Rapra* was a more accomplished recording and this time west coast G-Funk rhythms had replaced the samples of 70s funk, and Bushwick Bill's raps now boasted a clear-headed tone distinct from his debut.

● ALBUMS: *Little Big Man* (Rap-A-Lot 1992)★★★, *Phantom Of The Rapra* (Rap-A-Lot 1995)★★★.

BUSTA RHYMES

b. Brooklyn, New York, USA. Talented rapper Busta Rhymes became the toast of the American hip-hop community with the release of his Elektra Records debut, *The Coming*, in 1996. Although offering nothing outstanding in its lyrics, album tracks such as 'Everything Remains Raw' and 'It's A Party' highlighted Busta's compelling delivery to good effect. Rhymes had originally rapped as part of the highly praised Leaders Of The New School, with MC Charlie Brown, Dinco D and Milo In De Dance. He has also worked with a stellar cast of singers including Boyz II Men, Mary J. Blige, TLC and A Tribe Called Quest, and appeared in the movies *Higher Learning*, *Strapped* and *Who's The Man?*. Attempts to promote *The Coming* in the UK ended in disaster. His planned performance at the Kentish Town Forum in May ended in calamity when delays in securing a work permit prevented him from appearing. Outraged fans caused an estimated £75,000 of damage after they rioted in protest. Rhymes released the ambitious *When Disaster Strikes . . .* in September 1997, exploring pre-millennial fears and the future of rap. The album also included a powerful duet with Erykah Badu on 'One'.

● ALBUMS: *The Coming* (Elektra 1996)★★, *When Disaster Strikes . . .* (Elektra 1997)★★★.

C + C Music Factory

A production team comprising Robert Clivillés (b. *c.*1960, New York, USA) and David Cole (b. *c.*1962, Tennessee, USA, d. 1995), who first recorded as 2 Puerto Ricans, A Black Man And A Dominican with 'Do It Properly' on their own label in 1987. As C + C Music Factory they reached number 3 in the UK with 'Gonna Make You Sweat (Everybody Dance Now)', in 1990. Although this was credited to C + C Music Factory featuring Freedom Williams (b. *c.*1966; a rapper who also appeared on records by New Kids On The Block and Grace Jones), the duo were solely in charge of matters, hiring vocalists and musicians and programming the backbeat. Over the next two years guest singers included Zelma Davis (b. *c.*1967, Liberia), whose contribution was lip-synched, with the vocal actually provided by Martha Wash of the Weather Girls, Q Unique and Deborah Cooper (ex-Fatback Band; Change). Though they enjoyed six further US Top 40 hits during 1991 and 1992, including a re-recording of U2's 'Pride', only 'Things That Make You Go Hmmm', again jointly credited with Williams, reached the Top 10. It was later widely played during a television advertising campaign. They also worked as remixers on songs by Seduction, Sandee and Lisa Lisa & Cult Jam, examples of which were contained on their 1992 album, credited under their own names. Their first remix had been Natalie Cole's 'Pink Cadillac', which, in drastically altered form, broke the US Top 5. They released a final album in 1994, but the following year Cole died of spinal meningitis.
● ALBUMS: *Gonna Make You Sweat* (Columbia 1991)★★★, as Clivillés And Cole *Greatest Remixes, Volume 1* (Columbia 1992)★★★★, *Anything Goes* (Columbia 1994)★★.

Cabana

UK-based Latin house duo Cabana comprises vocalist Mirelle Diaz, daughter of leading Afro-Cuban percussionist Robin Jones, and her half-brother musician, Krystof Pietklewicz, formerly percussionist with the Style Council. The group made its debut in September 1994 with 'Bailondo Con Lobos', the second release on Polydor's newly formed dance offshoot, Hi Life (after Kim English's 'Nitelife'). The record was produced by Tom Frederikse, previously best known for his work with D:Ream, and was promoted by a subsequent tour. With remixes from Sasha, the Goodmen and Deep Recess, it became a minor club hit but failed to repeat the feat of Hi Life's first single by breaching the UK Top 40.

Cajmere

b. Curtis A. Brown, Chicago, USA. The house music artist Cajmere, with vocalist Dajae (real name Karen), first broke through in 1993 with the club hits 'Brighter Days' and the ragtime-themed 'U Got Me Up'. Cajmere abandoned his degree course to pursue his musical ambitions, and, establishing himself among local house music producers, he soon cut his first tracks, including 'The Percolator'. Influenced by the UK's A Guy Called Gerald as much as by Chicago house music, he settled on a successful combination of diva-style vocals and 'breakdowns'. Before working with Dajae, he was best known for his collaboration with Lidell Townsell on 'Get With You', plus the *Underground Goodies* EP for Clubhouse. He also remixed 'Feel It' for Italians Workin' Happily. He runs the Cajual record label, and its offshoot Relief, on which he aimed to develop new talent. He has recorded artists including Dajae, DJ Sneak, Gemini and Boo Williams, and 12-inch singles such as 'Preacherman', which owe an obvious debt to one of his idols, Lil' Louis.
● ALBUMS: *Brighter Days* (Emotive 1996)★★★.

Cake Records

Record label based in Birmingham, England, and run by DJ Richard Whittingham, Nigel Blunt and Groove Corporation. The set-up evolved from an 'illegal, irregular, underground little party called Cake'. From there it became a weekly event entitled Breathless, before all the parties involved pooled their resources to form Cake. Each, however, maintains their own individual profile, with support from the others. DJ Dick's pet project, the Original Rockers, had originally been remixed by Groove Corporation, which led to them joining forces: 'We have a simple manifesto - which is to put out great records, lose no money, and do what comes naturally.' Releases so far include Original

Rocker's 'Push Push', Groove Corporation and Bim Sherman's 'Need More Love (In The Ghetto)', and both parties' collaboration, 'Stoned'. Other signings included Bite Time Crime (hip-hop) and Sylophonic.

CALIKES, DAVID

b. c.1958, Scotland, d. 31 January 1996, Scotland. A professional DJ from the mid-80s onwards, Calikes gradually rose to become one of the most respected figures in dance music in Scotland. His first high-profile job came as resident DJ at Fat Sam's club in Dundee. By the late 80s he had begun his groundbreaking Sunday night sessions at the Metropolis club in Saltcoats, inviting dance acts and DJs as varied as Paul Oakenfold, Queen Latifah, Inner City, Seal and Adamski to Scotland for the first time. Later he concentrated on journalism, writing for publications including *M8* and *MixMag*. When he died in 1996 from complications arising from his diabetes, *M8* publisher David Foulds was among the first to pay tribute to his work: 'The guy *was* the Scottish dance scene - he founded it. Before him, Scotland was a wilderness.'

CAMP LO

Formed in the Bronx, New York, USA, hip-hop duo Camp Lo were heavily promoted by Profile Records at their launch in the mid-90s as an atypical, experimental rap act. With much of their musical influence derived from 70s disco culture, the group's sound defied the limiting preoccupation with east/west coast styles that had overtaken hip-hop. Despite this, some critics still vilified their 'retro' use of 'nostalgic grooves and beats'. Their debut album, the accomplished *Uptown Saturday Night*, comprised 15 tracks and demonstrated Emerald Geechie Suede (b. 1976) and Sonny Cheba's (b. 1974) affinity with contemporary hip-hop rhythms as well as a myriad of other styles. Guests included De La Soul and Digable Planets, groups with whom frequent comparisons were made in the press. Having signed with Profile in 1995, the duo had already toured with De La Soul during the winter of 1996. Their debut was produced by Ski, previously best-known for his work with Bahmadia, Lil' Kim and Jay-Z. Both the attendant singles, 'Coolie High' and 'Luchini (Aka This Is It)' attracted widespread attention among the hip-hop press's taste-makers.
● ALBUMS: *Uptown Saturday Night* (Profile 1997)★★★★.

CAMPBELL, LINSLEE

b. England. Birmingham-based Campbell's musical background came in gospel music. However, in the 90s he was influenced by the swingbeat of Teddy Riley, whom he met when Guy toured England in 1991. Afterwards Campbell sent a speculative demo tape to Steve Jervier's Jerv Productions. With Jervier's help he began to embark on a host of R&B remixes, including R. Kelly, Soul For Real, Aaliyah, Ultimate Kaos, Darkman, Nu Colours and Original Son. He was also behind a highly successful remix of the Lighthouse Family's UK chart hit, 'Lifted'.

CAMPBELL, LUTHER

Campbell grew up with four brothers in an area of Miami, USA, known as Liberty City. At 15 he joined the Ghetto Style DJs - seven teenagers who hung around at radio station WEDR and African Square Park. He graduated from Miami Beach High in 1978, going on to promote concerts by visiting rap groups such as Run DMC and Whodini. With the money generated he and the Ghetto Style DJs purchased the Pac Jam disco in the summer of 1985. While promoting a California group, 2 Live Crew, he suggested they sign to his new label. They assembled a single together, 'Throwing The D', based on a new dance move, and recorded it in front of Campbell's mother's house. Following the record's success, Luke Skywalker records was inaugurated on a more permanent footing. Later the title was shortened to simply Luke when *Star Wars* director George Lucas threatened to sue over copyright of the name. Campbell's career with 2 Live Crew continued through the late 80s and 90s in a blaze of publicity, until by 1993 he was recording solo, with or without the band's backing. In 1994 Campbell announced plans to launch his own girlie magazine, in an effort to redress the balance of this 'pro-white artistic genre'. Entitled *Scandalous*, the idea was that it should be along the lines of *Penthouse*, but using Afro-American 'models'. Campbell himself purchased a yacht to house the magazine's offices. As well as rapping exiles such as Professor Griff, Luke Records is also home to R&B outfits such as H-Town. For all his bad press it should be remembered that Luke Campbell is the official sponsor of the Miami Easter Egg Hunt in Liberty City.
● ALBUMS: as Luther Campbell Featuring The 2

Live Crew *Banned In The USA* (Luke 1990)★★★, *Luke In The Nude* (Luke 1993)★★.

CANDYMAN

b. 25 June 1968, Los Angeles, California, USA. Formerly a member of Tone Loc's backing posse of rappers and dancers, the rap artist Candyman emerged in 1990 with a Top 40 *Billboard* album success, *Ain't No Shame In My Game*. It was full of Loc's familiar party vibes, with the occasional more distasteful cut such as 'Melt In Your Mouth 69', although 'Knockin' Boots' reached number 9 in the charts. Subsequent releases, *Playtime Is Over* and *I Thought U Knew*, played down the pop element but offered diminishing returns.
● ALBUMS: *Ain't No Shame In My Game* (Epic 1990)★★★, *Playtime Is Over* (Epic 1991)★★, *I Thought U Knew* (IRS 1993)★★.

CAPELLA

Capella scored a major and somewhat unexpected success in 1989 when their 'Heylom Halib' crashed into the UK Top 20 (number 11). It was made by Gianfranco Bortolotti's Media Records empire, which soon became the dominant force in Euro dance/techno. Although their founder continued to release a number of records under various umbrella names, he has retained Capella as his priority act. Capella's first chart entry had come the previous year, when 'Push The Beat' was a minor hit. Bortolotti subsequently employed two Londoners, Rodney Bishop and Kelly Overett, as full-time members of the project. They continued to enjoy hits throughout the 90s, most notable of which was the number 25-peaking 'Take Me Away', licensed to PWL in the UK. This featured the guest vocals of Loleatta Holloway - ironic, since Capella's success instigated the Italo-house scene, the biggest commercial hit of which was Black Box's 'Ride On Time', on which Holloway's vocals were sampled. Hits through 1993 continued with the typically immediate and anthemic 'U Got 2 Know'. They followed it with the similarly styled but equally successful 'U Got 2 Let The Music' and 'Move On Baby', before the advent of their debut album. Specializing in unpretentious, hook-heavy synth pop, Capella are unlikely to change the winning formula.
● ALBUMS: *U Got 2 Know* (Internal 1994)★★.

CAPPADONNA

(see Wu-Tang Clan)

CAPTAIN RAPP

Rapp was an old-school US rapper, famed for 'Badd Times (I Can't Stand It)', a Los Angeles answer to 'The Message' (complete with Chic stylings). He grew up with LA's Uncle Jam's Army, where he fought for his turn on the microphone. He was transported over to New York to little effect, and subsequent record contracts never materialized. However, 'Badd Times' (released on Saturn in 1983) remains a keynote in the development of West Coast rap.

CAROUSEL

Swedish-born but of Scottish ancestry, Douglas Carr started writing songs at the age of seven. He formed his first band when he was 12, and has played everything from dance pop to punk in his musical career. In the 90s he wrote and produced a series of hits for Swedish artists, working with international stars such as Leila K. and Dr. Alban. In 1993 he joined with Latin American Paolo Toro to form Carousel. Toro had previously worked as a session singer, contributing backing vocals to Dr. Alban's huge international hit 'It's My Life', as well as recording material with Ace Of Base. The duo first met in a Stockholm studio in 1992, recording their debut single as Carousel, 'Enough Ain't Enough', at the end of the following year. A full album, showcasing the pair's diverse ethnic influences and rooted in a pop-dance vein, followed in 1994.
● ALBUMS: *Carousel* (Cheiron 1994)★★★.

CARTER, DERRICK

One of the biggest names in 90s Chicago house music, Carter was described by Richie Hawtin as 'America's last true underground DJ' in 1994. That seemed likely to change with his debut release, *The Sound Patrol* EP, on the local Organico label, which attracted rave reviews. A second EP, *The Music*, was another slice of pure house. It included excellent cuts such as 'An Open Secret', which utilized Chaka Khan's 'Ain't Nobody' at its base. Carter continues to work in a 'DJ commune' near the downtown skyscraper precincts of Chicago, equipped with a built-in studio. He had started life as part of the experimental outfit Symbols And Instruments, who scored an underground techno success for Network. He was only 16 at the time, and went on to a scholarship at engineering college MIT. Following the EPs he embarked on a project for David Holmes'

Exploding Plastic Inevitable label. He also founded two labels, Blue Cucaracha and Classic, and performed live with the Sound Patrol Orchestra.

● ALBUMS: as Sound Patrol *As Long As It's Groovy* (Organico 1995)★★★.

CASH MONEY AND MARVELLOUS

Among the earliest Philadelphia-based rap crews, Cash Money's 1988 set (produced by Joe 'The Butcher' Nicolo) was widely, and unjustly, ignored. With a strong funk undertow, the raps embraced the juvenile humour of Kid N Play in a wholly engaging manner. Money had previously won the 1988 DMC Mixing Championships. They disappeared from the rap scene before they were able to consolidate on their debut set.

● ALBUMS: *Where's The Party At?* (Sleeping Bag 1988)★★★.

CASUAL

b. *c*.1974. East Oakland, California, USA. This USA-based rapper specializes in old school lyrical battles, and the dissing of 'sucker MCs'. Hardly an engaging prospect, but the jazz flourishes (the result of his father's record collection) and light production offered a stylistic diversion to most of his neighbourhood's fare. Casual was the latest product of Del Tha Funkee Homosapien's Hieroglyphics enclave, alongside Souls Of Mischief, etc. He retained that spirit of combative rhyming that Hieroglyphics have done much to reinstate: 'I think that MCing should be a competitive thing, almost like a sport. The only way an MC can keep polishing and sharpening his skills is to test them against the competition and the up and coming young bloods.' Likewise, there was plenty of old school braggadocio, tempered by an occasional foray into more serious matters ('Chained Minds' and 'Loose In The End' being good examples from his debut set). The musical backing was the province of jazz-funk breaks from Roy Ayers and others.

● ALBUMS: *Fear Itself* (Jive 1994)★★★.

CAVEMAN

Based in Wycombe, England, this rap crew had scorn poured upon them by some critics who felt that their macho image was excessive given the atmosphere of their home-town. However, image aside, Caveman was an adept and engaging outfit with more skill than most UK-based hip-hop crews. Comprising MCM, Diamond J and the

Principle, songs such as 'Fry You Like Fish' (their second single) were justifiably lauded. They were willing to look outside of staple rap sources (choosing to sample Jimi Hendrix rather than James Brown), and signed to the US label Profile, but finally dissolved early in 1993. Their second album had been significantly weakened by the defection of the Principle. In truth splitting was also the only way out of their contracts with Profile, following disagreements within the band. The Principle's first post-Caveman project was *The Principle Presents 499*, again for Profile, in 1994.

● ALBUMS: *Positive Reaction* (Profile 1991)★★★, *The Whole Nine Yards... And Then Some* (Profile 1992)★★★.

CHALONER, SUE

In her youth Chaloner was awarded a scholarship by the BBC and attended a school for the performing arts, going on to spend several years in the UK stage production of *Hair*. In the mid-70s she went on to become half of the Spooky And Sue duo (who scored a novelty hit with 'Swinging On A Star'). By the early 90s she had become a hit with the club cognoscenti via 'Answer My Prayer' and 'I Wanna Thank You', with productions offered by the 3 Man Island/Band Of Gypsies team. 'I Wanna Thank You' name-checked black leaders Nelson Mandela, Marcus Garvey, Martin Luther King and Gandhi. She has been resident in Amsterdam for over 20 years, and appears live backed by her Soul Train team.

CHAMPION RECORDS

The UK's oldest independent dance label, Champion is a north London-based operation headed by Mel Medalie, with A&R support from Johnnie Walker. Since its inception Champion has enjoyed a steady stream of successes. Examples include Todd Terry Project's 'Never Give Up', Kelly Charles' 'Falling In Love' and Dee Dee Brave's 'So Many Roads' and 'There Is So Much' (all 1991). In 1992 they licensed tracks such as 'See The Day' (Ann Consuelo), 'Take Me Higher' (Hysteria) and 'Higher Degree' (Blast) from Sweden's Swemix/B-Tech set-up. They opened a New York office the same year, picking up distribution for labels including 111 East and Madhouse Records. In the meantime they continued to license from foreign labels, including Belgium's Dance Opera (picking up Atomizer 2's 'Liberty And Freedom'). Further big garage hits in 1994 arrived with Kristine W's (whom Medalie had spotted playing the Las Vegas circuit) 'Feel What You Want' and Third Nation's 'I Believe'.

CHEEKS, JUDY

b. Florida, Miami, USA. Of mixed black American and Cherokee ancestry, Cheeks is the daughter of gospel singer Rev. Julius Cheeks, cited by James Brown, Otis Redding and others as a pivotal influence in the development of black music. She grew up in Miami where her godfather was Sam Cooke, who once plucked her from the front row of a 6,000 audience and sang the rest of the set to her while cradling her in his arms. Before her solo career began in earnest her voice had been employed by Tina Turner, Betty Wright, Leon Ware, Georgio Moroder and Harold Faltermeyer, and she has long been a close friend of Stevie Wonder. Indeed, her recording career stretches back to the mid-70s, when she recorded a debut album with Ike and Tina Turner. She subsequently moved to Europe and Ariola Records, her first record for whom, 'Mellow Lovin', was an international success. After she had traversed the language barrier, she became a major German star, appearing in several movies and hosting a television game show with a hamster called Willie. She came to England in 1987, though an album for Polydor was never released outside of mainland Europe. Her career lapsed until she finally began recording demos again in the 90s. There was interest from the PWL stable, but she eventually settled on Positiva, a contract cemented by the release of 'So In Love', written by China Burton. Remixes from Frankie Foncett and Sasha added greatly to the cult status of this minor garage classic. The follow-up, 'Reach', capitalized on this and her tours of select dance venues, and this time employed the Brothers In Rhythm production team. She subsequently worked with Nigel Lowis (producer of Eternal and Dina Carroll) on tracks for her first Positiva album.

● ALBUMS: *Judy Cheeks* (United Artists 1973)★★, *Mellow Lovin'* (Salsoul 1978)★★, *No Outsiders* (Polydor 1988)★★★, *Respect* (Positiva 1996)★★★.

CHEEKY RECORDS

This UK label was set up in late 1991 by the house producer Rollo. Cheeky initially released two singles, Franke's 'Understand This Groove' and Gloworm's 'Lift My Cup', which were subsequently licensed to major labels, but soon folded owing to 'general business ineptitude and lack of organization'. A year later, with the backing of Champion Records, Rollo relaunched Cheeky and released a number of successful singles. Their first album was Faithless's *Reverence* in 1996.

CHEMICAL BROTHERS

Tom Rowlands and Ed Simons met while studying at Manchester University in the late 80s. Rowlands became a member of the Balearic group Ariel, which put out a number of releases on DeConstruction Records. At the same time the pair found a common interest in acid house, techno and hip-hop and began DJing at house parties, calling themselves the Dust Brothers after the west coast hip-hop producers. They subsequently played at a club called 'Naked Under Leather' and began writing their own material to use. One track, 'Song To The Siren', was picked up by Junior Boy's Own Records and released early in 1993. The pair were consequently invited to remix Lionrock's 'Packet Of Peace' and tracks by various other artists, including Leftfield/John Lydon, Republica and the Sandals. The next year the Dust Brothers released the EPs *14th Century Sky*, which became well-known for the track 'Chemical Beats', and *My Mercury Mouth*. Following the success of these records and the Sunday Social, a club that they ran in London in conjunction with Heavenly Records, they signed to Virgin Records in early 1995 as the Chemical Brothers, after the threat of legal action from the original Dust Brothers. Their first releases included the single 'Leave Home' and the album *Exit Planet Dust* on their own subsidiary, Freestyle Dust. As well as their trademark sound of guitars, heavy breakbeats and analogue noise, the album surprisingly included vocals from the Charlatans' Tim Burgess ('Life Is Sweet') and Beth Orton ('Alive: Alone'). During 1995 the group promoted the album with successful performances at many rock and dance festivals throughout the UK and Europe and also toured America alongside Orbital and Underworld. After remixes for Dave Clarke, the Manic Street Preachers and Method Man, in the autumn of 1996 the pair released 'Setting Sun', which featured Oasis's Noel Gallagher, and became their first number 1 single. The Chemical Brothers' huge popularity was confirmed with the release of their second album, *Dig Your Own Hole*, which also received critical acclaim, being nominated for Mercury and BRIT Awards in the UK,

while the number 1 single 'Block Rockin' Beats' won a Grammy for Best Rock Instrumental.
● ALBUMS: *Exit Planet Dust* (Junior Boy's Own 1995)★★★★, *Dig Your Own Hole* (Freestyle Dust 1997)★★★★.

CHERRY, NENEH

b. Neneh Mariann Karlsson, 10 March 1964, Stockholm, Sweden. Cherry is the step-daughter of jazz trumpeter Don Cherry. She joined English post-punk band Rip, Rig And Panic in 1981 as a vocalist, later performing with several ex-members of that band as Float Up CP. In the mid-80s she also sang backing vocals for the Slits and The The ('Slow Train To Dawn', 1987). In 1989, Cherry recorded a series of dance tracks for Circa, including the international hit single 'Buffalo Stance' (which was featured on the soundtrack of the film *Slaves Of New York*), 'Manchild' and 'Kisses On The Wind'. Her main co-writer was husband Cameron McVey. Her debut *Raw Like Sushi*'s eclectic blend of hip-hop rhythms and pop melodies earned Cherry excellent reviews and sizeable sales figures. In 1990 Cherry contributed to the AIDS-charity collection, *Red Hot And Blue*, singing Cole Porter's 'I've Got You Under My Skin', but was quiet again until the release of *Homebrew* in 1992. A noticeably mellower album, it featured production and writing collaborations with a pre-Portishead Geoff Barrow and cameo appearances by Gang Starr and Michael Stipe. Cherry reasserted herself as a commercial force in 1994 with the international hit single 'Seven Seconds', which saw her collaborating with African superstar Youssou N'Dour. Family commitments meant another lengthy recording hiatus before she released *Man* in 1996.
● ALBUMS: *Raw Like Sushi* (Circa 1989)★★★★, *Homebrew* (Virgin 1992)★★★, *Man* (Hut 1996)★★★.
● VIDEOS: *The Rise Of Neneh Cherry* (BMG Video 1989).

CHI-ALI

b. c.1976, New York, USA. At just 15 years of age, Chi-Ali (his real name) recorded his first single. Suitably entitled 'Age Ain't Nothin' But A Number', it announced his arrival as the youngest member of the Native Tongues Posse. Afrika Bambaataa, Black Sheep, the Jungle Brothers and Brand Nubian were all on hand to appear in the video. The song itself was, ironically, a little juvenile, recounting his ability to enter clubs and chat up women even though he was too young for either. Elsewhere on his debut album, things became less credible still, lines such as 'Are you going to be allowed to stay up and watch the Superbowl this weekend' notwithstanding.
● ALBUMS: *The Fabulous Chi-Ali* (Violator 1992)★★.

CHILL EB

An articulate, highly politicized US rapper linked with Jello Biafra's Alternative Tentacles label, the original home to pre-Disposable Heroes Of Hiphoprisy outfit the Beatnigs. Together with his DJing partner RD, Chill EB's harsh rhymes are tempered by sweet female vocal interludes, in an arresting combination. Chill grew up in Oakland, California, and, at 6 foot 5 inches tall, was a leading basketball player (a high-school colleague was Michael Jordan). Via singles such as 'Menace To Society', his profile was stamped large across American television screens, and he also won an award for his work with Los Angeles' homeless. 'Menace To Society', which revolved around the true story of a 13-year-old boy dealing in drugs to help to feed his sister and brother ('I only rob the rich to feed my family, and now they call me a menace to society'), inspired a film of the same name (though the cut was not included on its soundtrack), and was also dubbed on to two television films. Less nobly, however, Chill also found time to appear in five separate adverts for Sega games.
● ALBUMS: *Born Suspicious* (Alternative Tentacles 1994)★★★.

CHILL, ROB G.

b. Rob Frazier, Queens, New York, USA. Rob Chill remains best known for having his 'Let The Words Flow' hijacked by German house act Snap!. This was taken by producers Benito Benites and John Garrett Virgo III and revitalized with Penny Ford's distinctive vocals, bringing them a huge worldwide hit. Chill received little of the credit (although he was namechecked in the titles) and has so far proved unable to follow up this success.
● ALBUMS: *Ride The Rhythm* (Wild Pitch 1990)★★★.

CHIMES

UK soul/dance trio originating in Edinburgh, Scotland, in 1981, when they were initially put together by Mike Pedan (keyboards and bass) and the much-travelled James Locke (keyboards and

drums, ex-Heartbeat; Rhythm Of Life; Bathers; Hipsway; Indian Givers). The pair had met when they were backing former Parliament keyboard player Bernie Worrell at a local club. Deciding to form their own group, they set about writing material and auditioning female singers, eventually settling on Pauline Henry in 1987. With the duo's desperation mounting, her successful audition was held over the telephone, after which she was flown up from London for sessions. After signing to CBS in 1988 they finally released their debut single a year later. '1-2-3' was produced by Jazzie B (from Soul II Soul), a group to whom the Chimes were frequently compared. Their biggest UK breakthrough came in 1990 when they covered U2's 'I Still Haven't Found What I'm Looking For'. Apparently approved by Bono, the cover version was chosen when the band heard Henry singing it in the studio. Aided by an appearance on the mainstream television show *Wogan*, it eventually went Top 5 in both the UK and USA. The boys also contributed to old friend Paul Haig's solo LP during 1990, and produced several other artists. Subsequent minor hits included 'True Love' and 'Love Comes To Mind', before Henry left for a solo career midway through sessions for a second album.
● ALBUMS: *The Chimes* (Columbia 1990)★★★.

CHOCOLATE WEASEL

During the mid-90s Mark Royal worked with Cris Stevens on the dark, jazz-flavoured jungle of T-Power, before signing to Ninja Tune Records as Chocolate Weasel. After the sombre sounds of *The Self-Evident Truth Of An Intuitive Mind* and *Waveform*, Royal and Stevens wanted to move away, 'because you can't take the piss with drum 'n' bass', and create more funky, hip-hop-influenced music. They released their first single, 'Body Lockers', in 1998, followed by the album *Spagettification* the same year.

CHRIS AND COSEY

Chris Carter and Cosey Fanni Tutti (b. Christine Newby) became partners while with late 70s 'industrial' sound pioneers Throbbing Gristle. When the latter split in 1981, the couple decided to operate both as Chris And Cosey and as CTI (Creative Technology Institute). Their debut album, *Heartbeat*, credited to CTI, drew from Throbbing Gristle's rhythmic undercurrents, but the pair's next collection, *Trance*, was soured by a disagreement with Rough Trade Records over its

selling price. 1983 yielded two singles, the Japanese-only 'Nikki' (a collaboration with John Duncan) and the relatively mainstream 'October (Love Song)'. These were followed in 1984 by *Songs Of Love And Lust*. That year the duo also issued *Elemental 7* in collaboration with John Lacey on Cabaret Voltaire's Doublevision label and further projects, as CTI, with Lustmord's Brian Williams and Glenn Wallis of Konstructivitis. These projects were also accompanied by *European Rendezvous*. *Mondo Beat*, released in 1985, was originally conceived by Carter as a 12-inch single, but expanded beyond that format. By this time, the pair's relationship with Rough Trade had become strained and they left after *Techno Primitiv* and 'Sweet Surprise', a project with the Eurythmics. They then joined Vancouver label Nettwerk Productions, while in Europe they were handled by renowned Brussels label Play It Again Sam (who have also reissued much of their product). Since then, Chris And Cosey have gradually steered towards the 'New Beat' dance sound, with singles such as 'Obsession', 'Exotica' (both 1987) and 'Rise' (1989). Early 90s albums *Reflection* and *Pagan Tango* confirmed their adoption of hi-tech dance music.
● ALBUMS: *Heartbeat* (Rough Trade 1981)★★, *Trance* (Rough Trade 1982)★★, *Songs Of Love And Lust* (Rough Trade 1984)★★★, as CTI *Elemental 7 - The Original Soundtrack* (Rough Trade 1984)★★★, *European Rendezvous* (Doublevision 1984)★★★, *Techno Primitiv* (Rough Trade 1985)★★, *Action* (Licensed 1987)★★★, *Exotica* (Nettwerk 1987)★★★, *Trust* (Play It Again Sam 1989)★★★, *Reflection* (Play It Again Sam 1990)★★★, *Pagan Tango* (Play It Again Sam 1991)★★★, *Muzik Fantastique* (Play It Again Sam 1992)★★★.
Solo: Chris Carter *Mondo Beat* (Conspiracy International 1986)★★.
● COMPILATIONS: *Best Of Chris And Cosey* (Play It Again Sam 1989)★★★, *Collectiv 1, 2, 3, & 4* (Play It Again Sam 1990)★★★.

CHUBB ROCK

b. Richard Simpson, 28 May 1968, Jamaica, West Indies. The cousin of Hitman Howie Tee, Simpson moved to New York at an early age. A rap colossus, his ample frame has seen him compared with Barry White, with whom he duetted on his second album. Chubb Rock started his own band in New York, but after dropping out of college elected to set out on a solo career. The first results of this were a debut album that sank without trace. However, the promotional single for his second album, 'Caught Up', secured the public's interest. This introduced them to his most consistent effort so far, on which humour and reflections on urban violence sat side by side. By the dawn of the 90s and his third album, interest in Chubb had escalated to the point at which it spawned no less than three *Billboard* number 1 hits. He also appeared on film, in the movie *Private Times*, but fell from commercial grace following two further albums. *The Mind* was his comeback release, but its sound was too old school to make much of an impact.

● ALBUMS: *Featuring Hitman Howie Tee* (Select 1988)★★★, *And The Winner Is...* (Select 1989)★★★★, *Treat 'Em Right* mini-album (Select 1991)★★★, *The One* (Select 1991)★★★★, *I Gotta Get Mine Yo! - Book Of Rhymes* (Select 1992)★★★, *The Mind* (Select 1997)★★.

CHUCK D.

b. Carlton Douglas Ridenhour, 1 August 1960, Roosevelt, Long Island, New York City, USA. As the principal lyricist of Public Enemy, Chuck D. can lay claim to having written some of the highest-impact lines in the history of rock 'n' roll. However, as that group's vitality decreased, by the mid-90s a Chuck D. solo album seemed an obvious next step for the artist. *Autobiography Of Mistachuck* reinforced his credentials as rap music's most eloquent commentator. As he stressed on 'Free Big Willie': 'There once was a time we fought the power with a rhyme, Now the attitude goin' round, no use tryin'.' In fact, much of the album offered a critique on the rise of gangsta rap, its glamorization of violence and misogyny, and the rise of the car and clothes as consumer status symbols. One of the most effective tracks was 'But Can You Killer The Nigga In You?', a collaboration with Isaac Hayes that asked pertinent questions about the end result for those who invest in their own mythology rather than their own community. A further track, 'Horizontal Heroin', featured Professor Griff, the controversial former member of Public Enemy who left the group in 1989 after making allegedly anti-Semitic comments to the *Washington Times*.

● ALBUMS: *Autobiography Of Mistachuck* (Mercury 1996)★★★★.

● FURTHER READING: *Fight The Power - Rap, Race And Reality*, Chuck D. with Yusuf Jah.

CLAIL, GARY, AND THE ON U SOUND SYSTEM

The On U Sound System features a plethora of musicians drawn from Tackhead, Roots Radics, Akabu, Dub Syndicate and others. It was officially launched in 1980 by Adrian Sherwood for a one-off album by the New Age Steppers, who comprised various members of the Slits, Pop Group and Aswad. The second album was by the Mothmen (who are now the rhythm section for Simply Red), and over the years an impressive roster of collaborative productions took shape. These include works from the likes of Dr. Pablo, Prince Far I, Tackhead, Mark Stewart And The Mafia, Dub Syndicate and African Headcharge. Clail's bombastic vocal delivery was honed when he grew up in a predominantly black neighbourhood given rhythm by 'Toasting' Jamaican locals. He is of Irish descent, though his parents moved to Bristol when he was very young. After spells as a scaffolder and runner for the criminal fraternity, he joined Tackhead and became further involved with the On U Sound team. 'Human Nature' was something of a freak hit in 1991. The original intention to sample Billy Graham's 1958 speech of the same name over the beat was rejected by his representatives, forcing Clail to deputize. It also owed a great deal to Paul Oakenfold's production, and his knowledge of the dance clubs. His adaptation from On U Sound's resident misfit to pop star designate was quite remarkable. He still works mainly as a producer and mixer, and in the long term wants to emulate Sherwood by providing new talent with a forum for exposure. In interviews Clail constantly stressed that he is but one cog in a 32-person music-making machine.

● ALBUMS: *Emotional Hooligan* (On-U-Sound 1991)★★★, *Keep The Faith* (Yelen 1996)★★★.

CLARKE, LONI

b. New York, USA. Clarke originally sang in Harlem church choirs before joining with Luther Vandross in Listen My Brother, eventually striking out solo. She made her recording debut in 1981 for West End Records, enjoying a minor dance hit with 'Let's Go Dancing'. She returned to a singing career in the 90s, making the UK Top 40 with 'Rushing', and gaining a further success with the Lem Springsteen/John Ciafone-written and -produced 'U'. Now signed to A&M, the disc saw remixes by Mood II Swing and K Klass.

CLEVELAND CITY RECORDS

Wolverhampton, Midlands, England-based label, housed in the city's Ruby Red record shop, itself formerly home to the Plan B and Ruby Red imprints. The label was set up to feature local Midlands acts on a first-person basis, and has expanded rapidly, helmed by A&R man Lee Arnold. Their debut release was Chubby Chunks' 'Testaments 1, 2 and 3', a big-seller later remixed by Judge Jules and the Jungle Brothers. There is little of the preciousness usually associated with premier dance labels, as the small print on each release indicates: 'DJ warning - Music Is Fun'. Among their best received releases so far have been Direct 2 Disc ('Don't Stop', 'Excuse Me', *The Backstab* EP), Dig The New Breed ('Who's Number 1'), and Herbal Hand ('B Line'/'Come To It', 'Tripped'). Subsidiary labels cropped up early in the label's development, namely Cleveland City Blues (swingbeat and garage) and Cleveland City Imports (Alex Party etc.). Cleveland City Blue brought the empire an immediate success when Italian artist Tony Di Bart's 'The Real Thing' scaled the charts in May 1994.

CLUB ECSTASY

Singaporean dance group Club Ecstasy were formed in 1992 by keyboardist/vocalist Leonard Tan and lead singer Kevin Verghese. Eventually expanding to a trio, they submitted numerous demos to local radio stations before signing with the independent record label Valentine Music Productions. The group's debut album, *Midi Genetics*, mixed high-adrenaline house music with hip-hop beats and samples, winning them a huge audience among their country's more discerning young music followers. The follow-up, the impressively titled *Virtuosos Of The Infinite Acid Bath*, proved even more popular, attracting strong reviews from western journalists. A third collection, *Club E*, was promoted via the release of a cover version of Andy Gibb's disco classic, 'Shadow Dancing', as its attendant single.
● ALBUMS: *Midi Genetics* (Valentine 1994)★★★★, *Virtuosos Of The Infinite Acid Bath* (Valentine 1995)★★★, *Club E* (Valentine 1996)★★★.

COCO STEEL AND LOVEBOMB

Brighton, Sussex, England-based combo who scored in 1992 with the house/techno crossover hit, 'Feel It'. It was inspired by the Zap club's smouldering Saturday nights, a venue run by Chris 'Coco' Miller. It was followed by the 12-minute 'You Can't Stop The Groove', compiled so that it could be played as a whole or segmented by DJs, which included a sample of Hamilton Bohannon from 'Let's Start The Dance'. The rest of the band numbered Craig Woodrow (Lovebomb) and Lene (Steel). They had made their debut with 'The Crucifixion Of Danny', a cut-up of Donny Osmond's 'Puppy Love'. 1993's 'Work It Tough Bitch' was championed by Junior Vasquez at the Sound Factory in New York, as the trio's reputaton grew. Mellor maintains that CS&A is 'more of an idea than a fixed project', and continues to edit a specialist DJ magazine. 'I was writing about music and rapidly becoming one of those music journo bores that listen to a record and gripes 'I can do that', or 'I'd edit that there'. So I thought rather than moaning about it I'd get on with it'. Mellor also went on to remix for Underworld, Wild Planet and others.
● ALBUMS: *It!* (Warp 1994)★★★.

COLA BOY

Cola Boy is the name used by the Peterborough, England artist Andrew Naughtie. Cola Boy's '7 Ways To Love' was mailed out as a white label with a press release saying the record had been financed by a Hong Kong teenager who had sold his collection of rare Coke bottles to subsidise the project - one Jesse Chin, who was acknowledged on the sleeve of the stock release. Some people continue to give credence to the story to this day. Naughtie had previously worked with Bob Stanley and Peter Wiggs in the early days of St Etienne, who remixed the track. '7 Ways To Love' reached number 8 in the UK chart in 1991, after being widely bootlegged, with its subtle vocal contribution from Janey Lee Grace. The follow-up was 'He Is Cola', which featured Burundi drumming.

COLD CHILLIN' RECORDS

This record label, distributed through Warner Brothers Records, was overseen by that company's A&R man Ben Medina with Fly-T's Tyrone Williams, the label manager, and producer Marley Marl. Cold Chillin' grew quickly since it was first mooted as a possibility by Williams and Marl, signing with Warners in 1987. As well as recording, Marl went on to produce most of the label's output. The label quickly struck strong sales with material from Biz Markie, MC Shan and Big Daddy Kane.

COLD CRUSH BROTHERS

The Cold Crush Brothers traced their origins to the Bronx freestyle ethos of the late 70s, when the line-up was fronted by Kay Gee The All, EZ AD and Grandmaster Caz. The latter, who had been rumoured to be one of the lyricists behind the early Sugarhill releases, and also led the Mighty Force Emcees, opted out in the early 80s, at which point DJ Tony Crush climbed behind the decks. He provided the group with their distinctive brass and reed riffs, drawn from old Stax and soul classics. The Cold Crush Brothers were responsible for the 'Punk Rock Rap' single/novelty, on Aaron Fuchs' Tuff City label. They had formerly recorded for Elite and Smokin', but by the end of the 80s they had moved on to B-Boy, as a duo comprising simply Kay Gee and DJ Tony Crush. The double a-side 12-inch, 'Feel The Horns'/'We Can Do This', gave them a minor hit, but it proved to be a fleeting success.

● ALBUMS: *Troopers* (B-Boy Records 1988)★★★.

COLDCUT

Since the mid-80s ex-art teacher Jonathan Moore and computer programmer Matt Black have been responsible for a number of important innovations in the dance music arena. Like DJ Steinski, they realized the creative potential of sampling records, television, Walt Disney sounds and other non-musical sources, and in 1987 made their first records, 'Say Kids What Time Is It?', 'Greedy Beat' and 'Bits And Pieces'; a sample of 'Say Kids ...' was later used on MARRS' 'Pump Up The Volume'. With the acid house boom, Coldcut became a widely respected remix team, beginning with a mix of Eric B And Rakim's 'Paid In Full'. At the same time they were DJing on pirate radio stations, notably their *Solid Steel* show on Kiss, and at acid house parties such as Shoom. In 1988, with Yazz, Moore and Black (as the Plastic Population) produced groundbreaking pop that combined hip-hop and house styles on such tracks as 'Doctorin' The House' and 'The Only Way Is Up'. The following year they helped to launch the career of Lisa Stansfield with 'People Hold On', which was featured on their debut album, *What's That Noise?*. In 1990 they were voted producers of the year at the BPI awards, at which point it was conceivable that they would continue in a Stock, Aitken And Waterman mould, churning out more hits. However, their vision extended beyond the formulae of house and techno and, following diffi-culties with major labels, Moore and Black established Ninja Tune Records as a vehicle for their own experimentation. Coldcut released the album *Philosophy* for Arista Records in 1993 in order to fulfil contractual obligations, a number of singles including 'Autumn Leaves', and a number of tracks on Ninja Tune compilations. In 1997 'Atomic Moog 2000' and 'More Bits And Pieces' heralded *Let Us Play*, the CD release of which contained an 'interactive toybox full of Coldcut games, toys and videos', designed in collaboration with Hex. Like the DJ Food albums, *Let Us Play* explores the abstract hip-hop idea where funk beats underpin various textures, often based on dialogue, including poets, rappers and other pre-recorded segments, and other non-melodic sources. In the meantime, they developed the Ninja Tune concept and were involved in a range of projects linked with the label, including the DJ Food albums and various club nights. They have continued to broadcast on Kiss FM and to DJ worldwide. Like many of the most creative artists of the 90s, Moore and Black envisage a future that combines music with technology, where DJs may have any number of sources at their disposal, rather than two decks and a mixer.

● ALBUMS: *What's That Noise?* (Ahead Of Our Time 1989)★★★★, *Some Like It Cold* (Ahead Of Our Time 1990)★★★, *Philosophy* (Arista 1993)★★, *Let Us Play* (Ninja Tune 1997)★★★★.

COLLAPSED LUNG

All round entertainers from Harlow, Essex, England, Collapsed Lung utilise an unconventional hip-hop derived musical format, but also intersperse rowdy electric guitar and mid-song comedy banter. They formed in February 1992, and after their debut performance were invited to play an all-day festival in Harlow at which guitarist Steve Harcourt (formerly of heavy metal band Gethsemane and by day a toy shop assistant) first met the bespectacled Nihal Arhanayake, a rapper of Sri Lankan descent who opted out of a legal career to join the band. He was consequently invited to record some of his material over the existing trio's tracks. Nihal's co-rapper was Anthony Chapman, with the line-up completed by bass player Johnny Dawe. Members traced their roots back to several earlier Harlow bands including Pregnant Neck, Bombers and indie band Death By Milkfloat. The first Collapsed Lung single, 'Thundersley Invacar', eulogising the famous UK invalid car, brought comparisons to Cornershop. The follow-up, 'Chainsaw Wedgie', was about a particularly painful playground torture involving the victim's underwear being hoisted from behind. However, Arhanayake left the band in 1994, subsequently guesting on Fun-Da-Mental's debut album and joining the Maddie Funksters. Collapsed Lung replaced him with rapper Jim Burke and drummer Chris, while Chapman also bolstered his reputation with DJing work at a variety of London venues. He was also keen to reinstate Collapsed Lung's rap credentials, stating 'at the end of the day it's just hip-hop' while promoting the release of 1995's *Jackpot Goalie*. 'London Tonight'/'Eat My Goal' was a sizeable UK hit in 1996.

● ALBUMS: *Jackpot Goalie* (Dedicated 1995)★★★★, *C**ler* (Deceptive BLUFF 1996)★★★.

COLLEGE BOYZ

Based in Los Angeles, California, USA, this rap quartet consists of Rom, Squeak, the Q and DJ B-Selector. Their 1992 debut album for Virgin Records, an all too predictable collection of street narratives combined with funk and soul samples, made the lower reaches of the *Billboard* charts in that year, despite lukewarm reviews. A second album in 1994, *Nuttin' Less*, featured the minor hit single 'Rollin'', but again failed to break them into the mainstream.

● ALBUMS: *Radio Fusion Radio* (Virgin 1992)★★, *Nuttin' Less* (Virgin 1994)★★★.

COMBS, SEAN 'PUFFY'

b. 1970, Harlem, New York, USA. The most prosperous of a new breed of entrepreneurs in black music, Sean 'Puffy' Combs is a hugely successful hip-hop artist (under the name Puff Daddy) and noted producer for artists including TLC and Mary J. Blige. He also excels in business - the value of his Bad Boy empire was estimated at $170,000,000 during 1997. Although his sample-heavy sound has been criticised for taking hip-hop too far into the mainstream, it's commercial appeal is unquestionable, and has made Combs one of the most powerful players in American music.

Brought up in the contrasting New York districts of Harlem and Mount Vernon by a single mother, Combs was bright enough to secure a university place, before his musical instincts took over. He danced in a Fine Young Cannibals video, and

found a job at Uptown Records, run by Motown Records boss Andre Harrell. By the age of 18 he had been made head of A&R for Uptown, and was involved in successful albums by Mary J. Blige, Father MC and Heavy D And The Boyz. Having been fired from Uptown, Combs worked as a remixer before launching his own company, Bad Boy Entertainment, in 1993. There, he quickly assembled a pool of talented R&B and hip-hop artists around him. Craig Mack's 1994 'Flava In Ya Ear' single earned Bad Boy their first platinum record, and the label enjoyed huge success thereafter, notably with the controversial rapper Notorious B.I.G., and R&B/hip-hop acts including Faith Evans and Total. Combs also produced other prominent artists including Mariah Carey, Boyz II Men and Aretha Franklin. His involvement in the east coast/west coast gangsta rap feud, which pitched Combs and Notorious B.I.G. against Tupac Shakur and Marion Suge Knight's Death Row Records, was an unpleasant distraction from his seemingly unstoppable assault on both the pop and R&B charts. The untimely death of Notorious B.I.G. delayed Combs' own solo album while he mourned his long-time friend. Released in summer 1997, the single 'Can't Nobody Hold Me Down' was US number 1 for almost eight weeks, and was followed by the international number 1 tribute single 'I'll Be Missing You', a rewrite of the Police's 'Every Breath You Take', with new lyrics dedicated to Notorious B.I.G. The long-awaited *No Way Out* was almost inevitably a multi-platinum number 1 album, which earned Combs a 1998 Grammy for Best Rap Album. 'I'll Be Missing You' also won the Grammy for Best Rap Performance.

● ALBUMS: *No Way Out* (Bad Boy 1997)★★★.

COMMON

b. Lonnie Rashied Lynn, *c*.1971, Chicago, Illinois, USA. Originally recording under the expanded pseudonym Common Sense, Lynn is one of the more enlightened examples of contemporary hip-hop, proffering a heady mix of verbiage and syncopated hip-hop rhythms. He made his debut in 1992 with *Can I Borrow A Dollar?*, a series of tracts on consumer identity with the occasional lapse into X-rated anatomical detail to make it a hit with the hardcore hip-hop audience. Conversely, the best song was 'Take It EZ', a laid-back statement of identity and individuality. By the advent of *Resurrection* in 1994, Lynn had abandoned some of the bloated misogyny of the debut, and the results were excellent. Fuelled by the soul and funk beats of his DJ No.1 I.D., the album provided the rapper with a license to indulge his self-evident love of vocabulary and syntax (particularly affecting was his sketch of black economics - 'Chapter 13 (Rich Man vs. Poor Man)'). A follow-up set was then delayed as Lynn lost a court battle to retain the rights to his name Common Sense, eventually abbreviating it simply to Common. In the interim, he also completed classes in music theory, encouraging him to bring live instrumentation to the fore on his new recordings. *One Day It'll All Make Sense* (1997) also displayed further development in songwriting. Although it lacked the consistency of its predecessor, there were several stand-out cuts, notably the single 'Reminding Me (Of Sef)', which mourned the loss of a childhood friend.

● ALBUMS: as Common Sense *Can I Borrow A Dollar?* (Relativity 1992)★★★, as Common Sense *Resurrection* (Relativity 1994)★★★★, *One Day It'll All Make Sense* (Relativity 1997)★★★.

COMPTON'S MOST WANTED

Gangsta rap traditionalists whose naked aggression was only tempered by deft production. *It's A Compton Thing* contained enough obscenities to ensure that it was also made available in a censored version, but at least by *Music To Driveby* they had honed their punishing, forceful formula. Lead rapper MC Eiht's pseudonym, incidentally, stands for 'Experienced In Hardcore Thumpin''. The other pivotal member is DJ Slip, who has produced for other acts including DFC, with whom Eiht has also duetted.

● ALBUMS: *It's A Compton Thang* (Orpheus 1990)★★, *Straight Checkn'Em* (Orpheus 1991)★★★, *Music To Driveby* (Orpheus 1992)★★, *We Come Strapped* (Epic 1994)★★★.

CONDITION RED

Based in Orlando, Florida, USA, the 90s rap duo Condition Red consist of Sir Tron and Gangster Red. They made their debut in 1994 for the local O-Town label with the disappointing *Don't Get Caught Slippin'*. Tired, simplistic rhythm motifs drawn from the region's 'bass music' tradition, did little to substantiate the group's raps, in which safe sex was a recurrent theme (the album's title also alluded to this idea). Critically dismissed, the record also sold poorly.

● ALBUMS: *Don't Get Caught Slippin'* (O-Town 1994)★★.

CONSCIOUS DAUGHTERS

This rap duo consists of CMG and the Special One, from Oakland, California, USA, who both possess a powerful arsenal of vocal effects and characters, a combination that was ably backed on their debut by the production skills of Paris, for whose Scarface emporium they record. The Conscious Daughters had come across Paris in familiar fashion, thrusting a demo cassette into his hand, in the hope of him supporting their cause. Paris eventually came through with his promise to do something with the duo, albeit a long time after their initial meeting in 1991. When they did record, references to the treatment of women by gangsta rappers abounded, especially on tracks like 'Wife Of A Gangsta' and 'What's A Girl To Do', which saw them namecheck the Fu-Schnickens, with whom they toured. The attitude appears to be a direct response to gangsta mythology and misogyny, particular the brand traded on by local rapper Too Short: 'The bitch ho shit sells, but if that's all a man can talk about then we can do the same back.'

● ALBUMS: *Ear 2 Tha Street* (Scarface 1993)★★★.

CONSOLIDATED

Highly political funk/rap/rock trio from San Francisco, USA, comprising Adam Sherburne (vocals, guitar; the son of an American Two Star General), Mark Pistel (sampler/technician) and Philip Steir (drums). Their approach to rock music reflects the anti-establishment, left field approach of Crass or Minor Threat; their 'mission' is to agitate, to provide more than a passive spectacle for an audience to consume. At the end of gigs the microphone is turned open to the audience, a format which has annoyed as well as intrigued paying customers (witness 'Play More Music', on which they are berated by audience members for not doing just that). As a background to their generally impressive arrangements, projected visuals comprise various images of totalitarianism, linking such themes as animal abuse to men's treatment of women. Acknowledging themselves as 'Typical Men' despite their political stance, they also co-operate with the polemic of female cohorts the Yeastie Girlz (Cammie, Kate and Wendy). The latter achieved recognition for their frank exposition of the importance of cunilingus to a good relationship. They made a surprise move to a major label for 1994's *Business Of Punishment*, the wisdom of which was hinted at in the title of the delayed follow-up, *Dropped*. While Consolidated continue to tread a path on the right side of dogma, their status as artists of conscience serves as a reminder of the potential of music to inform and improve. Sherburne has also recorded solo as Childman.

● ALBUMS: *Consolidated* mini-album (Antler 1989)★★, *The Myth Of Rock* (Nettwerk 1990)★★★, *Friendly Fa$cism* (Nettwerk 1991)★★, *Play More Music* (Nettwerk 1992)★★★, *Business Of Punishment* (London 1994)★★★, *Dropped* (Roadrunner 1997)★★★.
Solo: Adam Sherburne as Childman: *Childman* (Nettwerk 1993)★★★.

COOK, NORMAN

b. Quentin Cook, 31 July 1963, England. This musical chameleon grew up in Reigate, Surrey, and began to DJ when he moved to Brighton to study for a degree. After playing bass guitar with the Housemartins, he had his first success as a solo artist with a remix of Erik B And Rakim's 'I Know You Got Soul', which reached number 13 in the charts in the late 80s. In the 90s he formed Beats International and later Freak Power, but achieved most success producing dance music under a number of different pseudonyms. In 1994 he turned to house music as Pizzaman and had a number of Top 20 hits, including 'Tripping On Sunshine' (Loaded Records). At the same time he began to write in a style that later became known as big beat, and purveyed this sound at the Big Beat Boutique (from which the movement took its name). Following the success of the club, he signed to Damian Harris's newly formed Skint Records as Fatboy Slim, releasing 'Santa Cruz' as the first single. He subsequently became big beat's best-known and most successful artist, with a number of hit singles including 'Everybody Needs A 303', the album *Better Living Through Chemistry* and various remixes including Wildchild's 'Renegade Master' (Hi-Life) and Cornershop's 'Brimful Of Asha' (Wiija). He has also recorded for Southern Fried Records as the Mighty Dub Katz, notably 'It's Just Another Groove' and 'Magic Carpet Ride'. In 1998 his success continued with a Fatboy Slim single, 'Rockafeller Skank', and Freak Power single, 'No Way', which he recorded just with Ashley Slater. Cook's success lies in his ability to blend funky breakbeats with the most catchy melodies and riffs, and he has reached a wider audience than much dance music by combining elements of

rock and dance. 'Everybody Needs A 303' mixes a funky bass guitar riff with various analogue effects, and 'Song For Lindy' features slide guitar, busy percussion, tubular bells and house-style piano, while 'Magic Carpet Ride' has a ska-edged feel. In this way he has coloured his music with a variety of styles and has been broad-minded enough to look further than the 'old-skool' hip-hop and acid jazz clichés that pervade much of the scene. While he admits that his music is simple, cheesy and obvious, describing himself as 'just a party fiend who nicks bits of other people's records', his light-hearted attitude and unashamedly amateurish approach, which also pervades Skint, could prove more important in the long run than the sound itself.

● ALBUMS: *Better Living Through Chemistry* (Skint 1996)★★★.

COOKIE CREW

This Clapham, South London rap duo consists of MC Remedee (Debbie Pryce, a former chef for the Ministry Of Defence) and Susie Q. (Susie Banfield, sister of the Pasadenas' Andrew Banfield), both b. *c.*1967. They put the act together in 1983, originally as a 13 piece collective entitled Warm Milk and the Cookie Crew, after which they were picked up by the Rhythm King label. The breakthrough followed when they recorded 'Rok Da House' with their producers, the Beatmasters. Originally to have been used as an advert for soft drink Ribena, it became a UK hit in December 1987, and is often credited with being the first 'hip-house' record. Signing to ffrr, they went on to work with producers such as Stetasonic, Gang Starr, Black Sheep, Davey D, Daddy 'O' and Dancin' Danny D (D-Mob), and later added Dutch singer MC Peggy Lee as a 'human beatbox'. Their DJs also included DJ Maxine and DJ Dazzle, who were among a succession of collaborators. 1989 proved their watershed year, with the hits 'Born This Way', 'Got To Keep On' and 'Come And Get Some'. They were also prominent as part of the Black Rhyme Organisation To Help Equal Rights (B.R.O.T.H.E.R.) along with Overlord X, Demon Boyz, She Rockers, and many other black rap acts in the UK. On their second album they teamed up with jazz fusion artist Roy Ayers for a new version of his 'Love Will Bring Us Back Together'. However, all was not well between the Cookie Crew and London. The latter wished to increase the duo's chart profile with more commercial material. The Cookie Crew, for their part, wanted to concentrate on more hardcore hip-hop. A bizarre compromise was reached in the summer of 1992 when two singles, 'Like Brother Like Sister' and 'Crew's Gone Mad' were released side by side. The former was a hip house pop tune, the latter a biting rap track, in an experiment to decide the direction of their future career. In the event, the group had run its course anyway, and Remedee would go on to form the New Wave Sisters with Trouble & Bass (another female rap duo) and Dee II, also setting up a concert and club agency - 786 Promotions.

● ALBUMS: *Born This Way!* (London 1989)★★★, *Fade To Black* (London 1991)★★★.

COOLIO

b. Artis Ivey, 1964, Compton, Los Angeles, California, USA. Boasting of a long, though infrequently recorded, career in hip-hop, rapper Coolio appeared alongside other west coast luminaries such as Dr. Dre when he was still with the World Class Wreckin' Crew. He even signed to Ruthless Records for a brief, unproductive spell. His debut release was 'Whatcha Gonna Do', one of the very first Los Angeles rap records, followed by 'You're Gonna Miss Me'. After attending rehabilitation classes in an attempt to kick his cocaine habit, Coolio started making music again, with WC and DJ Alladin as part of WC And The MADD Circle (one album for Profile Records). He then joined the 40 Theivz, a hip-hop community made up of producers, rappers and dancers. Along with a friend called Dobbs the Wino, Coolio signed to Tommy Boy Records who released the single 'County Line' about his experiences on welfare assistance. 'Fantastic Voyage', based on Lakeside's similarly-titled 1980 release, also made waves when released as a single, and Coolio's profile was further enhanced by an autumn tour with R&B megastar R. Kelly. *It Takes A Thief* became a major seller, going platinum and establishing Coolio at the forefront of mid-90s hip-hop. 'Gangsta's Paradise' was a resigned lament performed with the gospel singer 'LV' and a full choir that sampled Stevie Wonder's 'Pastime Paradise'. The single, featured in the film *Dangerous Minds*, went to number 1 in the US and the UK. In the UK this was the first time anything approaching true 'street rap' had achieved such sales. As the music business magazine *Music Week* commented, 'in Britain for such a record to reach number one is quite sensational'. It subsequently won a Grammy in 1996 for Best Rap Solo Performance.

● ALBUMS: *It Takes A Thief* (Tommy Boy 1994)★★★, *Gangsta's Paradise* (Tommy Boy 1995)★★★★, *My Soul* (Tommy Boy 1997)★★★.

COOLTEMPO RECORDS

One of the most prolific and identifiable dance music labels in the UK, Cooltempo is backed by the muscle of Chrysalis records, and operated under the A&R direction of Ken Grunbaum. Among their most notable acts have been Shara Nelson, Guru/Gang Starr, Arrested Development and Brand New Heavies. By the early 90s they had become a fixture of the dance music charts with hits such as 'Always' (Urban Soul), 'Everybody Jump' (DJ Power) and 'Don't Let It Show On Your Face' (Adeva). They also helped to set up Paul Oakenfold's Perfecto subsidiary in its original incarnation.

● COMPILATIONS: *Quality Produce* (Cooltempo 1994)★★★.

CORRIDOR

This UK techno band consists of the apparently surname-less Ashley and Chris whose origins lie in Tunbridge Wells, Kent, where in 1982 Chris bought his first synthesizer after seeing a Tangerine Dream gig. Both were originally in indie band the Merkins (the name taken from a pubic wig used by prostitutes who had been shorn following lice infestation). The name Corridor was taken from the Sam Fuller film about a mental asylum (*Shock Corridor*). Together with friends Nat and Grant they recorded a demo that was sent to Andy Weatherall at his Sabres Of Paradise label. The latter released Corridor's debut, 'Element', followed by 'X'. The first was dreamy, soundscape techno, the second a much harder regime. Afterwards, Nat and Grant took off to join Conemelt, who released their debut EP on Ashley's New Ground label. Chris and Ashley continued as a duo, their 'Two Days' cut, also on New Ground, providing them with a big club hit in late 1993. Their hard techno is informed by their love of the industrial genre - it was the Sabres' remix of Throbbing Gristle's 'United' that originally encouraged them to contact Weatherall.

COSMIC BABY

b. *c.*1966, Germany. Ambient sound sculptor whose methodology reflects his erudite philosophy on music - 'Trance isn't purely mind music. It's body and soul music and therefore cannot be

represented simply by sounds of the sea and mystical flutes. My own music is far too complex to be reduced to a label like trance. My music has nothing to do with creating a functional dance or ambient track'. His music conversely, has led to him being widely regarded as 'The Star Of Trance', or worse, 'The Modular Mozart' or 'Sir Trancealot'. He had actually been perfecting his technique since the late 80s, and even resisted approaches to sign him from Rhythm King in 1990. Cosmic Baby is a trained musician, who studied at the Nuremberg Conservatory at the age of seven. As well as classical music (notably Erik Satie) he was also heavily influenced by his native forebears such as Kraftwerk and Tangerine Dream. He has recorded widely in his own country since 1991, under the Energy 52 and Futurhythm monikers. Eventually he signed with the Berlin-based MFS label in 1992. He first graced the British club scene, and charts, with a collaboration with Paul Van Dyck under the name Visions Of Shiva, scoring with 'Perfect Day'. An appearance at the Eissenporthall in Cologne brought him many plaudits as a live entertainer, as did another PA at Club UK in London. On record he became widely noted for his 'Loops Of Infinity' cut, which prefaced a stylistically varied second album. Alongside the conventional trance of 'Cosmic Greets Florida' lay such splendours as a rewriting of Debussy's 'L'Apres-Midi D'Une Faune'.
● ALBUMS: *Stellar Supreme* (MFS 1992)★★, *Thinking About Myself* (Arista/Logic 1994)★★★.

COSMIC FORCE

Alongside Soul Sonic Force, Cosmic Force were the second arm of Afrika Bambaataa's Zulu Nation network. They joined with the latter for his debut release on Winley Records (see Paul Winley) 'Zulu Nation Throwdown', featuring the talents of female rapper Lisa Lee, herself an ex-member of Soul Sonic Force.

COSMOSIS

This psychedelic trance group was originally formed in the mid-90s by the guitarist Bill Halsey and Jez Van Kampen. Their first release was 'Cannabanoid' for Transient Records in September 1995, after which they brought out a number of singles including 'Deus', 'Morphic Resonance', 'Gift Of The Gods' and 'Howling At The Moon'. At the same time they recorded together as Laughing Buddha for TIP Records and released 'Infinite

Depth'/'Andromeda' in December 1995. The following year Cosmosis's debut album, *Cosmology*, received an enthusiastic response. After the Laughing Buddha release 'Karma/Earth Medecine/Megamorphosis' (TIP 1997) the pair decided to pursue individual projects, with Halsey working as Cosmosis and Van Kampen as Laughing Buddha. The second Cosmosis album, *Synergy*, was released on Transient in March 1998 and in the spring Halsey took part in a tour of South Africa, Australia, Japan and the USA organized by Transient and Phantasm Records. Cosmosis's music is characterized by funky, multilayered riffs and the most psychedelic, abstract noises and effects, which fade in and out and shoot around, lending a three-dimensional shape to the sound. As many psy-trance artists had moved towards a sparser sound that was less reliant on swirling effects and riffs, *Synergy* was not the most original trance album at the time of its release. However, the quality of production and arrangements combined with the sheer size of the tracks, overrides any bias one might have towards trends. Halsey sometimes employs guitar in his music, notably 'Down At The Crossroad', and recently he has been joined in live performances by the DJ Pied Piper or the guitarist Wei.
● ALBUMS: *Cosmology* (Transient 1996)★★★★, *Synergy* (Transient 1998)★★★★.

COWBOY RECORDS

UK Record label founded by Dean Thatcher and Charlie Chester in mid-1992, as a complementary operation to London's Flying Records. The turning point came when Thatcher grew tired of not being able to sign artists to Flying when tapes were brought into the shop for him, and Cowboy was used as a more 'street' label with the ability to release smaller-scale runs that would have been impossible on a bigger label. Chester and Thatcher had originally run Volante Records, through a licensing deal with Cooltempo (Audio Deluxe, Tyrrel Corporation, etc.). Chester is also manager of Secret Life and the Aloof, both of whom enjoyed early success for the label with 'As Always (Farley/Heller mixes)' and 'On A Mission (Fabio Paras mixes)', respectively. Cowboy went on to establish a strong reputation in their year of inception with releases such as Sona Lakota's 'Ice And Acid', Faith Department's (Phil Perry) 'Initiation' or Well Hung Parliament's 'We Can Be'. In 1993 Pulse 8 bought a substantial share in the operation, bringing over artists like Deja Vu (who had scored big club hits with 'Why Why Why', a cover of the balearic classic by the Woodentops, of whom Deja Vu leader Rollo was a member, and 'Never Knew The Devil') and Talisman, providing distribution through Pulse 8's deal with Sony/3MV in return. It was originally anticipated that the deal would be struck with Sony's Licensed Repertoire Division, through whom they had worked Secret Life's 'Love So Strong'. Chester made his own vinyl debut as Perks Of Living Society, which was the name he gave to his own club, which he runs alongside Back To Basics' Dave Beer. The track was a cover versio of 'Too Damn Free', previously a test pressing only by YB Experience. New vocals were added by Val Chalmers.

COX, CARL

b. 29 July 1962, Oldham, Lancashire, England. Cox is one of the UK's best-loved DJs; his reputation for playing up to 14 sets a week and being a permanent fixture on the rave circuit is well known. He became a full-time DJ in 1985. After serving an apprenticeship as host to a thousand private parties, he eventually graduated to weddings and finally clubs. He helped to pioneer the house scene in Brighton in the late 80s, and was highly involved in the development of acid house. He played at the first night of the Shoom club as well as other famous clubs such as Spectrum and Land Of Oz. He was the first to introduce a 'third' deck into a set at the 1989 Sunrise show. Cox remains a great advocate of European techno and house, which forms the basis of most of his live sets, and his celebrity fans include Laurent Garnier, whose Wake Up nightclub is apparently Cox's favourite venue. As his popularity grew, it became inevitable that he would release a record of his own. Following his 1991 hit single, 'I Want You (Forever)' (UK number 23), he attempted to woo the airwaves with 'Does It Feel Good To You'. His first 'mix' album arrived on the React label in 1995. Cox is also the managing director of Ultimate Music Management and MMR Productions.
● ALBUMS: *F.A.C.T. (Future Alliance of Communication and Technology)* (React 1995)★★★★, *At The End Of The Cliché* (A World Wide Ultimation 1996)★★★.

CPO

An acronym for Capital Punishment Organisation, CPO is the brainchild of rapper Lil'

Nation. Nation had formerly been an armed gang member in South Central Los Angeles, California, USA, from the age of 12 onwards, providing him with suitable gangsta rap credentials. However, his debut album *To Hell And Back*, on which he was aided by members of the Ruthless Records/NWA stable (notably MC Ren), was a poor imitation of those artists' street hip-hop élan. In particular his rapping carried neither the potency nor dexterity of his better-known peers.
● ALBUMS: *To Hell And Back* (Ruthless 1990)★★.

CRAIG, CARL

A prolific techno third columnist from Detroit, Michigan, Craig rose to prominence on Derrick May's Transmat imprint, releasing material under names including Psyche (famed for the pre-trance 'Crackdown' epic) and BFC (notably 'Static Friendly'). Originally he had been inspired by Kraftwerk and early Human League, but after supporting Derrick May as a component of Rhythim Is Rhythim his tastes broadened, taking a more ethno-centric view of his surroundings. Following recording sessions for 'Stringz Of Life '89' with May, he set up his own label, Planet E, before a six-month sabbatical to England in 1990 (at which time Fragile released his 'Galaxy'). Increasingly welcomed across two continents as a prime mover in the Detroit techno sound, Craig has issued a plethora of subsequent material. Most notable among these are his collaboration with Maurizio ('Mind') and his work as Paperclip People ('Remake Uno'), which were licensed from Planet E to Ministry Of Sound's Open label in the UK. He signed his 69 moniker to R&S in 1994. That name had first been employed for his epic 1991 12-inch, 'Ladies And Gentleman', which latterly found favour as a Sound On Sound reissue with DJs such as DJ Pierre, Andy Weatherall and Amsterdam's Dimitri. In the meantime the duo remixed 'Le Funk Mob' for Planet E, while Craig offered a new version of 'Throw' for Open. Craig has also performed remix work for prominent artists including the Orb, Yello and Tori Amos. He released his debut long-player (on Blanco Y Negro) in 1995, but the follow-up *More Songs About Food And Revolutionary Art* offered more compelling evidence of Craig's superb melodic talent.
● ALBUMS: *Landcruising* (Blanco Y Negro 1995)★★★, *More Songs About Food And Revolutionary Art* (SSR/Planet 1997)★★★.

CRAMMED RECORDS

Brussels, Belgium-based label distinguished by releases such as Avalon (aka Tim Handel)'s *Earth Water Air Fire*. They also released Geir Jenssen's (of Biosphere) *North Pole By Submarine* collection of late 80s ambient house cuts. On the singles front, 1991 was typified by material that included YBU featuring Jonell's 'Soul Music', which would be licensed to Mark Moore of S'Express's Splish label in the UK and Flying in Italy. Follow-up releases by YBU (essentially Hans Gottheim, b. Tromso, Norway) included 'Apache', which again found its way onto Splish. Otherwise, Crammed's main artists were Modulate, Bobuan and Solar Quest. Later material included Hector Zazov's remarkable 1993 set, *Sahara Blue*, which featured Bill Laswell, Tim Simenon (Bomb The Bass), Khaled, John Cale, Ryuichi Sakamoto and Gerard Depardieu. An Algerian/French composer, Zazov used this personnel and others to set the backdrop to a selection of Rimbaud's poetry, in six different languages - a finger in the eye to those who suggest that dance music is intellectually/artistically limited.

CRANIUM HF

This UK hardcore industrial dance trio consists of Fisheye (vocals), Kev and Ross. (The initials at the end of their name stand for 'Head Fuck'.) Fisheye was living on an abandoned fire engine on a waste disposal dump when he met the other two while they roadied for Daisy Chainsaw. On the tour Fisheye and Kev devised an impromptu supporting rap act. Kev had previously worked as sound engineer with Ross on projects involving Meat Beat Manifesto and Sheep On Drugs. The trio decided to attempt to make it as a professional act and settled in London for the release of *Nation Of Pinheads* (1992). They followed up a year later with a second EP, *The Deal*. The music is a mixture of old-style house, rap and industrial music.

CRASH CREW

US rap group Crash Crew recorded a solitary single for Sugarhill, 'Breaking Bells (Take Me To The Mardi Gras)', in 1982. This was a heavily restructured (basically utilising the break only) version of Bob James' cover of Paul Simon's 'Take Me To The Mardi Gras' original.

CREDIT TO THE NATION

Among the most commercially viable of new UK hip-hop groups, Credit To The Nation comprise Matty Hanson (b. 1971, Wednesbury, West Midlands, England, aka MC Fusion), with his dancers, Tyrone and Kelvin (aka T-Swing and Mista-G). Credit To The Nation broke through in 1993 after several months of sponsorship by agit-prop anarchists Chumbawamba, with whom they recorded their first, joint single. They also shared a lyrical platform which attacked racism, sexism and homophobia. Hanson took time out to point out the flaws in the gangsta philosophies of Ice-T, Onyx and the like, but received short shrift from hardcore hip-hop fans. Credit To The Nation broke through with 'Call It What You Want', which cheekily sampled the guitar motif used by Nirvana on 'Smells Like Teen Spirit'. This helped them find an audience in hip indie kids outside of the hardcore rap fraternity. There was a backlash to be observed: after threats to his life he was eventually forced to move out of his home in Wednesbury, West Midlands. The band continued with the release of the singles 'Teenage Sensation', which went into the Top 30, and 'Hear No Bullshit, See No Bullshit, Say No Bullshit' - often dedicated to the likes of East 17 and Kriss Kross on stage. Tracks on their debut album included pro-female tracks like 'The Lady Needs Respect', the anthemic 'Pump Your Fist', on which Tyrone enjoys a rare chance to rap, and 'Rising Tide', influenced by the election of BNP councillor Derek Beacon. Among the samples were Benjamin Britten, Glenn Miller, the Sex Pistols and even the Coldstream Guards.
● ALBUMS: *Take Dis* (One Little Indian 1993)★★★, *Daddy Always Wanted Me To Grow A Pair Of Wings* (One Little Indian 1996)★★★.

CUJO

(see Tobin, Amon)

CULTURE BEAT

Euro-dance sensations who were created by Torsten Fenslau (b. *c.*1964, Germany, d. November 1993, Darmstadt, Germany) in 1989 by putting together the more visual duo of Jay Supreme and Tania Evans. Fenslau had begun his career DJing at the Dorian Gray club at Frankfurt Airport, also working on Hessen State radio presenting the Club Night and Maxi-Mix shows. He subsequently moved into production, scoring a solo hit under the banner Out Of The Ordinary with 'Los Ninos Mix', although it did not find success outside of his native Germany. The same could hardly be said for Culture Beat, who quickly racked up huge overground dancefloor hits with 'No Deeper Meaning', 'Mr Vain' and 'Got To Get It'. In its wake Fenslau remixed for the Shamen ('Coming On Strong') and released a solo progressive trance single, 'Come Into My Heart', as Abfahrt, and was behind Cheery Lips' 'Das Erdbbermund'. 'Mr Vain' sold over two million copies, but sadly Fenslau did not live long enough to see his endeavours bear fruit. He was involved in a car crash in November 1993, dying from internal injuries when he reached hospital. The Culture Beat members informed the press of their intention to carry on in his absence, scoring another Top 10 hit with 'Anything' in 1994. Alex Abraham became Fenslau's replacement as musical guru to Culture Beat, alongside long-term collaborators Peter Zweier and Nosie Katzman.

● ALBUMS: *Horizon* (Epic 1991)★★★, *Serenity* (Epic 1993)★★★.

CURRENT 93

Current 93 - a name derived from the writings of Aleister Crowley is the brainchild of David Michael Bunting (aka David Tibet) with the assistance of fellow English maverick Steve Stapleton (Nurse With Wound). Tibet launched the name in 1983 with *Lashtal*, an EP issued on the Belgian label Laylah. The slow, trance-like drum patterns, droning electronics and tapes of chanting formed the basis of the first two Current 93 albums. *Nature Unveiled*, produced by Stapleton, possesses a terrifying intensity. Taking inspiration from the work of the author William Burroughs, Tibet plunders pre-existing music, reassembling it in a 'cut-up' method into which he adds distressing moans and screams. On *Dog's Blood Rising* he proved less reliant on sampling, employing treated vocals and keyboard figures to flail at the darkest side of human existence, conjuring up an aural hell. Perversely, the set closes with an a cappella medley of Simon And Garfunkel songs. Following a collaboration with Coil on *Nightmare Culture*, Tibet recycled material from *Nature Unveiled* and *Dog's Blood Rising*, added new electronics and issued *Live At The Bar Matador*. *In Menstrual Night* offered a gentler sound, combining passive sound effects, tape loops and English folk tunes. *Imperium* drew inspiration from Tudor and Elizabethan melodies, albeit with a disconcerting

mood, while *Dawn* showed Tibet's love of noise and distortion had not lessened. However, *Swastikas For Noddy* and *Earth Covers Earth* showed a continued passion for folk music themes. *Earth Covers Earth* even comes in a pastiche sleeve playing homage to the Incredible String Band. Although these releases are less challenging than earlier Current 93 recordings, Tibet had proved himself an imaginative performer.

● ALBUMS: *Nature Unveiled* (Laylah 1984)★★★, *Dog's Blood Rising* (Laylah 1984)★★★, with Coil *Nightmare Culture* (Laylah 1985)★★, *In Menstrual Night* (United Dairies 1986)★★★, *Live At Bar Maldoror* (Mi-Mart 1986)★★★, *Imperium* (Maldoror 1987)★★, *Dawn* (Maldoror 1987)★★★, *Swastikas For Noddy* (Laylah 1987)★★★, *Earth Covers Earth* (United Dairies 1988)★★★, *Looney Runes* (Durtro 1991)★★★, *All The Pretty Little Horses* (Durtro/World Serpent 1996)★★★.

CURTIN, DAN

b. c.1969. This second-generation US techno innovator comes from Cleveland, Ohio. Compressing Chicago house, breakbeats and loops into records since 1991's *Third From The Sun* EP, his style maintains an organic, human thread through its electronic beats. An entrepreneur as well as a recording artist, he runs his own label, Metamorphic, and record shop, Deep Sleep Records, in his native Cleveland, as well as undertaking traditional DJing activities. Much of his recorded material, including *The Planetary* and *Voices From Another Age* EPs (on Japanese label Sublime), reflects the artist's own interest in space and technology. This EP was remixed by Ken Ishii.

● ALBUMS: *The Silicon Dawn* (Metamorphic 1994)★★★, *Art & Science* (Peacefrog 1996)★★★, *Deception* (Sublime 1997)★★★.

CUT TO KILL

From Chelmsford, Essex, England, Cut To Kill were among the earliest UK rap groups. Established in the mid-80s, they comprised DJ 4 Tune and rapper Vision. The duo met in 1986 in their hometown. Vision had grown up with electro rap and old school DJs such as Grandmaster Flash, while 4 Tune's background was in 'rare groove'. The latter influence resulted in samples such as Bill Coday's 'Get Your Life Straight' being deployed throughout their early material. They signed to the independent label

Tam Tam Records (whose other artists included Silver Bullet), having been investigated on the basis of a four-track demo which circulated throughout London in 1985. Their debut single was the double a-side 'Talking Facts'/'Listen To The Bass Tone', the b-side produced by part-time member DJ Fame. However, in common with Silver Bullet they never fulfilled their potential, though 'Talking Facts' remains widely regarded as an important staging post in the development of UK rap and hip-hop.

CUTTING RECORDS

US label formed in 1984, originally as a side venture for record store owners Aldo and Amado Marin. Cutting has displayed a tremendous variety in its first decade of operation, having moved from hip-hop-related matters to the overground house movement. Huge commercial success arrived with Corina's 'Temptation' and Two In A Room's 'Wiggle It'. Other classics, such as Hashim's 'Alnaaflysh', were well regarded despite not breaking through to quite the same extent. Label boss Aldo Marin maintained that 'I don't like music labels, I just look for good music to keep people dancing.' This propensity to span genres from techno to house and garage has been continued by releases like Vibe Tribe's (Joey Beltram) 'Something Unreal', Pamela Fernandez's 'Kickin' In The Beat', Masters At Work's (featuring Jocelyn Brown) 'Can't Stop The Rhythm' or Praxis's (featuring Kathy Brown) 'Turn Me Out'.
● COMPILATIONS: *Cutting It To The X:Treme Volume 1* (Cutting 1994)★★★.

CYPRESS HILL

Another of the new rap breed to extoll the creative use of marijuana/hemp, Los Angeles-based Cypress Hill, with songs such as 'I Wanna Get High', 'Legalise It' and 'Insane In The Brain' all advocating marijuana as a cultural replacement for alcohol, are champions of NORML (National Organisation For The Reform Of Marijuana Laws). However, the reason for their widespread success lies instead with their blend of full and funky R&B, tales of dope and guns adding the final sheen to the rhythm. The band comprise DJ Muggs (b. Lawrence Muggerud, *c.*1969, of Italian descent) on the decks, and vocalists B-Real (b. Louis Freeze, *c.*1970, of Mexican/Cuban descent) and Sen Dog (b. Sen Reyes, *c.*1965, Cuba), a former running back for Los Angeles' Centennial High. An additional member is Eric Bobo - their sometime percussionist. Sen Dog had come to Los Angeles from his native Cuba at the age of 14. With his younger brother Mellow Man Ace, he had formed the prototype rap outfit, DVX, and claims to have invented the Spanglish 'lingo' style. After his brother left he hooked up with former 7A3 members DJ Muggs and B-Real, who was one of the same breakdancing crew as Mellow. Their debut set was only available in the UK on import for some time, though in the US it created a lot of interest almost immediately. Spanning two years' songwriting, it eventually went platinum. Longstanding B-boys, touring for free and opening for Naughty By Nature in 1991, Cypress Hill represented rap's new wave. After the militancy and radicalism of Public Enemy and NWA, Cypress Hill were advocating escapism via pot, and making it sound very attractive indeed. The second album, rather than pursuing a more commercial bent, was informed by the dark events in their home city *à la* Rodney King. *Black Sunday* debuted at number 1 in the US R&B and Pop charts, while the gun-touting 'Cock The Hammer' turned up on the soundtrack to Arnold Schwarzenegger's mega-flop, *Last Action Hero*. Their reputation for violent lyrics (a method they justified as: 'not promoting, more explaining what goes on') was underscored when they appeared on the soundtrack for another film, *Mad Dog And Glory*, in a scene that accompanies a drug killing. Their breakthrough in the UK came when they supported House Of Pain on dates through 1993. The latter group, and several others, benefited from the services of DJ Muggs' in-demand production skills (Ice Cube, Beastie Boys, etc.). Their most recent soundtrack appearance occurred when they recorded a track with Pearl Jam, 'The Real Thing', for the film *Judgement Night*. Sen Dog left the unit in February 1996 and was replaced by DJ Scandalous, who had already worked with the band.
● ALBUMS: *Cypress Hill* (Ruffhouse 1991)★★★★, *Black Sunday* (Columbia 1993)★★★, *III The Temples Of Boom* (Columbia 1995)★★★, *Unreleased And Revamped* mini-album (Columbia 1996)★★.

D*NOTE

The skills behind D*Note's brand of jazz, rap and rare groove belong chiefly to Matt Winn (Matt Wienevski), who is helped by scratcher Charlie Lexton and occasional keyboard player Matt Cooper (who records for Dorado in his own right as Outside). Their debut album housed the singles 'Now Is The Time', 'Bronx Bull', 'Scheme Of Things' and 'The More I See', each of which enjoyed good reviews in their original formats. Wienevski's first film, a 10-minute short entitled *Round The Block*, was shown on the UK's Channel 4. *Criminal Justice* built on the energy level of the debut, but *Coming Down* was a marked disappointment, with only the forceful 'Waiting Hopefully' standing out.

● ALBUMS: *Babel* (Dorado 1993)★★★, *Criminal Justice* (Dorado 1995)★★★, *Coming Down* (VC 1997)★★.

D-MOB

D-Mob is essentially the creative vehicle of 'Dancin'' Danny D (b. Daniel Kojo Poku), an ex-McDonald's employee. He found solace by DJing for three or four years in the evenings, at one point working with journalist James Hamilton at Gullivers in Park Lane, London. He subsequently started club promotions for Loose Ends (for whom he contributed his first remix), Total Contrast and Full Force, before taking up an A&R post at Chrysalis Records. This brought a number of further remixing opportunities, including Nitro Deluxe, Kid 'N Play, Adeva and Eric B And Rakim's 'I Know You Got Soul' in tandem with Norman Cook. By the time he had started using the name D-Mob he had already released two records, as the Taurus Boys, which were minor hits in the USA. Then came 'Warrior Groove', about the tribe (the Ashantis) from which his Ghanese parents came. The first D-Mob release was 1989's crossover hit 'We Call It Acieed', which featured Gary Haisman on vocals. It was a stirring acid house tune, bringing the underground scene a good deal of notoriety when politicians and papers determined its subject matter was drugs-related. BBC Television, in its wisdom, banned it from *Top Of The Pops*. However, as Poku confirmed to the press: 'I don't take any form of drugs. I don't even go the doctor to get something for my cold.' Follow-up hits included 'It Is Time To Get Funky' (with London Rhyme Syndicate), 'C'mon And Get My Love' and 'That's The Way Of The World' (with Cathy Dennis) and 'Put Your Hands Together' (with Nuff Juice). He also produced/remixed records for Adeva, Juliet Roberts ('Another Place, Another Day, Another Time'), Monie Love, Diana Ross ('Working Overtime'), Chaka Khan ('I'm Every Woman') and the Cookie Crew ('Love Will Bring Us Together'), plus dozens more. In 1993 he brought back Dennis (who had enjoyed huge subsequent solo success) for vocals on 'Why', his 'comeback' single as D-Mob. As an in-demand producer and remixer he had never been away.

● ALBUMS: *A Little Bit Of This, A Little Bit Of That* (ffrr 1989)★★★.

D-NICE

b. Derrick Jones, 19 June 1970, Bronx, New York, USA. An important member of the Boogie Down Productions crew, Jones became the group's DJ and beatbox having befriended Scott La Rock. D-Nice finally stepped out into the solo spotlight with 1990's *Call Me D-Nice*. KRS-1 kept tabs on his old partner by adding his vocals to cuts like 'The TR-808 Is Coming', which boasted of his familiar 808-derived sound. However, D-Nice also struck out on his own groove, straying into more commercial musical territory, and sticking to the self-aggrandisement themes of old school rappers rather than KRS-1's more socially aware themes. There were only two exceptions: 'Glory', which measured the role of the black man in the American Civil War, a theme touched on in the film of the same name, and 'A Few Dollars More', which painted a sympathetic portrait of inner city poverty. The album gave him two number 1 US rap singles with 'Crumbs On The Table' and the title track, 'Call Me D-Nice'. For his second album he invited Too Short, KRS-1, Naughty By Nature and funk guitarist Jean-Paul Bourelly along for the party. Though he was branching out musically, 'Rhyming Skills' continued the path laid by 'The Tr-808 Is Coming', with its bass-heavy, stomping arrangement. There were also cuts like the pro-feminist 'Get In Touch With Me' which contrasted with the 'bitch and ho baitin' 'Check

Yourself. Though he has found some commercial reward after stepping out from behind the turntable, the more pleasing aspects of his solo work remain his funk-based deck skills.

● ALBUMS: *Call Me D-Nice* (Jive 1990)★★★, *To Tha Resuce* (Jive 1991)★★★.

D-ZONE RECORDS

Based in Essex, England, D-Zone Records were set up and run by DJ Andre Jacobs, who started DJing in Romford at the age of 15 and has since been lumped in with the 'Essex techno scene', alongside other acts including Codeine and Ray Keith). D-Zone has thus far given the world Tekno Too (Jacobs' own recordings, such as 'Jet Star'), Turntable Symphony (Jazzy Jason and Aston Harvey of the Blaaps! Posse, responsible for 'Instructions Of Life' and other tunes), Is That It (again Jacobs), Toxic (Toxic EP), Easymo (Cut And Run EP), Artful Dodgers ('Pure Love - Pure Energy') and Greed (DJs Mike Gray and John Pearn - 'Love').

D., DONALD

The first artist to appear because of Ice-T's deal between the Rhyme Syndicate and Epic Records, Donald D's influence in the 90s was marginal. His anti-drugs stance was hammered home on his debut release, 'FBI (Free Base Institute)' although he showed a lack of sensitivity elsewhere on his debut album on tracks such as 'Just Suck', which gloried in the Rhyme Syndicate's gangbanging activities. Although he moved to the west coast, Donald D's roots were in the Bronx. He met Ice-T in 1985 when he was visiting California with *Notorious*'s eventual co-producer, Afrika Islam.

● ALBUMS: *Notorious* (Epic 1990)★★, *Let The Horns Blow* (Sire 1992)★★.

D., WILLIE

b. Willie Dennis, Houston, Texas, USA. Yet another member of the outlandish Geto Boys to hallucinate about having displayed enough talent in his efforts with that band to warrant a solo career. He left the group for good in 1992, having already released his misogynistic solo debut in 1989: 'It was very rewarding and a good experience for me to have been in the group, working with Bushwick Bill and Scarface. We were always dealing with controversy, and sometimes all we had was each other for support'. The 1992 single 'Clean Up Man' was backed by the controversial 'Rodney K', which he used as a platform for an attack on the black community leaders so incensed by the activities of the Geto Boys. Willie subsequently moved to Ichiban to set up his new Wize Up imprint, the first release on which was Sho's *Trouble Man* album. Willie also featured as a guest rapper on the collection. His own *Play Witcha Mama* featured a duet with Ice Cube on the title-track, but was otherwise undistinguished smooth rap. Willie D. reunited with the other two Geto Boys for 1996's *The Resurrection*.

● ALBUMS: *Controversy* (Rap-a-Lot 1989)★★, *I'm Goin' Out Like A Soldier* (Rap-a-Lot 1992)★★★, *Play Witcha Mama* (Wize-Up/Wrap 1994)★★.

D.A.F.

This German band, based in Dusseldorf, specialized in minimalist electro-dance music. The initials stood for Deutsch Amerikanische Freundschaft, a term first invoked on local posters to symbolize post-war American-German friendship, and the line-up comprised Robert Gorl (drums, synthesizer), W. Spelmans (guitar), Chrislo Hass (saxophone, synthesizer, bass) and Gabi Delgado-Lopez (vocals). *Die Kleinen Und Die Bosen* was their first album available in the UK (*Produkt* had only been available in Germany), released on the Mute Records label in 1980; the title translates as 'The Small And The Evil'. Recorded in London, the album was uneven and is generally considered as unrepresentative, dominated by 'songs' whose heritage combined *Pink Flag*-era Wire and Can influences. Afterwards, Gorl and Delgado-Lopez continued as a duo (Haas would later join Crime And The City Solution), recording three albums for Virgin Records in an 18-month period. These comprised a mixture of Teutonic fantasy, love songs, and social statements. Delgado-Lopez's refusal to sing in English condemned them to a minority international market. Contrary to their dour image, there was much to admire in the exemplary pop of singles such as 'Verlieb Dich In Mich'. Indeed, in 1981 they guested on the Eurythmics' first album, *In The Garden*. Later, Annie Lennox would return the compliment by adding vocals to Gorl's solo 'Darling Don't Leave Me' single and several tracks on the accompanying album.

● ALBUMS: *Ein Produkt Der D.A.F.* (Warning/Atatack 1979)★★★, *Die Kleinen Und Die Bosen* (Mute 1980)★★, *Alles Ist Gut* (Virgin 1981)★★★, *Gold Und Liebe* (Virgin 1981)★★★, *Für Immer* (Virgin 1982)★★★, *Live In London* (Music For Midgets 1984)★★.

Solo: Robert Gorl *Night Full Of Tension* (Mute 1984)★★. Gabi Delgado *Mistress* (Virgin 1983)★★★.

● COMPILATIONS: *DAF* (Virgin 1988)★★★.

D.O.C.

b. Tray Curry, *c.*1970, Texas, USA. D.O.C. was once one of the world's most promising rappers, before his career was cut short by a horrendous automobile accident that crushed his throat and left him unable to rap. Hanging out with Dr. Dre's Dogg Pound posse, he had regained enough use of his voice to contribute to Dre's classic 1992 set, The Chronic. On his debut album, future Dre protégé Michel'le was heard for the first time, alongside former NWA personnel Eazy-E, Ice Cube and MC Ren. There was a fluidity of rhythmic expression apparent on the record that could have predicted the runaway success of subsequent Dre protégé, Snoop Doggy Dogg. It also included D.O.C.'s killer rap, 'Portrait Of A Masterpiece', which would grace any collection of rap's greatest hits. D.O.C. returned in 1996 with *Helter Skelter*, but failed to match the commercial impact of his debut.

● ALBUMS: *No One Can Do It Better* (Ruthless 1988)★★★★, *Helter Skelter* (Giant 1996)★★★.

D.O.P.

West London artists Kevin Hurry and Kevin Swain, who met at Shoom in the late 80s, are the men behind the D.O.P. banner, an acronym for Dance Only Productions. Their first chance to DJ came at Gary Haisman's infamous Raid club. They have interspersed their regular sets at venues like Flying, Love Ranch and Sign Of The Times with their recordings as D.O.P. throughout the 90s (their first release was credited to Bliss on the *Live At The Brain* compilation set). D.O.P.'s first single, 'Future Le Funk', sampled Visage, and was picked up by Guerilla in the summer of 1991. The second, 'Get Out On The Dancefloor', used strings borrowed from a Japan record, while they also remixed stablemates React 2 Rhythm's 'Whatever You Dream'. They eventually dissolved in 1994, stating they had 'taken the band as far as we possibly can'. As further evidence of this they pointed out the way in which D.O.P.'s music had cropped up on compilations spanning garage, hardcore, progressive house and techno. However, they will be fondly remembered for singles such as 'Oh Yeah' and 'Groovy Beat'.

● ALBUMS *Musicians Of The Mind* (Guerilla 1992)★★★.

D:REAM

London pop-dance artists who crossed over from clubs to daytime radio, and won themselves impressive chart placings in the process. D:Ream originally comprised Al Mackenzie (b. Alan Mackenzie, 31 October 1968, Edinburgh, Scotland) and Peter Cunnah (b. 30 August 1966, Derry, Northern Ireland; ex-Tie The Boy, Baby June). Their first outing came at the JFK Bar in Great Portland Street, London, in February 1992. Four months later, Rhythm King released their debut single, 'UR The Best Thing' (the Prince-like spellings would become a regular feature of their titles). Although they failed to score many credibility points among their dance music peers (when asked in one survey who were their favourite DJs, Mackenzie included Steve Wright), they nevertheless became a sought-after remix team among mainstream pop artists (Deborah Harry, EMF, Duran Duran). Both 'UR The Best Thing' and, later, 'Things Can Only Get Better' were reissued in the wake of their higher profile and initial chart appearances. Their debut album, released in August 1993, was roundly rubbished by the press. MacKenzie too appeared less than happy with its new pop direction, and announced his decision to leave the band in October 1993 and return to DJing work. Shortly afterwards, the revitalized 'Things Can Only Get Better' enjoyed a long stay at the top of the UK pop charts, when there was some derision among the puritan dance community, with Pressure Of Speech lambasting the track for its potential to be: 'the next Tory Conference song' (ironically, the song was used by the Labour Party in their triumphant 1997 election campaign). MacKenzie, meanwhile, was embarking on a solo career as (among other things) Kitsch In Sync ('Jazz Ma Ass' for Global Grooves in 1994).

● ALBUMS: *D:Ream On Vol. 1* (Rhythm King 1993)★★★, *World* (Magnet 1995)★★.

DA BUSH BABEES

A New York, USA-based hip-hop trio, Da Bush Babees comprise Khaliyl (aka Mr. Man), Lee Major (aka Babyface Kaos) and Light (aka Y-Tee). The group had only been together for three months when they signed to Warner Brothers Records and released their 1994 debut album, *Ambushed*. This borrowed heavily from downtown reggae as well as the hip-hop tradition. The group were also keen to emphasise their positivity, writing a number of songs reacting angrily to the ghetto stereotypes propagated by gangsta rap. That theme continued on *Gravity*, the 1996 follow-up collection. Produced by the band alongside Posdnous (De La Soul), Sean J. Period and Ali Shaheed and Q-Tip (A Tribe Called Quest), Major told Billboard that it reflected the fact that 'we have grown and that we're new people. As individuals, for example, we know each other better now, because we had just gotten together [before *Ambushed*].' Among the album's strongest tracks was 'The Love Song', a freestyle hip-hop tune harking back to the old school values of Grandmaster Flash and Melle Mel.

● ALBUMS: *Ambushed* (Warners 1994)★★★, *Gravity* (Warners 1996)★★★.

DA HAPPY HEADZ

Comprising Big J, Grand Man and Angelo Smoove, Da Happy Headz dashed to prominence in the early 90s following an appearance on television on *The Oprah Winfrey Show*, on the premise of talking about hip-hop. Researchers for the show invited the trio to make an impromptu appearance, freestyling raps to give audiences an example of the genre. From Danville, Illinois, USA, they started life as the Street Corner Hustlers, with Da Happy Headz actually coalescing from a larger team of rappers and graffiti artists, called Da Happy Headz Nnjaz. However, despite their ghetto background they charted a more humane course which could easily be differentiated from gangsta rap which made them eminently suitable for such mainstream coverage. Bolstered by the impression they had created on the Oprah show, their typically humorous debut single, 'I'm Nappy', became a minor hit. However, their subsequent efforts failed to overcome their unfortunate image as 'Oprah's rap band'.

DA LENCH MOB

Hardcore gangsta rappers and protégés of Ice Cube, signed to his Street Knowledge label, Da Lench Mob were originally employed as backing musicians on their benefactor's first three solo recordings, before eventually seeing their own debut on *Guerillas In The Mist*. The title, an obvious pun on the film of similar name, was picked up by the band from a police report issued after attending a Los Angeles domestic incident. Although Da Lench Mob share many lyrical concerns with Ice Cube, there is a distinct moral tone stressed in their distrust of drugs and dealers.

Front person J-Dee numbers amongst the more articulate of rap's inner city spokesmen. He was joined by the backing duo of T-Bone (b. Terry Gray) and Jerome Washington (aka Shorty). However, after his arrest for attempted murder and subsequent imprisonment, J-Dee was dropped from the band at the end of 1993. This was caused, according to press statements, because of contractual obligations with which Da Lench Mob were enforced to comply. His replacement was Maulkley, ex-rap duo Yomo and Maulkley. Ironically, it was always Da Lench Mob's intention to recruit Maulkley, but contractual problems, once again, prevented this at the start of their career. His vocals were dubbed over their previously completed set, *Planet Of Da Apes*. However, T-Bone too would subsequently be charged with murder, and East West dropped the band in 1994. He was acquitted the following year.

● ALBUMS: *Guerillas In The Mist* (Street Knowledge 1992)★★★★, *Planet Of Da Apes* (Street Knowledge 1994)★★★.

DA LUNIZ

From Oakland, California, USA, rap artists Da Luniz consist of Yukmouth (b. *c*.1975) and Numbskul (b. *c*.1974). Their 1995 debut, *Operation Stackola*, featured guest appearances from Shock G of Digital Underground, plus DJ Fuse, N.O. Joe, Richie Rich, Gino Blackwell, E-A-Ski and Tone Capone. It reached number 1 in the US Billboard charts soon after release, taking many commentators, even within the hip-hop community, by surprise. The secret of their success lay in the duo's slick, empathetic performance, a theory endorsed by Yukmouth: 'Sometimes Numbskul will just be freestyling, and I'll damned know exactly what he's about to say next. We're like two halves of a whole.' They also found success with the attendant single, 'I Got 5 On It', built over a sample of the main riff from Timex Social Club's 'Rumours', and featuring a guest appearance from that group's Michael Marshall. The follow-up *Lunitik Muzik* was a sprawling and entertaining album, although the downbeat 'Y Do Thugz Die', which commented on the murders of 2Pac and Notorious B.I.G., was arguably the best track.

● ALBUMS: *Operation Stackola* (Noo Trybe/Virgin 1995)★★★, *Lunitik Muzik* (Noo Trybe 1997)★★★★.

DA YEENE

This duo of Swedish sisters made a substantial impact in UK dance clubs in the early 90s with two popular house tracks, 'Alright' and 'Body Action'. The originators, Dianne and Jeanette Söderholm, came from a strong musical background, and were the first act to be signed to the innovative Swedish dance label Swemix Records in 1989. The sisters' work combines sweet, harmonious garage vocals over the traditional sound of their label, which has long been acclaimed for its 'deep house' releases. However, their efforts have earned them scant respect in their native country: 'House is not that big here. Tempos are very slow. We're making music for other countries', they told UK dance magazines in 1993. Their debut album brought them their greatest domestic success, with the attendant single 'Big Bad World' becoming a minor national hit. A follow-up set was produced by Stonebridge, the man credited with revitalising the career of fellow dance artist Robin S. More recently they have recorded with Martin White, Denniz Pop and Douglas Carr - the latter two famous for their work with fellow Swedish exports Dr. Alban and Leila K.
● ALBUMS: *United Soul Power* (Swemix 1990)★★★, *Primetime* (Swemix 1992)★★★.

DA YOUNGSTA'S

A trio of young rappers from Philadelphia, USA who were visually distinguished by their closely shaved heads, but the appearance was deceptive. Far from the Onyx school of macho hardcore rap, Qu'ran, Taji and Tarik arrived with a much more scholarly view of things, from a profoundly Muslim perspective. Sadly, many of their lyrics were ghost-written for them, which in the world of rap, where self-expression is everything, led many to view them as contrived.
● ALBUMS: *Somethin' 4 Da Youngsta's* (East West 1991)★★, *The Aftermath* (East West 1993)★★★, *No Mercy* (Atlantic 1994)★★★.

DADDY-O

b. c.1961, Brooklyn, New York, USA. A founder member of Stetsasonic, and for some time one of hip-hop's most influential figures, Daddy-O is remembered fondly as the 'Quincy Jones' of rap. While still a member of the band he worked in communities furthering the A.F.R.I.C.A. programme - an anti-apartheid album and study guide. He has also spoken at several college seminars. When Stetsasonic broke up in 1990, Daddy-O was called in to provide remixes for swingbeat classics like Mary J. Blige's 'Real Love' and Shanté Moore's 'Love's Taken Over'. Before long everyone from Jeffrey Osbourne, Third World and They Might Be Giants to the Red Hot Chilli Peppers were on his casebook, as well as more conventional hip-hop concerns such as K9, Queen Latifah and Audio Two. Elsewhere he kept busy by producing jingles for Casio Electronics, Alka Seltzer and Pepsi, amongst others. His debut solo album, and promotional single 'Brooklyn Bounce', saw a welcome return to the freewheeling old school trickery which had been conspicuous by its absence in hip-hop. However, this was a 90s version, though a more politically directed album had been recorded but scrapped in deference to the one which eventually saw the light of day.
● ALBUMS: *You Can Be A Daddy But Never Daddy-O* (Brooktown/Island 1993)★★★.

DAFT PUNK

Guy-Manuel de Homem Christo (b. 8 February 1974) met Thomas Bangalter (b. 3 January 1975) when they both attended school in Paris, France, in 1987. In 1992, heavily influenced by the Beach Boys, they recorded a song under the name Darling, which in turn found its way onto a compilation single issued on Stereolab's Duophonic label. A review in *Melody Maker* described their effort as 'a bunch of daft punk', which depressed the pair but unwittingly gave them a name for their next project. Increasingly influenced by the house sounds filtering across from the UK and the USA, they signed with the Scottish label Soma Records and in 1994 they released the dance single 'New Wave'. However, it was their 1995 offering, an insanely catchy slice of techno-funk, 'Da Funk', that really set the Daft Punk bandwagon rolling, especially when the Chemical Brothers spotted its floor-filling potential during their DJ sets. One important factor in the duo's sound is that they are not dance purists; neither had been to a dance club until 1992 and their music is influenced as much by Roxy Music and the Ramones as it is by house and techno pioneers such as Laurent Garnier. There is also a strong streak of old-style disco running through their work; Bangalter's father wrote hits for Ottawan and the Gibson Brothers, and 'Da Funk' is based around a riff from a vintage R303 bass machine. The re-release of 'Da Funk' by Virgin

Records, and the subsequent *Homework* broke Daft Punk to an overground audience that had for too many years seen French pop as synonymous with Johnny Hallyday. Bangalter's alter ego, Stardust, was responsible for 'Music Sounds Better With You', one of the club anthems of 1998.

● ALBUMS: *Homework* (Virgin 1997)★★★★.

DAKEYNE, PAUL

A DJ since 1980, Windsor, Berkshire, England-based Dakeyne went on to become in-house producer to the DMC organization in 1986. Having remixed for Bass-O-matic, Erasure, James Brown and C + C Music Factory, Dakeyne became one of the resident DJs at U2's Kitchen club. He went on to establish the Zone club night in north London, and launched Zone Ranger, alongside Terri Heywood (vocals), Matt Eld (keyboards) and Suzanne (dancer). They made their debut with the double a-side '2 Be Reel'/'Kaleidoscope Girl', the latter remixed by 808 State's Eric Powell. '2 Be Reel' included a sample drawn from Echo And The Bunnymen's 'The Cutter'. However, for the stock release on Omen, Dakeyne was forced to recreate the keyboard section when he failed to gain clearance for the sample. It would not be the last time Dakeyne's career has suffered at the hands of the copyrighters. A side project, at first veiled in secrecy, saw Dakeyne introduce Tinman. Tinman became instantly famous for '18 Strings', inspired by Nirvana, which had a devastating effect when it was released as a white label at the end of 1993. His intention was to re-record the 'Smells Like Teen Spirit' riff, rather than sample it, like Abigail's 'Teen Spirit' on Klone Records, thereby simplifying sample clearance. The move backfired horribly. Though the 20 white labels mailed to DJs were hugely successful, changing hands for £150, Dakeyne was unable to get full permission on the track from Nirvana manager John Silva - which ironically would not have been required had it been merely 'sampled'. To make matters more complicated, after Kurt Cobain, Nirvana's singer, died, the track, though still hugely popular, was held in limbo and was ineligible for release on London. It finally emerged on 14 August 1994, by which time the Abigail version had already charted.

DALE, COLIN

Dale is the techno guru of London's Kiss FM radio station, where he took up a post in 1986 after abandoning his day job at a bank. He played a selection of music drawn from house, funk and garage, until visiting Detroit DJs Derrick May, Blake Baxter and Juan Atkins turned him on to techno. His first move into recording came in 1994 when he put together the Outer Limits compilation on Kickin' Records, featuring Luke Slater, Carl Craig and Peter Namlook. He also started his own Abstract Dance imprint (named after his show), with the intention of becoming 'the UK's Strictly Rhythm', a statement that was rapidly becoming a cliché among new label entrepreneurs. He also collaborated with Dave Angel on recording projects, and runs the Deep Space club with Colin Faver, and Knowledge with Jane Howard.

DANE, DANA

A graduate of New York's High School Of Music And Art, notable for being the first hip-hop star to offer his name to a fashion range or shop, which most major artists subsequently imitated, Dana Dane's reputation was also built on a solid musical platform (generally provided by DJ Clark Kent) of hard East Coast rhythms and smooth production. His humorous quasi-British accent customised unusual, pop-orientated songs like 'Cinderella', which became a huge crossover success. He has continued to release albums into the 90s, but has struggled to maintain the same level of success he achieved in the late 80s.

● ALBUMS: *Dana Dane With Fame* (Profile 1987)★★★, *Dana Dane 4 Ever* (Profile 1990)★★★, *Rollin' With Dane* (Maverick 1995)★★★.

DARKMAN

b. Brian Mitchell, *c.*1970. Rapper of West Indian heritage who grew up in Finsbury Park and Shepherds Bush, London, but also spent three years in the Caribbean. The reggae tradition in west London was very strong at the time and it was with the sound systems that he first learnt his craft as an entertainer, setting up his own system, Platinum. There he would alternate between Jamaican patois 'chatting' and a more conventional rap style, also learning production and helping out local groups Outlaw Posse and Cash Crew. He set up his own label, Powercut, in 1987. One of its earliest releases, One Love Sound featuring Joe 90's 'This Is How It Should Be Done', was widely appraised as the first to combine reggae and hip-hop. In its wake Powercut was signed to Warner Brothers Records' subsidiary

Slam Jam, via dance producer Dancin' Danny D (D-Mob). The deal never worked, with only one song from sixty demos submitted, the Powercut Crew's 'Firin'', seeing the light of day. It left Mitchell embittered, an anger expressed in his first release as Darkman, 'Whats Not Yours', included on the *Jus The Way* compilation. This largely featured acts housed on Darkman's new Vinyl Lab record label. Through this Beechwood collection Steve Jarvier, Darkman's partner in his north London record shop, was headhunted by Polydor Records. He was placed in charge of that label's ailing Wild Card subsidiary, to which he brought Darkman. His breakthrough disc, 'Yabba Dabba Doo', was another track to be inspired by anger, this time his impotent rage at watching a documentary on the killing of Stephen Lawrence. With its *Flintstone* rallying call (Mitchell is a big cartoon fan) it brought him overground approval, and sponsorship deals with Magnum Hi-Tech clothing and Vicious Circle. All this while he was still pursuing his performance arts and animation courses. The follow-up single, 'She Used To Call Me', maintained his commitment to the rap/reggae interface: 'Everyone should just dig into themself and then it would just come. A lotta people don't look back, they forget where they come from, just live for today...' Despite his protestations to the effect that UK hip-hop needs its own identity, there was some criticism of his gun-fixation as being irrelevant to indigenous audiences, but this was a minor carp.

● ALBUMS: *Worldwide* (Wild Card 1995)★★★.

DAS-EFX

Drayz (b. Andre Weston, 9 September 1970, New Jersey, USA) and Skoob (b. Willie Hines, 27 November 1970, Brooklyn, New York, USA; Skoob is 'books' spelled backwards) are two easy-natured rappers whose success story is of the genuine rags to riches variety. As college friends who had met during English classes, they entered a rap contest at a small Richmond, Virginia nightclub. Luckily for them Erick Sermon and Parrish Smith of EPMD were in attendance, and, despite not winning, they walked off with an instant record contract. The judgement shown by EPMD proved impeccable when Das-EFX's debut release, Dead Serious, charted strongly. Soon they were touring together, despite the fact that neither Drayz nor Skoob were old enough to legally enter the premises on some of the dates. As rap aficionados began to look once more to the old school and its freestyle vocals, Das-EFX were the perfect modern proponents, with their jagged, cutting rhymes and sweet wordplay. They developed a wonderful habit of making words up if they could not find something appropriate in the dictionary to shore up their rhymes: 'We're not too worried about really putting heavy messages in our records - we just try and make sure all the lyrics are super dope'. It was a style that was to be, in typical hip-hop fashion, quickly adopted and mimicked by a hundred other artists, and by the time of their follow-up some of its impact had been lost. Their debut self-production, 'Freak It', followed in 1993, and was the first release to see them drop their familiar tongue-flipping style, which detractors accused them of copying from UK rappers like the Demon Boyz. The advent of west coast gangsta funk saw the duo suffering a blow to their credibility, allied to criticisms that their style possessed only novelty value. Toughening up their stance, they silenced some of these detractors with 1998's streetwise *Generation EFX*.

● ALBUMS: *Dead Serious* (East West 1992)★★★, *Straight Up Sewaside* (East West 1993)★★★, *Hold It Down* (East West 1995)★★, *Generation EFX* (Elektra/Asylum 1998)★★★.

DAVEY D

b. David Reeves, Queens, New York, USA. Formerly titled Davey DMX, because of his use of the Oberheim DMX machine, Reeves started in a group, Rhythm And Creation, when he was just 16. He subsequently picked up on the DJ's art, importing the new 'scratch' style from the Bronx and becoming the first Queens DJ to incorporate the cut and mix template. He honed his technique playing neighbourhood parties, generally because he was too young to gain entrance to proper clubs. He formed a team called Solar Sound, but this broke up when he was given the opportunity to work with Kurtis Blow, an association which would last several years. At the same time he played guitar in Orange Crush, alongside Larry Smith and Trevor Gale, providing production for Run DMC. He has also recorded solo, debuting with 'One For The Table (Fresh)' on Tuff City, before moving over to Def Jam.

● ALBUMS: *Davy's Ride* (Def Jam 1987)★★★.

DAVIS, ROY, JNR.

Old school Chicago DJ and producer, who grew up with disco, purchasing his own turntables at the age of 15, before he started hanging around local celebrity DJ Pierre. He eventually progressed to a position as part of Pierre's Phuture production team, alongside first lieutenant Spanky, who also provided vocals, and Felix Da Housecat. His first solo recording was 'Twenty Below' for Jack Traxx, but it was again credited to the better-known Pierre. Unimpressed but undaunted, he continued to record under various guises, including an update of Phuture's 'Rise From Your Grave' (at Pierre's suggestion), before switching to New York and Strictly Rhythm, where he recorded the floor-filler 'Mental Behaviour'. A liaison with the UK's Ministry Of Sound saw the 1994 release of 'Who Dares Believe In Me' (credited to the Believers), which at last looked like bringing him out of the shadows of his mentor. He released a ten-track album on the Power label in 1995.
● ALBUMS: *Secret Mission* (Power 1995)★★★.

DC TALK

This inter-racial trio have cultivated a large and diverse audience in the USA through their sophisticated and adept blend of pop, soul and hip-hop. Primarily orientated towards the gospel/Christian market, they have done much to redress the balance of profanity and outrage expressed by the gangsta rappers. The group originally comprised Michael Tait and Toby McKeehan, who formed the band while at college in Washington, DC, in 1989. They were soon joined by Kevin Smith from Grand Rapids, Michigan. The name was alternatively stated to express either DC referring to the area of the group's origin or 'Decent Christian' talk. Using street poetry as their central mode of communication, they made their debut in 1991 for Heartwarming Records with *Nu Thang*, a title that accurately reflected the Christian pop/hip-hop style of its contents. More declamatory was the follow-up, *Free At Last*, which included cover versions of 'Jesus Is Just Alright' and 'Lean On Me', alongside the trio's original compositions. It was still a fixture on Billboard's Contemporary Christian chart at the end of 1995, having sold over a million copies. In the three years before the group entered the studio again each member concentrated on solo activities - Smith writing a poetry book, McKeehan launching Gotee Records

and Tait concentrating on songwriting. Released in December 1995, *Jesus Freak* took the band's Christian concerns into alternative pop/rock territory. Most impressive was the title track, an unashamed declaration of personal commitment set against dense guitar riffs. It saw them cited in *Billboard* as 'Christian music's most innovative and accomplished group'. Though the music was now as secular as it had ever been, the group's gospel background was still much in evidence. As McKeehan expressed, 'dc Talk has always been a pop group expressing our faith and we always will be, but we've followed our collective artistic pull a lot more on this project.' For example, the promotional single released from the album was targeted at MTV with a video produced by Nine Inch Nails collaborator Simon Maxwell. With sales of 85,000 copies in its first week of release, it became the biggest first-week seller in Christian music history.
● ALBUMS: *Nu Thang* (Heartwarming 1991)★★★, *Free At Last* (Forefront 1992)★★★, *Jesus Freak* (Forefront 1995)★★★.

DE LA SOUL

Formed in Long Island, New York, De La Soul consisted of Posdnous (b. Kelvin Mercer, 17 August 1969, Bronx, New York, USA), Trugoy the Dove (b. David Jude Joliceur, 21 September 1968, Brooklyn, New York, USA), and Pasemaster Mace (b. Vincent Lamont Mason Jnr, 24 March 1970, Brooklyn, New York, USA) were contemporaries of Queen Latifah, Monie Love and A Tribe Called Quest. With the aforementioned groups they formed the Native Tongues Posse, who were at the forefront of the black renaissance of the early 90s. Less harsh than many of their fellow rappers, De La Soul's pleasantly lilting rhythms helped them chart their debut LP - one of the first such acts to cross into the album market. Produced by Stetsasonic's Prince Paul, it revealed an altogether delightful array of funky rhythms and comic touches, presenting an influential alternative to the macho aggression of gangsta rap. As well as hit singles like 'Me Myself And I', and 'The Magic Number', they also charted in conjunction with Queen Latifah on 'Mama Gave Birth To The Soul Children' and guested on the Jungle Brothers' 'Doing Our Own Dang'. Some of De La Soul's more esoteric samples ranged from Curiosity Killed The Cat to Steely Dan, though their mellow approach belied difficult subject matter. *De La Soul Is Dead*, however, saw them return to tougher rhythms and a less whimsical melodic approach. Evidently they had grown tired of the 'hippies of hip-hop' tag dreamt up by their press officer. With over 100 artists sampled, they sidestepped injunctions by gaining clearance from all concerned artists, having previously been sued by the Turtles for sampling 'You Showed Me' on the 3 Feet High And Rising track 'Transmitting Live From Mars'. The painstaking procedure delayed the album for over a year. When it did emerge it was roundly denounced by critics, who were not taken by De La Soul's drastic gear change. However, infectious songs like 'Ring Ring Ring (Ha Ha Hey)' kept their profile high in the singles chart. *Buhloone Mindstate* saw them move back towards the stylings of their debut, and received better press, although by now the trio's fortunes had waned and the album quickly dropped off the charts. A similar fate befell 1996's *Stakes Is High*, which, despite returning to the tougher stylings of *De La Soul Is Dead*, struggled against the commercial ascendancy of gangsta rap.

● ALBUMS: *3 Feet High And Rising* (Tommy Boy 1989)★★★★, *De La Soul Is Dead* (Tommy Boy 1991)★★★, *Buhloone Mindstate* (Tommy Boy 1993)★★★, *Stakes Is High* (Tommy Boy 1996)★★★.

● VIDEOS: *3 Feet High And Rising* (Big Life 1989).

DEAD DEAD GOOD

Based in Whitton Walk Cheshire, England (not to be confused with Yorkshire label Dead Good), and founded by owner and managing director Steve Harrison. Dead Dead Good was the home of 1991's biggest dance single, Oceanic's 'Insanity'. It was a record that cost less than £1,000 to make yet netted some 365,000 sales. Their other acts included Bowa, Joy Salinas, Digital Orgasm ('Moog Eruption'), N Trance, Rig and That Uncertain Feeling. They enjoyed a further crossover hit with Italian-based, Los Angeles-born singer Katherine E's 'I'm Alright', and continued to release northern rave with tunes such as Rhythm Device's 'Pink Champagne'. However, they returned to total independence in 1992 after Warner Brothers Records pulled out when the label failed to replicate its 1991 success.

DEATH IN VEGAS

Formerly called Dead Elvis, Death In Vegas occupy similar ground to Andy Weatherall's Sabres Of Paradise, in that their aggressive, rock-edged dancefloor sound owes a huge debt to the punk ethos of 1977. Led by DJ Richard Fearless and producer Steve Hellier, the group announced itself with the release of a series of mesmerizing, bombastic singles, 'Opium Shuffle', 'Dirt', 'Rocco', 'GBH' and 'Rekkit'. All of these were included on their debut album, *Dead Elvis*, which was celebrated within both the mainstream and dance music communities for its intelligence, musical freshness and daring.

● ALBUMS: *Dead Elvis* (Concrete 1997)★★★★.

DEATH OF VINYL

Based in Toronto, Canada, this record label is run by Jerry Belanger, who describes himself as 'more of a scientist than a businessman'. Death Of Vinyl specializes in trance, hard house, acid, and various other sonic anomalies, and began in 1990. Three years later they picked up a distribution deal in the UK with the aid of Ninja Tune Records (Matt Black and Jonathon Moore of Coldcut). The back catalogue includes over a dozen collections of ambient, industrial, techno and mystic music. Among the artist titles on offer are 'Chaosphere' by Automata and DIN's 'Watersports'. Other groups include Digital Poodle, Infor/Mental and the Tape Beetles (who have appeared on material from the Orb and Positiva). The label also distributes albums from countries as far apart as Brazil and Croatia as part of an international networking exercise in weirdness.

DEATH ROW RECORDS

For a short time in the mid-90s Death Row was rap's most successful record company. The label was formed in 1991 by Dr. Dre of NWA after he complained bitterly about restraint of trade and monies owed by his previous employers, for whom he produced several million-sellers. Not content with cursing Ruthless General Manager Jerry Heller, and being sued by Eazy-E, he finally managed to find a deal with Jimmy Iovine at Interscope. Iovine agreed to finance Dre's own label, Death Row. Former bodyguard and Vanilla Ice publicist Marion 'Suge' Knight, who had warned Dre about his NWA contract, was the new label's co-founder. Unfortunately, Knight revealed a similar propensity for trouble that had already marred Dre's career. He was charged with assault with a deadly weapon in late 1993, and allegedly attacked two rappers, Lynwood and George Stanley, with a gun in July 1992, at Dr Dre's recording studio. The attack was witnessed by both Dre and Snoop Doggy Dogg, and concerned the use of an office telephone. The money Knight invested in Death Row was drawn from the publishing rights he partly owned for Vanilla Ice's hit album - a huge irony in the wake of the war of words between Vanilla and the west coast gangsta rappers a few years previously. Several months later Dr Dre's The Chronic justified his decision to back the rapper by becoming a huge crossover success. The label also released the big-selling soundtrack to the basketball film *Above The Rim*, ensuring that Death Row's first three albums all went multi-platinum. However, it was Snoop Doggy Dogg's phenomenally successful debut *Doggy Style* that really capped the label's multi-million status. Dogg had first come to prominence on Dre's *The Chronic*, but was already embroiled in a murder case that put his career on hold for a further two years. Other artists signed to the label include Dat Nigga Daz, Kurrupt, Lady Of Rage, Jewell and, infamously, hip-hop's brightest new star Tupac Shakur. A series of incidents then escalated the much-hyped east coast/west coast feud between Death Row and Sean 'Puffy' Combs' Bad Boy label, indirectly leading to the gangland-related murders of Shakur (September 1996) and Notorious B.I.G. (March 1997).

By 1997 the increasingly troubled label had received a series of body blows from which it seemed unlikely to recover. Dr. Dre left acrimoniously to form his own Aftermath label, Snoop Doggy Dogg filed a $10 million lawsuit against Death Row for alleged negligence and intentional misconduct, and Knight was sentenced to nine years' imprisonment for parole violations. The label was also the subject of a federal investigation and was facing numerous lawsuits. Time Warner relinquished their involvement with Death Row's distributor Interscope, and MCA Entertainment's $200 million share deal was swiftly rescinded following Knight's incarceration.

● COMPILATIONS: various artists *Above The Rim* (Death Row 1994)★★★, various artists *Greatest Hits* (Death Row 1997)★★★★.

DeConstruction Records

During the 90s DeConstruction was responsible for bringing dance music into the mainstream. It was co-founded in 1987 by Keith Blackhurst and Mike Pickering, who were later joined by Pete Hadfield, in order to release good house that was being overlooked by the major labels. They opened their account with Hot!House's 'Don't Come To Stay' in 1987 and achieved success with their three other records that year, T-COY's (Pickering and Richie Close) 'Carino', 'Nightrain' and 'Da Me Mas'/'I Like To Listen', which claimed to be one of the first British house tracks. Towards the end of 1987, they also released the country's first house compilation, *North*, although it mainly contained material by Pickering. While singles by Zuzan ('Girls Can Jack Too'), T-COY ('Nightclubbin'') and Hot!House in 1988 covered the same kind of territory, Black Box's 'Ride On Time' (1989), licensed from the Italian label Discomagic, introduced what became known as the Italian house sound, notable for its 'uplifting' piano lines, and was a UK number 1 for six weeks. At the same time, DeConstruction continued to foster such UK artists as Gina Foster, Annette and Dynasty Of Two. More success followed in 1990 with Guru Josh's 'Infinity' (supposedly the definitive rave track) and in 1991 with the compilations *Italia* and *Decoded And Danced Up*. Over the next few years they released material by Felix (notably 'Don't You Want Me'), Hyper Go-Go ('High'), N-Joi, M People, K Klass, the Grid, Kylie Minogue and the DJs Sasha, Justin Robertson (as Lionrock) and Danny Rampling (Millionaire Hippies). In 1995 DeConstruction signed a deal to become part of the BMG company and also formed an alliance with the commercial club Cream to produce a number of compilations, including *Cream Live* (1995), *Cream Anthems* (1995) and *Cream Live Vol. 2* (1996). Since then they have signed Robert Miles, Republica, Dave Clarke and Beth Orton, among others, in an attempt to broaden their range. Although DeConstruction insist their policy is concerned with originality and quality, and hope 'to stay at the cutting edge of youth culture', during the 90s they managed to produce some of the most unchallenging, middle-of-the-road dance music around, and have 'successfully' brought the sound of dance music into the mainstream.

Deee-Lite

Deee-Lite are a multiracial dance/pop trio who shot into the UK (number 2) and US (number 4) charts in August 1990 with the groundbreaking 'Groove Is In The Heart', blending 70s disco with house beats in an outrageously funky mix. The group was formed by Lady Miss Keir (b. Keir Kirby, Youngstown, Ohio, USA; vocals) and Super DJ Dmitry Brill (b. Kiev, Russia, his parents having defected from the East) after they met in a New York park in 1982. The pair, who later married, then added Korean-raised computer expert Jungle DJ Towa Towa (b. Towa Tei, Tokyo, Japan), who saw them perform in a nightclub in 1987 after moving to New York to study graphic design. His presence helped to make them a truly cosmopolitan act (another early member, Booty, left the band prior to their major success). 'Groove Is In The Heart' featured additional guest artists Bootsy Collins and Q-Tip (A Tribe Called Quest), though the follow-up, 'Power Of Love', and subsequent efforts failed to replicate their debut's impact. *Infinity Within* saw a band toned down in sound as well as visual garb. It included tracks such as the half-minute 'Vote, Baby, Vote', which served as an antidote to the aesthetics of the 'Second Summer Of Love' to which 'Groove Is In The Heart' had proved so pivotal. By the advent of their third album Kirby and Brill had been joined by new member On-e, while Towa left to work on a far more enjoyable solo album. Kirby also earned herself a niche market in computer graphics, designing covers for Deee-Lite and others, as a parallel career.

● ALBUMS: *World Clique* (Elektra 1990)★★★★, *Infinity Within* (Elektra 1992)★★★, *Dew Drops In The Garden* (Elektra 1994)★★, *Sampladelic Relics And Dancefloor Oddities* (East West 1997)★★★. Solo: Towa Tei *Future Listening!* (Elektra 1995)★★★.

DEEP FOREST

This ambient techno/new age group are based in France. Their 'Sweet Lullaby' track was one of the most popular of its kind during 1993, with its rich, warm tones and ethnic instrumentation. It was based on the sampled voices of Pygmies drawn directly from the African rainforest. The duo in charge of proceedings were Eric Mouquet and film composer Michel Sanchez. Based in Paris and Lille, their collaboration was the result of Sanchez returning from Africa with boxes of records from all over that continent. However, most of the actual sounds used on the track were taken from record libraries. Remixes of 'Sweet Lullaby' were made by both Apollo 440 and Jam And Spoon (Deep Forest in turn remixed Apollo 440's 1994 single, 'Liquid Cool'). Deep Forest are now massively popular, and their album went platinum in Australia, they won a Grammy for *Boheme* in February 1996 as Best World Music Album. *Comparsa* continued previous themes, visiting new areas of the world including Mongolia, Taiwan, India and Hungary.

● ALBUMS: *Deep Forest* (Columbia 1993)★★★★, *Boheme* (Columbia 1995)★★★★, *Comparsa* (Columbia 1997)★★★.

DEEP FRIED

Born in England, but based in Stockholm, Sweden, rapper Deep Fried released his debut single, 'Chanel Girl', for the Swedish Mega label in February 1994. It was dedicated to the model in the perfume advert for Chanel No. 9. He had previously enjoyed a varied background, having flown to Barbados when he was 16 years old, where he took various jobs including working in a bar. It was there he first began to rap and write his own lyrics. He signed to Polydor Records in the UK on his return but the limited success of 'Chanel Girl' saw him dropped from their roster soon afterwards.

DEÉRE, DARRON

b. c.1971, Birmingham, West Midlands, England. This Birmingham rapper made an immediate impact with his debut single, 'Just Watch Me', which was produced by Cox and Steele of the Fine Young Cannibals. A smooth jazz/R&B-based track, it was inspired more by dancehall reggae than Public Enemy or NWA. The track also featured a vocal contribution from singer Wincey - previously heard on Monie Love's 'It's A Shame'. Deére had turned down a career in professional football and a place at the Royal Academy of Dramatic Art to pursue music, signing with music publishers MCA Records and record label Eternal (Warner Brothers Records). He used his advance to build his own studio, but so far has been unable to follow-up the promise of his debut single.

DEF FX

This Australian techno-rock outfit claim to have chosen their name simply by throwing a pile of CDs into the air and examining the resultant mess. When a Def Jam Records recording was spied on top of a sound-effects compilation, Def FX were born. The group, the first signing to MCA Records Australia after releasing an independent debut set, offer a techno/metal fusion that is the result of their equal interest in the studio and the live arenas. *Witchcraft*, their MCA debut released in June 1995, was titled after singer Fiona Horne's abiding interest in that phenomenon. She was reportedly in the middle of writing a book on the subject, but Def FX were criticized by church bodies for what some saw as their propagation of the black arts. In truth, Horne was more committed to the holistic medicine aspect of witchcraft - she had already completed a degree in nutrition and remedial massage. The album, which was co-produced by Robert Taylor, was recorded in his 48 Volt studios next to the Pacific Ocean.

● ALBUMS: *Magick* (MCA 1995)★★★.

DEF JAM RECORDS

Russell Simmons (b. 1958, Hollis, Queens, New York, USA) and Rick Rubin's (b. Frederick Rubin, Long Island, New York, USA) noted New York, USA street rap label, Def Jam Records brought the world the skewed genius of the Beastie Boys and the militancy of Public Enemy. The label made its debut with T. La Rock and Jazzy Jay's 'It's Yours', a record released in conjunction with Partytime/Streetwise Records. Managing director Simmons (brother of Run DMC's Joe Simmons) was described as 'The mogul of rap' by *The Wall Street Journal* as early as 1984, following his early managerial coups. A year later Def Jam had netted a landmark distribution deal with Columbia Records, the first results of which were the LL Cool J smash, 'I Can't Live Without My Radio'. Simmons also concurrently managed the affairs of Whodini, Kurtis Blow, Dr Jeckyll And Mr Hyde and Run DMC, co-producing the latter's first two albums alongside Larry Smith. Rubin's credits included the label debut by T La Rock and Jazzy J. Together they produced Run DMC's platinum set *Tougher Than Leather*, before Rubin's productions of LL Cool J and the Beastie Boys' enormously successful debut sets. The biggest signing, however, would be Public Enemy, though Simmons was at first unconvinced of their potential. The Rubin/Simmons partnership dissolved in acrimony in 1987. As Rubin recalled: 'Russell's and my visions were going in different directions. My taste was growing more extreme, toward more aggressive and loud music, and Russell would say, like, "You made a hit record with the Bangles, why are you wasting your time with this stuff like Public Enemy?"'. Simmons would go on to head several other business ventures, including Rush Management, the Phat Farm clothing line and HBO's Def Comedy Jam, continuing to manage the careers of R&B artists including Alyson Williams, Oran' Juice Jones, Tashan and the Black Flames. However, he lost the Beastie Boys in liti-

gation over unpaid royalties on their debut album. Rubin, meanwhile, set up Def American Records in 1988. There he continued to enjoy success with a variety of artists, including several thrash metal outfits such as Slayer, then the Black Crowes. He earned himself a series of rebukes in hip-hop circles when he released a record by the latter with lyrics that gloried in allusions to an Aryan race war. He maintained his links with rap, however, via similarly outrageous concerns such as the Geto Boys. On 27 August 1993 Rubin officially dropped the 'Def' from the Def American imprint, reasoning that now the word Def had been incorporated into the latest edition of a major US dictionary, it no longer had the street value it once enjoyed. He 'buried' it via an elaborate New Orleans style funeral, complete with a dixieland jazz band. Def Jam continued in its own right, though it left its original deal with Columbia and is presently distributed through PolyGram Records. In 1992 Simmons opened a west coast subsidiary, DJ West, to follow the action there, signing Boss and MC Sugs. However, despite its continued presence, Def Jam never regained its standing of the 80s, when it became the most significant rap label ever and a vital musical outlet.

● COMPILATIONS: *Def Jam, The First Ten Years Volumes 1-4* (Def Jam 1995)★★★★, *The Box Set 1985-1995* 4-CD box set (Def Jam 1995)★★★★.

DEF JEF

b. Jeffrey Forston. Californian rapper who made a big impression with his 1989 debut set, but has largely disappeared from view in the interim. Decidedly on the Afrocentric trip, Def Jef's minimalist hip-hop beats propelled his consciousness messages with excellent clarity. Following the commercial failure of his second set he moved into films and production, appearing in the films *Deep Cover* and *Def By Temptation* and working with Shaquille O'Neal and Boss.

● ALBUMS: *Just A Poet With Soul* (Delicious Vinyl 1989)★★★★, *Soul Food* (Delicious Vinyl 1990)★★★.

DEF WISH CAST

Proving hip-hop's international appeal, Def Wish Cast are a Sydney, Australia-based quartet who are thoroughly enmeshed in the culture of graffiti and breakdancing as well as rap music. Their trademark relentless hardcore beats are composed by DJ Vame, while their most distinctive rapper is Latino Die C, whose approach is closer to that of dancehall reggae vocalists such as Daddy Freddie than Ice-T or Ice Cube. The group made its debut in 1993 with *Knights Of The Underground Table* for Random Records, a hard-hitting record that earned coverage in Europe and USA hip-hop magazines as well as their Australian equivalents. Rapping in 'ocker' (Australian working-class) accents, though their initial releases were confined to small pressings, they regularly played to audiences of around 1,000. *Knights Of The Underground Table* was billed as 'Australia's first hardcore hip-hop album', but songs such as 'Chris Missed The Point' and 'Perennial Cross Swords' would have benefited from more considered production.

● ALBUMS: *Knights Of The Underground Table* (Random 1993)★★.

DEFINITION OF SOUND

This London-based duo pair commercial raps with fully fledged pop songs, aided by soul cho-ruses and touches of psychedelia and reggae. Samples are scattered amongst rock hooks, with a lyrical focus that spans anti-drug messages and new age mysticism. The group comprise Kevwon (b. Kevin Anthony Clark, 1971) and The Don (b. Desmond Raymond Weekes, 1969). Kevwon is a former graffiti artist who guested on Krush's pio-neering UK house hit 'House Arrest' in 1987. He joined ex-body-popper The Don in 1988 to form Top Billin', a precursor to Definition Of Sound. Their two generic hip-hop singles ('Straight From The Soul' and 'Naturally') sampled the staple James Brown records then in vogue. As part of the Soul Underground tour of 1989 they became the last 'Western' group to play East Berlin before the wall came down. However, their career was scuppered when their label, Dance-Yard, col-lapsed. Under their new banner they have proved a much more decisive and durable act, with sam-ples now worked into arrangements with a greater degree of insight and ingenuity. Occasional outings with Coldcut, P.P. Arnold and X Posse have increased their profile, and they are also one of the few hip-hop/rap crews of their generation who tackle playing live with any flu-idity. Their debut album featured the singles 'Now Is Tomorrow' and 'Wear Your Love Like Heaven'. The former not only featured the soulful vocals of Elaine Vassell, but also boasted a notable b-side cut, 'Moira Jane's Cafe'. Whereas most rap/dance acts have found a remix or edit to be sufficient for the flip, the song, with its coded

drug references and use of Them's 'Gloria' riff, is among their finest moments. In the wake of the subsequent failure of 'Dream Girl', it was released as an a-side.

● ALBUMS: *Love And Life; A Journey With The Chameleons* (Circa 1991)★★★, *The Lick* (Circa 1992)★★★, *Experience* (Fontana 1996)★★★.

DEGREES OF MOTION

New York band (Kit West, Balle Legend, Mariposa) that enjoyed both underground cult status and overground success with singles such as the club classic 'Do You Want It Right Now' (number 31), featuring the vocals of Biti in 1992. It had origi-nally been released on the Esquire imprint in the USA, before transferring to ffrr. The song itself had first appeared on Taylor Dayne's *Tell It To My Heart* album in 1988. It was produced by Richie Jones with keyboards from Eric Kupper, and topped the *Record Mirror* Club Chart for no less than four weeks. Other hits included 'Shine On' (number 43, remixed by Farley & Heller, again originally on Esquire) and 'Soul Freedom - Free Your Soul' (number 64), on the ffrr imprint, while Jones remixed Sheer Bronze's 'I'm Walkin''.

● ALBUMS: *Degrees Of Motion* (Esquire 1992)★★★.

DEL THA FUNKY HOMOSAPIEN

Formerly a part of his cousin, Ice Cube's backing band, Da Lench Mob, Del (b. Teren Delvon Jones, 12 August 1972, Oakland, California, USA) earned his first, glowing reviews for his debut solo set in 1992. Far from the hardcore streak of his more celebrated relation (though there are definite sim-ilarities in musical inclination), Del offered a more detached viewpoint, laced with humour. Like many of his West Coast rap colleagues, there was a scarcely disguised debt to the rhythms of P-Funk and George Clinton in his work, acknowl-edged in its title. However, this approach was abandoned for the follow-up, a much more dour, self-consciously worthy affair (this time without Cube on production) that completely lost the magic of his debut, and placed him at a definite crossroads in his career. However, if Del has fal-tered, then the achievements of his Hieroglyphics crew (Casual, Souls Of Mischief) have gone some way to compensating.

● ALBUMS: *I Wish My Brother George Was Here* (Elektra 1992)★★★★, *No Need For Alarm* (Elektra 1993)★★★.

DELICIOUS VINYL

This highly prominent US label was co-founded by Mick Ross and Matt Dike in 1987, both DJs and promoters who were bored and frustrated by the dearth of good hip-hop records. Despite Delicious Vinyl being hailed by the media as the harbinger of the 'new West Coast sound', each partner originally hailed from New York. With Eric B and Rakim's laidback sampling/breakbeat technique in vogue, they set about finding artists who could provide them with similar, great cuts for their club nights. The label's offices were established next to a Thai restaurant in Melrose Avenue, Los Angeles. The first major artist they hooked up with was Young MC, who released the label's debut record ('Know How'). His career took off almost immediately, as did that of Tone Loc, whose hilarious narratives of sexual gratification made a nice bookend to Young MC's adolescent tales (even though Young MC was the writer behind both). *Wild Thing*, in particular, set up the label for the foreseeable future, going triple platinum. From there the ride was an easier, though still eventful one. The label's major success of the 90s has been the Pharcyde and Master Ace, though they also benefited from the US success of Brit-musicians Brand New Heavies. In 1994 the label signed a distribution deal with East West to make their product more readily available worldwide, marking the association with the release of a compilation album, *Natural Selections*. This introduced several of their new signings, including the Wascals, Born Jamericans (a dancehall/rap cross) and Angel. The latter was the first to sign to their new subsidiary, Brass Records. Ross is stoical about the label's evolution and success, suggesting its secret lies in the fact that 'all of the artists on the label that are creating music have good taste'. Dike is also known for his work with the Dust Brothers (alongside radio DJ's John Simpson and John King) - having produced/remixed for the Beastie Boys and Mellow Man Ace in addition to the aforementioned Young MC and Tone Loc.

● COMPILATIONS: *Natural Selections* (Delicious Vinyl 1994)★★★.

DELORME

This UK group comprises Chris Day, who is also a DJ at Club For Life, Martin Tyrell and Jason Hayward. They first recorded for the MFF label with 'Guitar Dance' and 'Physical Energy', before they broke through in 1993 with 'Beatniks'. The latter saw them signed to north London's Zoom enclave, although it was also licensed to European operation ZYX. Buoyed by their success, Delorme were invited to pick up remixing duties, initially on Lost Tribe's 'Gimme A Smile'. They also toured the USA alongside Mindwarp's Jon Debo, and recorded the *Spanish Fly* EP, which saw the introduction of vocalist Hayley Kay.

DEMON BOYZ

UK rap duo the Demon Boyz comprise Mike J. and Darren (nicknamed Demon due to his 'Spock-like ears'). An English underground phenomenon, the Demon Boyz rap owed a stylistic debt to reggae, notably on tracks like 'Sweet Jamaica'. This was housed on the belated follow-up to their 1989 debut album, which saw them switching to the Rebel MC's Tribal Bass label. This completed the circle for the duo, who had made their debut performing on the mic at the Rebel's Broadwater Farm sound system parties. They showed they were in touch with the club scene too by incorporating raps like the breakbeat-feast, 'Dett', and genre-defining single, 'Jungle-Ist'. Many have acknowledged the manner in which US artists such as Das-EFX have incorporated their 'wiggedy diggedy' delivery.

● ALBUMS: *Recognition* (Music Of Life 1989)★★★, *Original Guidance - The 2nd Chapter* (Tribal Bass 1993)★★★.

DENNIS, CATHY

b. 1969, Norwich, Norfolk, England. Dennis displayed early vocal poise and by the age of 13 she was singing in her father's Alan Dennis Band at Butlin's holiday resorts. Cathy started her career proper in the mid-80s singing in a covers band where she was spotted by Dancin' Danny D's manager, Simon Fuller, at the time looking for a female singer to work with the producer and remixer. She subsequently signed to Polydor and started writing her own songs and recording solo. She put this parallel career on hold to work with Danny D's D-Mob, between them achieving a chart hit with 'C'Mon Get My Love'. While other D-Mob tracks employed a variety of backing vocalists, Dennis was also featured on 'That's The Way Of The World'. By the end of 1989 she was able to resume her solo career with 'Just Another Dream' and her debut album. Her first significant success came in the USA, with three Top 10 hits including 'Touch Me (All Night Long)', after

which recognition in her native country followed. She was, in fact, the most successful UK singles artist in the US charts in 1991. *Into The Skyline* saw her team with Madonna's favoured producer, Shep Pettibone. She also reunited with Danny D for the 1993 D-Mob single, 'Why'. In 1995 she released the Japan-only single, 'Love's A Cradle', providing English lyrics to Japanese composer Ryo Aska's music (the track was later released on *One Voice - The Songs Of Chage And Aska*). The following year she released her new album, *Am I The Kinda Girl?*
● ALBUMS: *Move To This* (Polydor 1991)★★★, *Into The Skyline* (Polydor 1992)★★★, *Am I The Kinda Girl?* (Polydor 1996)★★★.

DEPTH CHARGE

Depth Charge is the name under which the former DJ Jonathon Saul Kane released his bizarre house singles, whose big beat rhythms prefigured the music of Chemical Brothers, Propellerheads and Bentley Rhythm Ace. The most memorable of these was undoubtedly 'Goal', which sampled an excitable Brazilian football commentator holding the 'Goooooaaaall' crow throughout its recording. Released at the height of World Cup '90 fever, it caught the imagination of the terraces after they had retired to the clubs of a Saturday evening. Other such releases included 'Depth Charge (Han Do Jin)' (sampling U-Boats from hoary old black-and-white films), 'Bounty Killers' (which did the same with cowboy films) and 'Dead By Dawn (horror movies). All were released on the Vinyl Solution imprint. Kane also records under other pseudonyms, including Octagon Man and Alexander's Dark Band. A new Depth Charge EP, *Disko Airlines*, was released in 1998.
● ALBUMS: *Nine Deadly Venoms* (Vinyl Solution 1994)★★★★.

DETROIT'S MOST WANTED

The rap duo Detroit's Most Wanted arrived on the hardcore hip-hop scene in 1991 with a strong-selling debut album propelled by singles like 'City Of Boom'. The album was nominated for album of the year in the Soul Train awards. The follow-up brought further singles chart success with 'The Money Is Made' and 'Pop The Trunk'. The third album in the series was previewed by a tribute single, 'Keep Holding On', which was dedicated to Motsi's nephew, Ja-Vanti Abrams, whose life ended after four months. The group is built around rapper Motsi Ski (b. Reginald Adams, c.1970, Detroit, Michigan, USA), who is actually the grandson of soul legend Jackie Wilson, who brought out the young Motsi to perform with him on occasion.
● ALBUMS: *Money Is Made* (Bryant/Ichiban 1991)★★★, *Tricks Of The Trade, Vol. II* (Ichiban 1992)★★★, *Many Faces Of Death, Vol. III* (Bryant/Ichiban 1993)★★★, *Bow The Fuck Down* (Push Play 1994)★★, *Ghetto Drama* (Push Play 1996)★★.

DFC

US rap group DFC comprising Al Breed, T-Trouble E, who backed MC Breed on his 1991 debut. DFC stood for the Dope Flint Connection. After their 1991 US tour they took time out to perfect a formula which was finally unveiled with the Top 5 success of their debut album, *Things In Tha Hood*. Reduced to a duo, the group subsequently advised interested parties that DFC now conferred the status 'Da Funk Clan'. Four of the songs on the debut were recorded in Los Angeles with Warren G., while the other tracks were culled from sessions in Atlanta, the remainder drawn from work with DJ Slip and MC Eiht (of Compton's Most Wanted), again in LA. MC Breed, Al's cousin, also returned to help out with advice and suggestions. 'Caps Get Peeled', a duet with MC Eiht, would give the group a major hit single.
● ALBUMS: *Things In Tha Hood* (Assault/Big Beat 1994)★★★, *The Whole World's Rotten* (Penalty 1997)★★★.

DIAMOND D

Not the white artist of the same name, who arrived on the scene much later but had copyrighted the name, Diamond D. is one of rap music's top flight production experts from the USA, who, although he really broke through in the 90s, started out as DJ back in 1979, going on to join Jazzy Jay's team in the early 80s. He followed that with engagements for Master Rob (who also appeared in the *Wild Style* film as one of the Romantic Fantastic Five) as a component of the Ultimate Force. They released one single on Strong City Records, 'I'm Not Playing', but it was not considered lyrically tough enough by prevailing hip-hop standards. Diamond D pressed on, teaching himself rhyming to add to his deck skills, making a debut appearance on A Tribe Called Quest's 'Show Business'. Together with his Psychotic Neurotics posse Diamond D made his 'solo' debut with 'Best Kept Secret' on Chemistry/Mercury Records. It was an attempt to reinstate the principle of the old school Bronx pioneers in lyrical showdowns and couplets. The album that followed saw co-production assistance from DJ Mark The 45 King and Large Professor (Main Source), and remains a classic of its kind. However, it is as a producer that Diamond D remains best known, and his client list is growing. These include Showbiz & AG (often working in tandem with the former), Lord Finesse, Apache, the Geto Girlz, Chill Rob G, Pharcyde, Run DMC, KRS-1, Fugees and Brand Nubian. His most acclaimed work came with A Tribe Called Quest's *The Low End Theory* (1991) and the Fugees' massive-selling *The Score* (1996). Several top rappers appeared on his second album, including Busta Rhymes and Pete Rock, another highly creative and enjoyable collection.

● ALBUMS: *Stunts, Blunts & Hip Hop* (Chemistry/Mercury 1992)★★★★, *Hatred, Passsion And Infidelity* (Mercury 1997)★★★.

DIGABLE PLANETS

US psychedelic jazz rappers who, along with Gang Starr, were hailed as the instigators of the genre. Contextually they are more accurately the legacy of De La Soul/PM Dawn's Daisy-age rap, as might be detected from their colourful pseudonyms; Doodle Bug (b. Craig Irving, Philadelphia, Pennsylvania, USA), Butterfly (b. Ishmael Butler, Brooklyn, New York, USA) and Ladybug (b. Mary Ann Vierra, Silver Springs, Maryland, USA). This conveyed their kooky, spaced-out philosophy, their names derived from an admiration for the community structures of ants and insects. Musically it was a delicious combination of wordplay and dreamy jazz backing utilising samples from artists as diverse as Art Blakey and Curtis Mayfield. The group admitted that 'We use a lot of the colloquialisms that came out of jazz'. However, there was an underlying political bent, as expressed on debut album cuts like 'La Femme Fetal', an attack on the Pro-Life lobby who firebomb abortion clinics. The trio then toured with live musicians in an attempt to recreate the jazzy atmosphere of the album. They returned to the recording studio for *Blowout Comb*, a strong follow-up that failed to match the success of *Reachin'*. Lacking a single track as catchy as the debut's hit single 'Rebirth Of Slick (Cool Like Dat)' partly explained the album's commercial failure.

● ALBUMS: *Reachin' (A New Refutation Of Time And Space)* (WEA 1993)★★★, *Blowout Comb* (Pendulum/EMI 1994)★★★★.

DIGI DUB

Digi Dub is a UK label, a studio, an occasional recording act and a Camberwell, south London squat collective, which provides its personnel. Spin-off bands include Mk3, RIP and LS Diesel & Launch Dat. Their manifesto is collected together on *South East Of The Thames*, a collection of tracks by those artists passing through the Digi Dub studios. An intriguing combination, they are a collective that combines the ideals of the Crass generation with the aesthetics of the club scene. In 1994 they also managed to pen a song about the joys of drinking Special Brew.

● COMPILATIONS: *South East Of The Thames* (Digi Dub 1993)★★★.

DIGITAL UNDERGROUND

Among rap's most faithful P-Funk advocates, Digital Underground, whose line-up perms up to seven members, were formed in the mid-80s in Oakland, California by Shock-G (b. Gregory E. Jacobs; keyboards/vocals) and Chopmaster J (samples/percussion). Other key members included DJ Fuze (b. David Elliot, 8 October 1970, Syracuse, New York, USA). Shock-G subsequently introduced his alter-ego, Eddie 'Humpty Hump' Humphrey, and Money B (b. Ron Brooks). According to Digital legends, back in 1987 Humphrey sustained severe burns in a freak kitchen accident. He was forced to continue his rapping career with the addition of a false nose. Instead of hiding the event surreptitiously, however, Humphrey chose a joke nose, leading to much merriment and a series of tribute records. Among these were 'the 'Humpty Dance' routine, wherein the protagonist extols his ability to still, despite such deformity, get his snout into the object of his desire's pants. Typically, there is a good-natured verve to the recording that militates against any possible offence. Their staple diet of P-Funk and Funkadelic samples is evident on most of their recordings, including a concept debut album. The subtext was the ruse of a mad scientist marketing a drug that caused the recipients to have wet dreams. Shock-G/Humpty Hump adopted the characters of two dealers, and despite the threadbare plot it actually managed to exceed its comic potential. Alongside the samples it also introduced live piano and musicians, which were also in evidence on the follow-up, *This Is An*

EP. The latter included two tracks from the dreadful *Nothing But Trouble* film in which Digital Underground appeared. However, *The Body Hat Syndrome,* its name alluding to prophylactics, paid simply too many compliments to the P-Funk coalition, ending up sounding highly derivative. 2Pac, formerly a full-time member, joined for a few verses on 'Wussup Wit The Luv', complaining about drug dealers selling to children, a rare outbreak of moral responsibility. There were three newcomers for *Body Hat*: DJ Jay Z, Clee and Saafir (aka the Saucy Nomad). The album also came with an invitation to vote in the Humpty Dance Awards, run by their fan club. In the grim world of hardcore rap Digital Underground offered a welcome release from corpses and curses. Money B and DJ Fuze also recorded two albums as Raw Fusion. Following their move from Tommy Boy the unit signed with a smaller label, Critique, and issued *Future Rhythm* after a three-year gap in 1996.

● ALBUMS: *Sex Packets* (Tommy Boy 1990)★★★, *Sons Of The P* (Tommy Boy 1991)★★★, *The Body-Hat Syndrome* (Tommy Boy 1993)★★, *Future Rhythm* (Critique 1996)★★★.
Solo: Saafir *Boxcar Sessions* (Qwest/Reprise 1994)★★.

DIGITALIS

One of the most exciting and original producers of psychedelic music in the mid- to late 90s, Seb Taylor began playing the guitar in a death metal band at the age of 15, inspired by such groups as Ministry, Nine Inch Nails and 808 State. He started recording electronic music around 1994 and the next year had his first release, 'Repeater', as Digitalis on Roost Records, which was followed by two releases as Shakta, 'Lepton Head Pt. 2' (Celtic Records) and 'Amber Mantra' (Psychic Deli). In 1996 he signed to Dragonfly Records as Shakta and released the single 'Cosmic Trigger'/'Spiritual Beings In Physical Bodies' to accompany his debut album, *Silicon Trip*, the following January. The album was well received on the trance scene and over the next year Taylor performed at parties in the UK and around the world. At the same time he continued to work as Digitalis and during 1997 released the single 'Rapid Eye'/'The Mind Gap' on 21-3 Productions, and contributed the tracks 'Double Helix' and 'Chaos By Design' (as CBD) to that label's *All Boundaries Are Illusion* compilation. In the same year he also produced the track '3rd State' for

Matsuri Productions' *Let It Rip* and continued to work with these two labels in 1998. For Matsuri he recorded the *Soma Junkies* EP and the track 'Teleprescence', which was released on *Forever Psychedelic*, while 21-3 included 'Not Human' and 'Waving Not Drowning' on their compilation *Elastic*. Taylor also records as Somaton for Phantasm Records and has released an album, *Future Memories*, and a single, 'Monogatari/Mutate And Survive'. He works in a slightly different area of the psychedelic techno sound under each pseudonym. *Silicon Trip* presents straightforward powerful, four-on-the-floor psychedelic trance characterized by excellent production, well-balanced arrangements and funky riffs. His work as Digitalis moves away from melodic-sounding, modal riffs to concentrate on abstract psychedelia and often rather metallic textures, combined with more varied rhythms that incorporate breakbeats and elements of drum 'n' bass. Taylor is distinguished from the majority of artists in the field of psychedelic music through his original choice of sounds, his arrangements and considerable production skills. He has also recorded material under the name Biotone, and has released material on Indica, Inspiral and Phantasm.

● ALBUMS: as Shakta *Silicon Trip* (Dragonfly 1997)★★★★, as Somaton *Future Memories* (Phantasm 1997), as Digitalis *The Third State* (Matsuri 1998)★★★★.

DIMITRI

Publicity-shy DJ (b. Amsterdam, Holland), who regularly hosts the Hi-Tech Soul Movement nights at the Roxy, and also plays the Richter club, both in his home-town. He began his DJ career on the radio in the early 80s, before graduating to clubs. Famed for his mix tapes and CDs, he has latterly hooked up with Carl Craig and Rhythim Is Rhythim (Derrick May) to set up a new record label. He is the part-owner of the Outland shop and label, and has founded two further labels, Spiritual and BeST. Some of this roster's better-known releases include Super Jazz's 'Hi-Tech Soul Anthem' and MDMA's 'Cerebral Asendence'. He has also worked with fellow-Amsterdam talent Eric Nouhan ('Tecnobility', etc.) and released his own material in conjunction with Jaimy ('Don't Be A Prisoner Of Your Own Style', which neatly encapsulates his own DJing principles). In 1994 he established the Outland imprint in the UK, commemorating the occasion with the release of a compilation, *The Best Of Outland And Spiritual*. He also licensed recordings such as Two Men Will Love You's 'Goodbye Thing' and remixed for Chanelle ('Work That Body').

● COMPILATIONS: Various Artists: *The Best Of Outland And Spiritual* (Outland 1994)★★★.

DIRT NATION

New York rap trio comprising JB (b. Brooklyn, New York, USA), KD (b. Jamaica, West Indies) and E Depp (b. New Jersey, USA). Specialising in smooth, easily palatable (at least musically) goods, Dirt Nation's debut 45, 'Khadijah', became a summer 1993 hit throughout urban America. Quoting Curtis Mayfield, Jimmy McGriff and Marvin Gaye, and alluding to the golden age of soul in its mellow rhythms too, 'Khadijah' was a tribute to the womenfolk often degraded as 'bitches' and 'ho's' in gangsta rhymes. The group met at school in Maryland, relocating to Manhattan in search of a record deal. There they recorded their debut single, plus a track with rapper Biggie Smalls (Mary J. Blige). Their debut album's title was lifted from the movie of the same name, while a collaboration with Guru of Gang Starr was also mooted.

● ALBUMS: *Three The Hard Way* (1994)★★★.

DISCO EVANGELISTS

The Disco Evangelists comprised Ashley Beadle (b. London, England), David Holmes (b. Belfast, Northern Ireland) and Lyndsay Edwards (b. London, England; ex-If?). Originally released on Beadle's Black Sunshine label before Positiva picked it up, their 'De Niro' hit referred to the eponymous actor's movie, *Once Upon A Time In America*. The follow-up, 'A New Dawn', also found a home on Positiva's release schedule. Beadle worked alongside the Stereo MCs' Nick and Rob as Axis ('Rollin' With Rai'), and as part of Workshy, Xpress 2, Black Science Orchestra and Marden Hill. In 1994 he formed Delta House Of Blues, which signed to Go! Discs. He has also undertaken remixes for Jodeci and East 17 ('Deep'). Holmes is one of the most interesting and prolific of England's DJ fraternity, working as part of Scubadevils (with ex-members of Dub Federation) and running the Sugarsweet/Exploding Plastic Inevitable club/label empire in Belfast.

DISCO FOUR

The Disco Four, who included in their number the son of Enjoy Records' president Bobby Robinson, were arguably most famous for their 'Country Rock Rap' cut for that label. Produced by early hip-hop innovator Pumpkin, it used cow horns and hoe-down instrumentation to arrive at a sound that inspired Malcolm McLaren's 'Buffalo Gals' novelty. The Disco Four, whose origins were in the Bronx sound system days (Troy B was in an early incarnation of the Fearless Four), didn't last much longer, though they did switch to Profile for a hit and miss mini-career.

DISCO MAGIC RECORDS

Italian label Disco Magic was the original home to Black Box's groundbreaking 'Ride On Time'. They also introduced artists such as rapper Tony Carrasco, who released a cover version of Adamski's 'NRG'. Disco Magic's popularity continued with Pierre Fieroldi's 'Moving Now', Hoomba Hoomba's 'Voice Of Africa' and Rhythm Orchestra's 'Such A Good Feeling', a revision of David Seaman and Steve Anderson's Brothers In Rhythm original, orchestrated by DJ Oliver. Marmalade contributed 'Mi Piace' in 1992.

DISPOSABLE HEROES OF HIPHOPRISY

A hugely innovative contemporary hip-hop band who comprised Rono Tse (percussion) and Michael Franti (vocals). Both residents of the Bay area of San Francisco, USA, the duo worked together for several years, most notably in *avant-garde* industrial jazz band the Beatnigs. Following their inception as the Disposable Heroes they won significant allies amongst press and peers; support slots to Billy Bragg, U2, Public Enemy, Arrested Development and Nirvana demonstrating the range of their appeal. Their sound recalled some of the experimental edge of their former incarnation, while Franti's raps were arguably the most articulate and challenging of his generation. Typically he broke down his subject matter beyond the black/white rhetoric of much urban rap, and was willing to place his own inadequacies as a person at the forefront of his manifesto. When he called himself a 'Jerk' in the intensely personal 'Music And Politics', Franti took rap into a whole new dimension. Examples of his skilled deployment of words litter the band's debut album; 'Imagination is sucked out of children by a cathode-ray nipple, Television is the only wet-nurse, that would create a cripple' (from 'Television The Drug Of The Nation', which also bemoans the amount of violence visited upon an average American child through his television set). 'Language Of Violence' took to task rap's penchant for homophobia, forging a link between that and a wider circle of prejudice. Franti was more effective still when dealing with subjects on a personal level; 'I was adopted by parents who loved me; they were the same colour as the kids who called me nigger on the way home from school' (from 'Socio-Genetic Experiment'). One unfortunate consequence of Franti's eloquence was that the Disposable Heroes became the token rap band that it was 'safe for white liberals to like'. Otherwise there was precious little to fault in them. In 1993 they recorded an album with *Naked Lunch* author, William Burroughs. However, as the year closed they informed the press that the Disposable Heroes were no longer a going concern, with both parties going on to solo careers. The first result of this was Franti's 1994 album *Home*, as Spearhead, with producer Joe 'The Butcher' Nicolo. There were also liaisons with the Disposables' live guitarist Charlie Hunter, and a projected dub album with Adrian Sherwood. Rono, meanwhile, has worked with Oakland rappers Mystic Journeymen.

● ALBUMS: *Hypocrisy Is The Greatest Luxury* (4th & Broadway 1992)★★★★, with William Burroughs *Spare Ass Annie & Other Tales* (4th & Broadway 1993)★★★.

DIY

Nottingham, England-based party collective, populated by numerous contributors, the best known of which are Harry, Damien, Digs and Woosh. 'Our main intention from the start was really to be able to do our own thing...rather than having to pander to club owners, record labels, managers or whoever'. Their releases include the *Duster* EP, and the acclaimed 'Shock Disco Invasion'. Their debut album numbered some 14 assorted DJs, remixers and musicians working in a spirit of collective adventure. The title of *Strictly 4 Groovers* also doubled as the name of their record company. In 1994 the group recorded a split single with Chumbawamba to protest at the Criminal Justice Bill, and launched a second imprint, Spacehopper, for hip-hop/funk projects.

● ALBUMS: *Strictly 4 Groovers* (Warp 1993)★★★.

DJ BIZNIZZ

b. Billy Ntimih. Alongside the Underdog DJ Biznizz is the UK's leading rap producer, with most of the important UK artists (Cookie Crew, London Posse, Caveman, Monie Love, MC Mell

'O' and Cash Crew) having sought his favours. He has also remixed for the Cookie Crew ('Love Will Bring Us Back Together') and House Of Pain ('Jump Around') and established his PD3 and Points Proven collectives. The floating personnel involved in these two rallying groups are fascinating in themselves. Byron the Greek is co-owner of the Hitt Recording Studio and had previously worked as a rock guitarist. Cutch is a session drummer, and Dego has worked with DJ Silk Worm of Digable Planets and is now part of the production team. Female vocalist Face has provided backing to Don-E and Gabrielle as well as rap artists Son Of Noise, MC Mell 'O' and London Posse. Fly was once in rap group Rap Conscious, while Niles Hailstones had previously worked with reggae artists like Misty In Roots, Mad Professor and Delroy Wilson. Ola The Soul Controller is an expatriate Canadian rapper. Together with DJ Biznizz this personnel has been responsible for a number of releases.

● ALBUMS: *Does Anybody Really Know What Time It Is?* (Syncopated Productions 1993)★★★.

DJ DAG

Frankfurt, Germany-based DJ/producer, with many classic dance music releases such as 'Sun Down' (released on Eye Q and credited to the Volunteer) to his name. One of the pre-eminent forces in the development of trance, he was originally based at the Dorian Gray club in Frankfurt before moving to Sven Vath's Omen club in 1993. Dag was behind the chart success of Dance 2 Trance, a collaboration with Jam El Mar (of Jam & Spoon) and vocalist Tony Clark, breaking the Top 40 with 'Power Of American Natives' and 'Take A Free Fall'. He worked with Jam El Mar on Peyote's 'Alcatraz' for R&S, and in 1994 was purportedly purchasing land in Dakota in order to give it back to the indigenous population.

DJ DUKE

An underground dance music DJ talent who exploded as a crossover proposition in the early 90s when 'Blow Your Whistle' became a chart fixture. Duke had served a long apprenticeship, however. He made his first record in 1990 on a white label, which sold out of its first 500 records shortly afterwards. Faced with rejection from every record company he approached, he set up his own label. This has eventually expanded to include four separate imprints - Power Music Records (vocal tracks), Power Music Trax (harder techno), Sex Mania (sexually inspired trance themes, such as Erotic Moments' 'Touch Me') and DJ Exclusive (for other artists) - housed under the collective Power Music umbrella. Group names exercised have included Inner Soul, Club People, The Music Choir, Tribal Liberation and The Pleasure Dome. As DJ Duke the follow-up to 'Blow Your Whistle' was 'Turn It Up', which again followed the route from club to chart.

DJ FLOWERS

One of the pioneering forces in the early 80s of the Brooklyn, New York, USA rap scene, DJ Flowers never progressed like peers such as Grandmaster Flash to recorded status. He was nevertheless an important presence in hip-hop's development as it grew from its base in warehouse club 'jams' and street-corner gatherings to an international pop medium. As legend has it, he would frequently perform live by hiring a friend to pedal a bicycle attached to his sound system, thereby acting as a generator, while he 'scratch mixed' old soul and R&B records on the record decks.

DJ FOOD

As part of Coldcut's DJing angle on creating music, Jonathan Moore and Matt Black released a series of albums entitled *Jazz Brakes*, beginning in 1990 when they formed Ninja Tune Records, under the name DJ Food. Containing mainly funk and hip-hop instrumentals, often cut up with samples of bizarre dialogue, it was partly intended as material for mixing, remixing and producing. Volumes 4 and 5 (1993, 1994) were co-written with the producer PC (Patrick Carpenter) and developed the abstract hip-hop sound by incorporating shades of Latin, dub, techno, ambient, jungle and non-western music. The two 12-inch records, *Refried Food*, in 1995, contained mixes by Autechre, Fila Brazilia and Ashley Beadle, among others, and were collected onto one album the following year. PC became more involved on *A Recipe For Disaster* (1995), and later took over the reins, still with the assistance of Coldcut. DJ Food present live sets during which PC works with Strictly Kev on four decks.

● ALBUMS: *Jazz Brakes Vols. 1 – 5* (Ninja Tune 1990–94)★★★, *A Recipe For Disaster* (Ninja Tune 1995)★★★, *Refried Food* (Ninja Tune 1996)★★★.

DJ GUSTO

b. 28 July 1971, Trenton, New Jersey, USA. After initially working as a care assistant for the elderly and disabled, Gusto secured his first DJing job at the Funhouse in Trenton in 1990, abandoning plans to become a rapper. By the mid-90s he had launched his career as a recording artist, with singles including 'Disco's Revenge' (Manifesto Records) and 'Move The Drum' (Bullet Records). His remixes include Shara Nelson's 'I Feel' for Chrysalis Records, and he also produced Roz White's 'Bad For Me'. In 1996 he began work on a full studio album for Manifesto, and played a number of European dates at venues including Amsterdam's Escape Club. His preferred medium is contemporary funk and soul, with his set list regularly including classics from Stevie Wonder and Diana Ross.

DJ HOLLYWOOD

Just like DJ Flowers and Kool Herc, Hollywood was one of the earliest DJ/MC rap artists, yet one whose legacy does not confer his true status because his performances predated rap recordings (the posthumous 'Um Tang Tum Tang' aside). His background was as a compere at the Apollo Theatre in Harlem, where he chatted over disco records between performers. Grandmaster Flash remembers him as 'one of the greatest solo rappers that ever there was', for his later performances at venues including Club 371.

DJ HURRICANE

b. USA. The Beastie Boys' long-standing musical collaborator, DJ Hurricane finally made his solo debut in 1995, but boasted a much longer history in hip-hop. Before joining the Beastie Boys in 1986, Hurricane had been part of the Solo Sounds - the first ever rap group in Hollis, Queens, New York (even predating Run DMC). While with the Beasties he was also a component of the entertaining Afros side-show. His debut solo album used more up-to-date moves, however, with the strong rhythmic influence being Cypress Hill (Sen Dog guested on one track, 'Feel The Blast'). Other guests included MC Breed ('What's Really Going On') and newcomer Tye Bud ('Comin' O-F-F'). The Beastie Boys themselves turned in a strong performance for the agenda-setting 'Four Fly Guys', while Beastie associate Mario Caldato Jr. provided production. DJ Hurricane returned in 1997 with the harder-hitting *Severe Damage*.

● ALBUMS: *The Hurra* (Grand Royal 1995)★★★, *Severe Damage* (Wiija 1997)★★★.

DJ INTERNATIONAL

Alongside Trax, DJ International was the pivotal label in documenting the rise of Chicago house music (priding itself on never releasing anything in a different musical category). The imprint was founded in the late 80s by DJ Rocky Jones, and picked up on DJ artists such as Mr Fingers ('Mystery Of Love', 'You're Mine') Tyree ('Tyree's Got A Brand New House' and, with Kool Rock Steady, 'Turn Up The Bass'), Joe Smooth ('Promised Land'), Sterling Void ('It's Alright'), Pete Black ('How Far I Go') and Fast Eddie ('Hip House', 'Get On Up', 'Let's Go', 'Yo Yo Get Funky'). The Chicago Music Pool, where promotional releases were distributed to DJs, was located on the ground floor of the label's premises, thereby ensuring that the label kept its ear to the ground for new talent. The backroom stalwarts included Frankie 'Hollywood' Rodriguez, who produced much of the label's output as well as his own solo projects (including the jokey Lincoln Boys). He also mixed for house radio show B96. Other prominent names were Julian Perez and Martin 'Boogieman' Luna, who recorded 'House Express'/'Pump It Up Homeboy', the latter forming the backbone of D-Mob's 'Come And Get My Love'. Like many of the label's releases, it became sample-fodder to the European masses.

DJ JAZZY JEFF AND THE FRESH PRINCE

The Fresh Prince (b. Will Smith, 25 September 1968, Philadelphia, Pennsylvania, USA) is now just as famous for his acting career, which started when he played the streetwise tough suffering culture shock when transplanted into the affluent Beverley Hills household of television series *The Fresh Prince of Bel Air*. However, this was initially very much a second career for Smith. Together with DJ Jazzy Jeff (b. Jeffrey Townes, 22 January 1965, Philadelphia, Pennsylvania, USA), this young duo had already cut a highly successful debut album in 1987, and charted with the hit single 'Girls Ain't Nothing But Trouble'. Musically the duo operated in familiar territory, working a variety of inoffensive, borrowed styles to good effect and in marked contrast to the threatening 'street style' of other rap artists.

Jazzy Jeff started DJing in the mid-70s when he was a mere 10 years old (though he is not to be confused with the similarly titled Jazzy Jeff who cut an album, also for Jive, in 1985). He was frequently referred to in those early days as the 'bathroom' DJ, because, hanging out with better-known elders, he would only be allowed to spin the decks when they took a toilet break. He met the Fresh Prince at a party, the two securing a recording deal after entering the 1986 New Music Seminar, where Jeff won the coveted Battle Of The Deejays. Embarking on a recording career, the obligatory James Brown lifts were placed next to steals from cartoon characters like Bugs Bunny, which gave some indication of their debut album's scope. In the late 80s they cemented their reputation with million-selling teen anthems like 'Girls Ain't Nothing But Trouble', which sampled the *I Dream Of Jeannie* theme, and was released three weeks before Smith graduated from high school. They became the first rap act to receive a Grammy Award for their second album's 'Parents Just Don't Understand', even though the ceremony was boycotted by most of the prominent hip-hop crews because it was not slated to be 'screened' as part of the television transmission. In its wake the duo launched the world's first pop star 900 number (the pay-phone equivalent of the UK's 0898 system). By January 1989 3 million calls had been logged. *He's The DJ, I'm The Rapper* contained more accessible pop fare, the sample of *Nightmare On Elm Street* being the closest they came to street-level hip-hop. The raps were made interesting, however, by the Prince's appropriation of a variety of personas. This is doubtless what encouraged the television bosses to make him an offer he could not refuse, and *The Fresh Prince Of Bel Air*'s enormous success certainly augmented his profile. He has since moved on to dramatic film roles, beginning with *Where The Day Takes You* and *Six Degrees Of Separation* (1993), and reaching a peak with *Independence Day* (1996) and *Men In Black* (1997), two of the highest-grossing films of all time. Jeff, meanwhile, formed A Touch Of Jazz Inc, a stable of producers working on rap/R&B projects. The duo picked up a second Grammy for 'Summertime' in 1991, before scoring a surprise UK number 1 in 1993 with 'Boom! Shake The Room', the first rap record (Vanilla Ice and MC Hammer aside) to top the British singles chart. The same year's *Code Red* was the duo's final album, with Smith concentrating on his acting career and releasing a solo debut in 1997.

● ALBUMS: *Rock The House* (Word Up 1987)★★,

He's The DJ, I'm The Rapper (Jive 1988)★★★, *And In This Corner* (Jive 1990)★★★, *Homebase* (Jive 1991)★★★, *Code Red* (Jive 1993)★★.
● COMPILATIONS: *Greatest Hits* (Jive 1998)★★★★.

DJ KRUSH

b. 1962, Tokyo, Japan. DJ Krush is a leading figure in the Japanese hip-hop scene and one of Mo' Wax Records' most influential artists. As a result of seeing a Tokyo screening of the rap film *Wild Style*, he began DJing to accompany breakdancers and in 1987 formed the Krush Posse. Several releases in the early 90s passed with little recognition until he met James Lavelle, who signed Krush to Mo' Wax. His first release for that label was the track 'Kemuri', which appeared on a double a-side with DJ Shadow's 'Lost And Found' in September 1994. This was followed the next month by the eagerly awaited *Strictly Turntablized*. A collection of laid-back hip-hop beats with abstract jazz inflections, it received an enthusiastic response from both the public and the press. At the same time, Krush was also featured on Mo' Wax's *Headz* compilation (1994), helping to establish the label's unique sound. Since this time he has collaborated on a number of projects. The album *Meiso* featured a number of American rappers, including C.L. Smooth and Malika B (The Roots), and the stark texture of *Strictly Turntablized* was replaced by a more accessible, vocal-orientated sound. On *Milight* Krush worked with the Japanese singer Eri Ohno, Deborah Anderson and others, producing a set of contemplative and positive tracks quite unlike much 'gangsta rap' of the time. *Ki-Oku* was an interesting collaboration with trumpeter Toshinori Kondo and included a version of Bob Marley's 'Sun Is Shining'. Krush released *Holonic*, a mixed compilation of some of his previous work, in 1998.
● ALBUMS: *Krush* (Nipon), *Strictly Turntablized* (Mo' Wax 1994)★★★★, *Meiso* (Mo' Wax 1995)★★★, *ColdKrushCuts* (Ninja Tune 1997)★★★, *Milight* (Mo' Wax 1997)★★★★, with Toshinori Kondo *Ki-Oku* (R&S 1998)★★★.
● COMPILATIONS: *Holonic* (Mo' Wax 1998)★★★.

DJ MAGIC MIKE

b. Michael Hampton, Orlando, Florida, USA. Critically and commercially ignored due to his south east location, Magic Mike is a talented rap producer and the executive vice-president of Cheetah Records. His most memorable moments arrived on his 1991 album, *Ain't No Doubt About It*, which featured highly commercial party raps like 'Suckers Frontin'' and 'Just Crusin''. Other cuts like 'Class Is In Session' were reprised for his collaboration with MC Madness a year later. All were flavoured with Hampton's distinctive use of house textures and Miami bass.
● ALBUMS: *Vicious Bass* (Cheetah 1988)★★★, with the Royal Posse *DJ Magic Mike And The Royal Posse* (Cheetah 1988)★★★, *Bass Is The Name Of The Game* (Cheetah 1988)★★★, *Ain't No Doubt About It* (Cheetah 1991)★★★★, as Vicious Base featuring Magic Mike *Back To Haunt You!* (Cheetah 1991)★★★, with MC Madness *Twenty Degrees Below Zero* (Cheetah 1992)★★★, *This Is How It Should Be Done* (Cheetah 1993)★★★, *Bass Is How It Shoud Be Done* (Cheetah 1993)★★★, *Bass: The Final Frontier* (Digital Master 1994)★★★, with the Royal Posse *Represent* (Cheetah 1994)★★★★, *Bass Bowl* (Magic 1995)★★★, *Back In Bass* (Newtown 1996)★★★, *Don't Talk Just Listen* (Cheetah 1996)★★★.
● COMPILATIONS: *The King Of The Bass' Greatest Hits, Volume 1* (Cheetah 1993)★★★★, *Foundations Of Bass, Volume 1* (Cheetah 1997)★★★.

DJ MARK THE 45 KING

Rap DJ Mark broke through in the early 90s with his production of Lakim Shabazz's debut set, *Pure Righteousness*, though Latee's 'This Cut's Got Flava' 12-inch had earned him his first production credit. He has gone on to become a hip-hop backroom guru ranking alongside Marley Marl and Hank Shocklee (Bomb Squad). As a young man he was the record boy for the Funky Four Plus One More, at which time he learnt the art of beatbox and turntable craft. He would also record solo, releasing an album for Aaron Fuchs' Tuff City label entitled *45 Kingdom*, which saluted the achievements of rappers on the smaller disc. The cut 'The 900 Number' was another tribute, in this case to the Akai 900 sampler. He has also produced numerous breakbeat albums, including *The Lost Breakbeats Vols. 1&2* (45 King Records).
● ALBUMS: *Rhythmical Madness* (Tuff City 1989)★★★, *45 Kingdom* (Tuff City 1990)★★★, *45 King Introduces The Flavour Unit* (Tuff City 1991)★★★.

DJ PETE JONES

One of the earliest US hip-hop DJs, enjoying a residency at the 371 club in the late 70s and taking Grandmaster Flash under his wing, he also introduced Afrika Bambaataa by allowing him to play on his system. The latter adapted his 'switch' mechanism for changing channels on the decks to great effect, to all intents and purposes inventing 'scratch' DJing in the process.

DJ PIERRE

Beginning his DJing career in 1983, Pierre was his second choice of name after hosting a disastrous set under his original title. He played at several early Lil' Louis parties, before he was credited with developing acid house, alongside his collaborator Spanky, in a Chicago basement in 1986. The duo had just purchased a bass machine, the Roland TB 303. Through a process of experimentation the 'acid squelch' sound came forth, which was recorded and passed on to DJ Ron Hardy to play at his Warehouse club. These quickly became known as Hardy's 'Acid Tracks' and the term stuck. Pierre went on to form Phuture Records, started in 1987, which consolidated on his invention with the hugely influential *Acid Trax* series. From there his name first became synonymous with the Acid House movement, before he tired of Chicago and moved to New York to help to establish the Strictly Rhythm empire. His work there in his capacity as A&R head, producer and artist was pivotal. Pierre's discography is a varied and prolific one, beginning with singles such as 'Annihilating Rhythm' (as Darkman), 'Masterblaster', 'Rise From Your Grave', 'Musik' and 'Generate Power'. In New York he perfected the 'Wyld Pitch' musical style, and in more recent years operated more as a free agent (releasing material such as 'More Than Just A Chance' on the UK's Vinyl Solution, and 'I Might Be Leaving U' for Moving, which featured a vocal from LaVette), though he maintains links with Strictly Rhythm. He has also remixed widely, his clients including Yo You Honey, Midi Rain and DIY. Not to be confused with the similarly titled DJ Pierre (Pierre Fieroldi) from Italy, who, along with Gianfranco Bortolotti, has been responsible for Euro hits by the 49ers, Cappella and others, plus his own cuts including 'We Gonna Funk'. Various heated letters were exchanged between the two as confusion increased.

DJ POGO

One of UK hip-hop's prime spinners of the early 90s, Pogo made his name through the World DJ Championships. From there he took on remix and production work for UK rap troupes such as London Posse, Demon Boyz, MC Mell 'O', and Monie Love, as well as US imports like House Of Pain and Cypress Hill and even the Fine Young Cannibals. This in addition to his regular stints on London's Kiss FM Radio Station. He was also the prime mover behind PLZ (Party A La Mazon), together with Brooklyn born and bred duo Regi and Fredi, who had been operating out of London since 1987. Regi is a former dancer while Fredi is a business student turned rapper. They met Pogo in 1990, releasing their first record as PLZ two years later ('If It Ain't PLZ...'/'Bad Person' on Go For The Juggler Records). Producing positive industry reaction, it was followed by the *Build A Wall Around Your Dreams* EP and a debut long-playing set.
● ALBUMS: as PLZ *Parables And Linguistic Zlang, Volume One* (Go For The Juggler 1993)★★★.

DJ PREMIER

The musical foundation of Gang Starr, DJ Premier (b. Chris Martin, Brooklyn, New York, USA) has also become one of hip-hop's most respected producers and remixers in his own right during the 80s. As a child his interest in music was demonstrated by the fact that he collected records from the age of four. Unlike many of the original producers, Premier learned his craft through technology and experimentation rather than the manual dexterity ethos of scratching ('I believe that sampling is an art form if you don't abuse it'). He recorded his first demos with Boston rapper MC Topski, and after Gang Starr's success there was no stopping him. Those artists who have benefited from the Premier production tradition include Jeru The Damaja, Nas, KRS-1, Branford Marsalis, Da Youngstas, Neneh Cherry, Heavy D, Subsonic 2, Cookie Crew, K-Solo and Lady Of Rage. His remix roster includes Shyheim, Boss, Loose Ends, MC Solaar, Fat Joe and MOP.

DJ QUIK

b. David Blake, 18 January 1970, Compton, California, USA. Artist whose deification of his home-town, where he had grown up the youngest of ten children, pervaded both his first two albums ('Born And Raised In Compton' on his

debut, and minor hit single 'Jus Lyke Compton' on the follow-up set). At the age of 12 he began to learn the art of DJing, but it wasn't until NWA exploded on the West Coast that he actually considered these skills might provide a career. He began recording cassettes, one of which found its way into the hands of Profile A&R man Dave Moss, head of their newly opened Los Angeles office. His debut set saw comparisons to Prince, though in mode of operation rather than musical terms: Quik writing, rapping, producing and arranging the set in its entirety. Rather than repeating the gangsta stance of his near-neighbours NWA (though he claimed to be a former member of the Bloods gang), Quik confirmed that 'There's a fun side to Compton, too', reflecting this in songs about sex (the rather too obvious 'Sweet Black Pussy' - I'm like Noah's Ark, My bitches come in pairs'), alcohol ('8 Ball') and marijuana ('Tha Bombudd'). His biggest hit, however, came with the Top 50-breaking 'Tonite'. He has also produced widely for Compton groups like 2nd II None and Penthouse. Quik signed to the influential Death Row Records for his 1995 set, *Safe + Sound*, which borrowed even more heavily from George Clinton's G-funk sound.
● ALBUMS: *Quik Is The Name* (Profile 1991)★★★, *Way 2 Fonky* (Profile 1992)★★★, *Safe + Sound* (Profile 1995)★★★.

DJ S THE KARMINSKY EXPERIENCE

In the mid-90s a bizarre development occurred within London, England's club scene. Eschewing the more abrasive delights of jungle and techno, several clubs sprang up to regale crowds with the delights of 'easy listening' music. Among the most popular DJ teams in this context were brothers Martin and James Karminsky, who proudly used old K-Tel Records and Matt Munro/Klaus Wunderlich albums to form the basis of their playlists at clubs including Sound Spectrum and the Bamboo Curtain. As Martin elaborated, 'Maybe there's a trend towards more relaxed music. When people get in from a techno club they want to explore other musical areas.' This underground scene was brought to the mainstream at the end of 1995 when Mike Flowers Pops recorded a version of Oasis's 'Wonderwall', which became a huge national hit. As a result London Records signed the brothers as DJ S The Karminsky Experience, releasing an album of their selections and mixes titled *In Flight Entertainment* in the early months of 1996.

Selections included Brigitte Bardot's 'St. Tropez', Max Gregor's 'Big Train' and a version of the Doors' 'Light My Fire' performed by the Edmundo Ros Orchestra.
● ALBUMS: *In Flight Entertainment* (London 1996)★★★.

DJ SHADOW

b. Josh Davis, c.1972, California, USA. Self-proclaimed 'vinyl-addict and beat-head' DJ Shadow was turned on to hip-hop by Grandmaster Flash's 'The Message' and later began compiling his own mix tapes. His first release on Mo' Wax Records, 'In Flux'/'Hindsight' (1993), was seen by some as a benchmark in instrumental hip-hop and helped to define that label's approach. His second Mo' Wax single, 'Lost And Found', was released together with DJ Krush's 'Kemuri' in 1994, and was followed by 'What Does Your Soul Look Like' the next year. Towards the end of 1996 he released his first album, *Endtroducing ...* , as well as the singles 'Midnight In A Perfect World' and 'Stem', which brought him to the mainstream consciousness through coverage in the national press. The album was widely acclaimed for the way in which Davis blends hip-hop grooves with elements of jazz, rock, ambient, techno and other styles to create a unique, coherent sound that never resorts to the formulae of these influences. As with some of the more melodic instrumental hip-hop, compared to the humorous abstract collages of artists such as DJ Food, much of the album seems deeply introspective and rather earnest, with its mournful cello, piano and organ melodies and sequences. This feeling is further emphasized by the raw production and the tendency towards slow tempos. In 1997 he released 'Hign Noon' and also DJed at the Verve's appearance at Wembley Arena in 1997, as a result of working with Richard Ashcroft on James Lavelle's *U.N.K.L.E.* album. Later that year, he released a set of his tracks performed by DJ Q-Bert (renowned for his technical mastery) entitled *Camel Bob Sled Race*. Davis has collaborated with other Mo' Wax artists, including Blackalicious and DJ Krush.
● ALBUMS: *Midnight In A Perfect World* (Mo Wax 1996)★★★, *Endtroducing . . .* (Mo Wax 1996)★★★★, with Q-Bert *Camel Bob Sled Race (Q-Bert Mega Mix)* mini-album (Mo Wax 1997)★★★, *Preemptive Strike* (Mo Wax 1998)★★.

DJ SPOOKY

b. Paul Miller, Washington, DC, USA. An experimental DJ working in contemporary electronica, Spooky is an energetic, as well as prolific, performer. His world view was partially shaped by his parents' involvement in the civil rights movement - his father was a lawyer for the Black Panthers and his mother a leading light in the Afro-Futurism fashion movement. He first became attuned to music when his father purchased a computer: 'The idea of sound becoming a way of creating text, or even code, really blew my mind.' As well as recording extensively, he exhibits his visual art, contributes articles to magazines such as the *Village Voice*, and writes books (covering music theory, intellectual property, and, bizarrely, science fiction). He defended his billing as a modern renaissance man thus: 'We're in an aesthetic that is so linked to all these different world cultures, the music that I'm trying to create celebrates that diversity. It's all in the mix.' As a continuation of this, his DJ sets routinely mix easy listening (Esquivel!), with reggae, drum 'n' bass and soul.

● ALBUMS: various *The Necropolis Dialogic Project* (Knitting Factory Works 1997)★★★, *Songs Of A Dead Dreamer* (Asphodel 1997)★★★.

DJ SS

b. Leroy Small, 1971, Leicester, Leicestershire, England. Small has been at the forefront of the UK hardcore dance movement since the early 90s. Before concentrating on building a profile as DJ SS, he had operated under a number of guises and aliases, including International Rude Boys, Rhythm For Reasons, Sounds Of The Future and MA1 and MA2. He was also the co-founder and in-house producer of Formation Records, the acclaimed Leicester-based label. This involved him in some capacity in the vast majority of the label's 60-plus releases. Small had first worked as a DJ at the age of 13, playing at school discos before specializing in commercial hip-hop nights. He soon transferred over to the nascent rave scene when his interest in rap waned with the advent of the gangsta groups. Conversely, his affection for hip-hop (the parent style of much of the hardcore phenomenon) has been rekindled since he began recording as DJ SS. Releases such as 'Hearing Is Believing', 'The Lighter', 'Smoker's Rhythm' and 'The Rollidge' in 1995 brought him to nationwide prominence as the leader of the 'hardstep' (or purist drum 'n' bass) sound. Despite being heavily rooted in jungle's rhythmic dynamism, this style eschewed the intimidatingly violent narratives of ragga-based jungle.

DJ TALLA 2XLC

One of Europe's most prominent producers and DJs, Talla had listened from an early age to the electronics of Kraftwerk and the Yellow Magic Orchestra. He rebelled against the pre-eminence of guitar and rock music by opening the Techno Club in Germany in 1984 - a club dedicated to preserving and propagating electronic music. Within five years he had also started his own label, Music Research. This developed two subsidiary outlets: Zoth Ommog, for electronic- and industrial-based acts, and New Zone, for electro dance. In the 90s further division occured. Suck Me Plasma was incorporated to cover hard trance and techno house releases, while Influence dealt with more melodic techno projects. Talitha pandered to electro goth fans, while Zoth Ommog continued to service the more experimental concerns. New Zone was effectively discontinued. As well as running the club and various imprints, Talla is also the creative force behind his own band, Bigod 20, who are signed to Warner Brothers Records. Other artists on his various labels include Armageddon Dildos, Leather Strip, X Marks The Pedwalk and Psychopomps.

● ALBUMS: as Bigod 20 *Steel Works* (Sire 1992)★★★, *Supercute* (Warners 1994)★★★.

DJ VADIM

Vadim was born in the Soviet Union but moved to London when he was three. After becoming interested in hip-hop, he began to DJ and in 1995 released his first EP, *Abstract Hallucinogenic Gases*, on his own Jazz Fudge label. Later that year he continued his abstract hip-hop experiments on the EP *Headz Ain't Ready*, after which he signed to Ninja Tune Records. His first release for Ninja was 'Non Lateral Hypothesis' in April 1996, and his debut album, *USSR Repertoire*, 'a crazy selection of minimal hip-hop, ansa machines, *musique concrete* and the old school', arrived towards the end of the year. His only release of 1997 was the EP *Conquest Of The Irrational*. While recording for Ninja Tune he has continued to develop 'audio research into minimal hip-hop' at Jazz Fudge, with a number of artists and collaborators such as Andre Gurov, Mark B, the Creators, Blade and the Bug. He also DJs around the world, with particular success in Japan, which prompted an album of remixes, *USSR Reconstrustion - Theories Explained* (1998), featuring work by the Prunes, Kid Koala, the Herbaliser and DJ Krush, among others.

● ALBUMS: *USSR Repertoire* (Ninja Tune 1997), *USSR Reconstrustion - Theories Explained* (Ninja Tune 1998).

DJAIMIN

b. Dario Mancini. Swiss DJ whose 'Give You' cut was discovered by Tony Humphries, who unveiled it at 1992's New Music Seminar. It was quickly picked up by Strictly Rhythm, and then licensed to Cooltempo in the UK. 'Give You' featured singers Mike Anthony and Alessandra. Djaimin himself had been a DJ from the age of 16. Born of mixed Italian and English parentage, he is based in Lusanne, the French-speaking region of Switzerland. He moved there in 1986, hooking up with Anthony, best known for his 1983 cover version of Timmy Thomas's 'Why Can't We Live Together'. Together they run a national Swiss radio show. The follow-up to 'Give You' was 'She's Ga Ga', again for Strictly Rhythm.

DJAX UP BEATS

House label esteemed by the critics and run by the similarly garlanded Dutch DJ, Miss Djax (aka Saskia Slegers). Voted Best DJ by German magazine *Frontpage* in 1992, she started DJing in her native Eindhoven in the mid-80s, establishing the record label in 1989. Djax Up has released records by the likes of Trance Induction, Terrace (aka Stefan Robbers, *The Turning Point* EP), Mike Dearborn (*Unbalanced Frequency* EP), Planet Gong (Dylan Hermeljin), Edge Of Motion, Acid Junkies and Random XS, just a few of the better examples in a very strong discography. However, the one thing that singles out Djax Up among other UK and European labels is its profligate release schedule (Paul Johnson's 'Psycho Kong' being its 200th release). Despite the extensive catalogue (and the fact that over 90% of sales originate from outside of Holland), there have been relatively few lapses of taste. For example, they conquered the rise of ambient house with releases from Optic Crux, a group from Utrecht whose output was engineered by Random XS.

DOCTOR ICE

b. *c.*1965, USA. Rapper thus named because he wanted to belong to the medical profession while at school. Ice was formerly a member of U.T.F.O., with whom he remained for five years, and before that Whodini, as a live dancer (one of the first such occurrences). Striking out solo he enlisted the aid of Full Force member Brain 'B-Fine' Lou to write new material. The record was completed within one month. Ice toured to support it, appearing in white coat and with a medical team as part of the 'theme'. His two dancers were presented as 'patients', and his DJ 'the surgeon'. Other songs traced different 'concepts' but were similarly narrative: in the single excerpt, 'Sue Me', Ice is depicted in the accompanying video driving a white Porsche until his alter ego, Doctor Dread, crashes into him in a taxi, with riotous court scenes and accusation and counter-accusation following. 'Love Jones' featured contributions from Full Force and Cheryl 'Pepsi' Riley, while the album closed with 'True Confessions', which featured a cameo from Lisa Lisa and Blair Underwood of *L.A. Law* fame, on a song concerning an unhappy married couple and their interceding lawyer. Renaming himself simply Doc Ice, he switched to Ichiban to set up his own Selph Records, which housed his *Rely On Selph* set. In the intervening years, rather than hanging up his stethascope as many had assumed, he had developed a career in acting and choreography, working on several high profile commercials and the feature film, *Don't Let Your Meat Loaf.*

● ALBUMS: *The Mic Stalker* (Jive 1989)★★★, *Rely On Selph* (Selph/Ichiban 1993)★★★.

DODGE CITY PRODUCTIONS

London-based duo who filter jazz and rap into a cohesive music, usually fronted by the voice of Ghida De Palma. Principal members Dodge (b. Roger Drakes) and I.G. also employ guest musicians such as the Young Disciples and jazzmen Ronny Jordan and Steve Williamson, as and when the need arises, alongside rappers like MC Bello (Of Brothers Like Outlaw/KLF fame) and MCM. Dodge and I.G. have also remixed for Gang Starr, Digital Underground and Naughty By Nature. Singles like 'Unleash Your Love' led to them being viewed as the new Soul II Soul in some corners, particularly the way in which they operated as a collective, with live shows usually featuring no less than eight people on stage at any given time.

● ALBUMS: *Steppin' Up And Down* (4th & Broadway 1993)★★★.

DOG, TIM

b. Timothy Blair, 1 January 1967, Bronx, New York, USA. A dropout from St John's University in Queens, Dog's 'Fuck Compton' single proved to be one of the most notorious releases in rap's chequered history. Yet this anti-NWA tirade (at one point he sings 'Shut up bitch/You can't sing' while simulating intercourse with Eazy-E's 'girlfriend') was an undeniably forceful manifesto, for all its wanton tribalism. Indeed, legend has it that it provoked death threats from members of the west coast rap community. Dog was also a guest member of Ultramagnetic MCs for a period, appearing on their 'Chorus Line' anthem. Dog's second album, *Do Or Die*, was a largely discredited offering, despite the presence of KRS-1 on 'I Get Wrecked'. Other tracks such as 'Silly Bitch' featured a refrain of 'Clean out the kitchen/And the bathroom sink', just in case listeners were unaware as to Dog's vision of women in the scheme of things. In 1994 Dog made a surprise signing to Phonogram Records' Talkin' Loud label, home to the likes of Incognito and Galliano. The first result of this deal was the single, 'Bitch Wid A Perm', dedicated to fellow canine rapper Snoop Doggy Dogg.

● ALBUMS: *Penicillin On Wax* (Ruffhouse 1991)★★★, *Do Or Die* (Ruffhouse/Columbia 1993)★★★.

DOMINO

b. Shawn Ivy, c.1972, St. Louis, Missouri, USA. From the new school of rappers hailing from Long Beach, California, Domino typified the area's preoccupation with cool, languid, almost sexual delivery. His hybrid accent was accounted for by the fact that he spent his first seven years in St. Louis. He had begun singing professionally in nightclubs like Marla Gibbs' Crossroads and Sir Alex in Compton before he embarked on a rap style. Just as contemporaries like Snoop Doggy Dogg spiced their rhymes with outbursts of actual singing, Domino repeated the feat, with slightly less contentious lyrics, with an arguably greater degree of success. After a childhood spent listening to soul and funk standards from the Stylistics and Funkadelic, he caught the rap bug and began writing words for himself and Snoop. According to Domino, Snoop could not resist the temptation to 'go gangsta' when it was offered to him on a plate by Dr. Dre, and the duo split. Domino's perseverence with a more cognitive

style was eventually rewarded. After several years of trying to get the major labels to listen, he signed with the small independent Outburst. 'Getto Jam' underlined his appeal: these were still tough-talking rap words, but sauntered through in an easy, inviting fashion. The buzz created by the track saw him and Outburst signed up for distribution by Def Jam. Samples from Kool And The Gang sat side by side with lines like: 'Everybody loves them dead presidents' on his debut album. This was combined with a more realistic overview of Domino's place in the scheme of things, with rhymes discussing his desire for sexual gratification ('Ass For Days') contrasting with morally tinged attitudes to safe sex ('Raincoat'), from which he even launched a condom range of the same name. Similarly, rather than the glorification of the drive-by shooting so evident in the work of others, there is a matter-of-fact discourse instead on the hassles of getting paid ('Money Is Everything'). Such platitudes saw him discussed in one magazine as 'a soft spoken businessman who will make an excellent bank manager when he gets sick of making records'. His own view: 'There's so much going on in the 'hood apart from guns and murder'. However, he did face criticism on his first British outing when misguided punters paid £10 to hear him perform three songs at a PA, when they had expected a full gig. Not to be confused with the production specialist Domino of Del Tha Funkee Homosapien's Hieroglyphics crew fame, he has failed to live up to his reputation on subsequent outings *Physical Funk* and *Dominology*.

● ALBUMS: *Domino* (Outburst 1994)★★★★, *Physical Funk* (Outburst 1996)★★, *Dominology* (Thug 1997)★★.

DOOF

b. Nick Barber, 1968. With a background in punk, reggae, rock and Indian music, Taylor's first release, the EP *Disposable Hymn To The Infinite*, was on Novamute Records in 1991. He has since recorded for a number of the top trance labels, including the *Born Again* EP (Matsuri Productions 1995) and 'Double Dragons' (Dragonfly Records). In 1995 he released 'Let's Turn On' (a collaboration with Simon Posford aka Hallucinogen) on TIP Records, followed in 1996 by 'Angelina' and 'Destination Bom' (also on TIP), which all became favourites on the trance scene. Towards the end of that year, TIP released Doof's eagerly awaited debut album, *Let's Turn On*, one of the most coherent and enduring releases in the 'Goa' trance style. On tracks such as 'Mars Needs Women' and 'Destination Bom', Barber distilled the rip-roaring, four-on-the-floor/Indian mode style in careful, restrained arrangements, while presenting a more tranquil, chilled-out trance sound on 'Sunshrine' and 'Star Over Parvati'. At the same time, the album is characterized as a whole by his focused collection of sounds. In 1997 he contributed 'The Tower And The Star' to the TIP compilation *Infinite Excursions II*; the following year 'Wormwhole' was released on TIP's *Beyond Colour*. He has also written tracks for the dub compilations *Dub Mashing Up Creation* and *Dubbed On Planet Skunk* for Dubmission Records. Barber frequently travels and performs around Europe and further afield. He has remixed for a number of artists including the Green Nuns Of The Revolution, Hallucinogen and The Infinity Project.

● ALBUMS: *Let's Turn On* (TIP 1996)★★★★.

DORADO RECORDS

Eclectic London imprint, easily recognizable from its gold and blue sleeve designs, which has had fingers in many musical pies since its inception. Primarily, however, it has been identified as the UK's number one jazz fusion outpost, with a predilection for the club sounds of that spectrum. The label was established by Ollie Buckwell in 1992, and quickly became pre-eminent in its field, particularly in mainland Europe where much of Dorado's output is revered. It debuted with Monkey Business's 'Ain't No Fun'. The main artists on the label include Matt Cooper, a hugely talented young artist who writes, composes and arranges his own material as Outside, and Matt Wienevski's ambitious D*Note (whom Buckwell managed). Other releases have included material by Jhelisa Anderson (ex-Soul Family Sensation and Shamen), Ceri Evans (former Brand New Heavies keyboard player), Mesh Of Mind ('Learn The Words'), Origin ('Music Man', which featured Jah Shaka), Ute ('Soul Thing'), and even hip-hoppers including Dana Bryant or Brooklyn Funk Essentials ('The Revolution Was Postponed Because Of Rain'). 'I like to think of Dorado as more progressive', summarized Buckwell. 'It's almost the second wave. Talkin' Loud and Acid Jazz kind of broke the market, and we're trying to develop it - push it forward'.

● COMPILATIONS: *A Compilation Volumes 1 - 3* (Dorado 1992-94)★★★★.

DOUBLE YOU?

European house group Double You? first came to prominence in the early 90s, largely through the public disagreements between their label, ZYX Records, and Network Records. Network had made overtures to obtain the licence for Double You?'s version of KC And The Sunshine Band's 'Please Don't Go', but their approaches were rejected. Network employed KWS to record a version instead, earning a five-week stay at number 1 in the UK charts in 1992 in the process. Double You?'s manager Robertson Zanetti collapsed of nervous exhaustion as a result of the disagreement and subsequent litigation. Despite this, the group continued to record, achieving limited success with another cover version, 'Run To Me'. 1994's 'What's Up', was a surprise hit, many having presumed the group to have folded, while 'Hot Stuff' in 1995 was uninspired, but confirmed Double You?'s continued presence in the elementary house cover version market.

DOUG E. FRESH

b. Douglas E. Davis, 17 September 1966, St. Thomas, Virgin Islands, though he grew up in the Bronx and Harlem districts of New York, USA. Self-proclaimed as The Original Human Beatbox, i.e. being able to imitate the sound of a rhythm machine, Fresh broke through in 1985 with the release of one of rap's classic cuts, 'The Show'. Joined by partner MC Ricky D (aka Slick Rick), the single matched rhymes with a bizarre array of human sound effects, courtesy of Fresh. It marked a notable departure in rap's development, and was so distinctive it began a small flurry of similarly inclined rappers, as well as Salt 'N' Pepa's answer record, 'Showstopper'. Despite its impact, it was a song that was hardly representative of Fresh fare: far too much of his recorded material was workmanlike and soundalike. A debut album included live contributions from Bernard Wright (synthesiser) and veteran jazz man Jimmy Owens (trumpet), as well as a dubious anti-abortion cut. The follow-up saw him allied to Public Enemy's Bomb Squad production team. To give him his due Fresh was very nearly rap's first superstar, but rather than capitalise on 'The Show', he would end up in court trying to sue Reality Records for non-payment of royalties on the song. He was also the first genuine rapper to appear at Jamaica's Reggae Sunsplash festival, stopping in the West Indies long enough to record alongside Papa San and Cocoa Tea. He made something of a comeback at the end of 1993 with the release of party record 'I-Right (Alright)', after he was reunited with Slick Rick (recently returned from a period of incarceration), and signed with Gee Street Records. Fresh has also enjoyed the distinction of seeing a 'Doug E. Fresh' switch added to the Oberheim Emulator, in order to provide samples of his human beat box talents. On *Play* Fresh employed Luther Campbell of 2 Live Crew to add a gangsta edge.

● ALBUMS: *Oh, My God!* (Reality 1985)★★★, *The World's Greatest Entertainer* (Reality 1988)★★★, *Doin' What I Gotta Do* (Bust It 1992)★★, *Play* (Gee Street 1995)★★, *Alright* (Gee 1996)★★.

● COMPILATIONS: *Greatest Hits, Volume 1* (Bust It 1996)★★★.

DOWN SOUTH

Richmond, Virginia-based rappers Shawn J-Period and Soda Pop (ably assisted by DJ Myorr) combined a winning mix of jazz, funk, reggae, bluegrass and salsa on their debut recordings for Atlantic. The smooth, lolling rhythms proved intriguing but too insubstantial in their own right to convey the mix of reality/party themes, despite production expertise from the Beatnuts, T-Ray and others. However, the promotional single, 'Southern Comfort', with a guest vocal by label mates Jomanda, was strong. Rather than being dedicated to the alcoholic drink, it was addressed to their former locale, the trio having shipped over to New York. Down South had formed in 1990 when Pop and J-Period, who are first cousins, met Myorr at high school. Myorr had formerly worked in a lowly position at Def Jam, and it was his connections that led to them signing with Atlantic.

● ALBUMS: *Lost In Brooklyn* (Big Beat/Atlantic 1994)★★★.

DR. ALBAN

b. Alban Nwapa, Nigeria. Swedish-based euro rapper who rose to prominence with his curious pot pourri of styles, christened 'jungle reggae hip-hop' by some commentators. Of all the artists who employ the title 'Doctor' in their names, Alban is one of the few to do so legitimately. He originally went to Stockholm, Sweden, to train as a dentist, and after qualifying, he started the Alphabet Club in the city, which eventually spawned a record and clothes shop of the same name. His attempts

to 'toast' over the records he played at the venue attracted the attention of the Swemix label. The first result of his work with the studio was the 1990 single 'Hello Afrika', which immediately launched him in the national and international charts. With the anti-drug 'No Coke' and pro-unity 'U & Mi', Dr. Alban continued to cut himself a large slice of credibility in the European mainstream dance market. The musical style combined techno with club vocals and African rhythms. Among the most notable traits were the Nigerian percussive effects and dancehall chanting. In September 1992 he enjoyed a huge European hit with 'It's My Life', which reached number 2 in the UK pop chart. His unique Afro-Swedish patois earned praise from a variety of quarters, reinforcing the fact that rap had become a universal currency. The man behind the production on the big hits was Denniz Pop, who also produced Ace Of Base's number 1, 'All That She Wants'. Dr. Alban started his own Dr. label, whose first release was the 'Alrabaiye Take Me Up' single by Amadin.

● ALBUMS: *Hello Africa - The Album* (Swemix 1990)★★★, *One Love* (Swemix 1992)★★★.

DR. DRE

b. Andre Young, 18 February 1965, South Central, Los Angeles, USA. Widely regarded, by Rolling Stone at least, as the chief architect of west coast gangsta rap, Dre's musical career began as a DJ at Los Angeles dance club, Eve After Dark. There he would splice up a mix of new records with soul classics like Martha And The Vandellas. The club had a back room with a small four-track studio where he, together with future-NWA member Yella and Lonzo Williams, would record demos. The first of these was 'Surgery', a basic electro track with a chorus of 'Calling Dr Dre to surgery'. These sessions, and nights at Eve After Dark, taught him the turntable techniques he would later bring to NWA, after forming the World Class Wreckin' Cru at the age of 17. Although other former members such as Ice Cube had laid the ground for rap's immersion into the mainstream, the success of Dre's debut solo effort, The Chronic, confirmed its commercial breakthrough. It also signalled a change in tack by modern gangsta rappers. The music now took its cue from the funk of George Clinton and Funkadelic, Dre freely admitting to the influence Clinton played on his life: 'Back in the 70s that's all people were doing: getting high, wearing Afros, bell-bottoms and listening to Parliament-Funkadelic. That's why I called my album *The Chronic* and based my music and the concepts like I did: because his shit was a big influence on my music. Very big'. To this end he created a studio band for the sessions, which included the R&B talents of Tony Green (bass) and Ricky Rouse (guitar). While Dre's lyrics were just as forceful as those that had graced NWA, there was also a shift in subject matter. *The Chronic* referred heavily to the recreational use of marijuana, taking its name from a particularly virulent, and popular, brand. Together with the efforts of Cypress Hill, cannabis was now the drug of choice for the gangsta rapper, with crack cocaine much discussed but rarely endorsed. *The Chronic* would go on to spend eight months in the Billboard Top 10. At least as important was Dre's growing reputation as a producer. As well as producing an album for one of his many girlfriends, Michel'le, his work with Eazy E, D.O.C., Above The Law and, most importantly, Snoop Doggy Dogg, broke new ground. Snoop had already rapped with Dre on the hit singles, 'Deep Cover' and 'Nuthin' But A 'G' Thang'. However, the Doggy Style opus would break box office records, bringing gangsta rap to the top of the album charts. Many sustained the belief that Dre was the driving force behind its success, the producer himself acknowledging: 'I can take a three year old and make a hit record with him'. At the same time he was dismissive of his own, pioneering efforts for NWA, particularly the epoch-making Straight Outta Compton: 'To this day I can't stand that album, I threw that thing together in six weeks so we could have something to sell out of the trunk'. During his involvement with the NWA posse he became the house producer for Eazy E's Ruthless Records. Seven out of eight albums he produced for the label between 1983 and 1991 went platinum, but he broke from Ruthless over what he alleged was under-payment. Dre's on-record sneers at Eazy E began shortly afterwards, including *The Chronic*'s 'Dre Day', a putdown which Eazy E would countermand for his reply, 'Muthaphukkin' Gs'.

Like many of rap's leading lights, Dre never strayed far from controversy, even after he bought into the comfort of a luxury home in San Fernando Valley. As if to reinstate himself as a 'true gangsta', Dre waged a war of attrition with authority. Television host Dee Barnes filed a multi-million dollar lawsuit against him for allegedly throwing her against the wall of a Hollywood nightclub in 1991. He was also convicted of breaking the jaw of a record producer (he was sentenced to house arrest and was fitted with a tracking device), and was detained by mounted police after a fracas in a New Orleans hotel lobby. Eazy E sued him, while Dre complained bitterly about restraint of trade and monies owed, cursed Ruthless General Manager Jerry Heller, and finally managed to find a deal with Jimmy Iovine at Interscope, who let him set up his own label, Death Row Records, co-founded with the controversial Marion 'Suge' Knight, Vanilla Ice's ex-publicist. The success of *The Chronic* and *Doggy Style*, and the signing of rap's biggest new star Tupac Shakur, briefly made Death Row one of America's most powerful labels. By 1996, however, its well documented problems culminated in Dre acrimoniously leaving to form his own Aftermath label. The label's first release was a various artists compilation, whose standout track was Dre's declamatory hit single 'Been There Done That', a kiss-off to gangsta rap and Death Row.

● ALBUMS: *The Chronic* (Death Row 1993)★★★★.

● COMPILATIONS: *Back N Tha Day* (Blue Dolphin 1994)★★, *Concrete Roots* (Triple X 1994)★★, *First Round Knock Out* (Triple X 1996)★★★, *Dr. Dre Presents The Aftermath* (Aftermath 1996)★★★★.

DR. JECKYLL AND MR HYDE

Consisting of the Bronx-born duo Andre Harrell (Jeckyll; b. *c*.1959) and Alonzo Brown (Hyde), alongside DJ Scratch On Galaxy (b. George Llado), Dr. Jeckyll and Mr Hyde enjoyed a steady stream of success in the early 80s. Their best-remembered song, 'Genius Rap', constructed over the Tom Tom Club's 'Genius Of Love', sold over 150,000 records for Profile in 1981. Previously Brown had recorded the label's second release, and first rap record, as Lonnie Love ('Young Ladies'). 'AM:PM', backed by the Kurtis Blow-produced 'Fast Life', also earned the duo healthy chart placings. However, when their debut album bombed both elected to concentrate on non-performing careers. Harrell established Uptown, scoring huge success with Heavy D as well as the New Jack Swing prime movers, notably Teddy Riley's creations. Brown would work in executive posts at Cold Chillin' and Warner Brothers before heading up A&R for A&M. The duo still remain good friends and suggest a reunion from time to

time, though nothing more tangible than their joint sponsorship of the Groove B. Chill act has yet to surface.
● ALBUMS: *The Champagne Of Rap* (Profile 1986)★★★.

DR. OCTAGON

b. Keith Thornton, New York, USA. Formerly known as Kool Keith while a member of groundbreaking New York, US rap group the Ultramagnetic MC's, Thornton has also travelled under a variety of other pseudonyms - Poppa Large, the Reverend Tom, Sinister 6000, Big Willie Smith and Mr. Gerbik. In the mid-90s, and now based in Los Angeles, Thornton unveiled his latest project, Dr. Octagon. In principle a band, it was effectively just his latest solo musical outlet. However, after attracting favourable reviews for his live shows, he alarmed his backers (including record label Dreamworks) by failing to appear for performances in support of Beck and refusing to answer messages. This all fuelled a reputation for esoteric behaviour that had been with him since his time in the Ultramagnetic MC's. For example, he was said to have spent his entire five-figure advance from Dreamworks on pornography. However, he was indulged because of a precocious talent and, when he could be persuaded to marshall it, a prolific output. Between 1995 and 1996 he recorded tracks with Dan 'The Automator' Nakamura, DJ Q-Bert (of Invisibl Skratch Piklz), DJ Shadow and appeared on a track with the UK's Prodigy. The ensuing *Dr. Octagonecologyst* album was initially recorded for an independent label and featured a dazzling mixture of vibrant textures filled with Moog synthesizer, violin, flute, bass and even classical samples (including Pachelbel's Canon) that strove to redefine the hip-hop genre. However, the lyrics were a different matter, reflecting Thornton's obsession with pornography in lustful anatomical detail. As he told Rolling Stone magazine, 'I wrote that album in one day. I was like, "Fuck it. I'll write the sickest shit ever, just to bug out on it."' He followed this with *Sex Style*, released on his own Funky Ass label. In the meantime, Thornton was finding further time to waste on his favourite distraction by launching his own pornography magazine, *All Flavors*.
● ALBUMS: *Dr. Octagonecologyst* (Bulk/Dreamworks 1996)★★★★, *Instrumentalyst: Octagon Beats* (Dreamworks 1996)★★★, *Sex Style* (Funky Ass 1997)★★★.

DR. PHIBES AND THE HOUSE OF WAX EQUATIONS

Formed in the late 80s at South Cheshire College of Further Education, England, where they all studied music, Dr. Phibes quickly became one of the north-west's most important dance bands. The name is taken from two separate Hammer Horror films. The band comprises Howard King Jnr. (vocals, guitars), Lee Belsham (bass), and Keith York (drums). Their recording debut came with the 1990 12-inch 'Sugarblast', which preceded their long-playing debut in April 1991. Topping the independent charts for two weeks, it generated significant media coverage and critical acclaim. Their music is an eclectic, but primarily rhythmic, mix of blues, funk and psychedelia. Recording sessions for their second album were interrupted when Belsham injured a shoulder. His colleague York drove off in their van, unbeknownst to Belsham who was lying on top of it.
● ALBUMS: *Whirlpool* (Seel 1991)★★★, *Hypnotwister* (1993)★★★

DRAGONFLY RECORDS

The DJ and producer Youth and Jazz Summers set up Dragonfly And Butterfly in 1992 as a subsidiary of Big Life Records to develop the techno trance sound the former had heard in Goa. After System 7's single, '777 Expansion', and album, *777*, in early 1993, Dragonfly released material from Drum Club (*Everything Is Now*), Heather Nova (*Glowstars*), Spiral Tribe (*Techno Terra*) and The Infinity Project ('Time And Space') over the next 12 months. At the same time the label fostered experimentation as a number of important artists worked in close collaboration in Youth's Butterfly Studios on a sound that became known as psychedelic trance (what the media termed 'Goa' trance), notably Simon Posford (Hallucinogen), Martin Freeland (Man With No Name), Nick Barber (Doof) as well as members of the Green Nuns Of The Revolution, Slinky Wizard and The Infinity Project. The label became associated with some of the best psy-trance around and helped to bring that style to a wider audience without entering the commercial mainstream, through releases from artists such as Doof ('Double Dragons' and 'Youth Of The Galaxy'), Hallucinogen ('Alpha Centauri'/'LSD', 'Astral Pancakes'/'Fluoro Neuro Sponge' and *Twisted*) and Man With No Name ('Sly-ed'/'Teleport' and 'Lunar Cycle'/'Neuro Tunnel') and a number of compilations, including the *Order Odonata* series and mix albums from Danny Rampling and Paul Oakenfold. Many of these artists have played at parties and clubs organized by the label in the UK and around the world. Although many of their best-known artists have gone on to form and record for other labels, Dragonfly have continued to produce some of the best new music, notably from artists such as Genetic (*We Are ... Genetic*), Muses Rapt (*Spiritual Healing*), Oforia (*Delirious*), Pleiadians (*IFO*), Shakta (*Silicon Trip*), UX (*Ultimate Experience*) and Zodiac Youth (*Devil's Circus*). In 1998 the subsidiary LSD Records released material from Youth's projects Dub Trees and Hicksville (also with Simon Posford and Saul), as well as Celtic Cross.

DREAD ZONE

This UK trance-dub club team comprises Greg Roberts (ex-BAD; Screaming Target), Leo Williams and Tim Bran. Roberts is responsible for rhythms and sampling, and Bran for programming and other feats of technology. Part of Dread Zone's distinctive charm is drawn from Roberts' appetite for cult films, many of his samples being taken from this field; dialogue from b-movies (often to avoid the problems of copyright clearance) is a particular favourite. However, their dub credentials were ensured by the arrival of the single 'House Of Dread'. This came complete with a 'Howard Marks' remix - the latter being among the world's most famous cannabis traffickers. 'Zion Youth' broached the UK Top 40 in 1995 and was followed by an excellent second album, *Second Light*.
● ALBUMS: *360˚* (1993)★★★, *Second Light* (Virgin 1995)★★★★, *Biological Radio* (Virgin 1997)★★.

DREAM FREQUENCY

On the back of popular club tunes such as 'Feel So Real' and 'Take Me', Debbie Sharp and Ian Bland have conquered a niche market, especially in being among the few dance acts to avail themselves of the live arena. They generated several column inches when they were originally sought out by Madonna's Maverick label (whose interest, they claim, dropped when it was realized that Sharp was pregnant). Further success, however, arrived with the stylish 'So Sweet', which became another club favourite. Bland has also worked with Martin Lever as Museka (the *M-Series* EP).

DREAM WARRIORS

A key part of the surprisingly active Canadian rap scene, West Indian duo King Lou (b. Louis Robinson, Jamaica, West Indies) and Capital Q (b. Frank Lennon Alert, 10 August *c*.1969, Port Of Spain, Trinidad, West Indies - so named because his father was a John Lennon fan) had to go to the UK to secure a record contract with 4th & Broadway. Previously, they had released a single, 'Let Your Backbone Slide', on a New York independent. Their blend of hip-hop superstructure with jazz tempo arrived via arch lyrics, overflowing with obscure mystic imagery, from the pen of King Lou. The sound was big and loose, often punctuated by samples from television themes and psychedelic and African chants. They secured a hit almost immediately with 'Wash Your Face In My Sink', and the success continued with 'My Definition Of A Boombastic Jazz Style', derived from a Quincy Jones television theme tune. They also charted when they moved into reggae with 'Ludi' in 1991 (Ludi is a West Indian board game), and they worked with jazz legend Slim Gaillard shortly before his death the same year. The follow-up album attempted the same fusion of jazz and hip-hop, and also introduced spoken word.
● ALBUMS: *And Now The Legacy Begins* (4th & Broadway 1991)★★★★, *Subliminal Simulation* (EMI Canada 1994)★★★.

DRIZABONE

Club trio from the USA who made a big splash in 1991 with the 'Real Love' cut. In its aftermath many record companies sought to wave chequebooks at the group - 'Real Love' having first emerged on a white label 12-inch - but they held out until they received an album offer from Island Records. The success of 'Real Love' had taken Drizabone by suprise, and it was not until 1994 that their debut album arrived. At the time of the single, Drizabone consisted of mainstays Vincent Garcia and Billy April plus vocalist Sophie Jones. She had performed the original demo versions of the song but was not really interested in a musical career. Dee Heron (b. Jamaica, West Indies) gave up her secretary's job to take over her role. However, she became the group's second casualty after a follow-up single, 'Catch The Fire'. Having decided that the latter's vocal range was too limited, the backroom duo spent several months auditioning for more suitable replacements, also filling their time by performing remix duties for Linda Layton ('Without You (One On One)'), Alison Limerick, Lisa Stansfield ('Change') and Shanice. They eventually met Atlanta, Georgia-based singer Kymberley Peer (b. Detroit, Michigan, USA), who had formerly worked with artists including Howard Hewitt and Freddie Jackson. She was also a partly established actress, having appeared alongside Marvin Winans and Vanessa Bell Armstrong in the musical *Don't Get Got Started*. She was on Drizabone's 'Pressure', which prefaced their long-awaited debut album.

● ALBUMS: *Conspiracy* (4th & Broadway 1995)★★★.

DRS

Their initials an acronym for 'Dirty Rotten Scoundrels', DRS were, predictably, a gangsta soul quintet. However, when Pic, Blunt, Endo, Deuce Deuce and Jail Bait finished with the hard-nosed rhymes, they offered a surprising, and by no means unwelcome, line in close harmony a cappella. Their early inroads into the R&B charts were credited largely to this; it was something of a novelty to hear such down-and-dirty reality tales sung rather than spat out. Based in Los Angeles, their debut album took its title from the preferred burial mode of their local gangster homeboys. The production company associated with the album, Roll Wit It Entertainment, boasted Hammer as a silent partner.

● ALBUMS: *Gangsta Lean* (Capitol 1993)★★★.

DRUG FREE AMERICA

Atmospheric Leeds, Yorkshire-based techno group who originally worked in a more funk-orientated vein for Blind Eye ('Throw A Crazy Shape', 'Day-Glo Pussycat', 'Heaven Ain't High Enough') and Concrete Productions ('Just Like Daddy's Gun') between 1988 and 1990. Afterwards the group - Brian Moss and Steve Dixon - split to travel around the globe. They reunited in 1991, along with female vocalist Goochie, and signed to York's Cybersound label, releasing 'Can You Feel' and 'Loud Everybody'. Moss had formerly worked with Soft Cell on their debut album and was also a member of Vicious Pink.

● ALBUMS: *Trip - The Dreamtime Remixes* (Dreamtime 1994)★★★.

DRUM CLUB

The Drum Club, named after a Sunderland nightspot that imported Balearic beat in 1983, and more recently Charlie Hall's own club night, comprised the duo of Lol Hammond (b. 7 January 1960, Stoke Newington, London, England) and Hall (b. 25 October 1959, Whitstable, Kent, England). The latter, self-effacing both on stage and off, and a former book reviewer for the *Catholic Herald*, was nevertheless perceived as the group's creative lynchpin. Before the Drum Club he was already a well-known London club DJ, and had also played in rock/pop bands the Apaches and London Cowboys. Hammond, meanwhile, had been part of the many and varied line-ups of Spizz (Spizz Oil, Athletico Spizz, etc.). The Drum Club's first recording arrived via the Spiral Tribe label in March 1992. 'U Make Me Feel So Good' was an instant club classic, and was re-released a few months later on the Guerilla Records imprint. A follow-up, 'Alchemy', was similarly well received. In the meantime, the Drum Club were becoming a favoured remixing stable, a variety of musicians seeking out their talents. These included Jah Wobble's Invaders Of The Heart, Meat Beat Manifesto, Psychick Warriors Ov Gaia and would-be progressive indie outfits Curve and Chapterhouse. Most notable, however, was their work on Killing Joke's alternative dancefloor staple, 'Change'. In addition to their studio wizardry, the duo were also keen to 'play out', making their debut at the Ministry Of Sound, London, in October 1992. Steve Hillage and Emma Anderson from Lush later guested on their live dates. Anderson also contributed guitar to *Everything Is Now*, and recorded a 1993 single, 'Stray', with the Drum Club, under the name Never Never. It was Hall who came up with the idea of the MIDI circus (to rival rock's Lollapalooza touring phenomenon), which also featured Orbital, Aphex Twin, Underworld, etc. By the time of their debut album they had moved on to Big Life Records, signifying the very real commercial status open to their mesmeric, shimmering music. The venue, The Drum Club, closed its doors on 30 June 1994, with farewell appearances from Fabio Paris, Justin Robertson, Billy Nasty and others. The Drum Club themselves would finally disintegrate in the early months of 1996. Hammond had contacted Hall in advance of projected sessions in Ireland for a fourth studio album, explaining that his commitments to the Slab project with Nina Walsh of Sabrettes precluded him from taking part. Hall was happy to end the collaboration, commenting to the press that 'I've ended up doing more sparse, minimal house and techno, while Lol has gone on to, dare I say it, the next fashionable thing.' Hall himself chose to concentrate instead on his MC Projects record label, whose releases include those by Phlex (his own pseudonym) and a remix of Consolidated's *This Is Fascism* album.

● ALBUMS: *Everything Is Now* (Butterfly 1993)★★★, *Drums Are Dangerous* (Butterfly 1994)★★★.

DUB FEDERATION

MERC recording artists whose career with that label saw the release of 'Space Funk' and 'Love Inferno'. The group, which split at the beginning of 1994, comprised Andy Ellison, Pete Latham and the surname-less Elton. After the band's demise Ellison and Latham would go on to work alongside David Holmes as part of the Scubadevils (who recorded a track for the *Trance Europe Express* compilation), while Elton relocated to Scotland, before guesting alongside the Grid on their UK television appearances on *Top Of The Pops* for 'Swamp Thing'.

DUB SYNDICATE

An On U Sound UK offshoot that Adrian Sherwood has used as a flag of convenience for various collaborations. The debut Dub Syndicate cassette, for example, saw contributions from Aswad, Roots Radics and Creation Rebel, while their 1993 LP, *Echomania*, included credits for U-Roy, Lee Scratch Perry, Akabu and Michael Franti. The group had previously made their name as dancefloor dub reggae/bass heavy tunesmiths, fostered under Sherwood's watchful eye. Personnel were recruited as the need arose: their *Vol. 2* selection was given focus by the voice of Andy Fairley, who also appeared on the 'Lack Of Education' single. More recent material has included ethnic chants and mantras, a nod to the global ambient school of club music.

● ALBUMS: *One Way System* (ROIR 1983)★★★, *Tunes From The Missing Channel* (On-U-Sound 1985)★★★, *Pounding System* (On-U-Sound 1988)★★★, *Classic Selection Vol. 1* (On-U-Sound 1989)★★★, *Strike The Balance* (On-U-Sound 1990)★★★, *Classic Selection Vol. 2* (On-U-Sound 1991)★★★, *Echomania* (On-U-Sound 1993)★★★★.

DUKE BOOTEE

b. Edward Fletcher. Bootee was formerly a New Jersey schoolteacher in Newark until the East Coast rap bug hit. As part of the Sugarhill house band/retinue, he wrote the chorus and several sections of 'The Message'. He also contributed to 'Message II', 'New York, New York' and sundry other label hits. His debut solo album comprised a rap side and a song side, with the former seeing further assistance from old Sugarhill friends. Though the song side was disappointing, he proved himself a talented rapper and maintained his reputation as an accomplished lyricist.

● ALBUMS: *Bust Me Out* (Mercury 1984)★★★.

DUST BROTHERS

One of the pre-eminent remix/production teams of the 90s, the Dust Brothers comprise radio disc jockeys Mike Simpson and John King, who first came to prominence with Matt Dike of the Delicious Vinyl label. In addition to fostering the career of Delicious Vinyl's major acts (Tone Loc, Young MC, etc.), they also afforded Mellow Man Ace and the Beastie Boys (1989's groundbreaking *Paul's Boutique*), among others, their skills and expertise. The Beastie Boys' album introduced their pioneering cut-and paste sampling technique, which in time saw them become among the most sought-after producers/remixers in music. There was some confusion when a UK-based duo sought to use the same name for their recordings, but when Dike and his colleagues objected, the other group became the Chemical Brothers. The original Dust Brothers subsequently worked with acts as diverse as Technotronic, Shonen Knife, Hanson (1997's UK/US chart-topping single 'MmmBop'), Beck (1996's highly acclaimed *Odelay*) and the Rolling Stones (tracks on *Bridges To Babylon*). They set up their own label, Nickel Bag, in 1996.

DYNAMETRIX

This London, England-based hip-hop trio comprised producer Ace Shazamme and rappers 0026 and the Phantom. Formed in the early 90s, their central appeal was the intoxicating beats and rhythms designed by Shazamme, including both 70s funk grooves and samples drawn from television and radio as well as the Doors. However, for many critics this served as scant compensation for misogynist lyrics conveyed by the group's MCs. Signed by emergent London rap label Kold Sweat, they released their debut album, *A Measure Of Force*, in 1994.

● ALBUMS: *A Measure Of Force* (Kold Sweat 1994)★★.

E-40

b. San Francisco, California, USA. Considered a natural successor to Too Short's reductionist thematic with his glorification of the 'player' hip-hop lifestyle, E-40 started his own independent label, Sic-Wid-It Records, in the Bay area of San Francisco in 1990. He enjoyed immediate success with records such as 'Captain Save A Hoe', 'Sprinkle Me' and 'Ballin' Out Of Control', which all featured his trademark stop-start delivery and the inclusion of heavy regional slang such as 'scrilla' (money) and 'broccoli' (marijuana). By 1994 and *In A Major Way* (which included 'Sprinkle Me'), he had signed a major distribution deal with Jive Records. Having sold over half a million copies of this record, the subsequent *The Hall Of Game* set was given a major international push. With producers including Studio Tone, Ant Banks and Rick Rock of the Cosmic Shop, the musical climate was more relaxed and smoother than had previously been the case. The first single from the album, 'Rapper's Ball', was a typical example, being an updated version of Too Short's 1987 single, 'Playboy Short'. This new version featured Too Short as well as Jodeci's K-Ci. Other highlights included 'On The One', featuring L'il Bruce, Digital Underground's Money B and Da Funk Mob's G-Note, and 'Things'll Never Change'. This reinterpreted Bruce Hornsby's 'That's The Way It Is' with a contribution from E-40's eight-year-old son, Li'l E.
● ALBUMS: *Mr Flamboyant* (Sic-Wid-It 1991)★★★, *In A Major Way* (Sic-Wid-It/Jive 1994)★★★★, *The Hall Of Game* (Sic-Wid-It/Jive 1996)★★★.

E-LUSTRIOUS

E-Lustrious comprises the Manchester duo Mike 'E-Bloc' Kirwin (nicknamed after the famed Eastern Bloc record shop at which he works) and Danny 'Hybrid' Bennett. Kirwin is among the north of England's most popular DJs, though his profile has been lessened by his refusal to attend events in the nation's capital. After learning the tuba at school he progressed to sundry hopeful punk bands such as Bastard Antelopes. Bennett, meanwhile, grew up on breakdancing and break-beats, and was an early scratch DJ. They began working together at the end of the 80s, when Kirwin and then fellow Eastern Bloc co-worker Justin Robertson planned to record a single. Bennett was hauled in due to his having access to rudimentary recording equipment. Though the track was never completed, Bennett and Kirwin continued as a duo. Their first major success came as the men behind the Direkt single, 'I Got The Feeling', which enjoyed a curious germination. *Mixmag Update* magazine invented a white label record entitled 'I Got Ya' by Direckt, giving it a magnicent review in order to gauge the reaction. As thousands assailed their local dance counters in the hope of finding this invisible disc, few noticed that Direckt was an anagram of 'Tricked'. When the scam was revealed the enterprising E-Lustrious made the most of the furore by hijacking the name for 'I Got The Feeling', enjoying instant record sales and notoriety. They have gone on to establish their own record label, UFG, which has subsequently housed tunes from the Luvdup Twins ('Good Time') and material from DJ EFX And Digit and DJ Tandoori. Under their principal name, E-Lustrious, they have established themselves with the success of 'Dance No More'. Just as notable was their second single as Direckt, 'Two Fatt Guitars', a fabulous piece of digifunk that became a party standard in 1993. They also record as Rolling Gear ('I've Got It').

EARTH NATION

This German ambient/new age rock project, masterminded by studio experts Markus Deml and Ralf Hildenbeutel, was released in 1994 on the Eye Q Records label. Hildenbeutel had already earned his reputation in the ambient dance community as co-producer to Eye Q founder Sven Vath. Deml was a guitarist and had worked with a number of rock bands. These diverse influences were channelled into their debut album, featuring meshed guitar and voices underpinned by a hypnotic, shifting backbeat. Their debut single, 'Alienated', quickly established an audience in the trance clubs of Europe.
● ALBUMS: *Thoughts In Past Future* (Eye Q/Warners 1994)★★★.

EARTHLING

Originating in London, England, in late 1994, Earthling, along with the Mo' Wax Records roster, Portishead and Tricky, were a core element of the new wave of 'trip hop' cross-genre experimentation. Led by rapper Mau (b. 1969, Ilford, Essex, England), the group's '1st Transmission' single for Cooltempo Records married the requisite dub rhythms with languid, occasionally inspired lyrics. It followed on from their debut white label 12-inch, 'Nothing', which won them their recording contract. The resultant album featured extended dub/jazz passages, courtesy of musical collaborator and former BBC kitchen staffer Tim Saul. Mau employed these as an anchor for his highly imaginative lyrics, which he stated are influenced as much by Leonard Cohen as conventional rap sources. The subject matter included issues as diverse as alcohol, news trivia, psychedelia and space travel, all related in cut and paste, stream of consciousness narratives. The release of 'Nefisa' later in the year provided the second great single to be associated with the album.

● ALBUMS: *Radar* (Cooltempo 1995)★★★.

EAST END

A UK-based remix team of the mid-90s who have closely protected their identity. However, it is known that they are a 'UK record company boss', 'an engineer who's worked on Eric Clapton and Phil Collins albums' and two A&R men. Their client list includes artists such as Dina Carroll, Judy Cheeks, Eternal and Pauline Henry. East End was unfortunately set up to remix dance music in a commercial manner, with the participants tired of the esoteric and wholly unmarketable remixes offered to their clients by 'name' producers.

EASTERN BLOC

Famed as the north of England's premier record shop, Eastern Bloc's in-house Creed imprint launched 808 State, K Klass, Ariel and Justin Robertson, The latter and Mike E-Bloc (see E-Lustrious) worked together on the counter before pursuing their own musical careers. Creed was brought under the generic MOS label banner in 1991 (MOS standing for More O' Same). Eastern Bloc inaugurated its own brand label in 1993. Peter Waterman (of Stock, Aitken And Waterman fame) was the unlikely purchaser of the establishment when it ran into financial difficulties. He then placed DJ and club owner Peter Taylor in charge of proceedings, with a brief to record strong, commercial dance music. Taylor had formerly worked with Waterman as part of the PWL set-up, notably remixing Kylie Minogue's 'Keep It Pumping'. He also runs the Angels club in Burnley, Lancashire. The label's first release was a licensed track, 'Waterfall', by Atlantic Ocean, the second, 'She', by Ideal - Manchester DJs Jon Dasilva and A.G. Scott. However, it was the 'Loveland Saga' that earned their biggest headlines. A band of that title, affiliated to Eastern Bloc, released their version of Darlene Lewis's 'Let The Music (Lift You Up)' without obtaining sample clearance. A legal tussle ensued, until both parties agreed to release a joint version, performing together on *Top Of The Pops*.

EAT STATIC

During the 80s, while they were performing with the Ozric Tentacles, Merv Pepler and Joie Hinton were inspired to start writing dance music after coming into contact with acts such as the Mutoid Waste Company at festivals and parties. They began by recording 'three weird acid house tracks' with the engineer Steve Everett and were soon performing live at Ozrics gigs. During the early 90s they developed their live shows at many of the legendary 'orbital' raves and free parties, as well as releasing three singles and a cassette album, *Prepare Your Spirit*, on their own Alien Records. In 1993, as a result of their connection with the Megadog parties, Eat Static signed to Planet Dog Records and released the *Lost In Time* EP, followed by the albums *Abduction* and *Implant*. These albums featured the group's unique brand of psychedelic electronic music which, while showing the influence of techno, trance, ambient and other dance styles, never simply regurgitated established formulae. They were as happy with straight four-on-the-floor beats (e.g., 'Prana' and 'Implant') as they were with more breakbeat-like grooves ('Abnormal Interference' and 'Dzhopa Dream'). Many of their titles were sci-fi and space-orientated, about which they commented: 'We can't take techno as seriously as some purists do so we've coated it in this sci-fi motif. And we're mad for all that anyway.' Over the next few years they performed live and released a number of EPs that pursued their eclectic sound, notably 'Dionysiac' (on the *Epsylon* EP), which combined an eastern-influenced string melody with ele-

ments of dub and drum 'n' bass. 'Bony Incus' (1996) included collaborations with Andy Guthrie and a remix by Man With No Name, while 'Hybrid' (1997) featured remixes by Yum Yum and Dave Angel. Towards the end of 1997 Eat Static released the single 'Intercepter' and the album *Science Of The Gods*, which proved to be their most focused and adventurous work to date. While presenting a kind of psychedelic drum 'n' bass on such tracks as 'Interceptor', 'Dissection' and 'Bodystealers', Pepler and Hinton often vary the grooves and textures throughout a track, notably 'Science Of The Gods' and 'Kryll' (a collaboration with Tangerine Dream's Steve Joliffe), thereby structuring and developing their music in a manner unlike the variations-on-a-groove approach of much dance music. With their unique, eclectic sound, attention to detail and outrageous production skills, Eat Static have gained the respect of a number of different camps in an increasingly fickle and narrow-minded dance music community. Their broad-minded attitude predicted the trend towards mixing styles that developed in the late 90s.
● ALBUMS: *Abduction* (Planet Dog 1993)★★★, *Implant* (Planet Dog 1994)★★★, *Science Of The Gods* (Planet Dog 1997)★★★★.

EAZY-E
b. Eric Wright, 7 September 1963, Compton, California, USA, d. 26 March 1995. There are those critics who did not take well to Eazy-E's 'whine', but his debut kept up NWA's momentum by managing to offend just about every imaginable faction, right and left. Attending a fundraising dinner for the Republican party and having lunch with police officer Tim Coon, one of the LAPD's finest charged with the beating of Rodney King, hardly helped to re-establish his hardcore credentials. His work as part of NWA, and as head of Ruthless Records (which he founded in 1985 allegedly with funds obtained from drug dealing) had already made him a household name. However, as a solo performer his raps lacked penetration, even if the musical backdrop was just as intense as that which distinguished NWA. His debut solo album contained a clean and dirty side. The first was accomplished with very little merit, cuts such as 'We Want Eazy' being self-centered and pointless. The 'street' side, however, offered something much more provocative and nasty. His ongoing bitter rivalry against former NWA member Dr. Dre has pro-

vided much of his lyrical subject matter, including his 1994 single, 'Real Muhaphukkin' G's', which was essentially a rewrite of Dre's 'Dre Day'. Ruthless also released an EP, *It's On (Dr. Dre 187UM) Killa*, in the same year. Eazy-E subsequently moved on to production for artists including Tairrie B and Blood Of Abraham. Having been a pivotal figure of gangsta rap, he succumbed to AIDS and died through complications following a collapsed lung after having been hospitalized for some time.
● ALBUMS: *Eazy-Duz-It* (Ruthless/Priority 1988)★★★, *Str.8 Off The Streetz Of Muthaphukkin' Compton* (Ruthless 1995)★★★.

ED.OG AND DA BULLDOGS
Boston, Massachusetts-based hip-hop duo who debuted with the singles 'Be A Father To Your Child' and 'I Got To Have It'. The latter, with its engaging horn lick, was quickly pilfered as a sample by many other artists, becoming the number 1 hit in *Billboard*'s Hot Rap chart. 'Be A Father To Your Child' was also widely revered for its strong moral sentiments. DJ Cruz and Ed.Og (b. Edward Anderson, Roxbury, Massachusetts, USA) are the main cogs in Da Bulldogs, who followed up the singles by cutting a well-regarded debut album. Samples from the set have been repeatedly recycled by other hip-hop artists, notably Heavy D. Anderson's lyrics span tales of the street and take on his own sexual chemistry, as advertised on the promotional singles for their second long-playing set, 'Skinny Dip (Got It Goin' On)' and 'Love Comes And Goes'. The latter was dedicated to those lost in street violence, who include Anderson's father. With production expertise thrown in by Joe 'Rhythm Nigga' Mansfield, Diamond D and the Awesome 2 (Special K and Teddy Tedd), it proved a certain east coast hit. The Ed.Og acronym stands for Everyday Day, Other Girls, while the Bulldogs suffix represents Black United Leaders Living Directly On Groovin' Sounds.
● ALBUMS: *Life Of A Kid In The Ghetto* (Chemistry/Mercury 1991)★★★, *Roxbury 02119* (Chemistry/Mercury 1994)★★★.

EDWARDS, SCOTT
Bristol, England-based electronic musician who, though he has never DJed, has become in the mid-90s a name on the dance circuit through his experimental approach. Recording for Out Of Orbit, a subsidiary of Italian label ACV (Annibaldi,

Armani, etc.), his work reveals a stylistic debt to the Detroit techno godfathers: 'There's nothing pretentious about what I do, it's just that I have ideas which are a little different to most other people. I'm not making music which says "take ecstasy all the time". I'm trying to think beyond that.'

● ALBUMS: *Distant Horizons* (Out Of Orbit 1994)★★★.

EFX AND DIGIT

San Francisco-based EFX (b. Raul Recinos) began his career in the early 90s overseeing the decks at funk and hip-hop parties, also playing hi-NRG in gay clubs by night. His partner, Digit (b. Jeremy Cowan), took an active role in a succession of funk and ska bands, and was a DJ at Powerplant in Chicago when that city experienced its famous house revolution. After meeting at a record shop they steadily built a reputation with their releases, which kicked off on Strictly Rhythm with two records as Politix Of Dancing. These were followed with a solo EFX record, 'Is It Like My Dil-Doe', before they reunited as Killa Green Buds. They were gradually invited into the lucrative world of remixing (although EFX complains of several unpaid invoices), often under the name Third Floor Productions. After a breakthrough rebuilding Rozalla's 'Everybody's Free', further big names followed, including Sting ('Demolition Man'), Deep Forest ('Sweet Lullaby') and even *Beavis And Butthead*, the MTV cartoon characters. They also produced a welter of productions for the N-Fusion label, before that was succeeded by their own operation, Freshly Squeezed. Credited with being the harbingers of musical movements such as San Trancedisco or San Frandisko, their style remains relentlessly buoyant, happy house.

EGE BAM YASI

b. *c*.1958, Edinburgh, Scotland. Mr Egg is a bald Scot and former plumber who took the name for his techno operation from a Can album. The group began as a band back in the mid-80s, touring a tacky cabaret show with onstage S&M and a papier mâché penis that squirted shaving foam. Despite such antics, he built his reputation with a series of increasingly successful acid tracks. These include the *Indigestion* EP (1991) and 'Highblow' (Groove Kissing 1991), though the then-group's career had first begun way back in 1986 with 'Circumstances' on Survival. His mini-album, *Ex Ovo Omnia* (meaning 'everything comes from the egg' in Latin), was released on Finitribe's Finiflex imprint, and included such delights as 'The Good, The Bad And The Acid'. It was distinguished by the fact that all the effects were played live, without the use of either a sampler or DAT machine. He uses his new-found fortunes to invest in vast quantities of his chosen passion: eggs. He has continued to develop his talents as a remixer for the likes of the Fugues ('Sensityzed').

● ALBUMS: *Ex Ovo Omnia* mini album (Finiflex 1994)★★★.

EGG

The Egg were formed in the UK from a conglomeration of various Oxford-based dub-influenced dance acts. The group consisted of Dave Gaydon (bass), Mark Revell (guitar) and twin brothers Maff Scott (drums) and Ned Scott (keyboards). They developed a unique sound combining hip-hop, psychedelia, ambient and house, resulting in what has been described as a 'fluid trance groove'. In 1995 they recorded their debut EP, *The Shopping*, through the iconoclastic Bristol-based Cup Of Tea Records. The release was greeted with critical acclaim, which resulted in the initial pressing selling out within two weeks. They maintained a high profile with notable performances at the Glastonbury and Phoenix festivals. By 1996 the group secured a contract with Indochina Records who endorsed the band's 11-track opus *Albumen*, which was co-produced by Joe Gibb. They continued performing on the live circuit throughout Europe and the USA, where the band made an appearance at the prestigious South X South West Festival. Beyond the music was the Egg's visual presentation, wherein the group dressed in white and performed as human cinema screens, with films and pictures being projected onto their outfits. In a review of their show, *Melody Maker* described the event as 'instant psychedelia meets Aunt Harriet's home movies'. The band achieved further notoriety when they performed a benefit gig for the people of the remote Scottish Isle Of Eigg on Glasgow's Renfrew Ferry, to help the residents to buy the island from an apathetic proprietor. Through to 1997 the band released the underground hit 'Bend', which featured a Steve Hillage sample, performed with Moby alongside Jah Wobble, and relished a triumphant appearance at the Third Post Apartheid Festival. The band were also engrossed in studio work remixing and subsequently releasing their second album. A UK tour featuring their unique stage presentation was arranged to promote the follow-up.

● ALBUMS: *Albumen* (Indochina 1996)★★★, *Get Some Mixes Together* (Indochina 1997)★★★★.

8 BALL RECORDS

New York, US record label famous for its mellow approach to house music, with offices on the 12th floor of a building in the Chelsea district of Manhattan. The label was established in 1991 by Alex Kaplan, then a video-maker, who still leads the company in association with A&R head Kevin Williams, a veteran of the New York club scene. It was Kaplan who recorded the label's debut single, Napoleon-Soul O's 'Come On Girl', a jazzy, funky house tune that set out 8 Ball's stall. Artists and producers were subsequently recruited and acquired by word of mouth. As well as stalwarts such as Williams' sister Joie Cardwell ('Goodbye', 'If We Try', 'Trouble') and Lectroluv (Fred Jorio), the label is equally famous for its T-shirt and merchandising, its emblem being among the most popular in the UK. Other prominent recordings arrived from African Dream, Groove Thing, Wall Of Sound, Screamin' Rachael, and Mack Vibe's 'I Can't Let You Go' (Al Mack, who had previously recorded as the Al Mack Project for Strictly Rhythm). 8 Ball also runs the Empire State deep house subsidiary label, and has its own record store in Greenwich Village. Kaplan returned to video-making by launching his own compilation video series.

808 STATE

Manchester's finest dance combo of the late 80s/early 90s, comprising Martin Price (b. 26 March 1955), owner of the influential Eastern Bloc record shop, Graham Massey (b. 4 August 1960, Manchester, Lancashire, England; ex-Beach Surgeon; Danny And The Dressmakers; Biting Tongues), Darren Partington (b. 1 November 1969, Manchester, Lancashire, England) and Andy Barker (b. 2 November 1969, Manchester, Lancashire, England). The latter two had already worked together as DJ double act the Spin Masters. Massey had previously worked in a café opposite the Eastern Bloc shop, while Partington and Barker had been regular visitors to the premises, proffering a variety of tapes in the hope of securing a contract with Price's Creed label. Together with Gerald Simpson, they began recording together as a loose electro house collec-

tive, and rose to prominence at the end of 1989 when their single, 'Pacific State', became a massive underground hit. It proved to be a mixed blessing for the band, however, as they were lumped in with the pervading Manchester indie dance boom (which they themselves despised). *Newbuild* and *Quadrastate* helped to establish them as premier exponents of UK techno dance, leading to a lucrative deal with ZTT Records. However, Simpson had left to form his own A Guy Called Gerald vehicle, and launched a series of attacks on the band in the press concerning unpaid royalties. *Ex:El* featured the vocals of New Order's Bernard Sumner on 'Spanish Heart', and then-Sugarcube Björk Gudmundsdottir on 'Oops' (also a single) and 'Qmart'. They also worked with Mancunian rapper MC Tunes on the album *North At Its Heights* and several singles. In October 1991 Price declined to tour the USA with the band, electing to work on solo projects instead, including managing Rochdale rappers the Kaliphz, and his own musical project, Switzerland. 808 State persevered with another fine album in 1993, which again saw a new rash of collaborations. Featured this time were Ian McCulloch (Echo And The Bunnymen) adding vocals to 'Moses', and samples from the Jam's 'Start', UB40's 'One In Ten' and even *Star Wars*' Darth Vader. Massey occupied himself with co-writing Björk's 'Army Of Me' single and other material on *Post*. Martin Price departed after being much sought after as a remixer (David Bowie, Shamen, Primal Scream, Soundgarden and many more). *Don Solaris* finally arrived after a gap of four years.

● ALBUMS: *Newbuild* (Creed 1988)★★★, *Quadrastate* (Creed 1989)★★★, *808:90* (Creed 1989)★★★★, with MC Tunes *North At Its Heights* (ZTT 1990)★★★, *Ex:El* (ZTT 1991)★★★, *Gorgeous* (Warners 1992)★★★, *Don Solaris* (ZTT 1996)★★★.

EIGHT RECORDS

Liverpool, England record label formed by the trio of Ian Wright, Peter Coyle and Steve Cummersome. They first started working together in 1989, originally envisioning licensing their work to the majors. Their debut, Morina Van Rooy's 'Sly One', was consequently placed on DeConstruction Records, but the trio soon decided to set up their own company. Since its inception, Eight Records has specialized in matching strong house tunes with unusual vocal-

ists. Among the best examples of this have been Connie Lush, a local pub blues singer ('Shame'), Van Rooy ('Sly One') and G Love (DJ John Kelly) featuring Jayne Casey's 'You Keep The Love', in 1991 (Casey was the former Pink Military/Pink Industry chanteuse). G Love is also the name of the club the trio run in association with Liverpool's other leading label, 3 Beat. Coyne, formerly of Lotus Eaters, also records on the label as Coloursex (*Deep And Devastating* EP).
● COMPILATIONS: *Give Love* (Eight 1991)★★★.

ELECTRIBE 101

Electro-dance band centred around the voice of female vocalist Billie Ray Martin (b. Hamburg, Germany). She moved to Berlin in the hope of setting up an R&B band with 60s influences, especially the Motown sound. However, following several unsuccessful attempts she moved to London in 1985. Two years later she met Joe Stevens, Les Fleming, Rob Cimarosti and Brian Nordhoff and formed Electribe 101. Their first two singles, 'Talking With Myself' and 'Tell Me When The Fever Ended', were instant hits with the acid generation and Martin's voice drew comparisons with Marlene Dietrich and Aretha Franklin. Despite the acclaim, Electribe 101 broke up shortly afterwards, with Martin pursuing a solo career, while the others formed Groove Corporation. Martin's 'Your Loving Arms', taken from *Deadline For My Memories*, was a major club hit and went on to reach number 6 in the UK charts in May 1995.
● ALBUMS: *Electribal Memories* (Mercury 1990)★★★.
Solo: Billie Ray Martin *Deadline For My Memories* (WEA 1995)★★★.

ELECTRO

Started by Afrika Bambaataa's 'Planet Rock', electro music was first heard in the USA in the early 80s and harnassed the video game craze and attendant appetite for electronica and tied it to a computerized beat. For some time it became *the* sound of hip-hop. In the wake of 'Planet Rock', rap's journeymen, new and old alike, hitched themselves to the bandwagon, as releases such as 'Magic Wand' (Whodini), 'Play At Your Own Risk' (Planet Patrol) and 'Hip-hop Be Bop (Don't Stop)' (Man Parrish) testify. More conventional dance music, too, was heavily influenced by these new techniques, notably the Peach Boys and D-Train. It took Bambaataa, however, to equal 'Planet Rock', when he unveiled 'Looking For The Perfect Beat'. Although electro held sway on the rap scene for a surprising length of time, it was blown away quickly and irrevocably with the arrival of Run DMC in the mid-80s and their more robust approach.

ELEVATE

Elevate are one of a clutch of Scandinavian bands formed to emulate the Euro house success of artists such as Ace Of Base and Dr. Alban. Comprising Yvette Palm (vocals), Stefan Bosson (vocals) and Robert Ahlin (keyboards), they made their debut in 1993 with a single, 'Easy To Believe', released on Virgin Records. Finding substantial popularity on the German club scene, it propelled the Stockholm, Sweden-based group to the top of many critics' tip sheets by the end of the year.
● ALBUMS: *The Architect* (Flower Shop 1996)★★★.

11:59

This Ladbroke Grove, London, England duo of DJ Daniel X and rapper Gian Carlo Morroco, formed when X heard Morroco chatting a reggae lyric, 'My Ambitions To Kill Mr Botha', at a blues party in 1987. Together they signed to Virgin Records subsidiary From A Whisper To A Scream, releasing two critically acclaimed singles, '3 A.M.' and 'Digi', the latter utilizing the O'Jays' 'For The Love Of Money' as the musical foundation for an anti-stardom rap. Despite the interest generated, Virgin soon pulled the plug on the label, and 11:59 elected to form their own Ticking Time imprint instead. Two more underground EPs followed, before they signed a licensing deal with China Records in 1994 because, as Gian states: 'As far as I'm concerned the whole UK underground rap scene is a dead-end road. A lot of us don't make the record companies want to know'. Daniel X took the argument further: 'White rock bands get a three album deal, massive advance, buy a house, chill out, set up a studio in the garage, and make music. There's no rap or soul example of that in this country. They'll back East 17 - now they're the biggest rap band in the country. UB40 are the biggest reggae band. Mick Hucknall is the biggest soul artist . . . what do you think it all means?'. 1995's 'Trouble On My Mind' was inspired by poverty and its frustrations, though Daniel X did at least have some property to his name, in the shape of a part-ownership of a hairdressing salon in Soho. Live they utilized a series of loops with live trumpet to produce a sound that offered a soulful counterbalance to the trio's hard, politicized diatribes.

ELLIOTT, MISSY

b. 1972, Portsmouth, Virginia, USA. Hip-hop/R&B songwriter Missy 'Misdemeanor' Elliott has become one of the most esteemed composers in the New York 90s hip-hop firmament, providing material for artists including MC Lyte, Adina Howard and Jodeci, as well as working as an arranger, producer and talent scout. Elliott first performed as part of a neighbourhood singing group, Sista, who were signed up by DeVante from Jodeci in 1992. Elliott was already writing with her long-time collaborator, Tim Mosley aka Timbaland, and with Sista's career terminally stalled (DeVante would not release any of their recordings) she concentrated on songwriting and production. Her distinctive 'hee haw' rap on Gina Thompson's 'The Things You Do' brought her wider exposure, and several offers from record companies. Fiercely independent and ambitious, Elliott signed to Elektra Records as a solo artist on the understanding that they would subsidise her own label, Gold Mind Records. In 1997, she launched her solo career with the album *Supa Dupa Fly* and attendant single 'The Rain (Supa Dupa Fly)'. The well-connected Elliott was provided with immediate exposure for the song via rotation play of its Hype Williams-directed video on MTV. Co-produced with long-time collaborator Timbaland and producer DJ Magic, the album received excellent reviews, though Elliott was reluctant to commit herself fully to a career as a performer: 'I don't want to get caught up and be an artist always on the go, because once you do that, it's hard to get into the studio and do what I do.' The album also featured cameo appearances from Aaliyah and Busta Rhymes (Elliott has written songs for both). Despite her growing reputation and success, Elliott is still based in her home-town in Virginia, where she lives with her mother. In September 1998 she collaborated with Melanie B from the Spice Girls on the one-off single, 'I Want You Back'.
● ALBUMS: *Supa Dupa Fly* (East West 1997)★★★.

EMERSON, DARREN

Also half of Underworld and Lemon Interrupt, Emerson is a very active and highly visible mid-90s DJ, who became a fan of electro as a 14-year-old, at which time he also bought his first decks.

He was in place for the rise of acid house, spinning at clubs in Southend, Essex, England, before emerging as a real talent at venues including the Limelight and Milky Bar. Stylistically his modern tastes favour trance and European hard house. His remixes include Simply Red's 'Thrill Me', Gat Decors' 'Passion', Björk's 'Human Behaviour' and Shakespears Sister's 'Hey You (Turn Up Your Radio)' and 'Black Sky'.

EMOTIVE RECORDS

New York dance label founded in January 1990 when their debut release was licensed from an Italian label. Emotive is one of the new breed of hip US imprints that have emerged in the 90s. Generally the label creed has been to promote new names and talent on their schedule, while the style encompasses garage and house in its myriad forms. The first release came from Toronto artist Matt Di Mario (M1's 'Feel The Drums', the same artist going on to release 'Dynamite' and the *Then And Now* EP for the label). He was joined by Smoke Signals ('I Want Your Love'), B-Town ('Weekend'), Insomnia ('I'll Be There'), Deep Expressions (*Deep Expressions* EP), Michael Lavel ('Do Me This Way') and Michael Ayres ('Share My Love'). James Howard's 'We Can Do It (Wake Up)' was arguably the biggest Emotive tune in its early stages, though Valerie Johnson's 'Step Into My Life' and 'Inside', and Jovonn's 'Out All Nite' were also key releases. The latter was the first 'established' artist on the roster, and ran his own Goldtone imprint through the parent label. The second James Howard release would be 'Feeling Good', again created by label mainstay Charles Dockins (who also contributed to Bobby Konders Jus' Friends project on 'As One'). Other 1992 releases included Producers On Wax (DJ Romain Gowe and Matt 'Keys' Echols El) with 'Feel The Piano' and Karen Pollack ('You Can't Touch Me'). Further material from Project 4007 ('It's Our Turn') appeared as Emotive continued its ascendancy.

ENIGMA

Ambient pop sculptors Enigma are the brainchild of Michael Cretu (b. 18 May 1957, Bucharest, Romania), who enrolled in the Lyzeum No. 2, a college for gifted young musicians, as a pianist, in 1966. After completing his studies Cretu moved to the Academy Of Music in Frankfurt, where Professor Philipp Mohler began to take an interest in him. Having passed his final exams in 1978,

Cretu immediately found work as a studio musician and arranger. By 1980 he had earned his first significant success as producer, and he released his debut solo album, *Legionare*, three years later for Virgin Records. He was then the architect behind the 1985 number 1 European success of Moti Special as writer, producer and keyboard player. Afterwards he devoted many of his efforts to the rise of Sandra, including masterminding 'Maria Magdelana', a number 1 in over 30 countries, and several successful albums. Further Gold Record status arrived in 1987 for his production work with Mike Oldfield, and in France he helped revitalize the career of Sylvie Vartan by writing and producing 'C'est Fatale'. He married Sandra Lauer in 1988 before putting together his most commercially successful project, Enigma, two years later, stating that 'old rules and habits have to be rejected and dismissed so that something new can be created'. Enigma's Gregorian chants and dance rhythms subsequently enchanted nearly all who heard them, with the meditative repetition giving it universal appeal. 'Sadness Part 1' hit the UK number 1 spot in December 1990, leading Cretu, who had now turned his back on a prospective career as a concert pianist, to remark, 'I started writing hits the day I sold my piano.' Almost every movement of the accompanying *MCMXC AD* album, which also topped the charts and spent no less than 57 weeks on the UK list, was used in some form of television or film production. Gold or platinum status was attained in 25 countries. Film director Robert Evans then invited Cretu to compose the title song to the film *Sliver* and this resulted in the release of 'Carly's Song' and 'Carly's Loneliness'. With the phenomenal success of Enigma's debut, it was no surprise that the artist took a full three years to produce a follow-up. Although it had pre-orders of 1.4 million units, it was hardly the expected blockbuster. However, the debut of a single, 'Return To Innocence' reached number 9 in the UK charts in 1994 and demonstrated his enduring appeal to the record-buying public.
● ALBUMS: *MCMXC AD* (Virgin 1990)★★★★, *The Cross Of Changes* (Virgin 1993)★★★★, *Le Roi Est Mort, Vive Le Roi!* (Virgin 1996)★★★★.

ENJOY RECORDS

One of the earliest US record labels to promote hip-hop, Enjoy Records was owned by Bobby Robinson, whose background in R&B stretched back to 1946, when he ran the Happy House Records' store. He elected to pursue a career in musical production when he realized that all the A&R men were coming to him for advice on what was marketable, and that he could cut out the middle man. Enjoy was actually inaugurated in 1963 with King Curtis's 'Soul Twist'. When rap arrived his Harlem-based operation was the first to record Grandmaster Flash And The Furious Five ('Superrappin') before their contract was bought out by Joe Robinson (not a relation, though an old sparring partner from R&B days) of Sugarhill Records. Other notable Enjoy releases included the Treacherous 3/Spoonie Gee's agenda-setting 'The New Rap Language'. 'Bodyrock' and 'Heartbeat' followed in 1981, before the Treacherous 3 also elected to join Sugarhill. Robinson's son was a member of the Disco Three, who also recorded on the label.

EON

Eon consists simply of Ian Loveday, whose interest in electronica and music was inspired by the theme to the BBC Television science-fiction programme *Dr Who*, which was created by the BBC radio workshop under the name Ray Cathode. Eon released a sequence of impressive singles: 'Light, Colour, Sound', 'Infinity', 'Inner Mind' (featured in the film *Buffy The Vampire Slayer*) and 'Spice'. The latter was remixed by Loveday's long-standing hero, Juan Atkins, and featured samples taken from the science-fiction epic *Dune*. He continued his association with Vinyl Solution for singles such as 1992's horror film-inspired 'Basket Case'.
● ALBUMS: *Void Dweller* (Vinyl Solution 1992)★★★.

EPMD

Erick 'E' Sermon (b. 25 November 1968, Brentwood, Long Island, New York, USA) and Parrish 'P' Smith (b. 13 May 1968, Brentwood, Long Island, New York, USA) are two rappers who did much to revitalize a flagging rap scene with an early outburst of controlled creative energy, *Unfinished Business*. Taking samples from rock sources such as Steve Miller, as well as underground dance music, they worked up a healthy, funk-fuelled groove. Particularly effective among their early recordings was the rap manifesto on 'So Whatcha Sayin'. Their early struggles to attract record company interest are best observed in the 1989 single, 'Please Listen To My Demo', which documents their malaise. By then, however, they

had recorded their first two albums. *Strictly Business* was distinguished by an idea for a new dance entitled 'The Steve Martin', while the fun continued on *Unfinished Business*, which in many ways sounded just like its title. Unrestrained anarchy in the studio appeared to be the order of the day, with improvised lines, interruptions and jokey singing forming the basis of proceedings. It included contributions from K-Solo (Kevin Madison), who had previously worked in a pre-EPMD band with Smith, and would go on to record a solo album under his tutelage They moved to Def Jam in time for their third album, a much more accomplished affair (at least musically) with tighter production and harder beats. Despite the prevailing ethos, they never felt the need to provide a direct political agenda like many rap groups, seeing music as a source of personal self-advancement. This is openly demonstrated by the titles of their LPs, and the fact that their initials stand for Erick And Parrish Making Dollars. However, the manner in which EPMD tried to accommodate new lyrical concerns was less than satisfactory. Their raps continued to chastise their peers as 'sucker MC's', which was by now little more than cliché. Ironically, one of the better cuts on *Business As Usual* was 'Rampage', a collaboration with LL Cool J, whose artistic fortunes had witnessed a similar decline in recent years. *Business Never Personal* simply continued in remorseless EPMD style. The duo split in 1993, Sermon being the first to embark on a solo career with 'Stay Real' and the *No Pressure* album. The latter's title reflected, wryly, on the fact that most considered Smith to be the 'talent' of the band. Yet *No Pressure* was an excellent collection that did much to lay that myth to rest. They reunited in 1997, releasing *Back In Business*, their first album of new material for five years.
● ALBUMS: *Strictly Business* (Fresh/Priority 1988)★★★★, *Unfinished Business* (Fresh/Priority 1989)★★★★, *Business As Usual* (Def Jam 1991)★★★, *Business Never Personal* (Def Jam 1992)★★, *Back In Business* (Def Jam 1997)★★.
Solo: Erick Sermon *No Pressure* (RAL 1993)★★★★. Parrish Smith *Shade Business* (PMD/RCA 1994)★★.

ERIC B AND RAKIM

This Queens, New York rap duo consisted of Eric Barrier (b. Elmhurst, New York, USA) and William 'Rakim' Griffin (b. William Griffin Jnr., Long Island, New York, USA), using additional musicians such as Sefton the Terminator and Chad Jackson as required. Rakim was the lyricist, Eric B the DJ, or, as Rakim himself put it in 'I Ain't No Joke': 'I hold the microphone like a grudge, Eric B hold the record so the needle don't budge'. They met in 1985 when Eric was working for the New York radio station WBLS and was looking for the city's top MC. They started working together before emerging with the demo, 'Eric B Is President'. Released as a single on an obscure Harlem independent, Zakia Records, in the summer of 1986, it eventually led to a deal with 4th And Broadway. Their long-playing debut was preceded by a stand-out single of the same name, 'Paid In Full', which inspired over 30 remixes. When the album arrived it caused immediate waves. Representatives of James Brown and Bobby Byrd took legal action over the sampling of those artists' works. Conversely, they helped to galvanize Brown's career as a legion of rap imitators drew on his back catalogue in search of samples. They also originated the similarly coveted 'Pump Up The Volume' sample. As well as Eric B putting the funk back into rap music, Rakim was responsible for introducing a more relaxed, intuitive delivery that was distinctly separate from the machismo of Run DMC and LL Cool J, and is probably the biggest single influence on current hip-hop artists such as Wu-Tang Clan, Nas and Dr. Dre.
The duo hit the UK charts in 1987 with 'Paid In Full (The Coldcut Remix)', though they themselves hated the version. Later hits included 'Move The Crowd', 'I Know You Got Soul', 'Follow The Leader' and 'The Microphone'. Label moves may have diminished their probable impact, though the band themselves never went out of their way to cross over into the mainstream. Instead, each of their albums offered a significant musical development on the last, Rakim's raps growing in maturity without sacrificing impact. The split came in the early 90s, with Rakim staying with MCA to deliver solo material like 'Heat It Up', produced by new co-conspirator Madness 4 Real, and included on the soundtrack to the Mario van Peebles vehicle, *Gunmen*.
● ALBUMS: *Paid In Full* (4th And Broadway 1987)★★★, *Follow The Leader* (MCA-Uni 1988)★★★, *Let The Rhythm Hit 'Em* (MCA 1990)★★★★, *Don't Sweat The Technique* (MCA 1992)★★★.

ESKIMOS AND EGYPT

This mid-90s group is a highly regarded, mellow groove coalition. Their name was originally invoked as a gesture in support of the Inuit people's struggle for their own homeland. The four-piece, Salford, Manchester-based band consists of Paul Cundall (b. 5 April 1963, Manchester, Lancashire, England; keyboards, sequencer), Christopher O'Hare (b. 13 October 1966, Manchester, Lancashire, England; vocals, keyboards), Mark Compton (b. 14 October 1963, Salford, Manchester, England) and David Pryde (b. David Cameron Pryde, 1967, Dublin, Eire). They made their vinyl debut in December 1987 with 'The Cold' on Village Records, shortly after appearing live for the first time at Manchester's Cloud Nine venue. After a succession of singles that built their dancefloor credentials, including the Axl Rose-slamming 'The Power Of G N'R', their breakthrough release came with the gangland-inspired 'US:UK' single. Typically, it was awash with sweet female harmonies, furious raps and a slice of rock guitar. Other singles such as 'Fall From Grace' followed, with remixes from Moby and the Beatmasters. However, by 1994 they had been dropped by One Little Indian Records (though the band itself insisted that they had walked).
● ALBUMS: *Perfect Disease* (One Little Indian 1993)★★★.

ESP

Leading Amsterdam techno record label with a release schedule featuring Nico, Ken Ishii (Rising Sun), Black Scorpion and Blake Baxter. The label was started in 1991 as the underground rave offshoot of Go Bang!, who had in turn scored hits with D-Shake, GTO and Turntable Hype. The ESP boss is Fred Berkhout, who describes the label's orientation as 'experimental'. Other artists on ESP include Orlando Voorn, who records as Format, the Nighttripper and the Ghetto Brothers (with Blake Baxter), Dr No No ('Paradise 3001') and Jeff Mills.

ESPIRITU

Latin-flavoured 90s dance duo from Brighton, Sussex, England, consisting of Vanessa Quinnones and Chris Taplin (ex-Frazier Chorus). Quinnones, half-Peruvian and half-French, grew up in an affluent suburb of Paris under the care of a South American nanny, whose name, Francisca,

was subsequently employed as the title of Espiritu's debut single in 1992. It was about her treatment at the hands of Quinnones' mother. The group's second single, 'Conquistador', was another slice of classy Latin dance. Its Andy Weatherall remix had originally taken the club scene by storm, with copies reaching extravagant prices of over £100, before the stock release arrived. Signed to Heavenly Records, the single was a continuation of the thoughtful approach to lyrics demonstrated by their debut. This time the subject was the exploitation of South American Indians in the name of civilization. A third single, 'Bonita Monana', continued the club/chart crossover in 1994.
● ALBUMS: *Espiritu Number One* (Heavenly 1997)★★★.

EUSEBE

One of a new wave of UK-based hip-hop acts in the mid-90s, London's Eusebe features rapper Steven Eusebe (Fatcat), sister Sharon (Saybe) and cousin Allison Ettienn (Noddy). Their debut came in 1994 with 'Pick It Up, Fuck It Up And Drop It', released on their own label, Mama's Yard. When Lee Haynes, A&R manager for EMI Records, signed them, he also took on board the Mama's Yard operation, a practice familiar in US rap circles but less so in Britain. Having briefly flirted with hip-hop with the Ruthless Rap Assassins, EMI's employment of Haynes (formerly at Wild Pitch Records in New York) signified a new recognition of the genre, with Eusebe an important first staging post in its attempts to update its roster. Two summer 1995 singles, 'Captain Of Love' and 'Summertime Healing', the latter sampling Marvin Gaye's 'Sexual Healing', were the first results of the partnership. Both showcased a mixed rap/singing approach in fully realized song structures, a distinct but commercial sound further refined on their debut album.
● ALBUMS: *Tales From Mama's Yard* (Mama's Yard/EMI 1995)★★.

EVANS, FAITH

Married to hardcore rapper Notorious B.I.G., urban R&B singer Faith Evans originally rose to prominence by singing background vocals and co-writing songs for Mary J. Blige, Color Me Badd and Tony Thompson. She broke through as a solo artist in the mid-90s with the release of her winning debut single, 'You Used To Love Me'. Mixing slightly lisped rap sections with soulful singing of

her predominantly romantic concerns, her self-titled debut album followed expertly in the tradition of Blige, with a wide cast of producers and collaborators. Without ever demonstrating the originality to separate her from a host of 'new jill swing' peers, *Faith* was sufficiently contemporaneous and lavishly executed to arouse interest throughout the R&B community. Following Notorious B.I.G.'s murder in March 1997, Evans appeared on the international number 1 tribute single 'I'll Be Missing You' by Sean 'Puffy' Combs.
● ALBUMS: *Faith* (Bad Boy/Arista 1995)★★★.

EVERLAST

b. Eric Schrody, USA. A former graffiti artist and protégé of Ice-T, US rapper Everlast was one of the few white members in the Rhyme Syndicate posse. Everything on his debut album was as might have been expected: hardcore visions of violence, extensive use of expletives, and puerile, anatomical descriptions of women. There was, at least, room for an anti-PMRC rap, and samples drawn from the diverse tangents of Sly And Robbie, Sly Stone and even Bananarama and the Knack. Everlast was introduced to hip-hop while at summer camp, a friend there teaching him both graffiti and elementary street rap. Everlast laid down a couple of tracks with the help of his friend's DJ partner, Bahal, and Ice-T liked what he heard. He released his first single as far back as 1988. Everlast toured the UK supporting Ice-T, but seems to have abandoned his solo career since joining House Of Pain.
● ALBUMS: *Forever Everlasting* (Warners 1990)★★.

EXIST DANCE

90s Los Angeles, USA-based trance/techno label run by Tom Chasteen and Mike Kandel, covering artists such as Merge (whose 'You Move Me' was their debut release), Tranquility Bass ('They Came In Peace'), High Lonesome Sound System ('Love Night', 'Were Go', 'Waiting For The Lights'), Eden Transmission ('I'm So High'), Odyssey 2000 ('The Odyssey'), Voodoo Transmission ('Voodoo Fire'), Up Above The World ('Up Above The World') and Freaky Chakra ('Freaky Chakra'). The latter was the first outside production to emerge on the label, but like the rest of their catalogue it was distinguished by an approach that cross-fertilized dance rhythms with tribal chants and environmental effects. Chasteen and Kandel met at art school, and began recording *avant garde* elec-tronica, heavy with loops and repetition, a style that is apparent in their modern output.

EXPERIMENTAL

90s US label based in Broadway, New York, noted for its deep house, trance and acid releases. The roster included the dark, Euro-flavoured house of Big Dreams, the hard house of The Rising Sons, and the effusive deep groove of Symphony Of Love. The operation was masterminded by Damon Wild, who names each of his releases after their catalogue number. Hence, 'EX17' by Bio Dreams, 'EX19' by the Lazer Worshippers and 'EX22' by Diffusions. He started DJing in the mid-80s, and was once half of the team behind Toxic Two's 'Rave Generator'. Experimental is part of New York's Northcott stable (run by Tommy Musto), which also includes the Sub-Urban imprint. However, Wild departed from Experimental, amicably, in March 1994, setting up the Synewave label with Tim Taylor, releasing material including Equinox's 'Pollox'.

EXPRESS

b. Simon Francis, *c*.1967, England. A bright new hip-hop talent from Northampton, England, Express has been rapping since 1981. However, his musical path took a different slant when he joined a local industrial dance unit. Eventually, following a major label débâcle, he and his partner Stuart left London to regroup. Together they elected to keep their music independent, setting up their own imprint, Expressive Records, to this end. In October 1993 Express's first record, the *Hit The Hook Heavy* EP, arrived. It quickly attained cult popularity, not least for its references to television fare like *Inspector Morse* and the absence of Chris Waddle from the England football squad. Even Ian Paisley got a namecheck, as the *New Musical Express* pronounced its verdict with a Single Of The Week award. Other songs also contained references to the footballer Andy Cole. However, if anyone had marked Express as a novelty act he brought about a quick rethink with 1994's follow-up, 'Gone To The Dogs'. This, as the title suggested, was a young black man's reflection on the election of a British National Party politician to the Isle Of Dogs (London) council.

F9s

This London, UK-based duo named themselves after the highest function button available to them on their computer keyboard. The F9s are technocrats with samplers, as might be suggested by the name, but Uncle B. Nice is also a confident rapper, who won the DMC UK rap championships in 1989. His messages are backed by DJ Mr Islam, aka Rizla. They began their career with a three-track EP in May 1991, after which they earned a reputation as powerful advocates of forward-thinking Christianity. This led them into conflict with some of the advocates of the Nation Of Islam, notably Professor Griff. They were similarly vocal about British hip-hop crews who did not use their platform to put forward a positive message, criticizing many of their peers: 'They're not gathering any white fans. They talk about racism, but they only talk to black people. Why do you need to be taught racism if you are already black.'
● ALBUMS: *The F-9's Are A Hip Hop Band* (Kold Sweat 1992)★★★.

Fab 5 Freddy

b. Frederick Braithwaite, Brooklyn, New York, USA. Freddy grew up with lawyer parents, his father managing jazz musicians like Max Roach and Clifford Brown. Nowadays best known for his hosting of *Yo! MTV Raps*, Freddy began life as a rap promoter and grafitti artist. He was responsible for the establishment of the Roxy, a former roller-skate rink turned hip-hop venue, alongside English-born Cool Lady Blue (he got Afrika Bambaataa his first gig there). After being namechecked by Blondie's 1981 hit 'Rapture', he was invited to make a rap record for the French Celluloid imprint, who had commissioned Bill Laswell and Michael Beinhorn to provide them with five 'rap' singles. 'Une Sale Histoire' duly emerged, while female rapper Beside, from California, but also rapping in French, took b-side duties. Freddy also appeared on the 'New York

City Rap Tour In Europe' line-up. This consisted of breakdancers, artists and rappers, a club of which Freddy has never really counted himself a member. He has gone on to a successful career as video director to KRS-1, Snoop Doggy Dogg and others.

Faithless

The prime mover behind Faithless is Rollo, one of the major forces in 90s UK house music. In 1994 he worked on two singles by Sister Bliss, 'Life's A Bitch' and 'Oh What A World', and the pair subsequently formed Faithless with the additional input of the vocalists Maxi Jazz (a former Acid Jazz Records artist) and Jamie Catto (from the Big Truth Band). They made their debut in 1995 with 'Insomnia' and 'Salva Mea' on Rollo's Cheeky Records, both of which became major European hits, before a reissued 'Insomnia' reached the UK Top 5 in late 1996, buoyed by extensive airplay from the Radio 1 DJ Pete Tong. Their debut album *Reverence*, originally released at the beginning of 1996, continued to sell steadily as a result and 'Salva Mea' also became a hit second time around. The album included 'Dirty Ol' Man', an excellent collision of reggae and funk, for which the group walked 'all over London in dirty raincoats with a DAT recorder to get those playground samples', and 'Baseball Cap', a typically intellectual rap from Maxi Jazz.
● ALBUMS: *Reverence* (Cheeky 1996)★★★, *Sunday 8pm* (Cheeky 1998)★★★★.

Family Foundation

Manchester, England-based jungle techno crew, made famous by their 'Express Yourself' white label single, which was selling for upwards of £100 to DJs in 1992. The leader is producer Johnny Jay, and the track was eventually given an official release a year later on Mancunian label 380. However, it was never originally intended to be a Family Foundation number. Jay had produced the track for an artist called Franschene Allea, but when BMG dropped Omen Records the title never saw the light of day. Instead he covered it when FF were doing demos, utilizing the services of Rachel (vocals) and Shine (ragga vocals). It proved a hugely winning formula. The debut album included 'Gunchester', a comment on Manchester's rising gang problems, and 'Red Hot'. This saw a guest appearance from ex-Smiths guitarist Craig Gannon, while over the top of the record Terry Christian and Johnny Rogan dis-

cussed the accusations of racism that had recently been directed at ex-Smiths singer Morrissey.
● ALBUMS: *One Blood* (380 1992)★★★.

FARLEY AND HELLER

London, UK-based DJs Terry Farley and Pete Heller first came to light in the early 90s, alongside the likes of Andy Weatherall, as part of the Boy's Own collective. Farley, an ex-gas fitter, was initially playing dub and reggae upstairs at Paul Oakenfold's Spectrum club when acid house arrived and changed everything. Afterwards he joined with Heller to become the simply titled Farley And Heller, a production/remix team. The Farm in the mid-80s had seemed an unlikely target for dancefloor adulation, but that was what they became when the duo took hold of their 'Groovy Train' single (later going on to remix 'Altogether Now'). It was a landmark almost as important as Weatherall's work on 'Loaded'. Their more indigenous dance projects included work with Espiritu ('Francisca'), K Klass ('Don't Stop'), Sunscreem ('Perfect Motion') and Secret Life ('As Always'). They additionally operate as Fire Island (releasesd on Boy's Own).

FARLEY JACKMASTER FUNK

The resident DJ at Chicago's Playground between 1981 and 1987 (often combining live drum machine with his selection of Philly soul and R&B), Farley was also one of the earliest house producers, with 'Yellow House' being the first record on Dance Mania Records. He was also a key component of the Hot Mix 5, the DJ group that provided Chicago's WBMX radio station with its groundbreaking mix shows. As Chicago backroom boy Mike 'Hitman' Wilson once stated: 'To me Farley started house. Because while Frankie [Knuckles] had an audience of 600, Farley reached 150,000 listeners.' He had a hit in 1986 with a cover version of 'Love Can't Turn Around', with a vocal from Greater Tabernacle Baptist Choir's Daryl Pandy (although this actually hijacked a Steve 'Silk' Hurley song). Other notable releases include 'Aw Shucks', 'As Always' (with Ricky Dillard) and 'Free At Last' (with the Hip House Syndicate).When WBMX went off air his career ground to a halt, an intermission he occupied by exploring rap and R&B. He returned to DJing in England in the 90s, where his reputation had not diminished, and started a new Chill-London label.

FAT BOYS

From the Bronx, New York, the Fat Boys were originally known as the Disco 3, before deciding to trade in the appellation in exchange for something more gimmicky. The bulk of their material dealt with just that, emphasising their size, and did little to avert the widely held perception of them as a novelty act. The trio consisted of Darren 'The Human Beatbox/Buff Love' Robinson (b. 1968, New York, USA, d. 10 December 1995), Mark 'Prince Markie Dee' Morales, and Damon 'Kool Rockski' Wimbley. They were discovered by Charlie Stetler (later manager of MTV's Dr. Dre and Ed Lover), whose interest was aroused by Robinson's amazing talent for rhythmic improvisation, effectively using his face as an instrument. It was Stetler who suggested they take the name-change, after winning a nationwide talent contest at Radio City Music Hall in 1983. Legend has it that this was prompted during an early European tour when Stetler was presented with a bill of $350 for 'extra breakfasts'. Their initial run of records were produced by Kurtis Blow, and largely discussed the size of the group's appetites. All their LPs for Sutra offered a consistent diet (a phrase not otherwise within the Fat Boy lexicon) of rock, reggae and hip-hop textures, with able if uninspiring raps. Their fortunes improved significantly once they signed up with Polydor Records, however. *Crushin'* is probably their best album, crammed with party anecdotes that stand up to repeated listening better than most of their material. It yielded a major hit with the Beach Boys on 'Wipe Out' in 1987. One year and one album later they scored with another collaboration, this time with Chubby Checker on 'The Twist (Yo' Twist)'. It peaked at number 2 in the UK chart, the highest position at the time for a rap record. In truth the Fat Boys had become more pop than hip-hop, though the process of revamping rock 'n' roll chestnuts had begun as far back as 1984 with 'Jailhouse Rock'. Also contained on *Coming Back Hard Again* was a strange version of 'Louie Louie' and 'Are You Ready For Freddy', used as the theme song for one of the *Nightmare On Elm Street* films. They also starred in another movie, *Disorderlies*, after appearing with Checker as part of Nelson Mandela's 70th Birthday Party at Wembley Stadium in June 1988 (they had previously been the only rap participants at Live Aid). The decade closed with the release of *On And On*. It proved a hugely disappointing set, overshadowed by its 'concept' of being a 'rappera', and offering a lukewarm adaptation of gangsta concerns. News broke in the 90s of a $6 million lawsuit filed against their former record company, while Robinson was put on trial in Pennsylvania for 'sexual abuse of a minor'. Prince Markie Dee went on to a solo career, recording an album as Prince Markie Dee And The Soul Convention. He also produced and wrote for Mary J. Blige, Christopher Williams, Father, El DeBarge, Trey Lorenz and others. Their career never recovered from the bad press after Robinson was found guilty and the Fat Boys' true legacy remains firmly in the era of rap party records, Swatch television ads and cameo appearances on television's *Miami Vice*. Robinson died in 1995 after a cardiac arrest following a bout of respiratory flu.

● ALBUMS: *Fat Boys* (Sutra 1984)★★★, *The Fat Boys Are Back!* (Sutra 1985)★★★, *Big & Beautiful* (Sutra 1986)★★★, *Cruisin'* (Tin Pan Apple/Polydor 1987)★★★★, *Coming Back Hard Again* (Tin Pan Apple/Polydor 1988)★★★, *On And On* (Tin Pan Apple/Mercury 1989)★★.
Solo: Prince Markie Dee *Free* (Columbia 1992)★★.

● COMPILATIONS: *The Best Part Of The Fat Boys* (Sutra 1987)★★★, *Krush On You* (Blatant 1988)★★.

FAT JOE DA GANGSTA

b. Bronx, New York, USA. This heavyweight rapper made a major impact in 1993 with the release of his debut album, *Represent*. Signed by Chris Lighty of Relativity Records' subsidiary Violator, his career began with a *Billboard* Rap Chart number 1 single, 'Flow Joe'. His self-projected image of 'worst kid in the neighbourhood', based on numerous scuffles with the Bronx police as a graffiti artist and 'hustler', endeared him to many. Though his lyrics often lacked poise there were no doubts about the smoothness of their delivery, a lugubrious drawl befitting his stature and origins. With strong sales of his debut album, Fat Joe used the proceeds to open up the Half-Time community store, named after his friend Nas's song. His second album, *Jealous One's Envy*, stuck squarely to the conventions of the first, celebrating his triumph in escaping a past of drug pushing and 'gang-bangin'.

● ALBUMS: *Represent* (Relativity 1993)★★★★, *Jealous One's Envy* (Relativity 1995)★★★.

FATBOY SLIM

A man of many musical faces, Norman Cook first rose to prominence as the 'jobbing' bass player in the Housemartins. However, that venture gave little clue as to his future direction. Following the dissolution of the '4th best band in Hull', he returned to his home in Brighton and scored a number 1 hit with Beats International's 'Dub Be Good To Me'. However, Beats International proved to be merely a temporary sidestep, and thereafter, he concentrated on his role as a club DJ and remixer, ostensibly under the guise of Pizzaman. His next collaboration as part of a group came with the launch of the acid jazz-inspired Freak Power, who reached number 2 in the UK charts after their 'Tune In, Turn On, Drop Out' single was featured in a jeans commercial. By 1997, Freak Power had been put on hold because of Cook's burgeoning dance music activities - in addition to remixing as Pizzaman, he had by now also adopted the pseudonyms Fatboy Slim (for club DJing and recording), Fried Funk Food, Might Dub Katz and Norman Cook Presents Wildski. This meant he was able to boast to the *New Musical Express* in 1997: 'I am going for a place in the *Guinness Book Of Records* - for having had the most Top 40 hits under different names. If Fatboy [Slim] gets in there, that'll be seven - a new record!'. This was achieved with 'Going Out Of My Head', his March 1997 single featuring samples of the Who. He enjoyed huge chart success in 1998 under the Fatboy Slim moniker with his remixes of Cornershop's 'Brimful Of Asha', Wildchild's 'Renegade Master' and his own 'Rockafeller Skank'.

● ALBUMS: *Better Living Through Chemistry* (Skint 1996)★★★.

FATHER

b. Timothy Brown, New York, USA. Father's debut album included the Top 20 US hit, 'I'll Do 4 U', and a powerful scene-setter between Father and Lady Kazan. On his return in 1994 for a belated third album, *Sex Is Law*, he dropped the MC suffix he had previously employed. It tied in with a switch in image too, from lovers rock hip-hop to down and dirty gangsta pimp. Gimmicky raps like '69' were the order of the day, as Father perved his way through a succession of saucy rhymes. There was a nod to the New Jack Swing movement with cuts produced by Teddy Riley and Pete Rock, who added an En Vogue sample to 'R&B

Swinger'. Other samples included the Jackson 5's 'I Want You Back'. The sexual lyrics were given a brief respite on his duet with Little Shawn, 'For The Brothers Who Ain't Here', a touching commemoration of loss in the ghetto.
● ALBUMS: as Father MC *Father's Day* (Uptown 1989)★★★, *Close To You* (Uptown 1992)★★★★, as Father *Sex Is Law* (Uptown 1994)★★.

FEARLESS FOUR

One of the earliest and more satorially challenged of rap's formations, the 80s group the Fearless Four consisted of MCs the Great Peso (b. Mitchell Grant, 5 December 1959), the Devastating Tito (b. Tito Dones, 27 May 1964), Mighty Mike C (b. Michael Kevin Clee, 10 March 1963) and DLB the Microphone Wizard (b. 25 April 1965), aided by two DJs; Master O.C. (b. Oscar Rodriguez Jr, 22 September 1962, Manhattan, New York, USA) and Krazy Eddie (b. Eddie Thompson, 25 July 1960). The band was originally started by Tito and Master O.C., when they were known as the Houserockers Crew, selling their tapes across Manhattan and the Bronx. They gradually picked up members, first Mike Ski, then the Great Peso and Troy B, who arrived fresh from the Disco Four. He was subsequently replaced by DLB, before Mike Ski also departed for marriage and a steady job. The line-up was completed by Mighty Mike C and Krazy Eddie, a second DJ who took his name from a local record store renowned for its zany commercials. They first struck for the Enjoy label in 1981 with 'Rockin' It' which, hot on the trail of Afrika Bambaataa's 'Planet Rock' success, used Kraftwerk's 'The Mean Machine' as well as excerpts from the horror film *Poltergeist*. The follow-up was 'It's Magic', based on a Cat Stevens song, before moving to Elektra. Their career there began with 'Just Rock', built on Gary Numan's 'Cars', and remixed by Larry Levan, which flopped. 'Problems Of The World Today' (1983), produced by Kurtis Blow, was an improvement. Master O.C., meanwhile, produced the Fantasy Three's 'Biters In The City'. The Fearless Four continued to plough a furrow into the mid-80s, but the hits had long since dried up.

FEHLMANN, THOMAS

b. Switzerland. An elder statesman of the German techno/house scene, with an intriguing history. Fehlmann originally met guitar wizard Robert Fripp in Hamburg in 1979, where he was studying art, and it was Fripp who inspired him to learn the synthesizer. Later he would make the acquaintance of the Orb's Alex Paterson while working on Teutonic Beats, a mid-80s dance project. Paterson tried to sign him to management company EG, but the deal fell through. Undeterred, the two remained firm friends. Before joining the Orb as an ambient DJ and electronics consultant, he recorded as Readymade and produced the *Sun Electric* LP, joining with Juan Atkins for the release of 'Jazz Is The Teacher' on Belgian imprint Tresor (licensed to Novamute in the UK). This was recorded under the group name 3MB, with Morris Von Oswald, an old friend whom he had known from the time they liaised on Palais Schaumburg's third album from a decade previously. They have worked together intermittently since then. His contributions to the Orb also include 'Towers Of Dub' on the latter's live double, *Orb Live 93*. Following touring commitments, he teamed up once more with old guru Fripp to put together the *ad hoc* project FFWD (Fripp, Fehlmann, Weston and Dr Alex Paterson). According to the latter, Fehlmann had also been 'the first person to put a house record out in Britain in 1986' - as Ready Made on Rhythm King.

FELIX

b. *c.*1972, Essex, England. UK house artist and alleged former tax inspector Felix represented something of an enigma - never talking to the press or appearing in his videos. He even took the stage at the DMC awards sporting a lion suit. However, his anonymity wasn't helped by the massive success of singles such as 'Don't You Want Me' and 'It Will Make Me Crazy', which sold nearly two million copies between them worldwide. Both predicted the rise of trance and hard house.
● ALBUMS: *One* mini-album (DeConstruction 1992)★★★.

FELIX DA HOUSECAT

b. Felix Stallings, Chicago, Illinois, USA. The childhood friend of house legend DJ Pierre, Stallings' youth was spent experimenting with electronic musical equipment. He taught himself keyboards by the age of 14, and a year later stepped into a studio for the first time. An early tape had been passed on to the elder Pierre by a mutual playground acquaintance. Intrigued, he decided to record it properly, and from those sessions 'Phantasy Girl' emerged. Based on the original keyboard motif from the demo tape, it became one of house music's biggest early cult smashes. Felix went on to release a steady stream of dance vinyl, establishing his name alongside that of Pierre, who remained his mentor. Unfortunately, as school ended so did his parents' tolerance of his extra-curricular pursuits, and he was ordered to attend college in Alabama. Three years later he returned to Chicago, taking up the house mantle once again. Numerous releases followed on all the major imprints: Strictly Rhythm, Guerilla ('Thee Dawn'), Nervous, D-Jax Up, Chicago Underground and Freetown. Under the title Thee Madkatt Courtship he also provided a long-player for Deep Distraxion, while as Afrohead he proferred 'In The Garden', a classic cut, much revered by DJs such as Darren Emerson.

● ALBUMS: *Thee Madkatt Courtship* (Deep Distraxion 1994)★★★.

FESU

Born in Greenspoint, Texas, USA, Fesu, his name a corruption of his real name Yusef, began his career with a single on his own label, Air-Run-Boy, 'Salt N Da Game'. The follow-up, 'Streets Of Greenspoint' picked up a lot of local radio coverage, but it was with the lauded 'Blind, Cripple And Crazy' single that he really made headway. *The Source* magazine was particularly impressed, promoting him as a major new talent. Although born a Muslim, it was not until he encountered the teachings of Louis Farakhan that Fesu found a spiritual direction and became a member of the Nation Of Islam, a process recounted in the single. He went on to record a 1994 duet with Bobby Womack entitled 'Going Round N' Circles'.

FFRR RECORDS

London records' (UK) dance label is headed by Andy Thompson, although BBC Radio 1 presenter Pete Tong provides A&R support. Tong joined London in 1983 after leaving his job as advertising manager for *Blues & Soul* magazine. He became the label's club promotions manager, and was the first to import the sound of the Chicago house explosion via Farley Jackmaster Funk and Steve 'Silk' Hurley. Tong 'began' ffrr in 1986. It had originally been a label launched as a subsidiary of Decca in 1946 to celebrate the advent of high fidelity recordings, and had been dormant for several decades. The original intention was to use the imprint to develop acts on a long-term basis. Hence the signing of major acts such as Brand New Heavies, Salt 'N' Pepa, L'il Louis and Degrees

Of Motion. A second outlet, ffreedom, was launched in 1991 by Thompson, who, like Tong, had progressed through the ranks as club promotions director, with former Hooj Choons employee Phil Howells as his partner. The idea was to specialize in rave culture, and be flexible enough to pick up on tunes as they broke in the club scene. They even took a bite out of the toy-town techno cake by providing the nation with Shaft's ridiculous 'Roobarb & Custard' in 1992. A second subsidiary, Internal, was launched in late 1992 for album-based techno projects. The main label ffrr played things a little more safely. As Thompson admitted during the recession of 1992: 'The doctrine of our company is that caution pays and we only believe in spending money where we think there is a reason to.' Nevertheless, ffrr's strict sense of discipline has not prevented it from being both prolific and successful. In the late 80s they boasted some of the cream of the acid house generation's music with artists like D-Mob, also picking up on commercial hip-hop with the Cookie Crew (since dropped). They also lost Orbital, who had given them a major hit in 1992 with the *Mutations* EP, but maintained relationships with a series of female house vocalists including Lisa B. Among the major hits of recent times have been DJ Duke's 'Blow Your Whistle', Good Men's 'Give It Up', Joe Roberts' 'Back In My Life' and the omnipresent Brand New Heavies' 'Back To Love', alongside sundry high-quality releases from Frankie Knuckles. ffrr has gone on to become the most credible and successful dance division of a major UK label.

FINITRIBE

Scottish dance unit, who shared the same One Little Indian label as their fellow countrymen the Shamen, but failed to replicate their success. It was not through want of effort, or, for that matter, talent. The band took their name from 'Finny Tribe', a name given to the entire fish species by Irish religious sect the Rosicrucians, as well as by the common people of that country. Originally a six-piece formed in Edinburgh in 1984, they founded their own label, striking out with a debut EP, *Curling And Stretching*, in October. One month later they played their first gig together supporting Danielle Dax at London ULU. By 1986 they had acquired their first sampler, and released 'DeTestimony', an influential cut in both the balearic and, later, house movements. The following year they began an ill-fated liaison with

Chicago's Wax Trax Records, releasing a version of Can's 'I Want More'. Following problems with the label, vocalist Chris Connelly eventually elected to remain, ostensibly as part of Ministry and Revolting Cocks, but also recording solo. Finitribe re-emerged in 1989 with the curtailed line-up of Mr Samples (b. John William Vick, 6 November 1965, Edinburgh, Scotland), Philip Pinsky (b. Philip David Pinsky, 23 March 1965, Appleton, Wisconsin, USA) and David Miller (b. David Francis Ashbride Miller, 20 July 1962, Moffat, Dunfrewshire, Scotland). Vick and Pinsky had previously been colleagues in Rigor Mortis, and Miller had served in Explode Your Heart. Their influences remained both traditional rock and indie giants (Dog Faced Hermans, Magazine) and a myriad of new and old dance innovators (Jah Wobble, Tackhead, Sparks, Sub Sub, Orbital). A succession of well-regarded releases on One Little Indian failed to deliver them much in the way of commercial reward. The first and most notable of these was the acidic 'Animal Farm', which sampled the 'Old McDonald' nursery rhyme and lay torrents of abuse at the door of the McDonald's hamburger chain. The ensuing fuss, hardly deflated by a 'Fuck Off McDonald's' poster campaign, brought the band significant media exposure for the first time. Entering the 90s they looked as though they might expand beyond cult tastes with a new, kitsch image (white boiler suits peppered with stars) and more pop-dance-orientated material. As critics pointed out, they resembled an underground version of the Pet Shop Boys. By 1992 they had resurrected the Finiflex label and opened their own studio complex in Leith.
● ALBUMS: *Noise Lust And Fun* (Finiflex 1988)★★★, *Grossing 10K* (One Little Indian 1990)★★★, *An Unexpected Groovy Treat* (One Little Indian 1992)★★★.

FINN, MICKEY

b. Michael Hearne. One of the 90s' more publicity-shy UK DJs, Finn's ambitions stretch to writing film soundtracks rather than desiring pin-up pieces in the popular music press. His musical inclinations were established at blues parties before he got hooked on Eric B & Rakim. He purchased his own decks and starting mixing, getting his first paid engagement at the Tunnel Club, near the Blackwall Tunnel (under the River Thames in East London), run by his sister Nancy, who first used the 'Finn' nickname. From such beginnings in 1988 he progressed to the Genesis and Biology nights. He recorded a solo track, 'She's Breaking Up', for US label Focus in January 1991, before going on to remix for a multitude of labels including Suburban Base, ffrr, Champion and PWL (Mandy Smith's 'I Just Can't Wait', of all things). A more representative example of his work would be his contribution to Urban Shakedown with friends Gavin King and Claudio Guissani on 'Some Justice', which enabled it to become a real chart contender (despite problems obtaining clearance for the sample of Ce Ce Rogers' 'Someday'). He remains a huge name on the UK DJ circuit.

FIRST CHOICE RECORDS

This record label and studio is based in Greenwich Village, New York, USA, and was founded in the mid-90s by DJ/remixer Andrew Komis in conjunction with Network. His intention to return dance music to the late 80s when the dramatic garage divas such as Adeva and Kym Mazelle held sway, was first attempted at the Big Shot label in Canada (see Hi-Bias). Among those involved are Pandella, the well-regarded house diva veteran, and Dyone, a highly touted disco diva whose upfront personality and sexuality have endeared her to many, including actor Robert De Niro, which sent rumour mills into a frenzy of activity. A former beauty queen, dancer and college graduate, Dyone has been heralded as a sussed Teena Marie of the 90s. Komis himself records under the *nom de plume* Komix And Co. Of the opinion that the 90s US dance scene is dead, he formed First Choice primarily to reach English and European markets, linking up with Network after they had opened a New York office in 1990.

FIRST DOWN

Comprising MCs King Arroe, Correkt, Baron Demus and DJ Hyste, UK rap group First Down originally formed in 1990. A full four years passed between the release of their debut single, 'Jawbreaker' (1990), and its follow-up, 'Let The Battle Begin' (1994). The debut single was a staple of pirate hip-hop shows, making their failure to capitalise on its success seem even stranger. Despite their US football-related name, their second release was a defiant slice of British rap fashioned on 'old school' precepts. It was released on their own Ill Gotten Gains label as a reaction to prevailing trends in American hip-hop culture.

Correkt gave this verdict to the press: 'When was the last time you heard a good American rap record with cutting on it, apart from Gang Starr or EPMD. Rap's become too commercialised . . . it's become too conformist.' However, delays in the release of the group's debut album again stalled their progress. When *World Service* did emerge in 1995, it was on the German label Blitz Vinyl, and the band were disappointed by its distribution and the financial details of the deal.

● ALBUMS: *World Service* (Blitz Vinyl 1995)★★★.

FLASH FACTION

UK techno outfit comprising Matt Nelmes, Richard Johnstone and Jake Davies. The three worked as engineers at Soho's Berwick Street Studios, before deciding to give it a go themselves with the help of DJ Sean Johnstone in late 1993. They began 1994 with two hard trance releases, 'Robot Criminal' on Labello Trax, and 'Repoman' on Andy Weatherall's Sabres Of Paradise label. The latter was envisioned as an 'alternative soundtrack' to Alex Cox's film of the same name. It was followed up with the release of 'Mad Moog Rising' for Third Mind.

FLAVOR FLAV

b. William Drayton, 16 March 1959, Roosevelt, Long Island, New York, USA. The sharp banter of Public Enemy had been both heightened and lightened by Flav's interjections as stoolpigeon to Chuck D. However, his personal life had won him some degree of infamy too. In February 1991 he was arrested at his Long Island home, and charged with assault on his girlfriend and mother of his three children, Karen Ross. After pleading guilty to third degree assault he was sentenced to 30 days' imprisonment and served with an exclusion order. Just as his debut solo album was announced in the press, he again hit the headlines when he was arrested in the Bronx after allegedly trying to shoot another man in a dispute over a woman. That album has yet to see a release.

FLOORJAM

This 90s UK techno act is the creation of one Nick Newell, a man whose dance records show a clear line of descent from Kraftwerk's computerized pop. His 'Stone Age' has become a widely venerated track, but it was not always a life of boundless techno experimentalism. In 1993 he returned to his former occupation, that of session musician, picking up lucrative contracts with Gary Glitter and Take That tours.

FLUKE

Purveyors of charismatic, electronic dance music, Fluke are both a stand-alone musical project and a mixing house for others. The band consists of Mike Bryant (b. Michael James Bryant, 1 May 1960, High Wycombe, Buckinghamshire, England), Michael Tournier (b. Michael James Tournier, 24 May 1963, High Wycombe, Buckinghamshire, England) and Jonathan Fugler (b. 13 October 1962, St Austell, Cornwall, England). Fugler and Bryant were both formerly in third-rate teenage punk bands the Leaky Radiators and the Lay Figures. Tournier and Fugler had more prominently been part of Skin. They emerged as Fluke in August 1989 with the white label 12-inch, 'Thumper!'. Other early singles included 'Joni' (complete with a sample from Joni Mitchell) and 'Philly', their debut release for Creation Records. Their first live performance was on the lawn of a Kent country house at a Boy's Own Records party - a set that subsequently became their second album release, *Out*, in November 1991. It arrived as part of a new contract with Virgin Records subsidiary Circa Records, with whom they released their third album, *Six Wheels On My Wagon*, in 1993. This was accompanied by a limited edition free vinyl copy of their long-deleted *Techno Rose Of Blighty* debut. *Six Wheels* also proffered a further significant club hit, 'Groovy Feeling'. The band maintain their own West London studio, and remain somewhat aloof from the dance music community. This has not stopped them from earning considerable plaudits as remixers: World Of Twist, JC001, Opik, Tears For Fears, Talk Talk, New Order and Frankie Goes To Hollywood numbering among their clients. Their notoriety continued in the mid-90s when Björk invited them to remix 'Big Time Sensuality', and was so impressed with the results she issued it in preference to the original version. This led to Fluke sharing a stage with the Icelandic singer at 1994's *Smash Hits* Poll Winners Party, after their own single, 'Slid', had just failed to break the UK Top 40. 'Bubble' finally took them there in April 1994, and preceded their first national tour. Their fourth album, *Oto* (Greek for 'of ear'), was released in the summer of 1995, preceded by another highly praised single, 'Bullet'. Barry Andrews, veteran of XTC and Shriekback, was involved in the sessions in an informal production capacity. It was followed by a remix album, *Risoto*, later in the year.

● ALBUMS: *Techno Rose Of Blighty* (Creation 1991)★★★, *Out* mini-album (Circa 1991)★★★, *Six Wheels On My Wagon* (Circa 1993)★★★★, *Oto* (Virgin 1995)★★★, *Risoto* remixes (Virgin 1995)★★★.

FLYING RECORDS

This Italian record label is also the country's biggest independent dance distributor, and also has a London arm that distributes its own product and that from Media, Ummm and other labels. The UK operation was set up by Dean Thatcher in association with Charlie Chester and Cooltempo. Their debut release was a Thatcher remix of 'Hit Me With Your Rhythm Stick' by Ian Dury And The Blockheads. The idea was taken from Glen Turner who played the original at the end of one of his 1990 sets at Ibiza. It had previously been remixed in 1985 by Paul Hardcastle, but it was the Flying version that received the chief Blockhead's blessing. Since its inception Flying has offered a consistent diet of quality dance for their many advocates in the media and the nation's club scene. Their signings include End ('Rebel Song'), Joy Salinas ('The Mystery Of Love'), Korda ('Move Your Body'), Ferrante & Co featuring Kay Bianco ('Breakin' Away'), Kwanzaa Posse ('Wicked Funk', which like many releases was Italian in origin), Digital Boy ('This Is Muthafucker', '1-2-3 Acid'), Nexy Lanton ('I Am'), Jamie Dee ('Memories, Memories'), Latin Blood ('Deseo', created by Italian brothers Max and Frank Minoia) and Lamott Atkins ('Communicate'). A series of background personnel, affiliates and colleagues were routinely involved, sometimes English, often Italian. For instance, Daybreak's 'Tomorrow' was created by Gino 'Woody' Bianchi and Corrardo Rizza and Dom Scuteri, and sung by Karen Jones. The label's major successes include Gat Decor's 'Passion', remixed for the label by Darren Emmerson, and Ami Stewart's 'Friends '91'.

FLYING RHINO RECORDS

This psychedelic trance label based in north London was formed in 1994 by the producers and DJs James Monro (of Technossomy), Dominic Lamb and George Barker (both of Slinky Wizard). It was initially established in collaboration with Zoom Records, but became independent the following year. Their first release was Slinky Wizard's *Wizard* EP in December 1994, since

which time they have put out work by artists including Technossomy, Green Nuns Of The Revolution, Kundalini, Process And Tristan, Blue Planet Corporation and Darshan. Flying Rhino pride themselves on the quality rather than quantity of their releases and most of their compilations, including *First Flight*, *Boyd In The Void*, *White Rhino* and *Black Rhino*, contain brand new material written especially for the label. As well as artists, the company's agency promote a number of successful trance DJs, notably Lamb, Monro and Sally Welch, who play at parties and festivals around the globe. They have expanded to include a range of Flying Rhino clothing, and in-house recording and design studios.

FONCETT, FRANKIE

b. England. A 90s UK disc jockey, producer and remixer, Foncett began his career by spinning hip-hop discs for the Rappatack sound system. In the mid-80s he switched to house music, playing at several of the major clubs of the period. In London he made appearances at the Black Market and Shoom clubs, and was also resident disc jockey alongside Norman Jay at High On Hope. He travelled to the USA in 1989 to play at New York's Payday, appearing alongside Larry Levan, before dates at Detroit's Music Institute with Derrick May. On his return to London he was among the original staff at the influential Black Market record shop, gradually earning his reputation by remixing several acts for major record companies, including the Chimes and Regina Belle. He made his solo debut at the end of 1995 with the *Streetfighter 2000* EP, which included one track, 'The Ride', dedicated to fellow UK disc jockey pioneer Paul Anderson. The intention was to 'represent the UK and London. We created our own vibe with house and I've always been big on individuality. We can listen to US music and let it influence us but we don't have to live or die by it. I wanted to show it's no big deal to do those kind of beats.' He followed its release with work on Lisa M's 1996 album, also writing and producing for the R&B act Sugar Tree.

FORCE MD'S

Often neglected next to the adventures of Afrika Bambaataa or Grandmaster Flash, Force MD's (from Staten Island, New York, USA) were nevertheless a vital component in the early 80s in rap's development. They were originally titled the LDs, working as a street-corner act in the manner of

the Jackson Five, with TCD, Stevie D and Trisco and Mercury holding the reigns. Alongside Planet Patrol, they were the first to instigate doo wop hip-hop, before changing tack to largely soul-based harmonies. They employed formation steps alongside breakdance routines as visual inducement, adding impersonations of television theme tunes and popular stars of the day, often performing on the Staten Island ferry. They became Dr. Rock And The MCs when they were joined by a DJ of that title, introducing scratching into their nascent act (in his absence a DJ Shock would deputise). Their later career is best aired on their hit single, 'Tender Love', a US number 10-peaking Jimmy Jam, Terry Lewis ballad, but elsewhere there is little to suggest historical reassessment is overdue. The MD component of the name is short for Musical Diversity.
● ALBUMS: *Love Letters* (Tommy Boy 1984)★★★, *Chillin'* (Tommy Boy 1986)★★★★, *Touch And Go* (Tommy Boy 1987)★★★★, *Step To Me* (1990)★★★, *For Lovers And Others* (1992)★★★.

FORMATION RECORDS

This UK dance record label specializes in hardcore/'darkside' techno. It was inaugurated by Leroy Small (aka DJ SS) and Eidris Hassam in 1992. They grew up as part of a breakdancing team before joining a DJ clique entitled Formation 5 in their native Leicester, Leicestershire, England. Formation was established as an outlet for their 5HQ shop in the city, to fill a gap for the region's underground dance fans. The records were distributed by their own F Project operation, which also released records just as frequently in its own right. They also run their own house and rap labels. 'Our music's made underground to appeal to a commercial crowd. We've survived because we've stayed versatile. The whole feel and vibe of the scene has gone so we've had to change with the times', noted Small. In just over a year, via their various networking operations, Formation released over 40 12-inch singles for their enthusiastic following, the best of which included several items from DJ SS (including his collaborations with EQ and Tango, who record in their own right), as well as Oaysis, Mastersafe, Darkman, Bizz and Mickey Finn.

FOUL PLAY

Foul Play consist of John Morrow and Steve Bradshaw and are one of the more interesting and long-standing teams in the UK's jungle/drum 'n' bass movement of the mid-90s. Their debut album recalled their back-catalogue to date, with only four wholly new items standing next to remixes of their earlier club hits (the best known of which was probably 1993's 'Open Your Mind'). The production guests included Andy C and Ant Miles under one of their many aliases, Desired State, Hopa And Bones and perceived rivals, Omni Trio. The new tracks included 'Ignorance', a massively complex rhythmic collage, and 'Artificial Intelligence', quiet jungle complete with classical string section.
● ALBUMS: *Suspected* (Moving Shadow 1995)★★★★.

4 HERO

A publicity-shy London, England duo of Dego McFarlane and Mark Clair, the roots of 4 Hero were established in the late 80s at the height of the acid house explosion. Together they established Reinforced Records, which became the foremost UK outlet for hardcore techno (at that time often referred to as 'dark hardcore'). Their releases for Reinforced included the devastating 'Mr Kirk's Nightmare', which provided a thematic bridge between hardcore and the embryonic jungle/breakbeat scene. Alongside Goldie, who joined Reinforced in the early 90s, 4 Hero became innovative members of a new aristocracy in the dance community, though unlike Goldie, McFarlane and Clair eschewed publicity. As well as 4 Hero the duo released singles as Manix, Tom&Jerry, Jacob (whose *Optical Stairway* EP was inspired by the writings of Nostradamus), Nu Era and McFarlane's solo project, Tek 9. The debut 4 Hero album, *Parallel Universe*, was considered by many to be the first album to showcase the full potential of 'drum 'n' bass' music. Its themes included science fiction television programmes and science fact (with references to author Stephen Hawking). It was followed by an album credited to Tek 9 and remix and production work for Nicolette, DJ Krush and Courtney Pine. As 4 Hero, collaborations with Josh Wink and Juan Atkins preceded their second album, *Two Pages*, which was nominated for the 1998 Mercury Music Prize.
● ALBUMS: *Parallel Universe* (Reinforced 1994)★★★★, *Two Pages* (Talkin' Loud 1998)★★★.

430 WEST RECORDS

One of the pre-eminent labels to host the much admired second-wave Detroit-techno sound of the early 90s, 430 West was formed in 1990 by brothers Lawrence, Lenny and Lynell Burden. The inspiration for the label came from their first release together as Octave One on Derrick May's Transmat Records. 'I Believe', recorded with Antony Shakir, became an instant agenda-setter with its tightly marshalled rhythms and harmonies, sung by Lisa Newberry. The Burden brothers elected to form 430 West Records thereafter, taking the label's name from its address at 430 West Eight Mile Road in Detroit. Its first release was another Octave One project, the *Octivation* EP, recorded with a budget of $500. The label grew rapidly, with its discography encompassing groundbreaking releases by artists such as Eddie 'Flashin'' Fowlkes, Terrence Parker and others. These producers were attracted to the group's low-key ethos. 'All our artists are treated like family', claimed Lawrence Burden, 'We sit around, shoes off, trippin' out and eating from the same table. That's basically the way we've tried to keep it from the start.' Distributed by Mike Banks' enterprising Submerge distribution company, the label has been largely responsible for keeping Detroit at the forefront of contemporary dance music. As well as hosting pivotal releases by artists such as Sight Beyond Sight ('Good Stuff', 'No More Tears'), Tokyo Gospel Renegades ('Tokyo Soul') and Unknown Force's self-titled EP, the brothers have also launched a subsidiary electro label, Direct Beat (Will Webb, Aux 88, etc.). Octave One have also continued to record with the label, and were most recently heard on the *Foundation* and *Point Blank* EPs.

FOWLKES, EDDIE 'FLASHIN''

b. 24 December 1962, Detroit, Michigan, USA. One of the less celebrated techno artists from the ever fertile Detroit region, Fowlkes began making mix tapes at the age of 14. His first booking as a DJ came in 1981 at a campus party. In the early 80s he built up his record collection and began to secure a reputation for both his live appearances and his mix tapes. His nickname, 'Flashin', came from his early prowess as a scratch and mix DJ. Fowlkes was a friend of many of the Detroit giants, DJing alongside Derrick May and Juan Atkins in the early 80s. He recorded his debut, 'Goodbye Kiss', on Atkins' Metroplex imprint. In

the 90s he began to build his recording profile, working with labels including Jump Street, React and Tresor Records. One of the best of these releases was 'Turn Me Out', produced by Graeme Park. Throughout the 90s he performed regularly at Detroit's The Alley club, and in 1991 released *Serious Techno Vol. 1*, featuring tough but soulful techno. As he reasoned, 'most Euro techno has no feeling because the makers haven't got the history'. He also recorded for Detroit label 430 West with 'Inequality', as well as UK label Back To Basics in 1996.

● ALBUMS: *Serious Techno Vol. 1* (Tresor 1991)★★★★, *Black Technosoul* (Tresor 1996)★★★.

FPI PROJECT

Principally Damon Rochefort (b. *c*.1965, Cardiff, Wales), a former law student, and Sharon Dee Clarke (b. *c*.1965), a part-time actor with minor roles in several television soap operas. They achieved an instant hit in late 1989/early 1990 when 'Going Back To My Roots' gatecrashed the UK Top 10. It was available in two formats, the first with a Paulo Dini vocal, the second version by Clarke. Following further singles 'Risky' and 'Everybody (All Over The World)', the two protagonists went on to enjoy further chart success as Nomad. However, Rochefort continued to use the FPI banner on occasion, such as the 1992 *Paradise* EP.

FREAKY REALISTIC

Based in Peckham, London, this 90s group was founded by Justin Anderson, whose cockney leer was the focal point for much of their press. He sang alongside Texan rapper Michael Lord and female Japanese vocalist Aki Omori. Four singles, 'Something New', 'Cosmic Love Vibes', 'Leonard Nimoy' and 'Koochie Ryder', all featured on their debut album, before Lord quit the band in the summer of 1993.

● ALBUMS: *Frealism* (Polydor 1993)★★★.

FREDDIE FOXXX

MC whose career has seen more highs and lows than most. By the age of 13 he had built his reputation as a talented freestyler in Westbury, Long Island, New York. He recorded a debut album in 1989, produced by Eric B, which promptly sank without trace. He was left to lick his wounds as the hip-hop populace forgot his name. However, a resurgence in his fortunes was kickstarted by collaborations with KRS-1 ('Ruff Ruff'), then Naughty By Nature ('Hot Potato'), before he was signed to Queen Latifah's Epic subsidiary Flavor Unit. It was his third record deal. His first release for his new home was 'So Tough'. This boasted his sharply observed lyrics about the ghetto, 'We went from African kings/ To Martin Luther King/ Now they wanna make us all Rodney Kings'. He also produced videos which reminded would-be gangstas about the realities of prison life, and helped found Dream House, a Brooklyn charity which helps local youths out of the negative downward spiral of poverty and homelessness.

● ALBUMS: *Freddie Foxxx Is Here* (1989)★★★, *Crazy Like A Foxxx* (Flavor Unit/Epic 1994)★★★.

FREEDOM OF SPEECH

Comprising Luke Losey, Mickey Mann and Stika, UK group Freedom Of Speech are proponents of what has come to be known in dance clubs of the mid-90s as 'darkside', a style of techno that attacks the conscious and subconscious with images culled from horror books, nursery rhymes and Kafka-esque noises. The trio met on the Shamen's Synergy tour in 1987, and each member has subsequently made a sizeable contribution to the evolution of dance music. Losey prepared lights for stage shows from the KLF and Curve, Mann co-produced an album with Orbital, and continued to organize warehouse parties, often in conjunction with the Mutoid Waste Company. The trio came together as part of the Midi Circus tour, and made their debut with 'Surveillance', which appeared on Planet Dog's *Feed Your Head* compilation. There was a big brother theme to back it up, with the single being built on samples of surveillance workers. They also released 'X-Beats', which preceded their debut album. 'We're into the kind of paranoia and bleakness of emotions which Joy Division used to put across', they noted. The 'negative vibes for the future of the world' syndrome was informed in part by a visit to Russia when supporting the Shamen on tour.

● ALBUMS: *Art Of The State* (1994)★★★.

FREEFORM

Welcomed in the UK dance music press in 1996 as a natural successor to the sonic experimentalism of the Aphex Twin, Freeform is the recording *nom de plume* of Croydon resident Simon Pike. Like the Aphex Twin he quickly established himself as one of techno's most prolific artists, his sound collages composed almost at daily intervals. His musical career started as a teenager when he acquired a second-hand set of record decks and a sampling keyboard. Within weeks he was composing his own material. Supporting Autechre on their 1996 UK tour, he concurrently released a series of excellent records that have drawn consistent praise from England's dance music press. These included a self-titled EP for Autechre's Skam label, a contribution to the *Elastic Speakers* ambient compilation and an EP for Warp Records, titled *Prowl*.

FREESTYLE FELLOWSHIP

From South Central Los Angeles, USA, 90s rap band Freestyle Fellowship were named after their rhyming abilities and dextrous word play. Comparisons to De La Soul and the Dream Warriors frustrated them, but the impressive thing about the group, as revealed on singles like 'Hot Potato', with its samples from Dizzy Gillespie and Kool And The Gang, was the dizzy speed of their delivery and appetite for innovation. The group comprised Mikah Nine, Mtulazaji (Peace), Self Jupiter, Aceyalone and DJ Kiilu, who grew from the Los Angeles Good Life Cafe collective. Mikah Nine had formerly recorded with Carmet Carter and the Wailers. However, the most important music in the Freestyle Fellowship cocktail was undoubtedly jazz, whose experimental edge was reflected in their lyrics.

● ALBUMS: *To Whom It May Concern* (Sun Music 1991)★★, *Inner City Griots* (Island 1993)★★★.

FRESH FRUIT RECORDS

After ESP, Fresh Fruit is Amsterdam's most important, slightly more underground dance label. The location of the enterprise, run by Rene 'DJ Zki' and Gaston Dobre, is a bedroom in Gaston's mother's house. From here emerged records by the Goodmen (the debut 'Give It Up', which brought them mainstream chart success), Klatsch ('God Save The Queer') and Rene Et Gaston ('Contes De Fees'), which are the three names the duo employ. They also use these names for their remixing activities, i.e., the Goodmen's work on Ricky Rouge's 'Strange Love'. The label started in November 1991, before which they had both already been active in the dance scene. Rene's string of Euro house credits included SiL and World Series Of Life ('Spread Love'), while Gaston operated as Trancesetters, Virtual Reality, Jark Prongo, Con-Am, Jamshed and 41 Days. Gaston takes responsibility for keyboards and computers, while Rene, with 15 years of DJing work behind him, furnishes ideas. Their mode of operation involves a week-long bedroom routine, with sampling a key, but invisible, component: 'We use records for sampling . . . we build a song around the sample, then we take the sample away'. 'Father In The Bathroom', the title track to the Goodmen's debut album, was in fact a sample of exactly that; Gaston's father cleaning the bathroom. Other names used by the duo include South Street Player.

● ALBUMS: As the Goodmen: *Father In The Bathroom* (Fresh Fruit 1994)★★★.

FRESH GORDON

Fresh Gordon was a popular early DJ in Los Angeles, California, USA, who rose to prominence as the hip-hop message spread from the Bronx in New York to America's west coast. His infamous early bootleg 12-inch, 'Feelin' James', combined samples of James Brown's 'Funky Drummer' and 'Sex Machine' long before Brown had become such a popular staple of rap samplers, as well as Aretha Franklin's 'Rock Steady'. The record was finally given an official release when Tommy Boy Records issued it in 1987, in a slightly diluted format because of the complexities of sample clearance. By this time Fresh Gordon had long since disappeared into obscurity.

FROST

b. Arturo Molina Jnr., 31 May 1964, Los Angeles, California, USA. This Mexican-descended 90s rapper was raised on military bases in Guam and Germany, but spent most of his youth in east Los Angeles, where he began writing his first rhymes in 1982. He was initially inducted into the ranks of break-dance crew Uncle Jam's Army, as west coast rap began to accommodate the innovations of the Bronx. He released a number of 12-inch singles during this period as well as competing in 'backyard parties'. His breakthrough came in 1989 with 'La Raza', a single typically demonstrating 'Chicano pride'. A major force in the establishment of Latin hip-hop, Frost (then working as Kid Frost) brought together several other Hispanic rappers for the Latin Alliance project in 1991. This came shortly after the release of his 1990 debut solo set, another important signpost in the development of Latin rap. His blend of Chicano social observation and breakbeats provided him with a considerable audience outside of his own social bracket. He subsequently signed to Virgin, for whom he continued to deploy the intelligence to sample not only from funk's back-catalogue, but also that of the salsa tradition of his own people. However, he received scant commercial recognition for his efforts. In 1995 Frost dropped the prefix Kid ('the kid's a man now') and became Eazy-E's final signing to Ruthless Records. An album, *Smile Now, Die Later*, and single, 'East Side Rendezvous', placed him firmly 'back on the block', as one reviewer observed.

● ALBUMS: *Hispanic Causing Panic* (Virgin 1990)★★★, *East Side Story* (Virgin 1992)★★★★, *Smile Now, Die Later* (Ruthless 1996)★★★, *When Hell A Freezes Over* (Ruthless 1997)★★★.

FU-SCHNICKENS

Brooklyn, New York rap trio who comprise Poc Fu (Prophet Overseeing Creativity), Chip Fu (Creative Harmony:Intertwine Perfection) and Moc (Manifest Culture) Fu. Not content with wearing ludicrous Oriental costumes, the band also claim to have descended on the world of rap via a mythical fireball. The Fu part of their names and the band's moniker indicates 'For Unity', while 'Schnickens' is a wholly invented term signifying 'coalition'. Raised in East Flatbush in Brooklyn, the trio were discovered at the Carwash club, a specialist showcase event. Soon after Phil Pabon took over their affairs as manager, and began to set up dates for the group all over New York. They finally earned their break with an appearance in Feburary 1991 at the 1st Annual Rap Conference, at Howard's University in Washington DC. An A&R representative from Jive saw and liked their performance, and asked them to submit a tape. They received a contract in return. Famed for their onstage humour and high-speed delivery (including perfectly executed backward raps), they opened their account for their new employers with the dancehall-flavoured 'Ring The Alarm!', the warmth and humour of which typified the contents of their well-received debut album.

● ALBUMS: *Don't Take It Personal* (Jive 1992)★★★.

FUGEES

New York crew whose name is shortened from Refugees, due to two of the three rappers being expatriate Haitians. Their style is that of dry, cushioning beats, matched by the clever wordplay of rappers Wyclef Jean (b. 1970, Haiti), Lauryn 'L' Hill (b. 1975, New Jersey, New York, USA) and

Prakazrel 'Pras' Michel (b. 1972, Crown Heights, Brooklyn, New York, USA). The sound is not exactly unfamiliar; and the title of their debut album, *Blunted On Reality*, seemed to suggest they were coming from a similar direction to Cypress Hill, Digable Planets. However, the group are all non-users, the title signifying instead their belief that they do not need to smoke the weed to induce a state of heightened perception and relaxation. Similarly, their lyrical concerns are somewhat different, as might be expected of a group where the majority of members also attended university courses. Some of their targets included America's perception of Haitians as 'Boat People' (Prakazrel intended to return to his native Haiti, using profits from his music to help build schools and decent roads on the island) and their own, mixed gender status. 'Our music is a paradoxical thing. We blend soft and hardcore elements into it'. Musically this included rapping over acoustic guitars, as well as more upbeat numbers, both modes in which the Fugees excel. *The Score* was a magnificent album, one of the musical highlights of 1996, and accessible enough to bring their soulful jazz-rap to a wider market. 'Ready Or Not' and reworkings of 'Killing Me Softly' (Roberta Flack) and 'No Woman No Cry' (Bob Marley) were all international hit singles, and the album has already sold over five million copies. Hill's pregnancy meant the trio were largely inactive during 1997, with Wyclef Jean taking the time to release a successful solo album.
● ALBUMS: *Blunted On Reality* (Ruffhouse 1994)★★, *The Score* (Ruffhouse 1996)★★★★, *Bootleg Versions* (Columbia 1996)★★★.
● VIDEOS: *The Score* (SMV 1996).
● FURTHER READING: *Fugees: The Unofficial Book*, Chris Roberts.

FULL FORCE

Six-piece rap, R&B ensemble from Brooklyn, New York, comprising the three George brothers, Brian 'B-Fine', Paul Anthony and 'Bowlegged' Lou, plus cousins 'Baby' Gerry Charles, Junior 'Shy Shy' Clark and Curt 'TT' Bedeau. In addition to their three hit albums (all placed in the lower reaches of the Billboard Top 200), the sextet also provided production for protégés Lisa Lisa & Cult Jam, as well as U.T.F.O., Cheryl 'Pepsi' Riley and even James Brown. Full Force's debut album saw their anthropology rewarded with friends like Lisa Lisa, U.T.F.O., Howie Tee and the Real Roxanne dropping in. B-Fine would also help ex-U.T.F.O. man

Doctor Ice write songs for his debut album. They also found time to appear in *Krush Groove*, *House Party 1* and *2*, and form their own independent label, Homegrown Records. The first signing to their new empire was rap group Scream. A more dubious honour was also being the only rap, hip-hop group ever to be lent vocal assistance by Samantha Fox (on *Smoove*). A serious car accident threatened their future for some time as two members were out of action. They returned to full strength in 1997.
● ALBUMS: *Full Force* (Columbia 1985)★★, *Full Force Get Busy 1 Time!* (Columbia 1986)★★★★, *Guess Who's Comin' To The Crib?* (Columbia 1987)★★★, *Smoove* (Columbia 1989)★★, *Don't Sleep* (Columbia 1994)★★★.

FUN FACTORY

A cosmopolitan 90s pop/dance group from Hamburg, Germany, Fun Factory comprise singer Marie-Annett (b. France), backing singer Smooth T. (b. Italy), dancer Steve (b. Germany) and rapper Rod D. (b. USA). Since their inception in the early 90s, and with the substantive help of producer Bulow Aris, they have successfully achieved a string of pop hits including 'Groove Me', 'Take Your Chance', 'Close To You' and 'Pain'. Though these have failed to cross over to either the USA or UK, such singles have enjoyed enormous success in mainland European countries including France, Holland and Sweden, as well as Germany. Promoting their debut album, *Non Stop!*, Rod D. described their appeal thus: 'The main thing is that it grooves, kicks and beeps, and that people have a good time.'
● ALBUMS: *Non Stop!* (Edel 1995)★★★.
● COMPILATIONS: *All Their Best* (Edel 1997)★★★.

FUN-DA-MENTAL

An Asian 'world dance' band, the original Fun-Da-Mental had formed in Bradford, Yorkshire, in August 1991, specifically to play the Notting Hill Carnival of that year. Though all the members of the initial four-piece were born in Pakistan or India, they had each grown up in cities in northern England. The initial line-up was Propa-Ghandi (b. Aki Nawaz: aka Prince Haq), DJ Obeyo, Bad-Sha Lalliman and Man Tharoo Goldfinger (b. Inder Matharu; also of Transglobal Underground). Their debut single was 'Janaam - The Message', which immediately brought them to the attention of the national music press, particularly the dance magazines. After a cassette-only release, they followed up with 'Gandhi's Revenge', before 'Sister India', initially recorded for a live John Peel Radio 1 session. On the back of such exposure they looked certain to be on the verge of a significant breakthrough - when they themselves broke in two in late 1993, during a video shoot in Pakistan. Industry conjecture suggested rows over royalty payments and allocations, as rappers Goldfinger and Bad-Sha Lallaman left to team up with DJ Obeyo, and attempted to take the name with them. Eventually they became Det-ri-Mental. Fun-Da-Mental carried on; their first release following the departures was 'Countryman', in November 1993. Fun-Da-Mental's leadership remained Propa-Ghandi, formerly a member of gothic bands Southern Death Cult and Getting The Fear, and who is also responsible for Nation Records, and DJ Blacka D. They joined with Pop Will Eat Itself for the 'Ich Bin Ein Auslander' anti-racism tirade. Another controversial single followed in 1994, 'Dog Tribe', which began with a recorded answer-phone message left at the offices of Youth Against Racism by a member of sinister far-right group Combat 18. Fun-Da-Mental themselves have been targeted by the likes of the British National Party - who were forced to apologize after printing their picture in one of their magazines with the caption 'a gang of Asian thugs'. Fun-Da-Mental also became one of the first bands to visit the post-apartheid South Africa, which left a lasting impression on them, prior to the release of their debut album. This, the title adapted from Black Panther Bobby Seale, included remixes of 'Wrath Of The Black Man' and 'Countryman', guest appearances by Neil Sparkes of Transglobal Underground, poet Subi Shah and ex-Collapsed Lung singer Nihal. On subsequent albums the band have relentlessly pursued their musical and political ideals.

● ALBUMS: *Seize The Time* (Beggars Banquet 1994)★★★, *With Intent To Pervert The Cause Of Injustice* (Nation 1995)★★★, *Erotic Terrorism* (Nation 1998)★★★.

FUNKDOOBIEST

One of the hardest working crews in hip-hop, mid-90s rap group Funkdoobiest comprise Son Doobie, DJ Ralph M the Mexican and Tomahawk Funk (aka T-Bone). From Los Angeles, USA, they are managed by Happy Walters, who also looks after Cypress Hill and House Of Pain. Prior to

their establishment as a band Ralph M had worked on the now defunct Los Angeles radio station KDAY, at only 13 years of age, going on to DJ for Kid Frost. Funkdoobiest's debut single was the incessant 'Bow Wow Wow', which instantly launched them into the hearts of a nation of B-boys. Typically, their debut album was a rein-statement of old school principles, as Son Doobie eulogised in interviews: 'I'm an old skool supremacist. I'm a hip-hop inspector, I'm a funda-mentalist, to me hip-hop is a religion. You know it can't be trivialised'. The title-track of their second album was released as a single, and as well as a Little Richard sample featured a guest first verse from Cypress Hill's B-Real. Unfortunately it proved to be the best segment on the single, which was in turn the best track on the album. Ralph M has gone on to produce tracks for both House Of Pain and Mellow Man Ace. Funkdoobiest are certainly not the most politically correct of rappers. Many of their lyrics are vividly pro-pornography, Son Doobie's alter ego being the 'Porno King'. At least their commitment to rap's history is as staunch as their fondness for exposed flesh.

● ALBUMS: *Which Doobie U B* (Immortal 1993)★★★, *Wopbabuloop* (Immortal 1993)★★★, *Brothas Doobie* (Epic 1995)★★★.

FUNKI PORCINI

He left England at the age of 19 and moved to California, later settling in Italy where he lived for 10 years. While there he began recording for Ninja Tune Records as 9 Lazy 9, releasing two singles and the albums *Paradise Blown* and *Electric Lazyland* (both 1994) on which he combined hip-hop and funk beats with jazz-influenced sounds. He later assumed the name Funki Porcini and returned to England, where he continued his association with Ninja Tune. His single 'Long Road/Poseathon' was released at the beginning of 1995 and was followed by the album *Hed Phone Sex* in May; the latter was described as 'a trip around a bedlam-addled musical sex asylum' and 'a lush voyeuristic fantasy'. 'Long Road' presents a chilled hip-hop groove, melodic dub bass, tinkling piano, sleazy saxophone, sampled voice and various other sounds, to create a lush, abstract texture. 'Big Pink Inflatable' (1995) and *Love, Pussycats & Carwrecks* (1996) pursued Funky Porcini's themes of sex, pornography and voyeurism. Tracks such as 'River Of Smack' move away from the hip-hop and drum 'n' bass rhythms of most of the album, creating a dark, psychedelic dirge, underpinned by double bass and shuffling percussion.

● ALBUMS: *Hed Phone Sex* (Ninja Tune 1995)★★★, *Love Pussycats & Carwrecks* (Ninja Tune 1996)★★★★.

FUNKMASTER FLEX

Funkmaster Flex is New York, USA's most prominent modern hip-hop disc jockey, appearing on the Hot 97FM show, which is also the number 1-rated rap outlet in Chicago and Los Angeles, where it is syndicated. Flex (aka Stretch Armstrong) has also turned his skills to production and remix work for other artists, as well as making his own recordings. He started in hip-hop as a disc jockey for the band Deuces Wild, before securing his first radio slots for Chuck Chillout at Kiss FM in 1987. He went on to play the Manhattan club circuit until the end of the decade, having already served his apprenticeship on block parties in the early 80s. Together with his 'Flip Squad', which started as a partnership with Big Kap but expanded to include DJ Enuff, DJ Boodakhan, DJ Riz, Frankie Cutlass and Biz Markie, he has gone on to become a prominent remixer. His own recording career began with 'Dope On Plastic', for Bobby Konders' label Massive B. It was followed by 'Six Million Ways To Die' and 'C'Mon Baby' for Nervous Records' subsidiary Wreck Records. A debut album followed in 1995 which comprised 'old school jams' as well as the artist's own creations. He subsequently broadcast in the UK as co-host of Tim Westwood's regular link-ups for the Radio 1 *Rap Show*. His second album, this time for RCA Records, featured freestyle raps by Method Man, Redman, Erik Sermon and Keith Murray. Again, it attempted to capture the atmosphere of the unofficial mix tapes sold widely on the streets of New York. Taken from it, 'Every Day & Every Night', sung by R&B singer Yvette Michelle, was released as a single.

● ALBUMS: *Bounce To Da Bat* (Wreck 1995)★★★, *Funkmaster Flex Presents The Mix Tape Volume One* (Loud/RCA 1996)★★★★, *The Mix Tape Volume II* (Loud 1997)★★★★.

FUNKY FOUR (PLUS ONE MORE)

The Funky Four's background is an interesting one, with Lil' Rodney Cee having been part of the street-jivers the Magnificent Seven between 1977 and 1978. The Funky Four were founded when KK Rockwell and DJ Breakout, adding first Keith Keith and then female MC Sha Rock. Rahiem joined, then departed to take up an engagement with Grandmaster Flash. Keith Keith also left. With the addition of Lil' Rodney Cee, then Jazzy Jeff, the group became the Funky Four. None of the group were older than 17 when they signed with the Enjoy label, opening that imprint's account (in rap terms) with 'Rappin' And Rocking The House'. This utilised the Cheryl Lynn break, 'Gotta To Be Real', over which a 16-minute rap commentary was placed. The drums were programmed by Pumpkin, arguably rap's first production hero, and it was an impressive overall introduction. Shortly afterwards they switched to Sugarhill, adding the Plus or + One More suffix. In addition to this cast DJ Mark The 45 King would act as Breakout's 'record boy', locating and passing records up to the decks as his DJ requested them. They made their debut for Sugarhill with 'That's The Joint', a song arranged by jazz-funk organist Clifton 'Jiggs' Chase. Their performances at Bronx house parties included full-blown dance routines, a rare precursor to the vibrant live hip-hop of Stetsasonic. After a clash album with the Cash Crew, their career petered out somewhat, though Jazzy Jeff would go on to a brief solo career with Jive. Lil' Rodney Cee and KK Rockwell would go on to be partners in fellow underachievers, Double Trouble. At the same time Cee married Angela 'Angie B' Brown of Sequence fame.

FUNKY POETS

Presenting one of the more positive images of young black men in the ghetto, mid-90s US rap group the Funky Poets are a four-piece whose intelligent lyrical trickery is defiantly old school, yet whose outlook has been unquestionably informed by the Afrocentricity noises of the Jungle Brothers and De La Soul. The group is made up of brothers Paul and Ray Frazier and their cousins Christian Jordon and Gene Johnson. Together they broke through on the hit single, 'Born In The Ghetto', on which they recounted the urban tale of a young sister learning that she is pregnant at the age of 14. The narrative was turned round, making the situation a positive, with the central character emerging renewed, defiant and proud. 'We're just telling young black people that there is hope, despite the negative things they face everyday living in neighbourhoods that resemble war zones'. Their lyrics are sharply focused to this end, notably on the self-explanatory 'Message To A Funky Poet' poem, which contains couplets relaying the black inner-city experience in its many shades, from crack-dealing to barbecues and fountains gushing from fire hydrants.

● ALBUMS: *True To Life* (Epic 1993)★★★.

FUTURE SOUND OF LONDON

Offered to dance punters as the 'intelligent way out of blind-alley hardcore', Future Sound Of London emerged in the 90s, the brainchild of Gary Cobain (b. Bedford, England) and Brian Dougans. They met at college in Manchester in 1985, but Cobain soon left in order to set up his own studio under an Enterprise Allowance scheme. Both went on to earn their spurs in the Manchester house scene, Dougans completing a groundbreaking Top 10 hit (as Stakker) with 'Humanoid', after it had been adopted by the BBC as the theme tune to a 'youth' television programme. Their other projects together spawned Semi Real ('People Livin' Today'), Yage, Metropolis (the industrial *Metropolis* EP), Art Science Technology, Mental Cube (the ambient 'So This Is Love'), Candese, Intelligent Communication and Smart Systems. However, as Future Sound Of London they enjoyed a major crossover success with 'Papua New Guinea', an enticing, beautifully orchestrated piece. Both 'Papua New Guinea' and 'Metropolis' can be found on *Accelerator*, a seamless collection of rhythmic tracks. Under the name Amorphous Androgynous the pair recorded *Tales Of Ephidrina*, which used imaginative samples from sources as diverse as Peter Gabriel's soundtrack to *The Last Temptation Of Christ* and the alien's voice from the film *Predator*. Back under the FSOL banner, the duo released the excellent 'Cascade' in October 1993, a 30-minute workout taken from their second album, *Lifeforms*, which combined breakbeats with rumbling bass and heavy atmospherics. Unfortunately, the album was, at times, disappointing. On several of the pieces, FSOL had the potential to allow an interesting groove to develop into a full-blown track, as with the 'Cascade' single. However, they were all too willing to allow the vibe to deconstruct to basic, although well-produced, chill-out fodder. FSOL expressed their desire to break into other media, and throughout 1994 they experimented with live broadcasts from their own north London studio, via ISDN telephone links to various national and international radio stations, inviting listeners to view accompanying video graphics on their home computers. They released a collection of these tracks on an (originally limited release) album, simply titled *ISDN*. Taken from various live radio broadcasts and electronic café sessions, *ISDN* proved to be an engaging and involving departure from their previous full-length work. In 1996 FSOL released *Dead Cities*, which offered fresh sounds, ranging from the furiously harsh 'Herd Killing', to the pure choral piece, 'Everyone In The World Is Doing Something Without Me'.

● ALBUMS: *Accelerator* (Debut 1992)★★★★, as Amorphous Androgynous *Tales Of Ephidrina* (Virgin 1993)★★★★, *Lifeforms* (Virgin 1994)★★★, *ISDN* (1994)★★★, *Dead Cities* (Virgin 1996)★★★.

G

G-Wiz, Gary

b. North Carolina, USA. A white hip-hop producer, who moved to Freeport, New York, at the age of six. Musically-inclined parents, who owned a nightclub and booked acts like the Coasters and Drifters, were an early influence. Teaching himself first drums then computer programming, he sat in on the decks behind two rappers as part of New York rap group 516. In 1985 he met Chuck D of Public Enemy for the first time, and the two struck up a friendship, as G-Wiz was invited to work alongside Eric Sadler and Keith Schocklee as part of the Bomb Squad. When Schocklee formed his S.O.U.L. label, G-Wiz brought him their first act, Young Black Teenagers, who he would go on to produce and manage. His own production credits had begun with Public Enemy's *Apocalypse '91: The Enemy Strikes Black* album, and 'Can't Truss It' single. He would subsequently work with Run DMC ('Oooh Watcha Gonna Do', '3 In The Head'). Further work with Public Enemy followed on *Greatest Misses*, while Aaron Hall's 'Don't Be Afraid', for the *Juice* film soundtrack, gave him a hit record. His remix client base has branched out beyond the hip-hop frontier, including work for Janet Jackson, Bel Biv Devoe, Peter Gabriel, Lisa Stansfield, Anthrax, Helmut and Sinead O'Connor.

G., Gilly

b. Birmingham, West Midlands, England. The debut album of this harsh-voiced rapper from Birmingham, combined the geographically strong tradition of reggae with funk and soul samples. The most effective track on 1992's *Brothers Of The Jungle Zone* was 'Push It Along', which employed the widely imitated 'shuffling' drum pattern from Massive Attack's 'Daydreaming'. Although lyrically astute, the rest of the album's tracks, especially 'State Of Self-Decline', were too obviously redolent of west coast gangsta rappers such as Ice-T and Ice Cube. In the light of poor sales MCA Records chose not to renew Gilly G.'s contract.

● ALBUMS: *Brothers Of The Jungle Zone* (MCA 1992)★★.

G., Gina

b. Queensland, Australia. Having moved to Melbourne, Australia, in 1987, Gina G. began work as a DJ in that city's dance clubs. Eventually, she joined the influential dance group Bass Culture. Signed to Mushroom Records, the group reached the Australian Top 40 with their first single in 1992. It was written and sung by Gina herself. Later she moved to the UK, where she became involved in several projects before recording '(Ooh Aah Just A Little Bit'. A trite, Euro-pop dance song, it was entered in the Great British Song Contest (a preliminary round preceding the Eurovision Song Contest), and progressed to the final four of the competition before becoming the official British entry. Written by Simon Tauber and Motiv8's Steve Rodway (previously responsible for remixing Pulp's 'Disco 2000' and 'Common People', as well as their own hits 'Searching For The Golden Eye' and 'Break The Chain'), it was released on Warner Brothers Records' dance subsidiary, Eternal, in March 1996. It also became the first Eurovision song contest entry to be voted Single Of The Week by *Melody Maker*.

● ALBUMS: *Fresh* (Eternal/WEA 1997)★★★.

G., Warren

b. Warren Griffin III, *c.*1971, Long Beach, California, USA. Half-brother to Dr Dre, Griffin's parents relocated to Long Beach from Tennessee and Oklahoma before he was born. He was raised in a staunchly Christian tradition, and despite affiliations with gangsta rap, he maintained his allegiance to 'Jesus' at the top of his list of dedications on his debut album. It was Dre's World Class Wreckin' Cru which inspired him to follow a musical path. He first began rapping and producing while working at the local VIP record store. Later he helped form Dre's Dogg Pound collective, with Nate Dogg and his best friend, Snoop Doggy Dogg. The trio also worked together as part of the unrecorded group, 213. His role in the development of west coast rap was crucial - he is credited with having introduced Snoop Doggy Dogg to Dre (a meeting recalled in his debut album's 'Do You See'). Having subsequently produced a track for MC Breed ('Gotta Get Mine'), and appeared on both *The Chronic* and *Doggy Style*, he then wrote, produced and guested on

Mista Grimm's 'Indo Smoke' and 2Pac's 'Definition Of A Thug'. 'Indo Smoke' appeared in the film *Poetic Justice*, while 'Definition Of A Thug' was included on the soundtrack album, *Above The Rim*, which hit the number 1 spot on the US R&B album charts. Griffin's own debut as Warren G., 'Regulate', was the keynote to that album's success. Built around a sample of Michael McDonald's 'I Keep Forgettin'', which his father had played constantly when he was a child, it also became his first single - the first release on Chris Lighty's Violator imprint. *Regulate*, also the title of his debut album, immediately achieved double-platinum status, and confirmed the accessibility of his approach. He also departed from rap norms with his employment of live musicians. 'I figured people could get a better feeling with live music, plus it's original. You don't hear none of that crackling on my record.' Following a US tour with R. Kelly and Heavy D, he concentrated on producing the debut of his protégés, Da Twinz, who were part of the collective involved with *Regulate*. In 1996 he scored further international success with 'What's Love Got To Do With It', a hit single from the soundtrack to *Super Cop* which topped the German charts and reached the UK Top 5. His second album, *Take A Look Over Your Shoulder (Reality)*, was released as part of a new contract with Def Jam Records in 1997. Incorporating cover versions of Bob Marley's 'I Shot The Sheriff' and the Isley Brothers' 'Coolin' Me Out' (with a chorus sung by Ron Isley), Gifford was again responsible for production and direction. Once again demonstrating a welcome sense of style and class amid gangsta-rap's increasingly murky indulgences, it nevertheless failed to match the commercial impact of his debut.

● ALBUMS: *Regulate ... G Funk Era* (Violator/RAL 1994)★★★, *Take A Look Over Your Shoulder (Reality)* (G Funk Music/Def Jam 1997)★★★★.

GAGE, MARK

b. *c*.1961, USA. From Rochester, New York, Gage can genuinely point to a lifelong commitment to his art. 'I've been possessed by music ever since I was a very little kid. I was collecting 45s when I was four or five years old. I had boxes for them, and I would go off to my Grandma's house and just play records the whole time I was there. So, in a sense, even at that age I was a DJ'. However, until the early 90s he subsisted entirely on wages from waiting tables. Two cult 12-inch successes,

the *Cusp* EP and Vapourspace's 'Gravitational Arch Of 10', both for Plus 8, changed that. 'Gravitational Arch Of 10', was, in fact, a misprint. The title was supposed to have read 'Arch of Lo', but a mix up at the pressing plant ensured that it passed into techno folklore under a slightly different title. He went on to tour as Vapourspace, which is also the name of his studio, and was quickly signed up to a multi-album contract with ffrr/Internal, gaining rave reviews from a US tour with the Aphex Twin, Moby and Orbital.

● ALBUMS: As Vapourspace: *Themes From Vapourspace* (Internal 1994)★★★.

GAINES, REG E.

Based in Los Angeles, California, USA, this hip-hop artist has laboured hard to escape critical comparisons with Gil Scott-Heron, though that artist has also been a useful advocate. Gaines shared the bill with Scott-Heron at his first concerts for several years, held at the Troubadour club in Los Angeles in 1994. The title of Gaines' debut album of the same year for Mercury Records, *Please Don't Steal My Air-Jordans*, gave notice of his sense of humour and cynicism at the preoccupation of modern rap with the trappings of fiscal success. The album, which sold particularly well in the UK, combined such rich humour with Gaines' deeply held philosophical convictions, narrated in thoughtful spiels which combined lyricism with a deep-seated realism forged by his own experiences of urban ghettos. Gaines subsequently toured as part of MTV's 'Free Your Mind' spoken-word tour, alongside Maggie Estep and John S. Hall of King Missile, before the release of his second album, *The Sweeper Don't Clean My Street*. Cited by *Mojo* reviewer Lloyd Bradley as 'blues for the new millennium', it was another critical triumph.

● ALBUMS: *Please Don't Steal My Air-Jordans* (Mercury 1994)★★★★, *The Sweeper Don't Clean My Street* (Mercury 1996)★★★.

GALLIANO

b. Rob Gallagher. New age rapper and jazz poet who was originally inspired by a school visit to see Linton Kwesi Johnson, and subsequently retraced rap's origins to the Last Poets. When he left school Galliano began broadcasting on pirate radio and made appearances on the underground poetry circuit. The most important of these dates was at Gilles Peterson's 'Babylon' club in Charing Cross. There he enthusiastically partook of the resident rare groove/jazz sounds, and incorporated these as his musical backing. He released his first record, 'Frederick Lies Still', a tribute to Curtis Mayfield and Last Poet Jalal Mansur Nuriddin, with Peterson, but his first vinyl as Galliano was to be 'Welcome To The Story'. Galliano became an intrinsic component in the rise of Acid Jazz, building a fruitful relationship with producer Chris Bangs. When Peterson was headhunted by Phonogram Records to set up the similarly-inclined Talkin' Loud label, Galliano was his first signing. Although his solo work had thus far been successful, he elected to extend his live and studio performances by adding musicians and collaborators. Thus vocalist Constantine Weir (who sang on S-Express' two major hits, and managed the 70s funk club, the Shack) and drummer Bro.Spry (b. Crispin Robinson, formerly a professional skateboarder and a session contributor to Soul II Soul, Yazz, Bananarama, Young Disciples etc.) became official members of Galliano, as well as occasional appearances from Jalal Nuriddin. Aided by former Style Council member Mick Talbot, this line-up completed Galliano's debut album. By the advent of the group's third album, the line-up boasted singer Valerie Ettienne, Ernie McKone, Talbot, Spry and Mark Vandergucht (guitar). This formation's May 1994 single, 'Long Time Gone', based on the David Crosby song, was their first release in over two years, by which time the line-up included drummer Crispin Taylor. The subsequent album *The Plot Thickens* was critically acclaimed and described as an acid jazz/funk/urban alternative. Even without the cumbersome label it was an excellent record.

● ALBUMS: *In Pursuit Of The 13th Note* (Talkin' Loud 1991)★★★, *A Joyful Noise Unto The Creator* (Talkin' Loud 1992)★★★, *The Plot Thickens* (Talkin' Loud 1994)★★★★, *4* (Talkin' Loud 1996)★★★.

GANG STARR

Arguably hip-hop's most literate, challenging act on both musical and lyrical fronts, comprising Guru Keith E (b. Keith Allam, 18 July 1966, Roxbury, Massachusetts, USA; vocals and lyrics) and DJ Premier (b. Chris Martin, 3 May 1969, Brooklyn, New York, USA; music). Guru was born the son of a Boston municipal and superior court judge, but moved to Brooklyn following graduation with a degree in business administration from Atlanta's Morehouse College. He had previously worked as a counsellor in a maximum detention home in Boston, an experience which would inform many of his lyrics. Gang Starr was in existence before DJ Premier joined, originally also consisting of fellow rapper Damo D-Ski and DJ Wanna Be Down. Their early labours are recalled on cuts like 'The Lesson' and ' Bust A Move', both of which were produced by DJ Mark The 45 King. However, they were at that time still Boston based, and in the end opted to pursue more geographically convenient projects. Premier, meanwhile, had relocated to Texas to attend college, but left demos of his work with various labels before his departure. In Texas he put together the Inner City Posse, who finally saw their demo get some attention. Premier was offered a deal with Wild Pitch, but only on the condition he lost his original rapper. The label put him in touch with Guru instead, who had chanced upon one of Premier's demo tapes in their offices, and a marriage made in hip-hop heaven was born. However, Premier had to return to college in Texas, and so the duo's liaison took place largely over the phone, and by sending each other tapes. The fruits of their labour were unveiled on a debut album, *No More Mr Nice Guy*, completed in ten days while Premier was on vacation. 'Manifest', taken from the album, picked up airplay on *Yo! MTV Raps*, and caught the attention of film director Spike Lee. In the process of completing his new film, *Mo Better Blues*, Lee was greatly impressed by album track 'Jazz Thing', and asked his musical director, Branford Marsalis, to track Gang Starr down. Marsalis urged the duo to cut a recording of Lotis Eli's poem about the history of jazz to a hip-hop rhythm, for inclusion on the film's soundtrack. The song they eventually came up with would see release as 'Jazz Thing'. Not only one of rap's most crucial moments, 'Jazz Thing' also gave Gang Starr a manifesto for their subsequent career. Credited with popularising jazz-rap, they took the form to its logical conclusion with *Step In The Arena*, before retreating to hardcore pastures for *Daily Operation*. Both Guru and Premier have strived to be seen as individuals outside of the Gang Starr hallmark. A joint collaboration with the Dream Warriors on 'I've Lost My Ignorance' aside, each has increased their profile with solo projects. Premier has produced widely for KRS-1, Fu-Schnickens, Big Daddy Kane and Heavy D among many others, while Guru set up the winning Jazzamatazz situation. The latter comprised his distinctive rap style with the best of modern freeform jazz. An interesting departure considering that Premier has always used samples rather than live instruments, though since *Daily Operation* he has been forced to credit and clear them. Though such forays encouraged speculation that Gang Starr were about to split, the duo belied the critics with a storming return on *Hard To Earn*. Back to his freestyle, flowing best, it was the second outing for the posse of rappers that Guru had formed into the Gang Starr Foundation: Jeru The Damaja, Big Shug (who was a collaborator with Guru in his early days in Boston), Little Dap and Felachi The Nutcracker. Over four albums Gang Starr proved themselves to be rap's most consistent, dynamic team. After a prolonged absence they returned to the scene in 1998 with the inventive and diverse *Moment Of Truth*.

● ALBUMS: *No More Mr Nice Guy* (Wild Pitch 1990)★★★, *Step In The Arena* (Chrysalis 1991)★★★★, *Daily Operation* (Chrysalis 1992)★★, *Hard To Earn* (Chrysalis 1994)★★★, *Jazzmatazz Volume II - The New Reality* (1995)★★★, *Moment Of Truth* (Cooltempo 1998)★★★.

GANGSTA PAT

b. Patrick Hall, Memphis, Tennessee, USA. Gangsta Pat is the son of Willie Hall, who had played with R&B greats like Isaac Hayes, and continues his family's musical traditions by playing all the instruments on his releases. He is also responsible for their writing, composition and production. He quickly rose to prominence with his debut album and single (the introductory 'I Am The Gangsta'). Both became hot items in the south west of America, while a second set spawned hit singles in 'Gangsta Boogie' and 'Stay Away From Cali'. The video for the former was particularly well received, capitalised on the then vogueish hip-hop dance craze of the same name. Transferring to Wrap/Ichiban, Pat has continued to hone his skills and, despite the critical backlash against gangsta rap, maintains that his music is about 'talent, cool rhymes and doin' things on your own'.

● ALBUMS: *#1 Suspect* (Atlantic 1990)★★★, *All About Comin' Up* (Wrap/Ichiban 1993)★★★★, *Sex, Money And Murder* (Wrap/Ichiban 1994)★★★, *Homicidal Lifestyle* (Power 1997)★★.

GANJA KRU

One of the collectives at the forefront of UK jungle in 1997, Ganja Kru comprise the pseudonymous trio of Pascal, DJ Zinc and leader DJ Hype (b. *c*.1967, England). Releases such as the 'Super Sharp Shooter' 12-inch (which sampled LL Cool J) and *New Frontiers* EP helped to establish a reputation for intelligent but unrelenting drum 'n' bass. With a major label contract with RCA Records (through its Parousia Records dependent), the group are also responsible for running the Frontline and Tru Playaz independent labels. The latter has brought artists including DJ Swift and MC Fats to vinyl. Before Ganja Kru's breakthrough, Hype could already boast of a significant past in dance music, beginning with a stint as a DJ on the early 90s rave scene. Despite the growing success of the band, he continues to work most evenings as a DJ.

GANXSTA RID AND THE OTHA SIDE

One of the least appetising and gifted of the new breed of west coast rap collectives, Ganxsta Rid and his backing group, the Otha Side, made their debut in 1996 with *Occupation Hazardous*. The album was released in the UK on the predominantly hard rock-based Music For Nations label. The only other rap group to have made much of an impression on that label were fellow Los Angeles group Boo-Yaa Tribe, leading many critics to suspect that the groups were one and the same. It was later confirmed that Ganxsta Rid And The Otha Side were indeed an attempt by the Tribe to adopt a new persona and pick up on some of the commercial possibilities granted by the breakthrough of Dr. Dre's G-Funk style. It was an attempt that failed miserably.

● ALBUMS: *Occupation Hazardous* (Music For Nations 1996)★★★.

GARAGE

A musical term that, in the dance world, is generally taken to indicate smooth house music with female diva vocals, rather than the ragged guitar bands it represented in the late 60s and 70s. It took the name from the success of its principal early venue, Larry Levan's Paradise Garage, in New York. Levan (b. *c*.1954, d. 8 November 1992) was the producer behind 'electro' standards from the Peach Boys ('Don't Make Me Wait'), and produced Taana Gardner's 'Heartbeat', Instant Funk's 'I Got My Mind Made Up' and Skyy's 'First Time Around'. Best of all, arguably, was his remix of Gwen Guthrie's 'Ain't Nothing Goin' On But The Rent'. This lent him obvious 'disco' credentials, which proliferate in the garage music of the 90s.

Levan ran the Paradise Garage from opening to closure (1976 to 1987), but died in the early 90s after a heart attack brought on by cocaine addiction. Others had already accepted the torch, with Junior Vasquez (an early attendee at Paradise Garage) launching the hugely popular Sound Factory night, and producers such as David Morales perfecting the formula. Much generic garage music has come and gone, its origins in disco ensuring that it is the staple output of many mainstream pop dance acts. At its best (Crystal Waters, the aforementioned Morales) it can be an elegiac, uplifting art form; at its worst it is all too often predictable, formulaic and stiflingly unadventurous.

GARNIER, LAURENT

b. 1 February 1966, Boulogne sur Seine, near Paris, France. Influential European DJ figurehead Garnier enjoyed a previous life as a restaurant manager, then footman at the French Embassy (where he claims to have served UK dignitaries including the Queen, Princess Diana and Margaret Thatcher). Regarded as France's finest techno DJ, Garnier, who started behind the decks at the Hacienda in October 1987, insists that his musical spectrum is much wider. Although he has been a powerful advocate of all things Detroit for some time, he has also had a hand in the establishment of the European hard trance movement. A typical evening will see him mixing standbys from Rhythim Is Rhythim (Derrick May) and Joe Smooth ('Promised Land') against classic Salsoul and disco records (typically Donna Summer's 'I Feel Love'), in addition to the hottest new underground sounds. His reputation is built on a punishing schedule, performing five nights a week in up to four different countries within Europe. He also runs a club in Paris called Wake Up, whose free-ranging music policy was reflected on the 'Wake Up' remix of Moby's 'Hymn'. The latter was just one of many remixing projects that have brought him to the forefront of the dance world. Similarly, his label, FNAC, established with Eric Morand (his PR), has pioneered French dance music. It has been superseded by a new imprint, F-Communications. However, before they bowed out of their involvement with FNAC, they put together a compilation, *La Collection*, which was extraordinarily well received by dance critics and pundits. Many of the acts featured followed Garnier and Morand to their new label.

● ALBUMS: *RawWorks* (F Communications 1996)★★★, *30* (F Communications 1997)★★★.

GEE STREET RECORDS

Established at the end of 1987 by managing director Jon Baker, who had lived in New York in the early 80s, fixing his roots in black music, hip-hop and electro. He returned to London but tired quickly of music industry machinations within the majors and elected to set up a separate entity. He enrolled his co-conspirator DJ Richie Rich as his partner and Gee Street was born. The label began with the 'Scam 1 & 2' record, but soon built up an eclectic dance/rap roster, gaining a distribution deal through Rough Trade. They immediately set up a sister office in New York to allow them to gauge and exploit both markets, their first US signing being the Jungle Brothers. The label also licensed material from US labels including Warlock and Idlers. However, the most succesful act would prove to be the Stereo MC's and their Ultimatum remix arm (Birch and 'The Head' having played a prominent role in establishing Gee Street studio). Other early acts included Outlaw Posse and Boonsquawk. Rich, who also recorded for the label, went on to found Happy Family Records in 1992 and become a video jockey for MTV. He split with Baker when Island bought out Gee Street, but agreed to offer their artists his remix skills. Simon Quance took over as label manager, while the label also grew an extra tentacle with the Gee-Zone subsidiary (Doi-ing, Spooky, etc.).

GENERAL KANE

b. Mitch McDowell, 1954, San Bernadino, California, USA, d. January 1992. McDowell took the professional name General Kane (formerly General Caine) in tribute to an officer who had supported his artistic ambitions when he was at military school. After leaving that institution, he formed the group Booty People with several future members of War, before assembling an eight-piece rap group and signing with Motown in 1986. The group's debut single, 'Crack Killed Applejack', was an uncompromising reflection of drug addiction on the inner city streets, and reached number 12 in the black music charts despite being barred from airplay. Subsequent releases have mellowed General Kane's approach, without losing their commitment to the basic rap sound of the late 80s - though the group's album, *Wide Open*, does include a romantic ballad, 'Close Your Eyes', which features vocals from two of the group's less prominent members, Cheryl McDowell and Danny Macon. Mitch McDowell was murdered in January 1992. Their catalogue has remained in print through the efforts of their former producer, Grover Wimberly III, who runs his own label, King Bee Records.

● ALBUMS: *Let Me In* (1978)★★★, *Get Down Attack* (Groove Time, 1980)★★★★, *Girls* (Taboo, 1982)★★, *Dangerous* (1984)★★★, *In Full Chill* (1986)★★★, *Wide Open* (1987)★★★.

GENIUS

The Genius (aka GZA) is one of the many talents who comprise the Wu-Tang Clan, the chess-playing, martial arts hip-hop posse whose ranks include Raekwon, Method Man, Ol' Dirty Bastard and RZA, among others. Like his compatriots he is a native of Staten Island, New York, USA. In common with Prince Rakeem, another member of the Wu-Tang Clan, the Genius had already released a solo album for Cold Chillin' Records before becoming part of the collective. However, when the Clan as a whole signed with BMG Records, provision for each member to work solo was enshrined in the contract, and the Genius used the opportunity to link with his third record company, Geffen Records. The Genius's recent solo work closely mirrors that of the Wu-Tang Clan - the musical backing is one of stripped down beats, with samples culled from martial arts movies and film dialogue. This came as little surprise given that RZA - the production mastermind behind both the collective Wu-Tang Clan and several associated solo releases - was again involved in *Liquid Swords*. Lyrically, Genius continued to concentrate on what he knew best, down at heel scenarios concerning blue collar crime and drug smuggling. The chilling true story tale of 'Killah Hills 10304' offered a perfect example of the measures his acquaintances on the street would undergo to get paid - 'He tried to smuggle half a key/He even underwent surgery/They say his pirate limp gave him away as the Feds rushed him/Coming through US Customs'. Among many to be impressed by Genius's transition from group member to solo stardom was *Select* magazine, whose reviewer wrote '*Liquid Swords* sneaks under the tape to qualify as rap album of the year.'

● ALBUMS: *Words From The Genius* (Cold Chillin' 1991)★★★, *Liquid Swords* (Geffen 1996)★★★★.

GERARDO

b. Gerardo Mejia III, 16 April 1965, Guayaquil, Ecuador. This popular Latin rapper has based his career in Los Angeles since he moved to Glendale, California, USA, at the age of 12. From the outset of his career Gerardo has specialised in both Spanish and English rhymes, though it is his athleticism in jumping between the two languages which has most distinguished him. In 1985 he won two separate televised street-dance competitions, leading to roles in the films *Colors*, playing a gang leader, and *Can't Buy Me Love*. He would enjoy his first major crossover success in April 1990, with 'Rico Suave' making number 7 in the US charts. 'We Want The Funk' was also successful. His debut album, released the following year, included an appearance by 'rap grandfather' George Clinton. The title of this collection, *Mo' Ritmo*, translates as 'more rhythm'. Though his rapping style is well-heeled, it is somewhat lacking in innovative subject matter. He is notorious for taking the stage bare-chested and with his zip undone to tantalise his female followers, which has ensured the popularity of his videos on MTV.

● ALBUMS: *Mo' Ritmo* (Interscope 1991)★★★.

GET SET VOP

This mid-90s US rap duo consist of brothers Infinite Kundalini and Kwabena The Triumphant, or Mark and Scott Batson as their mother knew them. Raised in the Bushwick sector of Brooklyn, New York, the group were first spotted while playing support for Maverick recording artist Me'Shell during the Washington Area Music Association's 1990 convention. Leotis Clyburn of Polydor was in attendance, but lost touch until two years later when he saw their name under the live listings. The first result of a long-term deal was the single, 'Pretty Brown Babies (Pro Seed)', and live dates with Jazzamatazz, with whom they have frequently been compared thanks to their mellow, jazzy groove.

● ALBUMS: *Voice Of The Projects* (Polydor 1993)★★★.

GETO BOYS

Houston, Texas-based gangsta rappers, led by the notorious Bushwick Bill (b. Richard Shaw, Jamaica, West Indies), Brad 'Scarface' Jordan and Willie 'D' Dennis, alongside DJ Ready Red (b. Collins Lyaseth). The latter had left the band by

early 1991. In fact the Geto Boys had originally started with a completely different line up in 1988; featuring Jukebox, Ready Red and Johnny C, with Bushwick a dancer. When Johnny C and Jukebox quit (Jukebox was subsequently jailed for murder) former Rap-A-Lot solo artists Scarface and Willie D were added by the record company. It was this line-up which made the headlines. In 1990 the David Geffen company refused to distribute *Grip It! On That Other Level*, following the controversy over some of its lyrics (which included allusions to necrophilia). The group returned to Rap-A-Lot, but shortly afterwards Bushwick Bill forced his girlfriend to shoot him after threatening their baby (he lost an eye). Their next album was bedecked with a picture of him being pushed through a hospital by his two pals after the incident. A fair introduction into the world of the Geto Boys, characterised by thoroughly nasty, sensationalist tales, which made their work difficult to evaluate objectively. Some of the most vile sequences of words ever used in popular music appear on their debut album, glorying in rape, mutilation and violence. Though at first appearance a cocktail of pure hatred, hidden beneath their more self-serving statements were tiny vignettes filled with persuasive detail - 'Life In The Fast Lane' on their debut, and 'Mind Playing Tricks On Me' on the follow-up being the best examples. Not that this is nearly enough to forgive them their otherwise dangerously stupid attitudes. Certainly though, the defence of 'reporting from the front-line' would seem to be more honourable in their case than many others, bearing in mind Bushwick Bill's aforementioned partial blinding, and the alarmingly high gun profile of the deep south. The group have gone on to concentrate more on their solo careers, following internal friction (Bushwick and Willie D at several points refusing to appear on stage at the same time). On *The Resurrection* the oriiginal three Bushwick, Willie 'D' and Scarface were back together.
● ALBUMS: As the Ghetto Boys: *Grip It! On That Other Level* (Rap-A-Lot 1990)★★★. As the Geto Boys: *The Geto Boys* (Def American 1990)★★★, *We Can't Be Stopped* (Rap-A-Lot 1991)★★★, *Best Uncut Dope* (Rap-A-Lot 1992)★★, *Till Death Us Do Part* (Rap-A-Lot 1993)★★, *The Resurrection* (Virgin 1996)★★★.

GHETTO MAFIA

An Atlanta, Georgia-based crew, The Ghetto Mafia are, as their name implies, a hardcore rap outfit, relentlessly exploring the life cycle of the young, alienated black man. The group is fronted by the twin rapping talents of Nino and Wicked. The lead-off single for their debut album, 'Everday Thang In The Hood', introduced guest vocals by MC Breed, who also produced the album. These were nothing if not controversial songs - 'Mr President' talking about not only assasinating the President, but wiping out his whole family for good measure.
● ALBUMS: *Draw The Line* (Funktown 1994)★★, *Straight From The Dec* (Down South 1997)★★.

GIFTED

The Gifted are a religiously-motivated hip-hop trio from London, England, led by rapper Prince Gilbert Okyere. He had originally released a debut solo EP on his own GBR Recordings label, which introduced his advocacy of Christian 'street ministry'. A debut album followed, credited to the Gifted and provocatively titled *Transformation Of The Mind*. Much of the interest surrounding its release could be attributed to the unusual presence of Christian imagery in a rap community now dominated by Muslim principles. Despite the record's unorthodoxy within its own genre, there was little else about *Transformation Of The Mind* to distinguish the Gifted from other under-achieving UK rap acts of the period.
● ALBUMS: *Transformation Of The Mind* (GBR 1994)★★.

GINUWINE

b. Elgin Lumpkin, *c.*1974, Washington, D.C., USA. Talented R&B performer Ginuwine began his musical apprenticeship at the age of 12, performing at parties and (illegally) at bars with his friends in the neighbourhood group, Finesse. From this he graduated to a solo act, which was initially built around impersonations of his childhood idol, Michael Jackson. At the age of 21 he chose to sign with the New York-based Sony subsidiary 550 Records, despite interest from several other parties. He enjoyed immediate success with the release of 'Pony', an unusual, synthesizer-infused R&B effort, which reached number 4 on *Billboard's* Hot R&B Airplay chart. As a result, his debut album, which included a cover version of Prince's 'When Doves Cry', was assured of mainstream media attention. To promote it, Ginuwine set out on a national tour in support of labelmate Aaliyah.

● ALBUMS: *The Bachelor* (550/Sony 1997) ★★★★.

GLAMOROUS HOOLIGAN

Comprising Dean Cavanagh, Enzo Annechianni and Martin Diver, and based in Bradford, Yorkshire, England, Glamorous Hooligan took their name from the members' past experiences 'running with a local football firm'. Their breakthrough release came with 1994's *Wasted Youth Club Classics*, a collision of breakbeats with disparate samples and trip-hop-inspired 'otherness'. Part of the record's ethos was a rebuttal of the way the modern club scene has evolved. The bleak but realistic mood of the album was further explored with the release of the attendant 10-inch single, 'Stone Island Estate'.

● ALBUMS: *Wasted Youth Club Classics* (Delancey 1994)★★★.

GLOWORM

Group fronted by Sedric Johnson (b. Alabama, USA). The leader of the 100-strong Long Beach Choir, he was spotted at a soul revue by Englishman Will Mount, who was searching for a singer. After an impromptu performance Mount, who together with producer/remixer Rollo forms the musician team behind Gloworm, was won over. They anchored Johnson's gospel-inspired vocals to a club beat to produce records including 'Lift My Cup' and 'Carry Me Home', both based on traditional songs. The result was reviewed as 'spiritual hard house', and was widely admired. 'Lift My Cup' was unveiled on Hooj Tunes at the end of 1992, before the group switched to Go! Beat.

GOATS

This Philadelphia, USA rap trio consists of Oatie Kato, Madd and Swayzack. From early in their career they made a conscious decision to play live (without DAT, often rapping freestyle) whenever possible, and earned immediate notoriety by playing at a celebration of Columbus' discovery of America - educating their audience about the degradation native Americans consequently suffered. They were snapped up by Columbia subsidiary Ruffhouse on the basis of their first, four-track demo. Their debut album was a joy, with alter-egos Chickenlittle and his kid brother Hangerhead acting as tour guides through the strange world of 90s America. Their political targets included Dan Quayle, while 'Drive By Bumper Cars' parodied hardcore rap. Their puns were incisive, sometimes almost funny: ('Hey Mr Columbus! You took all my money/No I didn't kid, I discovered it'). Singles such as 'Do The Digs Dug?' again returned to the rights of the oppressed, singling out Leonard Peltier, a community leader in South Dakota in 1973, as 'Our Mandela'. However, their UK appearances in 1993 without founder member Oatie fuelled rumours of a split, which were confirmed on the advent of a second album on which Swayzack took the lead on a less-politicised set.

● ALBUMS: *Tricks Of The Shade* (Ruffhouse/Columbia 1993)★★★★, *No Goats, No Glory* (Ruffhouse/Columbia 1994)★★★.

GOLDIE

b. *c.*1964, Wolverhampton, Warwickshire, England. A distinctive visual as well as aural presence, graffiti artist, hardcore and jungle innovator Goldie is distinguished by the gold-inlaid front teeth from which many assume he takes his name. In fact, Goldie is an abbreviation of 'Goldilocks', a nickname he earned from his gold-dreadlocked hip-hop days. Though he jealously guards his true identity, his origins can be fixed in Wolverhampton, England, though he currently spends much of his time at clubs in London. In his youth he travelled to Miami and New York but returned to subsidize his musical activities as a (somewhat unsuccessful) mugger. Possibly his most famous graffiti illustration was his 'Change The World' mural at Queens Park Rangers' Loftus Road football ground in London. Later, his paintings, which had once been the main source of his criminal record, were sold for over £3,000 each. His early musical experiences were most notably conducted as part of the Metalheads collective (later Metalheadz) on hardcore imprint Reinforced Records. He had previously recorded a white label EP under the name Ajaz Project and then 'Killer Muffin' as a solo artist. The Metalheads' *Angel* EP was a major breakthrough for 'intelligent hardcore', and when offshoots of hardcore (an extreme hybrid of techno) mixed with reggae and evolved into jungle in 1993/4, Goldie found himself at the centre of the new movement. However, he had little time for General Levy and other artists he saw as 'bandwagon jumpers'. His own 'Inner City Life' single maximized the possibilities of the drum 'n' bass sound of jungle, using them as a framework for melodious vocals and other musical innovations. Similarly, the sounds contained on *Timeless*, the first jungle album released on a major label and to find mainstream approval, eschewed any notion of observing dance music convention. He admitted to influences as diverse as the Stranglers (notably Jean Jacques Burnel's bass), 10cc and hip-hop behind this multilayered recording. His compatriots in the project were Moving Shadow Records boss Rob Playford, keyboard player Justina Curtis, singers Diane Charlemagne and Lorna Harris, plus jazz musicians Cleveland Watkiss and Steve Williamson. This array of talent ensured a multi-dimensional sound, underpinned by breakbeats and rolling cycles of rhythm. The press had finally found a figurehead for the previously anonymous jungle movement, a role Goldie subsequently lived up to in sometimes reckless style.

● ALBUMS: *Goldie Presents Metalheadz: Timeless* (London 1995)★★★★, with Rob Playford *The Shadow* (Moving Shadow 1997)★★★, *Saturnz Return* (London 1998)★★★.
● COMPILATIONS: *Platinum Breakz* (Metalheadz/London 1996)★★★★.

GOOD BOY RECORDS

Mark Auerbach and Steve Travell's London-based operation. The company was formed in December 1992. Auerbach and Travell were already well known in dance circles for their work as Bump (whose 'I'm Rushin'' graced the label). They have their own studio, and elected to start Good Boy because they were squandering too many of their own ideas on remixes for other people. A 'classy New York style' is the intention, based on their admiration for the Strictly Rhythm empire. Distributed through the Network umbrella, they certainly started well with releases such as Wax Factor's 'Only Love'.

GOOD LOOKING RECORDS

This label was set up in 1991 by the DJ LTJ Bukem and helped to pioneer and develop drum 'n' bass. After four of Bukem's own singles, including 'A Demon's Theme' (1991) and 'Music' (1993), Good Looking began to release material by other artists, including Aquarius, Blame, Intense, Peshay and PFM. Following the success of the club Speed in central London, in 1995 Good Looking began promoting Bukem's touring club Logical Progression, which featured the label's

artists and was accompanied by a series of albums of the same name; it has since completed trips to Germany, Japan and America as well as several tours of the UK, including nights at the Ministry Of Sound and Cream. One side of each *Logical Progression* album featured material, generally by Good Looking artists, selected by Bukem. The first two also included mixed sides, by Bukem and Blame, respectively, while the third contained a recording of Bukem DJing with the nine-piece drum 'n' bass band Intense at Brixton Academy. In 1995 Tony Fordham joined as a business partner and helped to develop the label into an umbrella for a number of subsidiaries, including Looking Good, Nexus, Ascendant Grooves, Diverse, 720° and Cookin'. Much of the sound associated with Good Looking revolves around high tempos and busy drums, contrasted with slow-moving dubby bass and impressionistic chords and patterns. Other releases include the two *Earth* compilations and the *Progression Sessions* albums. The label has also developed a range of clothing and merchandise.

GRAND PUBA

b. Maxwell Dixon, New Rochelle, New York, USA. A founder member of Brand Nubian, and before that Masters Of Ceremony, Puba kicked off his solo career with a track, 'Fat Rat', on the *Strictly Business* soundtrack. When his debut album was unveiled, the smooth reggae backing was subjugated by Puba's by now familiar lyrical subject matter. Born the son of a Five Percent Nation Islamic father, Puba's raps reinstated that doctrine just as forcefully as he had done with Brand Nubian, but it was generally a more playful set. It included a guest appearance from Mary J. Blige. Puba guested on Fat Joe's *Represent* album, on 'Watch The Sound'.

● ALBUMS: *Reel To Reel* (Elektra 1992)★★★.

GRANDMASTER FLASH

b. Joseph Saddler, 1 January 1958, Barbados, West Indies, but raised in the Bronx, New York. This pivotal force in early rap music grew up in the South Bronx, studying at Samuel Gompers Vocational Technical High School, spending his leisure time attending DJ parties thrown by early movers such as Grandmaster/DJ Flowers, MaBoya and Peter 'DJ' Jones. The latter took him under his wing, and Flash intended to combine Jones' timing on the decks with the sort of records that Kool Herc was spinning. Hence in the early

70s Saddler set about discovering the way to 'segue' records (commonly pronounced segway) smoothly together without missing a beat, highlighting the 'break' - the point in a record where the drum rhythm is isolated or accentuated - and repeating it. With admirable fortitude, Saddler spent upwards of a year in his apartment on 167th Street experimenting. The basis of his technique was to adapt Herc's approach, using two turntables each spinning the same record. He would then interrupt the flow of the disc offering the basic rhythm by overlaying the 'break', repeating the process by switching channels on the mixer, as necessary. The complexity and speed of the operation (the second desk would have to be rotated backwards to the beginning of the 'break' section) earned him the nickname Flash when he brought the style to his public, owing to the rapid hand movements. However, attention grabbing though this was, the style had not yet quite gelled into what Flash required. He decided, instead, to invite a vocalist to share the stage with him. He worked in this respect with first Lovebug Starski, then Keith Wiggins. Wiggins would eventually come to be known as Cowboy within Grandmaster Flash's Furious Five, in the process becoming one of the first 'MCs', delivering rhymes to accompany Flash's turntable wizardry. Flash continued in the block/park party vein for a considerable time, often illegally by hooking up his sound system to an intercepted mains cable until the police arrived. One person, at least, saw some commercial potential in his abilities, however. Ray Chandler stepped up and invited Flash to allow him to promote him, and charge an entrance fee (previous hip-hop events had always been free). Initially incredulous at the thought that anyone would actually pay to see them, Flash nevertheless accepted.

Flash put together a strong line-up of local talent to support him: Grandmaster Melle Mel (b. Melvin Glover) and his brother Kid Creole (b. Nathaniel Glover) joining Cowboy, this line-up initially titled Grandmaster Flash And The 3 MCs. Two further rappers, Duke Bootee (b. Ed Fletcher) and Kurtis Blow subsequently joined, but were eventually replaced by Rahiem (b. Guy Todd Williams; ex-Funky Four) and Scorpio (b. Eddie Morris, aka Mr Ness). The Zulu Tribe was also inaugurated, with the express purpose of acting as security at live events: with Flash popularising the rap format, rival MCs sprang up to take their mentor and each other on. These head to heads often had the result of garnering the participants equipment as prizemoney. A crew who were not popular could expect to see their turntables and sound system rehabilitated for their troubles. Just as Jamaican sound system owners like Duke Reid and Coxsone Dodd had done in the 60s, Flash, Kook Herc and Afrika Bambaataa would hide their records from prying eyes to stop their 'sound' being pirated. Similarly, record labels were removed to avoid identifying marks. The Furious Five, meanwhile, made their debut proper on September 2nd, 1976. Shortly afterwards they released their first record, 'Super Rappin'', for Enjoy. Although hugely popular within the hip-hop fraternity, it failed to make commercial inroads, and Flash tried again with 'We Rap Mellow' (as the Younger Generation on Brass) and 'Flash To The Beat' (as Flash And The Five for Bozo Meko). However, it would be Joe Robinson Jnr. of Sugarhill Records who finally bought out their Enjoy contract. He had seen the Grandmaster in action at Disco Fever, 'hip-hop's first home', which had opened in the Bronx in 1978. His wife, Sylvia, wrote and produced their subsequent record, a relationship which kicked off with 'Freedom'. On the back of a major tour, certainly the first in rap's embryonic history, the single sold well, going on to earn a gold disc. The follow-up 'Birthday Party' was totally eclipsed by 'Grandmaster Flash On The Wheels Of Steel', the first rap record to use samples, and a musical *tour de force*, dramatically showcasing the Flash quick-mixing and scratching skills. Memorable enough, it too was overshadowed when Sugarhill brought the band in to record one of Robinson's most memorable compositions (written in tandem with Bootee): 'The Message'. The single, with its daunting, apocalyptic rumblings, significantly expanded not just rap but black music's boundaries, though the Furious Five had been less convinced of its worth when it was first offered to them in demo form. In just over a month the record achieved platinum sales. In the wake of the record's success Flash enquired of his Sugarhill bosses why no money was forthcoming. When he did not receive satisfactory explanation, he elected to split, taking Kid Creole and Rahiem with him, signing to Elektra Records. The others, headed by Melle Mel, would continue as Melle Mel and the Furious Five, scoring nearly instantly with another classic, 'White Lines (Don't Do It)'. Bearing in mind the subject matter of Mel's flush of success, it was deeply ironic that Flash had now become a freebase cocaine addict. In the 80s Flash's name largely retreated into the mists of rap folklore until he was reunited with his Furious Five in 1987 for a Paul Simon hosted charity concert in New York, and talk of a reunion in 1994 eventually led to the real thing. Back with the Furious Five he hosted New York's WQHT Hot 97 show, 'Mic Checka', spinning discs while prospective rappers rang up to try to pitch their freestyle rhymes down the telephone. Unfortunately the reunion would not include Cowboy, who died on 8 September 1989 after a slow descent into crack addiction. Flash also helped out on Terminator X's *Super Bad* set, which brought together many of the old school legends.

● ALBUMS: As Grandmaster Flash And The Furious Five *The Message* (Sugarhill 1982)★★★★, *Greatest Messages* (Sugarhill 1984)★★★, *On The Strength* (Elektra 1988)★★. As Grandmaster Flash *They Said It Couldn't Be Done* (Elektra 1985)★★, *The Source* (Elektra 1986)★★, *Ba-Dop-Boom-Bang* (Elektra 1987)★★★.

● COMPILATIONS: Grandmaster Flash And The Furious Five/Grandmaster Melle Mel *Greatest Hits* (Sugarhill 1988)★★★★, *The Best Of ...* (Rhino 1994)★★★★, *The Greatest Mixes* (Deepbeats 1998)★★★.

GRANDMASTER SLICE

b. c.1967, South Boston, Virginia, USA. 90s US rap artist Slice began to flex his rapping skills at the age of 11, going on to DJ and dance for a group titled Ebony Express by his teenage years. He subsequently formed his own combo, playing at parties in and outside of his hometown, taking his talents seriously enough to record his first demo tapes. It was while attending Halifax County Senior High School that Slice hooked up with Scratchmaster Chuck T. (b. Charles Fulp), who became his road manager and DJ. They had known of each other's rapping interests, having previously gone head to head in an after-school talent show. Together they released a debut album on independent distributor Selecto Hits Records, which was subsequently picked up by Jive. They had been suitably impressed by one of the album cuts, 'Thinking Of You', a slow-climbing hit throughout the US.

● ALBUMS: *The Electric Slice (Shall We Dance)* (Selecto Hits/Jive 1991)★★★.

GRANDMIXER DST

b. Derek Howells, 23 August 1960, New York, USA. Born and raised in the South Bronx - the tough spawning ground of many of the finest first-generation hip-hop artists - scratch DJ DST was a member of Afrika Bambaataa's street gang/sound system crew the Zulu Nation, before quitting to carve out a solo career in 1982 with the single 'Grandmixer Cuts It Up' on French label Celluloid, backed by the Infinity Rappers (KC Roc and Shahiem). With a formidable underground reputation behind him, he achieved international breakthrough in 1983 as the scratcher on Herbie Hancock's 'Rockit', and was also prominently featured on other tracks from Hancock's album *Future Shock* the same year. It was the first collaboration between jazz and hip-hop, until then seen as mutually exclusive forms. In 1984 he enjoyed an international dancefloor hit with his own single, 'Crazy Cuts'.

He raised his profile further with a series of collaborations with avant-funk/jazz producer Bill Laswell, producer of *Future Shock* and 'Rockit', appearing on a wide range of Laswell-produced tracks by Deadline, Manu Dibango, Foday Musa Suso and Material. A supremely talented, musical scratcher, DST's star faded in the late 80s as new generations of DJs replaced him in hip-hop's notoriously short-shelf-life marketplace. (DST derived his tag from the New York garment district's Delancey Street, where the young DJ was often to be found in the late 70s adding to his collection of fashion wear.)

● ALBUMS: *Crazy Cuts* (Celluloid 1984)★★★. With Herbie Hancock: *Future Shock* (Columbia 1983)★★★★. With Deadline: *Down By Law* (Celluloid 1984)★★★.

GRAVEDIGGAZ

A 90s New York, USA rap 'supergroup', the Gravediggaz feature ex-Stetsasonic personnel Prince Paul (b. Paul Huston, USA) and Fruitkwan, renamed the Undertaker and the Gatekeeper respectively, plus Poetic the Grym Reaper and RZA the Ressurector. Poetic was formerly a member of Two Poetic, while RZA the Ressurector also attends the record decks for the Wu Tang Clan. Prince Paul started the group after his Doo Dew label collapsed, needing a new venture to express his frustration. He had originally contacted his fellow band members with the intention of putting together a compilation album. The group's debut single was 'Diary Of A Madman', in the gothic/horror style the group had evolved, which utilised loops donated by producer RNS (famed for his work on Shyheim's debut set). The band toured in the US with the Wu Tang Clan, while Prince Paul went back to production work for Soul II Soul (having already made the groundbreaking *3 Feet High And Rising* with them) and Living Colour. Further singles such as the *6 Feet Deep* EP and 'Nowhere To Run, Nowhere To Hide' embossed a growing reputation for the group's 'horror core hip-hop'.

By 1995 they were also considered by many to be the nearest US approximation of the UK's trip hop scene. This impression was cemented by *The Hell* EP, their collaboration with Tricky, which entered the UK top 40.

● ALBUMS: *Niggamortis* (Gee Street 1994)★★★, *Six Feet Deep* (Gee Street 1994)★★, *The Pick, The Shovel & The Sickle* (Gee Street 1997)★★★★.

GREEN NUNS OF THE REVOLUTION

The Green Nuns was initially formed in 1994 when Matt Coldrick and Sev Burden were sharing a flat. Coldrick was working as a session guitarist and composing soundtracks for natural history films, while Burden was a psychedelic trance DJ. Together they made their first recording, 'The Whirling Dervish', which was produced by Pete Smith (The Hypnotist) and released on Triumph Records, before Burden left the country to travel. In the meantime, Burden had introduced Coldrick to the sound engineer Dick Trevor, who had been on the techno/trance scene since the days of Castle Morton.

Having established their Blaglands Studios, Coldrick and Trevor released a series of recordings that began with 'Cor/Conflict' (TIP Records 1995) and included 'Atomic Armadillo' (on Flying Rhino's compilation *Boyd In The Void*). Radio exposure from such DJs as Danny Rampling, Annie Nightingale and John Peel broadcast their sound around the UK before the Green Nuns played a number of live shows, including the Brixton Academy, the Trinity Centre in Bristol and the Liberty Science Centre in New York. While performing on a session for soul singer Gabrielle, Coldrick met the keyboard player Neil Cowley (who has also played with the Brand New Heavies), who soon joined the group to work on new tracks for a debut album.

Released in October 1997, *Rock Bitch Mafia* featured more of the band's muscular psychedelic trance. Straight-ahead rockers such as 'Cor' and 'Rock Bitch' feature chunky sledgehammer riffs, while 'Octofunk' has more quirky, funky melodies and 'Klunk' includes fragments of cartoon noise.

The group have also produced a number of excellent remixes for other artists, notably Prana ('Scarab') and Tufaan ('Tufaan').

● ALBUMS: *Rock Bitch Mafia* (Flying Rhino 1997)★★★.

GRID

The Grid comprises Dave Ball (b. 3 May 1959, Blackpool, Lancashire, England) and Richard Norris (b. 23 June 1965, London, England). Ball's name was familiar to many through his work as part of another highly successful pair, Soft Cell. Having split from Marc Almond, Ball worked with Psychic TV and Jack The Tab before linking with Norris, a veteran of several outfits including the Fruitbats, Innocent Vicars, East Of Eden and Mr Suit. He was also well known among the dance cognoscenti through his writing in *Boy's Own* magazine, and also the b-movie and 60s-fixated periodical *Strange Things*.

Like many of techno's new breed, the Grid have not limited themselves to their own releases, clocking up an impressive array of remixes for other artists. These have included several major names, including Brian Eno, Happy Mondays, Pet Shop Boys, the Art Of Noise and Ball's old friends, Soft Cell. Even Vic Reeves ('Abide With Me') came in for the Grid treatment. Their own recording career has attracted plenty of praise in both the mainstream and specialist dance press, who have even tolerated the band playing live behind screens. However, since their debut, 'On The Grid', in June 1989, their CV has been chequered by short tenures with their record labels. Following four singles and an album for East West, the group joined Rhythm King for a one-off single ('Timothy Leary Meets The Grid'), before departing for Virgin. Their eclectic *456* set for the latter included collaborations with Robert Fripp, Yello and Sun Ra. Singles like 'Crystal Clear', however, revealed a return to the stripped-down, meaner techno sound.

They departed for DeConstruction in late 1993, their debut single for the label being 'Texas Cowboys'. However, it was 'Swamp Thing' that provided the real fanfare, predicting the hoedown sound that was creeping into house with its use of banjos, and catapulting them into the UK Top 10.

Norris subsequently set up his own label, Candy Records.

● ALBUMS: *Electric Head* (East West 1990)★★★, *456* (Virgin 1992)★★★, *Evolver* (Deconstruction 1994)★★, *Music For Dancing* remixed singles (Deconstruction 1995)★★.

GROOVE CORPORATION

Based in Birmingham, England, Groove Corporation are essentially the remainder of Electribe 101 minus the original vocalist Billie Ray Martin. After they had buried their former incarnation, Joe Stevens, Les Fleming, Robert Cimarosti and Brian Nordhoff retreated to their Birmingham studio complex (Elephant House Sound Laboratory) to regroup. They re-emerged in 1993 with a new, reggae-influenced club sound. They also hooked up with Birmingham independent label Cake, joining DJ Dick and Nigel Blunt (aka the Original Rockers) on a 'dub-clash' 12-inch, 'Stoned'. They worked with local reggae movers such as Captain Animal and Bim Sherman, as well as the soulful techno of Kevin Saunderson's Reese Project. Their own account was opened with the *Passion* EP and the club hit, 'Summer Of Dub'. A debut album was the result of sessions with local rappers and singers working as a collective, in a manner that echoed Massive Attack's Bristol operation. 'As people walked in and heard the music, we would just say "go on, have a go yourself", and they'd add whatever they liked to it.' The album, complete with static interference and dialogue, was structured around the concept of a fictional radio programme, dubbed Skunk FM. A single, 'Ghetto Prayer', was released from the set in February 1995, while Groove Corporation set about working on projects with some of the guests they had involved in the aptly titled *Co-Operation*.

● ALBUMS: *Co-Operation* (Network 1994)★★★.

GROOVERIDER

Best known for his DJ partnership with Fabio, Grooverider's work has seen him proclaimed by at least one UK magazine as 'the Godfather' of contemporary dance music. A major contributor to both the hardcore and jungle phenomena (frequent collaborator Goldie rates him as a pivotal influence), Grooverider has been active as a DJ at house parties since the mid-80s. He was particularly associated (alongside Fabio) with the outdoor rave movement of the late 80s when he was one of the few recognizable champions of a music

that matched huge popularity with barely concealed hostility from the mainstream press. The base element of his music has always been exclusive dub plates, from whose breakbeats he fashioned what subsequently became known as drum 'n' bass music. His partnership with Fabio started in the early 80s when both were invited to DJ on a pirate radio station called Phase One. The show's creator was sufficiently impressed to invite the duo to host a new club he was opening in Brixton, south London. His recording career began much later, with tracks such as 'Sinister' and 'Dreams Of Heaven' (credited to Inta Warriors). However, rather than ride his current boom in popularity, Grooverider has remained almost exclusively a performance DJ, earning his reputation by playing sets at venues throughout the country and also appearing regularly on the Kiss FM radio station and at Goldie's Metalheadz Sunday Sessions at the Blue Note club in London. He also launched his own label, Prototype Records, in the early 90s, working with a new wave of breakbeat artists such as Photek, Dillinja and Lemon D.

GTO

One of the many bands to feature the talents of London-based former video artist Lee Newman, one of the few women involved in the evolution of techno. Influences primarily came from the industrial sector, and groups such as Test Department and the output of the Wax Trax label. Newman has spent several years DJing, remixing and programming, and contributes a column to *DJ* magazine under the title Technohead. She worked with her partner, Michael Wells. GTO was an acronym for Greater Than One, the original title of their band in the mid-80s, which released a string of experimental albums. Together they have contributed some of the essential modern techno cuts ('Pure' for Go! Bang, 'Listen To The Rhythm Flow' for Belgium label Jumping Man), the best of which were compiled on their debut album. However, instead of the anticipated rigid, hard beat techno experience, it circumvented expectations by partially adopting the innovations of the trance movement.

It was preceded by another excellent single, 'Love Is Everywhere'. Later came 'Dub Killer', which went further still and slowed down the pace to a crawl. As Tricky Disco they released two singles, 'Tricky Disco' (1990) and 'Housefly' (1991) for the Warp empire, and also recorded as John & Julie (hardcore) and Church Of Ecstasy (for Rising High). There have also been collaborations with Germany's DJ Tanith and the USA's Underground Resistance.

GUERILLA RECORDS

Record label formed by William Orbit and Dick O'Dell (previously owner of Y Records) in London in 1990, in furtherance of their mutual devotion to house music. Guerilla was originally set up as an outlet for Orbit's Bass-O-Matic project, who gave the label their debut release, 'In The Realm Of The Senses'.

In the wake of that track's success several offers came from major record labels, and Guerilla eventually signed to Virgin. The label managed to maintain its own image and identity, however, not least through their now-famous 'camouflage' sleeves. The most successful of Guerilla's artists include Spooky, Moody Boyz, Outermind, D.O.P, React 2 Rhythm, Trance Induction and others. The sound of the label has most frequently been described as 'progressive' house, though this hardly pleases the protagonists: 'What we do has been hijacked and turned into this thing called progressive house, which I absolutely loathe. It's possible that people might say we're following a trend that we started!'. Guerilla has successfully built its own audience with its generic cover designs and fully realized, polished recordings, which are just as suitable for home listening as for the club scene. As O'Dell notes: 'Unlike the majors we don't have to keep releasing records at a breakneck speed. If we don't feel we have any material ready to release in any particular month then so be it'. The label signed a US deal with IRS to licence their (increasingly popular) product in that territory.

● ALBUMS: Various: *Dub House Disco* (Guerilla 1992)★★★★, *Dub House Disco 2000* (Guerilla 1993)★★★★. React 2 Rhythm: *Whatever You Dream* (Guerilla 1992)★★★. Spooky: *Gargantuan* (Guerilla 1993)★★★. Moody Boyz: *Product Of The Environment* (Guerilla 1994)★★★.

GUMBO

Following Arrested Development's success, their singer Speech's first venture as a producer created considerable media interest. Gumbo had several things in common with Arrested Development, notably the affable but politicised Afrocentric vision, and the lolling, unhurried pace. Gumbo comprised three principals; Deanna Dawn (raps, vocals), percussionist and dancer Gichii Gamba and lead rapper Faluke Kele Fulani (b. *c*.1976), the latter writing the group's lyrics, .Although the comparisons to Arrested Development and PM Dawn were not easy to shed, they were greeted with enthusiasm by an audience already worked up on the idea of black cultural rap which does not romanticise an urban base. Signed to Cooltempo in the UK, their debut album was soaked in funk and Afro-Cuban rhythms, with jazz samples culled from John Coltrane and Charles Mingus.

● ALBUMS: *Droppin' Soulful H20 On The Fiber* (Chrysalis 1993)★★★.

GUNSHOT

Based in London, England, this mid-90s rap trio consist of MC Mercury, Alkaline and DJ White-Child Rix. Raised on a diet of reggae, 2-Tone and the Jam, the school friends came together in early 1990. Although their breakthrough did not come until *Patriot Games* in 1993, which saw them heralded as one of the UK's few legitimate answers to US hip-hop, they had released a steady stream of quality singles; 'Battle Creek Brawl', 'Crime Story' and 'Clear From Present Danger'. 'Mind Of A Razor' in late 1993 also featured some metal guitar riffs courtesy of Napalm Death's Shane, while 'Killing Season' boasted a sample of Bob Hoskins dialogue in *The Long Good Friday*. The title of their album is a reference to their own view that UK rap has a lot more to offer than hanging on to the coat-tails of its cousins across the Atlantic. It also chose to tackle domestic issues rather than glamorise the life of the rapper, celebrate the size of his phallus or chuck insults at lady friends. The band continued their associations with alternative guitar bands by remixing material for S.M.A.S.H. in 1994.

● ALBUMS: *Patriot Games* (1993)★★★★.

GURU JOSH

b. Paul Walden, *c*.1964, England. Noted for his goatee beard, flailing live performances and three-word songs, Guru Josh nevertheless helped to kick-start the DeConstruction success story. He had originally run a club night in Putney entitled the Happy House, and sang in a rock band, Joshua Cries Wolf. 'Infinity' was propelled by a great saxophone sequence, and 'Whose Law (Is It Anyway?)' also had its fans. The title might have given the impression that this was some sort of rave 'mission statement', but in fact the 'lyrics' made absolutely no sense whatsoever. If Guru Josh was, as *Smash Hits* magazine delcared, 'spokesman for the warehouse generation', he was an embarrassingly inarticulate role model. Singles such as the earlier asinine 'Time For The Guru' caught him at his 'peak', but when critics spotted a cover of 'Louie Louie' on his debut album the game was definitely up.

● ALBUMS: *Infinity* (DeConstruction 1990)★★★.

GUTHRIE, ANDY

b. 20 January 1965, Camberwell, London. During the 90s Guthrie was involved with some of the most interesting and enduring dance music of the time. At school he learned classical music and later played rock, funk, reggae, bhangra and other styles in a number of bands. He began writing his own tunes on a sequencer and four-track recorder at home and subsequently did some work programming for Island Records. During the late 80s Guthrie became interested in dance music and in 1989 co-founded Banco De Gaia with Toby Marks. He worked on the first Planet Dog Records release, the EP *Desert Wind* (1993), and subsequently on the albums *Maya* (Planet Dog 1994) and *Last Train To Lhasa*. (Planet Dog 1995), after which he began to concentrate on his own work. He had formed Medicine Drum with Chris Dekker around 1993 and was producing such bands as Children Of The Bong and Senser. As 100th Monkey he made his solo debut with 'Spiritus' on Matsuri Productions in 1995. The following year, with Jaki Kenley (of 21-3 Productions), Guthrie put together the charity compilation *Earthtrance* for Positiva Records, for which he contributed the track 'Invocation' (with Medicine Drum) and a remix of Banco De Gaia's 'Kincajou' (with Si Wild). At the same time he worked with Eat Static (*Bony Incus* EP) and with Tsuyoshi Suzuki for the Prana album *Geomantik*. He has continued to record with Medicine Drum and Prana and in 1997 released his first EP (*Skwirm/Skweel*) for 21-3 Productions, as Funkopath. With Medicine Drum Guthrie draws on 'world music' sources, while Funkopath and Prana have a purer psychedelic trance sound with a funky edge.

Unlike much dance music that revolves around repetition and established formulas, his work is often characterized by varied textures and grooves, and the most detailed, original production. Other work includes remixes for Bentley Rhythm Ace and Digitalis, and collaborations with Mark Allen, Manmademan, Tristan and Process. As well as writing and producing, he teaches music technology and DJs dub and trip-hop sets as 100th Monkey.

GYPSY

Among Limbo Records' most prestigious recordings acts, Gypsy is the Glasgow-born musician Graham Drinnan (also referred to by some as 'the hardest working man in house music'). His recordings include the wonderful 'I Trance You', released when he was just 18 in 1992, which has remained a standby in many DJs' playlists ever since. 1994 material included 'Funk De Fino', while he also mixed the 17-track *Transend* compilation for Rumour. He formed Sublime in 1992 with Circa DJ Matt Brown, and has gone on to release a slew of hugely impressive dance cuts for Limbo: 'Fight The Feeling', 'Theme', 'Trans American' (one of 1993's most popular club cuts) and 'TGV'.

HAÇIENDA

Perhaps the most famous dance music venue in England, Manchester's Haçienda Club was opened in Whitworth Street in May 1982. It was owned jointly by New Order and their then record label, Factory Records. Indeed, it was given its own catalogue number by that ever esoteric company. It styled itself as a 'post-industrial fantasy venue', but quickly became known for its pioneering sponsorship of house music imported from the USA. Among the venue's best-known disc jockeys were Dave Haslam and Mike Pickering. The latter was responsible for inviting Madonna to England for her first UK appearance in 1985, and later enjoyed enormous success as the creative engine behind M People. With the rise of 'Madchester' and bands such as the Stone Roses and Happy Mondays in the late 80s, Manchester enjoyed massive exposure and the Haçienda was regularly mentioned as the area's most successful/chic club. Its success led to the opening of celebrity haunt the Dry Bar, but in 1991, with ecstasy culture at its height, the venue became the victim of a press witch-hunt after a paying customer succumbed to a drugs overdose in the toilets. It was closed for six months after a serious firearms incident (allegedly drugs-related), and its ownership then became the subject of conjecture when Factory collapsed in 1992. However, though Factory entered liquidation, the Haçienda has continued to thrive since, its reputation enhanced by internationally renowned clubs such as the 'Flesh' night and a roster of top-flight DJs.
● ALBUMS: *15 Years Of Nights At The Haçienda* (DeConstruction 1997)★★★★.

HADDAWAY

b. Nester Alexander Haddaway, *c*.1966, Tobago, West Indies. A lightweight techno pop artist licensed to Arista Records from his German home at Coconut/Logic Records, Haddaway enjoyed a huge crossover hit throughout Europe with the anthemic 'What Is Love' in 1993, followed by the equally strident 'Life'. The artist grew up in Washington, DC, USA, before relocating to Cologne, Germany, to find employment as a singer and dancer. There he formed a band, Elegato, with keyboard player Alex Trime, before embarking on solo work with the production duo of Dee Dee Halligan and Junior Turello in 1992. Halligan and Turello are also known as Tony Hendrik and Karin Hartmann, respectively, and jointly head the Coconut record label. They had previously produced Bad Boys Blue, Chypnotic and the Hollies. Backed by the songwriting and production expertise of Trime, Halligan and Turello, 'What Is Love', originally written as a ballad, eventually reached number 2 in the UK charts in April 1993. 'Life' also earned the same chart position a few months later, ensuring Haddaway's status as Europe's most successful solo artist of 1993. His debut album, however, was little more than a roster of fillers sandwiching the hits, even if 'What Is Love?' and 'Life' remain as good as commercial hip house comes. The album achieved gold status and reached number 8 in the UK charts in November 1993. Haddaway himself, though often bracketed with the Euro dance fare of 2 Unlimited and Cappela, is a far more sophisticated proposition. He has a college degree in marketing, his own business career, his own fashion company (Energy) and until 1994 was completely self-managed. Prior to his chart residencies he was also a professional American footballer for the Cologne Crocodiles. In 1994 he again achieved significant success with two further singles, 'I Miss You' and 'Rock My Heart'.
● ALBUMS: *Haddaway - The Album* (Arista 1993)★★, *The Drive* (Logic 1995)★★.

HAMILTON, JAMES

b. 25 December 1942, England, d. 17 June 1996, Blyth, Nottinghamshire, England. While many music journalists have built substantial literary or media reputations, James Hamilton was an entirely different breed to other celebrated music writers such as Nick Kent or Lester Bangs. While better-publicized writers embraced the energy and lifestyle of the rock breed, Hamilton made his name within soul and dance music through his meticulous attention to detail and the unmatched accuracy of his writing. A large, imposing man whose knowledge of food was as awe-inspiring as his affinity with his subject area, his love affair with music and his subsequent career path were in sharp relief to his privately educated, almost aristocratic origins. He began working as a disc jockey in 1962, and among his first jobs was a spell as the resident disc jockey in the Kray Twins' Knightsbridge, London venue. By 1965 he had moved on to the Scene Club in Soho, which became the mecca for the emerging mod scene with its famed Saturday all-nighters. He regularly worked abroad, befriending the Beatles on their first US tour and helping to arrange James Brown's first UK shows. After over 10 years of work as one of the pioneering 'mobile DJs' he took a 1979 residency at Gulliver's Club in the capital's West End. He also began to appear regularly on the radio, working with mix partner Les Adams (of LA Mix) on Capital Radio's *New Year's Eve Mix* shows. The duo used these shows to combine together a wide variety of musical styles into one seamless, continuous mix. Tapes of these shows continue to proliferate as bootlegs. They also served notice of Hamilton's personal innovation in dance and soul music - the BPM (beats per minute). As a disc jockey of several years' standing he had noted the possibility of mixing differing styles of music in the same set as long as the rhythmic tempos were compatible. These counts, minutely detailed to include fractions of bpms, became the basis for his famed *Record Mirror* columns. His journalistic career had begun in 1964 when he first wrote for that music paper under the sobriquet Dr. Soul (covering US soul and R&B records). *James Hamilton's Disco Page* followed in 1976. This was the first weekly dance music column to include 'club return' charts - a more accurate, sophisticated response system that allowed disc jockeys to assess how well a particular record was received at his/her venue. Such charts have become the staple taste barometer of every subsequent dance music publication. He began presenting BPM counts in 1979, interspersing factual information that relied on his own peculiar review language. Over a period of time, his disciplined, economic appraisal of dance music inculcated a distinct but highly informative language that allowed disc jockeys and record shop owners to purchase new releases unheard, knowing they would suit their audiences. For example, one of his latter-day reviews cited Pro Active's 'Culthouse' release as 'galloping progressive bounder with a "clap your hands" breakdown in terrific acidically building Wink-ish twittery percussive scampering 134.8 bpm Cult House T.I.M Remix, chunkier lurching 129.8 bpm Cult

House Original Mix, long eerily started swirly pulsing 0-130 bpm Tevendale & McCreery Remix.' The density of information communicated in just a few words gave some indication of the concise, disciplined nature of Hamilton. What some have described as his 'pedantry' in going so far as to bpm to fractions was also a clue to his obsessive perfectionism. Hamilton only married late in life and it is easy to understand why - many anecdotes after his death described bizarre instances of Hamilton not sleeping for three days in order to review the latest batch of 12-inch records. As well as his writing, Hamilton continued to work as a disc jockey at one-off events and his knowledge of 60s and 70s music was so encyclopedic that Bruce Springsteen invited him to Oslo to be disc jockey at his end of tour party in 1995. However, by this time Hamilton had publicly acknowledged that he suspected his fight with cancer of the colon was drawing to a close. He died on 17 June 1996, leaving behind his new wife and over a quarter of a million records.

HAMMER, MC

b. Stanley Kirk Burrell, 30 March 1962, Oakland, California, USA. Immensely popular rap artist, later working only under the Hammer name, who synthesized the street sounds of black cultural alienation, or his interpretation thereof, to great commercial gain. After failing in professional baseball and attending a college course in communications, Hammer (named after his likeness to Oakland A's big hitter Henry 'Hammerin' Hank' Aaron) joined the US Navy for three years. Indeed, his first forays into music were financed by baseball players Mike Davis and Dwayne Murphy, allowing him to form Bustin' records and release the solo single, 'Ring 'Em'. He had previously been part of religious rap group The Holy Ghost Boys. Together with a backing band consisting of two DJs and singers Tabatha King, Djuana Johnican and Phyllis Charles, he cut a 1987 debut set, *Feel My Power*. A minor hit, it did enough to bring Hammer to the attention of Capitol Records. After contracts were completed, including a reported advance of $750,000 (unheard of for a rap artist), the album was reissued under the title *Let's Get It Started*. Such success was overshadowed, however, by that of the follow-up, *Please Hammer Don't Hurt 'Em*. Following massive exposure due to sponsorship deals with British Knights footwear and Pepsi Cola, the album began a residency at the top of the US charts for a record-breaking 21-week run. The single, 'U Can't Touch This', embodied his appeal, with near constant rotation on pop channel MTV, and dance routines that were the equal of Michael Jackson. The single sampled Rick James' 'Super Freak', creating a precedent for follow-ups 'Have You Seen Her' (the Chi-Lites) and 'Pray' (Prince; 'When Doves Cry'). Whilst an on-going duel with white rapper Vanilla Ice raged, critics pointed out the plagiarism that underpinned both artists' most successful work. Unperturbed, Hammer was being praised as a suitable role model for black youth (not least by himself), and was honoured by 'MC Hammer Days' in Los Angeles and Fremont.

His first single to be free of sampling, 'Here Comes The Hammer', became an unexpected failure by stalling at number 51 in the US charts, despite its appearance on the soundtrack to *Rocky V*. A multitude of awards, including Grammys, Bammys and International Album Of The Year at the Juno awards in Canada, reflected the global success of the album. Its long-awaited successor, *Too Legit To Quit*, featured a direct challenge this time: 'I'm taking on Michael Jackson from a spirit of competition . . . You've had Ali and Frazier . . . so why not Hammer versus Jackson?'. The sleevenotes to the album expanded on his desire for black youth to rid themselves of drugs and resurrect their Christian morality through self education. His exposure to US audiences already included the television adventures of cartoon hero 'Hammerman', and a Mattel Hammer doll and attached ghetto blaster. However, his ability to sustain a challenge to the Jackson crown would inevitably be limited by his own admission that: 'I'm not a singer. I'm a rapper'. Despite a soundtrack hit with 'The Addams Family', heavily promoted in the film of the same title, Hammer's fortunes declined. In 1992 *The San Francisco Examiner* reported that Hammer faced financial ruin after poor attendances for his *Too Legit To Quit* tour, promoting an album that had seen him tracing a more R&B-based groove. Though Hammer denied there was any truth in such stories, it was obvious a re-think was needed. By 1994 there was a huge image switch, from harem pants and leather catsuits to dark glasses and a goatee beard. The resultant album pulled in producers G-Bomb from Grand Jury Records, the Hines brothers from Detroit, Teddy Riley and members of the Dogg Pound, and specifically went after the Oakland G-Funk sound of artists like Too Short. Hammer as a gangsta rapper? As Simon Price of the *Melody Maker* bluntly pointed out: 'Please Hammer, don't hurt me. My sides are killing me'. Hammer reverted to using the MC prefix for his 1995 album *Inside Out*.

● ALBUMS: As M.C. Hammer *Feel My Power* (Bustin' 1987)★★★, *Let's Get It Started* (Capitol 1988)★★★, *Please Hammer Don't Hurt 'Em* (Capitol 1990)★★★, *Inside Out* (Giant 1995)★★. As Hammer *Too Legit To Quit* (Capitol 1991)★★, *The Funky Headhunter* (RCA 1994)★★.

● FURTHER READING: *M.C. Hammer: U Can't Touch This*, Bruce Dessau.

HANNANT, BEAUMONT

b. *c*.1970. York, England-based Hannant boasts Austrian, English and Yugoslavian ancestors. Working during the day at the Depth Charge record shop in York, he also DJs at local techno and jazz/hip-hop clubs. He began recording for the first time in 1992, releasing one EP before a mini-album, *Basic Data Manipulation*, was unveiled on General Productions Recordings. He principally came to prominence via the compilation *Positiva Ambient Collection*, with 'Awakening The Soul'. Predicted by no lesser a tipster than Andy Weatherall as techno's great white hope, his first full album in 1994 arrived in two completely separate versions: one intended for CD consumption, the other a vinyl variant. It was a clear indication of the different requirements of dance fans in the 90s. Hannant also talked widely about future projects mixing his current Detroit-derived techno flair with the music of prominent 'indie' bands such as Madder Rose and Screaming Trees, his own personal listening favourites.

● ALBUMS: *Basic Data Manipulation: Tastes And Textures Vol. 2* mini-album (General Production 1993)★★★, *Texturology* (General Production 1994)★★★.

HARD 2 OBTAIN

H20, as they prefer to be abbreviated, hail from Long Island, New York, with a sound that combines the local influences of Public Enemy, EPMD and De La Soul. The three man crew is made up of Taste, DL and DJ Six Seven, the latter's title derived from his physical height. Their debut album revealed them to be competent freestylers, with a mature, reflective edge on titles like 'Shit We Do'. Production help was offered by the Stimulated Dummies, previously behind Grand Puba. The jazzy samples and cool

groove placed the record as a direct descendent of the former's work, minus the Islamic references.
● ALBUMS: *Ism And Blues* (1994)★★★.

HARDBAG

A collaborative project launched by Red Marc, a resident UK DJ with the Drum Club, and Matt Early, formerly of Bumble, who once enjoyed a club hit via a celebrated Andy Weatherall remix of 'West In Motion'. Their debut release together, 'Ceasefire', was recorded with sampled sounds from the war in the former Yugoslavia, to raise money for the Serious Road Trip charity. This was no idle conscience-appeasing effort, but an attempt to ship food and medical supplies directly to Sarajevo. The samples were collected personally by Early on a visit in 1993, and as well as the sounds of conflict embraced library recordings of many years of native Yugoslavian music. The project was designed to portray ravers and dance music fans as something more than mere hedonists and consumers. Early has also lectured to the British Council on the positive, unifying nature of club music. 'Ceasefire' was released on the Drum Club's Midi Circus Projects imprint, only their second release.

HARDCASTLE, PAUL

b. 10 December 1957, London, England. Hardcastle is a producer, mixer, composer and keyboard wizard specializing in dance-orientated product. He first worked in a hi-fi shop and developed an interest in electronics in his teens. His first group was First Light, alongside Derek Green, whose output included the deplorable 'Horse With No Name'. After four minor solo hits in 1984, '19', a record about the Vietnam conflict utilizing spoken news reports, went straight to number 1 in the UK in 1985. The follow-up, 'Just For The Money', was based on the Great Train Robbery and boasted the voices of Bob Hoskins and Sir Laurence Olivier. Further singles were progressively less successful before he scored with 'Papa's Got A Brand New Pigbag' under the pseudonym Silent Underdog. He also wrote the *Top Of The Pops* theme, 'The Wizard', in 1986, before switching to production for young funk band LW5, providing remixes for everyone from Third World to Ian Dury. Another production credit was the last ever Phil Lynott single, coincidentally called 'Nineteen'. Other engagements came with Carol Kenyon (previously vocalist on Heaven 17's 'Temptation') most notably on her

1986 Top 10 hit 'Don't Waste My Time'. Recently Hardcastle has 'retired' to his Essex home studio and releases records under pseudonyms such as the Def Boys, Beeps International, Jazzmasters and Kiss The Sky (the last of which is Hardcastle and Jaki Graham). He is also founder of his own label, Fast Forward, and composes theme music for a number of BBC Television series.
● ALBUMS: *Zero One* (Blue Bird 1985)★★, *Paul Hardcastle* (Chrysalis 1985)★★★, *No Winners* (Chrysalis 1988)★★, *First Light* (Connoisseur 1997)★.
● COMPILATIONS: *Soul Syndicate* (K-Tel 1988)★★.

HARDFLOOR

Oliver Bandzio and Ramon Zenker from Germany are the duo behind these Dusseldorf-based acid house revivalists. Typically, Bandzio's life was changed by 1988's flourishing acid scene. Unlike many, however, he was determined to recreate the excitement of those heady days, and spent no less than three years attempting to track down his own Roland 303, responsible for much of the sound of that period. After having finally traced one he made the acquaintance of studio wizard Zenkler, and together they debuted with 'Hardtrance Acperience', on Sven Vath's Harthouse label late in 1992. Some critics questioned whether the track contained the longest snare roll ever committed to vinyl, while its stylings were inextricably those of the summer of 1988 (it became arguably the most important post-acid house acid house record ever). The follow-up 12-inch sampled hunting horns, hence its name, 'Into The Nature', on which production was orchestrated by 303 guru Richie Hawtin.
● ALBUMS: *Funalogue* mini-album (Harthouse 1994)★★★★, *Home Run* (Harthouse 1996)★★★.

HARDKISS

Based in San Francisco, California, USA, Scott Hardkiss grew up in the area's house music subculture, although he was primarily inspired by hip-hop. He DJed at Tenerife in 1989 and the Glastonbury Festival in 1990, a performance fondly remembered for his determination to incorporate a live 303 synthesizer. He had formed the Hardkiss trio with disc jockeys Robbie Hardkiss and label manager Gavin Hardkiss after meeting them at college on the east coast. After studies they moved to San Francisco, and made their name on the warehouse scene there.

Continuing the high-profile Sunny Side Up nights, they also moved into label management and recording, the *Magic Sounds Of San Francisco* EP being their debut release. A major cult success, it boasted samples drawn from both the Beatles and Shamen, pinned to a hip-hop backdrop. Under the title Hawke, their third release, '3 Nudes In A Purple Garden', was similarly inventive. 'Raincry' and 'Phoenix' by God Within (aka Scott Hardkiss) arrived in typically glossy packaging and psychedelic 'new age' artwork. Meanwhile, their highly personalized, off-centre live sets continued, with Robbie typically dropping 'Radio Clash' into appearances at the Ministry Of Sound. Scott also remixed One Dove's 'White Love' in an acid version, and turned the Drum Club's 'Drums Are Dangerous' into 'Shrubs Are Dangerous' for US consumption. 1995 found the trio signed to Phonogram Records, who issued a singles compilation which immediately ran into trouble over an uncleared ELO sample on 'Phoenix'.

● COMPILATIONS: *Delusions Of Grandeur* (L'Attitude/Phonogram 1995)★★★.

HARDKNOCKS

An early 90s hip-hop band from New York City, New York, USA, Hardknocks' debut album was distinguished by several tracks denouncing the police ('A Dirty Cop Named Harry', 'A Nigga For Hire' and 'Road To The Precinct'), all strongly advocating good reasons why young black men should not join the police force. Released on noted New York label Wild Pitch Records, *School Of Hardknocks* additionally comprised messages concerning black separatism akin to the Five Percent Nation philosophy popularised by Brand Nubian and others. This no-compromise lyrical package was allied to tough rhythmic cycles indebted to the Bomb Squad's work with Public Enemy.

● ALBUMS: *School Of Hardnocks* (Wild Pitch 1992)★★★.

HARRIS, SIMON

b. England. Although Harris, at one time the 'world yo-yo champion', became synonymous with house music in the late 80s, his connections with the hip-hop movement are just as strong. His big hit, 'Bass (How Low Can You Go)', which reached number 12 in the UK charts in March 1988, was an idea based on the first line of Public Enemy's 'Bring The Noise'. As Harris explained to the press 'Originally the line was going to be

'black race, how low can you go?' . . . When I first heard that line I thought it was really good. And Public Enemy gave permission to use it and helped out in the final mix too.' Alongside Derek B., Harris also signed several early British hip-hop acts to his Music Of Life label, including Overlord X, MC Duke, Hijack, She Rockers and Demon Boyz. His own follow-up singles were less spectacularly successful. 'Here Comes That Sound' reached number 38 in October 1988 and '(I've Got Your) Pleasure Control' number 60 in June of the following year. However, when 'Another Monsterjam' failed to reach even the Top 60 it proved to be the artist's last release for ffrr Records. March 1990's 'Ragga House (All Night Long)', which reached number 56, proved to be his last chart hit.

HARTHOUSE RECORDS

German label overseen by Heinz Roth and Sven Vath. As Harthouse's popularity grew in the 90s, they signed some of their Eye Q/Recycle Or Die product compilations through Warners for superior distribution, also giving a long-awaited UK release for the Vernons' 'Wonderland' 12-inch in the process. Other releases included Marco Zaffarano's 'Minimalism', and Spicelab's eponymous EP. Most impressive of all, however, was Hardfloor's 'Hardtrance Acperience', which reopened the acid house scene with its pumping delivery.

HARVEY

b. *c*.1963, England. Famed for his seven-hour-long DJ sets, especially his acclaimed New Hard Left nights at London's Blue Note club, Harvey's interest in music developed at the same time as his passion for skateboarding. He was exposed to a wide variety of music in his youth, his initial appetite for punk, metal and electronica eventually overtaken by his interest in the burgeoning dance scene. This background accounts for the eclecticism of his DJ sets, which can incorporate anything from the Clash and Led Zeppelin to up-to-the-minute Masters At Work remixes. He is certainly one of the few house DJs prepared to admit to being a fan of Deep Purple. He formed the Tonka DJ collective in the early 90s before establishing the Moist night at Covent Garden's Gardening Club. From there he became a resident DJ at the Ministry Of Sound. It was here that his 'live edits' of rock and dance songs won him a reputation as an innovator behind the decks.

HAWTIN, RICHIE

b. 1973, Windsor, Ontario, Canada. Just over the border from Detroit, Hawtin grew up under the influence of Detroit's recent stars, Juan Atkins, Derrick May and Kevin Saunderson. A DJ since 1987 and a recording artist since 1990, Hawtin is perhaps better known for operations under two separate guises, F.U.S.E. and Plastikman. His first releases as a solo artist came as F.U.S.E. on his own label, Plus 8, an acronym for Future Underground Subsonic Experiments. F.U.S.E. kicked off with the still fresh-sounding 'Approach And Identify', quickly gaining further popularity and respect with the 1991 release 'F.U.', which launched Plus 8's harder offshoot, Probe Records. These early releases were usually limited to between 500 and 800 copies, thereby ensuring that they were quickly circulated and collected by DJs. F.U.S.E. tends to encompass Hawtin's more disparate solo projects, with sounds ranging from these harsher early releases to beautifully blissed-out 'home-listening' music (the atmospheric 'Train Trac' was even likened to 'having sex in a bubble in space with someone you trust'). This range of styles was perhaps best captured on the album *Dimension Intrusion*, part of Warp Records' highly collectable *Artificial Intelligence* series. As Plastikman, Hawtin debuted with the 'Spastik' 12-inch, an unreservedly harsh and abrasive cut, followed by the album *Sheet One*, on his own Plus 8 label. The tail-end of 1993 saw the release of 'Krakpot' on Novamute, another intense house workout. The Plastikman title allows Hawtin to indulge his love of the 'acid' sound of the 303: 'a lot of the 303 tracks got very noisy and un-funky and against what I believed it was all about . . . that's why I came back with Plastikman. To me it reflects what the 303 was designed to do. It's a beautiful machine . . . "sexy"'. More recently, Hawtin achieved major acclaim with the Concept series, 12 releases over 12 months of minimally packaged, almost dublike techno, reminiscent of much of the work of Maurizio. Hawtin is still releasing records on Plus 8 and has a busy DJing schedule. He still hosts his Hard, Harder And Hardest warehouse parties in Detroit.

● ALBUMS: As Plastikman: *Sheet One* (Plus 8 1993)★★★, *Recycled Plastik* (Plus 8/Novamute 1994)★★★, *Mixmag Live Volume 20* (Mixmag Live 1995)★★★.

HEAVY D AND THE BOYZ

Self-proclaimed 'overweight lover of rap from money earnin' Mount Vernon', Heavy D (b. Dwight Myers, 24 May 1967, Jamaica, West Indies) fronted a mainstream rap outfit which has been considered the genre's equivalent of Luther Vandross. Though the vast majority of his material represents rap's familiar call to procreation, Heavy D's rhymes are imbued with warmth rather than breast-beating machismo. Similarly, though he makes much of his muchness (titles like 'Mr. Big Stuff' are frequent), there is more to Heavy D than novelty. His debut album, helmed by Teddy Riley, comprised funk alongside hints of the New Jack Swing sound the producer was in the process of creating. Riley was also in tow for the follow-up, though this time he was in the company of fellow rap production legend Marley Marl, among others. Q-Tip (A Tribe Called Quest), Big Daddy Kane and Pete Rock And CL Smooth all featured on 'Don't Curse', a posse cut from *Peaceful Journey*. The album also included a tribute to former band member T-Roy (b. Troy Dixon, c.1968, d. 15 July 1990). One of his trio of backing vocalists (the Boyz), the singer was killed in an accident on their 1991 tour. The other 'Boyz' are G. Whiz (b. Glen Parrish) and DJ Eddie F (b. Edward Ferrell). Success continued unabated when 'Now That We've Found Love' became a UK number 2 in July 1991, profiling a fresh, Jamaican DJ influenced style. He also made a high profile guest appearance on Michael Jackson's 'Jam' single and sister Janet's 'Alright With Me'. Strangely, despite this success MCA did not see fit to offer *Blue Funk*, which saw Heavy return to hardcore territory with guest production from Pete Rock and DJ Premier an immediate UK release. His 1994 set *Nuttin' But Love* saw him reunite with rap's top rank of producers, including old hands Marl, Riley and Rock, alongside Erick Sermon, Trickmasterz and Troy Williams. It was another superb package. He shares the same management company as Hammer and has become one of rap's heavyweights in more than the literal sense.

● ALBUMS: *Living Large* (MCA 1987)★★★, *Big Tyme* (Uptown 1989)★★★★, *Peaceful Journey* (Uptown 1991)★★★, *Blue Funk* (Uptown 1992)★★★, *Nuttin' But Love* (Uptown 1994)★★★★, *Waterbed Hev* (Uptown 1997)★★★.

HECKMANN, THOMAS

b. Mainz, Frankfurt, Germany. Acid/techno DJ who first became interested in music through his father's collection of electronica - Jean Michel Jarre, Kraftwerk, Tangerine Dream and Pink Floyd - via the early innovations of bands such as the Human League and Throbbing Gristle in the late 70s. Afterwards he listened to more guitar-oriented bands until the acid scene of 1988 and the work of 808 State returned him to his first love. Although he himself had recorded as early as 1980, buying his first synthesizer four years later, it was not until 1991 that he began to record acid cuts, the first of which was 'Liquid' (recorded under the name Exit 100). Since then, as well as his regular club spots throughout Europe, Heckmann has collaborated on a number of projects. His pseudonyms include Age, Skydiver, Spectral Emotions, Parot Torture, and he has also worked with Hoschi of Labworks as Purple Plejade. Having previously worked with D-Jax Up Beats, Sony and Edge, in 1993 he set up his own label, Trope Recordings, which became famed for a series of recordings under the Drax banner: 'Interior', 'Section 2' and 'Phosphene'. Other projects on the label include tracks from Christian Vogel and Mono Junk. Exit 100 separated from Sony in mid-1994, just before his first album proper on Trope as Drax.
● ALBUMS: *Age* (Sony 1994)★★★. As Drax: *Drax Red* (Trope 1994)★★.

HEDNINGARA

This Swedish dance band were signed to China Records in the UK. Their musical motifs generally encompassed a feel for traditional folk music as much as new technology. Hedningara translates as 'the Heathens', and embraces five people: Anders Stake (string and wind instruments), Björn Tollin (string and percussion, programming), Hallbus Totte Mattsson (string), Sanna Kurki-Suoni (vocals), and Tellu Paulasto (vocals). They formed in 1987 when the three male members became disillusioned with the traditional folk music scene and travelled around various Scandinavian museums searching for newer means of expression. Based on historical documents, they constructed their own instruments with which to conduct these experiments. They were joined by their two vocalists after a trip to Finland. The vocalists themselves were conducting research into the musical properties of the former Finnish (now Russian) state of Karelia. The two strands of music sat together well, yet instead of regaling folk audiences with it, a more natural market was found within the world of dance - the energy of their performances reflecting communal club culture more than any personality-led, secular music. In 1992 they were awarded with a Swedish Grammy for Best Folk Music, which came in addition to two consecutive awards as Best Festival Band.
● ALBUMS: *Hedningarna* (MNW 1989)★★★, *Kaksi!* (Xource 1992)★★, *Tra* (Silence 1994), *Hippjokk* (Silence 1997)★★★.

HEIDI OF SWITZERLAND

Also known simply as HOS, this is a Swiss operation that relocated to London in January 1993. Headed by owner/producer Hilary, the label has quickly become popular for its underground dance records, generally located in the fields of techno or trance. Other styles of music are diverted through HOS's sister labels, Budgie (Euro techno), Flash Your Tits (progressive) and De'Crust (ambient and dub). The label's most famous advocate is probably German artist Kinky Roland, whose material permeates through the label via several different pseudonyms, a good example being Dinge Queen In The Mist's 'Let Me Be Your Tupperwear' for the FYT subsidiary. Other artists include Trance Uber Alles, who work techno in a dramatic Teutonic style (notably 'Ich Shalte'), Innersystem (mainstream dance) and Tranceparents (a highly regarded soulful techno team). HOS also operates its own distribution, exporting under the title Wasp.
● ALBUMS: *Erotic Tracks Vol. 2* (HOS 1994)★★★.

HENRY, PAULINE

The former vocalist with Scottish band the Chimes, whose solo work brought about a reassessment of her career: 'After the Chimes, I took a while to think about what I really wanted to do with my career. I got my head down writing and had 25 songs. I learned my craft live, as opposed to being 'created' in the studio'. As she idolizes Tina Turner, it was doubtless no accident that her debut album included compositions such as 'Can't Take Your Love', co-written with Terry Britten, who had penned many of Turner's biggest hits. There was also a cover version of Bad Company's 'Feel Like Making Love.
● ALBUMS: *The Harder They Come* (Sony 1993)★★★, *Pauline* (Soho Square 1994)★★★.

HERBALISER

The Herbaliser is led by Jake Wherry and DJ Ollie Teeba, who work from the former's TrainTrax studio in Twickenham. Wherry grew up in south London interested in jazz, funk, rare groove and hip-hop, and played the bass and guitar in several jazz, funk and rock bands. Teeba began DJing when he was 15 and later played hip-hop, electro and funk in clubs and warehouses around London. After Wherry had built his studio in 1992, the pair began working together; they later met DJ Food at a club and signed with Ninja Tune Records. Their first release, 'The Real Killer'/'Blowin' It' (1995), was recorded with keyboards, percussion and horns to produce an abstract blend of jazz instrumental sounds and hip-hop beats, created in a repetitive, sample-orientated manner. After a second single, their first album, *Remedies*, arrived in October 1995. During 1996 they performed live around the UK and Europe with a band that included drums, bass, keyboards, percussion and horns. The following year they toured again to promote further singles, including 'New and Improved'/'Control Centre', and a new album, *Blow Your Headphones*.

● ALBUMS: *Remedies* (Ninja Tune 1995), *Blow Your Headphones* (Ninja Tune 1997).

HERMELJIN, DYLAN

Dutchman Hermeljin was still studying business economics part-time when his first brace of 2000 And One records were released on Fierce Ruling Diva's Lower East Side label in 1989 preceding 1992's 'Focus', which arrived on fellow countryman Stefan Robber's Eevolute imprint. It was a typical slice of passionate techno. Much of his output remains mysterious, though 100% Pure is him and Sandy, his partner at the Black Beat Record Store. Their tribal techno opus 'My Life In The Bush' arrived on his own 100% Pure label. Other monikers include Planet Gong ('Planet Gong', a Djax Up Beats dose of Detroit techno, actually recorded two years before release in 1994), Babies From Gong and Edge Of Motion. After just four releases 100% Pure were rewarded with an installment on Beechwood's New Electronica series, an album entitled *The Lowlands* emerging.

● ALBUMS: *New Electronica Presents: The Lowlands* (Beechwood 1994)★★★.

HEX

Hex started as the multimedia side of Ninja Tune Records, firstly with Rob Pepperell in charge and later Stuart Warren Hall. Working closely with Jonathan Moore and Matt Black, Hex has created a number of projects aimed at developing the role of the DJ, and has evolved into a 'multi-armed posse manipulating multiple sound and vision sources'. Some of their software applications are based around sampling and remixing ideas, while two installations, 'Synopticon' (TRADEMARK) at the Barbican and 'Generator' (TRADEMARK) at the Glasgow Gallery of Modern Art, allowed visitors to create and mix sounds and visuals simultaneously. As a live attraction Hex has become an exciting VJ team working at Ninja Tune's club nights, Stealth and Kungfusion. Attempting to expand the established formats, Hex created a scratch video, *Natural Rhythm*, to accompany Coldcut's 'Atomic Moog' (1998). It was the first in a trilogy of collaborations that also included 'More Bits And Pieces' and 'Timber' (as Hexstatic). They also contributed a number of games, creative tools and videos to Coldcut's album *Let Us Play*. By 1998 Hex were signed to Ninja Tune as artists, no longer just the multimedia arm of the label.

HI-BIAS RECORDS

A dance label based in Toronto, Canada, Hi-Bias Records was widely proclaimed as 'the DJ's label' in the early 90s. The imprint grew out of the collapse of Big Shot Records (which had released material by Index, Dionne, Amy Jackson, Dream Warriors, etc.) in 1990, with producer and co-founder Nick Anthony Fiorucci describing his new label as 'the next progression to the Big Shot sound'. Fiorucci's partner was Michael Ova. The term Hi-Bias was first used by an artist title on Big Shot for the single, 'Wanna Take You Home'. Hi-Bias began with three releases in 1990 that were later accredited by *Record Mirror* as 'putting Canadian dance music on the map'. The label's high-profile releases, which were often extravagantly packaged, included Z Formation's *Brutal EP* in 1991, a typically collaborative project which featured remixes from Ova, Fiorucci, Jason 'Deko' Steele and Nicky Holder. The 'Rhythm Formula Team' which formed the production basis for the label also produced material by artists such as Red Light (*Rhythm Formula* EP), Oval Emotion ('Do It', sung by Cissy Goodridge and created by her producer brother Kenny Moran and Fiorucci) and

DJs Rule. Fiorucci's influence was celebrated in the 90s when he was invited to the UK to play sets at the Ministry Of Sound. 1992 releases included Syndicate 305's 'I Promise' and Groove Sector's 'The Love I Lost', but, following the death of Ova, the label endured a period of reduced activity. However, the label signed a distribution deal with BMG Canada and concentrated on building their profile there rather than on export markets. That situation changed again in the mid-90s when Hi-Bias was invited to perform at the Ministry Of Sound to celebrate five years of activity in December 1995. As well as Fiorucci the label's major acts - Oval Emotions, DJ Rules, Shauna Davis, Furry Freaks and Temperance - took part. By this time the label had released nearly 60 records, with 34 more on its Toronto Underground subsidiary. It also distributes seven other labels.

HI-C

b. Louisiana, USA. From Compton, California, Hi-C is some way short of the in-yer-face gangsta rap made famous by that area: 'I'm into music first, messages later. I'm not hardcore and I don't constantly say "black this" or "black that"'. Hi-C introduced his pleasant, personable fare to a national audience in 1990 when singles such as 'I'm Not Your Puppet' rose high in the *Billboard* charts. He also took roles in movies, including *Encino Man*, *South Central*, and *CB4*. In the latter it was Hi-C who provided the voice and lyrics for the Chris Rock character's on-screen raps. He is backed on record by DJ Tony A from Wilmington, California.
● ALBUMS: *Skanless* (Skanless 1991)★★★, *Swing'n* (Skanless 1993)★★.

HIGHER INTELLIGENCE AGENCY

Higher Intelligence Agency are Dave Wheels and Bobby Bird, part of the Birmingham Oscillate Collective, who first set up their own ambient/dub club in the back of a local pub in 1992. Next to London's Megadog, the Oscillate night soon emerged as one of the leading such establishments, with a strong reputation built on HIA's 'non-DJing' live sets plus appearances from Autechre, Biosphere, Orbital, Banco De Gaia, Drum Club and others, plus DJ sets from Mixmaster Morris and the Orb's Alex Paterson. They released their debut album in 1993, and a remix EP, *Re-Form*, the following year. This featured the imprints of Autechre, The Irresistible Force, Pentatonik and labelmates, A Positive Life. However, playing live remained their forte, using an improvised set and state-of-the-art equipment to produce a powerful fusion of dub and club music.
● ALBUMS: *Colourform* (Beyond 1993)★★★.

HIGHER STATE RECORDS

London-based record company formed in 1992 and run by Mark Dillon and Patrick Dickens, whose backgrounds were resolutely in the funk and soul traditions. As such they played out live as DJs in these genres, before the upsurge of house finally swept them up. However, the 20 or more releases in their first two years revealed a strong residual flare for digifunk aesthetics. They soon cut out a niche with releases by Disco Biscuit, Spacebase and Sound Environment. There was also evidence of wider listening tastes, including dub reggae, new wave experimentalism (early Simple Minds) and proto hip-hop (Mantronix): 'I could never listen to one particular kind of music all night in a club - it'd get too monotonous'. By 1994 they were still going strong with releases such as 'My Geetar Hertz' by Roller Coaster and Lafferty's 'Thinkin' Bout'.

HIJACK

British hip-hop crew who garnered attention via their debut, 'Style Wars', on Simon Harris' Music Of Life label, going on to record for Ice-T's Rhyme Syndicate. Ice-T had been doing a interview for Capitol Radio when the band's 'Hold No Hostage' was played to him. Reactions to the voice of Kamanchi Sly, a powerful MC, have often been positive, and their stage show is very effective. They also earned themselves a little celebrity via their 'Don't Go With Strangers' warning to young children. DJ Supreme from the band (who also include DJ Undercover, Agent Clueso, Agent Fritz and Ulysees) also released superior breakbeat albums like 1992's *Stolen Beats And Ripped Off Samples*.
● ALBUMS: *The Horns Of Jericho* (Rhyme Syndicate 1993)★★★.

HIP-HOP

Although rap is the obvious focal point, the black urban culture of hip-hop manifested itself in terms of graffiti and break dancing as well as music. The term, originally denoted in the Sugarhill Gang's 1979 release 'Rapper's Delight', was born in the Bronx district of New York, USA, in the 70s. At street parties DJs such as Grandmaster Flash, Kool Herc and Afrika

Bambaataa spun an eclectic mix of records while encouraging their dancers to aspire to ever greater feats. Flash was responsible for the development of 'scratch-mixing', moving discs backwards and forwards under the stylus, and switching between two turntables. Like his fellow DJs he would improvise dialogue over the resultant sounds in the manner of Jamaican toasting DJs. The dancers developed innovative new steps to keep up with the quick changes, including break-dancing, body-popping and robotics (best depicted in the film *Wildstyle*). At the same time New York subway trains were decorated with spray-cans in elaborate graffiti murals - an explosion of creativity which took as much joy in outraging authorities as it did in its own expression. Hip-hop has continued to be viewed as the 'mother culture' behind the commercial explosion of rap music in the 80s and 90s - with microphone artists keen to announce their credentials in other related fields such as graffiti.

HITHOUSE RECORDS

Label and studio, a subsidiary of ARS, founded by Dutch DJ and producer Peter Slaghuis, whose surname literally translated as Hithouse (hit as in 'strike' rather than in the pop chart sense). He used the same name to score a hit in 1988 with 'Jack To The Sound Of The Underground', one of a rash of such records utilising the 'jack' word following the breakthrough success of Steve 'Silk' Hurley. Hithouse would host a slew of Dutch and Belgian techno acts, including Global Insert Project, Problem House, Holy Noise and Meng Syndicate ('Artificial Fantasy'). Slaghuis died in a car crash on 5 September 1991.

HOEZ WITH ATTITUDE

Whilst taking gangsta rap's misogynist attitudes to task may be a positive move, adopting the latter's agenda to do so seems less well-advised. All in all Hoez With Attitude (HWA) ('Baby Girl' Kim Kenner, Goldie and Jazz) are a tragic concept stretched ever thinner over scuttling Miami-bass rhythms. Emigrating from Chicago to Los Angeles in the late 80s, within a year they had unveiled an album that would sell nearly 400,000 copies. A group destined to earn their notoriety off skimpy stage wear rather than anything constructive they might have to offer, musically or lyrically.
● ALBUMS: *Livin' In A Hoe House* (Ruthless 1990)★★★, *As Much Ass Azz U Want* mini-album (Ruthless 1994)★★.

HOLMES, DAVID

b. Belfast, Northern Ireland. House mixer, DJ and recording artist David Holmes is a former member of the Disco Evangelists. After the latter group's successes for Positiva Records ('De Niro', 'A New Dawn'), he recorded his first solo effort, 'Johnny Favourite', for Warp Records. An enormously popular DJ, Holmes also found time to collaborate with former Dub Federation musicians Andy Ellison and Pete Latham as one third of the Scubadevils. The latter two met him while performing at the Sugarsweet nightclub. Together they recorded 'Celestial Symphony' for the *Trance Europe Express* compilation, which was also remixed for a Novamute Records 12-inch release. This was backed by Holmes solo on 'Ministry' (credited to Death Before Disco). He has also recorded as the Well Charged Latinos ('Latin Prayer') and 4 Boy 1 Girl Action ('The Hawaian Death Stomp'). Holmes' remixing projects include commissions for the Sandals ('We Want To Live'), Robotman ('Do Da Doo'), Fortran 5 ('Persian Blues', 'Time To Dream'), Freaky Realistic ('Koochie Ryder'), Secret Knowledge ('Sugar Daddy'), Abfahrt ('Come Into My Life'), Bahia Black ('Capitao Do Asfolto') and Sabres Of Paradise ('Smokebelch'). He was also partially behind Sugarsweet Records, the Belfast dance label, run with Ian McCready and Jim McDonald. As Holmes explained at the time: 'It's more of a front to feed our obsession with music, to put out what we like, when we like.' Releases on the label included the Arabic house excursions of Wah Wah Warrior (essentially Ian McCready), plus Holmes' Death Before Disco. However, when it was clear that Sugarsweet was not going to take off it was replaced by the Exploding Plastic Inevitable imprint. In 1994 Holmes signed with Sabres Of Paradise as a solo artist, but when that label's Andy Weatherall decided to rethink his strategy, he found a new home at Go! Discs. His debut album emerged in 1995, with Sarah Cracknell (ex-Saint Etienne) contributing to the quasi-James Bond theme, 'Gone', while elsewhere Holmes luxuriated in the possibilities of the long-playing format by incorporating cinematic elements, Celtic flavours and ambient guitar (provided by Steve Hillage). 1997's *Let's Get Killed* featured samples of street interviews with New Yorkers.
● ALBUMS: *This Film's Crap, Let's Slash The Seats* (Go! Discs 1995)★★★, *Let's Get Killed* (Go! Beat 1997)★★★★.

HOLY GHOST INC

One of a number of groups picked up from the underground and hoisted on to a major in the early 90s, in this case Island Records subsidiary Blunted, Holy Ghost Inc were formed in 1989 and produced two EPS, *The Word*, and the widely praised *Mad Monks On Zinc*, prior to the move. *The Megawatt Messiah* EP, a slower techno piece continuing their religous themes, was their first release for Blunted in January 1994. There are other associated projects run in conjunction with the group, under the titles Saucer Crew ('Andromeda', etc.) and Ouija Board, though the participants continue to shroud their identities in mystery.

HONKY

Honky were formed from the ashes of Club St Louis, a small time rap duo who attracted some music business attention in the early 90s. That outfit signed to East West Records, releasing a solitary single. When they lost their contract in 1992 they returned home to Doncaster, Yorkshire, England, disillusioned. Matt, responsible for the group's music, soldiered on as a studio engineer, before teaming up once more with his old rapping partner, Kyle, the line-up completed by Stu, Joloise and Rosa. Together they wrote the song which would become the debut Honky release. 'KKK (Koffee Koloured Kids)' emerged on ZTT in 1993. It concerned Kyle's alienation at being the son of a white mother and black father, and his exclusion from both societies. A follow-up, 'The Whistler', proved similarly thoughtful. Again it concerned Kyle's parentage, this time discussing his father's temper, which could always be detected by his whistling before an impending act of violence.
● ALBUMS: *The Ego Has Landed* (ZTT 1994)★★★, *Kuljit* (Columbia 1996)★★★.

HOOJ TOONS

One of the more upfront UK house record labels, whose *esprit de corps* seems to rise from knowing how to spot a breaking tune - rather than veiling themselves in clique mystique. Among their many notable releases were Simon Sed's 'Wigged Criminal', Felix's 'Don't You Want Me' (which made the UK Top 10), Hyper Go Go's 'High', Dis-Cuss's 'Pissed Apache' (a gay anthem from DJ Malcolm Duffy, Jonathan Blanks and DJ Kenny Clarke), Gloworm's 'I Lift My Cup', Andronicus's (Blanks again) 'Make You Whole' and DCO2's 'Do What You Feel', all of which were included on the listed sampler album. They were also the first to release JX's 'Son Of A Gun', before licensing it to the London-affiliated Internal Dance imprint. The label originally grew out of Greedy Beat Records, which was set up by an accountant, before A&R man Jerry Dickens joined after leaving college. Dissatisfied with the small returns on his imput, Dickens spent most of 1993 trying to disentangle himself from the relationship, eventually setting up his own studio and gaining his own publishing deal. With slightly more solid financial footing, 1994 saw Dickens sign his first act for more than a one-off deal, JX (Jake Williams and vocalist Billie Godfrey). He also set up a subsidiary operation, Prolekult.
● ALBUMS: Various: *Some Of These Were Hooj* (Hooj Toons 1994)★★.

HORIZON 222

Horizon 222 are Ben and Andy, who keep their surnames a closely guarded secret. From Whitley Bay in Tyneside, England, they run their own Charm Records label, taking their neo-ambient music on the road via a camper-van: 'Never mind all this stuff about ambient music being designed to send you to sleep. As far as we're concerned, it should be a wake-up call.' The music employed on their 1994 debut album included samples that echo their interest in social justice and politics: Oliver North admitting he lied to Congress, and samples taken from news coverage of the release of the Guildford Four.
● ALBUMS: *The Three Of Swans* (Charm 1994)★★★.

HOUSE

Chicago was the kindergarten of the warm, feel-good music in the late 80s that came to be known as house, although its actual birthplace was New York, and the Loft. House was built on the innovations of disco but with less of the 'flash' and even less of a reliance on lyrics. In 1983/4 dance music was, indeed, essentially disco, although hybrids such as electro, go go and rare groove also existed. The term was invoked due to the warehouse parties at which it was to be heard during its infancy. The music arrived in Chicago when DJ Frankie Knuckles relocated to the region and inaugurated the original Warehouse club. The scene was confined to the gay clubs until Farley Jackmaster Funk began to play it on the radio. As the house scene evolved its early stages were chronicled by records such as Colonel Abrams' 'Music Is The Answer' (the first to press a record was Jesse Saunders). The trickle became a river as Chicago releases including J.M. Silk's 'Music Is The Key' (an answer record to the aforementioned Colonel Abrams release), Jack Master Funk's 'Aw Shucks' and Jamie Principle's 'Waiting On My Angel' piled up. Many of these were housed on imprints such as Trax and DJ International, which ably documented the era. Following Farley important early mixers and movers on Chicago radio included Julian Peruse, Frankie Rodriguez, Mike 'Hitman' Wilson, Bad Boy Bill, Tim Shomer and Brian Middleton. It would be Steve 'Silk' Hurley's 'Jack Your Body' that finally brought the new music commercial recognition and reached the number 1 slot in the UK charts. Variants like acid house were also given birth in Chicago via DJ Pierre, while Detroit took the electronic elements to forge techno. Frankie Rodriguez arguably has the best answer to a rigid definition of house: 'If I go out the country, the first thing anyone asks is "What Is House?". Who cares? Put the record on, enjoy it'.

HOUSE OF PAIN

Hardcore Irish American hip-hoppers whose origins can be traced to Taft High School in Los Angeles (former students of which include Ice Cube). The band comprise lead rapper Everlast (b. Eric Schrody, USA), his co-lyricist Danny Boy (b. Daniel O'Connor, USA), and DJ Lethal (b. Leor DiMant, c.1974, Latvia). Everlast was originally signed to Warner Brothers, and was often to be seen 'hanging' with Ice-T and his Rhythm Syndicate at that time. With House Of Pain he scored a debut Top 10 hit with the impressive 'Jump Around', a good example of the street poetry hybrid which they branded 'Fine malt lyricism'. 'Jump Around' seemed to offer the pinnacle in House Of Pain's career, however. Their debut album gloried in self-styled Gaelic dressing. 'Shamrocks And Shenanigans', an ode to their spurious links with the Emerald Isle, contained a novelty sample of David Bowie's 'Fame'. Elsewhere the album's grooves were populated with familiar, dumb macho lines, delivered with a quite singular lack of dexterity: 'I feel blessed, I'm casually dressed, I wear a gun, But I don't wear a vest'. No strangers to controversy, House Of Pain were involved in two near riots on their 1993 tour with Rage Against The Machine; once in Baltimore when they refused to take the stage, and again when a member of the band's road crew was assaulted by security staff at a Manchester Academy gig. This was only a matter of days after the rapper had been arrested at JFK Airport in New York for illegal possession of a handgun. Such incidents led to his being subject to a tracking device and house arrest for three months in 1994. The press were also starting to ask awkward questions about Sinn Fein tattoos. Everlast has ventured in to the world of films, appearing in both the US rap movie, *Who's The Man* (alongside Public Enemy, Heavy D etc), and the Dennis Leary flick, *Judgement Day*, where, unsurprisingly, he played a gangster. House Of Pain also opened a pizza restaurant, in partnership with Mickey Rourke (House Of Pizza). *Same As It Ever Was*, despite the title, proved to be a much more impressive outing, with Everlast unleashing his frustration with his 'imprisonment' and the media in tracks like 'Back From The Dead'
● ALBUMS: *House Of Pain* (Tommy Boy 1992)★★★★, *Same As It Ever Was* (Tommy Boy 1994)★★★, *Truth Crushed To Earth Shall Rise Again* (Tommy Boy 1996)★★★.

HUBBA HUBBA RECORDS

Falkirk, Scotland label, formed in late 1992, whose eclectic release schedule quickly established the name. Among their earliest releases were Ohm's 'Tribal Zone' and Sheffield-based techno crew the Forgemasters' *Quababa* EP. The latter outfit were picked up after spells at Warp and Network. Other signings included Scotland's Dub Commission ('Lost In House'), and Bamboo ('Coney Island'). Their product was licensed to Murk subsidiary Vibe, while Hubba Hubba also housed material from US label MegaTrend (run by Photon Inc's Roy Davies Jnr.). The label is run by Utah Saints manager John MacLennan.

HUMPHRIES, TONY

Legendary for his shows on New York's Kiss FM, New Jersey-born Humphries was a hugely influential figure in the development of the east coast dance scene. His support for Adeva's 'Respect', for instance, was the essential ingredient in her winning a record contract. Humphries gained access to the radio after meeting Shep Pettibone in 1981, who approved of his demo cassette. His break as a live DJ was offered in the same year by Larry Patterson. Previously he had been a mobile jock and worked for the *New York Daily* newspaper.

Patterson gave him his opportunity at the Zanzibar club, which became New Jersey's premier nightspot. Humphries has gone on to produce and remix for a huge variety of clients, just a smattering of which include Mass Order ('Lift Every Voice'), Alison Limerick ('Make It On My Own', 'Hear My Call'), Bananarama ('Movin' On'), KLF ('3AM Eternal'), Cure ('Love Cats'), Jungle Brothers ('What Are You Waiting For'), Steel Pulse ('Rollerskates') and Evelyn King ('Shakedown') - which represents a mere fraction of his client list. He moved to the UK in 1992 to start a residency at the Ministry Of Sound, while in 1994 Romanthony's 'In The Mix' (on Azuli) celebrated his status by building a song out of the repetition of Tony Humphries' name.

HURLEY, STEVE 'SILK'

Formerly a DJ at Chicago station WBMX, Hurley's first recordings, like many of his peers, were originally cut specifically to augment his DJ repertoire. One such track, 'Music Is The Key', enjoyed a particularly warm reception, and Hurley borrowed money from his father and placed it on his friend Rocky Jones' DJ International label. It made number 9 in the US dance charts, though no royalties were forthcoming. He was similarly dismayed when his 'I Can't Turn Around' was hijacked by Farley Jackmaster Funk, and turned into 'Love Can't Turn Around', with new vocals by Daryl Pandy, in 1985. It became a hit without any of the credit being extended to Hurley. However, his reward was just around the corner. After recording the mighty 'Baby Wants To Ride' with Jamie Principal he scored the first house number 1 with 'Jack Your Body' on 24 January 1987. Later he would create Kym Sims' 'Too Blind To See', and was invited to remix Roberta Flack's 'Uh Uh Ooh Ooh Look Out' - which he saw as a great personal achievement. Other remix projects came thick and fast, including Paula Abdul (*Vibeology* EP), Yasmin ('Sacrifice'), Simply Red ('Something Got Me Started'), Ce Ce Peniston ('We Got A Love Thang') and Rodeo Jones ('Get Wise'). At one time in the 90s it seemed that a dozen such remixes were appearing on the market at the same time, and in truth they were all relatively similar, albeit polished and accomplished. Hurley had few complaints, raking in the money at a reported $20,000 per throw, and working with heroes such as Stevie Wonder. In addition he established his own production company ID (signed to Sony in the UK and Europe, its remix roster including Chicago DJ

Ralphi Rosario and Juan Atkins). A previous such venture, JM Silk (formed with famous house vocalist Keith Nunnally) had proved ill-fated.
● ALBUMS: *Work It Out* (Atlantic 1989)★★★.

HUSTLERS CONVENTION

A duo of Mike Gray and John Pearn. Mike had been a DJ for 14 years, spinning old school disco from labels such as Prelude and Salsoul, playing various gigs around Croydon, Surrey, England. He met Pearn when he was operating the lights at a local pub. They started to collaborate together, bringing in samplers for live mixes with drum machines and records. Although John did not at that time possess Mike's experience, he quickly became a self-taught engineer, and offered megamixes and remixes for DMC. Hustlers Convention is essentially 'Mike's baby', and is disco-based, with samples culled from old disco records from Chic to more obscure Prelude 12-inches. A good example was the well-received *Groover's Delight* EP for Stress in 1992. They also record as Greed, for Virgin, as a more vocal-orientated group. In addition to their own output, the Hustlers have also remixed for mainstream star Kenny Thomas ('Trippin' On Your Love').

HUSTLERS HC

Three young Sikhs from west London, England, fronted by Hustler MC, who confront those factors relevant to their ethnic and geographical societies via a hip-hop beta beat. Touted as part of the new 'Asian Cool' alongside Trans-global Express and Fun-Da-Mental, their debut single, 'Big Trouble In Little Asia', came out at the same time as Gurinder Chadha's groundbreaking film, *Bhaji On The Beach*. It was a similarly themed address to the cross-cultural problems facing the Asian community. They also run the Bombay Jungle nightclub, a mixed bhangra/hip-hop venue, in London. They are managed by Simon Underwood (ex-Pop Group and Pigbag).

HYPE·A·DELICS

Rap crew, based in the Templehof region of Berlin, though only DJ Derezon (b. Berlin) is a native German. The two MC's, Rodski (b. New York, USA) and BMG the Funky Funktioneer (b. Flint, Michigan, USA) are both relics of America's armed presence in West Germany, where their fathers were in the services. Both, however, are now married and settled in their adopted country. Derezon and Rodski had worked together under

different names for several years, signing to Ariole as the Hype-A-Delics in 1991. After one single they departed and added BMG - who had formerly worked with his own crew back in Flint (Rodski had also been a friend of Doctor Ice in his Brooklyn days). They have subsequently inaugurated their own Juiceful Records, now home to several German hip-hop crews including Cheeba Garden and Islamic Force. This imprint released their debut album in 1994, which reflected their concerns over the rise of the right wing in Europe, as well as dissing the police and praising the herb.
● ALBUMS: *More Funk For You Ass* (Juiceful 1994)★★★.

HYPER GO-GO

Never regarded as strikingly original, Hyper Go-Go are nevertheless one of the most commercially prominent UK house acts, a fact confirmed when their early singles, including 'High' (UK number 30) and 'Never Let Go' (number 45), both crossed over into the UK charts. The team, James Diplock and Alex Ball, have been working together since they left school in the mid-80s. They have their own studio, a converted warehouse in the middle of a disused airfield, in the heart of the Essex countryside. 'High' was originally released on Hooj Toons before being picked up by DeConstruction. For 'Never Let Go', a typical 'storming piano house tune', they switched to the Positiva label on a more permanent footing. 'Raise' used the familiar 'Raise Your Hands' vocal line as its core, with guest vocals from Brian Chambers. Other contributors have included Sally Anne Marsh, currently of Hysterix. Bell and Diplock are also one half of techno/rave sideline Electroset (whose 'How Does It Feel?' was their 'rave thing') and experimental electronic outfit Compufonic ('Ecstacy 0376' for Ocean Records in 1992, now signed to Mute for whom they debuted with the *Make It Move* EP).

HYPNOTIST, THE

Comprising UK's Rising High Records owner Casper Pound (b. *c*.1970; once the 'hippie' in A Homeboy, A Hippie And A Funki Dred), and in the early stages Pete Smith. Pound rejoiced in statements such as: 'I wanna scare people on the dancefloor. I wanna use sounds that are disturbing to the mind and really freak people out when they're tripping'. He seemed determined to prove his mettle with cuts including the debut 12-inch 'Rainbows In The Sky' and 'This House Is

Mine', the latter a Top 75 hit single in September 1991. More notorious was *The Hardcore* EP, which included the neo-legendary 'Hardcore U Know The Score'. Follow-ups included 'Live In Berlin' (The Hypnotist were celebrated as pop stars in Germany) and 'Pioneers Of The Universe'. Pound also works as part of Rising High Collective with former Shamen vocalist Plavka, and records under the name New London School Of Electronics and several more. He is also a distant relative of the US poet Ezra Pound.
● ALBUMS: *The Complete Hypnotist* (Rising High 1992)★★★.

HYPNOTONE

Hypnotone revolves around Tony Martin, who had previously worked with Creation Records with a different line-up featuring the vocals of Denise Johnson on releases such as 'Dream Beam' (remixed by Danny Rampling and Ben Champion). The modern Hypnotone included vocalist Cordelia Ruddock, discovered by Martin at a fashion show, Lee Royle, whom he met through a computer bulletin board and Cormac Fultan, a pianist and organist, who met Martin in the more conventional environment of a bar.

HYSTERIX

Formed when the principal members met up on the Tokyo dance music scene, where Tony Quinn was DJing at the Gold club for Yohji Yahamoto, Hysterix are not yet the most renowned of DeConstruction's acts. However, they have not been absent through want of trying. A typical act of anarchy came in 1993 when, via a live pirate broadcast, they illegally interrupted terrestrial television to transmit the slogan 'You've been Hysterixed!'. Dance magazine columns regularly overflowed with tales of their clubland ligging. They blew their record advance on tequila during an all-expenses trip to Mexico to shoot a video, which never materialized. Another five-day jaunt to Florida was arranged when they pretended to be a completely different band. They joined Technotronic on their Eastern European tour, demanding payment in champagne and caviar, and persuaded Jean-Michel Jarre to let them mix his work, staying at a hotel drinking Dom Perignon at his expense and completely forgetting to deliver the tape. They have also kidnapped their manager and booking agent and left them tied up at Skegness railway station, among many other pranks. Influenced by the original disco sounds of T Connection and Earth, Wind And Fire as much as late 80s house, they were signed to their label for a full three years before a debut single, 'Must Be The Magic', emerged. DeConstruction had originally been impressed by the 'Talk To Me' 12-inch, which later saw a tremendously popular, but elusive, Sasha remix. The nucleus of the group is 'Tokyo' Tony Quinn, Darren Black and Richard Belgrave. Their numerous female vocalists have included ex-KLF singer Maxine, though from October 1993 the band featured Sally Anne Marsh and Marie Harper. Marsh had originally been part of Tom Watkins' (manager of Bros, East 17, etc.) pop act Faith Hope And Charity when she was 14, alongside television 'presenter' Danni Behr. She also sang on Xpansions' Top 10 hit, 'Move Your Body', in 1991, and has worked with Hyper Go Go and Aerial. Harper, meanwhile, formerly operated on the jazz circuit. Hysterix finally looked as though they were getting their house in order for 1994, supporting D:Ream on their UK tour and garnering good press for the single.

IAM

One of the more impressive of a new wave of French hip-hop groups expanding throughout the 90s, Iam were formed in Marseilles at the beginning of the decade. After an independent debut that was not released internationally, they signed with Virgin Records for their second album. *Oembre Est Lumiére*, the title translating as 'Shadow Is Light', was a sprawling, 40-track package conducted over a double album, featuring a cocktail of American-derived, funk-based hip-hop. Alongside the work of MC Solaar, it became the first French rap album to sell significantly outside of mainland Europe, aided by strong reviews in the USA and UK. These included a five-star rating from *H.H.C.* magazine, who described it as 'a colossal feast of a record. Open your mind and feed your ears.' Taken from the album, 'Je Danse Le Mia' won an award for Iam as the best band of the year during the Victoires De La Musique ceremony.
● ALBUMS: *Oembre Est Lumiére* (Virgin 1994)★★★★.

ICE CUBE

b. O'Shea Jackson, 15 June 1969, Crenshaw, South Central Los Angeles, California, USA. Controversial hardcore rapper who formerly worked with the equally inflammatory NWA. Following a relatively stable background, with both his mother and father working at UCLA, Cube entered the homeboy lifestyle: 'One day I was sitting in class with a friend called Kiddo and we had some time on our hands, so he said let's write a rap'. At the age of 16 he penned his first important rap, 'Boyz 'N The Hood', which was later recorded by Eazy-E. He subsequently spent time with CIA, an embryonic rap outfit produced by Dr Dre. As guest lyricist, he brought NWA '8 Ball' and 'Dopeman', which would comprise the opening salvo from the band. After studying architectural draughtsmanship in Phoenix, Arizona, he returned to the NWA fold in time for the ground-breaking *Straight Outta Compton*. He would leave the group at the tail-end of 1989, amid thinly veiled attacks on NWA's Jewish manager Jerry Heller. His debut album, recorded with Public Enemy producers the Bomb Squad, drew immediate mainstream attention with its controversial lyrical platform. As well as homophobia and the glamorization of violence, his work was attacked primarily for its overt sexism, raps about kicking a pregnant girlfriend ('You Can't Fade Me') notwithstanding. Conversely, Ice Cube overlooks a production empire (Street Knowledge) run for him by a woman, and he also fostered the career of female rapper Yo Yo (who appears alongside him defending her gender on *AmeriKKKa's Most Wanted*'s 'It's A Man's World'). The politicization of his solo work should also be noted; in his NWA days he had once written, 'Life ain't nothing but bitches and money', but his words since then have incorporated numerous references to black ideology that add up to something approaching a manifesto. His defence against critical discomfort with his rhymes, 'I put a mirror to black America', has been hijacked by many other, less worthy cases. To Ice Cube's credit, he went on to produce two excellent sets, *The Predator* and *Lethal Injection*. The former, in particular, boasted a much more discursive approach to the problems of the ghetto, including reflections on the Los Angeles riots and the Rodney King beating. Perhaps it was marred by the blunt sexism of tracks such as 'Cave Bitch', but it was certainly an advance. Musically it was typified by a stirring 'One Nation Under A Groove', with a lead vocal by the song's writer, George Clinton. In 1993 he also teamed up with fellow rapper Ice-T, with whom he shares more than a similarity in name, to launch a fashion range incorporating a gun logo. No stranger to controversy, Ice Cube became better acquainted with commerce too. His 1992 film *Trespass*, retitled after the LA Riots deemed original moniker *Looters* unsavoury, saw him team up with Ice-T once more. He had already starred in John Singleton's 1991 hit film, titled after his first rap, *Boyz 'N The Hood*, and later appeared in the same director's *Higher Learning*. Having completed four million-selling albums, Ice Cube's career attracted the attention of those outside the hip-hop fraternity. 'It Was A Good Day' gave him a massive profile via MTV. Like Ice-T, Cube was targeted on right wing assassination lists discovered by the police in 1993. However, his career has continued unabated.

Street Knowledge has provided Da Lench Mob and Kam with successful albums on which Cube has acted as executive producer, and he has set up a second subsidiary, titled after his posse, Lench Mob, and written several screenplays. The soundtrack to his 1998 directorial debut, *The Player's Club*, was a Top 10 success in the USA. The film itself, set in a strip club, was one of the year's suprise successes, having grossed $20 million at the box office only six weeks after its April release.

● ALBUMS: *AmeriKKKa's Most Wanted* (Priority 1990)★★★★, *Kill At Will* mini-album (Priority 1990)★★★, *Death Certificate* (Priority 1991)★★★, *The Predator* (Lench Mob/Priority 1992)★★★, *Lethal Injection* (Lench Mob/Priority 1993)★★★, *Bootlegs & B-Sides* (Lench Mob/Priority 1994)★★.

ICE-T

One of the most outspoken rappers on the west coast, Ice-T (b. Tracy Marrow, *c*.1958, Newark, New Jersey, USA) boasts (sometimes literally) a violent past in which he was shot twice - once whilst involved in an armed robbery. His name, fittingly, is taken from black exploitation author Iceberg Slim, and he is backed on record by Afrika Islam and DJ Aladdin's hardcore hip-hop. His first record was actually 'The Coldest Rapper' in 1983, which was improvised over a Jimmy Jam And Terry Lewis rhythm, and made him the first Los Angeles hip-hop artist. Unfortunately, he was subsequently held under contract by mogul Willie Strong for several years. Disillusioned, he made his money from petty and not so petty crime, and also appeared in the breakdance film *Breakin'*, which included his 'Reckless' cut on the soundtrack. He followed it with the faddish 'Killers' single. The breakthrough, however, came with 'Ya Don't Know', which was widely credited with being the first west coast hip-hop artefact (although the honour was undoubtedly Ice-T's, the real beneficiary should have been the obscure 'The Coldest Rapper' cut). Four LPs in just three years created something of a stir in the USA, based as they were largely on his experiences as a gang member in Los Angeles. In 1989 he reached the lower end of the UK charts with 'High Rollers', but did better the following year teaming up with Curtis Mayfield on a remake of 'Superfly'. He is married to Darlene who normally appears semiclad on his record sleeves, and owns a pit pull terrier affectionately titled Felony. For a time, too, he delighted in inviting journalists to his luxury

Beverly Hills home to show them his personal armoury of semi-automatic weapons. Success has also enabled him to start his own record company, Rhyme Syndicate. His vision of the black man as sophisticated and articulate (being hard as nails is, of course, *de rigeur*) ranks him among the most potent forces in contemporary black culture. His refusal to engage in a white liberal agenda (he was the first rap artist to have warning stickers placed on his album sleeves) has irritated many, but helped to establish him as an authentic spokesperson for dispossessed black youth. His debut album, *Rhyme Pays*, with an Uzi emblazoned on the cover, served as a mission statement: hardcore raps on street violence and survival being the order of the day. By the time of its follow-up, there was demonstrably greater imagination displayed in terms of backing music. Like many of his west coast brethren, Ice-T had rediscovered funk. Notable tracks included 'Girls L.G.B.N.A.F., which the PMRC later discovered stood for 'Let's Get Butt Naked And Fuck'. Their reaction to this (arguably among the least offensive statements on Ice-T's records) was so overheated that the debate heavily informed his follow-up set. However, his crowning glory so far was *OG* (an acronym for Original Gangster that has passed into rap's lexicon) which ranks alongside the best work of Ice Cube, Public Enemy or NWA in terms of sustained intensity, yet managed to maintain a little more finesse than his previous work. In 1991, with appealing irony, he starred as a cop in the movie *New Jack City*. He had earlier contributed the title track to the LA gangster movie *Colors*, rapping the title song. He also appeared with former NWA and solo artist Ice Cube in the Walter Hill film *Looters*. (renamed *Trespassers* due to its release at the same time as the LA riots), as well as *Surviving The Game* and the cult comic hero movie, *Tank Girl*. His other soundtrack credits include *Dick Tracy*. Ice-T's hobbies include his own thrash metal outfit, Body Count, who released an album in 1992 and stirred up immeasurable controversy via one of its cuts, 'Cop Killer' (detailed under Body Count entry). Little wonder that he was targeted on right-wing assassination lists discovered by the police in 1993. His album from that year, *Home Invasion*, saw him take on the mantle of agent provocateur in the young white male's home, a theme reinforced in its cover and title - Ice-T was a threat in your neighbourhood, with another manifesto of spiteful intent ('I'm takin' your kids' brains, You

ain't getting them back, I'm gonna fill 'em with hard drugs, big guns, bitches, hoes and death'). Then he went and spoiled all the good work by writing a book, the *Ice-T Opinion*, which was so full of dumb ideas that it largely discredited such achievements. On 22 March 1994 he introduced Channel 4's *Without Walls*, a documentary on the rise of the blaxploitation movies. His own life would make an excellent documentary subject. He continues to fascinate those on both sides of the rap lobby, and, as he notes in *Home Invasion*'s 'Ice Muthafuckin' T': 'Every fucking thing I write, Is going to be analysed by somebody white'.
● ALBUMS: *Rhyme Pays* (Sire 1987)★★★, *Power* (Sire 1988)★★, *The Iceberg/Freedom Of Speech . . . Just Watch What You Say* (Sire 1989)★★★, *OG: Original Gangster* (Syndicate/Sire 1991)★★★★, *Home Invasion* (Priority 1993)★★★, *Born Dead* (Priority 1994)★★★.
● VIDEOS: *O.G. - The Original Gangster Video* (1991).
● FURTHER READING: *The Ice Opinion*, Ice-T and Heidi Seigmund.

ICHIBAN

Ichiban is a Georgia corporation that was founded in Atlanta in 1985 by John E. Abbey (London-born former proprieter of *Blues & Soul* magazine) and his wife, Nina K. Easton, who took the company title from the Japanese for number one. Their goal of providing an outlet for black music, be it blues, gospel, jazz, R&B or rap, has remained constant. Since its inception Ichiban has grown to become the distributor of some 20 to 30 labels. The company first came into contact with rap music when approached to distribute Vanilla Ice's *To The Extreme* album in 1990 (later picked up by SBK). As Abbey admitted, 'We literally stumbled into rap'. Their next project was MC Breed's 'Ain't No Future In Yo' Frontin', via Swamp Dogg's SDEG label. Buoyed by these initial successes, Ichiban launched its primary rap stable, Wrap Records. Product included a second MC Breed album, plus music from Success-N-Effect, Kilo and Gangsta Pat. Other releases filtered through on subsidiary rap imprints such as 380 Recordings, Easylee and Mo' Money, and for a time the Nastymix operation was also distributed through Ichiban's offices. The company's catalogue has extended to a point at which over 60% of its releases are in the rap/hip-hop field, and they possess one of the most talented rosters of new artists in the US. Apart from the aformentioned artists, some of these include Detroit's Most Wanted, Kid Sensation, Kwamé, Menace To Society, 95 South, Treacherous 3, Snoman and MC Shy D.

IF?

If? emerged in the UK during 1990's Summer Of Love, graduating from the backrooms of the Brain Club, which was co-managed by the group's Sean McLusky. They hit the rave scene in turn, before organizing a London Calling tour with Airstream, Natural Life and others. With vocals from Paul Wells, If? peddled a straightforward Balearic model of 90s dance culture. Member Lyndsay Edwards went on to join the Disco Evangelists.
● ALBUMS: *English Boys On The Love Ranch* (MCA 1992)★★.

IGNORANCE

A London hip-hop duo comprising Mark Martin and Trevor, who formerly found fame and fortune as dancers for the Pet Shop Boys. They started off their own career at Polydor with 'Phat Girls', a politically correct attempt to redress hip-hop's attitudes to women. They also took a non-conventional approach to their music, choosing a ska mix over the more preferred funk/jazz stylings of their American neighbours. This was done primarily to reinstate the Black British experience, reflecting the sounds of reggae and calypso. And there was no cussing of bitches and ho's to be found on their debut album, either: 'I mean, when we went to school we never had rucksacks with Uzis in 'em! To me, all that infatuation with being a hard superhuman with a gun by your side is bollocks. It's just a weak excuse for people that are insecure.'
● ALBUMS: *The Epitome Of Ignorants* (Polydor 1994)★★★.

ILL (FEATURING AL SKRATCH)

aka Big Ill The Mack, who first came to prominence in his home-town of Brooklyn, New York, by appearing on a freestyle tape that was circulated after a performance at a Big Daddy Kane birthday party (where he successfully 'dissed' both the birthday boy and other 'sucker MCs'). He made an impressive debut, backed by DJ Al Skratch, with the anthemic 'Where My Homiez?' 12-inch for Mercury. The track was produced by LG, brother of Easy Mo Bee (Rappin' Is Fundamental).
● ALBUMS: *Creep Wit' Me* (Mercury 1994)★★★★.

ILLEGAL

Illegal are two diminutive youngsters from the USA, Lil' Malik Edwards and Jamal Phillips. Far from the cutesy Kriss Kross school of teen-rappers, Illegal won a degree of notoriety when curtailing an interview with a US rap magazine and offering to 'smoke' the interviewer. Their debut album boasted production from heavyweights like Erick Sermon, Diamond D, Lord Finesse, Biz Markie and others. Having subsequently split, Malik featured as part of Snoop Doggy Dogg's Dog Pound, appearing on albums by the latter and Warren G.
● ALBUMS: *The Untold Truth* (Rowdy 1993)★★★.
Solo: Jamal *Last Chance, No Breaks* (Arista 1995)★★★.

ILLEGAL SUBSTANCE

From New South Wales, Australia, this three-piece rap group comprises MCs Micke and Flip (both b. *c*.1976), alongside DJ/producer ESP. The trio met in a record store and each had a long history of activity in Sydney's fledgling hip-hop scene, including graffiti and breakdancing. They recorded their debut album, *Off Da Back Of A Truck*, in a bedroom in a single day, using live takes of music that reflected their devotion to the hard funk sounds of west coast American rappers such as NWA and Dr Dre.
● ALBUMS: *Off Da Back Of A Truck* (Illegal Substance 1994)★★★.

INFINITE WHEEL

North London-based ambient techno duo who consist of former Pigbag percussionist/guitarist James Johnstone and Mark Smith. Their first recording, 'Segun International', was unveiled on cult New York label Nu Groove in 1991 after the duo simply sent them a tape in the post. They followed it with the *Dharma Sunburst* EP in 1992 for Brainiak. They described the latter thus: 'We wanted to use sounds that had some sort of depth to them, rather than pure bleeps. So it's a mixture of deep and shallow'. They made an appearance on Positiva's Ambient Collection ('Digi Out'), as well as releasing 'Gravity Attack' on R&S. Their other releases have graced imprints like Tomato, marking an effective sweep of the very best in international record labels.
● ALBUMS: *Blow* (Brainiak 1996)★★★.

INFINITY PROJECT, THE

Raja Ram (Ron Rothfield), who had trained as a jazz flautist in the 50s and played in the band Quintessence in the 60s, began making music with Graham Wood as The Infinity Project in 1989. Over the next few years they experimented with a kind of abstract techno gradually forming a sound that became known as the psychedelic or 'Goa' trance, often in collaboration with Simon Posford (Hallucinogen), Nick Barber (Doof) and Martin Freeland (Man With No Name). After producing material on DATs and white labels, in 1992 they started to release their music via the labels Fabulous ('Freedom In The Flesh'), Spiritzone ('Telepathy/Binary Neuronaut') and Dragonfly ('Bizarro', 'Time And Space', 'Super Booster' and 'Feeling Very Wierd'). In 1994 with Ian St. Paul they formed TIP Records and launched the label with 'Stimuli/Uforica'. At the same time they worked on projects with Posford and others, including the *Mystery Of The Yeti* album (TIP 1996) and various releases as Total Eclipse. After an ambient album *Mystical Experiences* (1995) for Blue Room, they released 'Alien Airport / Hyperspaced' on TIP followed by the album *Feeling Wierd* which was mostly made up of their previous releases. In the spirit of the 'Goa' scene *Feeling Wierd* was steeped in psychedelic hippie/sci-fi imagery. While tracks such as 'Telepathy', 'Stimuli' and the Doof remix of 'Hyperspaced' successfully blend the rigid four-on-the-floor rhythms, modal riffs, mysterious dialogue and abstract electronic phasing and filter sweeps that characterize the early psy-trance sound, 'Noises From The Darkness' and the early track 'Freedom From The Flesh' (written 1992) sound rather limp in comparison. In 1997 the group released the single 'Overwind / Incandescence' and contributed the excellent, but rather dark 'Mindboggler' to the TIP compilation *3D* Wood also began recording as Excess Head for TIP's subsidiary 10 Kilo while Ram continued to work with Posford. By 1998 The Infinity Project had split up to concentrate on individual projects.
● ALBUMS: *Mystical Experiences* (Blue Room 1995), *Feeling Wierd* (TIP 1995)★★★ .

INFONET RECORDS

The dance label subsidiary of Creation Records, managed by Chris Abbott who enjoys total creative freedom in his selection of artists. This has resulted in a refreshing lack of 'house style' (in both senses), with Infonet regaling its followers with a variety of shades of electronic music. Their premier acts include Bandulu and Reload, while among their most significant releases were the *Thunderground* EP (Thunderground), 'Better Nation' and 'Guidance' (Bandulu), 'Terminus' (Syzygy), 'Liquid Poetry' (Subterfuge), 'Phase 4' (Reload) and 'I'm A Winner, Not A Loser' (Eddie 'Flashin'' Fowlkes). New signings in 1994 included Sons Of The Subway, Indika and Kohtao.
● COMPILATIONS: various artists *Beyond The Machines* (Infonet 1993).

INKY BLACKNUSS

A highly regarded new techno duo comprising Alex Knight, a DJ and proprietor of London's Fat Cat record store, fellow DJ Andrea Parker and engineer Ian Tregonim. The latter, who handles production, was for many years responsible for Yello's engineering. Parker takes charge of mixing, while Knight looks after percussion. Together they made a strong impression on their debut 1993 release, 'Blacknuss', on the Sabrettes imprint, which was awarded the *New Musical Express*'s hastily improvised 'Filthy, Dirty, Techno Thing Of The Week' award. Dark and foreboding, its menacing ambience was recreated by a follow-up release, 'Drumulator'. Utilizing backwards synthesizer sounds and 'natural noises', Parker described her interests as being 'anything that blows the speaker up'.

INNER CITY

Dance team built around the prolific genius of Kevin Saunderson (b. Kevin Maurice Saunderson, 9 May 1964, Brooklyn, New York, USA; programming), and the vocals of Paris Grey (b. Shanna Jackson, 5 November 1965, Glencove, Illinois, USA). Saunderson, who is also widely revered for his remix and recorded work under the title Reese Project, is brother to a member of Brass Connection, and his mother was a member of the Marvelettes. He went on to study telecommunications at university, firing an interest in technology that would quickly become obvious in his musical leanings. Saunderson is the creative powerhouse of the unit, a studio denizen who writes all the songs and plays all the instruments. Grey is responsible for writing her own melodies. Their first single together, 'Big Fun', was lying around unissued in Saunderson's home base in Detroit until a friend discovered it while looking for tracks for a compilation LP. The record-buying public homed in on the strength of the tune (arguably one of dance music's all-time top five anthems), and with its follow-up, 'Good Life', Inner City had discovered a commercial career, with their debut album going on to worldwide sales of six million. Further singles have included 'That Man (He's Mine)', while the album that housed it, *Fire*, even boasted a token effort at rap. Other notable singles included 'Back Together Again', a stylish 1993 cover of Roberta Flack and Donnie Hathaway's standard. Saunderson runs his own label, KMS, through Network, whose Neil Rushton is his manager. This led to Network also picking up the Inner City name when Virgin allowed the group to run out of contract in the 90s.

● ALBUMS: *Paradise* (Ten 1989)★★★, *Paradise Remixed* (Ten 1990)★★★, *Fire* (Ten 1990)★★.
● VIDEOS: *Paradise Live* (1990).

INNOCENCE

Comprising brother/sister combination Mark and Anna Jolley (guitar and vocals, respectively), plus Brian Harris (percussion), Mattie (synthesizer) and Phil Dane (production) - although Gee Morris also featured heavily on their debut album. Innocence scored a UK Top 20 hit in 1990 with 'Natural Thing', a good part of the notoriety surrounding the release caused by one of the mixes featuring a sample of Pink Floyd's 'Shine On You Crazy Diamond'. Since then they have released 'Silent Voice', 'Let's Push It' and 'A Matter Of Fact' (all 1990), 'Remember The Day' (1991), 'I'll Be There', 'One Love In My Lifetime' and 'Build' (1992) all charting but none breaching the Top 20.
● ALBUMS: *Belief* (Cooltempo 1990)★★★.

INOUE, TETSUO

b. Japan, but based in New York, USA, where he settled because of the greater opportunities for techno artists. Inoue has recorded for New York's Mik Mak and, more prolifically, Germany's Fax label. In 1993 he released two LPs for the latter, and has also collaborated with German producer Atom Heart on the acid-inspired 'Datacide' project.
● ALBUMS: *Shades Of Orion* (Fax 1993)★★★, *2351 Broadway* (Fax 1993)★★★, *Ambient Otaku* (Fax 1994)★★★.

INTELLIGENT HOODLUM

b. Percy Chapman, *c.*1968, Rikers Island, USA. The Hoodlum grew up on the same street as Marley Marl, whom he pestered every day to try and get a record out, after having picked up the rap bug from his cousin Kadiya. Finally Marl acquiesced, and Hoodlum had his first record released, 'Coke Is It'. It was later retitled 'Tragedy', after the Hoodlum's own sorry tale. He was only 14, but instead of further releases he pursued a life of crime to support his crack habit. Inevitably, he found himself in prison on a one- to three-year sentence. However, the prison term gave him the chance to cool off, and he spent his time reading avidly. Having got through black-consciousness standards by Malcolm X and Elijah Muhammed, he was paroled just as Public Enemy arrived on the scene. Chuck D's bleak messages struck a chord with Hoodlum, and although he returned to the drug trade to support himself, he also attended college to learn more about his new heroes, Marcus Garvey and Malcolm X. Eventually he met up with Marley Marl again, by now a major hip-hop talent, who invited him to perform some more raps. The eventual results were the improvised 'Party Pack' and 'Vitally Tragic'. The Intelligent Hoodlum moniker indicated a path for the future, renouncing his illegal activities but acknowledging the necessary part his criminal past had played in his development. The intelligent prefix inferred his desire to learn, and use his new-found wisdom for the benefit of himself and others. This attitude was clearly demonstrated on his debut album by the ferocious protest of 'Black And Proud' or 'Arrest The President'. Now a practising Muslim, and affiliated to the Nation of Islam, Hoodlum also set up his own organization, MAAPS - Movement Against the American Power Structure.
● ALBUMS: *Tragedy* (A&M 1990)★★★, *Saga Of A Hoodlum* (A&M 1993)★★★★.

INTERNAL RECORDS

A connoisseur's UK dance label formed in 1992 by Christian Tattersfield, the former Marketing Manager of London Records, with whom the label is financially linked. They struck immediately; their first signings were Orbital, whose second album, having moved over from sister label ffrr, went on to sell over a million copies. Zero B's *Reconnections* EP followed, before an album of Yellow Magic Orchestra remixes which featured the work of the Orb, 808 State, Shamen and Altern 8 among others. Vapourspace also recorded for the label, before the unexpected, runaway success of Capella on the Internal Dance subsidiary. On the same imprint JX's 'Son Of A Gun' also hit, though the Outthere Brothers' 'Fuk U In The Ass' was probably a little risqué even for underground dance punters. More recent signings include Cisco Ferreira and Salt Tank.

● ALBUMS: Orbital: *Untitled 2* (Internal 1993)★★★.

INTERNATIONAL FOOT LANGUAGE

Comprising Noel McKoy (vocals) and Steve Spiro (keyboards), International Foot Language, based in London, England, came together in 1990 when the duo met and elected to join forces, though each was already heavily implicated in their own separate projects. McKoy is a veteran of his own band, McKoy, plus the James Taylor Quartet, co-writing most of their 1993 album *Supernatural Feeling* and singles such as 'Love The Life' and 'Brighter Day'. He has also worked with the Pasadenas, Snowboy and Steve Williamson. Spiro made his name in production and writing, working with artists including East 17 and the Pet Shop Boys. His remixes include work for MC Hammer, the Farm and Talk Talk. He had previously been commissioned by BBC Television to provide music for its sports programmes, including the 1992 Olympics, Grand Prix coverage, *Ski Sunday* and *Match Of The Day*. This connection led to International Foot Language's first single, 'The Brave', being used as the theme to the BBC's coverage of the 1994 Commonwealth Games. 'The Brave' was written and produced by the duo with the use of Canadian Indian chants and recordings of tribal music form north-west Canada, where the Games were being held. Underpinning the vocals were western dance beats, sampling and production technology.

IQ PROCEDURE

This London, England, hip-hop trio specialize in mixing dub reggae with more conventional hip-hop rhythms. Rapper and programmer Baron Smith, the group's guiding hand and spokesman, was among the many discoveries of British rap svengali MC Duke. Alongside fellow rapper Mr Million and ragga disc jockey DJ Danger, IQ Procedure (a name they translate as a desire 'to constantly strive for and pursue new forms of intelligence') made their debut with the EP, *U Can Get With This*, in 1993. Like many of their UK rap peers, however, its potential audience was restricted by both poor distribution and press coverage.

IRVINE, WELDON

b. *c*.1944, USA. Publisher Irvine Weldon rose to prominence in the 90s when his extensive catalogue became widely sampled by prominent rap and hip-hop artists. A Tribe Called Quest, Boogie Down Productions, Leaders Of The New School, Ice Cube, 3rd Bass, Too Short and Snoop Doggy Dogg are among those who have featured samples of Irvine's Nodlew Music catalogue in their work. However, music publishing is just one of his musical interests. Irvine was inspired into following a musical career by the rock, soul and jazz sounds that surrounded him in his youth. In the 50s he sang as leader of several big bands, and also worked as Nina Simone's musical director. He also wrote musicals, the most famous of which was *Young, Gifted And Broke*, which won an Audelco Award for Achievement in Black Theater in 1977. He became immersed in hip-hop in the 80s when one of his students asked where he saw its place in the continuum of black music. When he investigated rap, he quickly discovered that some of its participants had been borrowing liberally from his own catalogue. However, he was keen to take on a mediating role rather than simply pursue legal action. 'When sampling began, I thought it was viable and that its potential was unlimited in terms of the kinds of music that could be created that way. But I did have a concern about the matter of compensation to the creators and owners of the original works.' The first of his works to be widely sampled was 'Sister Sanctified'. This tune, which he originally wrote for saxophonist Stanley Turrentine, eventually turned up, in amended form, in songs by Ice Cube, 3rd Bass and Boogie Down Productions. Other popular samples of Irvine's authorship include the Fatback Band's 'Fatbackin'' (sampled by Leaders Of The New School), Rhythm Combination And Brass's 'Mr. Clean' (sampled by Casual) and his own recording of 'We Gettin' Down' (sampled by A Tribe Called Quest on 'Award Tour').

ISHII, KEN

b. *c*.1970, Tokyo, Japan. Ishii's early infatuation with music arrived via the electronica of Yellow Magic Orchestra, Kraftwerk and DAF. It was a fixation he would follow until it led him to the work of Derrick May. Impressed and inspired, he subsequently immersed himself in what little dance culture and recordings made it over to Japan. His modern tastes include the Black Dog and D-Jax Up Beats empires, whose experimental edge is reflected in his own works. These began with 'Rising Sun' for Dutch label ESP, before a double-pack R&S release, 'Garden On The Palm', and the *Utu* EP for Richie Hawtin's Plus 8 label. Nominally a daytime office worker, Ishii's wild and bracing material, often reflecting the keyboard undulations of his earliest influences, have made him Japan's first and biggest techno export.

● ALBUMS: *Innerelements* (R&S 1994)★★★, *Jelly Tones* (R&S 1995)★★★★.

ISOTONIK

UK-based Isotonik is essentially Chris Paul, helped out by DJ Hype and Grooverider, who claims to have remixed everyone from 'Mozart to Yazz'. He is also an efficient multi-instrument musician, especially adept at keyboards and saxophone. As well as working widely as a session musician he has DJed at venues including Camden Palace, and ran the Orange Club in north London. His first record came out in 1986 - 'Expansions '86'. However, there was a long gap before his next major success with 'Different Strokes', on ffrr in 1992, which sampled the Ten City song of the same name. This had been picked up following release on his own label, again titled Orange Records, in 1991. It was succeeded by an eponymous EP the following year.

IZIT

Rare UK groove revivalists of the early 90s whose name stemmed from a technological mishap; when they were sampling the word 'music' their sequencer messed up and looped 'Izit' instead. They enjoyed breakthrough success with 'Stories', on their own Pig & Trumpet label in 1989, a version of the rare groove staple originally recorded by Chakachas. The group, who comprise former Tarzan-a-gram Tony Colman (guitar, keyboards; ex-Pulse, who once appeared on *Wogan*), Peter Shrubshall (flute, tenor saxophone) and sister Catherine Shrubshall (soprano, alto and baritone saxophone) were originally a studio-based enterprise. However, they added drummer Andrew Messingham and a bass player to the line-up for their first live shows. A huge hit in 1989, Messingham had actually scratched 'Acid Free Zone' onto the run-out grooves of 'Stories'. Despite their avowed wish to slow the pace of the summer's soundtrack, the single was widely adored by the acid crowd after the track was ini-

tially bought on import (Izit having licensed its release in Italy). Eventually it transferred to Paul Oakenfold's Perfecto label where he produced a popular remix, before the group joined Maze on a tour of the UK and Europe. They eventually followed up with 'Make Way For The Originals', again on Pig & Trumpet, before electing to sign with the independent Optimism. However, when the latter neglected to pay the studio bill for Izit's debut album the tapes were retained, though the set did emerge under the name Main Street People in late 1993. Disillusioned, original members of the band drifted away, though Colman beavered away in the background, setting up a new Tongue & Groove imprint, which eventually saw Izit return on 'Don't Give Up Now' and 'One By One', featuring vocalist Sam Edwards. Later material introduced Nicola Bright, who co-wrote much of *The Whole Affair*. Other guests/semi-permanent members include Byron Wallen (trumpet), Andy Gangadeen (drums), Steven Lewinson (bass) and Haji Mike and MC Mell 'O' (rappers).

● ALBUMS: *The Whole Affair* (Tongue & Groove 1993).

J

J-BLAST AND THE 100% PROOF

One-off spoof merchants notable for their articulate 'dissing' of De La Soul. 'Break Ya Dawn' was a specific attack on Prince Be and his cohorts, released, tellingly enough, on the Geek St label, in 1992. It was introduced by a sample of UK disk jockey Bruno Brookes using entirely forced language such as 'peace' and 'respect', before the outfit waylay Prince Be and a host of other 'pseuds'. Alhough of UK origins, the protagonists' identities remained hidden, until J Blast went on to join the Scientists Of Sound.

J., OLLIE

b. Oliver Jacobs, c.1975, London, England. One of techno's new breed of studio operators, who first locked horns with a control panel at the age of 13. His education fell by the wayside as a result, as he devoted every waking hour to his consoles. Nevertheless, by the age of 19 he had remixed for Adamski, Frankie Goes To Hollywood, D:Ream and Take That, and provided full production for Rozalla, East 17 and Deja Vu. As well as engineering for Leftfield and Delta Lady, he helped on sessions at Rollover Studios in Kilburn, owned by his father Phil Jacobs. The studio has seen notable works recorded by Sure Is Pure, Paul Gotel, Qui 3, the Sandals and the Leftfield/Lydon collaboration ('Open Up'). Jacobs has a big future ahead of him; judged on the terms of an age to output matrix, there is nobody to touch him.

J.T. THE BIGGA FIGGA

b. San Francisco, California, USA. The most popular northern Californian to record in the hip-hop vein patented as 'G-Funk', J.T. is also the owner of Get Low Records, his record label, and Paper Chase Management, run by his mother Pearl. His reputation was built on several small-scale releases for Get Low in the early 90s which achieved successively greater sales, particularly within San Francisco where his rise coincided with the breakthrough of fellow artist and friend

E-40. Together with long-standing collaborators San Quinn and D-Moe, J.T.'s debut album, *Don't Stop 'Til We Major*, established his credibility as a street artist. It was followed by *Playaz N The Game*, a superior collection of ghetto recriminations and personality-enhancing boasts, the best track, 'Peep Game', featuring D-Moe. Better still was 1994's *Straight Out The Labb*, though by this time J.T. had converted to the Nation Of Islam and that new spiritual base reflected in his lyrics.
● ALBUMS: *Don't Stop 'Til We Major* (Get Low 1992)★★★, *Playaz N The Game* (Get Low 1993)★★★★, *Straight Out The Labb* (Get Low 1994)★★★★.

JACKSON, CHAD

Larger-than-life UK cult DJ who in 1987 won the World DJ Championships. Like so many others behind the decks in the house boom, Jackson's origins were in hip-hop, though his other interests included reggae and punk. He enjoyed a surprise number 3 in the UK charts with 'Hear The Drummer (Get Wicked)', before going on to remix for numerous clients including Gang Of Four ('Money Talks'), De La Soul ('Magic Number'), Beats International ('Dub Be Good To Me'), Public Enemy ('Bring The Noise'), Prince ('Sign O' The Times') and Kraftwerk ('Tour De France').

JAM AND SPOON

Duo credited by some as the originators of the 'trance' style. Based in Frankfurt, Germany, the faces behind the team are producer Jam El Mar and DJ Mark Spoon. Their groundbreaking work on a remix of Alex Lee's 'The Age Of Love' was the first track to set the ball rolling, followed in quick succession by work with Moby, Cosmic Baby and Frankie Goes To Hollywood. The latter was a difficult but rewarding project, as it had been this band and the production work of Trevor Horn in general that had originally inspired Jam El Mar to pursue a career in music. Another key reference point are the soundtrack recordings of Tangerine Dream. Only one single under their own name, 'Stella', preceded the release of their debut double album in the early months of 1994. This time they had moved away from the fast, pumping backbeat and acid tones which had flavoured their remixes, opting instead for a much more commercial slant. A sleeve-note written for R&S label boss Renaat wryly declares: 'I hope this is not too commercial for your uncommercial label'. Perhaps not, but it did see them crossover into the pop charts proper. Other singles such as 'Follow Me' were considered to be bona fide trance classics. Mark Spoon was also head of A&R for Logic and is boss of Frankfurt's XS Club.

● ALBUMS: *Tripomatic Fairytales 2001/2002* (1994)★★★, *Kaleidoscope* (Sony 1997)★★★.

JAMAL-SKI

b. Jamal Mitchell, New York, USA. By the time he released his debut solo album, Jamal-Ski's name had already cropped up on several high profile releases. Most notable among these were Boogie Down Production's *Edutainment* and the Brand New Heavies' *Heavy Rhyme Experience Vol. 1*. Jamal-Ski grew up in Manhattan, and was a product of the hip-hop cultural experience, from rapping through to sound system parties, graffiti and breakdancing. He originally hung around with the Rocksteady Crew and Afrika Bambaataa's Zulu Nation. His chosen path mixes traditional, old school rap with the rhythms of reggae. His musical heritage is certainly impressive, his father a jazz drummer who appeared alongside Stan Getz and Chet Baker, which allowed him to meet luminaries such as Thelonious Monk, ensuring that music remained in his blood through adolescence. He attended New York university for a year before moving to Oregon to play with reggae and ska bands, eventually returning east to take up the hip-hop cudgels.

● ALBUMS: *Rough Reality* (Columbia 1993)★★.

JARRE, JEAN-MICHEL

b. 24 August 1948, Lyon, France. This enigmatic composer and keyboard wizard has long been hailed as the premier exponent of European electronic music. From the age of five he took up the piano, and studied harmony and structure at the Paris Conservatoire, before abandoning classical music and joining Pierre Schaeffer's Musical Research group. Becoming gradually more fascinated with the scope offered by electronics, his first release comprised the passages 'La Cage' and 'Eros Machine' on EMI Pathe in France. He then contributed 'Aor' for the Paris Opera ballet, and the soundtrack for the film *Les Granges Bruless*, among others. After marrying actress Charlotte Rampling, he set about composing his first full-scale opus, *Oxygene*. This reached number 2 in the UK charts, signalling Jarre's arrival as a commercial force. The subsequent *Equinoxe* continued in familiar style, exploring the emotive power of orchestrated electronic rhythms and melody. The first of several massive open-air performances took place in Paris at the Place De La Concorde, with a world record attendance of over one million. However, it was not until 1981 and the release of *Magnetic Fields* that Jarre undertook his first tour, no small task considering the amount of stage equipment required. His destination was China where five concerts took place with the aid of 35 traditional Chinese musicians. A double album was released to document the event. 1983's *Music For Supermarkets* proved his most elusive release, recorded as background music for an art exhibition. Just one copy was pressed and sold at an auction for charity before the masters were destroyed. The *Essential Jean Michel Jarre*, compiled from earlier albums, proved more accessible for Jarre's legion of fans. *Zoolook* utilized a multitude of foreign language intonations in addition to the familiar electronic backdrop, but an unexpectedly lethargic reaction from the public prompted a two-year absence from recording. He returned with another outdoor extravaganza, this time celebrating NASA's 25th anniversary in Houston. Viewed by over one million people this time, it was also screened on worldwide television. The release of *Rendezvous* the following month was hardly coincidental. His first concerts in the UK, advertised as 'Destination Docklands', were also televised in October 1988. Whatever the size of audience he attracted, he was still unable to woo the critics. *Revolutions* appeared in the shops shortly afterwards, while one of its two singles, 'London Kid', featured the Shadows' Hank B. Marvin on guitar. *Waiting For Cousteau* anticipated his most recent update on the world record for attendance at a music concert. This time two million crammed into Paris on Bastille Day to witness 'La Defence'. While Jarre continues to bewilder and infuriate music critics, statistical evidence shows he is far from short of advocates in the general public. *Odyssey Through O2* featured DJ Cam, Apollo 440 and Hani, revisiting and remixing *Oxygene 7-13*.

● ALBUMS: *Oxygene* (Polydor 1977)★★★★, *Equinoxe* (Polydor 1978)★★★, *Magnetic Fields* (Polydor 1981)★★★, *Concerts In China* (Polydor 1982)★★★, *Zoolook* (Polydor 1984)★★★, *Rendezvous* (Polydor 1986)★★, *Houston/Lyon* (Polydor 1987)★★, *Revolutions* (Polydor 1988)★★★, *Live* (Polydor 1989)★★, *Waiting For Cousteau* (Polydor 1990)★★, *Oxygene 7-13* (1997)★★.

● COMPILATIONS: *The Essential* (Polydor

1983)★★★, various artists *Odyssey Through O2* (Epic/Dreyfus 1998)★★★.
● FURTHER READING: *The Unofficial Jean-Michel Jarre Biography*, Graham Needham.

JAYDEE

b. Robin Alders, *c.*1958, Netherlands. Alders is a regular DJ at Utrecht, Holland's Vlanen venue. Jaydee's beautiful trance cut 'Plastic Dreams' crossed over massively on the Belgian R&S label in 1993, with its distinctive Hammond B3 organ signature. It was his first release; previously he had been three-times winner of the Dutch arm-wrestling championship, and a member of the national baseball team. Since the early 80s he had worked on Dutch radio, proffering a critically lauded selection of house music. He turned to recording when his radio show was axed. After 'Plastic Dreams', the first release on the reactivated UK arm of R&S, he also released the 'Acceleration By Trance' 12-inch as Graylock on Logic's Save The Vinyl imprint. Far from usual rave convention, this contained the ominous 'Everybody Feel Free' warning on the flip-side. This boasted a spoken word narrative on the dangers of E, which also plotted Alders' semi-autobiographical downfall through the drug. A second Graylock release, 'The Movement', emerged on Belgium's Mental Radio Records, before he returned as Jaydee for 'The Hunter' for Dutch label Clubstitute

JAZZIE B.

b. Beresford Romeo, 26 January 1963, London, England. The larger-than-life svengali Jazzie B. began his musical apprenticeship on the London sound system circuit before helming the enormous international success of Soul II Soul. As such, Jazzie B. is widely credited with having pioneered a renaissance in British soul and dance music in the late 80s - certainly his group were the first of their generation to make a serious impact on the US R&B charts. By the advent of Soul II Soul's fifth album, Jazzie B. had signed a new contract with Island Records' subsidiary 4th And Broadway, following six successful years with Virgin Records. Island also provided a home for his record label, production and publishing company, Soul II Soul Records, and an artist roster including Yorker, Backroom, the Funki Dreds and EFUA. Although his publishing agreement with EMI Publishing for the Jazzie B. Music, Soul II Soul and Mad Music catalogues also

expired in 1996, his music remained omnipresent in the UK media, including advertisements for Renault and Levi's. Indeed, his only significant setback has been the clothes stores opened in the late 80s under the Soul II Soul banner, which have since closed. While waiting to conclude record company business and begin work on the new Soul II Soul album, Jazzie B. continued to occupy himself by running his studio complex in Camden, north London.

JAZZMATAZZ

A collaboration between seasoned jazz exponents and Guru (b. Keith Allam, Roxbury, Massachusetts, USA) of Gang Starr. Some of the names involved included N'Dea Davenport (Brand New Heavies), Carleen Anderson, Courtney Pine, Branford Marsalis, Roy Ayers, Donald Byrd, Lonnie Liston Smith and French rapper MC Solaar. An inventive combination, highlighted by a single, 'No Time To Play', featuring the vocals of Paul Weller's missus D.C. Lee, which in turn helped relaunch the latter's career. The Jazzmatazz project's roots were undoubtedly laid in Gang Starr's 'Jazz Thing', a collaboration with Marsalis which Spike Lee has used to theme his film, *Mo' Better Blues*.
● ALBUMS: *Jazzmatazz* (Chrysalis 1993)★★★★.

JAZZY JASON

UK artist of the early 90s who first emerged with Epitome Of Hype's 'Ladies With An Attitude', which sampled Madonna, and was first released on his own Pure Bonhomie label before being licensed to Big Life. Further funky rave tunes, dominated by breakbeats, followed. As part of Blapps Posse! he was also behind 'Bus It'/'Don't Hold Back', which sold some 10,000 copies on white label before being picked up by Rebel MC's Trible Bass label. He moved over to Essex's rave central HQ - D-Zone Records - for Turntable Symphony's 'Instructions Of Life', created with fellow Blaaps Posse! member Aston Harvey.

JAZZY JAY

b. *c.*1963, Bronx, New York, USA. Bronx studio-based DJ who was one of the early movers in Afrika Bambaataa's Zulu Nation movement, travelling with his mentor from early park and block parties to the stadia of the Roxy and the *Planet Rock* tour. In a less-publicised role he was also Rick Rubin's original partner in Def Jam, and co-produced the label's first single, T La Rock's 'It's

Yours' (with lyrics written by his brother, Special-K). His own label (with Rocky Bucano) Strong City, would unveil records by Busy Bee, Ultimate Force, Ice Cream Tee, Don Baron and Grand Puba's first outfit, Masters Of Ceremony. Regular visitors and pupils of his Bronx studio have included Diamond D, Fat Joe Da Gangster, Showbiz and AG and Skeff Anslem. Jazzy Jay grew up in the Bronx River region, and started DJing in his early teens. Kid Cassidy and Sundance were his first two MC recruits, playing together in the park by Soundview Houses, distributing tapes of the shows to other early hip-hop fans. After working with the Chuck City Crew from Bronxdale he received the call from Bambaataa, and debuted with them in 1977. He was promoted to the head of the Jazzy 5 enclave, and was partially behind the 'Jazzy Sensation' cut. He had already hooked up with Rubin whom he had met at the Club Negril, before 'Planet Rock' took off. Though neither the liaison with Rubin nor his Strong City venture actually afforded him great fininacial reward, Jay has gone on to maintain the respect afforded him by the hip-hop community with a series of productions which have never been less than competent, and often much more.

JAZZY JEFF

A former member of the Funky Four, Jazzy Jeff should not be confused, as frequently and quite naturally happens, with DJ Jazzy Jeff. The latter, alongside The Fresh Prince, shares not only his name, but also his label and producer. Though the original Jazzy Jeff has largely been eclipsed by the duo, he is a rapper of some historical note. His able, clear rhymes decorated a likeable album for Jive in the mid-80s, aided by Bryan 'Chuck' New and Phil Nicholas of the Willesden Dodgers. Eschewing the macho delivery and breast-beating more familiar at the time, *On Fire* included the vulnerable tribute 'My Mother (Yes I Love Her)' alongside material that frowned upon the ghetto's drug problems. 'King Heroin (Don't Mess With Heroin)' is actually one of rap's few lyrics about that drug in a subculture sadly obsessed with cannabis, crack and cocaine.

● ALBUMS: *On Fire* (Jive 1985)★★★.
● COMPILATIONS: *Greatest Hits* (Jive 1998)★★★★.

JAZZY M.

UK DJ who started out on that career's familiar route to stardom by working at a record shop counter, before appearing on the LWR pirate radio station, playing early Detroit techno and Chicago house on his *Jackin' Zone* shows. After DJing at his own Mania nights and various club appearances he joined with Pete Tong to compile ffrr's *The House Sound Of London Vol. 4*, which featured his first recording, 'Living In A World Of Fantasy', a collaboration with Fingers Inc. He ran his own shop, Vinyl Zone, and launched his first label, Oh Zone Records, the first release on which was Orbital's 'Chime', licensed to ffrr. It sold 66,000 copies after being passed to Jazzy M on a TDK cassette. His second label was Delphinus Delphis which dealt with more garage-house themes. It saw the release of the well-received 'Hold On' by Cuddles, before a third label was mooted, Spankin'. This produced several notable cuts, such as the *Rubberneck* EPs and Dub Nation's 'I Can't Help Myself', produced with partner Doug Martin. Jazzy continued to play out all the time, feeding back the results into his recordings and *vice versa*. Not surprising then that the Spankin' releases were held in high regard by the DJ fraternity in the early 90s, similar to Tony Humphries and C + C. He continues to play regular sets at Release The Pressure.

JC001

b. 16 June 1966. Rapper JC001 boasts one of the world's most fearsome, animated rap deliveries. His maniacal rants adorn a mixed hip-hop/ragga backing, with samples lifted from classic Jamaican fare (Dave And Ansell Collins' 'Double Barrel' on the 'Cupid' 45, etc.). Born of part Indian/Catholic parentage, he first listened to ragga rhymes on David Rodigan's *Roots Rockers* radio programme, but he bought into rap with the advent of electro and 'Planet Rock'. After performing at blues parties and carnivals he joined the pirate radio stations. His first record emerged in 1987, 'I Diss Therefore I Am', built on the Ethiopians' 'Train To Skaville', before collaborating with others for 'Bad Place To Get Hit'. Though his press image is one of devilish intensity and spite, his lyrics trace strong anti-racism sentiments. He collaborated with the Beatmasters on 'Boulevard Of Broken Dreams'.

● ALBUMS: *Ride To The Break* (Anxious/East West 1993)★★★.

JEFFERSON, MARSHALL

One of the legends of US acid house music, Jefferson claims to have invented the familiar 'squelch' of the Roland TR 303 (a claim hotly countered by DJ Pierre). Jefferson's reputation rests more squarely on records such as Reggie Hall's 'Music', Richard Rogers' mighty 'Can't Stop Loving You', and Ce Ce Rogers' epic 'Someday'. Afterwards he would move on to helm production for Ten City, but was criticized at the time of their arrival for what some critics observed to be a fixation with nostalgia in the latter's soulful house grooves. Jefferson preferred the description deep house, and was quick to proclaim the death knell for acid. Nevertheless, Ten City hit with singles such as 'That's The Way Love Is' and 'Right Back To You', with Byron Stingily's distinctive vocals providing an excellent outlet for Jefferson's studio craft. He has also worked with Tyrrel Corporation and Kym Mazelle ('I'm A Lover') among many others, and recorded as Jungle Wonz ('Time Marches On') and Truth ('Open Your Eyes'). 1994 saw him record only the second track under his own name, 'I Found You', for Centrestage Records, as well as continuing to produce artists of the calibre of Tom Jones, System 7 and Keith Thompson.
● ALBUMS: Ten City: *Foundation* (East West 1988)★★★.

JELLYBEAN

John 'Jellybean' Benitez, a native of the Bronx and renowned Manhattan club DJ, made his mark in the early 80s as one of the post-disco dance scene's most favoured remixers/producers. Eventually he would earn his own record contract, though his *modus operandi* did not change; maintaining instead a largely supervisory role on his output. His debut release under his own name was the 1984 EP, *Wotupski!?!*, which included two minor dance classics, 'The Mexican' and 'Sidewalk Talk', the latter penned by Madonna (he had significantly enhanced his own personal reputation by working on earlier tracks for her, including her breakthrough hit 'Holiday'). It was not until *Spillin' The Beans*, however, that Jellybean actually recorded his own voice, alongside guest vocalists including Nikki Harris, who, ironically, had last been seen on Madonna's tour.
● ALBUMS: *Just Visiting This Planet* (Chrysalis 1987)★★★, *Jellybean Rocks The House* (Chrysalis 1988)★★★, *Spillin' The Beans* (Atlantic 1991)★★★.

JERU THE DAMAJA

His stage name in full reading Jeru The Damaja: D Original Dirty Rotten Scoundrel, Jeru (b. Kendrick Jeru Davis, c.1971) is a native New Yorker, whose name refers to the 'first god', son of Egyptian deities Osiris and Isis (his father was a Rastafarian). Having at one time earned a living changing tyres for Greyhound buses, he made his first demos with his homeboy/DJ PF Cuttin', before meeting up with Guru of Gang Starr at their 'Manifest' video shoot. His hardcore, Brooklyn style was thus premiered on Gang Starr's *Daily Operation* album (on 'I'm The Man'). Jeru also worked freestyle on their live shows. In turn DJ Premier would produce Jeru's debut cut, 'Come Clean'. This had been originally issued as a promo single entitled 'Gang Starr Doundation Sampler', on Gang Starr's own label, Illkid Records. His approach was resolutely old school: 'A long time ago rhyming was about having some skills, and what I tried to do is say let's bring it back to the skills and forget about the guns, take it to the skills level and then we'll see who the real men are'. His debut album was widely venerated in both the specialist and general music press, not least due to one of Premier's most effective productions and Jeru's clear, heavily enunciated style.
● ALBUMS: *Ths Sun Rises In The East* (Payday/Double Vinyl 1994)★★★, *Wrath Of The Math* (Payday 1996)★★★.

JIMMY JAM AND TERRY LEWIS

Based in Minneapolis, Minnesota, USA, Jimmy 'Jam' Harris and Terry Lewis are prolific producers of contemporary R&B The two first worked together in the early 80s as members of Time (formerly Flyte Time), and subsequently, Harris (keyboards) and Lewis (bass) became black music's most consistently successful production duo. They formed their own record label, Tabu, in 1980, which enjoyed enormous success with artists such as the S.O.S. Band throughout the 80s. Among the other early bands and artists to benefit from the duo's writing and production skills were Change, Cherrelle, the Force MD's, Johnny Gill and the former Time singer Alexander O'Neal. Their greatest success, however, came as the creative catalysts behind Janet Jackson's career. The first album they recorded with her, *Control*, included five hit singles, and the follow-up, *Rhythm Nation 1814*, was similarly successful. In

1990 Jam and Lewis recorded once again with Time, who had re-formed to make *Pandemonium*, which was released on Prince's Paisley Park Records. Though the reunion was not widely regarded as a success, the duo's productions remained in the higher reaches of the charts. Their continued association with Jackson was never surpassed commercially but many others benefited from their expertise, especially with their pioneering work in what would become known as swingbeat, and cross-genre productions with artists ranging from the Human League to Sounds Of Blackness. In the 90s they also established a new record label, Perspective Records, distributed by A&M Records.

JIVE BUNNY AND THE MASTERMIXERS

A throwback to the medley craze of the early 80s, with a similarly repetitive disco beat cushioning the samples, Jive Bunny are single-handedly responsible for making recent generations believe that rock and pop classics of yesteryear are only 10 seconds long. A UK male production/mixing group comprising John Pickles and disc jockey Ian Morgan, they became UK chart-toppers with their first three singles 'Swing The Mood', 'That's What I Like', and 'Let's Party' during 1989. This equalled the record held by Gerry And The Pacemakers (1963) and Frankie Goes To Hollywood (1984). The idea was conceived by Pickles, previously the owner of an electrical shop. The concept for 'Swing The Mood' had originally come from an ex-miner living in Norway called Les Hemstock. John's son Andy Pickles also helped out. They appeared on 'It Takes Two Baby' by Liz Kershaw and Bruno Brookes in December 1989. Subsequent hits saw progressively lower chart placings, doubtless to the relief of many: 'That Sounds Good' (number 4), 'Can Can You Party' (number 8) and 'Let's Swing Again' (number 19). More recently they seem to have disappeared up their own bobtails, although Pickles has become highly successful as head of Music Factory, which controls a number of dance labels such as trax, Defcon and Energize.
- ALBUMS: *Jive Bunny - The Album* (1989)★★★, *It's Party Time* (1990)★★.
- COMPILATIONS: *The Best Of ...* (Music Collection 1995)★★.

JIVE RECORDS

A subsidiary of the UK Zomba group, founded by chairman Clive Calder, Jive was established in the UK in 1981. In response to the growing base of its US rap roster, Jive Records US was inaugurated three years later, where it has gained a significant market-share. The first rap single to emerge on the label (which also covered sundry other musical styles, including dance and pop) was Whodini's 'Magic Wand'. Whodini also presided over the imprint's first rap album, a self-titled set from 1983. Although steady success continued with artists like Kool Moe Dee, Boogie Down Productions, Wee Girl Papa Rappers, A Tribe Called Quest and others, the label's real commercial breakthrough act would be DJ Jazzy Jeff And The Fresh Prince. Although already several albums into their career (including a debut set, *He's The Rapper And I'm The DJ*, which would be Jive's biggest seller), 'Boom! Shake The Room' gave the duo a surprise UK number 1. The group had formerly won the first ever Grammy for rap with 'Parents Just Don't Understand' in 1988.
- ALBUMS: Whodini: *Whodini* (Jive 1983)★★★. DJ Jazzy Jeff And The Fresh Prince: *He's The DJ And I'm The Rapper* (Jive 1988)★★★★. Boogie Down Productions: *By All Means Necessary* (Jive 1988)★★★, *Ghetto Music: The Blueprint Of Hip Hop* (Jive 1989)★★★. A Tribe Called Quest: *People's Instinctive Travels And The Paths Of Rhythm* (Jive 1990)★★.

JJ FAD

The breakdance fad in the USA between 1985 and 1988 was known as the B-Boy period. This Los Angeles female rap trio, comprising M.C.J.B. (b. Juana Burns), Baby D (b. Dania Birks) and Sassy C (b. Michelle Franklin) came into fashion towards the end. Protégées of Eazy-E, their collective name stands for 'Just Jammin' Fresh And Def'. Boosted by an eponymous Top 30-peaking single, their debut album made a small dent in the album charts.
- ALBUMS: *Supersonic - The Album* (Ruthless 1988)★★.

JOEY NEGRO

b. David Lee, Essex, England. A remixer, producer and artist, and champion of the garage/disco revival, Negro's work on cuts from Adeva and Kym Sims is among the most representative of his style. The media-labelled 'England's David Morales' can trace his heritage back to M-D-Eemm (the chemical formula for acid) in the late 80s. He is a fanatical record collector who often works alongside DJ Andrew 'Doc' Livingstone. Together

they have worked on remixes by Brand New Heavies, the Reese Project and Negro's own album. Negro's career began at the Republic label, where he was taught the art of remixing by a friend. Together with Mark Ryder, he produced a number of cuts for the same label, using production team names ranging from Quest For Excellence to Masters Of The Universe. Republic was responsible for classics such as Phaze II's 'Reachin'' and Turntable Orchestra's 'You're Gonna Miss Me'. However, Negro ran into trouble when he created the persona Kid Valdez of Mystique. Under that name they mixed the club hit 'Together' for Raven Maize. The track was licensed to an American label, but when the single topped the dance charts journalists tried to hunt down Mr Maize. He was of course, totally fictional, the figure on the cover having been scanned in and adapted from an old rap record. Negro also licensed tracks to Republic, including several house classics, and compiled the *Garage Sound Of New York/Chicago* series. From this point on he picked up the Negro moniker and began to establish an identity as a talented disco remixer. Negro's own material reflects the tastes of his record collection; a penchant for US labels such as Prelude and West End, 70s funk (Brass Construction, Cameo), jazz fusion and disco (notably the latter's 'syn drums'). His debut album additionally includes a version of the Gibson Brothers' 'Oooh What A Life', featuring Gwen Guthrie. Recent mixing work has included Hue & Cry, Sister Sledge, Fortran 5 ('Look To The Future'), Soul II Soul ('Move Me No Mountain') and Take That ('Relight My Fire'). In 1994 he teamed up with Andrew 'Doc' Livingstone to become half of the Hedboys.
● ALBUMS: *Universe Of Love* (Virgin 1993)★★★.

JOHNNY VICIOUS

The proprieter of New York's Vicious Muzik label, Johnny Vicious is one of the most exciting up-and-coming producer/remixers on the circuit. A rock 'n' roller who became bored of rock music after he heard Tony Humphries on Kiss FM, he was championed by Junior Vasquez in his early days. His career proper began with tunes like 'Liquid Bass' and 'Frozen Bass', before reworking the Loletta Holloway standard 'Dreaming' as 'Stand Up' (released in the UK by Six By Six, the label being licensed to the Network umbrella organisation). This demonstrated his technique, which was essentially slicing up old disco classics

in an alarmingly cavalier fashion and producing a punk disco hybrid. 1994 records like JV verus MFSB's 'TSOP' (another disco chestnut) continued his ascendancy and cult status.

JOHNSON, DENISE

b. 31 August 1966, Manchester, Lancashire, England. Former backing vocalist on some of Primal Scream's finest moments, Johnson has also worked with A Certain Ratio, Electronic and sundry other more minor local projects like the Jam MCs' 'Ironweed'. She had initially been discovered by Maze's Frankie Beverley singing in Fifth Heaven, who supported Maze on their Wembley dates in the UK. She was subsequently enlisted as backing vocalist for Maze. Johnson's solo career began in 1994 with the marvellous 'Rays Of The Rising Sun'. Produced by David Tolan of the Joy (for whom she was also a vocalist). Eventually she settled on East West/Magnet, who invited K Klass to remix the song. It gave her a sizeable club hit, though this time the version somewhat diminished Johnson's vocal input. A radio mix also featured Johnny Marr (Smiths) on guitar, presumably through his previous liaisons with K Klass.

JOI

Long before the fashion for Asian-influenced dance music took off in the mid- to late 90s, Farook and Haroon Shamsher were fusing the sounds of traditional Bengali music with hip-hop and contemporary dance styles. In the mid-80s they were part of a youth movement in east London called Joi Bangla, which aimed to promote various aspects of Bengali culture. Wishing to concentrate on the music side, the brothers formed a sound system with the same name and began playing around local community centres. At the same time they wrote their own material and in 1988 recorded a promo, 'Taj Ma House' (BPM Records), which coincided with the acid house movement. As they continued to write, they produced DATs that they played out on the sound system, with additional live percussion and samples, in the same way as dub plates. In 1992 they released 'Desert Storm' on Rhythm King Records as Joi, which was also the name of a club night they hosted the following year that ran weekly at London's Bass Clef. Over the next few years they continued to play their own material, and tracks recorded by like-minded artists, as the Joi sound system at various clubs and parties, including Bar Rumba, the Big Chill, Megatripolis, Ministry Of Sound and Return To The Source. They developed a live act and have since performed at such events as Tribal Gathering, Whirl-Y-Gig and WOMAD, as well as others around Europe. In October 1996 the *Bangladesh* EP was released on Nation Records to raise awareness of disastrous Western interference in that country's affairs. 'High Times' and 'Nargin' are typical of the group's unique, melodic sound, which blends Asian and Middle Eastern sounds with various styles of dance music.

In 1998 they contributed a remix of Nusrat Fateh Ali Khan's 'Sweet Pain' to the tribute album *Star Rise*, and signed to Real World Records with plans to release an album later that year. While they have not had many releases in their own right, they have contributed tracks to a large number of compilations, notably 'Goddess' on Sony's *Eastern Uprising* (1997), 'India' on Zip Dog's *Global Explorer* (1997) and 'Shanti' on Law And Auder's *Further East* (1998). Perhaps more important than the group's releases is their sound system, through which they have promoted their fusion ethic regardless of trends within the music industry. Over the years they have been involved with various other artists and DJs, including Asian Dub Foundation, Athletico, Mixmaster Morris, Plaid and Spring Heel Jack.

JOMANDA

New Jersey trio who enjoyed chart action in the late 80s and early 90s with sweet vocals embodying what those in dance circles affectionately term 'girlie house', or New Jill Swing. Cheri Williams, who started singing from the age of 14, met Joanne Thomas in 7th grade at college, though they lost contact when each went to high school. They reunited in 1987, when they were joined by Renee Washington, whose youth was spent singing in Baptist church choirs. She had also attended the Newark School Of Performing Arts. Their recording career began in 1988, when they enjoyed hits with 'Make My Body Rock'.and 'Gotta Love For You'. The combination of swing and house with soulful hip-hop vocals was instantly popular. 'Make My Body Rock' would also provide the sample around which Felix's huge hit, 'Don't You Want My Love' was built. *Nubia Soul*, referring to the skin pigmentation of 'blackness', was more R&B-based, as Washington explained: 'The reason why we're heading for an R&B market is that we feel club music is very lim-

ited and I personally fell we've done all that we could as a group as far as club music is concerned'. Nevertheless, that did not stop them from employing Sasha for a very well-received remix of 'Never'. On the album they worked with Buff Love (ex-Fat Boys), Dave Hall and Kenny Kornegay of the Untouchables, and the Band Of Gypsies.
● ALBUMS: *Nubia Soul* (East West 1993)★★★.

JON PLEASED WIMMIN

b. *c.*1969, London, England. Transvestite DJ who has built his reputation on the dexterity of his deck technique and record selection, rather than his dress sense He began his adult life attending a four-year course in fashion design, eventually running his own shop in Kensington Market. He started out as a DJ at clubs such as Glam, Kinky Gerlinky and Camp in the capital, before opening up his own nightspot, Pleased, in Sutton Row, London, in October 1993. The Pleased Wimmin transvestite posse was first sighted as live backing on Linda Layton PAs. Their leader's first major appearance on record came with the dancefloor hit 'Passion', released on Southern Fried in 1990. A cover of Bobby Orlando's Hi-NRG classic from 1980, it was produced by Norman Cook. He went on to record further ambivalent gender/genre classics like 'Hammer House Of Handbag'.

JORDAN, MONTELL

b. Los Angeles, California, USA. Montell Jordan made a huge impact in both the US and UK charts in 1995 with the runaway success of his Def Jam Records' single 'This Is How We Do It'. Including a sample from Slick Rick, this celebration of life in South Central, Los Angeles, struck a chord with both hip-hop fans and modern R&B audiences. Within weeks of release it entered the US R&B Top 10 and then the pop charts, preceding a debut album of the same title. This included several B.B. King samples and a guest rap from Coolio on the excellent 'Payback'. The lyrics also diverged somewhat from typical Californian swing subjects - 'Daddy's Home' addressing the importance of black fatherhood in the ghettos. He attributes his development in an otherwise hostile environment to the rare presence of both a father and mother as he grew up. Rather than running with the gangs in the 'South Central 'hood', Jordan attended both church and school regularly, eventually graduating from Pepperdine University in Malibu with a degree in Organisational Communication. However, his growing interest in music eventually diverted him from a projected career in law.

● ALBUMS: *This Is How We Do It* (Def Jam 1995)★★★, *More* (Def Jam 1996)★★, *Let's Ride* (Def Jam 1998)★★★.

JOY

Built around the production duo of David Tolan (b. 3 May 1967, Dublin, Eire; programming, percussion) and Ali Fletcher (b. Alistair Fletcher, 27 May 1968, Newcastle, England; drums, programming), the Joy additionally number Gavin O'Neill (b. 20 September 1965, Worcester, England; vocals), Denise Johnson (b. 31 August 1966, Manchester, Lancashire, England; vocals) and Andy Tracey (b. 11 September 1965, Harehills, Leeds, Yorkshire, England; guitar). Johnson is best known to club-goers for her contributions to Primal Scream's epoch-making *Screamadelica*, but Tolan also produced her debut solo single. He and O'Neill had initially worked together in Perspex Spangles, while Fletcher had been part of the Canoe Club and Tall Americans. The Joy took their name as a revolt against the rejection offered to them by record companies in their early days. They played their first gig at the Buzz Club in Manchester in September 1992, and kicked off their new contract with Compulsion Records in 1994 with a re-release of 'Shine', previously a minor club hit in April 1993 for Playground Records. As Joy Productions Tolan and Fletcher have also contributed remixes, most notably for the Dub Disciples' 'Hyperphoria Parts One And Two'.

JU JU SPACE JAZZ

Sydney, Australia-based Daniel Conway and Alexander Nettelbeck worked together in the mid-90s on various projects, including music for contemporary dance and films. Around the beginning of 1996 they began to record material together around the concept of Ju Ju, which is 'about the unexpected, the spooky, the ridiculous, the fantastic - all that makes your hairs stand up and wiggle'. Consequently, their first album, *Head Over Heels In Dub*, released towards the end of 1996 on the Australian label Fluid Records, incorporated a variety of styles without adhering to any particular established genre. In 1997 they signed to Matsuri Productions who released 'Pizza' on the *Sympathy In Chaos* compilation and the EP *Mermadium Palladium*, followed by the group's UK debut album, *Shloop*, early the next year. Ju Ju Space Jazz's eccentric, experimental music incorporates unusual combinations of sound with funky, relaxed beats, underpinned by a solid, dubby bass. Familiar electronic noises and effects of dance music sit together with jazz-inspired chords and improvised lines played on various live instruments, including saxophone, trombone and violin, to create the most unusual abstract textures. Some tracks feature guest vocalists including Edwina Blush, Mr Thankyou Very Much, MC Zen, Dr Karshnoofdibah and Miguel Valens. Conway and Nettelbeck often present live performances of their material.

JUAN TRIP

Versailles-based French team built around Basil, who mortified several commentators with their 1994 *Masterpiece Trilogy* EP. The controversy centred on the main track, 'Louis' Cry'. This used a sample of a particularly unhappy one-year-old of the author's acquaintance who died shortly after the record was made. One of his screams was used, alongside a loop of organist Jimmy Smith, to punctuate the track. When the newshounds rang round to confirm the existence of the 'dead baby track', Basil, who had formerly promoted the hugely successful Fantom nights in France, confirmed its origins (though it was conceived more as a tribute to the child's life than anything more exploitative). Released on F Communications in France, many DJs refused to play it because of the unsettling nature of the scream, including Darren Emmerson, who even asked permission to re-record the masterful backing track without it.

JUDGE JULES

b. Julius O'Rearden. Together with partner Michael Skins, Jules has become one of the UK's leading remixers. He was originally bedecked with the Judge prefix from Norman Jay during the mid-80s house/rare groove scene, at which time he was studying law. Apparently he proved exceedingly useful when police raided parties, tying the officers up in legal jargon while his friends extinguished their herbal cigarettes. Together with Jay (nicknamed Shake And Finger Pop, while Jules was Family Function) they performed at about 30 warehouse parties between the years 1984 and 1987. He earned a living from buying up rare house records on trips to America and bringing them back to England to sell at exorbitant prices. As house turned to acid he remained a prominent figure in the rave scene, playing at many of the larger events such as Evolution, Sunrise and World Dance, after which he earned his first remixing credits. The clients included Soft House Company, Fat Men, Big Audio Dynamite and, bizarrely, the Stranglers. In 1991 he reacquainted himself with an old school-friend, Rolo. They set up a studio together, and learned how to produce and engineer properly, an aspect through which they had previously bluffed their way. A studio was slowly established in the basement of his house, before he teamed up with ex-reggae drummer Michael Skins. By remixing a version of M People's 'Excited' in 1992, the team was established, with guesting musicians such as guitarist Miles Kayne adding to the musical melting pot. Having set up Tomahawk Records Jules has gone on record his own work. This has included Datman (licensed to ffrr), the All Stars ('Wanna Get Funky', which sampled from Andrew Lloyd Webber's *Jesus Christ Superstar*) and 290 North ('Footsteps'), as well as guest appearances from ex-KLF singer Maxine Hardy (Icon's 'I Can Make You Feel So Good') and ex-O'Jays singer Ronnie Canada ('Heading For Self-Destruction'). Other remixes have included T-Empo's handbag house classic 'Saturday Night, Sunday Morning' , Melanie Williams ('Everyday Thing'), BT Express ('Express'), Jeanie Tracy ('Is This Love'), Our Tribe ('Love Come Home'), plus the big money-spinners Doop ('Doop') and Reel 2 Real ('I Like To Move It'). This has ensured that he can now practically write his own cheque for remixing engagements, of which he is offered at least 10 a week. He also records two radio shows a week for Radio 1.

JUNGLE

The evolution of jungle is hard to pin down exactly. However, the term 'junglist' is Jamaican patois for a native of Trenchtown, the ghetto area of Kingston from where Bob Marley came. Despite this, controversy persists over the use of the name, with some commentators insisting it is a derogatory term. Musically jungle rides on a combination of breakbeats and samples, with ragga's staccato rhythms, and subsonic bass. The tempo is roughly double that of ragga, clocking in at around 160bpm. The use of the hardcore breakbeats neatly completes a circle - they were originally a derivation of hip-hop, which in turn leaned heavily on the reggae culture. It is a music widely perceived to be created by and for black people who are disaffected with the sound of 'white techno' (another anomaly considering that all of techno's originators were themselves black). The sound was pioneered in clubs by DJ Ron, Randall, Bobby Konders and on radio by Jumping Jack Frost (on Kiss FM) and pirates such as Kool FM, Transmission One and Don FM. The earliest sighting of it outside of the underground came when SL2's 'On A Ragga Tip' broke through in 1993. There had been antecedents, however. Singles like Genaside II's 'Narra Mine', material by Shut Up And Dance and even Rebel MC's Comin' On Strong', built on a riot of breakbeats, all predicted the jungle sound. Recent innovations in the sound have arrived from more traditional reggae acts including General Levy ('Incredible' on Renk Records) who have begun 'voicing' words over the rhythms, where previously sampled chants sufficed. Amongst the better modern proponents, who tend to be anonymous even by dance music's standards, are Blame and Bubbles.

● FURTHER READING: *State Of Bass - Jungle: The Story So Far*, Martin James.

JUNGLE BROTHERS

Rap innovators and precursors to the sound later fine-tuned by De La Soul, PM Dawn *et al*. Following on from Afrika Bambaataa, the Jungle Brothers: Mike G (b. Michael Small, *c*.1969, Harlem, New York, USA), DJ Sammy B (b. Sammy Burwell, *c*.1968, Harlem, New York, USA) and Afrika Baby Bambaataa (b. Nathaniel Hall, *c*.1971, Brooklyn, New York, USA) were unafraid of cross-genre experimentation. The most famous demonstration being their version of Marvin Gaye's 'What's Going On', though their incorporation of house music on 'I'll House You' is another good example. They made their debut for Warlock/Idlers Records in October 1987, before signing to Gee Street Records. As part of the Native Tongues coalition with Queen Latifah, A Tribe Called Quest and others, they sought to enhance the living experiences of black men and women by educating them about their role in history and African culture. In many ways traditionalists, the Jungle Brothers carefully traced the lines between R&B and rap, their admiration of James Brown going beyond merely sampling his rhythms (including the basis of their name - which shares the godfather of soul's initials). A second album was slightly less funky and more soul-based, particularly effective on cuts like 'Beyond This World'. It has been argued that the

Jungle Brothers' failure to break through commercially had something to do with the fact that they were initially signed to a New York dance label, Idlers. More likely is the assertion that audiences for macho skulduggery greatly outnumbered those for which intelligent, discursive hip-hop was a worthwhile phenomenon in the late 80s. By the time of 1993's *J Beez Wit The Remedy*, they had unfortunately succumbed to the former. They charted again in 1998 with the Stereo MCs' remix of 'Jungle Brother', taken from the one-dimensional *Raw Deluxe*.

● ALBUMS: *Straight Out The Jungle* (Idlers/Warlock 1988)★★★, *Done By The Forces Of Nature* (Warners 1989)★★★★, *J Beez Wit The Remedy* (Warners 1993)★★, *Raw Deluxe* (Gee Street 1997)★★, *Raw Deluxe* with bonus remix album (Gee Street 1998)★★.

JUNIOR BOY'S OWN RECORDS

This label was founded in 1992 by Steven Hall and Terry Farley (who records with Pete Heller and Gary Wilkinson as Fire Island) from the ashes of Boy's Own Records, which they had formed in 1990 with Andrew Weatherall. Junior Boy's Own became one of the most important independent dance labels of the 90s, with strong releases from the Ballistic Brothers, Black Science Orchestra, the Dust Brothers (who later became the Chemical Brothers), Underworld, X-Press 2 and others. Among their first singles were Fire Island's 'In Your Bones' and 'Fire Island', Black Science Orchestra's 'Where Were You', Known Chic's 'Dance' and Outrage's 'That Piano Track'. During the same period Underworld released two early singles, 'Big Mouth' and 'Dirty', as Lemon Interrupt. In 1993 the label signed the Dust Brothers on the strength of their track 'Song To The Siren', which, with its reliance on prominent hip-hop beats, helped to kick off the movement that became known as big beat. After more singles from Fire Island ('There But For The Grace Of God'), Roach Motel ('Movin' On' and 'Transatlantic'), Underworld ('Spikee'/'Dogman Go Woof' and 'Dark And Long') and X-Press 2 ('Rock 2 House'/'Hip Housin''), Junior Boy's Own achieved widespread success in 1994 with their first album release, Underworld's *Dubnobasswithmyheadman*. Their compilation *Junior Boy's Own Collection* was followed by the Ballistic Brothers' *London Hooligan School*, Underworld's *Second Toughest In The Infants* and Black Science Orchestra's *Walter's Room*. At the

same time they have continued to release a number of hit singles, notably Underworld's 'Born Slippy', Fire Island's 'If I Should Need A Friend' and the Farley And Heller Project's 'Ultra Flava'. In 1998 the label changed their name to JBO Music when they signed a distribution agreement with Virgin Records' dance subsidiary V2. With their roots in the Balearic movement, Junior Boy's Own has always had an array of sounds: such artists as the Dust Brothers, Underworld and, more recently, Sycamore have blended a broad range of influences in their music to make what could sometimes only loosely be described as dance music.

JUNIOR MAFIA

Junior MAFIA is a 90s rap collective featuring four acts from the Brooklyn, New York, USA area - Clepto, the Sixes, the Snakes and Lil' Kim. Most attention surrounded the latter artist, widely hailed as a natural successor to MC Lyte via her considerable dexterity on the microphone. Their debut single together, 'Player's Anthem', became a major R&B hit in 1995 with sales certified gold. On the album which accompanied it the rhythms were located at a mid-point between hip-hop and soul, with 'Backstabbers' proving particularly articulate in this musical climate. The Notorious B.I.G. made a guest appearance on the more predictable 'Get Money', though again Lil' Kim earned critical plaudits for her ability to stand shoulder to shoulder with the favourite son of New York ghetto rap.

● ALBUMS: *Conspiracy* (Undeas/Atlantic 1995)★★★.

JUNO REACTOR

Led by Ben Watkins and Mike MacGuire, who had previously worked with Youth, Juno Reactor has at various times included Johann Bley (who records for Blue Room Released as Johann), Stephane Holwick (of Total Eclipse) and Jans Waldenback. They grew out of the early Goa vibe in the early 90s, playing at the Full Moon parties on the travellers' circuit around the world, and with their album *Transmissions*, they became one of the first trance groups to gain widespread recognition. However, they have always stood apart from that sometimes formulaic scene: from an early stage Watkins employed heavy rock guitar in combination with techno ideas for their live shows. After signing to Blue Room, they released the single 'Guardian Angel'/'Rotorblade' and *Beyond The Infinite* in 1995. The following year, 'Conga Fury'/'Magnetic' gained Juno Reactor widespread praise for its innovative sound. In 1997 the group enjoyed a Top 40 hit with 'God Is God', which featured Natasha Atlas on vocals and was taken from their *Bible Of Dreams*. This album perhaps best represents Juno Reactor's varied sound, which presents a more melodic slant on the familiar riffs and rhythms of trance in unusual combinations and situations, with live percussion ('Conga Fury' and 'Kaguya Hime'), vocals ('God Is God') and slide guitar and triple time ('Swamp Thing'). Following the policy of Blue Room, the group have been marketed more like a rock band and moved further from the media's perception of how a dance act should function. In an attempt to integrate more live performance and improvisation into their sound, Juno Reactor performed with the South African band Amampondo on a tour of the USA in 1997, supporting Moby. During the same year they also made a seven-date tour of Japan and played at various festivals around the UK and Europe. The group have also provided music for a number of film soundtracks, notably *Barb Wire*, *Eraser*, *Mortal Kombat*, *Showgirls* and *Virtuosity*.

● ALBUMS: *Transmissions* (Mute 1993)★★★, *Beyond The Infinite* (Blue Room 1995)★★★, *Bible Of Dreams* (Blue Room 1997)★★★.

JUST-ICE

b. Joseph Williams Jnr., Ft. Greene, Brooklyn, New York, USA. Just Ice (aka Justice) was thrust to prominence in 1987 when his name was attached to the headline 'Murder, Drugs and the Rap Star'. The caption was emblazoned on the cover of the Washington Post. The text revealed that the rapper had been held and questioned in connection with the murder of a drug dealer (at no time were charges laid against him). Members of the Washington black community were so outraged by the implied racism and lack of factual reporting in the story that they picketed the newspaper's offices for several months. This has overshadowed the artist's recording career for Fresh and Sleeping Bag.

● ALBUMS: *Kool & Deadly* (Fresh 1987)★★★, *The Desolate One* (Sleeping Bag 1989)★★★, *Kill The Rhythm (Like A Homicide)* (In A Minute 1996)★★★.

JUSTIFIED ANCIENTS OF MU MU

Also known as the JAMS, this coalition saw Bill Drummond and Jimmy Cauty engage in some startlingly imaginative methods of undermining the prevailing pop ethos. Drummond had cut his teeth in the Liverpool scene of the early 80s and played a large part in setting up Zoo Records. By 1987 he was working with Cauty and exploiting the techniques of sampling and computers. Their liberal use of other artists' material within the framework of their own songs resulted in a court case with Abba, following which all remaining copies of the JAMS' album, *1987 (What The Fuck Is Going On?)*, were legally bound to be destroyed. However, a handful of copies escaped annihilation and ended up on sale for £1,000 each. The following year the duo switched guises to become the Timelords, enjoying a worldwide hit with 'Doctorin' The Tardis', with Gary Glitter. A manual on how to have a number 1 single was written, to be succeeded by work on their own movie. By this time Drummond and Cauty were calling themselves the KLF and enjoying yet more global success with the 'Stadium House' trilogy of singles. In 1991 the JAMS moniker was reactivated for 'It's Grim Up North', a dance single that owed several musical moments to composer William Blake. Subsequently, Drummond and Cauty slipped back into KLF mode to record with country singer Tammy Wynette.

● ALBUMS: *1987 (What The Fuck Is Going On?)* (KLF Communications 1987)★★★, *Who Killed The JAMS?* (KLF Communications 1987)★★★.

● COMPILATIONS: *The History Of The JAMS aka The Timelords* (TVT 1989)★★★.

JX

Based in south London, JX is the reclusive Jake Williams who established the name with 'Son Of A Gun', a UK Top 20 hit in April 1994 that featured the vocalist Billie Godfrey. This was followed by 'You Belong To Me' and 'Can't Take My Hands Off You'. Each single was originally issued on the cult house label Hooj Toons before being licensed either to London Records or its subsidiary dance outlet, ffrr Records. In May 1996, 'There's Nothing I Won't Do' entered the UK Top 10 in its first week of release. JX is less prolific than most house artists as Williams insists that 'quality control is very important' in order to gain the respect of his audience.

K

K KLASS

Carl Thomas and Andy Williams, who had previously been part of the band Interstate in Wrexham, met Russ Morgan and Paul Roberts, who were from Chester, at various clubs around Manchester in the late 80s. They began to write music together in 1989 and subsequently sent a demo to Martin Price's Eastern Bloc Records, who released the EP *Wildlife* the following year on their label Creed Records. The title track employed the theme to the BBC children's television programme *Animal Magic* and the EP became a hit in the dance charts. At the same time the band gained further exposure when they supported 808 State on tour that summer. In April 1991 K Klass released 'Rhythm Is A Mystery' which, with its Italian-style piano lines and singer Bobby Depasois, had more of a commercial edge. This uplifting house track became popular in clubs throughout the north of England and Scotland, as the band undertook a series of promotional gigs throughout the summer. However, it achieved national success and eventually reached number 3 in the charts when the band signed to DeConstruction Records and released a remix towards the end of 1991. K Klass's popularity was confirmed when 'So Right', 'Don't Stop' (both 1992) and 'Let Me Show You' (1993) continued to sell well. In 1994 they released their debut album, *Universal*, accompanied by the single 'What You're Missing'. In 1996 DeConstruction released an album of remixes, *Remix And Additional Production*. K Klass have become popular as remix artists and have completed work for a number of artists, including Carleen Anderson, Denise Johnson, New Order and Oceanic.

● ALBUMS: *Universal* (DeConstruction 1994)★★★, *Remix And Additional Production* (DeConstruction 1996)★★★.

K-9 POSSE

K-9 Posse were the unhappy result of Arista Records attempting to gatecrash the hip-hop party in the late 80s. The group were formed at Fairleigh Dickinson University in Teaneck, New Jersey, by Wardell Mahone and Vernon Lynch. The two rappers were in need of a DJ and up to the decks stepped Terrence Sheppard in 1988. Conscious rhymes about 'Someone's Brother' were present on their debut album, but no hit singles were forthcoming and the band soon disappeared from the face of the rap world.

● ALBUMS: *K-9 Posse* (Arista 1989)★★.

K-SOLO

b. Kevin Maddison, Central Islip, New York, USA. K-Solo is a part of the Hit Squad, the EPMD clique whose other members include Das EFX and Redman. Maddison had been involved in a pre-EPMD band with Parrish Smith, before providing vocals to the group's *Unfinished Business*. Parrish was on hand to provide production tutelage for K-Solo's debut album, a perfunctory demonstration of his story-telling skills highlighted by the stylish 'Tales From The Crack Side'. K-Solo is an acronym for Kevin Self Organisation Left Others.

● ALBUMS: *Tell The World My Name* (Atlantic 1990)★★★, *Spellbound* (Atlantic 1991)★★, *Times Up* (Atlantic 1992)★★★.

K., LEILA

b. Leila El Khalifi, c.1972, Gothenburg, Sweden. Frequently but somewhat erroneously compared to Neneh Cherry, Leila K. comes from an Arabic Muslim background and is one of hip-hop's more glamorous rappers. At the age of 16 she ran away from her parents in Gothenburg. On her travels she saw an advert in a newspaper for a rap contest in the capital, Stockholm, and decided to try her luck. Two of the judges, who were impressed enough to reward her with the title, were Rob'N Raz. They were looking for a 'visual front' for their own recordings, and together the trio recorded the single 'Got To Get'. It topped domestic charts and brought a major label contract, the success quickly repeated with the international hit 'Rok The Nation'. Afterwards Leila split from Rob'n Raz to establish a solo career, signing with Swedish label Mega Records. There has been a certain novelty value to this secondary career so far, which began in earnest with a cover version of Plastic Bertrand's 'Ca Plane Pour Moi'. Other singles such as 'Glam', which sampled Gary Glitter's 'Rock & Roll Part 1', with the Beastie Boys providing production assistance, did little to dispel this notion. Her debut album did, however, include collaborations with Euro techno wizards Denniz Pop and Douglas Carr (Ace Of Base, Dr. Alban etc.).

● ALBUMS: *Carousel* (Polydor/Urban 1993)★★★.

K7

This Latin-flavoured hip-hop unit from Manhattan, New York, USA found chart success in 1993 with the addictive and anthemic 'Come Baby Come'. The quintet combine energetic R&B arrangements with clean raps, a style which has been unkindly referred to as 'The Hispanic Take That'. Led by K7, who gives the group their name, they also feature DJ Non-Stop, Prophet, Tre Duece and LOS. K7's attitude to labelling is unequivocal: 'My music is male bonding on a hip-hop level. It's not rap music'. The party-jam spirit of their debut single was present alongside more of the same on their debut album, which included the bilingual 'Zunga Zeng' cut, as well as a rather embarrassing attempt at 'A Little Help From My Friends'.

● ALBUMS: *Swing Batta Swing* (Tommy Boy 1994)★★.

KALEEF

After an abortive experience with a major label, Manchester, England hip-hop act Kaleef rose to prominence at the end of 1996 with a UK Top 40 single for an independent label. The group originally signed to London Records in 1993 as the Kaliphz (their name translating as 'King' or 'Messenger' in an Arabic tongue). They were pulled together after 2Phaaan (pronounced Dufarn, b. *c.*1967) and Jabba Da Hype (aka The Alien) saw the Rocksteady Crew performing at the Runcorn Ideal Homes Exhibition in 1982 and became embroiled in the breakdancing and graffiti movements in their neighbourhood, forming breakdance crew Dizzy Footwork the same year. They were soon joined by Hogweed, and the trio began hanging out together, before finally adding Chokadoodle and SniffaDawg (b. *c.*1974) to complete the line-up.The group were backed by a production team entitled Funk Regulators, a junior back-up rap squad the Underhogs, an all-female troupe the Berserkers, a mixed race group Freaks Of Nature, and a freestyle solo rapper, Paraphinalia. They were paid a great deal of attention by a media fascinated with their predomi-

nantly Asian origins, and the deal with London was rumoured to involve a large advance. However, the group's debut album, *Seven Deadly Sins*, stalled commercially, as did a sequence of singles. Their record label having lost interest, the Kaliphz career seemed set to decline until Radio 1 disc jockey Pete Tong (who had been an early supporter of the group) put them in touch with Manchester independent, Unity Records - the label formed by Pete Waterman of Stock, Aitken And Waterman fame. They made a demo recording of the Stranglers' 1982 hit 'Golden Brown' at Waterman's Manchester studio, The Church. Their revision featured a rap by the group's Twice Born about the dangers of heroin - ironic, given the Stranglers' long-term refusal to admit the song was a paean to the drug.

● ALBUMS: as Kalphiz *Seven Deadly Sins* (Payday 1995)★★★.

KALIPHZ

(see Kaleef)

KAM

b. Craig Miller, *c.*1971, Watts, California, USA, before settling in Compton with his mother and brother. With his lyrical worldview drawn from the inter-gang arena of Los Angeles, Kam chose to call for unity rather than glorify the bloodletting of the Crips and Blood brotherhoods. Unfortunately, though his rhymes were deftly weighted tracts against the dissolution of the ghetto, generally arguing for his Muslim beliefs ('So it's hard to keep calm, When I'm accused of being racist, For Loving my people first...'), Kam's delivery lacked the heavyweight impact of Messrs Ice-T and Cube. The latter was the major influence in his career, picking him up as the first artist on his Street Knowledge empire. He made his debut with 'Every Single Weekend' on the *Boyz N The Hood* soundtrack, before guesting on 'Colorblind', a cut from Cube's *Death Certificate* set. He has also written for Yo Yo.

● ALBUMS: *Neva Again* (East West 1992)★★★, *Made In America* (East West 1995)★★★.

KANE, BIG DADDY

Self-styled 'black gentleman vampire' who followed his cousin in to hip-hop by rapping in front of a beatbox for his first shows on Long Island, New York. Aided by his DJ Mr Cee, he has released several albums of laconic, fully-realized songs pitched halfway between soul and rap. His tough but sensual work is best sampled on the hit singles 'Ain't No Stoppin' Us Now' (McFadden And Whitehead) and 'Smooth Operator' (Sade). Obvious similarities to Barry White are given further credence by the duet he shares with that artist on 1991's *Taste Of Chocolate*. He straddled the rap and mainstream R&B markets with his most recent, decidedly mellow album.

● ALBUMS: *Long Live The Kane* (Cold Chillin' 1988)★★★, *It's A Big Daddy Thing* (Cold Chillin' 1989)★★★★, *Taste Of Chocolate* (1991)★★★, *Prince Of Darkness* (1992)★★★, *Looks Like A Job For...* (1993)★★★, *Daddy's Home* (MCA 1994)★★★.

KATCH 22

British *avant garde* rap troupe headed up by MC Huntkillbury Finn (b. Andrew Ward) and producer Mad Marga (b. Steven Andre), whose additional personnel include DJ Killerman Twice (b. Nicholas Swaby), Cavey (b. Ian Williams; producer), Malika B Poetess (b. Malika Booker) and singer Ann Gray. Their imaginative utilisation of beats and rhythms appropriated from a variety of sources like jazz, dub and ska, place them squarely in the Black British underground tradition. They have also operated in an admirably collective manner, handing the mic over to a number of contributors (including a healthy female ratio) and collaborating with other groups like Cookie Crew, Hijack and Son Of Noise. The mainstays have also given production assistance to several other Kold Sweat outfits, including Rude Boy Business, Superb C and Ambassadors Of Swing.

● ALBUMS: *Diary Of A Black Man Living In The Land Of The Lost* (1991)★★★, *Dark Tales From Two Cities* (Kold Sweat 1993)★★★.

KAYO

b. Kayode Shekoni, Sweden. Of African heritage, Swedish dance music artist Kayo began her musical career at the age of 14. She was signed by the Swedish dance music label Swemix Records in 1989, releasing her self-titled debut solo album a year later. *Kayo* featured 'pure dance-orientated pop', while tracks such as 'Another Mother' and 'Change Of Attitude' demonstrated her ability as a songwriter. Both achieved national airplay and confirmed her as one of the most singular talents on a widely acclaimed record label. 'Another Mother' also established her as a successful artist in mainland European countries such as Germany. However, if commercial approbation

beckoned, Kayo bucked expectations with her 1993 album, *Karleksland*. Rather than the English-language lyrics that had dominated earlier releases, this record was recorded entirely in the Swedish tongue. The lyrics were written by Swedish pop star Orup, while the music, produced by Grammy-winner Dan Sundqvist, largely encompassed a sophisticated blend of pop and soul. Still to the forefront, however, was Kayo's distinctive, uninhibited vocal persona. Throughout 1993 she toured in support of the album, although she also devoted time to her first feature film, *The Pillmaker*. Kayo had previously appeared in the Creeps' satirical video for 'Ooh I Like It', which won an award in 1990 as MTV viewers' favourite video.

● ALBUMS: *Kayo* (Cheiron 1990)★★, *Karleksland* (Cheiron 1993)★★★.

KIANI, MARY

Prior to the start of her solo career 90s UK pop-dance vocalist Mary Kiani was the singer with Glasgow, Scotland-based techno/house group the Time Frequency (often abbreviated to TTF). That group was enormously successful in Scotland, reaching number 1 in the charts with 'Real Love', which also peaked at number 8 in the main UK charts. Their other successful singles included 'New Emotion' and 'The Ultimate High', both of which also charted in the UK Top 40. She made her debut *Top Of The Pops* appearance with TTF and also supported Prince at Edinburgh's Meadowbank Stadium. Later she worked with the Welsh band Waterfront, who toured the USA to strong acclaim and reached number 6 in the *Billboard* charts with 'Cry'. She signed a solo contract in 1995 with the management team behind Dina Carroll, MN8 and Eternal, and released her first single, 'When I Call Your Name', in August. It reached number 18 in the UK charts in its first week of release. The follow-up single, 'I Give It All To You'/'I Imagine', followed in December. This was a double a-side release, featuring a ballad and a rhythmic techno-house number, with remixes from producers including Tony de Vit and Eddie Fingers. Once again it was a hit.

● ALBUMS: *Long Hard Funky Dreams* (Mercury 1997)★★★.

KICKIN' RECORDS

Record label originally established in 1988, at that time under the name GTI Music (the Great Techno Institution), based in Notting Hill Gate in

West London (still its current home). At first the label supplied a demand for tough street soul, with April 1988's 'Good Living' from Dave Collins their first release. However, there was an immediate musical shift afterwards, with label boss Peter Harris signing Shut Up And Dance after hearing a demo track (eventually releasing '5678'). The Kickin' Records name was first invoked in 1990 when the Scientist's 'The Exorcist' arrived. This, claimed to be the first record with a bpm above 130, became a *de rigeur* accessory among followers of the burgeoning rave scene. The follow-up, 'The Bee', also sold strongly, and the Scientist would go on to join Kickin' at 1991's 'first ever Russian rave'. 1991 saw the label signing a second, hugely successful rave act, Messiah. Two years later the label began its popular *Hard Leaders* compilation series, which has become a favourite among hardcore fans. In the meantime a new roster of artists had been assembled, including Wishdokta, Xenophobia (a front for former members of Rubella Ballet), PMA, Kicksquad (Scientist with DJ Hype), Flat 47, Noodles & Wonder, Giro Kid and Green Budha. Kickin' also set up two subsidiary operations, Slip 'n' Slide (house/garage) and Pandemonium (indie guitar), as well as liaising with Colin Dale for his *The Outer Limits* series.
● COMPILATIONS: Various: *Hard Leaders 1-4* (Kickin' 1994)★★★.

KID 'N PLAY

Among rap's most innocuous outfits, Kid 'N Play came to light in 1988 through an album that to date represents their best work; and typified their happy-go-lucky style. So much so that the group were offered their own cartoon series, following their appearance in *House Party* (Kid 'N Play's *Funhouse* is a spin-off from the film, including actual dialogue). Kid (b. Christopher Reid) and Play (b. Christopher Martin) concentrate heartily on a youthful style of braggadocio, typified on their debut album by the two-timing morality sequence, 'Undercover' (which featured guest vocals by the Real Roxanne), or the self-explanatory 'Rollin' With Kid 'N Play'. Their music is underpinned by the production of mentor Hurby Luv Bug, while their practical messages like 'Don't do drugs' and 'Stay in school' are unlikely to offend middle-class American sentiments.
● ALBUMS: *2 Hype* (Select 1988)★★, *Kid 'N Play's Funhouse* (Select 1990)★★★, *Face The Nation* (Select 1991)★★★.

KID FROST

b. Arturo Molina Jnr., 31 May 1964, Los Angeles, California, USA. Mexican-descended rapper who was raised on military bases in Guam and Germany, but did most of his growing up in East Los Angeles, where he began delivering rhymes in 1982. He was inducted into the ranks of Uncle Jam's Army, as the west coast began to accommodate the innovations of the Bronx. A major force in the establishment of Latin hip-hop, Frost brought together several other Hispanic rappers for the Latin Alliance project in 1991. Before then he had made strides with his 1990 solo set, another important signpost in the sub-genre's development. His blend of Chicano social observation and pulsing rap breakbeats provided him with a considerable audience outside of his own socio-genetic bracket. Now signed to Virgin, Kid Frost deploys the intelligence to sample not only from funk's back-catalogue, but also that of the salsa tradition of his own people.
● ALBUMS: *Hispanic Causing Panic* (Virgin 1990)★★, *East Side Story* (Virgin 1992)★★★.

KID SENSATION

b. Steven Spence, Seattle, Washington, USA. Rapper who first came to fame as Sir Mix-A-Lot's DJ and keyboardist, before scoring a minor success with his own debut album. After graduating in 1988, he became part of the Sir Mix-A-Lot posse behind 1988's platinum-selling *Swass* set. It encouraged him to embark on his own career, which was soon rewarded when his debut album provided three hit singles, 'Back To Boom', 'Seatown Ballers' and 'Prisoner Of Ignorance'. His self-aggrandising title was reflected in the cool braggadocio of much of the material on offer, but by the advent of a follow-up album there was a message behind the rhymes. 'I'm trying to show I'm a down to earth guy, it's more of what I'm all about'. The b-side of the album's promotional single, 'Ride The Rhythm', was 'The Way I Swing'. This was a duet with the Seattle Mariner's all-star centerfielder, and Sensation's sporting idol, Ken Friggy Jnr.
● ALBUMS: *Rollin' With Number One* (Nastymix 1990)★★★, *The Power Of Rhyme* (Nastymix 1992)★★★.

KILLAH PRIEST
(see Wu-Tang Clan)

KILO

b. c.1972, Atlanta, Georgia, USA. Prolific young artist who was raised by his grandparents in the north-west projects of Atlanta, known as Bowen Homes. Turned on to hip-hop, he recorded his first demos at the age of 15 with the help of his DJ Red Money. These recordings eventually crystallised into a debut set that was released on the local Arvis imprint. The album would sell over 40,000 copies in the South East region, its sales profile buoyed by the attendant hit single, 'Cocaine'. A-Town Rush was similarly successful, again almost entirely on the back of local sales. Kilo went on to win Atlanta's Coca Cola Music Awards for the best Rap Artist in March 1992, prompting a bidding war within the rap label community. Wrap/Ichiban won out, and promptly re-released and re-promoted the artist's first and second albums. The duo returned to the studio in 1993 with a less commercial approach making the resultant album less airplay-friendly, but it was again highly regarded by critics (and spawned the hit single 'Tick Tock'). Kilo's second album from the same year was granted the production expertise of Carl Cooley, 'C' Dorsey and Craze, and was another ample demonstration of his resonant, high-pitched delivery and lyrical skill. As Kilo Ali he released Organized Bass in 1997.

● ALBUMS: America Has A Problem...Cocaine (Arvis Records 1991)★★★, A-Town Rush (Arvis Records 1992)★★★, Bluntly Speaking (Wrap/Ichiban 1993)★★★★, Git Wit Da Program (Wrap/Ichiban 1993)★★★, as Kilo Ali Organized Bass (Interscope 1997)★★★.

● COMPILATIONS: The Best And The Bass (Wrap/Ichiban 1994)★★★★.

KINCHEN, MARK

In 1988, together with Terrence Parker, Mark 'MK' Kinchen was part of the US duo Separate Minds for the techno/soul cut, 'We Need Somebody'. Kinchen went on to engineer on many of the early Inner City Records, and most of Kevin Saunderson's associated KMS label product, having been adopted as 'studio mascot' by Saunderson from the age of 17 onwards. He began to make records on his own as MK - including 'Mirror Mirror'. However, he was still eclipsed by his boss, and he elected to relocate to New York, recording songs like 'Play The World'. This was somewhat removed from the traditional Detroit sound, confounding expectations. A good example

was the 'Burnin'' single (featuring vocal support from Alana Simon), given a UK release after success as an import on Kinchen's own Area 10 label in 1992. He returned to the Separate Minds name for '2nd Bass' in 1992, a full three and a half years after recording '1st Bass'. Among other noms de plume he also records as 4th Measure Men. He has also remixed for Bizarre Inc and Masters At Work ('Can't Stop The Rhythm').

KING JUST

b. c.1974. Another of the new crop of Staten Island (aka Shaolin), New York, USA, rappers, whose appropriation of the 'Shaolin' martial arts ethos saw him compared to neighbours the Wu-Tang Clan. He made his debut with the 'Warrior's Drum' 12-inch, which became a huge underground hit in 1994. Backed by his crew/gang, Blackfist (also the title of his label, operated through Select), it was competent hardcore but seemed somewhat unoriginal in the context.

KING SUN

Mediocre artist whose records contain the over-familiar self-deifying advocacy of a rash of other rappers, alongside Afrocentric/Islamic concerns. Matters began more promisingly in 1987 when he teamed up with D Moe for the 'Hey Love' minor hit, which borrowed liberally from 'Moments In Love' by the Art Of Noise. Nothing in his more recent work has proved other than dispensable, however, and he remains best known for his bravery in dissing Ice Cube while the latter was peforming.

● ALBUMS: XI (Profile 1989)★★, Righteous But Ruthless (Profile 1990)★★, King Sun With The Sword (Profile 1991)★★.

KING TEE

b. Los Angeles, California, USA. Based in Compton, King Tee made his first entrance into music as a mixer for Houston's KTSU and KYOK radio stations. Through his radio connections he recorded his first record, 'Payback's A Mother', for Greg Mack's Mackdaddy Records. A contract with Capitol brought two albums together with producer DJ Pooh, but negligible success. However, he did have his moments. The first album was distinguished by jokey cuts like 'I Got A Cold', on which he delivered a remarkable impression of a vexed sinus. The follow-up was harder, tracks like 'Skanless' extolling the joys of bedding his friend's wife. 'Time To Get Out' was a rare flash of insight, and by far the best track on show. Tee did at least introduce the world to the potentially far more interesting Tha Alkaholics.

● ALBUMS: *Act A Fool* (Capitol 1989)★★★, *At Your Own Risk* (Capitol 1990)★★★.

KING, MORGAN

Alongside Nick E, the London-based King was responsible for over 90% of Sweden's B-Tech label output in the 90s. Some of his flags of convenience include Clubland (soulful garage), Soundsource ('Take Me Up' and other Balearic moments), Al Hambra ('Al Hambra'), Maniac Tackle ('Bass FU'), Technoir ('Logic And Knowledge'), Control E ('The Power Of Freedom'), Bassrace ('Futurama') and Full On Sound ('Mayhem') - all housed on B-Tech. King also remixed Moodswings' 'Spiritual High' for Arista Records and played a part in establishing London label Om Records.

KIRK

b. *c*.1964, USA. This teetotal, drug-free rapper, who recorded his debut album for East West Records in 1994, reminded many critics of the old school rappers of the Bronx, New York. Concentrating on the African-American experience as postulated by Afrika Bambaataa and others, his 1994 debut album, *Makin' Moves*, was marred by inferior production and a lack of musical dexterity. Many of his melancholy raps, which included subjects such as the difficulty of getting started in the rap business (though he was still only 19), were effective narratives reminiscent of the work of Leaders Of The New School and other rappers retreating to rap's 70s beginnings for inspiration.

● ALBUMS: *Makin' Moves* (East West 1994)★★.

KIRK, RICHARD H.

Founding member of Cabaret Voltaire whose releases under his own name in the 90s have seen him increasingly accommodated by the rave generation. Kirk released his first solo set in 1981, following it with the double album *Time High Fiction* two years later. His taste for dance music was probably most obviously previewed by the release of Cabaret Voltaire's 'James Brown', before further solo work in 1986 with *Black Jesus Voice*, a mini-album, and *Ugly Spirit*. This was followed a year later by a collaborative project, *Hoodoo Talk*, with the Box's Peter Hope. Further expansions in Cabaret Voltaire's dance sound were refined by

the 1989 single 'Hypnotised', after the duo had visited Chicago. A year later Kirk released 'Test One', an excellent example of the acid house style, under the guise of Sweet Exorcist. It launched what became known as the 'bleep' sound, which was widely imitated and dominated clubs for almost a year. A second hugely popular 12-inch arrived with 'Clonk'. Kirk currently enjoys his own Western Works studio in Sheffield, and looks to be one of the true survivors of the late 70s industrial scene centred in that town.

● ALBUMS: *Disposable Half Truths* (Rough Trade 1981)★★★, *Time High Fiction* (Rough Trade 1983)★★★★, *Black Jesus Voice* (Rough Trade 1986)★★, *Ugly Spirit* (Rough Trade 1986)★★★, with Peter Hope *Hoodoo Talk* (Native 1987)★★, as Sweet Exorcist *Clonk's Coming* (Warp 1991)★★★, *Virtual State* (Warp 1994)★★★, *The Number Of Magic* (Warp 1995)★★★.

KLF

Since 1987 the KLF have operated under a series of guises, only gradually revealing their true nature to the public at large. The band's principal spokesman is Bill Drummond (b. William Butterworth, 29 April 1953, South Africa), who had already enjoyed a chequered music industry career. As co-founder of the influential Zoo label in the late 70s, he introduced and later managed Echo And The Bunnymen and the Teardrop Explodes. Later he joined forces with Jimmy Cauty (b. 1954), an artist of various persuasions and a member of Brilliant in the mid-80s. Their first project was undertaken under the title JAMS (Justified Ancients Of Mu Mu - a title lifted from Robert Shea and Robert Anton Wilson's conspiracy novels dealing with the *Illuminati*). An early version of 'All You Need Is Love' caused little reaction compared to the provocatively titled LP that followed - *1987 - What The Fuck Is Going On?* Released under the KLF moniker (standing for Kopyright Liberation Front), it liberally disposed of the works of the Beatles, Led Zeppelin *et al* with the careless abandon the duo had picked up from the heyday of punk. One of the disfigured supergroups, Abba, promptly took action to ensure the offending article was withdrawn. In the wake of the emerging house scene the next move was to compromise the theme tune to well-loved British television show *Dr Who*, adding a strong disco beat and Gary Glitter yelps to secure an instant number 1 with 'Doctorin' The Tardis'. Working under the title Timelords, this one-off coup was achieved with such simplicity that its originators took the step of writing a book - *How To Have A Number One The Easy Way*. Returning as the KLF, they enjoyed a big hit with the more legitimate cult dance hit 'What Time Is Love'. After the throwaway send-up of Australian pop, 'Kylie Said To Jason', they hit big again with the soulful techno of '3 A.M. Eternal'. There would be further releases from the myriad of names employed by the duo (JAMS - 'Down Town', 'It's Grim Up North'; Space - *Space*; Disco 2000 - 'Uptight'), while Cauty, alongside Alex Paterson, played a significant part in creating the Orb. Of the band's later work, perhaps the most startling was their luxurious video for the KLF's 'Justified And Ancient', featuring the unmistakable voice of Tammy Wynette. The song revealed the KLF at the peak of their creative powers, selling millions of records worldwide while effectively taking the michael. They were voted the Top British Group by the BPI. Instead of lapping up the acclaim, the KLF, typically, rejected the comfort of a music biz career, and deliberately imploded at the BRITS award ceremony. There they performed an 'upbeat' version of '3AM Eternal', backed by breakneck-speed punk band Extreme Noise Terror, amid press speculation that they would be bathing the ceremony's assembled masses with pig's blood. They contented themselves instead with (allegedly) dumping the carcass of a dead sheep in the foyer of the hotel staging the post-ceremony party, and Drummond mock machine-gunning the assembled dignitaries. They then announced that the proud tradition of musical anarchy they had brought to a nation was at a close: the KLF were no more. Their only 'release' in 1992 came with a version of 'Que Sera Sera' (naturally rechristened 'K Sera Sera', and recorded with the Soviet Army Chorale), which, they insisted, would only see the light of day on the advent of world peace. The KLF returned to their rightful throne, that of England's foremost musical pranksters, with a stinging art terrorist racket staged under the K Foundation banner. In late 1993, a series of advertisements began to appear in the quality press concerning the Turner Prize art awards. While that body was responsible for granting £20,000 to a piece of non-mainstream art, the K Foundation (a new vehicle for Messrs Drummond and Cauty) promised double that for the worst piece of art displayed. The Turner short-list was identical to that of the KLF's. More bizarre still, exactly £1,000,000 was withdrawn from the National Westminster bank (the biggest cash withdrawal in the institution's history), nailed to a board, and paraded in front of a select gathering of press and art luminaries. The money was eventually returned to their bank accounts (although members of the press pocketed a substantial portion), while the £40,000 was awarded to one Rachel Whiteread, who also won the 'proper' prize. The K Foundation later cemented its notoriety by burning the aforementioned one million pounds, an event captured on home video. Since that time, Drummond and Cauty have made several pseudonymous returns to the singles charts, including the 1996 tribute to footballer Eric Cantona, 'Ooh! Aah! Cantona', as 1300 Drums Featuring The Unjustified Ancients Of Mu, and in 1997 as 2K for the charmingly titled 'Fuck The Millennium'. Urban guerrillas specializing in highly original shock tactics, the KLF offer the prospect of a brighter decade should their various disguises continue to prosper.

● ALBUMS: *Towards The Trance* (KLF Communications 1988)★★★★, *The What Time Is Love Story* (KLF Communications 1989)★★★, *The White Room* (KLF Communications 1990)★★★, *Chill Out* (KLF Communications 1990)★★★.
● VIDEOS: *Stadium House* (PMI 1991).
● FURTHER READING: *Justified And Ancient: The Unfolding Story Of The KLF*, Pete Robinson. *Bad Wisdom*, Mark Manning and Bill Drummond.

KMD

Long Beach, Long Island, New York-based rap outfit who have allied their breakbeats to a strong moral and political stance. This was made evident by their commitment to be a 'positive Kause (sic) in a Much Damaged Society', on their 'Rap The Vote' college tour of the US, an attempt to encourage young people to vote. They were a key element in 3rd Bass's RIF production roster, whose MC Serch (who discovered them) and Pete Nice handled executive production duties on *Mr Hood*. The fluid sound of the latter featured twisted riffs and hip-hop holding together a barrage of samples. However, the following years would not prove easy ones for the band. Their DJ, Subroc, brother to lead rapper Zevlove X, was killed in a car accident in 1993. The band were just readying themselves for the release of a promotional single ('What A Niggy Know'), when they were called into a meeting with label bosses on 8 April 1994, where chairman Bob Krasnow informed them that they were not happy with the artwork for *Black Bastards*. This featured a 'Sambo' character being hung by the noose. The thinking, on KMD's part, was to 'execute the stereotype'. However, R&B *Billboard* columnist Terri Rossi had already taken issue with the image, without really understanding the statement. It was a classic case of Time Warner paranoia in the wake of the 'Cop Killer' issue, dropping the band even though they were prepared to discuss changes, and hardly the tonic a recovering Zevlove needed. Ironically, the music on the second long-playing venture was a more sober affair, in a more reflective mode *à la* A Tribe Called Quest. It was lyrically informed by Last Poet Gylan Kain's spoken jazz (notably the *Blue Guerilla* set).

● ALBUMS: *Mr Hood* (Elektra 1991)★★★, *Black Bastards* (Elektra 1994; withdrawn).

KMS RECORDS

One of the original Detroit techno stables, and home to Kevin Saunderson's Inner City/Resse Project family, with its title taken from the proprietor's full name (Kevin Maurice Saunderson). Its important releases during the late 80s included Inner City's 'Big Fun' and Reese & Santonio's 'Truth Of Self Evidence'. However, by the 90s, in tandem with the Reese Project's more soulful approach to techno/house, Saunderson was using the label for more vocal-based tracks. A new subsidiary imprint, Transfusion, was planned to house any idiosyncratic excursions into techno. Just to confirm what he has always said: 'If its dance music, I do it all'. The label was also home to Saunderson projects including E-Dancer's 'Pump The Move', which was remixed by Joey Beltram and Tronik House ('Straight Outta Hell') while guest artists included Chez Damier ('Can You Feel It', which also featured Mark 'MK' Kinchen). In 1994 the label unveiled a triple compilation set featuring tracks from Inner City, Esser'ay, Members Of The House, Chez Damier and Ron Trent. KMS product is licensed in the UK through Network.

KNIGHT, MARION 'SUGE'

(see Death Row Records)

KNIGHTS OF THE OCCASIONAL TABLE

South-east London multiracial dance band, comprising Steve, Nygell, Moose, Andrew and vocalist Aquamanda. Their debut album was initially released on their own label before being picked up by Club Dog. Its title - *Knees Up Mother Earth* - offered a big clue to their sound, wherein modern technological means (programmes, drum machines, samplers) were employed to deliver a primal beat with varied ethnic stylings. The Knights have not been as immediately successful as stylistic counterparts Fun-Da-Mental or Trans-Global Underground, ensuring Steve and Andy continue their daytime jobs as psychiatric nurse and journalist for *Stage And Television Today*, respectively.

● ALBUMS: *Knees Up Mother Earth* (Club Dog 1993)★★★.

KNUCKLES, FRANKIE

b. *c*.1955, New York, USA. Knuckles is often credited with 'creating' house music while a Chicago DJ at venues such as the Warehouse and Powerplant. As a child he was inspired by his sister's jazz records, and took up the double bass. He attended the Dwyer School Of Art in the Bronx and F.I.T. in Manhattan to study textile design. However, he was soon lured into DJing at $50 a night at the Better Days emporium. Eventually Larry Levan of the Paradise Garage asked him to work at the Continental Baths club, and he was subsequently invited to travel to Chicago for the opening of the Warehouse. At the time he played mainly Philadelphia soul and R&B, bringing back hot records from New York for his shows. According to Knuckles, the term 'house' had not yet been coined. 'One day I was driving in the South Side and passed a club that had a sign outside that read 'We Play House Music'. I asked them what it meant and he told me that they played the same music as I did'. Into the 90s he was still to be found orchestrating the dancefloor until 10am at New York's Sound Factory on a Saturday night. The Powerplant, which he set up after the Warehouse, lasted for three years before outbreaks of violence and the criminal fraternity appeared on the fringes. Knuckles moved into production and recording work with DJ International, recording 'Tears' with the help of Robert Owens and also producing 'Baby Wants To Ride' for Jamie Principle on Trax. However, DJ International's Rocky Jones was singularly unimpressed, obtaining a tape of the latter record and pressing it up in competition, though Knuckles reasoned he was only signed to DJI as an artist. He had first started to remix records for

his own DJing purposes, and later would go on to become an in-demand remixer for everyone from Chaka Khan to the Pet Shop Boys and Kenny Thomas following his unofficial peerage by dance cognoscenti. He even remixed Nu Colours' version of his own classic, 'Tears'. He also recorded as a solo artist for Ten/Virgin. Knuckles became the partner of David Morales in Def-Mix Productions, one of the most high-profile remix and production teams ever. Morales was present on Knuckles' 1991 album, along with frequent co-conspirators Satoshi Tomiie, Ed Kupper (who wrote the hit single, 'The Whistle Song') and Danny Madden. Brave attempts to tackle ballads proved misguided, although back in the familiar territory of house Knuckles can usually be relied upon at least to pull muster, and at best pull the foundations down. His collaboration with Adeva on *Welcome To The Real World* enhanced and spread his reputation.
● ALBUMS: *Frankie Knuckles Presents: The Album* (Westside 1990)★★★★, *Beyond The Mix* (Ten 1991)★★★, *Welcome To The Real World* (Virgin America 1995)★★★.

KOKANE

Kokane was previously premiered as the dancehall DJ featured on NWA's *Efil4Zaggin'*. He moved over to more traditional rapping for his solo debut, which featured guest appearances from Above The Law's Cold 187um (who also produced, and was responsible for giving Kokane his nickname), Tha Alkaholics (on 'All Bark And No Bite'), while 'Don't Bite The Phunk' continued Ruthless' 'house policy' of lambasting Dr Dre. Like much of the rest of the album's tired G-funk formula, it was a somewhat misplaced and unoriginal move.
● ALBUMS: *Funk Upon A Rhyme* (Ruthless 1994)★★.

KOLD SWEAT

Innovative and highly regarded UK hip-hop operation, who initially made their name by staking over £6,000 of studio time in the embryonic Katch 22, allowing them to spend a month recording their *Diary Of A Blackman*. Their other artists include the F9s, SL Trooper's (who began the catalogue with 'Knowledge...Put Your Brain in Gear'), Rude Boy Business, Unanimous Decision, Korperayshun, Black Prophets and Son Of Noise.
● ALBUMS: Various: *Raw Flavours Volume 1* (Kold Sweat 1994)★★.

KONDERS, BOBBY

b. c.1962. New York DJ whose mixture of dancehall reggae with house and hip-hop breakbeats is widely acknowledged as a harbinger of the nascent jungle scene. Konders is a white boy from Philadelphia who ended up mixing it up for WBLS and living in the Bronx. He started DJing at the age of 15 at house parties, playing funk and reggae back to back. By 1986 he had started the Saturday Lunch Mix for WBLS. With singles such as 'Mack Daddy' he successfully combined the new rap language with dance stylings. Konders also worked on mixes for Maxi Priest, Shabba Ranks, Papa Dee and Shinehead and used dancehall vocalists such as Mikey Jarrett on his own recordings. His *Massive Sounds* set saw him teamed with artists including Connie Harvey, Monyaka's Raphael and soulstress Lisa Makeda.
● ALBUMS: *Cool Calm And Collective* (Desire 1990)★★★, *Massive Sounds* (Mercury 1992)★★.

KOOL G RAP AND DJ POLO

New York-based protégés of the omnipresent Marley Marl, Kool G (b. Nathaniel Wilson, 20 July 1968, Elmhurst, Queens, New York), so called to represent 'Kool Genius Of Rap', has yet to build a commensurate profile following three rich, undervalued albums. This despite hardcore benchmarks like 'Streets Of New York', and a marvellous debut single, 'It's A Demo'. 'Streets Of New York' was housed on a second album produced by Eric B and Large Professor and featuring guest appearances from Big Daddy Kane and Biz Markie. Their third album was passed over by Warners when they saw the sleeve - which merrily depicted the duo in balaclavas feeding steak to a pair of Rottweilers, while in the background stand two white males on chairs with nooses around their necks. As if to send the censorship lobby into further frenzy there was a guest appearance for Ice Cube, one of their oldest enemies, on the enclosed record. The best of their admittedly patchy first three albums were pieced together for *Killer Kuts*.
● ALBUMS: *Road To The Riches* (Cold Chillin' 1989)★★, *Wanted: Dead Or Alive* (Cold Chillin' 1990)★★, *Live And Let Die* (Cold Chillin' 1992)★★, Kool G Rap *4,5,6* (Epic 1995)★★★.
● COMPILATIONS: *Killer Kuts* (Cold Chillin' 1994)★★★.

KOOL HERC

b. Clive Campbell, 1955, Kingston, Jamaica, West Indies, moving to New York in 1967. Kool Herc (aka Kool DJ Herc) owns the rights to the accolade 'first hip-hop DJ', though his talent was never captured on record. Illustrating the connections between reggae and rap which have largely been buried by successive hip-hop generations, Herc brought his sound system to block parties in the Bronx from 1969 onwards. By 1975 he was playing the brief rhythmic sections of records which would come to be termed 'breaks', at venues like the Hevalo in the Bronx. His influence was pivotal, with Grandmaster Flash building on his innovations to customise the modern hip-hop DJ approach. Herc's methods also pre-dated, and partially introduced, sampling. By adapting pieces of funk, soul, jazz and other musics into the melting pot, he would be able to keep a party buzzing. With his sound system the Herculords, he would tailor his sets to the participants, most of whom he knew by name. He would call these out over improvised sets: 'As I scan the place, I see the very familiar face...Of my mellow: Wallace Dee in the house! Wallace Dee! Freak For Me!'. Grandmaster Flash himself admits he would often be so embarassed when Herc picked him out of the crowd and offered him elementary lessons in the art of DJing that he would have to leave. Nevertheless, the pack eventually caught up and his influence was dying down when his career was effectively aborted by a knife fight. He was an innocent bystander when three youths attempted to push past his house security and he was stabbed three times, twice in the side and once across his hands. After that his club burned down and, as he himself recalls: 'Papa couldn't find no good ranch, so his herd scattered'. As one of hip-hop's founding fathers, Kool Herc's reputation and influence has outlasted the vagaries of musical fashion. A status no doubt boosted by the fact that he has not attempted to launch a spurious recording career on the back of it. It is a shame, however, that he has never seen the commercial rewards of his innovations, though he was the subject of celebration at the Rapmania Festival in 1990.

KOOL MOE DEE

Once of original rap pioneers Treacherous 3, Kool Moe Dee (b. Mohandas DeWese, Harlem, New York, USA) has carved a solo career bracing his old school style against the more urbane concerns of the new wave. He originally started rapping in his native Harlem by grabbing the mic at house parties, soon hooking up with his Treacherous colleagues L.A. Sunshine and Special K. However, with interest in the group waning following the arrival of Run DMC *et al*, he elected to leave the group: 'Rap is repetitous. It gets to the pont where you wana hear hard beats, then it goes back to where you wanna hear melodies. You just gotta be on the right vibe at the right time'. He would go on to graduate from SUNY at Old Westbury, before his solo CV started in earnest when he joined up with Teddy Riley for the crossover hit, 'Go See The Doctor', a cautionary account of the dangers of AIDS. Released on Rooftop Records, it won him a fresh contract with Jive. Much of his notoriety as the 80s progressed involved a long-running duel on record with LL Cool J, the first flowering of which was the title track to his second, platinum-selling album. A succession of minor hit singles has ensued, including 'Wild, Wild West', 'They Want Money' and 'Rise And Shine', the latter featuring Chuck D (Public Enemy) and KRS-1 on complementary vocals. He also became the first rap artist to perform at the Grammy Awards (following the success of *Knowledge Is King*), and continued to fight back against gangsta rap's misogynist vocabulary: 'When you get funke funke wisdom, then you'll understand, The woman is the driving force for any powerful man, From birth to earth to earth to rebirth, it ain't a curse, Put your thoughts in reverse'. This from a man who has already written over half a dozen screenplays.

● ALBUMS: *Kool Moe Dee* (Jive 1986)★★★, *How Ya Like Me Now* (Jive 1987)★★★, *Knowledge Is King* (Jive 1989)★★, *Funke, Funke Wisdom* (Jive 1991)★★★.

● COMPILATIONS: *Greatest Hits* (Jive 1993)★★★★.

KOOL ROCK JAY

b. Leo Dupree Ramsey Jnr., Oakland, California, USA. A rapper whose depictions of urban reality were addressed with a detached, almost resigned air. He began to freestyle at the age of 10, when his radio first picked up rap on the Californian airwaves. He adopted the style, and wrote his own words to the beats he heard, competing with the neighbourhood boys to perfect his delivery. His principal influences were the political heavyweights Public Enemy and KRS-1. He hooked up with his DJ, Slice (b. Michael Brown, though he was known in Oakland circles as the 'Beat Fixer'), at a party in Fresno, adding Nate The Great (b. Jonathon Matthews) and Chuck Nice (b. Charles Johnson). As they built a strong local reputation the final jigsaw piece arrived in the shape of producer Lionel 'The Super Duper Dope Hook Man' Bea. Through him the group won a contract with Jive Records. Their debut album was premiered by their best-known cut, 'It's A Black Thing', released as a single. Decidedly on the Afrocentricity theme, it was critically well received but afterwards their camp remained comparatively quiet.

● ALBUMS: *Tales From The Dope Side* (Jive 1990)★★★.

KRAFTWERK

The word 'unique' is overused in music, but Kraftwerk have a stronger claim than most to the tag. Ralf Hutter (b. 1946, Krefeld, Germany; organ) and woodwind student Florian Schneider-Esleben (b. 1947, Düsseldorf, Germany; woodwind) met while they were studying improvised music in Düsseldorf, Germany. They drew on the influence of experimental electronic forces such as composer Karlheinz Stockhausen and Tangerine Dream to create minimalist music on synthesizers, drum machines and tape recorders. Having previously recorded an album with Organisation (*Tone Float*), Hutter and Schneider formed Kraftwerk with Klaus Dinger and Thomas Homann and issued *Highrail*, after which Dinger and Homann left to form Neu. Their first two albums, released in Germany, were later released in the UK as an edited compilation in 1972. Produced by Conny Plank (later to work with Ultravox and the Eurythmics), the bleak, spartan music provoked little response. After releasing a duo set, *Ralf And Florian*, Wolfgang Flur (electronic drums) and Klaus Roeder (guitar, violin, keyboards) joined the group. *Autobahn* marked Kraftwerk's breakthrough and established them as purveyors of hi-tech, computerized music. The title track, running at more than 22 minutes, was an attempt to relate the monotony and tedium of a long road journey. An edited version reached the Top 10 in the US and UK charts. In 1975, Roeder was replaced by Karl Bartos, who played on *Radioactivity*, a concept album based on the sounds to be found on the airwaves. *Trans-Europe Express* and *The Man-Machine* were pioneering electronic works that strongly influenced a gener-

ation of English new-wave groups, such as the Human League, Tubeway Army (Gary Numan), Depeche Mode and OMD, while David Bowie claimed to have long been an admirer. The *New Musical Express* said of *The Man-Machine*: 'It is the only completely successful visual/aural fusion rock has produced so far'. Kraftwerk spent three years building their own Kling Klang studios in the late 70s, complete with, inevitably, scores of computers. The single 'The Model', from *The Man-Machine*, gave the band a surprise hit when it topped the UK charts in 1982, and it led to a trio of hits, including 'Showroom Dummies' and 'Tour De France', a song that was featured in the film *Breakdance* and became the theme for the cycling event of the same name in 1983. *Electric Cafe* was a disappointment, but the group were now cited as a major influence on a host of dance artists from Afrika Bambaataa to the respected producer Arthur Baker. Bambaattaa and Baker's pioneering 1982 'Planet Rock' single was built around samples of both 'Trans-Europe Express' and 'Numbers' (from 1981's *Computer World*).

Hutter and Schneider have remained enigmatically quiet ever since *Electric Cafe*. In 1990, a frustrated Flur departed to be replaced by Fritz Hijbert (Flur later collaborated with Mouse On Mars under the name of Yamo). Kraftwerk's best-known songs were collected together in 1991 on the double *The Mix*, aimed chiefly at the dance market by EMI Records. 'I think our music has to do with emotions. Technology and emotion can join hands . . .', said Hutter in 1991. They made a surprise return to live performance with a headline appearance at the UK's Tribal Gathering in the summer of 1997.

● ALBUMS: *Highrail* (1971)★★, *Var* (1972)★★, *Ralf & Florian* (Philips 1973)★★★, *Autobahn* (Vertigo 1974)★★★★, *Radioactivity* (Capitol 1975)★★★, *Trans-Europe Express* (Capitol 1977)★★★★, *The Man-Machine* (Capitol 1978)★★★★, *Computer World* (EMI 1981)★★★★, *Electric Cafe* (EMI 1986)★★★.

● COMPILATIONS: *Kraftwerk* a UK compilation of the first two releases (Vertigo 1973)★★, *The Mix* (EMI 1991)★★★★.

● FURTHER READING: *Kraftwerk: Man, Machine & Music*, Pacal Bussy.

KRISPY 3

Chorley, Lancashire, England-trio comprising Mr Wiz, Sonic G and Microphone Don, who made their reputation with two strong 1991 cuts,

'Destroy All The Stereotypes' and 'Don't Be Misled', both of which showcased their jazz/rap leanings. Their debut album, however, only included three tracks not released on their initial brace of 12-inches, which lessened its impact. Much more representative was a subsequent set for Kold Sweat, which included an attack on music business nepotism in 'Who Ya Know' while the title track argued against the virtual ending of the vinyl format (ironic given that their debut was on CD only).

● ALBUMS: *Krispy 3* (Gumh 1992)★★★, *Can't Melt The Wax* (Kold Sweat 1993)★★, *Head Out Da Gate* mini-album (Kold Sweat 1993)★★★.

KRISS KROSS

Two youths from Atlanta, Georgia, USA, who topped the *Billboard* charts with 'Jump', a song anchored by the bass line to the Jackson 5's 'I Want You Back'. Chris 'Mack Daddy' Kelly (b. 1978) and Chris 'Daddy Mack' Smith (b. 10 January 1979) were both just 13 years old when they scored with 'Jump', the fastest-selling single the USA had seen for 15 years. In the process they instigated a batch of 'kiddie rap' clones. They were discovered in 1991 by writer/producer Jermaine Dupree, himself only 19, when he was shopping for shoes in Atlanta. Influenced by the likes of Run DMC and Eric B And Rakim, their visual character was enhanced by their determination to wear all their clothes backwards. Strangely enough, considering their natural teen appeal, they were signed up to the genuinely hardcore New York label Ruffhouse, home of Tim Dog and others. *Totally Krossed Out* sold over four million copies and spawned another hit, 'Warm It Up'. *Young Rich & Dangerous* stalled, and fell far short of its predecessor's success and critical acclaim.

● ALBUMS: *Totally Krossed Out* (Ruffhouse 1992)★★★★, *Da Bomb* (Ruffhouse 1993)★★★, *Young Rich & Dangerous* (Sony 1996)★★★.

KRS-1

b. Lawrence Krisna Parker, 20 August 1965, New York, USA. The kingpin of Boogie Down Productions and a genuine hip-hop pioneer, KRS-1's standing is reflected not only in terms of his music, but also his lecture tours of the US, appearing at Yale, Harvard, and countless other institutions to the dismay of some members of those establishments. His list of achievements is hardly limited to this, however. He has been given the keys to Kansas City, Philadelphia and Compton, California. He was nominated for the NACA 1992 Harry Chapman Humanitarian Award, and holds the Reebok Humanitarian Award, and three Ampex Golden Reel Awards. He inaugurated the Stop The Violence Movement, and recorded 'Self-Destruction', which raised over $600,000 for the National Urban League, and the human awareness single, 'Heal Yourself'. He has collaborated with R.E.M. (rapping on 'Radio Song', Michael Stipe returning the favour by assisting on the HEAL project), Sly And Robbie, Shelley Thunder, Shabba Ranks, Ziggy Marley, Billy Bragg, the Neville Brothers, Kool Moe Dee, Chuck D of Public Enemy and Tim Dog, among many others, and taken part in several important benefit shows for Nelson Mandela, Earth Day etc., as well as attending rallies with Jesse Jackson. Following the death of his erstwhile partner, Scott La Rock (whose violent exit played a significant role in KRS-1's anti-violence tracts), he has been joined on recent recordings by DJ Premier and Kid Capri. His post-BDP work combines hints of ragga with strong, bass driven funk and beatbox samples. He remains one of the philosophically more enlightened rappers: in particular fighting against the use of the terms 'ho' and 'bitch' when discussing women. His first album to be released outside of the Boogie Down Productions banner was *Return Of Da Boom Bap*, though many references to his past remained. 'KRS-One Attacks', for instance, looped part of the *Criminal Minded* title-track, and 'P Is Still Free' updated his 1986 anti-crack opus, 'P Is Free'. KRS-1 remained as arrogant as they come: 'I'm not a rapper. I am rap. I am the embodiment of what a lot of MCs are trying to be and do. I'm not doing hip-hop, I am hip-hop'. The early 90s also saw some words and actions that would seem to contradict earlier statements, notably his physical attack on Prince Be of PM Dawn. 'The way I stop the violence is with a baseball bat and beat the shit out of you . . . If negativity comes with a .22, positivity comes with a .45. If negativity comes with .45, positivity comes with an Uzi: The light has got to be stronger than darkness'. An adequate rebuttal, but apparently all PM Dawn had done to diss KRS-1 was to suggest in a copy of *Details* magazine that: 'KRS-1 wants to be a teacher, but a teacher of what?'. In retaliation KRS-1 and his posse invaded the stage during the following night's PM Dawn gig at the Sound Factory Club in New York, throwing Prince Be offstage and commandeering the microphone for his own set. The whole event was filmed live by *Yo! MTV Raps*. Though he later apologised publicly, in private KRS-1 was telling the world that he was tired of MCs and hip-hop crews disrespecting him. That he felt it necessary so piously to protect it is the only real blemish on his reputation.

● ALBUMS: *HEAL: Civilization Versus Technology* various artists (Elektra 1991)★★★, *Return Of Da Boom Bap* (Jive 1993)★★★, *KRS-One* (Jive 1995)★★★, *I Got Next* (Jive 1997)★★.

KRUSH

Commercial house artists from Sheffield who achieved a big breakthrough hit with 'House Arrest', which rose to UK number 3 in 1988, featuring the vocals of later Definition Of Sound member Kevwon (Kevin Clark). The band comprises Mark Gamble and Cassius Campbell, who lace their standard house/disco rhythms with a quicksilver backbeat that was actually less obtrusive than many similar outfits. The unobscured vocals belonged to Ruth Joy, the veteran house diva. The follow-up material was less effective largely because it lacked the hypnotic, catchy tone of 'House Arrest'. Following record company problems Gamble went on to work with Rhythmatic. The Krush name was revived in 1992 with a cover of Rockers Revenge's 'Walking On Sunshine', by which time they had moved from Fon to Network records.

KURIOUS

b. Jorge Antonio Alvarez, *c.*1969. Of Puerto Rican descent, Kurious broke big in late 1992 with the underground smash, 'Walk Like A Duck'. Based in uptown Manhattan (as described in the single, 'Uptown Shit'), Jorge and his Constipated Monkey crew won their reputation as talented freestylers, Jorge himself earning the title 'Freestyle King'. Despite the kudos his name inspired in the early 90s, by 1994 he was making a staunch bid to crossover with the radio-friendly 'I'm Kurious', originally written as long ago as 1991. His debut album, too, was three years in the making, eventually emerging as the debut platter on Prime Minister Pete Nice's Hoppoh Records. It was titled *Constipated Monkey* because of protracted negotiations between Hoppoh and Def Jam, who he had originally signed a contract with. He had worked as a messenger for Def Jam Records in 1988, before Russell Simmons offerred him a contract. However, after he rose to prominence because of

his open mic dexterity, he decided to honour a verbal arrangment with Nice instead. His debut album was produced in conjunction with the Stimulated Dummies and the Beatnuts. It featured excellent, thoughtful rhymes of the ilk of 'Spell It With J (Yes, Yes Jorge): 'Malt liquor got me trapped so my rap is controversial, Might drink the brew but I won't do the commercial'. It revealed the depth of the education his single parent mother had encouraged him to pursue at Farleigh Dickinson University.

● ALBUMS: *A Constipated Monkey* (Hoppoh 1994)★★★.

KWAMÉ

b. Kwamé Holland, East Elmhurst, Queens, New York, USA. Mild-mannered rapper whose relatively sunny disposition enshrines his recording profile. Something of a welcome change to the OG's and their attendant posturing, he is supported on stage and record by his backing band A New Beginning, variously credited in the titles of his first three releases. Growing up in and around the New York jazz set, he mingled happily with musicians of the order of Stevie Wonder and Lionel Hampton, the latter giving Kwamé his first set of drums. His debut album was produced by Hurby Luv Bug Azor, while the second was something of a 'concept' affair. This and his third set, *Nastee*, brought a string of hit singles in 'Only You', 'The Rhythm', 'The Man We All Know And Love', 'One Of The Big Boys', 'Nastee' and 'Sweet Thing'. He moved to Wrap/Ichiban in 1994 for *Incognito*, recorded alongside partners DJ Tat Money and A-Sharp in Atlanta, Georgia. 'This record is growth', he eulogised, 'It's my reincarnation, and I return Incognito'.

● ALBUMS: *The Boy Genius* (Atlantic 1989)★★★, *A Day In The Life - A Pokadelic Adventure* (Atlantic 1990)★★★, *Nastee* (Atlantic 1991)★★, *Incognito* (Wrap/Ichiban 1993)★★★.

KWS

This dance team from Nottingham, who originally signed to Network Records as B-Line, featured Chris King and Winnie Williams with a series of guest vocalists. They had a big commercial hit with the KC And The Sunshine Band cover version, 'Please Don't Go', following the success in Europe of a dance version by Double You? (on ZYX Records). KWS's version, which featured Delroy Joseph on vocals and supposedly took only a couple of hours to complete, stayed at number 1 for five weeks. The follow-up, 'Rock Your Baby', was a another KC composition and once again it jumped in front of a proposed ZYX label release, a Baby Roots version of the same track. Following the release of the album *Please Don't Go (The Album)*, the members of KWS left Network in 1994 to form X-Clusive.

● ALBUMS: *Please Don't Go (The Album)* (Network 1992)★★.

KYPER

b. Randall Kyper, Baton Rouge, Louisiana, USA. This rapper achieved a one-off hit single in 1990 when his appealing 'Tic-Tac-Toe' peaked at number 14 in the *Billboard* charts. His debut album was also titled after that track, but disappointed many who had expected some variation on the single's formula. The impetus behind Kyper disappeared and Atlantic Records did not renew his contract.

● ALBUMS: *Tic-Tac-Toe* (Atlantic 1990)★★.

L'TRIMM

Cutesy rappers whose 'Grab It!' was a literal answer to Salt 'N' Pepa's 'Push It'. As the pun might suggest, their records were dominated by a locker-room approach to sexuality, and anatomical revelry of the old school. The duo are Tigra (b. 1970, New York, USA) and Bunny D. (b. Chicago, Illinois, USA).

● ALBUMS: *Grab It!* (Time X/Atlantic 1988)★★★, *Drop That Bottom* (Atlantic 1989)★★, *Groovy* (Atlantic 1991)★★.

L.A. MIX

Despite the title, this is a British concern, L.A. standing for frontman Les Adams, a long-term disco mixer and club DJ, and his production partner and wife, Emma Freilich. Adams has earned a weighty crust in the late 80s/early 90s releasing pop-house singles including 'Check This Out' (UK number 6) and 'Get Loose', a hit after the team had been diagnosed by Stock, Aitken And Waterman as being 'unlikely to score another hit'. They were not without their detractors but, as Adams insisted: 'We never said we set out to break new ground or deliver a message. We just want to make dance records that people will enjoy and buy'. He had already taken Maurice Joshua's 'This Is Acid' to the top of the US club charts in 1988. However, chart placings for subsequent singles, 'Love Together', 'Coming Back For More', 'Mysteries', etc., were comparatively poor. His 1991 album for A&M was a familiar blend of old school British soul dance, including Juliet Roberts on 'All Mine' and Beverley Brown on 'Mysteries Of Love'. Another of his sometime vocalists, Jazzie P, would embark on a solo career for the same record label. Adams continued to concentrate on production work, including 'Baby Love' for Dannii Minogue.

● ALBUMS: *On The Side* (A&M 1989)★★★, *Coming Back For More* (A&M 1991)★★.

LA BOUCHE

A duo of D. Lane McCray Jnr. and Melanie Thompson, German pop/dance act La Bouche achieved instant success when their debut single, 'Sweet Dreams', became a European bestseller and topped the German charts, selling over half a million copies in the process. An accompanying album of the same title was also released in 1995, and rose to number 5 in the German charts. A second single, 'Fallin' In Love', was then released in the USA in an attempt to breach international markets. The group is produced by Uli Brenner and Amir Saraf, who have also enjoyed considerable success and international acclaim as the creative force behind Le Click.
● ALBUMS: *Sweet Dreams* (Hansa 1995)★★★★, *S.O.S.* (RCA 1998)★★★.

LADY B

Lady B's debut single was originally released in the mid-80s on the Tec label, based in Philadelphia, USA. Afterwards it was picked up by Sugarhill, who re-packaged it in a slightly re-recorded version. Entitled 'To The Beat Y'All', it told of Jill (from the nursery rhyme scenario of Jack and Jill fame) falling pregnant, rather than just down the hill, and advising her of her stupidity in not using contraception. Fellow Sugarhill act Sequence would come back at her with the answer record 'Simon Says', extending the onus of responsibility to the man.

LADY OF RAGE

Coming to prominence via her engaging support/crowd-warmer spot on tours with Snoop Doggy Dogg and mentor Dr. Dre, the Lady Of Rage also part-times as hairdresser to the stars of the Dogg Pound. She was living in New York when Dre called her at her job at Chung King Studios, where she was the receptionist. He had heard her guesting on the LA Posse album, having also performed with Chubb Rock and Branford Marsalis. She did not believe it was Dre until he sent her an air ticket in the post in 1990. Part of the Dogg Pound alongside luminaries like Snoop Doggy Dogg, and signed to Dre's Death Row Records, her debut release was the ruffhouse 'Afro Puffs' cut, also featured on the basketball movie, *Above The Rim*.
● ALBUMS: *Necessary Roughness* (Death Row 1997)★★★.

LAMB

A Manchester, Lancashire, England-based duo of Louise Rhodes (songwriting, vocals) and Andrew Barlow (production), Lamb were signed to Fontana Records in 1995 before A&R manager Richard O'Donovan had heard any proper demo recordings. Instead he was impressed by Rhodes' vision and personality, and the four songs they played him at a hastily arranged meeting in Manchester convinced him of their star qualities. The group were formed in 1994 shortly after Barlow's return from a three and a half year spell attending high school in Philadelphia. He had come back to attend a sound engineering course, eventually becoming in-house remixer for the So What management stable. He met Rhodes, the daughter of a folk singer, through a mutual friend. They set about working on songs together almost immediately. Their debut for Fontana, 'Cotton Wool', proved popular on the underground club scene with its dextrous employment of jazz and drum 'n' bass textures. It was followed by the similarly impressive 'Gold'. Remixers involved in these two singles included Fila Brazilia, Mr Scruff and Autechre. Their own remix work includes collaborations with UK indie band Space.
● ALBUMS: *Lamb* (Mercury 1996)★★★.

LAQUAN

b. c.1975, Los Angeles, California, USA. Rapper whose debut set was surprisingly mature, especially in its grasp of social issues, considering he was barely 16 when he recorded it. Though the harmonies were gentle, Laquan's words were not, accusing President Bush of 'Living large while others starve', among other charges. His debut album featured a live band and backing singers, orchestrated by Bell Biv Devoe studio crew Richard Wolf and Bret Mazur, adding a soulful sheen to proceedings.
● ALBUMS: *Notes Of A Native Son* (4th & Broadway 1990)★★★.

LARKIN, KENNY

b. c.1968, USA. A popular DJ through his European travels, Larkin began his musical career in 1989 after having served two years in the US Airforce. Returning back home to his native Detroit, he discovered the underground techno scene by attending the Magic Institute and Shelter clubs. He subsequently met Plus 8 proprietors Richie Hawtin and John Aquiviva, for whose label he recorded his debut 12-inch, 'We Shall Overcome', in 1990. A year later he returned with the *Integration* EP. He formed his own label, Art Of Dance, in June 1992, going on to record 'War Of The Worlds', as Dark Comedy, on Transmat/Art Of Dance in the USA, and on Belgium label Buzz Records in Europe. He also provided the latter with the *Serena* EP, under the guise of Yennek, and the *Vanguard* EP, as Pod.

LAST POETS

Coming out of the poverty-stricken ghetto of Harlem, New York, in the mid-60s, there are many who claim the Last Poets to be the first hip-hop group proper. Comprising Suliaman El Hadi, Alafia Pudim, Nilijah, Umar Bin Hassan (aka Omar Ben Hassan - as with other personnel name alterations occurred frequently) and Abio Dun Oyewole, the Last Poets formed on 19 May 1968 (Malcolm X's birthday). Hassan was not actually an original member, joining the band after seeing them perform on campus and insisting on membership. Together, the Last Poets recorded powerful protest gems like 'Niggas Are Scared Of Revolution' and 'White Man's Got A God Complex'. Their legacy, that of the innovative use of rap/talk over musical backing, has born obvious fruit in subsequent generations of hip-hop acts. Oyewole left after their debut album. They re-formed in 1984, with two 12-inch singles, 'Super Horror Show' and 'Long Enough', although the group was still split into two separate camps. Hassan released a solo LP featuring Bootsy Collins, Buddy Miles and others, after a period of seclusion, and drug and family problems. He also kept company with rap stars like Arrested Development and Flavor Flav, and starred in John Singleton's *Poetic Justice* film. While not bitter about failing to reap the financial rewards that subsequent rappers have done, Hassan remained philosophical: 'As far as I'm concerned we made a market, for those young boys to have their careers . . . I understand that some brothers are still trying to find their manhood. But it ain't about drive-by shootings. That's madness. Self-destruction. Real gangsters don't go around shooting everybody'. Another former Last Poet, Jalal Nuridin, who released an album alongside Kool And The Gang and Eric Gale under the title Lightnin' Rod, went on to become mentor to UK acid jazzers Galliano. Incidentally, this is a different Last Poets to the one comprising David Nelson, Felipe, Luciano and Gylan Kain who titled themselves the

Original Last Poets and recorded an album for Juggernaut in 1971.

● ALBUMS: *The Last Poets* (Douglas 1970)★★★, *This Is Madness* (Douglas 1971)★★★, *Oh My People* (Celluloid 1985)★★★, *Freedom Express* (Acid Jazz 1989)★★★, *Scattarap/Home* (Bond Age 1994)★★★, *Holy Terror* (Ryko 1995)★★★. Solo: Umar Bin Hassan *Be Bop Or Be Dead* (Axiom 1993)★★★. Jalal Nuridin As Lightnin' Rod *Hustlers Convention* (Douglas 1973)★★★. Oyewole *25 Years* (Rykodisk 1995)★★★.

● COMPILATIONS: *Right On!* (Collectables 1986)★★★.

LATIN ALLIANCE

A consortium of Latin and Hispanic hip-hop artists formed by Kid Frost in October 1989, which included other luminaries such as Mellow Man Ace and A.L.T. Topics such as slavery in Puerto Rico and other ethno-centric concerns such as exploitation and alienation dominated. The most effective track was 'Latinos Unidos', which celebrated the cultural and social identity of the race. It produced one Top 60 single, 'Low Rider (On The Boulevard)'.

● ALBUMS: *The Latin Alliance* (Virgin 1991)★★★.

LATOUR

b. William LaTour, Chicago, Illinois, USA. House producer made famous by his US crossover success, 'People Are Still Having Sex'. Unfortunately, he was never able to follow this up successfully, despite further wacky song titles such as 'Allen's Got A New Hi-Fi'. He was described as 'a poor man's Baby Ford, without the stylings or passion for the music'.

● ALBUMS: *Latour* (Smash 1991)★★★.

LAUGHING BUDDHA

(see Cosmosis)

LAVELLE, JAMES

(see Mo' Wax Records)

LAYTON, LINDA

b. Belinda Kimberley Layton, 7 December 1970, Chiswick, London, England. Renowned for her vocal contribution to Beats International's 'Dub Be Good To Me', Layton's mother was a professional dancer, responsible for choreographing West End productions of *The King And I* and *The Sound Of Music*. Layton's solo album was a disappointment, with a limp cover of Janet Kay's 'Silly

Game' notwithstanding. An MOR club sound was engaged that did little to bolster the flimsy song structures, even though Norman Cook from her old band and Jolly Harris Jolly were still on hand as part of the backroom set-up.

● ALBUMS: *Pressure* (Arista 1991)★★★.

LAZY, DOUG

More widely known for his production work, Lazy's own recorded output betrays not only a love of hip-hop energy, but also an eye for house music's pulsing rhythms. As a producer he is one of the more credible exponents of the hip house movement, while his solo hits include 'Let It Roll' and 'Let The Rhythm Pump', the latter based on Funkadelic's 'One Nation Under A Groove'. He also appeared on Raze's 1991 single, 'Bass Power'.

● ALBUMS: *Doug Lazy Gettin' Crazy* (Atlantic 1990)★★★.

LEADERS OF THE NEW SCHOOL

Uniondale, New York-based hip-hop troupe, combining aggressive vocals with loping bass beats, who, like many of the newer rap artists of the 90s, deployed lyrics which extolled the joys of marijuana. However, they retained an experimental edge - particularly in their complex rhythmic structures and 'mysticism'. Fronted by the giant Busta Rhymes (b. 1972, Brooklyn, New York, USA), an impressive rapper who served a long apprenticeship freestyling before cutting his first record, and backed by Charlie 'The Freestyle Wizard' Brown, Dinco 'The Rhyme Scientist' D and Milo In De Dance (aka The Cut Monitor), the Leaders concerned themselves not only with the current problems facing black culture in general and hip-hop in particular, but also its immediate past: 'Leaders Of The New School learnt from the old school and groups like the Cold Crush Brothers. We then developed our own unique style which a lot of people have started to copy'. It was certainly true that the band had etched a real impression with their debut, with three tracks produced by Eric Sadler of the Bomb Squad. The temptation to make their second set a facsimile of the winning formula was avoided, subtitling the album 'The Inner Mind's Eye - The Endless Dispute With Reality'. The group broke up in 1994, with Rhymes going on to a successful solo career.

● ALBUMS: *A Future Without A Past* (Elektra 1991)★★★, *T.I.M.E.* (Elektra 1993)★★★.

LEBLANC, KEITH

LeBlanc was previously an anonymous drummer and keyboard player as part of the Sugarhill Gang's house band in New Jersey, New York, USA, but cut himself a slice of the action in 1983 when he recorded the innovative Malcolm X anthem, 'No Sell Out', for Tommy Boy Records. This fused sections of the black leader's speeches with a cut-up dance groove. It led to disputes between Tommy Boy and Sugarhill Records over ownership of the speeches (LeBlanc had defected when he learned that Sugarhill were not going to pay any royalties to the Malcolm X estate), while LeBlanc was also questioned on his part in the process - he was, after all, white. However, the record was sanctioned by Betty Shabazz, Malcolm X's widow, and the song played no small part in pushing the name of the black leader back into the political firmament. It was also released a year later, intended as a tribute to the UK's striking miners.

By 1986 LeBlanc had assembled an album, *Major Malfunction*, which included contributions from his old and future sparring partners Doug Wimbush and Skip McDonald. They too had been part of Sugarhill's house band, and would go on to join LeBlanc as Tackhead took shape. They were also present for LeBlanc's second 'solo' album, *Stranger Than Fiction*, which again spanned boundless experimentation and styles, but maintained a strong political edge. By 1991 Leblanc had joined with Tim Simenon (Bomb The Bass) in a new project, entitled Interference (singles included 'Global Game').

● ALBUMS: *Major Malfunction* (World 1986)★★★, *Stranger Than Fiction* (Nettwerk/Enigma 1989)★★★, *Time Traveller* (Blanc 1992)★★.

LEFTFIELD

Leftfield originally comprised just Neil Barnes, formerly of Elephant Stampede and, bizarrely, the London School Of Samba. He released a solo track, 'Not Forgotten', on Outer Rhythm, before Leftfield were expanded to a duo with the addition of former A Man Called Adam contributor Paul Daley. Barnes first met him through a poetry group who wanted live backing. However, as 'Not Forgotten', a deeply resonant song, broke big, disputes with Outer Rhythm followed. Unable to record due to contractual restraints, they embarked instead on a career as remixers to the

stars. This first batch included React 2 Rhythm, Ultra Nate and Inner City. They were profligate in order to keep the Leftfield name prominent in the absence of their own brand material. Later remixes for David Bowie, Renegade Soundwave and Yothu Yindi would follow, but by now the duo had already established their Hard Hands imprint. This debuted with the reggae-tinted 'Release The Pressure' (featuring Earl Sixteen), then the more trance-based 'Song Of Life', which gave them a minor chart success in 1992. They subsequently teamed up with John Lydon (Sex Pistols/PiL) for what Q magazine described as the unofficial single of 1993, 'Open Up'. Remixed in turn by Andy Weatherall and the Dust Brothers, it was an enormous cross-party success - especially for Barnes, whose primary musical influence had always been PiL. It might have risen higher in the charts had it not been pulled from ITV's *The Chart Show* at the last minute because of the line 'Burn Hollywood, burn', as parts of Los Angeles were by coincidence affected by fire. They also produced a soundtrack for the film *Shallow Grave*, and recorded as Herbal Infusion ('The Hunter'), alongside Zoom Records boss Dave Wesson. Gaining favour with a mainstream audience, 1995's *Leftism* paved the way for the later crossover success of the Chemical Brothers and the Prodigy.
● ALBUMS: *Backlog* (Outer Rhythm 1992)★★★, *Leftism* (Hard Hands/Columbia 1995)★★★★.

LEINER, ROBERT

b. c.1966, Gothenburg, Sweden. One of the first techno artists actually to appear, in soft focus, on his album sleeves, robbing the genre of its usual anonymity, Leiner was formerly the in-house engineer for the Belgian-based R&S Label. He had relocated to Ghent after establishing himself as a DJ in Gothenburg. His own output reflects his prolific nature: 'I have ideas all the time, it never ends. I just wish I could put something into my head and record direct from there'. He started making music at the age of 14, and keeps a stock of old tapes, sounds or sequences to which he constantly returns to extract samples. Hence, his second album was titled *Visions Of The Past*, as it included snapshots from several eras of his life. His first dancefloor manoeuvres were conducted under the name the Source, and included two double-pack 12-inches, 'Organised Noise' and 'Source Experience'. Both showcased Leiner's trippy, engaging work, redolent in tribal, spacey

rhythms, which have also characterized his work under his own name.
● ALBUMS: *Organised Noise* (R&S 1993)★★★, *Visions Of The Past* (Apollo 1994)★★★.

LESHAUN

b. c.1973. US female rapper whose debut album was an acclaimed, thoughtful variant on the gangsta rap trip. LeShaun had become a single mother at the age of 18, experiences recalled in tracks like 'Young Girlz', and brought maternal widom to bear on a number of her better cuts. The influence of Queen Latifah, her stated idol, was undeniably strong. She also collaborated on the Lords Of The Underground cut, 'Flow On'.
● ALBUMS: *Ain't No Shame In My Game* (Tommy Boy 1993)★★★.

LEWIS, DARLENE

Garage diva from the USA in the early 90s whose original 'Let The Music (Lift You Up)', licensed in England through the London-based duo Network, started a strange and influential chain of events in dance music. Manchester band Loveland (affiliated to the Eastern Bloc record shop/label) released their own version of the record without obtaining sample clearance. A major war of legal attrition looked sure to ensue, until both parties agreed to release a joint version, performing together on *Top Of The Pops*. The case was hailed in turn as a perfect example of inter-artist co-operation and goodwill. Lewis herself is a former music student who was spotted as a waitress 'humming' by producer Hassan Watkins. Asking her to put words to the tune, a few minutes later she received a standing ovation from the clients of the restaurant. Not surprising, perhaps, as she was already engaged in the process of winning more than 40 awards for her opera singing. Although she also loves country, rock and opera, she has an instinct for club music that was honed in the Chicago house party scene. Following the success of 'Let The Music (Lift You Up)', she was signed to Kevin Saunderson's KMS Records.

LFO

Among the most unrelenting and popular exponents of hard techno, LFO's output on Warp Records represents everything an outsider might fear about the music: harsh, crashing, thumping 'bleep' music. When forced to play their debut single, 'LFO', on Radio 1, DJ Steve Wright described it as the worst record in the world. Gez

Varley and Mark Bell are the mainstays, though extra keyboard players Simon Hartley and Richie Brook were drafted in for occasional live outings. The pair met at college in Leeds, where they discovered mutual interests in music and technology, as well as partying in the city's clubs, where Nightmares On Wax worked. The duo gave the DJs a demo of a track they had recorded on a Casio SKI keyboard called 'LFO', and it proved a success in the Leeds clubland. Among the audience were the fledgling Warp team, who decided to release 'LFO' and were rewarded when it became a Top 20 hit in the summer of 1990. Along with NOW and the Forgemasters, LFO helped to pioneer the sound that became known as 'bleep'. Almost a year later, the single 'We Are Back' heralded their first album, *Frequencies* (Warp 1992), and 'What Is House' followed in early 1992. Their next album, *Advance*, did not arrive until the beginning of 1996, with only 'Tied Up' in November 1994 in between. However, during this time the duo had remixed and collaborated with a number of other artists, notably Kraftwerk (for their *Elektrik Music* recordings), Afrika Bambaataa, the Yello Magic Orchestra and the Art Of Noise. Bell also teamed up with Simon Hartley of Wild Planet, releasing the acid techno EP *I'm For Real* under the name Feedback. Since *Advance*, the group have split up to concentrate on individual projects, with Bell retaining the name and a contract with Warp. In 1997 he was involved in the production of Björk's album, *Homogenic*, and later toured with her around Europe. He also remixed tracks by Radiohead, Gus Gus and Sabres Of Paradise, among others.
● ALBUMS: *Frequencies* (Warp 1991)★★★★, *Advance* (Warp 1996)★★★.

LIBERTY GROOVES

Notable UK record label/shop run in Tooting, south London by Johnny F, a long time collector of hip-hop music, which opened in May 1992. Liberty Grooves began by releasing breakbeat albums and material from UK artists including the Gutter Snypes and Sniper, and also signed a licensing deal with American label Dolo. The first fruits of this marriage have been two acclaimed albums, *Freestyle Frenzy 1* and *2*, which showcased artists such as Nas, Large Professor, Q-Tip (A Tribe Called Quest), Wu Tang Clan, freestyling on DJ Stretch Armstrong's New York radio show.
● ALBUMS: *Freestyle Frenzy 1 & 2* (Liberty Grooves/Dolo 1993/94)★★★★.

LIEB, OLIVER

b. *c.*1970, Frankfurt, West Germany. A well-known and highly regarded member of Sven Vath's Eye Q/Harthouse stable and Omen Club, Lieb's most popular work thus far came out under the Spicelab moniker, which varied between hard house, acid and trance cuts. Contrastingly, he utilized the name Mirage for the more spacey, transcendental theme of 'Airborn'. Other *noms de plume* employed include Ambush, whose debut album was an enchanting collection of 'world techno' tracks, dominated by a thorough exploration of drums and rhythm: 'I programmed it in the way that I would lay the drums, the way I would feel them, and then I took vocals from CDs and old records'. Lieb also works as Superspy, Infinite Aura, LSG, Psilocybin and Azid Force. He is half of Paragliders with Torsten Stenzl ('Paragliders (The Remixes)'), and has remixed for Sven Vath, Vapourspace and Messiah among others. Together with Dr Atmo he recorded *Music For Films*, for Peter Namlook's Fax label, an alternative score to Philip Glass's ambient documentary *Koyaanisquatsi*.
● ALBUMS: as Ambush *The Ambush* (Harthouse 1994)★★★★, with Dr Atmo *Music For Films* (Fax 1994)★★★.

LIEBRAND, BEN

b. Netherlands. A well-known Dutch house remixer (though he claims his work is more geared to genuine cover versions because of the re-recording process he utilizes), Liebrand recorded in his own right in the 90s with 'Eve Of The War' and 'Black Belly'. His remixes include high-profile work for Phil Collins and Hot Chocolate. Within a more conventional dance format he also produced the Crystal Palace featuring CP's 'Son Of Godzilla'. His solo album featured British vocalist Carol Kenyon (of Heaven 17's 'Temptation' fame) and rapper Toni Scott. 'I've always enjoyed being a bit in the background', he maintained. His chart successes include Jeff Lynne's 'Eve Of The War', Bill Withers' 'Lovely Day', Phil Collins' 'In The Air Tonight', Vangelis's 'Puls(t)ar' and the Ram Jam Band's 'Black Berry'. All were created originally for his own radio show on Radio Veronica in Holland.

LIFERS GROUP

A rap troupe culled from the bowels of the US criminal underworld, namely Rahway State Penitentiary in East Jersey. Put together by the thinking of inmate 660604 (Maxwell Melvins), this was an intriguing project that gathered together the incarcerated 'lifers' to discourage those who still had their freedom from living the gangsta rap lifestyle to the full. The nightmare vision of prison life was revealed in intimate, gory detail on tracks like 'The Real Deal', while the cover rammed home the message with pictures of the criminals and the cells they were forced to occupy. The set was recorded in three months after the Disney-funded Hollywood Basic Records, ever sensitive to a good cause, had heard of the scheme.
● ALBUMS: *Belly Of The Beast* (Hollywood Basic 1991)★★.

LIL' KIM

b. Brooklyn, New York, USA. Having survived some time on the streets as a teenager, Lil' Kim was aided by Biggie Smalls (Notorious B.I.G.) who helped her team up with the New York rap collective Junior MAFIA. A strong response to her contributions to their 1995 debut single, 'Player's Anthem', and the ensuing *Conspiracy*, earned her comparisons with MC Lyte for her adept microphone skills. She then worked on albums by artists including Skin Deep and Total, before launching her own career in 1996 with *Hard Core*. This sexually explicit hardcore rap album came as something of a shock in the male-dominated world of hip-hop, but an aggressive marketing campaign and strong reviews helped *Hard Core* reach number 11 in the *Billboard* charts. The album featured an array of star producers, including Sean 'Puffy' Combs, with whom Lil' Kim dueted on the number 1 rap single 'No Time'.
● ALBUMS: *Hard Core* (Undeas/Big Beat 1996)★★★.

LIL' LOUIS

b. Louis Sims. Lil' Louis is the son of Bobby Sims, one of Chicago's premier blues guitarists who has played with B.B. King and Bobby 'Blue' Bland. The most notable moment in his son's career came with 'French Kiss' in 1989, peaking at number 2 in the UK charts, reportedly having been licensed from Diamond Records to ffrr for a figure in the region of £30,000. It was banned by the BBC because of its female 'vocal' (heavy breathing) being too near the knuckle. The censorship was not merely a British invention, however. New York DJ Frankie Bones was sacked for playing it at his club night in breach of prior warnings. Other hits in the piano-house mould followed, notably 'I Called U But You Weren't There'. Again this was no ephemeral dance tune, concerning instead a disastrous relationship with an ex-girlfriend that became so out of hand he was forced to take out a restraining order. His debut album was a surprisingly pleasing and varied selection, with tracks spanning soul and jazz (and including contributions from his father). Louis was responsible for singing, producing and much of the instrumentation. He returned after a long break in 1992 with 'The Club Lonely' and 'Saved My Life', having relocated from Chicago to New York, and taken time out to update his keyboard skills and reacquaint himself with the jazz records of his youth. Another long break preceded 1997's R&B-orientated 'Clap Your Hands' single.
● ALBUMS: *From The Mind Of Lil' Louis* (London 1989)★★★, *Journey With The Lonely* (London 1992)★★★.

LIMBO RECORDS

Emergent record label based in Bath Street, Glasgow, Scotland. Since the release of Havanna's 'Schtoom' in August 1992 Limbo has built an enviable profile as a home to underground house. The label was inaugurated by Billy Kiltie (b. *c*.1973) and Davey Mackenzie through the auspices of their 23rd Precinct shop. Both had been involved in DJing and running clubs in the area over several years. Originally titled 23rd Precinct, the label was launched in early 1992, at which point dozens of demo tapes flooded in through the doors (not least owing to the fact that a dance newsletter was distributed to Scotland from the premises). One was passed to Kiltie by local act Q-Tex, and their *Equator* EP consequently became the first release. By the time of Q-Tex's second, *Natural High* EP, they had national distribution through Revolver. Soon Limbo emerged, with most of the tracks released in its short history centring on funky, accessible house with distinctive breakbeats. Their success is founded, according to the label's proprietors, on the fact that every record features the involvement of DJs: so that each is geared to ensuring a strong club reaction. Other staples in its schedule have included Gipsy ('I Trance You'), Mukkaa, Deep

Piece (Kiltie himself with releases like 'Bup, Bup, Birri, Birri' and 'Torwart', in association with Stuart Crichton) and Sublime ('Sublime'). They have also added the experimental Out On A Limb subsidiary for material such as Space Buggy's eponymous debut (a side project from one of the Havanna team).

● ALBUMS: Various: *House Of Limbo Vol. 1 & 2* (Limbo 1993/94)★★★★.

LIMERICK, ALISON

b. *c.*1959, London, England. The first part of Limerick's entertainment career was spent on roller skates in the stage production of *Starlight Express* in London's West End. Her recording work, predictably, kicked off with sumptuous garage tunes, notably 'Where Love Lives (Come On In)', which showcased a simplistic but well executed musical approach, and was voted dance record of 1991 by *Billboard* magazine. This despite the fact that it was never released in the USA. Alongside fellow Top 20 singles 'Make It On My Own' (co-written and produced by Steve Anderson of Brothers In Rhythm, and featuring Limerick's boyfriend jazzman Roger Beaujolais) and 'Come Back (For Real Love)', it was housed on an impressive debut album. The presence of David Morales and Frankie Knuckles on her second album, *With A Twist*, added further spice to the formula.

● ALBUMS: *And Still I Rise* (Arista 1992)★★★, *With A Twist* (Arista 1994)★★★.

LIN QUE

Previously known as Isis, Lin Que is a tough-talking New York rapper who rose to fame as part of Blackwatch, the militant consciousness movement that also spawned X-Clan. She was joined on several tracks of her debut album by Professor X of the former outfit, who offered priceless interjections of a religious/moral nature. However, not everyone found the production values to be up to scratch, and she became vulnerable to the 'Blackwatch hype' backlash that has also affected the career of X-Clan. She has since joined MC Lyte's Duke The Moon management where she works in an A&R capacity.

● ALBUMS: *Rebel Soul* (Island 1990)★★★.

LIONROCK

Lionrock is one of the many vehicles used by Manchester disc jockey/remixer/artist Justin Robertson (b. *c.*1968, England). Robertson had risen to prominence in 1990 by launching the Spice club session, a meeting place for like-minds such as the Chemical Brothers (at that time the Dust Brothers). Alongside Andy Weatherall, Robertson subsequently became among the most prominent of a new wave of DJs, with his sets at Manchester's Heavenly club making him well known within the dance community. This impression was confirmed by remixing credits for Björk, New Order, the Shamen, Sugarcubes, Inspiral Carpets, Stereo MC's, Erasure and many others. Lionrock, a name synonymous with uplifting house music and originally featuring keyboard player Mark Stagg, was formed in 1992 for the release of a self-titled 12-inch single on Robertson's own MERC Records. The following year's 'Packet Of Peace' included a rap from MC Buzz B and saw the group transfer to DeConstruction Records. It entered the UK charts and became a staple of house clubs throughout the UK. 'Carnival', which sampled from the MC5, again secured several Single Of The Week awards, from both dance magazines and more mainstream publications. 'Tripwire' was released in 1994 and again reached the UK Top 40. Robertson described the contents of Lionrock's 1996 debut album as 'Coxsone Dodd meets Ennio Morricone', a statement that indicated that earlier experiments with reggae and dub were continuing. MC Buzz B again guested, with samples of dialogue taken from old Sherlock Holmes films. Lionrock's line-up now included Roger Lyons (keyboards, electronics), Paddy (bass), Mandy Whigby (keyboards) and Buzz B (vocals) as the album was promoted with a full-scale national tour. Release of the follow-up was delayed, allowing Robertson the opportunity to record new tracks and rework the album, which was finally released in early 1998. *City Delirious* eschewed the guitar riffing of the debut to return to Robertson's dance roots on tracks such as 'Push Button Cocktail' and 'Best Foot Forward'.

● ALBUMS: *An Instinct For Detection* (DeConstruction 1996)★★★★, *City Delirious* (DeConstruction 1998)★★★★.

LIQUID

This group originally comprised Eamon Downes and Shane Honegan. Downes' early influences included such dub maestros as Barrington Levy and Scientist. In 1992 they became one of the first progressive house acts to reach the Top 20 with 'Sweet Harmony', which was recorded in reaction to the 'louder faster' sounds of hardcore. It cost only £200 to record, yet saw them grace UK television's *Top Of The Pops* stage. After Honegan had left, Downes re-emerged in 1993 with the *Time To Get Up* EP on XL Records. He maintains that he calls himself Liquid because he 'likes the odd drink'.

LIROY

b. Kielce, Poland. Proof of the increasing globalization of rap and hip-hop culture, Liroy is Poland's most prominent rapper. According to his self-aggrandizing record company biography, his youth was spent in a constant maelstrom of drunkenness, fights and reform schools, claims made to substantiate his billing as a gangsta rapper comparable with his heroes Ice-T and LL Cool J. He had originally joined several rock bands in the mid-80s before becoming a local DJ, making his live debut as a rapper in the late 80s. In 1991 he moved to France and founded Leeroy And The Western Posse with French and English friends, the group performing widely on the burgeoning French hip-hop scene. After his return to Poland he secured a contract with BMG Ariola in 1994, leading to the release of the mini-album *Scyzoryk* (literally 'pocketknife') in 1995. The brutal themes included street violence and hardcore sex, with backing rhythms drawn from rock, pop and jazz.
● ALBUMS: *Scyzoryk* mini-album (BMG Ariola 1995)★★★.

LITTLE LOUIE VEGA

A New York-based DJ, Vega's career began at high school at the age of 18, after watching his friends spin records. He played high school parties before eventually establishing his own label. He went on to DJ at the Devil's Nest (regarded as the birthplace of the New York 'freestyle' approach, alongside TKA and Sa-Fire), then Hearthrob and 1018. By the time he had reached the 4,000-capacity Studio 54 Todd Terry would pass Vega his new mixes to try out on the crowd. His first remix job was 'Running' by Information Society, then Noel's 'Silent Morning'. He even worked on Debbie Gibson's first record. He began his own-name productions with the instrumental 'Don't Tell Me' for SBK in 1989 and 'Keep On Pumpin' It Up' (as Freestyle Orchestra), before signing to CBS subsidiary WTG Records with singer Mark Anthony. He had previously been commissioned to write songs for the movie *East Side Story*, where he first met the singer. Together they hooked up for a Latin R&B-flavoured album and single, 'Ride On The Rhythm'. He also worked with his girlfriend, 'India', and Todd Terry for the latter's 'Todd's Message'. Together with Barbara Tucker, Vega runs the Underground Network Club in New York, and he has also produced 'Beautiful People' for that artist. Despite this background as an established house star, he is probably best known now for his work alongside Kenny 'Dope' Gonzalez as half of the Masters At Work remix team. He is not to be confused with Chicago house veteran Lil' Louis, or, for that matter, with the Louie Vega who remixed for Lakim Shabazz, despite the fact that both shared the same management. Vega's most recent remix clients include Juliet Roberts and Urban Species.

LIVIN' JOY

At a time when the simple joys of Eurodisco had been reduced to the MOR noodling of Robert Miles and the naff behemoth that was 'Macarena', Livin' Joy provided some hope for the much-maligned form. This was mainly due to the efforts of singer/lyricist Tameka Star, a US forces brat and a fan of Natalie Cole. After a childhood spent on numerous army bases throughout Europe, Tameka met the Visnadi brothers, Paulo and Gianni, major Italo-house producers, and the trio began to work together as Livin' Joy. The anthem 'Dreamer' was a decent club hit but it was 'Don't Stop Movin'' that dominated the airwaves. Tameka's soulful vocals gave guts to the brothers' infectious backing, creating a major UK hit in the second half of 1996, although the act's Continental origin has so far denied them the critical credibility that US and British dance outfits can command.
● ALBUMS: *Don't Stop Movin'* (MCA 1996)★★★.

LL COOL J

b. James Todd Smith, 16 August 1969, St. Albans, Queens, New York, USA. Long-running star of the rap scene, LL Cool J found fame at the age of 16, his pseudonym standing for 'Ladies Love Cool James'. As might be inferred by this, LL is a self-professed ladykiller in the vein of Luther Vandross or Barry White, yet he retains a superior rapping agility. Smith started rapping at the age of nine, after his grandfather bought him his first DJ equipment. From the age of 13 he was processing his first demos. The first to respond to his mail-outs was Rick Rubin of Def Jam Records, then a senior at New York University, who signed him to his fledgling label. The first sighting of LL Cool J came in 1984 on a 12-inch, 'I Need A Beat', which was the label's first such release. However, it was 'I Just Can't Live Without My Radio', which established his gold-chained, bare-chested B-boy persona. The song was featured in the *Krush Groove* film, on which the rapper also performed. In its wake he embarked on a 50-city US tour alongside the Fat Boys, Whodini, Grandmaster Flash and Run DMC. The latter were crucial to LL Cool J's development: his *modus operandi* was to combine their beatbox cruise control with streetwise B-boy raps, instantly making him a hero to a new generation of black youth. As well as continuing to tour with the trio, he would also contribute a song, 'Can You Rock It Like This', to Run DMC's *King Of Rock*. His debut album too, would see Rubin dose the grooves with heavy metal guitar breaks first introduced by Run DMC. LL Cool J's other early singles included 'I'm Bad', 'Go Cut Creator Go', 'Jack The Ripper' and 'I Need Love' (the first ballad rap, recorded with the Los Angeles Posse), which brought him a UK Top 10 score. Subsequent releases offered a fine array of machismo funk-rap, textured with personable charm and humour. Like many of his bretheren, LL Cool J's career has not been without incident. Live appearances in particular have been beset by many problems. Three people were shot at a date in Baltimore in December 1985, followed by an accusation of 'public lewdness' after a 1987 show in Columbus, Ohio. While playing rap's first concert in Cote d'Ivoire, Africa, fights broke out and the stage was stormed. Most serious, however, was an incident in 1989 when singer David Parker, bodyguard Christopher Tsipouras and technician Gary Saunders were accused of raping a 15-year-old girl who attended a backstage party after winning a radio competition in Minneapolis. Though LL Cool J's personal involvement in all these cases was incidental, they have undoubtedly tarnished his reputation. He has done much to make amends, including appearances at benefits including Farm Aid, recording with the Peace Choir, and launching his *Cool School Video Program*, in an attempt to encourage children to stay at school. Even Nancy Reagan invited him to headline a 'Just Say No' concert at Radio City Music Hall. Musically, Cool is probably best sampled on his 1990 set, *Mama Said Knock You Out*, produced by the omnipresent Marley Marl, which as well as the familiar sexual braggadocio

included his thoughts on the state of rap past, present and future. The album went triple platinum, though the follow-up, *14 Shots To The Dome*, was a less effective attempt to recycle the formula. Some tracks stood out: 'A Little Something', anchored by a sample of King Floyd's soul standard 'Groove Me', being a good example. Like many of rap's senior players, he has also sustained an acting career, with film appearances in *The Hard Way* and *Toys*, playing a cop in the former and a military man in the latter. *Phenomenon* celebrated Cool's remarkable longevity on the rap scene, and featured guest appearances from Keith Sweat and Ralph Tresvant.

● ALBUMS: *Radio* (Columbia 1985)★★★, *Bigger And Deffer* (Def Jam 1987)★★, *Walking With A Panther* (Def Jam 1989)★★★, *Mama Said Knock You Out* (Def Jam 1990)★★★★, *14 Shots To The Dome* (Def Jam 1992)★★★, *Mr. Smith* (Def Jam 1995)★★★, *Phenomenon* (Def Jam 1997)★★★★.
● COMPILATIONS: *Greatest Hits All World* (Def Jam 1996)★★★.

LOADED RECORDS

Record label that is also the home of the Brighton-based remix team of JC Reid and Tim Jeffreys (also a *Record Mirror* journalist), who operate under the name Play Boys. Their first production work together was for the London Community Gospel Choir in 1992 with 'I'll Take You There' and 'Ball Of Confusion', before they set up the Loaded imprint. Titles such as 'Ransom' and 'Suggestive', co-produced with Pizzaman, aka Norman Cook, emerged. Their next work was on a hot reactivated version of 'Love So Strong' by Secret Life which proved more than merely a remix, with re-recorded Paul Bryant vocals. Other remix projects included Brother Love Dub's 'Ming's Incredible Disco Machine', PM Dawn's 'When Midnight Says' and Talizman. As the Play Boys they also released in their own right, including 'Mindgames' from 1992. They also returned the compliment to Norman Cook by remixing his Freak Power track, 'Turn On, Tune In, Cop Out'. The Loaded release schedule continued apace too, with records including those from Key Largo (Eddie Richards) and the garage house of Wildchild Experience (the *Wildtrax* EP, which ran to several volumes, created by Southampton-born DJ Roger McKenzie). Other artists included Jason Nevins ('The Upper Room').

LOCUST

In the accelerating flurry of ambient dance releases following the Orb's breakthrough, at least the work of Mark Van Hoen contained a snatch of humour. The track 'Xenophobia', for example: 'I started with this Japanese vocal sample, and began thinking I'd have to surround it with five-note Japanese pentatonik scales. Then I gave up and called myself xenophobic'. Elsewhere the musical territory on his debut album was mapped out in traditional genre style, eerie mood pieces with more than a passing nod to composers like Steve Reich. Diverting enough, but hardly a substantial listening experience. He originally came to prominence through the heavily imported *Skyline* EP, before a contract with R&S Records subsidiary Apollo for six albums. Unlike many similar artists, however, Van Hoen has no ambitions to remix other people's music, preferring instead to concentrate on his own.
● ALBUMS: *Weathered Well* (R&S 1994)★★★, *Truth Is Born Of Argument* (R&S 1995)★★★, *Morning Light* (R&S 1997)★★★.

LOGIC RECORDS

Founded in Frankfurt, Germany, in the early 90s by Luca Anzilotti and Michael Munzing, Logic Records provided the original home for their enormously successful Euro-techno creations, notably Snap!'s 'Exterminate'. The label was set up because: 'With Logic we have total creative control over every aspect of a record: the mixes, the artwork, the promotion, everything'. They operate Logic in addition to their interests in the highly popular Omen club in Frankfurt. Mark Spoon of Jam And Spoon held an A&R post at Logic for a number of years, before choosing to concentrate fully on his own music. In addition to high-profile Euro techno, the label has also released high-profile techno material from Blake Baxter ('One More Time') and Rapination featuring Kym Mazelle ('Love Me The Right Way'). Other successes included Pressure Drop's 'Release Me' and Durga McBroom's (ex-Blue Pearl) solo debut. Logic is equally well known for its impressive compilations which include *Logic Trance 1 & 2*. A subsidiary imprint, Save The Vinyl, which produces work on vinyl only, was established in 1993. It was then overhauled and relaunched at the end of 1995 at which time it was run by Logic's senior product manager, Wendy 'K'. The release schedule of one 12-inch per month

began with material by artists such as High Stepper, the Angel and Anacoeic Void.

LOÏS LANE

Taking their name from *Superman*'s female foil, this eclectic Dutch dance music band added an umlaut to their moniker to reinstate their European origins. Led by sisters Monique and Suzanne Klemann, they were originally signed to a publishing contract in 1985 by Andre de Raaff, at that time working at Warner Brothers Records but now the head of their present label, CNR Records. They gained an international profile in 1992 with their album for Polydor Records, *Precious*, which featured a collaboration with Prince and entered several European Top 30s. However, they were not able to build on this impact, and had to wait until 1995 for their next major hit, 'Tonight'.
● ALBUMS: *Precious* (Polydor 1992)★★★★.

LONDON POSSE

One of Britain's first credible rap acts, utilising rhymes built over expertly executed ragamuffin breaks, with cockney accents thrown in for good measure. Unfortunately, London Posse were not free of the misogyny made more explicit by the gangsta rappers (tracks like 'Sexy Gal' and 'Living' implied that the entire female gender was out *en masse* to rob them of their money). London Posse at least possessed wit and a nose for rhythm to dilute their urban warnings. Stylistically, the album was notable for its Eric B And Rakim-styled delivery.
● ALBUMS: *Gangster Chronicles* (Mango/Island 1990)★★★★.

LOOK TWICE

This Swedish hip-hop duo comprised Wincent (aka Vinny) and Crazy G., backed by their friend, writer and producer Håkan Libdo. Look Twice formed in 1992 to offer the Scandinavian world their 'positive' brand of rap music, promoting strong humane messages in their lyrics rather than self-aggrandisement or the chastising of rap peers common to American hip-hop. They specialised in a fast verbal delivery reminiscent of the UK reggae MC 'chatting' style. This was highlighted on their initial two singles for the Swedish MNW dance label, 'Shake That Rump' and 'Good Thing', released in 1993.

LOOP GURU

The listening tastes of spokesman Jal Muud (South American pipe music, Moroccan indigenous sounds) has informed the career of Nation Records' Loop Guru. Together with Salman Gita he forms the core of the band, aided by up to 10 guest musicians for various events (who include former Pigbag drummer Chip Carpenter and percussionist Mad Jym). The duo have been involved in music since 1980 when they were early members of the Megadog enclave, meeting through mutual friend Alex Kasiek (Trans-Global Underground). It was at this time that Jamuud: '. . . stopped listening to Western music altogether. I found that the wealth of sound and mood in Asian and African music was vastly more alive than its Western counterparts.' Offering their listeners 'total enlightenment through music', Loop Guru have perfected a package of chants, laments, tablas, Eastern religion and ethnic samples, which was first brought to the public's attention via their *Sus-San-Tics* EP, which featured the guest vocals of Sussan Deheim (b. Iran). A debut album was recorded, its title, *Duniya*, translating from Urdu as 'The World'. Part of the methodology evolved from Brian Eno's 'Choice Cards' ethos, wherein different instructions on musical structure are carried out via the turn of a set of cards. It placed them at the forefront of the 'world dance' movement. Arguably their most effective and popular single to date is 'Paradigm Shuffle', which included at its core Martin Luther King's 'I Have A Dream' speech.

● ALBUMS: *Duniya* (Nation 1994)★★★, *Amrita ... All These And The Japanese Soup Warriors* (North South 1995)★★★, *Catalogue Of Desires Volume 3* (North South 1996)★★★, *Peel To Reveal* (Strange Fruit 1996)★★★, *Loop Bites Dog* (North South 1997).

LORDS OF THE UNDERGROUND

Based in Newark, New Jersey, USA, Lords Of The Underground came to prominence via tours with Cypress Hill and Funkdoobiest, with whom their music shares more than a passing acquaintance. The group first met at college where all the band were majoring in radio communication. The frontmen are Doitall and Mr Funke (aka Mr Funky). The former also has acting interests, taking his first role in the film *The School Game*. They are backed by their DJ, Lord Jazz. Doitall and Mr Funke were originally solo artists, collab-

orating for the first time on a cut called 'Psycho'. 'Flow On' was eventually issued as a single, remixed by Pete Rock, while the debut collection was produced by Marley Marl. They have also been responsible for fostering the career of Rated R.

● ALBUMS: *Here Come The Lords* (Pendulum/Elektra 1993)★★★.

LORDS, TRACI

US actor Traci Lords made her recording debut as guest vocalist on the Manic Street Preachers' 'Little Baby Nothing'. For her solo career she signed to the Los Angeles, California-based Radioactive Records label, enlisting some high-profile musical personnel to back her on her debut album, *1000 Fires*. The participants included Mike Edwards (Jesus Jones), Tom Bailey and Alannah Currie (Thompson Twins) and Ben Watkins (Juno Reactor). The latter penned 'Control', which reached number 2 in the *Billboard* Dance Charts before the album's release. Lords' peculiar story began in the late 80s with an under-age porn career that ended in a well-publicized drug overdose. She emerged from the wreckage with the help of therapy and began to attend acting and vocal classes. Appearances in a variety of film and television shows, including *Roseanne* and *Melrose Place*, saw her re-establish herself, though journalists were reluctant to let her escape the shadow of her past completely. Rather than pursue the mainstream direction that her standing now warranted, Lords and her A&R director, Brendan Bourke, opted for a techno-dance slant for *1000 Fires*. This decision followed the artist's own conversion to dance music when she came to London in 1992 on a modelling assignment.

● ALBUMS: *1000 Fires* (Radioactive 1995)★★★.

LORDZ OF BROOKLYN

With an obvious stylistic debt to fellow New York, USA white rappers the Beastie Boys, the Lordz Of Brooklyn emerged in 1995 with an impressive debut album, *All In The Family*. There were several features to distinguish the group - their Italian heritage and lyrics which betrayed a passion for the 50s rather than 90s gang culture. Their name was chosen deliberately to reflect their territorial devotion to Brooklyn, with nearly all their songs offering everyday narratives attributed to growing up in the area. A quintet of lead rapper Kaves, brother and producer Admoney,

Scotty Edge, Dino Bottz and Paulie Two Times, their debut single, 'Saturday Nite Fever', typified the album's approach. Borrowing from both the Robert De Niro and Quentin Tarantino school of urban cinema, 'Saturday Nite Fever' used a sample of the Bee Gees' 'Staying Alive' (as well as a more traditional rap staple, Schoolly D's similarly named 'Saturday Night'). The gritty simplicity of their collages of second-generation immigrant working class life were bolstered by a rough but effective musical delivery akin to DJ Muggs' work with Cypress Hill or House Of Pain. Kaves, a renowned graffiti artist, had previously acted as warm up man for the latter group.
● ALBUMS: *All In The Family* (American 1995)★★★★.

LOST TRIBE

This group from New York City, New York, USA, escape easy categorization, their armoury spanning funk, soul, hardcore punk and hip-hop. 'Our music is a reflection of who we are, where we live, and what we've been through. That has an effect on the kind of music we play. It's a very intense environment.' Comprising David Benney (alto saxophone), Fima Ephron (bass), David Gilmore (guitar), Ben Perowsky (drums) and Adam Rogers (guitar), each contributes to the group's songwriting platform, bringing diverse personal influences to bear. Lost Tribe began by jamming in local New York clubs and Central Park, with members involved in sundry side projects. It was not until 1988 that the core of the group was cemented when Ephron, Perowsky and Rogers decided to put previous collaborations on a more permanent footing. By 1989 Binney and Gilmore had cemented the line-up. By this time members had amassed considerable and varying experience playing with John Cale, George Russell, Me'shell NdegéOcello, Roy Ayers, Steve Coleman, Rickie Lee Jones and Walter Becker, among others. The latter produced their self-titled debut album at his Maui studio. This mesh of contrasting influences was quickly followed by *Soulfish*. This time working with Joseph Marciano at Brooklyn's Systems Two, guests included Benny Nitze and Joe Mendelson of Rise Robots Rise, with whom Ephron, Rogers and Gilmore had formerly participated. *Soulfish* duly included several memorable songs, not least Perowsky's 'Daze Of Ol'' and Rogers' 'Steel Orchards'.
● ALBUMS: *Lost Tribe* (High Street 1994)★★, *Soulfish* (High Street 1995)★★★.

LOVE CITY GROOVE

The UK's entrants in the 1995 Eurovision Song Contest, dance/rap collective Love City Groove originally entered the competition 'for a bit of a laugh'. Certainly their stylised but effusive distillation of the Stereo MC's formula proved an unexpected hit in the qualifying stages. Led by Beanz (b. Stephen Rudden), with fellow rappers Jay Williams, Paul Hardy and 'Reason', the song, a half rapped/half sung affair also titled 'Love City Groove', found favour in the UK charts. It also served to give the competition some unexpected credibility and became a staple of the UK's summer 1995 pop radio schedules. There was some controversy over the single in the press, however, when runners-up Dear Jon argued that the single had already been released to club DJs in January 1995 (though this did not infract standing rules). Speculating on its Eurovision chances, Jonathan King commented that the song would 'either win or come last'. It did neither, managing a respectable UK Top 5 placing. Prior to the group's Eurovision success the members had all been struggling fruitlessly as musicians, but now found the opportunity to record their debut album at London's Nomis Studios, with all of the group members contributing to the writing process.
● ALBUMS: *Hard Times* (Planet 1996)★★★.

LOVE TO INFINITY

UK garage production duo comprising the brothers Andrew and Peter Lee, who have been working together since the late 80s. Both were trained in classical music, while their modern work recalls the heyday of disco, with strings, diva vocals and up-tempo rhythms. Peter is responsible for programming, while Andrew acts as engineer. In addition to remixing for the Other Two, Melanie Williams, D:Ream and Grace Jones, they have also worked as a band in their own right, notably with Bruce Forest in 1990. They co-wrote with Boy George, and released their own album in Japan. They also released a 12-inch for Big Life, before eking out a living with engineering work for Sub Sub and the Mock Turtles. They returned to their own recording work in the early 90s, alongside vocalist Louise Bailey, on singles such as 'Somethin' Outta Nothin'' for Pigeon Pie.

LOVE, MONIE

b. Simone Johnson, 2 July 1970, Battersea, London, England. Monie Love is a female rapper who has lived in New York since 1989. Her first recordings were with childhood friend MC Mell 'O', Sparki and DJ Pogo, under the banner Jus Bad Productions, who formed in 1987. They released a solitary single 'Freestyle'. Love started recording solo with DJ Pogo in 1988, releasing 12-inch singles on obscure underground labels which were eventually spotted by DJ Tim Westwood, who asked them to do a single for his Justice label. There were several delays in releasing it, so instead they approached Cooltempo with 'I Can Do This', which became a hit in early 1989. Love has since worked with many other rap groups including the Jungle Brothers, who she met at a London gig in September 1988. They subsequently introduced her to the Native Tongues Posse, while Afrika Baby Bambaataa would produce her debut album. There have also been collaborations with Andy Cox and David Steele of the Fine Young Cannibals on the summer 1990 single 'Monie In The Middle', and with the band True Image, who are best known for performing the theme to the *Cosby Show*. They featured on Monie's Christmas 1990 single, 'Down To Earth'. Previous hits included 'I Can Do This', 'Grandpa's Party' (a tribute to the original Afrika Bambaataa), and her biggest hit, the Spinners' cover - 'It's A Shame (My Sister)'. In 1991 she teamed up with Adeva, as well as working with Queen Latifah and Almond Joy on the Bold Soul Sisters feminist project. Tracks on her debut album like 'RU Single' were intelligent attacks on the expectations and stereotypes of black women. Despite maturity beyond her years, she recognised that this phase of her career was still an apprenticeship; 'To me, rap is a school. The heads are split between Public Enemy and KRS-1's Boogie Down Productions. The students are me, Jungle Brothers, De La Soul... but the best thing about it is that the classroom is open to all'. She would go on to appear in Forest Whittaker's Harlem film, *Strapped*.
● ALBUMS: *Down To Earth* (Warners 1990)★★★, *In A Word Or 2* (Cooltempo 1993)★★.

LOVEBUG STARSKI

b. Kevin Smith, 13 July 1961, New York, USA. One of the pioneering forefathers of hip-hop culture, Starski has seen commerce move rap away from what he originally envisioned. Still remembering the days in the Black Spades when 'we used to push refrigerator-size speakers through the blocks', his role in the developmental parties was pivotal. At the age of 13 he began spinning records on the playground of the Forrest Housing Project (at which time he also adopted his stage name, from the popular television show *Starsky & Hutch*). The *modus operandi* would be to set up two turntables in the South Bronx parks, or mix live at parties. He was among the first to begin 'rapping' over the records he played. Although technically too young, Starski would sneak into a West Bronx club, 371, where his friends DJ Hollywood and Peter 'DJ' Jones worked, initially under the guise of roadie. From there his reputation brought him prestige placements at upmarket venues like Dancetaria and Stardust Ballroom, before eventually being offered a residency at Disco Fever - rap's first proper home. In 1981, he released his first single, 'Positive Life', followed by 'Funky Pledge', a typical Lovebug message rap preaching the virtues of education, responsibility and self-respect. By 1983, with hip-hop showing signs of moving overground, Starksi cut his first proper record deal with Fever Records, owned by Sal Abatiello, the manager of Disco Fever. 'You Gotta Believe', on which he collaborated with producer Larry Smith (Whodini etc) would go on to sell nearly a million copies. It also became the theme for WABC-television's *Big Break Dance Contest*. It was followed by the masterful 'Do The Right Thing' (produced by Kurtis Blow) and the title theme for the movie, *Rappin'*. In 1986 he enjoyed crossover hits with 'House Rocker' and 'Amityville'. For a period in the mid-80s it looked as though Starski would truly break through, signing an album deal with Epic. Unfortunately, the resulting record sunk without trace, and Starski became another hip-hop pioneer to fall by the wayside. He slid into cocaine dependency and returned to the streets until he was busted for possession in 1987. He was finally released in December 1991. He returned, fittingly, to his old haunt, Disco Fever.
● ALBUMS: *House Rocker* (Epic 1986)★★★, *Lovebug* (Epic 1987)★★.

LTJ BUKEM

b. 1969, Croydon, Surrey, England. During the 90s Bukem played a significant part in the development of drum 'n' bass. He grew up around Harlesden and then Watford, where he learned the piano and listened to the Jam, the Police and

the 2-Tone bands. He later became interested in rare groove, soul, funk and jazz, and in the mid-80s began DJing with the Sunshine Sound System; he subsequently became interested in dance music and made his DJing breakthrough in 1990 when he played at Raindance in Essex. His first release was 'Logical Progression' on Vinyl Mania in 1991, which was followed by 'Demon's Theme', 'Bang The Drums' (featuring Tayla; both 1991), 'Return To Atlantis' (1992) and 'Music' (1993), on his own label Good Looking Records. 'Demon's Theme' introduced the strings and mellow ambience that characterizes much of Bukem's work and was one of the first records to feature the sound that became known as drum 'n' bass. Rather than sampling old breakbeats, like many jungle and hardcore artists of the time, Bukem preferred to create his own rhythm tracks in this style, thereby creating a more varied beat for his recordings. In 1993 with Fabio, he brought his sound to a wider audience with the launch of the club Speed in central London, which featured such DJs as Adam F., Alex Reece, Deep Blue and Goldie, and led to widespread media coverage of this new English cultural phenomenon. His success continued with a remix of Jodeci's 'Feenin'' (1995), and the development, along with Tony Fordham, of Good Looking. He has since presented his touring club, Logical Progression, and its associated albums, and the *Earth* compilations. In 1997 Bukem contributed a version of 'Thunderball' to David Arnold's album of *James Bond* theme remakes, *Shaken And Stirred*.
● ALBUMS: *Mixmag Live Vol 21* (MML 1996)★★★, *Presents: Earth Volume One* (Good Looking 1996)★★★, *Presents: Earth Volume Two* (Earth 1997) ★★★.

LUCAS

b. *c*.1970, Copenhagen, Denmark. His mother an artist and his father a writer, Lucas moved around the world from an early age, finding his most permanent port of call in New York. There he immersed himself in the prevailing hip-hop culture on the Lower East Side, rubbing shoulders with old school crews like Kid Crush as he became a breakdancer, a DJ, and finally a rapper. By 1990 he was signed to Uptown Records as part of Key West, billed as the label's 'first white artist'. When that band fell from favour Lucas worked briefly with Chubb Rock and Kool Keith (Ultramagnetic MCs), DJing for The Lifers Project, before leaving New York for England. His debut single for WEA, 'Wau Wau Wau'/'Work In Progress', revealed the experience he had gained. While the a-side was an easily likeable jazz-tinged affair, distinguished by a sample left on his answerphone by a drunken kid, the b-side cut, featuring the vocals of Fay Simpson (Nu Colours) and Junior Dangerous, spanned rap, soul and ragga. Lucas also became prominent in UK hip-hop circles for his production skills (Nu Colours, Shara Nelson).
● ALBUMS: *Living In A Sillicone Dream* (WEA 1994)★★★, *Lucacentric* (WEA 1994)★★★.

LUCKY PEOPLE CENTER

Proclaiming themselves 'dance terrorists', the samples used on this Swedish trio's debut album built on the traditions of Test Department and others by using speeches from world leaders, in this case marrying George Bush and Saddam Hussein to a backbeat on 'It's Still Cloudy In Saudi Arabia'. The group were formed in 1992 by Johan Söderburg (percussion), Lars Åkerlund (samples) and Sebastian Öberg (electric cello). The relentless barrage of samples was adopted in a vein more prevalent within hip-hop than the dance scene, though Lucky People Center are firmly placed in the latter by the dominance of rhythm over lyrics.
● ALBUMS: *Welcome To Lucky People* (MNW 1993)★★★.

LUVDUP TWINS

Twins Mark and Adrian Luvdup, who won numerous UK music press Single Of The Week plaudits with their debut 12-inch, 'Good Times'. This was released on Manchester's UFG label (set up by E-Lustrious), and featured mixes from Jon Dasilva and John McCready. The duo play out at the Jolly Roger night in their native Manchester's Paradise Factory venue, review for *Mixmag Update* (having formerly run the well-regarded Luvdup fanzine), and have remixed for Awesome 3 among others.

M PEOPLE

The key component of M People is Mike Pickering (b. March 1958, Manchester, England; keyboards, programming), a former disc jockey at the Factory Records-owned Hacienda club in Manchester. His activities there once encouraged *The Face* magazine to proclaim him 'England's most revered DJ'. After leaving school, Pickering worked in a fish factory and engineering warehouse, becoming a big fan of northern soul. He played saxophone and sang for mid-80s indie dance forerunners Quando Quango, and had various connections with New Order, including sharing a flat with their manager, Rob Gretton. He also had the distinction of having booked the Smiths for their first Manchester gig, and having signed both James and Happy Mondays in his role as Factory's A&R representative. After leaving Factory he became a junior director at DeConstruction Records, to whom he brought Black Box and Guru Josh, the label's two most important early successes. He also provided DeConstruction with *North - The Sound Of The Dance Underground*, cited by many as the first UK house music compilation, though in truth it was Pickering and his band T-Coy behind seven of the eight songs. He is also the founder-member and songwriter for M People - the M standing for his Christian name - who also record for DeConstruction. The band includes ex-Hot House vocalist Heather Small (b. 20 January 1965, London, England) and Paul Heard (b. 5 October 1960, Hammersmith, London, England; keyboards, programming), formerly of Orange Juice and Working Week. They made their debut in May 1991 with 'Colour My Life', achieving major success with the club hit 'How Can I Love You More' at the end of the year. These singles promoted a first album that took its name from Pickering's early musical leanings, *Northern Soul*. 1993 was M People's breakthrough year. On the back of colossal UK hits such as 'Movin' On Up' (later used as a campaign tune by the UK's Labour Party), they were awarded a BRIT Award for Best UK Dance Act. The album that contained the hits, *Elegant Slumming* (the title was taken from a Tom Wolfe book), included a cover version of Dennis Edwards' 'Don't Look Any Further', and vocal support from Nu Colours. In 1994 it won them the Mercury Prize for best UK act in any category, much to the chagrin of hotly tipped pretenders Blur. Meanwhile, their highly polished, commercial sound (omnipresent on car stereos and commercial radio) was being cited as the perfect example of 'handbag house', a term the group themselves despise. *Bizarre Fruit* and attendant single, 'Search For The Hero', were greeted with mild disappointment, but with the addition of new bongo/percussion player 'Shovel' the group nevertheless embarked on a tour of the world's stadia to ecstatic receptions. Their love affair with the critics had cooled, the media taking special pleasure in poking fun at Small's choice of boyfriend - rugby league player Shaun Edwards. *Bizarre Fruit II* merely compiled several remixes and edits as a prelude to a new album, though an ill-advised cover version of the Small Faces' 'Itchycoo Park' managed to irritate the critics further. *Fresco* proved to be another smooth slab of easy-listening dance music, with the single 'Just For You' the stand-out track.

● ALBUMS: *Northern Soul* (DeConstruction 1992)★★★, *Northern Soul Extended* (DeConstruction 1992)★★★, *Elegant Slumming* (DeConstruction 1993)★★★, *Bizarre Fruit* (DeConstruction 1994)★★★★, *Bizarre Fruit II* (DeConstruction 1995)★★, *Fresco* (BMG 1997)★★.

● VIDEOS: *Elegant TV* (1994), *Live At G-Mex* (BMG 1995), *One Night In Heaven* (Eagle Rock 1998).

M&S PRODUCTIONS

M&S Productions was formed in London, England, in 1994, when former Catch-A-Groove shop assistant Ricky Morrison teamed up with Fran Sidoli. Both had been listening to US garage house since their school days together, and Morrison had already made his name as a garage DJ. M&S Productions subsequently remixed for artists including Urban Discharge (their UK hit, 'Drop That House On That Bitch'), as well as Kenny Thomas, Beverly Brown and Soul Corporation. Also employing other names including Street Sense, the group then recorded singles for high-profile US labels including

Cutting, Todd Terry's Freeze and Strictly Rhythm Records, as well as UK imprints including Public Demand and MCA Records. The decision of Strictly Rhythm to release M&S Productions' 'Justify', was an honour particularly cherished by the partners. The duo also established their own UK dance imprint, 1001 Records, early in 1996.

M.O.P.

Their name standing for Mash Out Posse, Lil' Fame and Billy Danzenie were the faces behind one of Select Records' freshest hardcore arrivals of 1994. They came to prominence when 'How About Some Hardcore', included on the *House Party 3* soundtrack, took off. Fame had already made his debut with three tracks on 4th & Broadway's *The Hill That's Real*. After a projected solo deal with the label fell through, he hooked up with old friend Danzenie, then fresh out from a prison stretch. When 'Hardcore' succeeded they elected to make the partnership a permanent one. Both had grown up in Brownsville, Brooklyn, New York, and brought a sense of justice to their summaries of urban life. M.O.P. was the title of the gang they ran with, who in turn descended from the Tomahawks. M.O.P. thus started life as an 11-piece, but, according to legend, four of that number were cut down in gang fights, and five more are in jail. The sole remainder numbered Fame and Danzenie, alongside producer/manager Lazy Laz. Their debut album, produced by Darryl D, included the predictable put-downs of 'F.A.G.'s (fake-ass gangstas), while 'Blue Steel' confirmed that 'Nowadays shit is for real - so I'm packin' blue steel'.
● ALBUMS: *To The Death* (Select 1994)★★★, *Firing Squad* (Relativity 1996)★★★.

MACKINTOSH, C.J.

One of the UK's most widely revered DJs and remixers, with whom major record companies regularly indulge their A&R budgets. Chris 'C.J.' Mackintosh's standard approach, that of radio-friendly, lush garage arrangements, is too MOR for many of the nation's more underground clubbers, but his technique has become the epitome of taste in the mainstream. Clients have included Whitney Houston, Lisa Stansfield and Janet Jackson. Mackintosh actually started out as a hip-hop DJ, going on to win the 1987 finals of the DMC mixing championships. After this initial success he provided hip-hop megamixes for labels such as Champion. His first venture into remixing

proved even more rewarding. Together with Dave Dorrell, he mixed MARRS' 'Pump Up The Volume', one of dance music's seminal moments. Mackintosh happily continues his daytime job, that of club DJ, and on this basis is one of the first of the UK's 'names' to play in the USA. However, it is as a remixer that he has won fame and fortune, although he also sees the dangers inherent in a DJ-led music scene: 'With remixing, everyone's doing it and it's wrong, but I think it'll go on because there's nothing to stop it . . . All sorts of bands are depending on it, they all want a dance mix . . . remixing's easy because you're using someone else's ideas. Production, and writing, is a totally different thing.' A list of his credits could fill a small book, but some of the most important include Inner City ('Good Life'), Dina Carroll ('Ain't No Man'), PM Dawn ('Reality'), A Tribe Called Quest ('Bonita Applebum'), De La Soul ('Ring, Ring, Ring'), Digital Underground ('Packet Man'), Simple Minds ('Sign Of The Times), Gang Starr ('Take A Rest'), Whitney Houston ('Queen Of The Night') and Luther Vandross and Janet Jackson ('The Best Things In Life Are Free').

MAD PROFESSOR
(see Ariwa Sounds)

MAESTRO FRESH WES

Until the release of his self-proclaiming 1994 album, Fresh Wes had been one of the Canadian hip-hop fraternity's most closely guarded secrets. With production aid from DJ Showbiz (of Showbiz and AG fame), the MC's rhymes were delivered in old school New York style, emphasising a punning ability and freestyle approach, which was competent though hardly innovative. The introduction of jazzy overtones too, was not exactly revolutionary by this stage, though the single 'Fine Tune Da Mic' was well-received.
● ALBUMS: *Nah! Dis Kid Can't Be From Canada* (LMR 1994).★★★

MAGNETIC NORTH

This UK techno record label run by Dave Clarke is distinguished by releases by Woody MC Bride ('Rattlesnake'), who also works under the title DJ ESP. The label's first two releases were from the acid-fixated Directional Force and Graphite ('Pure'), in 1993. By 1994 the roster included material by DJ Hell and Christian Vogel.

MAIN

This UK ambient dance band was formed in the 90s by Robert Hampson, formerly of Loop. Taking the repetitive motifs from that band, Main refined the formula to accentuate the aesthetics of post-rave dance 'chill'. They drew heavily on environmental sounds on which they dubbed guitars, synths and electronically generated effects. Their first EP, *Hydra*, was dedicated to the German composer Karlheinz Stockhausen, and was followed by 'Dry Stone Feed' and 'Firmament'. The six-EP box-sets, *Corona*, *Maser*, *Neper*, *Terminus*, *Haloform* and *Kaon*, enable the listener's imagination to run wild, but no two people will come to the same conclusion.
● ALBUMS: *Firmament III* (Beggars Banquet 1997)★★★.

MAIN SOURCE

There has been much swapping and shifting in the constantly evolving line-ups of the rap band Main Source, formed in Toronto, Canada, but based in New York. The original MCs were K-Cut and Sir Scratch, though Large Professor (b. Paul Mitchell) excused himself after their first album, which included choice cuts like 'Just A Friendly Game Of Baseball'. Professor would go on to work with A Tribe Called Quest, Nas, who had first arrived on the debut album's 'Live At The BBQ' cut, and others. He was replaced by Mikey D, who was chief rapper on their second set, the invitingly titled *Fuck What You Think*, on which they were also joined by Shaheem, a female MC straight from high school (on the title-track and 'Set It Off'). Their fresh, jazzy platform was well served by the indignant, often complex lyrical matter they pursued. In the light of delays over the release of their *Fuck What You Think* set they parted company with label Wild Pitch, and Mikey D also broke ranks - claiming he did not get along with K-Cut and Scratch, looking for a solo deal instead.
● ALBUMS: *Breaking Atoms* (Wild Pitch 1990)★★★, *Fuck What You Think* (Wild Pitch 1994)★★★★.

MAMA RECORDS

Underground house DJ Chris Long first employed his Rhythm Doctor alias at the Rock City club in Nottingham, England, in 1986. In the 90s he established his own label, Mama Records, alongside partner Phillipe Lavena, which specializes in jazz/deep house projects. It was set up after the duo had provided cult US independent label 8 Ball Records with Wave's 'Enjoy Life', which gave 8 Ball its first Top 10 *Billboard* dance hit. Subsequent hits housed on Mama have included Love Tribe's *Sundance* EP and Batamania's 'Jazzy Notions' (which featured regularly at the Ministry Of Sound and also on the club's *Late Night Sessions* album). These records featured Mama's established proclivity for mixing live instrumentation (such as saxophone and flute) with rhythms, as did their late 1995 release, Nature Boys' *Drummer* EP.

MAN PARRISH

One of the earliest hip-hop acts who broke through in 1983 with 'Hip Hop Be Bop (Don't Stop)'. His only other UK hit was 'Boogie Down (Bronx)' in 1985. However, his biggest slice of success came in 1987 through a joint venture with Man 2 Man, 'Male Stripper'. After heavy exposure in gay clubs, it rose to number 4 in the UK.
● ALBUMS: *Man Parrish* (1983)★★★.

MANTRA, MICHAEL

A California-based musician/experimentalist who has sought to advance on the ambient ethic of Brian Eno and more recent 'chill-out' arists such as the Orb. Mantra describes his methods as 'Brain Hemisphere Harmonic Healing', which spells out his intention to create sound structures that 'induce a meditative state that synchronises brain wave frequencies'. After synchronizing the mind and the body, Mantra's work claims to release endorphines (part of the human body's natural pharmacy that work at the level of opiates). To achieve this, electronics are combined with field recordings of the Pacific sea, seagulls, and natural instruments such as the didgeridoo. Such experiments in the neural effects of sound could well represent a previously unchartered future for music.
● ALBUMS: *Sonic Alter* (Silent Records 1994)★★★.

MANTRONIX

DJ Curtis Mantronik (b. Kurtis Kahleel, 4 September 1965, Jamaica, West Indies, moving to Canada at age seven, then to New York as a teenager) is the creative force behind these New York-based hip-hop innovators, a multi-instrumental talent whose knowledge of electronics is instrumental to the band's sound. That sound, electro rap in its purest form, as suggested by the band's name, was highly popular in the mid-80s. Kahleel's use of samplers and drum machines proved.pivotal to the genre's development, not least on tracks like 'Music Madness', which used a snippet of 'Stone Fox Chase' by Area Code 615 (better known in the UK as the theme to *The Old Grey Whistle Test*). Indeed, the raps of MC Tee (b. Tooure Embden) often seemed incidental to the formula. The duo met at Manhattan's Downtown Record Store in 1985, where Mantronik was mixing records behind the turntables and introducing customers to new releases. A few weeks later, they made a demo tape and started looking for a label. Soon afterwards, William Socolov, the astute founder of independent label Sleeping Bag, was in the store and was sufficiently impressed with the demo tape Mantronik played him to offer a deal. The group's first single, 1985's 'Fresh Is The Word', was a huge street and dancefloor hit, as was their production of Tricky Tee's 'Johnny The Fox'. In late 1985 they released their first album, the adventurous *Mantronix*, which included the hit singles 'Bassline' and 'Ladies', and took the marriage of street rhyme and electronic studio wizardry to new heights. Mantronix further built their reputation with their production of Joyce Sims' 'All And All' and 12.41's 'Success Is The Word', before going on to record their second album, the competent but relatively disappointing *Music Madness*. The duo were one of the most popular acts at the historic UK Fresh hip-hop festival at London's Wembley Arena in the summer of 1986, but were dropped by Sleeping Bag a year later. Mantronix appeared to have run out of fresh ideas and had been overtaken by a new generation of rappers/studio maestros. In the late 80s Tee signed up to the USAF, to be replaced by two stand-in rappers, Bryce Luvah (b. *c*.1970; cousin of LL Cool J) and DJ Dee (b. *c*.1969, Mantronik's cousin). They did hit the UK charts with *This Should Move Ya*'s promotional single, 'Got To Have Your Love'. The latter featured the vocal sheen of Wondress, while the attendant album featured a cover of Ian Dury And The Blockheads' 'Sex And Drugs And Rock 'n' Roll'. The distinctive Mantronix bass lines were still in place, though by now Kahleel was branching out into soul and R&B horizons. Possibly their best material in this format is 1991's *The Incredible Sound Machine*, which saw the introduction of singer Jade Trini. Kahleel continues to produce for others, notably English

vocalist Mica Paris. He composes all his music on an Apple Macintosh computer, a trait he shares with many of techno's leading lights.
● ALBUMS: *Mantronix* (Sleeping Bag 1985)★★★★, *Music Madness* (Sleeping Bag 1986)★★, *In Full Effect* (Capitol 1988)★★, *This Should Move Ya* (Capitol 1990)★★★, *The Incredible Sound Machine* (Capitol 1991)★★★★.
● COMPILATIONS: *The Best Of (1986-1988)* (1990)★★★★.

MARIE, KELLY

b. Jacqueline McKinnon, 23 October 1957, Paisley, Scotland. The disco/Hi-NRG singer Kelly Marie won the *Opportunity Knocks* talent competition on British television at the age of 15, but it was in France that she first enjoyed any success on vinyl when 'Who's The Lady With My Man?' was awarded a gold disc. However, 'Feels Like I'm In Love' topped the UK singles chart in 1980. The song, written by former Mungo Jerry leader Ray Dorset, had originally been intended for Elvis Presley who died before he could record it. Minor hits followed with 'Loving Just For Fun', 'Hot Love' and 'Love Trial', before Kelly's chart career came to an end. She made a part-time return to the club circuit in the 90s generally to appreciative gay Hi-NRG audiences, such as those at the G.A.Y. venue. Her last record was a cover of Billy Fury's 'Halfway To Paradise' in 1989.
● ALBUMS: *Who's That Lady With My Man* (Pye 1977)★★★, *Feels Like I'm In Love* (Calibre 1980)★★★.

MARKY MARK AND THE FUNKY BUNCH

The younger brother of New Kids On The Block's Donald Wahlberg, Mark Wahlberg (b. *c*.1971, Boston, Massachusetts, USA) was once proclaimed as the 'thinking rapper's Madonna' upon his entrance into the music industry in the early 90s. Also employed as an underwear model for Calvin Klein, Marky Mark's two albums did little to dispel his image as a clothes horse for white rap, even though all of his Funky Bunch (who include DJ Terry Yancey and five mixed gender dancers) are black. One notable hit came with 'Wildside', a revision of Lou Reed's urban mantra, 'Walk On The Wild Side'. The cover treatment brought further rewards when 'Good Vibrations' topped the charts in the USA. The attendant debut album, *Music For The People*, achieved platinum sales in 1991. He was subsequently widely

attacked in the UK by gay activists for what they described as a conspiratorial silence during Shabba Ranks' homophobic outbursts on *The Word*. Marky Mark would go on to star in his first film, alongside Danny DeVito and Wesley Snipes, titled *Renaissance Man*, and completed a rap/reggae crossover single with Prince Ital Joe, 'United'. However, his second album failed to provide significant sales and like New Kids On The Block, Marky Mark's association with the *Billboard* charts had ended by the mid-90s. He received excellent reviews for his starring role in Paul Thomas Anderson's acclaimed *Boogie Nights*, a 1997 homage to the 70s porn industry.
● ALBUMS: *Music For The People* (Interscope 1991)★★★★, *You Gotta Believe* (Interscope 1992)★★★.

MARLEY MARL

b. Marlon Williams, 30 September 1962, Queens, New York, USA. Widely revered for his considerable production skills, notably for his cousin MC Shan, Big Daddy Kane, Master Ace, Roxanne Shanté and Biz Markie, Marl's work is inhabited by a spirit of accessible, old school gusto. He has been widely congratulated for his innovative sampling techniques, using the SP1200 on hip-hop landmarks like *Eric B For President*. He also acts as host on the weekly *Rap Attack* radio programme on the WBLS-FM station in New York. The selected albums listed below sample some of this work, including contributions from Shanté and Kane, plus Kool G. Rap, Chuck D., LL Cool J, King Tee and Chubb Rock.
● ALBUMS: *In Control Volume 1* (Cold Chillin' 1988)★★★, *In Control Volume II* (Cold Chillin' 1991)★★.

MARRS

A collaboration between two 4AD bands, Colourbox and AR Kane, which, though a one-off, was enough to set alight the independent, dance and national charts during autumn 1987. 'Pump Up The Volume' was augmented on the a-side by UK champion scratch mixer C.J. Mackintosh and London disc jockey/journalist Dave Dorrell. Primarily aimed at the dance market, the record was originally mailed to the 500 most influential regional club and dance DJs on an anonymous white label, in order that it received exposure six weeks prior to its stock version. On official release it entered the charts at number 35, a figure attained on 12-inch sales only. Daytime radio play

ensured the single was the next week's highest climber, rising 24 places to number 11. The following two weeks it stayed at number 2 before reaching the number 1 spot on 28 September 1987. Originally the idea of 4AD supremo Ivo, the single featured samples of James Brown, a practice already common in hip-hop that would soon come into vogue for an avalanche of dance tracks: 'We've used a lot of rhythms and time signatures from old records, classic soul records, but mixed that with modern electronic instruments and AR Kane's guitar sound', was how the single was described. The single was never followed up, apparently due to acrimony between the involved personnel over finance, which was a great shame. As such, the MARRS discography is a brief but blemishless one. Dorrell would go on to manage Bush while Mackintosh returned to the club circuit.

MASS ORDER

A Baltimore-based duo of Mark Valentine and Eugene Hayes, who grew up listening to the O'Jays and soul standards. Mass Order scored a huge autumn 1991 'hit' with their gospel house cracker, 'Take Me Away', a popular but elusive disc. It was actually a bootleg that had been pirated from a DAT tape at New York's New Music Seminar. It was eventually given a proper release (under its full title, 'Lift Every Voice (Take Me Away)') with remixes from the Basement Boys and Tony Humphries. As a footnote the bootlegging incident went to court, but the miscreants, David Cooper and William Lynch, still escaped justice. They were acquitted because they 'did not know they were breaking the law'.
● ALBUMS: *Maybe One Day* (Columbia 1992)★★★.

MASSIAH, ZEITIA

b. c.1974, Barbados. Dance vocalist Zeitia Massiah initially rose to prominence singing alongside Kim Wilde as live support to Michael Jackson. Her powerful vocals subsequently saw her signed by Virgin Records in the UK. Her debut single, 'This Is The Place', was playlisted by BBC Radio 1 and became a club hit in 1995. Her second release, 'Sexual Prime', was released in March 1996 and featured remixes from Tony De Vit and production duo Sharp (George Mitchell and Steven React). Both showcased her expressive and animated delivery. She also toured as backing vocalist to Tom Jones.

MASSIVE ATTACK

This loose Bristol collective has grown to become one of the premier UK dance/rap outfits. The group features the talents of rapper '3D' Del Najo (b. *c.*1966), and Daddy G (b. *c.*1959) and Mushroom (b. *c.*1968, Knowle West, Bristol, England). They started in 1988 having spent several years working on various mobile sound systems, as well as releasing records under the Wild Bunch moniker ('Fucking Me Up', 'Tearing Down The Avenue'). Nellee Hooper, a former member of the Wild Bunch, left to work with Soul II Soul, while another original member, Milo Johnson, began work in Japan. 3D is also a well-respected graffiti artist, having had his work exhibited in art galleries and included in a television survey on Channel 4. Liaisons with Neneh Cherry eventually led to a meeting with Cameron McVey, who produced Massive Attack's debut album. The resultant *Blue Lines* boasted three hit singles: 'Daydreaming', 'Unfinished Sympathy' (which also featured an orchestral score) and 'Safe From Harm'. The blend of rap, deep reggae and soul was provocative and rich in texture, and featured singing from Cherry and Shara Nelson. An outstanding achievement, it had taken eight months to create, 'with breaks for Christmas and the World Cup'. 'Unfinished Sympathy' was particularly well received. *Melody Maker* magazine ranked it as the best single of 1991, and it remains a perennial club favourite. One minor hiccup occurred when they were forced, somewhat hysterically, to change their name during the Gulf War in order to maintain airplay. It was duly shortened to Massive. Their philosophy singled them out as dance music's new sophisticates: 'We don't ever make direct dance music. You've got to be able to listen and then dance.' That status was confirmed when U2 asked them to remix their single 'Mysterious Ways'. Despite *Blue Lines* being widely acclaimed, the band disappeared shortly afterwards. Shara Nelson pursued a solo career, with Massive Attack put on hold until the mid-90s. Another early contributor, Tricky, launched himself to considerable fanfare, with Massive Attack widely credited as an influence on fellow-Bristolians Portishead. A second Massive Attack album finally arrived in 1994, with former collaborator Nellee Hooper returning as producer. The featured singers this time included Tricky, Nigerian-born Nicolette, Everything But The Girl's Tracey Thorn and Horace Andy (who had also contributed to the debut) on a selection of tracks that sadly failed to recapture the magic of *Blue Lines*. Many critics suggested that others had now run so far with the baton handed them by the collective that the instigators themselves were yet to catch up. Apart from a dub remix of *Protection* recorded with the Mad Professor, little was heard from Massive Attack until 'Risingson' was released in autumn 1997. The single's menacing atmosphere was a taster for the downbeat grooves of *Mezzanine*, which was released to wide critical acclaim in April 1998.

● ALBUMS: *Blue Lines* (Wild Bunch/EMI 1991)★★★★★, *Protection* (EMI 1994)★★★, Vs the Mad Professor *No Protection* (Circa 1995)★★★, *Mezzanine* (Virgin 1998)★★★★.

MASTER ACE

Raised in Brooklyn, Master Ace (aka Masta Ace) became a hip-hop DJ in the 70s before adjusting to MC status by 1983. He won a rapping competition two years later which earned him studio time with producer Marley Marl, before a collegiate interlude followed. He contributed to the *In Control Volume 1* set by Marl, and the latter's label, Cold Chillin', offered him a deal. His debut album, *Take A Look Around*, was fuelled by Marley Marl's funk throb and was to include a duet with Biz Markie. Biz never made it to the recording session for 'Me And The Biz' and Ace mimicked Biz for what should have been his part on the track. Songs like 'Brooklyn Battles' attempted to look through the blood and rage circus of urban decadent rap. He had earlier contributed to the Brand New Heavies' *Heavy Rhyme Experience*. His second album was better yet, the title-track, 'Slaughtahouse', a clever parody on the absurd machismo of gangsta rap: '99 rappers wanna kill to sound ill, You couldn't find their brains with a drill'. However, the graphic presentation of the video failed to impress MTV who banned it. He enjoyed more success with the Crooklyn Dodgers project (alongside Special Ed and Buckshot of Black Moon), scoring with the Spike Lee soundtrack single, 'Crooklyn'. He describes himself as a hip-hop purist, and certainly his wordy, considered narratives owe a debt to Gil Scott-Heron.

● ALBUMS: *Take A Look Around* (Warners 1990)★★★, *Slaughtahouse* (Delicious Vinyl 1993)★★★★.

MASTERCUTS SERIES

A Beechwood subsidiary UK record label master-minded by Ian Dewhirst, Mastercuts was launched in 1991 to document some of dance music's most essential moments, in all its myriad forms. Initial releases such as *Jazz Funk 1* sold 25,000 copies, while *New Jack Swing* climbed as high as number 8 in the *Music Week* compilation chart, showing well against much better-funded, television-advertised albums. The first record in the series had been Classic Mix, but other formats were explored in the following order: Jazz-Funk, Mellow, New Jack Swing, Funk, Salsoul, Rare Groove, P-Funk, 80s Groove, Electro and House. Each came complete with insightful sleeve-notes and anecdotes, in a manner that suggested that at last dance music might be taking its history as seriously as other forms of music. In 1994 the label also reluanched the legendary Streetsounds label.

MASTERS AT WORK

aka Lil' Louie Vega and Kenny 'Dope' Gonzalez, who marked the inception of their partnership by releasing 'Ride On The Rhythm' in 1991. On the back of that and their well established personal reputations (appearances as extras in Spaghetti Westerns notwithstanding), they subsequently undertook a vast array of remix projects. These began with Saint Etienne ('Only Love Can Break Your Heart'), plus Chic, Debbie Gibson, Melissa Morgan, BG The Prince Of Rap ('Take Control Of The Party'), Lisa Stansfield, Deee-Lite ('Bittersweet Loving') plus legendary Latin jazz player Tito Puente's 'Ran Kan Kan'. In turn Puente contributed three times to Louie's 1992 album with singer Marc Anthony. They also recorded, in their own right, material including 'Can't Stop The Rhythm (with Jocelyn Brown) for US label Cutting. Widely regarded as the cream of the profession, not everybody was clamouring for their wares - Jamiroquai's 'Emergency On Planet Earth' remix was rumoured to be hated by the artist concerned. His was a rare dissenting voice, however.

MASTERS OF CEREMONY

Nowadays chiefly remembered for the exploits of lead rapper Grand Puba (b. Maxwell Dixon), who would go on to front Brand Nubian before selecting a solo career. Masters Of Ceremony's singular album release was a pedestrian affair, divorced of the religious dogma, or indeed the musical precision, which characterised the work of Brand Nubian. Without which their attempts to fascimile a Public Enemy sneer wore fatally thin. However, it did include a major hit in 'Sexy'.
● ALBUMS: *Dynamite* (4th & Broadway 1988)★★.

MATSURI PRODUCTIONS

John Perloff and Tsuyoshi Suzuki set up Matsuri (Japanese for ritual or ceremony) in November 1994, since which time it has become one of the most innovative and respected labels in its field. The latter's intention was to introduce more people to psychedelic techno (what the media termed 'Goa' trance) when it was more of an underground scene. They kicked off with Prana's *Scarab* EP, the title track of which appeared on the first album release, Prana's *Cyclone*, and over the next few years they brought out EPs by Manmademan, Doof and Transwave, among others. A number of compilations, notably *The Truth Of Communication*, *Abstract Phaze* and *Resonance Mood*, established Matsuri as a leader in the psy-trance field, producing quality tunes from a range of respected names from around the world, as well as one-off collaborations. By 1997 the label was turning towards a psychedelic sound that embraced genres such as techno, breakbeat, drum 'n' bass and electronica as well as trance, a move heralded by the excellent compilations *Let It Rip* and *Sympathy In Chaos*. *Let It Rip* combined some elements of four-on-the-floor trance with more varied funky ideas, including breakbeats and slap bass which, blended with the most crazy noises and textures, produced fresh, exciting, psychedelic sounds, less turgid than much riff-based psy-trance. *Sympathy In Chaos* presented a more chilled set. In 1998 EPs from Digitalis (*Soma Junkies*) and Sandman (*Nostradamus*), and albums from Quirk (*Machina Electra & Fornax Chemica*) and the Australian Ju Ju Space Jazz (*Ju Ju Space Jazz*) confirmed Matsuri's broad-minded, truly experimental approach. The label's sound, together with their distinctive artwork, developed by Mark Neal in London and Organix in Tokyo, illustrates Tsuyoshi's philosophy, which espouses artistic expression applied with the latest technology.

MAURIZIO

Berlin DJ and recording artist who runs the Basic Channel label. He is famed for placing only a large M on the centre of his records, then pressing them in America so they are presumed to have emerged from Detroit. Cuts such as 'Domina' (1994) highlighted his experimental but accessible craft, while collaborations with genuine native Detroit man Carl Craig ('Mind') proffered further cult status.

MAX-A-MILLION

Based in Chicago, Illinois, USA, the dance act Max-A-Million consist of A'Lisa B., Duran Estevez and Tommye. They are one of several bands to emerge from the city's 20 Fingers collective, which has also spawned Gillette and Roula. Their debut album, *Take Your Time (Do It Right)*, took its title from the inclusion of a cover of the S.O.S. Band song, which was updated with deep bass/hip-hop production values. An ill-advised version of Marvin Gaye's 'Sexual Healing' was also included, alongside originals such as 'Fat Boy' and 'Hangin' On'. With accomplished songwriting and a marriage of traditional soul construction with hip-hop and urban R&B stylings, *Take Your Time* attracted widespread praise within the black music community.
● ALBUMS: *Take Your Time (Do It Right)* (S.O.S./Zoo 1995)★★★.

MAY, DERRICK

b. *c*.1964, USA. If one name crops up again and again in discussions of techno, it is that of Derrick 'Mayday' May. Alongside Juan Atkins, Carl Craig and Kevin Saunderson, May is regarded as one of the kings of the Detroit sound. Inspired by Yello and Kraftwerk, he began to make electronic music with Atkins and Saunderson while studying with them at Belleville High, Detroit. Recording either as Mayday or Rhythim Is Rhythim (occasionally in conjunction with Carl Craig) and generally on his own Transmat Records label, he went on to carve out a new vein in dance music that synthesized the advances of the electro movement with the more challenging end of the house movement - a music that defined 'techno'. Early cuts such as 'Nude Photo' and 'The Dance', both on Transmat, were inspirational to many. However, it was the release of 'Strings Of Life' in 1987, which, with its wide appeal to the house music fans of the late 80s, simultaneously brought May his deserved acclaim and Detroit techno to European clubgoers. However, May has never proved prolific in his recordings. After the success of 'Strings Of Life' he largely fled the dance scene, aside from a remix of Yello's 'The Race'. Rhythim Is Rhythim did not follow up 'Strings Of Life' until

1990, when 'The Beginning' was released.
May went on to cut three disappointing tracks on System 7's debut album, before Network released *Innovator: Soundtrack For The Tenth Planet* in 1991, a six-track EP that comprised some of May's definitive moments to date. In the same year May was responsible for what Carl Craig has called the finest remix ever, Sueño Latino's 'Sueño Latino', itself a reworking of Manuel Goettschring's epic 'E2-M4'. It was followed in 1992 by *Relics*, a double album of Transmat's finest moments, heavily featuring Rhythim Is Rhythim, which coincided with a re-release of 'Strings Of Life' on the Belgium label Buzz, this time in a drumless version reminiscent of May's 'Sueño Latino' remix. More recently, Transmat has been revived following its signing to Sony, resulting in the long-awaited release of Rhythim Is Rhythim's 1991 recordings, 'Kao-tic Harmony' and 'Icon', and the Japanese (and subsequent American) release of a comprehensive Derrick May retrospective, *Innovator*, which contains all May's work for the Transmat label including remixes and tracks released for the first time.
● COMPILATIONS: *Relics: A Transmat Compilation* (Buzz 1992)★★★★, *Innovator* (10th Planet 1998)★★★★.

MC 900FT JESUS

Dallas, Texas-based Mark Griffin is one of the more credible examples of white hip-hop. His pseudonym was taken from a statement made by US 'televangelist' Oral Roberts. Roberts once reminisced about how he was wandering in the Colorado desert, distraught at being unable to raise the money to build a sanctuary, when a huge Jesus appeared in front of him to reassure him. Alongside his musical collaborator DJ Zero, Mark Griffin explores a wide variety of styles including jazz and industrial dance as well as hip-hop. The lyrics, especially on his second album, track a more personal, introspective path than many of his peers.
He made his debut in 1989 with the self-titled *MC 900ft Jesus With DJ Zero* EP, which highlighted his distinctive vocal style, which could hardly be described as rap in conventional terms, and reflected more the spoken word narratives of the beat poets. However, he had certainly been listening to the rise of hip-hop on the East Coast, as the influence of Public Enemy testified. His debut album centred on club-orientated material, though again the interest centred on his lyrics

('The faces on the covers of all the magazines are me/Only cleverly airbrushed to look like someone else' from 'The Killer Inside Me'). Later, his single 'The City Sleeps Tonight' caused an outcry in Baltimore, where its inflammatory lyrics coincided with an outbreak of arson. Griffin moved to Rick Rubin's American label in time for his third album, *One Step Ahead Of The Spider*. Its title was inspired by, 'this dream that I was standing in a field and a guy in front of me turned round and threw spiders on me. It was the first time a dream had literally woke me up in fright.' His vivid imagination was again in full bloom here, blurring reality with his sneering delivery and sparse hip-hop beats, produced by his new, eight-piece backing band.

● ALBUMS: *Hell With The Lid Off* (Nettwerk/CIR 1990)★★★, *Welcome To My Dream* (CIR 1991)★★★, *One Step Ahead Of The Spider* (American 1995)★★★.

MC BRAINS

b. James De Shannon Davis, *c*.1975, Cleveland, Ohio, USA. MC Brains' early career was fostered by Michael Bivins (of New Edition and Bell Biv Devoe fame), who first brought him to the attention of Motown Records. His debut album, recorded when he was only 17, introduced his catchy, unassuming blend of commercial rap, and included two singles, the minor hit 'Brainstorming', and the US Top 30 success, 'Oochie Coochie'. He has failed to follow-up his breakthrough, however, while Bivins has moved on to discovering fresh talent.

● ALBUMS: *Lovers Lane* (Motown 1992)★★.

MC BREED

MC Eric Breed (b. *c*.1972, Flint, Michigan, USA) was originally supported by his cousin Al Breed (of DFC fame) in the early 90s, before that artist would go solo with the aid of T-Trouble E. Both Breeds would, however, remain firm friends, Eric going on to a support/advisory capacity on the latter's debut album. Under the title MC Breed And DFC, he had scored a crossover hit single (US number 66) with the debut album's 'Ain't No Future In Yo' Frontin'', a typical slice of hard-nosed gangsta vanity (a theme revisited on the second set's 'Ain't To Be Fucked With', retitled 'Ain't To Be Flexed With' for single consumption). 'Ain't No Future In Yo' Frontin'' continues to enjoy a healthy half-life and has been much sampled by other rap artists. The album which bore it was produced with the aid of Bernard Terry, of Ready For The World fame. The follow-up set again saw him working with Terry and his DJ/Producer Flash Technology, its chart profile buoyed by a further three successful singles. After sessions for a third set were completed, he was invited to join George Clinton for his 'Paint The White House Black' ensemble single. When *The New Breed* emerged it brought a harder-edged sound, as might have been anticipated by its title. It featured guest appearances from 2Pac ('Gotta Get Mine'), Clinton (on the video to 'Tight') and D.O.C. Production was assisted by Warren G and Colin Wolfe. Long-term friend D.O.C. would also contribute a song to Breed's fourth set, entitled 'B.R. Double E. D'. Other guests included DFC and Jamal of Illegal fame on an album whose high watermark was set by the 'Teach My Kids' track.

● ALBUMS: *MC Breed & DFC* (S.D.E.G. 1991)★★★, *20 Below* (Wrap-Ichiban 1992)★★, *The New Breed* (Wrap-Ichiban 1993)★★★★, *Funkafied* (Wrap-Ichiban1993)★★★, *Big Baller* (Ichiban 1994)★★, *MC Breed* (Flatline)★★★.

● COMPILATIONS: *The Best Of MC Breed* (Ichiban 1995)★★★★.

MC BUZZ B

b. Shorn Braithwaite. Eco-conscious UK rapper who allies his intelligent, highly wordy raps to a jazz/soul-funk melange which is characterised beyond anything else by its cool, restrained vibe. He debuted for Manchester independent Play Hard with the 12-inch only 'Slaphead' in May 1988, following it with 'How Sleep The Brave' and 'The Sequel' the following year. It was enough to procure a contract from Polydor Records, who released his ironically titled debut album in 1991. However, a series of singles, 'The Last Tree', 'Never Change' (delayed due to problems in obtaining clearance on a sample from Bruce Hornsby's 'That's Just The Way It Is') and 'Don't Have The Time' during that period failed to break him, as he became yet another UK hip-hop under-achiever. He made a comeback in 1993 by providing the vocal to Lionrock's 'Pocket Of Peace'.

● ALBUMS: *Words Escape Me* (Polydor 1991)★★★.

MC DUKE

Together with his DJ Leader One, this British MC released 'The Final Conflict' in 1990, which left substantial imprints in the relatively virgin soil of UK hip-hop. Raised in east London, MC Duke made his recorded debut on Music Of Life's compilation, *Hard As Hell*. Later he would make his home there, releasing two relatively succesful solo albums. He picked up *Hip Hop Connection* magazine's 1990 award for Best British Recording Artist, and even broke the Top 75 of the UK charts with 'I'm Riffin'/'English Rasta', before the recession cut in. Despite two solid singles for the Shut Up And Dance label, his fortunes declined. Duke has gone on to produce the 90s compilation series *The Royal Family*, to showcase new British rap talent. In turn he set up his own label, Bluntly Speaking Vinyl, formed in conjunction with Dan Donnely (Suburban Base Records). The initial releases included a 12-inch by Phat Skillz (essentially MC Duke) and material from a new group, IQ Procedure.

● ALBUMS: *Organised Rhyme* (Music Of Life 1989)★★, *Return Of The Dread-I* (Music Of Life 1991)★★★.

MC ERIC

b. Eric Martin, 19 August 1970, Cardiff, Wales. MC Eric, aka Me One, is of Jamaican descent, though he grew up in Wales as the youngest of twelve brothers and sisters. It was via his stint in Technotronic (notably the 'This Is Technotronic' refrain, appearing in said video with his notorious 'skyscraper' hairstyle) that he first graced television screens and stereos. He had been introduced to the band via his girlfriend, Ya Kid K. 'I was 18 and Ya Kid K was 17 when we came into Technotronic and we knew that the money wasn't good'. He has also contributed to material from artists as diverse as Madonna and Jazzy Jeff. His debut solo album, promoted by a single, 'Jealous', was an artistic success, with deceptively subtle shades to its musical spine, buoyed by piano motifs and lolloping bass. Following its release, however, he seems to have became another of rap's many yesterday men. In the meantime he had a child with Ya Kid K, one Eric Jnr.

● ALBUMS: *I Beg Uno Ceasefire* (Polydor 1991)★★★.

MC J

b. Jens Mueller, *c.*1971, Berlin, Germany. This renowned anti-fascist rapper and political activist currently resides in Paris, France, due to fears for his safety. He has certainly given the extreme right reason to silence him. He is behind an internationally distributed newsletter, *Germany Alert*, which catalogues racist incidents, an objective to

which his lyrics are also tuned. This has pushed him to the top of many organisations' hate lists. Typically, the final date of his 1993 British tour at Goldsmiths College in London saw an increased police presence due to threats that skinheads would attempt to halt his performance. He has been condemned by his own government as 'an alarmist', but even the briefest perusal of *Germany Alert* gives a very different impression. Sadly, *We Are The Majority*, for all its noble intentions, remained too deeply rooted in rhetoric to secure an international audience.

● ALBUMS: *We Are The Majority* (Germany 1993)★★.

MC KINKY

b. Caron Geary. This UK female ragga chat artist grew up in north London, England, on a diet of reggae, David Essex, Marc Bolan and Kate Bush. After being expelled from sixth-form college, she worked in children's playcentres by day and in nightclubs after dark. MC Kinky met Boy George while working as a DJ at Fred's in Soho, London, and was signed to his More Protein label in 1989. Her first release was in conjunction with the E-Zee Posse - 'Everything Starts With An E' - which became an instant UK club hit and eventually, after several attempts, went high in the charts. Once mistakenly arrested by police for soliciting (she was actually window shopping) her first solo single, 'Get Over It', was released in 1991 - after which the trail runs cold.

MC LYTE

b. Lana Moorer, 11 October 1970, Queens, New York, USA, but raised in Brooklyn. The daughter of First Priority boss Nat Robinson, and sister to the Audio Two brothers, Lyte began her career in fine style with the 45 'I Cram To Understand U (Sam)', released when she was still a teenager. The story told of personal deceit in a relationship, the narrator unable to compete for her boyfriend's attentions with his new mistress - crack. It was delivered with such force that it still has few peers in terms of adult, hardcore female rap. Lyte has gone on to underscore her patent scouring wit, often referring to the out-of-control egos of her male counterparts, with synthesizer and funk beats coalescing beneath. Her debut album additionally sampled Ray Charles, Helen Reddy and the Four Seasons. Her songs are populated by fully realised characters, though it is an unfortunate truism that they often end up dead (via

AIDS, lung cancer, violence or drugs). Despite the contributions of Grand Puba on her second album, which was musically solid, there was a lack of lyrical progression which limited its appeal. *Ain't No Other* included attacks on fellow rappers Roxanne Shanté ('Steady F. King') and an answer record to Apache's 'Gangsta Bitch' ('Ruffneck', which went gold when released on single). Rap forerunner KRS-1 introduced the tracks in a pseudo ragga style. Like Queen Latifah and others, she has founded her own management company, Dupe The Moon Productions, which also handles Isis and Brooklyn rappers Born In Hell. *Bad As I Wanna Be* and the follow-up remix album featured a more mature style.

● ALBUMS: *Lyte As A Rock* (First Priority 1988)★★★, *Eyes On This* (First Priority 1989)★★★, *Act Like You Know* (First Priority 1991)★★★, *Ain't No Other* (First Priority 1993)★★★, *Bad As I Wanna Be* (East West 1996)★★★★, *Badder Than B-fore* remix album (East West 1997)★★★.

MC MELL 'O'

b. Battersea, London, England. One of the earliest members of the UK's indigenous rap clan, Mell 'O' began his career in the best traditions of hip-hop by breakdancing and body-popping in the streets of Covent Garden during the early 80s. He modelled himself on Grandmaster Melle Mel, calling himself Grandmaster Mellow in tribute, eventually abbreviating it to MC Mell 'O'. These activities would be followed by improvised jam sets at the Charing Cross Centre youth project. He also cruised with sound systems like First Class and Young Lion, and reggae remains a strong component in his Cockney-delivered rhymes (he was among the first British rappers to reject the process of imitating East or West Coast American accents). Together with fellow pupils Monie Love, DJ Pogo and Sparkie D, he formed the DETT (Determination, Endeavour and Total Triumph) collective, based on the New York Native Tongues principle. Together they released a solitary record, 'Freestyle', in 1987. This underground jamming scene lasted for several years, and it was not until 1989 that he released his first records. After a well-received debut album for Republic, he swiched to Jazzie B's (Soul II Soul) Funki Dred label. However, he fell victim to record company politicking (when Motown pulled their finanical backing for Funki Dred). A completed album, due for release in 1992, was scrapped. Worse, Jazzie B

held on to his contract meaning he was not released until December 1993. In the meantime his only sighting was as part of Island Records' *The Rebirth of Cool* set, with 'Open Up Your Mind'. Freed from Funki Dred at last, he signed to the Stereo MC's' Natural Response label in 1994. He had at least spent some of the intervening period working - notably on projects with Izit and the Young Disciples. His debut release for his new home was *The First Chronicles Of DETT*, in the summer of 1994. The first track on the record was 'I Hear Voices', which tackled the problem of mental illness in immigrant black generations, and was another intelligent, illuminating epistle from one of the genuine talents of the British hip-hop scene.

● ALBUMS: *Thoughts Released* (Republic 1989)★★★.

MC POOH

b. Lawrence Thomas, USA. Rapper who emerged in the 90s with lyrical preoccupations including sex, money and murder (his debut album even housed one cut of that title). Other songs included the socio-political 'The Projects', but elsewhere the tasteless sexual jibes continued on 'I Eat Pussy' and 'Your Dick'.

● ALBUMS: *Funky As I Wanna Be* (Jive 1992)★★.

MC REN

b. Lorenzo Patterson, Compton, Los Angeles, USA. Another of NWA's personnel to launch a solo career. He opened his slate with the *Kizz My Black Azz* EP, the title of which was a thinly veiled reference to the actions of Vanilla Ice. For his debut album Ren joined up with a slew of producers, including Rhythm D, the Whole Click (which featured Ren's brother Juvenile) and Denmark-based crew Solid Productions. A deal with the latter was first mooted when Ren met them while they were working on the soundtrack to the *CB4* film, on which they encouraged Ren to participate. However, Ren has proved unable to replicate the lyrical incisiveness of Ice Cube nor the satisfying musical stance of Dr. Dre. Allusions to the wisdom of the Nation Of Islam have revealed little in the way of insight or character.

● ALBUMS: *Kizz My Black Azz* mini-album (Ruthless 1992),★★★ *Shock Of The Hour* (Ruthless 1993)★★★, *Da Villain In Black* (Ruthless 1996)★★★★, *Ruthless For Life* (Ruthless 1998)★★★.

MC SERCH

b. Michael Berrin, Queens, New York, USA. After splitting from white rap trio 3rd Bass, Serch remained with Def Jam for the launch of his solo career in 1992. Shortly afterwards he would take up a position as A&R Vice President for Wild Pitch Records. His sole solo hit thus far proved to be 'Love Will Show Us'.

● ALBUMS: *Return Of The Product* (Def Jam 1992)★★★.

MC SHAN

b. Shawn Moltke, 8 September 1965, Queens, New York, USA. Moltke enjoyed an unusual start to his hip-hop career. Rather than the drudgery of demo cassettes and auditions, he was first spotted by his future Cold Chillin' boss as he attempted to steal his car. Nevertheless, with the early guiding hand of cousin Marley Marl, Shan has gone on to provide an inconsistent but occasionally interesting legacy. His debut album was the archetypal B-boy artefact, replete with Marl's stripped down production and conscious and party rhymes (the best example of the former being the anti-drugs track 'Jane, Stop This Crazy Thing!', the worst instance of the latter 'Project 'Ho'). The follow-up was more musically varied, but Shan's voice lacked the agility to compete with some exquisite samples. He dispensed with Marl in time for *Play It Again, Shan*, which, as the title might suggest, saw a bid for more mainstream territory. Apart from the instructional 'It Ain't A Hip Hop Record', there was little to distinguish this collection and its lacklustre Heavy D-styled performance.

● ALBUMS: *Down By Law* (Cold Chillin' 1987)★★★★, *Born To Be Wild* (Cold Chillin' 1988)★★★, *Play It Again, Shan* (Cold Chillin' 1990)★★.

MC SHY D

b. Peter Jones, Bronx, New York, USA. Shy D is the cousin of Afrika Bambaataa, and grew up with the sounds and philosophy of the Zulu Nation. Moving to Atlanta in 1978, he made his name via his debut single 'Rapp Will Never Die' in 1985, before joining Luke Skywalker (now Luke) Records for 'I've Gotta Be Tough' and 'Shake It'. These releases, some of the first on the label, featured the prominent 'Miami bass' sound. After two well-received albums he set up his own Benz Records imprint in 1990, but his fortunes declined thereafter, 1991 being spent in the Georgia State

Penal System. More fruitful was his liaison with Wrap/Ichiban Records, which saw the release of a quality single ('True To The Game') and album which re-acquainted him with the hip-hop public.

● ALBUMS: *Gotta Be Tough* (Luke Skywalker 1987)★★★, *Comin' Correct* (Luke 1988)★★★, *Don't Sweat Me* (Benz Records 1990)★★★, *The Comeback* (Wrap/Ichiban 1993)★★★★.

MC SOLAAR

b. Dakar, Senegal, but raised in Cairo and Paris, MC Solaar is the most prominent of the new breed of French rappers. His debut album (translating as Who Sows The Wind Will Reap The Beat) gave him four Top 10 French singles, the album itself moving over 200,000 copies. It brought him to the attention of the UK's Talkin' Loud imprint. They, like many others, were impressed by his free-flowing, relaxed style, and its easy musical backdrop, formulated by his DJ/producer Jimmy Jay. Gang Starr were so taken with the album that after a single hearing they asked if they could remix the title-track. Solaar also took part in many collaborative projects for the Talkin' Loud stable (United Future Organization, Urban Species) and the Guru of Gang Starr-orchestrated Jazzamatazz project. His own material most often concerns sad stories about malcontents in the stream of French life. The wordplay and nuances do not translate easily, but the musicality of the French language does. As well as rappers like Big Daddy Kane, Solaar draws his inspiration from the French literary tradition of Baudelaire and Jaques Prevert.

● ALBUMS: *Qui Seme Le Vent Recolte Le Tempo* (Talkin' Loud 1993)★★, *Prose Combat* (Talkin' Loud 1994)★★, *Paradisiaque* (Mercury 1997)★★★.

MC TROUBLE

b. Latasha Rogers, *c*.1972. MC Trouble became Motown's first female rapper when she appeared in 1990 with a debut album and attendant singles ('High Roller' etc) at the tender age of 18. Backed by the soul undertow more familiar with the label, her rhymes were contrastingly harsh and cutting. Trouble's talents were obvious to many. Above and beyond being a talented contemporary rapper, she was also responsible for writing, arranging and producing her debut set. Her conscious raps included the likes of 'Black Line', which parodied black talk shows, while in a romantic mode cuts like 'Make You Mine' were

offered a smooth, soulful sheen. A guest appearance by Full Force was pleasing but incidental. She passed away in the early 90s.
● ALBUMS: *Gotta Get A Grip* (Motown 1990)★★★★.

MC TUNES

b. Nicky Lockett, Manchester, England. This rapper rose to fame by collaborating with local dance music stars 808 State, and later appeared on A Guy Called Gerald's 'Juicebox' single (A Guy Called Gerald also being a former member of 808 State). Whenever Tunes recorded solo, however, he seemed to possess a talent for over-estimating his own abilities. 'This is a concept of exceptional musical talent', he rapped on the single, 'Primary Rhyming'. It was not. His sole album was completed with strong musical backdrops provided by 808 State, but the fierce rendering of tales of inner-city violence and the perils of drink and drugs failed to gel. 808 State moved on to greater achievements while their former sparring partner was banished to obscurity. MC Tunes finally returned in the mid-90s with a new Manchester band, Dust Junkies. Featuring four musicians and a more guitar-orientated style, they were signed by Polydor Records in 1996.
● ALBUMS: with 808 State *The North At Its Height* (ZTT 1990)★★.

MCM

b. England. A former member of the well-regarded British hip-hop group Caveman, rapper MCM left that band due to internal friction and problems with their record company, Profile Records. MCM was the first of the former members to secure a solo contract, this time through BMG Records. He made his debut with the 1994 single, 'I Got Soul', produced by DJ Biznizz, which was stylistically familiar to the work of Caveman and their largely imported US style, but with a rawer, funkier edge. However, delays in the release of his debut album ensured he was unable to convert the positive reviews for 'I Got Soul' into artistic momentum.

MEAN MACHINE

Though somewhat unfairly consigned to the wastebasket of musical history, Mean Machine deserve their place in the hip-hop hall of fame by dint of being the first crew to rap in Spanish, in 1979. As such they would serve as a signpost to subsequent generations of Latino rappers, from Kid Frost to Mellow Man Ace, to Cypress Hill and K7.

MEAT BEAT MANIFESTO

Their name a grotesque reference to masturbation, London, England's Meat Beat Manifesto are a post-industrial dance group comprising multi-instrumentalist/vocalist Jack Dangers and programmer Jonny Stephens, aided by non-musical contributors Marcus Adams (dancer and choreographer) and Craig Morrison (stage and costume design). Taking their theme as the modern information/consumer society, the group combines samples drawn from television and commercials, combined with hip-hop beats and dub grooves to create mesmerizing aural soundscapes. The group began releasing a series of 12-inch singles (still their best medium) in the late 80s, which were later anthologized on *Storm The Studio*. Herein the 'cut-up' techniques pioneered in literature by William Burroughs were transposed to diverse musical cultures, a process confirmed by the fact that the title *Storm The Studio* was adapted from a statement made by Burroughs' character Uranian Willy in *The Soft Machine*. Enigmatically, none of the songs were given individual titles. The tapes for a debut album proper had been lost during a fire at their London studio, thus *Armed Audio Warfare* again comprised largely dated material. Their first studio album proper, *99%*, was less visceral and more attuned to the burgeoning house movement, though the group's lyrics were no less challenging. That was especially true of 1992's *Satyricon*, on which such subjects as consumerism ('That Shirt') and animal rights ('Untold Stories') were addressed without the band's sound becoming too didactic. In the 90s Dangers also became a celebrated remixer, working with artists including Consolidated, the Shamen, David Byrne and MC 900ft Jesus. After a four-year gap Meat Beat Manifesto returned in 1996 with their fifth studio album, *Subliminal Sandwich*.
● ALBUMS: *Storm The Studio* (Wax Trax! 1989)★★★, *Armed Audio Warfare* (Wax Trax! 1990)★★★, *99%* (Play It Again Sam/Mute 1990)★★★, *Satyricon* (Mute 1992)★★★, *Subliminal Sandwich* (Mute 1996)★★★, *Actual Sounds & Voices* (Play It Again Sam 1998)★★★.

MEDIA RECORDS

(see Bortolotti, Gianfranco)

MEGABASS

Comprising Darren Ash (b. c.1968, Sussex, England) and Martin Smith (b. c.1968, Sussex, England), Megabass grew as an offshoot of the Music Factory (a team, including Andy Pickles and Ian Morgan of Jive Bunny who are well known for their 'megamixes' for nightclub DJs). The intention to record as a duo arose from a commission to provide a whole album of remixes titled *Megabass*, plus an excerpted single to promote the album. In 1990 their 'Time To Make The Floor Burn' single reached number 16 in the UK charts. A medley of mixes featuring artists such as Kid N' Play, Rebel MC, Black Box, Inner City, Technotronic and others, it was their sole chart hit.

● ALBUMS: *Megabass* (Megabass 1991)★★★.

MEKON

90s jungle artist Mekon is the pseudonym of John Gosling, formerly a member of both Psychic TV and William Orbit's Bass-O-Matic. His debut solo single was 'Phatty's Lunch Box'. The genesis of the follow-up single, 'Revenge Of The Mekon', was extremely unusual. Gosling had just finished reading the biography of Frankie Fraser, a friend of the London gangsters the Kray brothers, when, coincidentally, he met Fraser on the streets of Islington, London. He later contacted Fraser through his publishers and set up a recording session at which three hours of Fraser talking were recorded. The single was then mixed from these tapes, with Fraser's reminiscences of the underworld underpinned by Gosling's dub-heavy orchestration. Gosling was reportedly not frightened by Fraser's reputation, but certainly respectful of it: 'There's not gonna be any arguing about the publishing splits on the track. He can have what he wants.'

● ALBUMS: *Welcome To Tackletown* (Wall Of Sound 1997)★★★.

MELENDES, LISA

b. East Harlem, New York, USA. This tiny Puerto Rican singer found immediate success in 1988's soul/dance scene when she made her debut with 'Make Noise', assisted by producer Carlo Berrios. 'Make Noise' was the result of her experiments with a new hybrid of street/dance music, which she christened 'new school'. A second hit single, 'Together Forever', sold nearly half a million copies, and topped the *Billboard* Dance and Hot 100 charts. Afterwards her career stalled, though an attempt to revive her fortunes was made in 1994 with *True To Life*, produced by hip-hop artist Greg Nice (Nice And Smooth). Preceded by the single 'Goody Goody', it heralded Melendes's new image - sultry looks and free-flowing dresses contrasting with heavy combat boots.

● ALBUMS: *True To Life* (Fever 1994)★★.

MELLE MEL AND THE FURIOUS 5

Melle Mel (b. Melvin Glover, New York City, New York, USA) was a typical black 'ghetto child' whose interest in music originally stemmed from the Beatles. He soon embraced the earliest sounds of hip-hop in the mid 70s, becoming a breakdancer with the D-Squad. As a DJ with his brother Kid Creole he was influenced by others in the profession like Klark Kent and Timmy Tim who used to talk rhymes whilst playing music. The pair started their own brand of rapping and around 1977 set up with another DJ, Grandmaster Flash - who gave Melle Mel his new name. Flash already had one MC - Cowboy - with him, and so the new team became Grandmaster Flash and the 3MCs. Over the next couple of years they were joined by Scorpio and then Rahiem. Spurred by the success Of 'Rapper's Delight' by the Sugarhill Gang, Flash's team recorded 'We Rap More Mellow' under the name The Young Generation. Both it and a second single ('Sugar Rappin') flopped but then they signed to Sugarhill Records as Grandmaster Flash and the Furious Five. Together they recorded one of rap's greatest standards, 'The Message'. A hugely significant record which took hip-hop away from braggadocio into social commentary, the featured vocalist was Melle Mel. Subsequent releases over the next few years came out under a wide variety of names and the battle for best billing plus squabbles with management and record company eventually led to the group splitting in two in 1984. A deep rift between Flash and Mel came about because, according to the latter: 'We'd known that Sugarhill was crooks when we first signed with 'em, so the plan had always been to build it up to a certain point where . . . they couldn't keep on taking the money that they was taking! That's what I'd been banking on, but those that left didn't seem to see it the same way'. Mel retained Cowboy and Scorpio and recruited another of his brothers King Louie III plus Tommy Gunn, Kami Kaze, and Clayton Savage. Flash had inaugurated a $5 million court action against Sylvia Robinson's

Sugarhill label to attain full rights to the Grandmaster Flash name, which he lost. The group's new operating title was thus Grandmaster Melle Mel & The Furious Five. The name was forced on the band by Sugarhill, though it infuriated Flash and Mel himself was unhappy with it. Singles like 'Beat Street Breakdown Part 1', and 'We Don't Work For Free' would fail to break the upper echelons of the charts, though Mel did appear on the intro to Chaka Khan's worldwide smash 'I Feel For You'. There was also a UK Top 10 hit with 'Step Off', after which his popularity cooled. By 1987 the mutual lack of success encouraged the separated parties to reunite as Grandmaster Flash, Melle Mel And The Furious Five for a Paul Simon hosted charity concert in New York. The intervening years between then and Mel's appearance on Quincy Jones' 'Back On The Block' were lost to drug addiction - painfully ironic, considering that Mel's best known record remains 'White Lines (Don't Do It)', an anti-drug blockbuster which was credited to Grandmaster Flash and Melle Mel. It first hit the charts in 1983 and re-entered on several occasions. Originally targeted specifically at cocaine, it was revamped in 1989 by Sylvia Johnson because of the crack boom. Its pro-abstinence stance was not physically shared by the protagonists. When Mel was in the studio in 1982, laying down the vocal track, he admits that the 'only thing I was thinking about in that studio was listening to the record, joking and getting high'. In 1994 news broke that Mel was back and fighting fit (taking the trouble to perform press-ups for interviewers to prove the point), and working on a new album with former Ice-T collaborator Afrika Islam. He also linked with Flash for his 'Mic Checka' radio show, but the 1997 comeback album, *Right Now*, proved to be a disappointing collection.
● ALBUMS: *Work Party* (Sugarhill 1984)★★★, *Stepping Off* (Sugarhill 1985)★★★.

MELLO K

Of West Indian descent, rapper Mello K was brought up a native of New York, and first emerged as a serious artist in 1990. It was then that he was given the opportunity to work with Keith Sweat and Charlie Wilson from the Gap Band, subsequently forming his own posse, 40 Deep, hooking up with producer Monti Blues and reggae DJ Shawnie Ranks. Through Ranks Mello K debuted on his L.A. Boy Records. He also guested on the single 'Do Me', a slow-burning narrative reminiscent of lovers rock. It is this sort of material which gives Mello K his name, but he is equally capable of gruff, hard-nosed raps.
● ALBUMS: *Hard & Mello* (L.A. Boy 1993)★★★.

MELLOW MAN ACE

b. Ulpiano Sergio Reyes, 12 April 1967, Havana, Cuba, though he moved to the US at the age of four. Ace was brought up in Los Angeles, where he made his entrance in 1990 with a debut rap LP on Capitol that swticned between his native Spanish and English. With production offered by the Dust Brothers and Def Jef (among others), the most successful exposition was a bilingual rap over Santana's 'Evil Ways', entitled 'Mentirosa'. This was released as a single (US number 14), and he was among the key participants in the Latin Alliance project, but younger, more capable brothers have largely taken up the mantle of hispanic rap these days. These include his own blood brother, 'Sen Dog', of Cypress Hill.
● ALBUMS: *Escape From Havana* (Capitol 1990)★★★, *Brother With 2 Tongues* (Capitol 1992)★★★.

MELODIE MC

b. Kent Lövgren, Sweden. This rapper began his career as a breakdancer at the age of 12 - proving good enough to be entered in major championship events throughout his native Sweden. He maintained his allegiance to the hip-hop cause thereafter, releasing two moderately successful singles, 'Feel Your Body Movin'' and 'Take Me Away', in 1992. His breakthrough came the following year with 'Dum Da Dum', whose 'hip-house' stylings proved popular throughout Europe, especially in Germany where it sold over 200,000 copies. The follow-up single, 'I Wanna Dance', was less strong, but repeated the chart success, and acted as a prelude to a debut album for the Sidelake Virgin label.
● ALBUMS: *Northern Wonderland* (Sidelake Virgin 1993)★★★.

MENACE TO SOCIETY

Not related to the film of the same name, Menace To Society offer reality or slice of life raps about their immediate surroundings in Inkster, a suburb of Detroit, Michigan. The group's lead rapper is AGQ (b. Kevin Riley; AGQ being an acronym for American Genuine Quality) alongside Rhythm Layer Riccola (b. Andre Brintley) and Frank Nitty (b. Franchot Hayes). Their debut single, 'Streets

Of Hell', set out their agenda: 'Although some of our lyrics appear to be harsh, they come to you with the reality of today's street life.'

● ALBUMS: *Life Of A Real One* (Cush/Ichiban 1993)★★★.

MERCEDES LADIES

A very early hip-hop group, the first all-female such aggregation, which featured Zena Z, Debbie D, Eva Deff, Sherry Sheryl, alongside DJs RC and Baby D. Their origins in the Bronx, they were often to be found supporting the Funky Four at house parties and jams. Baby D, whose sassy 'frontin'' earned her lessons at the hands of Grandmaster Flash himself, would go on to a contract for East West, then Polydor, recording the LPs *Dream About You* and *ESP*.

MERLIN

b. London, England. Hardly the 'new rap messiah' that his second album proclaimed him to be, Merlin nevertheless cut an intriguing figure in the British rap scene of the 90s. He was still a teenager when the record was released, but he had already chalked up a fair reputation for his late 80s releases on Rhythm King (including being arrested for stealing cheques from Mute Records just before he made an appearance on *Top Of The Pops*. One of the most notable examples of his craft was the single, 'Born Free', with its prototype UK hip-hop lyrics.

● ALBUMS: *Merlin* (Rhythm King 1989)★★, *The New Rap Messiah* (MCA 1991)★★★.

MESSIAH

Ali Ghani and Mark Davies, from Hounslow, Middlesex, England and Barnet, Hertfordshire, England, respectively, met while students at the University Of East Anglia. They represent the talent behind the Messiah name, which moved from the independent Kickin' Records to WEA in 1993. The major doubtless saw Messiah as accessible rave that they could market. Their debut album was completed with the aid of Def American's Rick Rubin, who saw the group as the perfect embodiment of dance with which to convert an American audience. Old habits died hard, however, and he hooked them up with Ian Astbury of the Cult to produce one of their debut album's tracks. He had picked up the band from their previous American base, Moby's Instinct label. Their debut for WEA arrived with the aid of Precious Wilson's vocals, and included re-runs of

their previous club favourites, '20,000 Hardcore Members', 'Temple Of Dreams' (based on This Mortal Coil's 'Song To The Siren'), 'I Feel Love' and 'There Is No Law'. The second and third of that quartet had given the band Top 20 crossover hits. In addition they unveiled the impressive 'Thunderdome', with remixes from Spicelab, Secret Knowledge and Gods Underwater.

● ALBUMS: *Beyond Good And Evil* (Kickin' 1991)★★★, *21st Century Jesus* (WEA 1993)★★★.

METALHEADZ

Metalheadz rose to prominence in the early 90s as home to jungle's first global superstar - Goldie. He makes up the nucleus of Metalheadz in collaboration with Fabio and Grooverider, two DJs who made their name on the hardcore rave scene of the early 90s, and Ronnie Randall, the more elusive fourth member. Together they have fashioned Metalheadz into an all-conquering drum 'n' bass collective. Their *Angel* EP was one of the first records to invoke the 'intelligent techno' description in the mid-90s, before 'jungle' or 'junglist' had been coined to describe their employment of dubplates and frenetic breakbeats. While that effort was Goldie's own work, other releases under the Metalheadz banner come from disparate sources, such as 'Here Come The Drums' (by extended family member Doc Scott) and 'Predator' (by Photek collaborator Peshay). With Goldie's brief relationship with Björk dominating the headlines, Metalheadz adopted the Blue Note club in London's Hoxton Square as their new residency in 1995. This has subsequently become jungle's first home, with a fleet of celebrities including Tricky, Malcolm McLaren, recent drum 'n' bass acolyte David Bowie and former members of Duran Duran among those who have attended. The team has expanded to include female DJs Kemistry And Storm (who were responsible for first introducing Goldie to hardcore) and MC Cleveland Watkiss in addition to the core quartet. As well as the club, there is also a Metalheadz label, run on a day-to-day basis by Kemistry And Storm.

METROPLEX

Juan Atkins' Detroit record label, which housed several of his greatest moments as Model 500 ('No UFO's', 'The Chase', 'Off To Battle', 'Interference'). In the 90s it has gone on to be operated under the aegis of Mike Banks' Submerge organisation.

MICHEL'LE

b. Michele'le (pronounced Me-Shell-Lay) Toussaint, c.1972, Los Angeles, California, USA. One time girlfriend and protégée of Dr. Dre, Michel'le's career exploded and then disappeared with equal velocity, after she retired to have a baby. She first came to prominence as a backing vocalist for Dre's World Class Wreckin' Cru, before guesting on the D.O.C.'s remarkable debut album. Her own 1990 set brought immediate platinum status, preceded as it was by the US Top 10 single, 'No More Lies'. She also appeared on the pro-awareness single 'We're All In The Same Gang' alongside other members of the NWA posse with Hammer, Tone Loc, Digital Underground and Young MC.
● ALBUMS: *Michel'le* (Ruthless 1990)★★★.

MILES, ROBERT

Miles was born to Italian parents in Fluerier, Switzerland, in 1969 and later moved to Italy. As a child he learned the piano and began DJing when he was 13. Four years later he took his first job at a local club, around the same time as he set up a pirate radio station. After a few years he was playing at various clubs throughout northern Italy and by the time he was 22 he had become one of the most successful broadcasters in the region on account of his show on Radio Supernetwork. He subsequently invested in a studio to concentrate on writing his own material, while continuing to DJ at clubs and parties. After a number of minor successes in Italy he achieved widespread success with his single 'Children' (1996), which was initially signed to Platypus Records in the UK from the Italian independent DBX, before being picked up by DeConstruction Records. Inspired by the sounds he had heard while DJing in Goa, Ibiza, Bali and other such places, while aiming to create a contrast to the hard techno that was popular in Italy at the same, 'Children' created a rather sickening ethereal atmosphere, blending a basic trance sound with live instruments, including strings, guitar and its famous piano hook. With its commercial melodic sound, it was extremely successful, particularly in Europe and brought Miles's name into the mainstream. The follow-ups 'Fable' and 'One & One' and his debut album *Dreamland* were equally popular and led to Miles winning various industry awards, including the BRITS' Best International Newcomer and the World Music's Highest-Selling Male Newcomer. In 1997 he released the single 'Freedom' and a second album, *23am*, which extended his sound to incorporate breakbeats and elements of drum 'n' bass as well as vocalists and jazz musicians. In the same year he mixed one side of the compilation *London* for the 'superclub' Rennaissance. He has remained a popular DJ throughout Europe.
● ALBUMS: *Dreamland* (DeConstruction 1996)★★★, *Dreamland II* remixes (DeConstruction 1996)★★★, *23AM* (DeConstruction 1997)★★★.

MILLER, DUNCAN

The studio boffin behind such 90s UK dance chart regulars as Esoterix (whose product includes 'Void', the first release on Positiva, and 'Come Satisfy My Love' for Union) and Monica De Luxe ('The Temperature's Rising' and 'Don't Let This Feeling Stop'). This is only the tip of the Miller iceberg, however. He garnered an *Echoes* Single Of The Week award for 'South By South West', from his jazz-based project As One, on Wow Records, and another creation, Feelgood Factor's 'Jump Up In The Air' also showed strongly in several club listings. Miller operates out of his own West London studio, working alongside various DJs and musicians. In this role he produced 'U Don't Have To Say You Love Me' for React Records, and 'Bonour M. Basie' for Wow. He has also produced a track for Robert Owens and provided keyboard services for remixer Frankie Foncett. His own remixing projects included working with Paul Gotel on the Well Hung Parliament takes of Nu Colours' 'The Power', McKoy's 'Fight' and Monie Love's 'Never Give Up'.

MILLS, JEFF

Hugely respected US techno DJ who relocated from his native Detroit (where he set up the Underground Resistance empire with 'Mad' Mike Banks) to the New York region. After the split he formed Axis, licensing the *Tranquilizer* EP to Network. Other releases on Axis include his 1994 single 'Cycle 30'. Robert Hood, who worked on several of Mills' productions, recorded his second EP, *Minimal Nation*, for Axis that year too. *Live At The Liquid Room - Tokyo* sounded more like a heavy metal excursion than techno and the (dubious) live audience adds little to an otherwise excellent record.
● ALBUMS: *Live At The Liquid Room - Tokyo* (React 1996)★★★.

MINISTRY OF SOUND

London club whose unique atmosphere has led to a series of highly successful releases. The first of these was a compilation mixed by Tony Humphries in August 1993. Heralded by promotions man Jason Hill as 'a natural progression', it was among the fastest-selling items in dance shops throughout the UK in 1993, selling over 35,000 copies. This first set compiled a series of club classics, such as Mother's 'All Funked Up', X-Press 2's 'London X-Press' and Gabrielle's 'Dreams', the latter a staple at the club long before it scaled the national charts. A second, similarly successful, set followed in 1994. This time there were remixes from Paul Oakenfold, who helmed a live touring version of the club through 1994. The club also rose to prominence by projecting their logo onto the Houses Of Parliament as part of their second birthday celebrations, despite police objections. The club launched its own dance magazine, *Ministry*, in December 1997.

● COMPILATIONS: various artists *The Ministry - Volume1* (MOS 1993)★★★★, *The Ministry - Volume 2* (MOS 1994)★★★.

MIX TAPES

An attempt in the UK during the early 90s to recreate the 'buzz' of live DJ performances, mix tapes are a musical format whose ancestry can be traced back to reggae's yard tapes. Often of similar dubious origins and quality, very few are cleared through copyright, bearing in mind the number of samples and tracks involved in a single one- or two-hour set (however, the official lines, such as those promoted by *Mixmag*, have undergone this process). It is a noble but inherently flawed medium, but also the closest recorded approximation of a night clubbing or raving.

MIXMASTER MORRIS

UK house guru, who arrived in the early 90s at the height of hardcore techno's domination (he titled his own music weirdcore), and whose name has subsequently graced dozens of releases, both as a producer and remixer. Morris's first live performances were at the ICA Rock Week in 1980, before he began to work with samplers in 1983. He has since claimed the honour of being 'the first to play a house set in the UK', at the Fridge in London in 1987 at his Madhouse nights. He also prepared pirate radio tapes for his 'Mongolian Hip Hop Show', and worked with experimental pirate TV. He met Colin Angus of the Shamen via mutual Psychic TV acquaintants, and began DJing on their Synergy tours. His musical style was certainly unique, often building a set to the centrepiece section, which would as likely be a This Heat track as anything more conventional. He also stressed the importance of providing DJs with label information, not just bpms but also the key in which a track was played. In addition to his sampling and rhythmic wizardry, he has gone on to record in his own right. The first such release was 'Space Is The Place' on the Rising High label, a relationship with whom prospers to this day. Following late 80s singles 'Freestyle' and 'I Want You', his debut album arrived, also credited to The Irresistible Force, in 1992. It boasted a splendid holographic label, and was filled with samples taken from obscure and obtuse sources. A more detached, ambient-based project, after a brief Kraftwerk parody on the intro it branched out into seamless 'chill-out' territory. This was the man, after all, who invented the phrase 'I think, therefore I ambient'. He has gone on to record with the new king of chill, Peter Namlook, as part of the latter's Dreamfish project, and remixed for Spiritualized among others.

● ALBUMS: As the Irresistible Force *Flying High* (Rising High 1992)★★★, with Peter Namlook *Dreamfish* (Rising High 1993)★★★.

MLO

A collaboration between UK-born Jon Tye and Pete Smith through the Rising High imprint, MLO's debut album was also the soundtrack to a film of the same name - shown as live accompaniment to Pink Floyd gigs in 1994. The project was put together in an intensive two-week period inside one of the world's most advanced multimedia studios. The term ambient was almost inevitably invoked, though the duo opted to disassociate themselves from the bulk of the artists working within that genre. The album was titled after the seventh moon of Jupiter, the only entity in the solar system, aside from the earth, known to be volcanically active. As well as recording a film for use alongside their debut album, and producing videos for other artists, Tye has also recorded solo as Flutter ('Flutter').

● ALBUMS: *Io* (Rising High 1994)★★★.

MO' WAX RECORDS

This label was formed by James Lavelle (b. 1975, Oxford, England) in 1992 and helped to develop the abstract hip-hop sound. As a child Lavelle heard jazz at home and later developed an interest in hip-hop through artists such as Grandmaster Flash and Doug E. Fresh. He began DJing when he was 14 and while working in specialist jazz and dance record shops in London, he developed his broad tastes in music. In 1992 he formed Mo' Wax Records, with the aid of £1,000 from his boss at Honest Jon's record shop, to 'bring together all the different types of music that I've grown up with'. The first release was 'Promise', from the New York jazz group Repercussions, followed in 1993 by tracks from Raw Stylus, Palmskin Productions and DJ Takemura. However, it was DJ Shadow's 'In Flux'/'Hindsight' that really established the Mo' Wax approach, helping to introduce hip-hop to the techno community and vice versa. In 1994 Mo' Wax pursued this idea with releases from DJ Krush, Attica Blues and Lavelle's own project, U.N.K.L.E. La Funk Mob's 'Tribulations Extra Sensorielles' included remixes by Ritchie Hawtin and Carl Craig, while the excellent compilation *Headz*, as well as containing material from Mo' Wax artists, featured Howie B. and Autechre, further highlighting the label's aim to unite artists and sounds from supposedly disparate backgrounds. After turning down offers from London Records and other major labels, in 1996 Lavelle signed a distribution agreement with A&M Records. The two *Headz II* compilations (1996) included tracks from the Beastie Boys, Black Dog Productions, Photek, Alex Reece, Roni Size, the Jungle Brothers and Massive Attack. Other artists who have released material on the label include Air, Deborah Anderson, Innerzone Orchestra (Carl Craig), Major Force, Money Mark, Dr. Octagon, Andrea Parker and Sukia.

MOBB DEEP

Mobb Deep, a duo of rappers Havoc (b. *c*.1975, Queensbridge, New York, USA) and Prodigy (b. *c*.1975, Queensbridge, New York, USA), made a colossal impact in 1995 with their hardcore hip-hop single 'Shook Ones Part II'. Compared in the music press to the experience of hearing Schoolly D for the first time, it saw the Queensbridge, New York, USA rap team propelled to the top of the *Billboard* charts and national fame. It accompanied the release of their second album, *The Infamous*, which offered a succession of bleak inner-city narratives such as 'Survival Of The Fittest' and the Q-Tip-produced 'Drink Away The

Pain'. Mobb Deep had first received attention in 1991 when US rap magazine *The Source* praised them in its 'Unsigned Hype' column. Both partners were just 16 years old, but their first demo possessed obvious maturity and skill, boosted by their experience of watching MC Shan and Roxanne Shante rapping in local parks. They met in 1988, Havoc having been tutored by his rapping cousin MC Tragedy. By 1992 they had secured a recording contract with Island Records' subsidiary 4th And Broadway, recruiting Large Professor and DJ Premier to help with the production of their somewhat listless debut album. Despite the initial momentum, however, the deal fell apart amid squabbles with an unethical manager. The duo regrouped in time for *The Infamous*, which was much-improved in terms of both production and lyrics. 'Survival Of The Fittest' was promoted by a 'paintball' competition in Long Island, with competing teams including members of the Wu-Tang Clan and Loud Records' staff.

● ALBUMS: *Mobb Deep* (4th And Broadway 1993)★★★, *The Infamous* (Loud/RCA 1995)★★★★, *Hell On Earth* (Loud/RCA 1996)★★★.

MOBY

b. Richard Melville Hall, *c*.1966, New York, USA. A New York DJ, recording artist, Christian, vegan and philosophy graduate, Moby is so nicknamed because of the fact that he can trace his ancestry back to Herman Melville, the author of the famous Captain Ahab whaling story. This is by no means the only interesting aspect of his idiosyncratic artistic life. He refuses to travel anywhere by car because of the environmental considerations, and generally displays little of the public anonymity that is the creed of the underground DJ. In 1991 he took the *Twin Peaks* theme, under the guise of 'Go', into the Top 10. Although that appealed to the more perverse natures of both mainstream and club audiences, the release of 'I Feel It'/'Thousand' in 1993 was yet more bizarre. The latter track was classified by the *Guinness Book Of Records* as the fastest single ever, climaxing at 1015 bpm. It was typical of Moby's playful, irreverent attitude to his work. In his youth he was a member of hardcore punk outfit the Vatican Commandos, and even substituted as singer for Flipper while their vocalist was in prison. He has brought these rock 'n' roll inclinations to bear on the world of dance: at the 1992 DMC/Mixmag Awards ceremony he trashed his keyboards at the end of his set. His introduction to dance music began in the mid-80s: 'I was drawn to it, I started reading about it, started hanging out in clubs. For me house music was the synthesis of the punk era.' He collected cheap, second-hand recording equipment, basing himself in an old factory/converted prison in New York's Little Italy. He signed to leading independent Mute in 1993. *Ambient* was a collection of unissued cuts from 1988-91, composed of barely audible atmospheric interludes. *Story So Far* gathered together a series of tracks he cut for Instinct Records. The following year Moby released 'Hymn', a transcendental religious techno odyssey, distinguished by a 35-minute ambient mix and a Laurent Garnier remix. His own remix catalogue includes Brian Eno, LFO ('Tan Ta Ra'), Pet Shop Boys, Erasure ('Chorus'), Orbital ('Speed Freak'), Depeche Mode and even Michael Jackson. He moved away from his techno/dance base in 1996 with *Animal Rights*, and in turn sounded more like Johnny Rotten.

● ALBUMS: *Ambient* (Mute 1993)★★, *The Story So Far* (Mute 1993)★★★, *Everything Is Wrong* (Mute 1995)★★★, *Animal Rights* (Mute 1996)★★★★, *I Like To Score* (Mute 1997)★★★.

MONEY MARK

b. Mark Ramos Nishita, USA. Money Mark first rose to prominence as keyboard player in the Beastie Boys' powerful stage show of the late 80s and early 90s. However, from his base in Los Angeles, California, he maintained a desire to write and perform his own material. Rather than use the Beastie Boys' own imprint, Grand Royal Records, Nishita was recruited by England's Mo Wax Records, whose proprietor, James Lavelle, travelled to California to persuade him to sign. His debut album was recorded with Lavelle's help, and followed the Mo Wax house style of mellow, deep hip-hop with jazz flourishes, over which Nishita added keyboard motifs and laconic narratives. He repeated the process on 1996's *Third Version EP*, but broadened the range for the follow-up album. *Push The Button* took in hip-hop, dub, funk, soul, art-rock and pop styles and shaped them into an endlessly inventive and dazzling 18-track epic .

● ALBUMS: *Mark's Keyboard Repair* (Mo Wax 1995)★★★★, *Third Version EP* (Mo Wax 1996)★★★, *Push The Button* (Mo Wax 1998)★★★★.

MOOD II SWING

A house production duo tipped by many to challenge the traditional supremacy of Clivilles And Cole and Masters At Work, Mood II Swing were formed when Lem Springsteen and John Ciafone met in an ill-fated R&B group in Brooklyn, New York, USA. When that group dissolved in 1989 the duo elected to remain working together, specifically on projects concerned with the burgeoning house music scene. Inspired by Masters At Work's Little Louie Vega, with whom they would subsequently work, they first broke through into the club scene with the release of Urbanised's (Featuring Silvano) 'Helpless'. Wall Of Sound featuring Gerald Latham's 'Critical' for 8 Ball Records, and Loni Clark's 'Rushing' confirmed their production expertise. A further Wall Of Sound single, 'Run To Me', followed at the end of 1995. Their collaboration with Vega came on Barbara Tucker's 'Beautiful People' and 'I Get Lifted', which they co-wrote. They have remixed for Indigo ('Fly To The Moon'), DoublePlusGood ('Conga Te') and India ('I Can't Get To Sleep' and 'Whenever U Touch Me'), and collaborated with esteemed New York singer Fonda Rae ('Living In Ecstasy').

MOODSWINGS

Formed by indie stalwarts JFT 'Fred' Hood, a drummer and friend of Johnny Marr (Smiths), plus producer Grant Showbiz (the Fall, Smiths), this was still a decidedly house-aimed project. They first interceded in the dance scene with the release of 1990's 'Spiritual High', a cover of the Diana Ross song with additional lyrics interspersed from the Beatles' 'Tomorrow Never Knows', with vocals from Chrissie Hynde. After appearing on a blue label it was snapped up by Zoom before Arista gave it a big push and stock release in 1991. However, instead of building on the acclaim they slaved over their debut album for several years before release.

● ALBUMS: *Moodfood* (Arista 1993)★★★, *Psychedelicatessen* (Arista 1997)★★★★.

MOODY BOYZ

Tony Thorpe's incarnation of the dub-house ethic, his most high-profile banner since 80s experimentalists 400 Blows. After the demise of that tempestuous outfit he formed Warrior Records. This was superseded by his BPM label, which won its spurs releasing compilations including *Acid*

Beats (1988), the musical tastes determined by Thorpe's immersion in the club scene (the legendary Spectrum nights in particular). Later he became in-house remixer for the KLF, before the Moody Boyz' name was first employed on a series of acid-inspired 12-inch releases such as 'Boogie Woogie Music', 'King Of The Funky Zulus' and the *Journey Into Dubland* EP. His debut long-playing set as the Moody Boyz combined his traditional love of reggae bass with a strong philosophy of black emancipation, particularly on 'Fight Back (27-4-94)', dedicated to the democracy movement's victory in South Africa. There were also intriguing collaborations with Black Dog on 'Elite Doodz Presents Snooze', and the Italian Vibraphone set-up. Thorpe has also recorded as Voyager, House Addicts and Urban Jungle, and remixed for Joi, Bocca Juniors and Fun-Da-Mental. He also provides Channel 4 with much of its incidental music.

● ALBUMS: *Product Of The Environment* (Guerilla 1994)★★★. As Voyager: *Transmission* (Underworld/Virgin 1993)★★★.

MORAES, ANGEL

b. 7 August 1965, Brooklyn, New York, USA. One of the more prominent of a new wave of New York DJs and remixers of the mid-90s, Moraes is also one of the most prolific. Before his first appearances as a DJ in the mid-80s he had worked as a Manhattan truck driver. By the 90s he had secured bookings at many of the premier New York clubs, including the Sound Factory, where his notoriously 'smooth and soulful' mixing pleased large clienteles. As an artist, all his records have been mastered by the producer Tom Moulton, a close friend and adviser. In 1996 alone he released three albums - *Burnin' Up*, *Time To Get Down* and *New York In The Mix* for three separate record labels. He has also remixed for London, Subversive and Tribal Records.

● ALBUMS: *Burnin' Up* (Strictly Rhythm 1996)★★, *Time To Get Down* (Hot 'N' Spicy 1996)★★★, *New York In The Mix* (Subversive 1996)★★★.

MORALES, DAVID

b. c.1961, Brooklyn, New York, USA. Born and bred in the capital, and of Puerto Rican parents, David Morales is the leader of the pack in terms of his country's premier remixers. His style, melodic garage house with a strong disco influence, belies his personal physique and presence,

that of a pencil-bearded, tattooed body-builder. Married with a son, he works out for two hours every day, though he also employs a bodyguard for his regular evening shows (he was shot in his youth). As a young man he attended both the Loft and Paradise Garage, before being invited to play at the latter through Judy Weinstein's For The Record organization. His other stomping grounds included all the major New York clubs, including the Ozone Layer, Inferno and Better Days. The Morales style has graced literally hundreds of records, his first remix being Insync's 'Sometimes Love'. He possibly works best in tandem with a strong garage vocalist (Alison Limerick, Ce Ce Penniston, Yazz, Jocelyn Brown, Chimes, etc.). A good selection of his greatest work might be permed from the following: Robert Owens' 'I'll Be Your Friend', Clive Griffin's 'I'll Be Waiting', Black Sheep's 'Strobelite Honey', Pet Shop Boys' 'So Hard', Thompson Twins' 'The Saint' or Limerick's 'Where Love Lives'. Many other remixes have been completed with long-standing friend Frankie Knuckles (as Def-Mix), whom he also met through For The Record (Weinstein going on to manage both artists). His productivity is made possible by the fact that he is happy to churn out up to two remixes a week under his own auspices. His live sets, however, are often less glossy than the productions for which he is best known: 'When I DJ I'm not as pretty as a lot of the records I make'. He has had trouble in constructing solo hits on his own account, though his debut album included guest appearances from Sly Dunbar and Ce Ce Rogers.

● ALBUMS: *The Programme* (1993)★★.

MORCHEEBA

Morcheeba, popularly known as the 'trigger hippie' UK trip-hop combo, consists of Paul Godfrey, Ross Godfrey and Skye Edwards. The Godfrey brothers began working from their hometown of Hythe, Kent, around the early 90s, drawing on a number of influences including 30s blues and 90s hip-hop. This fusion resulted in a complex sound that is difficult to categorize. Their quest for acclaim led the brothers to relocate to Clapham, London, where they continued recording, meeting Edwards at a party in Greenwich, London. The trio discovered a mutual affinity for songwriting, marijuana and soundtracks, and Edwards was enlisted to add her debonair vocals to their recording sessions. In the winter of 1995 they released their debut, 'Trigger

Hippie', a huge underground hit. The success of the single led to the release of *Who Can You Trust*, which was selected by *DJ* magazine as one of the top 100 dub albums. The band were as astonished as the hardcore reggae fraternity, although the album did display clear traits of dub, notably on the title track. In 1996 the band released a remix of the album track 'The Music That We Hear', and also the crossover hit 'Tape Loop'. The latter led to a triumphant US tour, collaborations with David Byrne and major critical acclaim. In 1997 the band played the Phoenix Festival and A Day At The Races, followed by the release of 'Shoulder Holster'. The single included a mix by DJ Swamp with added vocals from Spikey T. The group embarked on the promotional circuit with television appearances and an acclaimed tour supported by Zion Train. Skye also performed alongside Burning Spear *et al* on the 'Perfect Day' single which topped the UK chart in 1997/8. In the spring of 1998 the group released their eagerly anticipated follow-up, *Big Calm*. Among the mellifluous matchless melodies was the reggae-styled 'Friction', featuring the horn section from Zion Train.

● ALBUMS: *Who Can You Trust* (Indochina 1996)★★★, *Big Calm* (Indochina 1998)★★★★.
● COMPILATIONS: *Who Can You Trust/Beats And B Sides* (Indochina 1997)★★★.

MORILLO, ERICK 'MORE'

b. *c*.1971, USA. Morillo started DJing at the age of 11, playing sets in his local New Jersey that matched ragga with techno (a precursor to the sound of Reel 2 Real). As a student at New York's Centre For The Media Arts, he started collecting studio equipment, and became a self-taught maestro. He graduated to recording his own material by sampling Jamaican toasters onto DAT. One night a gentleman enquired as to the source of a particular sampled voice, and it transpired that the man, known as General, was the owner of said larynx. Together they went on to record 'The Funky Buddha' and *Move It* album for RCA. Influenced by old school Chicago house such as Lil' Louis, Todd Terry and Kenny 'Dope' Gonzalez, Morillo has gone on to build his own studio, Double Platinum, where Little Louie Vega's *Hardrive* EP and Barbara Tucker's 'Deep Inside' were recorded. His own productions included Deep Soul's 'Rhythms' (which featured future Smooth Touch collaborator Althea McQueen). He tried to get work at Nervous but was continually turned down by A&R head Gladys Pizarro. On the day he tried Strictly Rhythm instead, Pizarro had just been installed in their offices, and this time she relented. He has gone on to become one of the leading lights of the Strictly Rhythm empire, for whom he released over 25 records, under nearly as many pseudonyms, within 1993 alone (his first release on the label having been Reel 2 Real's debut). Among his productions were Deep Soul's 'Rhythm', RAW's 'Unbe', Smooth Touch's 'Come And Take A Trip' and Club Ultimate's 'Carnival 93'. He was also represented by albums in 1994 by Deep Soul and Reel 2 Real (whose 'I Like To Move It' and 'Go On Move' were both massive worldwide hits), and recorded his own *More* EP. Part of the secret of Morillo's success may lie in his refusal simply to sample current rhythms and beats, preferring instead to write his own drum patterns and arrangements. He is nicknamed 'More' due to everybody connected being astonished at the number of different mixes he would put onto each of his releases.

MOTHER SUPERIA

b. Miami, Florida, USA. A formidable female rapper in the vein of MC Lyte, this refreshingly principled hip-hop artist spent some nine years in the wilderness before the release of her debut album in 1997. Inspired by the old-skool rapping of KRS-1, Melle Mel and Eric B. And Rakim, she signed with Island Records subsidiary 4th & Broadway because of the label's widely-acknowledged history with some of rap music's pioneering forces. Her hardcore lyrics, meanwhile, carrying hardcore social messages through metaphor, were widely compared to those of Queen Latifah. She came to the attention of 4th & Broadway through the independently-released local hit, 'Rock Bottom'. The biggest rap song to come from Miami since 2 Live Crew were at their peak, it led to hip-hop writers referring to the city itself as 'The Bottom' in rap parlance. Superia stayed true to her local heritage by employing an all-Miami production team to work on her debut album, *Levitation*.

● ALBUMS: *Levitation* (4th & Broadway 1997)★★★.

MOVEMENT EX

A Los Angeles, California-based duo combining Lord Mustafa Hasan Ma'd and DJ King Born Khaaliq, whose Afrocentric/Muslim opinions (they support the Five Percent Nation Islamic creed) are frankly and sharply put. The production of their debut, recorded when they were still teenagers, was dense and tightly-wrought, engaging the listener with its austere atmosphere. Subjects included drugs, gun-running, ecology, history and sexually transmitted diseases. Light listening for a saturday evening.

● ALBUMS: *Movement Ex* (Columbia 1990)★★★.

MOVIN' MELODIES

A label founded in March 1993 by DJ's Rob Boskamp and Patrick Prins. Boskamp had started as a mobile DJ at the age of 14 in his native Amsterdam, joining DMC Holland in 1986. He worked with Go! Bang and ESP before releasing his own material on MTMT Records. Boskamp's other labels include Urban Sound Of Amsterdam, Gyrate, Weekend, Dutch Volume, Looneyville, Ces, Dutch Club Culture, Mulatto, Fast Food and Red Skins. Prins started DJing in Vegas, learning drums and keyboards before taking a course in production/engineering, building up his own studio. The two partners were introduced in January 1993 by a Dutch dance magazine. The Movin' Melodies name was first invoked for an EP on Urban Sound Of Amsterdam in March 1993. The label was inaugurated properly by July's *French Connection* EP, then 'Bailando Guitarra' a month later. 1994 brought Peppermint Lounge ('Lemon Project') and Artemsia ('Bits & Pieces').

MOVING SHADOW RECORDS

Rob Playford's hardcore label, founded in 1990 ('Hardcore is totally different from the rest of the music industry, cos it's not showbiz. There's no band loyalty and nothing to read about in teeny mags'). Playford comes from a hip-hop DJ background, and records on the label with various guest personnel as 2 Bad Mice (including 'Waremouse' and 'Bombscare', both of which featured the label's distinctive, heavy snare sound which was widely imitated/sampled subsequently). The label found its stride in 1992 with major releases from 2 Bad Mice ('Hold It Down'), Cosmo & Dibs ('Sonic Rush' - Playford and 'Little' Stevie 'T' Thrower's follow-up to 'Oh So Nice' and 'Star Eyes') and Blame ('Music Takes You'), which went to the top of the dance lists. By 1993 the roster included 'intelligent techno/ambient tunes like Omni Trio's 'Mystic Stepper' and 'Renegade Snares', Four Play's 'Open Your Mind' and Hyper-On-Experience's 'Lords Of The Null Lines'. The label also started the *Two On One* series of EPs,

where two artists were encouraged to experiment on either side of one record. The label's biggest record in the first half of 1994 would be Deep Blue's 'The Helicopter Tune'. Playford also promotes parties and raves (Voodoo Magic, etc.), runs a record shop (Section 5) and the compilation label Reanimate.

● ALBUMS: Various *Renegade Selector Issue 1* (Reanimate/Moving Shadow 1994)★★★★.

MR. FINGERS

b. Larry Heard. The house music DJ Larry Heard, based in Chicago, Illinois, USA, was given the nickname 'Fingers' because of his dexterity when spinning records. Before this Heard had played percussion in several bands, until he became fascinated by the musical possibilities of electronics. He made his recording debut in 1985 with Fingers Inc's 'Mystery Of Love' (the original copies credited it solely to Mr Fingers) on DJ International Records, following it a year later with 'You're Mind'/'A Path'. He also formed the It with Harry Dennis, releasing two further singles, 'Donnie' and 'Gallimaufry Gallery', named after a Chicago club. It has been suggested that Fingers invented acid house music in 1986 on the track 'Washing Machine', which was included on the three-track single, 'Can You Feel It?' (on Trax Records), but others suggest that DJ Pierre and Marshall Jefferson got there first. There can be no dispute, however, about the strength of his mid-80s releases such as 'Slam Dance', or his production of Robert Owens' 'Bring Down The Walls' and 'I'm Strong'. Owens had also sung on 'Washing Machine' and other Fingers Inc tracks. Fingers then established Alleviated Records, and in 1988 under the name of the House Factors released 'Play It Loud', and his first album, this time under the name Fingers Inc. In 1989 he produced records by Kym Mazelle ('Treat Me Right'), Lil' Louis ('Touch Me'), Blakk Society ('Just Another Lonely Day') and Trio Zero ('Twilight'), and as Mr Fingers he released 'What About This Love?' on ffrr Records. He also remixed and/or produced other artists, including Adamski, Electribe 101 and Massive Attack. Mr Fingers' second album included the singles 'Closer' and 'On A Corner Called Jazz'. *Back To Love* was a restrained and mature collection of mellow house tracks, which broke few musical barriers but cemented Fingers' reputation as one of house music's pivotal forces.

● ALBUMS: *Amnesia* (Trax 1989)★★★, *Introduction* (MCA 1992)★★★★, *Back To Love*

(Black Market International 1994)★★★. As Fingers Inc: *Fingers Inc* (Jack Trax 1988)★★★. As The It: *On Top Of The World* (1990)★★★.

MR. LEE

b. Lee Haggard, *c*.1968, Chicago, Illinois, USA. Haggard's introduction to music came via his elder brother, who taught him bass, drums and keyboards in the tradition of James Brown, Parliament and Funkadelic. By the time he was 18 he was to be found DJing at local clubs and recording demo tapes at home, perfecting his own sound. Confident of his new-found abilities, he approached a friend, who brought him to the attention of Mitchball Records. A few singles emerged from the deal, but failed to sell. More success was to be found with the Trax label, for whom he recorded the hip house cut 'Shoot Your Best Shot'. Popular in his native Chicago, it paved the way for the follow-up, 'I Can't Forget', on which he sang for the first time, to become an international hit. However, from then on he changed his vocal delivery to that of a rapper, releasing singles like 'Pump Up Chicago' and 'Pump Up England'. While promoting these in the latter territory he was the subject of intense bidding by the majors, finally signing with Jive. Following singles including 'Do It To Me' (which featured an all-star cast, being produced by Mr Fingers, part-penned by Stevie Wonder and featuring samples of Quincy Jones' 'Betcha'), his debut album would sell over one million copies worldwide, the title track reaching number 1 on the Billboard dance chart when released as a single. By the time of his second collection he was experimenting with the New Jack Swing sound, a new way of maintaining the blend of R&B/house and rap that had served him so well previously. His adoption of the style was made explicit on album cuts such as 'New House Swing'. The first single taken from it, 'Hey Love', featured label-mate R. Kelly, though there was a return to hip-hop roots with the samples of Chuck D's (Public Enemy) 'Bring The Noise' chant on 'Time To Party'.

● ALBUMS: *Get Busy* (Jive 1990)★★★, *I Wanna Rock Right Now* (Jive 1992)★★★.

MS MELODIE

b. Ramona Parker, Flatbush, Brooklyn, New York, USA. Gruff female rapper whose self-written rhymes and couplets were aided and abetted by the production skills of her (now ex-) husband KRS-1, on her debut album. The conscious lyrics were occasionally insightful, with 'Remember When' added a fitting testimony to the growth of the hip-hop movement: 'The street is the root of the tree that branches out to R&B'. Melodie had formerly served time on Boogie Down Productions' roster of artists. She came from a musical family; her father played saxophone and clarinet, while her mother and sisters were regulars in the local church choirs. Though her first love was soul, Melodie was immediately drawn into the emerging hip-hop world when it hit her native Brooklyn streets. In additon to her work with BDP, she had also made a film appearance in the blaxploitation movie parody, *I'm Gonna Git You, Sucka*, in 1987. Her abilities also extended to fashion design which incorporated her 'sophiticated B-girl' look.

● ALBUMS: *Diva* (Jive 1989)★★★.

MURK

US record label, based in Miami, who are probably best known for club hits such as the Funky Green Dogs From Outer Space's 'Reach For Me' (voted third best dance song of 1992 by the *New Musical Express*) and Coral Way Chiefs' 'Release Myself'. Ralph Falcon and Oscar Gaetan also remixed D.O.P.'s 'Oh Yeah' for Guerilla, and Karen Pollack's 'You Can't Touch Me' for Emotive. The group behind the majority of the label's product is also known as the Deep South Recording team, who were responsible for providing Warp with their *Miami* sampler EP. In 1992 they bowed to consumer demand and released a three-track DJ sampler that combined the hard-to-find trio of Funky Green Dogs From Outer Space ('Reach For Me'), Liberty City ('Some Lovin'') and Interceptor ('Together'). In the wake of their cult success the label's product was licensed to Network in the UK.

MURRAY, KEITH

b. USA. Rapper Keith Murray made an immediate impact with his debut for Jive Records, 1994's *The Most Beautifullest Thing In The World*. As well as his trademark tongue-twisting delivery, a throwback to old-school hip-hop which won him many fans, many critics were impressed by the similar dexterity employed in his writing style. However, despite good early press and sales, its final turnover figure of just over 300,000 was a major disappointment both to the artist and his record label. It left Murray to concede: 'People were telling me they couldn't understand what I was saying, so I had to slow it up a bit.' Despite this, he continued to enjoy a high media-profile by appearing on a Coca-Cola advertisement and guesting on remixes of Mary J. Blige's 'Be Happy', Total's 'Can't You See' and LL Cool J.'s 'I Shot Ya'. For 1996's *Enigma*, Murray once again employed Eric Sermon's hard-edged funk, but this time much of it drew riffs from the work of Maze/Frankie Beverly rather than the G-funk staples, Parliament and George Clinton.

● ALBUMS: *The Most Beautifullest Thing In The World* (Jive 1994),★★★★ *Enigma* (Jive 1996)★★★★.

MUSTO AND BONES

A highly successful, albeit brief, liaison between Tommy Musto and Frankie Bones, which resulted in success with singles such as 'Dangerous On The Dance Floor' and 'All I Want Is To Get Away'. In retrospect, 'Dangerous' might well have achieved more significant crossover success had it been more fully backed by the duo's record company, with a long time delay between its UK and domestic release. The partnership eventually dissolved after a solitary album as Bones spent more of his time DJing, while Musto remained in New York to oversee their company and studio projects: 'Basically, we also grew apart musically' is how Musto remembers this period. He would go on to become a hugely successful remixer to the stars, while his former partner persevered on the live circuit. The duo were still contracted to Beggars Banquet for another album, however, and subtle, but amicable, litigation proceeded until Bones could be removed from the contract, Musto offering instead his collaboration with Victor Simonelli, Colourblind.

● ALBUMS: *The Future Is Ours* (Citybeat 1990)★★★.

MUSTO, TOMMY

b. *c*.1963, New York, USA. Formerly recognized for his hit singles as part of Musto And Bones, under his own steam Musto has grown to become one of dance music's prime remixing talents, with close to half a century of projects under his belt. These include many major artists attempting to dip a toe into the world of dance (Michael Jackson, Gloria Estefan, Cyndi Lauper, Erasure). Musto grew up on a diet of Philly soul, before going on to present his own mix show on WAKT alongside the then-underground talents of Shep Pettibone and Tony Humphries on Kiss FM. He began remixing for other artists, the first example of which was Junior Byron's 'Woman' for Vanguard Records, and also taught himself keyboard skills. His first major label commission was S'Express's 'Nothing To Lose' in the early 90s. His biggest commercial break, however, was the opportunity to remix Michael Jackson's 'In The Closet', which went gold. In 1994 he formed Colourblind with Victor Simonelli, partially to satisfy a contract that was still extant between his former Musto And Bones partnership and Beggars Banquet. After removing Bones from the contract, he teamed with Simonelli and added first Barbara Tucker then Dina Roche. They initially provided a single, written and produced by Musto, 'He's So Fine', before an album scheduled for late 1994. He also runs the Northcott Productions empire, home to Experimental Records.

μ-ZIQ

Based in South London, England, μ-Ziq is effectively studio musician Mike Paradinas, though he has also worked in tandem with Francis Naughton. Both were students when they first met the Aphex Twin, Richard James, who invited them to join his new Rephlex Records imprint. Unlike the aforementioned ambient guru, neither were technocrats, preferring an organic, untutored approach to the creation of cerebral dance music. Their debut double album was recorded using only synthesizers, a beatbox, and a four-track mixer. Within a few months of studio time μ-Ziq claimed to have over 300 completed tracks sitting on the shelf, an output that threatened to eclipse even their mentor's notorious profligacy. By 1995's *In Pine Effect*, the first result of a new distribution deal for Paradinas' own label within the Virgin Records empire, he was effectively a solo artist. He had also found time to record as Gary Moscheles And The Badass Motherfunkers (in a jazz funk vein) and Jake Slazenger (for the underground dance label Clear Records).

● ALBUMS: *Tango N' Vectif* (Rephlex 1994)★★★, *In Pine Effect* (Planet μ/Virgin 1995)★★.

N

N-JOI

This group consists of the Essex, England-born 'brothers of hardness' Mark Franklin and Nigel Champion, who were originally joined by the singer Saffron. Their five minutes of fame came in 1991 with 'Adrenalin' (on DeConstruction Records), an overwrought affair much admired by Liam Howlett of the Prodigy. This was quickly followed by the UK Top 10 success of the re-released 'Anthem'. They released a recording of their stage set, *Live In Manchester*, for the same label in February 1992, which lasted over 28 minutes and included over a dozen separate tunes in the mix. They followed up with a more conventional EP that included a Moby remix of their 'Mindflux' single for RCA Records in the USA. Saffron attempted a solo career with garage singles such as 'One Love' for WEA Records in 1992.
● ALBUMS: *Inside Out* (DeConstruction 1995)★★★.

N-TENSE

The raps of this 90s New York, USA hip-hop duo are conducted against the surprising and rather fetching backdrop of an off-the-wall, ecologist philosophy. Dion Blue (aka Woodbanga) and his partner Taylor Schofield (aka Big Rallo) use the physical and metaphysical qualities of trees and forests to inform their sound: 'What we represent is the backwoods of the industry, the deep, dark section.' They began their career with the single 'Raise The Levels Of The Boom', on which lyrical references to woodsmen and trees abounded, aided by a video clip filmed in the woods of Central Islip, Long Island, New York. On its b-side, 'Wash His Back', the theme was stretched to indicate a sense of community between young black men, somewhat akin to the relationship of 'a copse of trees growing together'. It certainly made a change from the outrageous boasts normally associated with gangsta rap. The album from which the two songs were drawn, *If Trees Could Talk*, continued to address a similar theme.
● ALBUMS: *If Trees Could Talk* (Tree 1994)★★★.

N-TROOP

Touted as the new protégés of Soul II Soul and Jazzie B, London, England band N-Troop comprises DJ Dessie D, Yvonne (vocals; Dessie D's sister) and Stuart OV (rapper). They met Jazzie B when they were recording in the studio next door in the early 90s, and the renowned producer was so enamoured with N-Troop's 'Matter Of Fakt' that he had a contract drawn up for them the next day. The song extolled the names and achievements of a roster of black people and artists. The brother and sister team grew up singing in the gospel churches of the West Midlands, while Stuart OV's delivery was informed by the reggae sound systems of south London, where he grew up. As a dancehall DJ (equating to MC in rap terms) he had begun recording in 1985 for Smiley Culture's Happening label, making his debut with 'Save Me Your Love'. As N-Troop there was a conscious effort to reflect rap from a black British perspective, rather than American. Rather than drive-by shootings, lyrics touched on the 'joy-riding' craze and the murder of James Bolger. 'Matter Of Fakt' was released as only the second single on Jazzie B's newly inaugurated Funki Dred Records, but the band's career was disrupted when the label suffered problems caused by the withdrawal of its backers' funding.

N2-DEEP

A white rap trio based in Vallejo, Calfornia, USA. They were formed by their DJ and producer, Johnny 'Z' Zunino, who introduced MCs Jay 'Tee' Trujillo and TL Lyon. The title track of their debut gave them a substantial crossover hit (reaching US number 14), though their legitimacy as an act within the hardcore Profile fraternity was confirmed with cuts like 'What The Fuck Is Going On?'.
● ALBUMS: *Back To The Hotel* (Profile 1992)★★.

NAMLOOK, PETER

German-born Namlook is comfortably the most prolific and arguably the best of the new wave of ambient/house artists of the early 90s. Before his immersion in the world of dance, he had experimented with the sitar and new age jazz. His early solo EPs were shrouded in mystery, the labels distinguished solely by the contact number Fax +49-69/454064 - which later transpired to be the title

of the label. Since then his output has been fantastic, in both the literal and accepted senses of the word. From his base in Frankfurt, Germany, two or three collaborations emerge every week on 12-inch, via a stable of co-conspirators who include Dr Atmo, Craig Peck, DJ Hubee, DJ Brainwave, DJ Criss, Pascal FEOS and Mixmaster Morris (the latter also recording with Namlook as Dreamfish on the Faxworld subsidiary). Releases are colour-coded to differentiate between the types of music - yellow for trance, black for hardcore, green for house and blue for ambient - the most popular genre in terms of sales reaction. Each is also recorded in a cycle of eight - one each with each collaborator, always beginning with DJ Criss (as Deltraxx). Only five or six hundred copies of any given release ever emerge, quickly selling out, before the 'cycle' is reissued on a compilation CD. As if that were not enough, Namlook also records ambient 'solo' records as Air, Sin or Silence (with Dr Atmo). These recordings are symptomatic of the 'chill-out' factor that hit European clubs in the early 90s. On several of the tracks it can take up to 10 minutes for a distinctive beat or rhythm to appear, spending time building its atmospheric, neo-filmic musical soundscapes. Namlook has also found time for the Sequential project. Released in the UK via Rising High, this allows him to work with any of his roster, ironically, out of sequence. Namlook is now perceived to be at the forefront of what has been termed the 'ethno-trance' movement. Rather than riding the ambient bandwagon, he has an overview of this new music's place and purpose: 'I think it's very important to enhance the notion of a global ambient movement, and to realise that a lot of music which we didn't expect to be ambient is in fact very, very ambient. When you examine other cultures you discover that what we recognise as a very new movement is in fact incredibly ancient'.
● ALBUMS: with Dr Atmo *Silence* (Rising High 1993)★★★, *Air 2* (Fax 1994)★★★★, with Bill Laswell *Psychonavigation* (Fax 1994)★★★★, with Laswell, Klaus Schulze *Dark Side Of The Moog IV* (Fax 1996)★★★.

NAS

b. Nasir Jones, *c.*1974, Long Island, New York, USA. From the tough Queensbridge housing projects which brought the world Marley Marl, MC Shan and Intelligent Hoodlum, Nas is a highly skilled hip-hop artist whose music is crafted with a degree of subtlety and forethought often absent from the genre. He was heavily influenced by his jazz-playing father, and started rapping at the age of nine, graduating to a crew entitled the Devastatin' Seven in the mid-80s. He met Main Source producer Large Professor in 1989, in the course of recording his first demo tape. The producer introduced him to the group itself, and he would see his debut on Main Source's 1990 album *Breaking Atoms*, guesting on the cut 'Live At The BBQ', where he was part of a skilled chorus line, alongside Large Professor and Akinyele. However, though he was widely applauded for his contribution he failed to build on the impact, drifting through life and becoming disillusioned by the death of his best friend Will, and the shooting of his brother. He may well have stayed on the outside of the hip-hop game had not MC Serch (Nas had guested on his 'Back To The Grill') searched him out, to provide a solo track for the *Zebra Head* film. 'Half Time', again recorded with the Large Professor, was the result. A debut album followed, with contributions from the cream of New York's producers: Premier (Gang Starr), Pete Rock and Q-Tip (A Tribe Called Quest). A hefty unit for which Columbia were happy to pay the bill, judging Nas to be their priority rap act for 1994. Nas, who had by now dropped his 'Nasty' prefix, honed a rapping style that was at once flamboyant, but with a lyrical armoury that far surpassed the expected humdrum 'bitches and ho's' routines. Serch, now A&R head of Wild Pitch, once declared Nas: 'Pound for pound, note for note, word for word, the best MC I ever heard in my life'. There was now evidence to suggest he may have been correct. *It Was Written* debuted at number 1 on the Billboard album chart in July 1996. In 1997 Nas collaborated with Foxy Brown, AZ and Dr Dre as The Firm.
● ALBUMS: *Illmatic* (Columbia 1994)★★★★, *It Was Written* (Columbia 1996)★★★.

NATION RECORDS

This label was formed by Kath Canoville and Aki Nawaz (Propa-Ghandi from Fun-Da-Mental) in 1988 when they had had trouble convincing major labels there was a place for their concept of multiracial 'world-dance' fusion. One of the strongest, most distinguished independent labels, Nation Records has since promoted such artists as Asian Dub Foundation, Natasha Atlas, Fun-Da-Mental, Loop Guru, TJ Rhemi and Transglobal Underground. Its first release, the compilation *Fuse* (1989) introduced artists including Mahatma

T (Talvin Singh), Pulse 8 (including Jah Wobble) and !Loca! (featuring Natasha Atlas) whose cross-cultural mix blended bhangra and Latin with house and techno. Aided by the success of the bigger acts (especially Transglobal's 'Temple Head'), Nation has attracted more artists with sympathetic tendencies, maintaining the 'creative, innovative, uncompromising' philosophy of their logo: 'We hear something great and we want other people to hear it as well. That's our main driving force rather than wanting to sell bucketloads of records'. Brushes with the dance fraternity have included the *Global Sweatbox* compilation (1993) which contained mixes of Nation's back catalogue by Youth, Drum Club, Sabres Of Paradise and Fabio among others. In the event of the rise in popularity of the Asian scene in the mid-90s it might have tempting to concentrate on that area, but Canoville and Nawaz are more concerned with true cross-cultural fertilization and its power to bring people from different backgrounds together. Like Planet Dog Records, Nation have stuck to their concept rather than trying to promote a particular sound, with the result that their music is really quite varied, from the political hip-hop of Fun-Da-Mental and ADF to Loop Guru's chilled 'ethno-techno', Transglobal's rich blend of dub, house and techno to TJ Rhemi's more focused drum 'n' bass style. Since its foundation they have organized a number of clubs and showcases for their artists, sometimes under the name Global Sweatbox.

NATIVE TONGUES POSSE

An informal gathering in the late 80s of artists based in New York, USA, which set about to confirm and celebrate the history of black women and men. Intrinsic to the rise of 'Afrocentricity' in rap music, the coalition included the Jungle Brothers, De La Soul, A Tribe Called Quest, Queen Latifah and Monie Love. A critical backlash ensued in due course, with some of the proponents, or at least some of their adherents, criticised for their obsession with 'Afrocentric trinkets'. However, the movement as a whole was one imbued with positivity and intelligence, and the Native Tongues Posse played no small part in shifting rap's agenda from the self to the society.

NATURISTS

Seven-piece UK techno group led by Wilmott Doonican, who claims to be a relative of Val Doonican, and Sid Raven. Following the release of a mini-album (which despite the 'Gimmick' was well received in the press), they released an appropriate cover version in Blue Pearl's 'Naked In The Rain', in mid-1994. 'We were all into naturism before we started making records', they claim, 'in fact we all met at a small naturist reserve near Reading'. Their lack of clothing apparently acts as a key ingredient in the recording process too: 'When we went into the studio and recorded naked we found that the sound was much better because the top end frequencies weren't absorbed by our clothes'.

● ALBUMS: *Friendly Islands* mini-album (1993)★★★.

NAUGHTY BY NATURE

From New Jersey, New York, USA, the trio of Treach (b. Anthony Criss, 27 December 1970, East Orange, New Jersey, USA), Vinnie (b. Vincent Brown, 17 September 1970, East Orange, New Jersey, USA) and DJ Kay Gee (b. Keir Gist, 15 September 1969, East Orange, New Jersey, USA) are a rap troupe utilizing the funkier rather than darker aspects of gangsta hip-hop. Heavily influenced by the patronage of Queen Latifah, the language was blue but not always in the overtly sexual sense. 'Ghetto Bastard', for example, was a master stroke, pickled in the atmosphere of the street and exact in its execution of ghetto vernacular. Unlike many other hardcore outfits, Naughty By Nature were not afraid of injecting a touch of soul into the mix (once more, *à la* Queen Latifah), which makes the best of their work all the more endearing. They gave Tommy Boy their biggest ever hit with the 12-inch 'OPP', the largest-grossing authentic rap single in the USA in 1990, selling over a million copies ('OPP' stands for 'Other People's Pussy', incidentally, though that did not prevent several generations enthusiastically singing along to 'I'm down with OPP', making the record an American equivalent to the Shamen's 'Ebeneezer Goode'). A second album upped the sleaze factor with some lyrics, but still maintained the group's best traditions elswhere. The single lifted from *19 Naughty III*, 'Hip Hip Hooray', became another monster hit, helped in no small part by a Spike Lee-filmed video. Treach himself was to be found in Houston acting in the film *Jason's Lyric*, though he had appeared previously in the widely ridiculed *Meteor Man*. He has written his own film treatments, in-between bungie jumping sessions in Daytona with close friend Pepa (Salt 'N' Pepa). He also launched the

Naughty Gear clothing line. Kay Gee, meanwhile, earned a production deal with Motown, intial fruit from which was characterized by Zhane's debut album and hit single, 'Hey Mr. Deejay'.

● ALBUMS: *Naughty By Nature* (Tommy Boy 1991)★★★, *19 Naughty III* (Tommy Boy 1993)★★★★, *Poverty's Paradise* (Tommy Boy 1995)★★★.

NAVARRE, LUDOVIC

b. *c.*1967, Saint-Germaine-En-Laye, France. French techno/ambient artist who records as Modus Vivendi, Deepside, Hexagone, Soofle, LN's, Deep Contest, DS and Saint-Germaine-En-Laye (titled after his home-town). A mainstay of Laurent Garnier's FNAC and F imprints of the early 90s, Navarre has contributed to over 90% of both labels' output as a musician/technician. Each of the names he has employed for his own recordings see him adopt a different house style, from techno to electronic jazz. Among his more impressive outings have been his work as Saint-Germaine-En-Laye ('Alabama Blues', 'My Momma Said', 'Walk So Lonely'), Modus Vivendi ('Modus Vivendi') and DS (Volume 1, Volume 2).

NEARLY GOD

(see Tricky)

NEFERTITI

b. *c.*1973, Chicago, Illinois, USA, but raised in Los Angeles. Hardcore Islamic rapper, who as a baby was held in the arms of none other than Elijah Muhammed himself. Both her grandparents were employed by the founder of the Nation Of Islam, and their views have found a new conduit in Nefertiti. She began rapping at the age of 14, but this is just one of the means of expression and communication employed by her. She also works alongside Californian activist Jim Brown on the Amer-I-Can programme, to stabilize inter-gang violence and maintain truces in Los Angeles. She also lectures widely on self-awareness and improvement. Her first recorded messages came as guest appearances on records by Professor Griff and King Tee, and from an early age she was warming up crowds before Public Enemy and Louis Farrakhan shows. Although she signed to a major label, she insisted on a far-sighted contract stipulation: that Mercury pay to put her through college. The first results of this was the *LIFE* set, standing for Living In Fear Of Extinction. This included controversial calls for repatriation to Africa, never mind an Islamic State. She was joined on the record by MC Lyte, with whom comparisons have most frequently been made. She is not to be confused with the UK rapper of similar name.

● ALBUMS: *LIFE* (Mercury 1994)★★★.

NELSON, SHARA

b. London, England. Nelson, formerly vocalist for Massive Attack, began her solo career with 'Down That Road' on Cooltempo Records in July 1993 after returning to London from Bristol. Both Paul Oakenfold and Steve Osbourne were involved in remixing the single, which marketed her as the 'new Aretha Franklin'. She readily admitted to her Motown influences, and the arrangements on her debut album were sumptuous affairs, with heaped strings and gushing choruses. However, she did not desert her dance/hip-hop roots entirely, with co-writing credits for Prince B of PM Dawn ('Down That Road'), Adrian Sherwood (the title track) and Saint Etienne ('One Goodbye In Ten') offering a good balance. The latter track was the second single to be taken from the album, bringing her first major hit. *What Silence Knows'* commercial performance was something of a breakthrough for British R&B, and it was among the nominations for 1994's Mercury Music Prize and two categories in the BRIT Awards. In 1995 *Friendly Fire* firmly established her as an international soul artist, a fact at least partly attributable to Nelson's ability to write lyrics of much greater depth than is generally associated with the genre. The production assistance of Tim Simenon (Bomb The Bass) and Mike Peden (ex-Chimes) and musicianship of Skip McDonald (Sugarhill Gang, etc.), Pressure Drop, Ashley Beadle and the ubiquitous Jah Wobble also contributed greatly to an exemplary collection of cool, resonant soul songs.

● ALBUMS: *What Silence Knows* (Cooltempo 1993)★★★, *Friendly Fire* (Cooltempo 1995)★★★★.

NEMESIS

This rap trio are from Dallas, Texas, comprising The Snake, Big Al and MC Azim. Their first single, 'Oak Cliff', appeared in 1987, but it would be four years down the line before their debut long-player, *To Hell And Back*. It was promoted by the single 'I Want Your Sex'. As their spokesman Azim was happy to point out, 'To be young gifted and black is a blessing that has been treated as a sin'. Undoubtedly this has played a part in holding back their career, as too has prejudice against Texan rappers generally.

● ALBUMS: *To Hell And Back* (Profile 1990)★★★★, *Munchies For Your Bass* (Profile 1991)★★★.

NERVOUS RECORDS

New York-based record label almost as familiar to its adherents via a range of clothing merchandise emblazoned with its distinctive cartoon logo, as it is for its bouncing house tunes. Nervous came into being in the summer of 1990, through the efforts of Michael Weiss and Gladys Pizarro (who would subsequently split to form Strictly Rhythm). The label was launched onto New York's club underground via three specially selected releases - Niceguy Soulman's 'Feel It' (Roger 'S' Sanchez), Swing Kids' 'Good Feeling' (Kenny 'Dope' Gonzalez) and Latin Kings' 'I Want To Know (Quiero Saber)' (Todd Terry). Since then the label, and its merchandising arm, has been run on the basis of continuous throughput. New music is recorded and released week after week, and clothes lines are changed on a similar timescale. The philosophy is that this is the one way in which the label can maintain its link to the street, although it doubtless also increases profit margins. Trinidad's 'Philly'/'The Blunt' was produced on either side by Frankie Feliciano and Todd Terry, while Just Us's 'You Got It' was created by Frankie Cutlass and Andy Marvel, typifying the depth in talent employed by the label. Garage mainstay Paul Scott also chipped in with Sandy B's 'Feel Like Singing'. Some of the label's better-known later cuts include Nu Yorican Soul's output and Loni Clark's 'Rushin'' and 'You'. However, Nervous's ambitions do not end at merely providing high-quality dance material from established stars. There are already three subsidiary labels, Wreck, Sorted, Weeded and Strapped. Wreck covers hip-hop, scoring immediately with the signing of Black Moon (whose 'Who Got The Props' single moved over 200,000 units). Sorted documents more trance- and ambient-focused material, while Weeded hosts underground reggae and dub artists. The newest offshoot is Strapped, which is more funk-orientated. Despite a number of instant successes, the Nervous empire continues to maintain its commitment to its original vision.

NETWORK RECORDS

Birmingham dance label that originally grew out of the underground success of Kool Kat Records. Kool Kat was formed in 1988 by the partnership of Neil Rushton and Dave Barker. Rushton was a well-known northern soul DJ in the 70s and a journalist for *Echoes* and other periodicals, and in the 80s managed the Inferno record label which re-released northern soul records and material by psychedelic soul group Dream Factory. He stumbled on Detroit techno through his northern soul connections in the USA, and met leading lights Derrick May then Kevin Saunderson, in time becoming the latter's manager. He subsequently compiled an album of Detroit techno for Virgin (the first in the UK, later packaging similar collections like the *Retro Techno/Detroit Definitive* sets for Network). His partner Dave Barker's background was as a jazz-funk DJ in the Midlands. Kool Kat began with a number of underground records (experimental techno, psychedelic techno and Chicago house). The policy from the outset was to combine the cream of US releases with plenty of upfront British material. They consequently took on board several local groups, the best-known early example of which were Nexus 21/Altern 8. Proclaimed as one of the hip record labels of the day, funds still remained in short supply and the label was on the verge of collapse. The team had a rethink and formed a new label, Network. From the start Network has employed its own, hard imagery and defined, generic sleeves. The musical range, however, was much broader than had been the case with Kool Kat. The first record to be released was Neal Howard's 'Indulge', while the honour of first chart appearance came with Altern 8's 'Infiltrate'. 'Activ8', by the same group, would do even better, reaching number 3. Network's money problems were easing, and with the advent of KWS and 'Please Don't Go' they disappeared altogether. Neil Rushton had heard the track in a Birmingham club and saw the potential in making a pop record out of it. He approached ZYX who held the rights to the Double You? version of the KC & The Sunshine Band song, only available in Europe, but was turned down unceremoniously. Rushton arranged for KWS, then recording for Network as B-Line, to re-record it. It stayed at number 1 for five weeks. The follow-up, another KC cover, 'Rock Your Baby', was also hugely successful, and soon a lawsuit from ZYX, still unresolved years later, was underway. After KWS the label delivered Altern 8's debut, which effectively summarized the high watermark of the rave generation, with Network personnel taking a full hand in the various pranks and schemes that became synonymous with the group. However, they ran into trouble in June 1992 over Manchester rave band Rhythm Quest's *The Dreams* EP, which used expletives to criticize police procedures in closing down raves. The police expressed their fears to Network that the record, which featured ex-boxer Mark Hadfield, could incite violence, and it was subsequently reissued in a 'cleaned up version', narrowly missing the Top 40.

By the end of 1992 the label had grown unhappy with their distribution set-up with Pinnacle, and at great expense bought themselves out with two years of the contract to run. They initially contacted Sony with a view to distribution only, but in the end the notion of a bigger tie-in was mooted. After eight months of negotiations Sony bought 49% of the shares in the company in August 1993, and Network officially became (on the headed notepaper rather than record labels) Best Beat Dance Limited. It immediately allowed the company far greater freedom. Disenchanted with the reputation given to Network by KWS, they launched SiX6 (most commonly referred to as Six By Six) for street level house. Again a strong generic look was invoked with different colours to distinguish releases. The first product for the imprint was 'Hell's Party' by Glam, an immediate success, which secured the more underground vibe and credibility that Six By Six had been searching for. The Sony deal had also given the company the power to distribute records themselves, and thus help out younger labels by offering them distribution (as long as they passed the Network taste barometer). Some of these 'third party'-distributed labels include Bostin' (which is owned by a band called Mother, led by DJ Lee Fisher), Other Records, the 'Journeys By DJ' series, Good Boy, DiY/Strictly 4 Groovers, Sure Is Pure's Gem, the Ritmo Rival's Planet Four, Hott Records from London and Manchester's UFG and Silver City. In addition there are several labels that Network actually owns. In 1990 the company opened an office in New York, and the First Choice garage/disco label (also a recording studio based in Greenwich Village) grew out of that set-up. Baseroom Productions is similar to First Choice in that it grew out of a recording studio, based in Stoke On Trent. Artists including Sure Is Pure, Bizarre Inc, Altern 8 and MC Lethal had been recording there, and with the name cropping up so frequently Network investigated. They eventually bought out the Baseroom as part of their deal with Sony, and launched a label around the studio, specializing in techno and experimental ambient/non-vocal material. The label's principal artists include Aquarel and the System, and Laurent Garnier has also collaborated on projects emanating from there. As if that were not enough, there are additionally three or four labels with whom deals have been done where Network handle all the rights for releases in the UK. KMS UK was inaugurated via Rushton's management of Saunderson, which made the move inevitable. The label specializes in strong vocal house while spin-off label Eclipse offers the non-vocal techno for which Saunderson is famous. Another Detroit label is Serious Grooves, an underground techno/disco imprint pioneered by Terrence Parker. It is overseen by DJ Tone (b. Antonio Echols), a well-known underground DJ and the keyboard player in Inner City's live band. Vicious Muzik in New York is a label owned and run by Johnny Vicious, one of the most exciting new arrivals on the dance scene of the 90s. Other labels under the Network umbrella include Vinyl Addiction (underground house, and the outlet for the highly regarded Stereogen), Stafford South (named after the motorway junction, where Mark Archer, who A&Rs the label, lives - the label logo being a photograph of that sign), Stafford North (a more hardcore sister label), Eu4ea (for trance releases), Hidden Agenda and One After D. Not bad for a company with a staff team of seven. Intriguingly, bearing in mind the label's early sponsorship of modern techno, the team work in Birmingham's oldest building (a 'haunted Elizabethan house').

● ALBUMS: Various: *Retro Techno/Detroit Definitive* (Network 1991)★★★. Altern 8: *Full On...Mask Hysteria* (Network 1992)★★★.

NEURO PROJECT

UK-born Simon Sprince, Dave Nicoll and Stewart Quinn originally introduced themselves on R&S Records with the sublime techno hit, 'Mama', in the early 90s. Their 90-minute long-playing debut arrived shortly afterwards on 3 Beat Music, and retained the promise of their first release, offering a wide array of styles and structures.

● ALBUMS: *The Electric Mothers Of Invention* (3 Beat Music 1994)★★★.

NEUROPOLITIQUE

Detroit-influenced mannah often credited as 'organic techno'. This, the work of Matt Cogger, was first premiered by two limited edition EPs for London label Irdial. By the time a full-length album emerged its creator was still engaged in the ceaseless exploration of percussion patterns, though never to the detriment of a strong tune. His work was thus compared to that of Carl Craig.
● ALBUMS: *Menage A Trois* (Irdial 1994)★★★, *Beyond The Pinch* (New Electronica 1997)★★★.

NEVINS, JASON

A top New York producer/remixer of the 90s, whose first involvement with music was at his college radio station at Arizona State University, where his sets were primarily composed of techno. He went on to release product as Plastick Project, Crazee Tunes, the Experience and Jason Nevins Movement. 'The Viper Rooms', licensed to Loaded Records, a UK record label in Brighton, Sussex, England, was typical of his output, being completely unabashed in its use of samples. He has since recorded with Nervous, Logic, Strictly Rhythm and Tribal. He has also remixed Ann Consuelo for Champion, and signed to MCA as Analogue. His 1998 remix of Run DMC's 'It's Like That' provided the rap trio with an unexpected international hit.

NEW KINGDOM

Hardcore hip-hop duo from Brooklyn, New York, comprising rapper Nosaj (his real name Jason, backwards) and DJ Sebastian. Their debut single was 'Good Times', a rock hip-hop crossover effort on Gee Street Records which used a sample of Joe Walsh (of James Gang)'s guitar playing and looped it. Their major influence is Curtis Mayfield, and their output reflects a good deal of his social vision. 'Good Times', for example, was written about their desire not to lose their appetite for life as they grow older. They take a full band on tour with them and have live skateboarding at their events, much in the mode of hardcore punk bands. There is certainly a 'cartoon' element to the band, their lyrics generally being abstract, non-linear collages. Their beats, however, are more restrained, as pointed out in the self-explanatory lyric: 'Pouring no lies, no suits, no ties, No need to rush, we love to fuck time'. A genuine return to the old school aural values, their debut album was produced by the band in conjunction with Scott Harding of the Lumberjacks.
● ALBUMS: *Heavy Load* (Gee Street 1993)★★, *Paradise Don't Come Cheap* (Island 1996)★★★.

NEW ORDER

When Joy Division's Ian Curtis committed suicide in May 1980 the three remaining members, Bernard Sumner (b. Bernard Dicken, 4 January 1956, Salford, Manchester, England; guitar, vocals), Peter Hook (b. 13 February 1956, Manchester, England; bass) and Stephen Morris (b. 28 October 1957, Macclesfield, Cheshire, England; drums) continued under the name New Order. Sumner took over vocal duties and the trio embarked on a low-key tour of the USA, intent on continuing as an entity independent of the massive reputation Joy Division had achieved shortly before their demise. Later that same year they recruited Morris's girlfriend, Gillian Gilbert (b. 27 January 1961, Manchester, England; keyboards, guitar), and wrote and rehearsed their debut, *Movement*, which was released the following year. Their first single, 'Ceremony', penned by Joy Division, was a UK Top 40 hit in the spring of 1981, and extended the legacy of their previous band. Hook's deep, resonant bass line and Morris's crisp, incessant drumming were both Joy Division trademarks. The vocals, however, were weak, Sumner clearly at this stage feeling uncomfortable as frontman. Much was made, in 1983, of the band 'rising from the ashes' of Joy Division in the music press, when *Power, Corruption And Lies* was released. Their experimentation with electronic gadgetry was fully realized and the album contained many surprises and memorable songs. The catchy bass riff and quirky lyrics of 'Age Of Consent' made it an instant classic, while the sign-off line on the otherwise elegiac 'Your Silent Face', 'You've caught me at a bad time/So why don't you piss off', showed that Sumner no longer felt under any pressure to match the poetic, introspective lyricism of Ian Curtis. As well as redefining their sound they clearly now relished the role of 'most miserable sods in pop'. 'Blue Monday', released at this time in 12-inch format only, went on to become the biggest-selling 12-inch single of all time in the UK. In 1983 'disco' was a dirty word in the independent fraternity and 'Blue Monday', which combined an infectious dance beat with a calm, aloof vocal, was a brave step into uncharted territory. As well as influencing a legion of UK bands, it would be retrospectively regarded as a crucial link between the disco of the 70s and the dance/house music wave at the end of the 80s. New Order had now clearly established themselves, and throughout the 80s and into the 90s they remained the top independent band in the UK, staying loyal to Manchester's Factory Records. Their subsequent collaboration with 'hot' New York hip-hop producer Arthur Baker spawned the anti-climactic 'Confusion' (1983) and 'Thieves Like Us' (1984). Both singles continued their preference for the 12-inch format, stretching in excess of six minutes, and stressing their lack of concern for the exposure gained by recording with mainstream radio in mind. *Low Life* appeared in 1985 and is perhaps their most consistently appealing album to date. While the 12-inch version of *Low Life*'s 'Perfect Kiss' was a magnificent single, showing the band at their most inspired and innovative, the collaboration with producer John Robie on the single version of 'Subculture' indicated that their tendency to experiment and 'play around' could also spell disaster. Their next album, 1986's *Brotherhood*, although containing strong tracks such as 'Bizarre Love Triangle', offered nothing unexpected. It was not until the UK Top 5 single 'True Faith' in 1987, produced and co-written by Stephen Hague hot on the heels of his success with the Pet Shop Boys, and accompanied by an award-winning Phillipe Decouffle video, that New Order found themselves satisfying long-term fans and general public alike. The following year Quincy Jones's remix of 'Blue Monday' provided the group with another Top 5 hit.

If the recycling of old songs and proposed 'personal' projects fuelled rumours of a split then 1989's *Technique* promptly dispelled them. The album, recorded in Ibiza, contained upbeat bass- and drums-dominated tracks that characterized the best of their early output. Its most striking feature, however, was their flirtation with the popular Balearic style, as in the hit single 'Fine Time', which contained lines such as 'I've met a lot of cool chicks, But I've never met a girl with all her own teeth', delivered in a voice that parodied Barry White's notoriously sexist, gravelly vocals of the 70s. Meanwhile, the band had changed significantly as a live act. Their reputation for inconsistency and apathy, as well as their staunch refusal to play encores, was by now replaced with confident, crowd-pleasing hour-long sets. In the summer of 1990 they reached the UK number 1 position with 'World In Motion', accompanied by the England World Cup Squad, with a song that earned the questionable accolade of best football record of all time, and caused a band member to observe, 'this is probably the last straw for Joy Division fans'. Rather than exploiting their recent successes with endless tours, the group unexpectedly branched out into various spin-off ventures. Hook formed the hard-rocking Revenge, Sumner joined former Smiths guitarist Johnny Marr in Electronic and Morris/Gilbert recorded an album under the self-effacing title the Other Two. The extra-curricular work prompted persistent rumours that New Order had irrevocably split, but no official announcement or press admission was forthcoming. In the summer of 1991 the group announced that they had reconvened for a new album, which was eventually released in 1993. *Republic* consequently met with mixed reviews reflecting critical confusion about their status and direction. While retaining the mix of rock and dance music successfully honed on *Technique*, the tone was decidedly more downbeat, even sombre. Sadly, it arrived too late to help the doomed Factory label, and afterwards the band's membership would return to varied solo projects. Hook formed Monaco in 1996.

● ALBUMS: *Movement* (Factory 1981)★★★, *Power, Corruption And Lies* (Factory 1983)★★★, *Low Life* (Factory 1985)★★★★, *Brotherhood* (Factory 1986)★★★★, *Technique* (Factory 1989)★★★, *Republic* (London 1993)★★★.

● COMPILATIONS: *Substance* (Factory 1987)★★★★, *The Peel Sessions* (Strange Fruit 1990)★★★, *Live In Concert* (Windsong 1992)★★★, *(The Best Of) New Order* (London 1995)★★★★, *(The Rest Of) New Order* (London 1995)★★★.

● VIDEOS: *Taras Schevenko* (Factory 1984), *Pumped Full Of Drugs* (Ikon Video 1988), *Substance 1989* (Virgin Vision 1989), *Brixton Academy April 1987* (Palace Video 1989), *Neworderstory* (1993), *The Best Of New Order* (1995).

● FURTHER READING: *New Order & Joy Division: Pleasures And Wayward Distractions*, Brian Edge. *New Order & Joy Division: Dreams Never End*, Claude Flowers.

NEXUS 21

Namely, Mark Archer and Chris Peat, more famous (in some quarters) for their work as Altern 8. They began their career as Nexus 21 - their 'core' project - with the 'Still Life' 12-inch for

Blue Cat in September 1989, following it a few months later with 'Rhythm Of Life', this time for Blue Chip. After a 12-inch promo, 'Self-Hypnosis', they delivered *Logical Progression* in October 1990 on R&S, a second EP, *Progressive Logic*, following two months later. The duo have also released two singles ('Another Night' and 'Flutes') under the name C&M Connection. Archer has also recorded solo for the Stafford North Imprint as DJ Nex (the *DJ Nex* and *Poundstretcher* EPs) and Xen Mantra (the *Midas* EP). In 1994 he formed Slo-Moshun with Danny Taurus, scoring immediately with the Top 30 'Bells Of New York' cut.

NICE AND NASTY THREE

As hip-hop began to enter the mainstream in the early 80s, there were many businessmen from the black community, whose previous association with music had been in R&B and soul, prepared to take advantage. One such was Danny Robinson, just as had his brother Bobby at Enjoy Records. He reopened his Holiday label to record the Nice And Nasty Three's 'Ultimate Rap' in 1980. He had previously enjoyed success on the imprint with the Bop Chords and others. The Nice And Nasty single, however, proved to be one of the rap's earliest aesthetic victories, though it was never followed-up.

NICE AND SMOOTH

Based in New York City, Gregg Nice (b. Greg Mays) and Smooth Bee (b. Daryl Barnes) emerged in the late 80s with an album for independent concern Fresh Records, a matter of weeks before the label closed its doors. Their self-titled album did emerge, however, as did the two singles it yielded, 'More & More Hits' and 'Funky For You'. They switched to Def Jam for an album and hit single, 'Sometimes I Rhyme Slow', which made US number 44. Album tracks like 'Hip Hop Junkies' suggested they were authentic converts to the history of the movement, and indeed they spanned several of its styles and lyrical concerns. For their second collection they enlisted the help of some of rap and dance music's biggest heavyweights: Bobby Brown ('Return Of The Hip Hop Freaks'), Slick Rick ('Let's All Get Down'), Everlast ('Save The Children') and Jo Jo Hailey of Jodeci ('Cheri'). The duo had been trying to arrange a collaboration with Brown for some time, Barnes having previously written lyrics for his *King Of Stage* album, singing back-up vocals on

tours by the latter and New Edition. Despite the supporting cast it was a set that maintained Nice And Smooth's traditions of deep funk and lyrical pyrotechnics.

● ALBUMS: *Nice & Smooth* (Fresh 1989)★★★, *Ain't A Damn Thing Changed* (Def Jam 1991)★★★★, *The Jewel Of The Nile* (Def Jam 1994)★★★.

NICOLETTE

b. Nicolette Okoh, *c*.1964, Glasgow, Scotland. Though born in Scotland, Nicolette was raised in Nigeria, France, Switzerland and Wales. She originally rose to prominence as singer on the sampled-based house hits of Shut Up And Dance in the early 90s. Their first female signing, her approach to singing was more blues-based and less shrill than many of the 'garage' divas. She also wrote her own songs, demonstrating a keen talent on singles such as 'Wicked Mathematics'. Other collaborations with the Shut Up And Dance duo, such as 'I'd Like To Wake You Up' and 'Dove Song', are regarded by many as forerunners of the jungle and drum 'n' bass sound. Later she toured with Massive Attack, featuring on their *Protection* album, before signing a solo deal with Talkin' Loud Records. She was keen to affirm that 'I really do see myself as a dance act', despite her second album featuring more political material such as 'No Government', released as a single. On *Nicolette* she was joined by some of the cream of the UK production teams, including 4 Hero, Plaid (ex-Black Dog Productions) and Felix Da Housecat.

● ALBUMS: *Now Is Early* (Shut Up And Dance 1992)★★★, *Nicolette* (Talkin' Loud 1996)★★★★, *Let No-one Live Rent Free In Your Head* (Talkin' Loud 1996)★★★.

NIGHTCRAWLERS

The Nightcrawlers are a cover organization for the activities of house producer John Reid (b. Glasgow, Scotland). As he summarizes it, 'I see us as a collective of people and I'm the mouthpiece and the driving force behind it.' The Nightcrawlers' first single was 'Living Inside A Dream', but that failed to ignite significant interest. Much more successful was the subsequent effort, 'Push The Feeling On'. This became a major club success but only reached the UK charts when re-released for the third time. Originally issued in 1993, it finally reached the

UK Top 30 in October 1994. Previously Reid had been involved in several successful musical projects. After being dropped from his original contract with Island Records, Reid had been contacted by producer/writer Ian Levine and asked whether he would be prepared to write songs for him. The results included 'Whenever You Need Me' for Bad Boys Inc., his first major hit, and material for Eternal, Gemini and Optimystic. The Nightcrawlers' follow-up to 'Push The Feeling On', a repetition of the formula entitled 'Don't Let The Feeling Go', was marginally less successful but became another club hit.

● ALBUMS: *The 12" Remixes* (Arista 1996)★★★.

NIGHTMARES ON WAX

Based in Leeds, England, they began as a duo of George Evelyn (DJ EASE) and Kevin Harper. In the early 80s Evelyn spent time breakdancing with the Soul City Rockers, alongside future members of Unique 3, and as Nightmares On Wax he began DJing with Harper at parties and then clubs in the mid-80s. At the same time they recorded three tracks, 'Let It Roll', 'Stating A Fact' and 'Dextrous', which they sent out as a demo to various record companies in the UK and New York. Having been turned down, they released 'Let It Roll' on their own Positive Records, which went on to sell 2,000 copies. In the meantime, they had met Steve Beckett, who asked them to join Warp Records who made 'Dextrous' their second release in 1989. Together with the work of such groups as LFO, Unique 3 and the Forgemasters, this track and 'Aftermath' (a UK Top 40 hit in 1990) helped to create the sound known as bleep. 'Aftermath' was unique in that its rhythms, although built on a solid four-on-the-floor foundation, sound like an embryonic drum 'n' bass track. Their next release, 'A Case Of Funk' (1991), was a successful club hit. According to many, the group's first album, *A Word Of Science* (1991), created a blueprint for the trip-hop movement of the 90s as it merged funk and hip-hop rhythms with stark electronics, but at the time of its release it seemed to confuse those who had eagerly consumed NOW's straight dance singles. Subsequent releases, including 'Set Me Free' and 'Happiness', continued to gain critical acclaim. In 1992 Harper left to concentrate on his career as a DJ. Evelyn spent several years collecting samples, recording demos and co-running the club Headz in Leeds and released a few jazzy house tracks on the Warp subsidiary Nucleus. He eventually made his comeback as NOW in 1995 with the album *Smoker's Delight*, on which he worked with a guitarist, bassist, keyboard-player, rapper and singer. This low-tempoed, abstract hip-hop album embraces a broad range of influences, including funk, soul, jazz, dub and even touches of C&W. The following year, Evelyn released 'Still Smokin'' and in 1997 remixed Omar's 'Sayin' Nothin''.

● ALBUMS: *A Word Of Science* (Warp 1991)★★★★, *Smoker's Delight* (Warp 1995)★★★★.

9 LAZY 9

(see Funki Porcini)

95 SOUTH

From the Chill Deal Boys (who recorded albums for Quality Records) stable, and part of Toy Productions, 95 South were credited with starting a mini-revival in electro hip-hop with their huge 1993 hit, 'Whoot! There It Is'. Sampling Afrika Bambaataa's epic 'Planet Rock', the single returned to goodtime, basic beat-box tunes, with lyrics concentrating on the party angle, underpinned by the mighty Florida/Miami Bass sound. It was released in competition with Tag Team's similarly themed record. and was followed by an album that, good as it was in its own right, offered more of exactly the same. The group comprises Bootyman, Church's, Black and DJ Marcus. Together they created a monster in 'Whoot!' that refused to die; after high-profile appearances on programmes like *The Arsenio Hall Show* it was adopted by both the New Orleans' Saints and Philadelphia Fillies as their theme tune. All of this was lapped up by the protagonists: 'We are a group with a simple message. We are positive, not political or controversial. We make fun music that anyone can get into'.

● ALBUMS: *Quad City Knock* (Wrap 1993)★★★.

NINJA TUNE RECORDS

This London-based label was conceived in 1990 by Coldcut's Jonathan Moore and Matt Black, as a response to the intransigence of major record companies whose vision extended only to the formulae of house and techno. With its roots in their DJing philosophy, they set out to provide a vehicle for their own experimentation, taking pride in an eclectic DIY approach that drew from every kind of source, quite literally including the kitchen sink. With its mixture of breakbeats, hip-hop, jazz, funk, ambience and amusing samples, Ninja Tune has established itself as a source of self-consciously interesting, humorous music. Their first releases included Bogus Order's *Zen Brakes* (1991), the DJ Food *Jazz Brakes* series, and albums by Hex and 9 Lazy 9. With the rise of the Bristol scene they were unfortunately branded with the trip-hop tag by the press, which did nothing to express the real diversity and eccentricity behind the label: 'We regard ourselves as scientists of sound . . . getting back to that sense of wonder you feel as a child when everything seems incredibly weird . . . Complex systems and non-linear behaviour are actually about the real world, as opposed to Newtonian simplifications of the real world'. They have since released most varied music by Amon Tobin, Kid Koala, Chocolate Weasel, Coldcut, the London Funk Allstars, Funki Porcini and the Herbaliser, among others. Ninja Tune continue to produce an impressive range of compilations, notably *Funkjazztickle Tricknology* (1995), *Flexistentialism* (1996) and *Funkungfusion* (1998). Various related projects have included Coldcut's *Solid Steel* show on Kiss FM, the club nights Stealth (at the Blue Note) and later Kung Fusion (Turnmill's and 333), and Hex Media DJ and VJ activities. The subsidiary label N-Tone was created to cater for artists with more of an electronic sound, including Journeyman, Neotropic and Override, while Big Dada concentrated on a pure hip-hop sound.

NO FACE

A US rap duo purveying the ribald humour of Digital Underground or Naughty By Nature, No Face signed to CBS Records in 1990, but like so many of the hip-hop crop of 1990/91, failed to make a significant impact. Their only release in the UK was the 12-inch single 'Half', while their debut album, *Wake Your Daughter Up*, failed to interest either the critics or record buyers.
● ALBUMS: *Wake Your Daughter Up* (CBS 1990)★★.

NOMAD

This band's press largely revolved around two facts. First their vocalist, Sharon Dee Clarke (b. *c*.1965), had played the role of a nurse in Dennis Potter's *The Singing Detective*. She was also filmed in the bed next to the character Michelle Fowler when the latter was giving birth in *Eastenders*. Secondly, their single, 'Devotion', comprised sam-

ples from the British Poll Tax Riots and even transferred one of Margaret Thatcher's more rabid outbursts onto tape. It was also a huge hit, reaching number 2 in the charts and becoming the biggest dance single of 1991 in the process. It was co-written and produced by future Undercover producer Steve Mac. The other personnel in the band were rapper MC Mikee Freedom (b. *c*.1969, Bristol, England) and Damon Rochefort (b. *c*.1965, Cardiff, Wales). Freedom was discovered by former law student Rochefort while rapping on a song entitled 'Love Don't Live Here Anymore' by Fresh Connection. Rochefort himself had worked with Clarke on the FPI Project's 1990 hit, 'Going Back To My Roots'. Unfortunately their debut album was thin on original songs, comprising three versions of 'Devotion', while elsewhere formulaic Euro dance pop held sway. Though the follow-up single, 'Just A Groove', made the Top 20, subsequent efforts ('Something Special' - originally recorded by Clarke solo for a compilation album, 'Your Love Is Lifting Me' and '24 Hours A Day') failed to replicate their original success. Rochefort also embarked on a side project, Serious Rope, again featuring Clarke, who scored a 1993 hit with 'Happiness', recorded as a tribute to the Flesh club in Manchester. Freedom would go on to a solo career with TEK, beginning with 'Set You Free' for Dave Pearce's Reachin' label.
● ALBUMS: *Changing Cabins* (Rumour 1991)★★★.

NOOKIE

b. Gavin Chung, *c*.1971. In 1994 Nookie arrived from Hitchin in Hertfordshire at the forefront of the new jungle movement sweeping through the UK's dance scene. Singles such as 'Only You' (1994) and 'The Sound Of Music' (1995) attempted to add spiritual resonance to the drum and bass formula, and added keyboard, piano and vocals to crunching rhythms and breakbeats. Nookie had served a long apprenticeship in jungle and its two main antecedents, hardcore and reggae. Aged 17 he made his vinyl debut, remixing Flourgon and Ninjaman's ragga track 'Zig It Up', as a member of the hip-hop crew Main Attraction. His first release under his own steam (as 2 Boasters) was 'Large Southend Donut', which revealed his stylistic hallmarks of piano melding into a rhythmic onslaught. As well as Nookie, Chung also records under the name Cloud Nine for the hardcore stable Moving Shadow. He runs

his own record shop, Parliament, in Hitchin and label, Daddy Armshouse, with partner Pedro, as well doing a lot of remixing.
● ALBUMS: *The Sound Of Music* (Reinforced 1995)★★★.

NOTORIOUS B.I.G.

b. Christopher Wallace, 21 May 1972, New York, USA, d. 8 March 1997, Los Angeles, California, USA. A large, imposing figure in contemporary rap before his murder in 1997, Wallace grew up in the tough district of Bedford-Stuyvesant, in Brooklyn, New York. He soon graduated to a life modelled on the activities of those around him, selling drugs and acting as a teenage lookout. He first rapped, under the name Biggie Smalls, as part of the neighbourhood group the Old Gold Brothers. He also experimented with his own demo recordings, a copy of which was eventually passed to Mister Cee, Big Daddy Kane's DJ. Cee passed the demo on to *The Source*, America's best-selling rap periodical, which gave it a glowing review in its 'Unsigned Hype' column. This attracted the attention of Sean 'Puffy' Combs of Bad Boy Entertainment, who signed Wallace. Having now adopted the stage name Notorious B.I.G., Wallace made his recording debut in 1993 backing Mary J. Blige on 'Real Love'. He also made a guest appearance on Supercat's 'Dolly My Baby'. His first solo effort was 'Party And Bullshit', included on the soundtrack to the film *Who's The Man*. His debut album followed in 1994. *Ready To Die* became a major hit thanks to the inclusion of singles such as 'Juicy', 'One More Chance' and 'Big Poppa', the latter voted *Billboard*'s rap single of the year. He scooped a number of end-of-year awards in *The Source*, as the album achieved platinum sales. He went to the UK to support R. Kelly at Wembley Stadium in London, and also guested on Michael Jackson's *HIStory - Past, Present And Future Book 1*. However, despite his elevation to such exalted company, Notorious B.I.G. never left the ghetto behind. He formed a group, M.A.F.I.A., with some of his former hustler colleagues, who released an album, *Conspiracy*, in 1995. He was also involved in sundry episodes involving violence, such as a fracas with a promoter in New Jersey and his attempt to take a baseball bat to autograph hunters (for which he received a 100 hours' community service sentence). There was also a running feud between B.I.G. and Tupac '2Pac' Shakur - who was convinced of B.I.G.'s involvement in a 1994 robbery in which he was injured. Their disagreement soon festered into a bitter feud between the east and west coast American rap scenes. When Shakur was murdered, B.I.G.'s non-attendance at a rap peace summit in Harlem was widely criticized. Instead he began work on a second album, entitled, prophetically, *Life After Death*. He never lived to see its official release. He was gunned down after leaving a party in California in March 1997. Subsequent conjecture indicated that his murder may have been in retaliation for Shakur's killing.
● ALBUMS: *Ready To Die* (Bad Boy/Arista 1994)★★★, *Life After Death* (Bad Boy/Arista 1997)★★★★.

NOVAMUTE

The dance/techno arm of Mute Records' independent empire, launched in January 1992 with Mick Paterson (promotions, subsequently departed), Pepe Jansz (A&R) and Seth Hodder (production). Unlike many other established record companies trawling the backwaters of club music angling for financial reward, Mute had established its own tradition in commercial dance with Depeche Mode and Erasure, or more particularly Renegade Soundwave and Nitzer Ebb. They had also supported the fledgling Rhythm King for several years, before that label branched out on its own in the 90s. The step to the burgeoning house/techno scenes was a natural one, particularly as the parent label had already released Exit 100's 1991 12-inch 'Liquid', the Underground Resistance mini-album *X101*, and licensed a Black Market compilation set. The original plan for Novamute then, was to license 12-inch white labels and imports and give them a proper release. In the US this was achieved via a distribution deal with independent rap label, Tommy Boy. Three compilations were crucial in establishing Novamute: *Tresor 1 (The Techno Sound Of Berlin* and *Tresor II (Berlin-Detroit: A Techno Alliance)* - from the Berlin-based Tresor label, and *Probe Mission USA* - drawn from Canada's Plus 8 Records. Their roster of artists has grown to include Moby, Richie Hawtin/Plastikman, 3Phase, Juno Reactor, Spirit Feel ('Forbidden Chant'), 3MB ('Jazz Is The Teacher'), Compufonic (aka Hyper Go-Go: 'Make It Move') and Doof ('Disposable Hymns To The Infinite').
● ALBUMS: Various: *Version 1.1* (Novamute 1993)★★★.

NSO FORCE

The NSO Force are a UK-based hip-hop crew featuring the vocal skills of Melodee and Ola the Soul Controla. While Melodee was London-born and bred, Ola came from Nigeria via Baltimore and Brooklyn. This influenced the band's international flavour, and their acknowledged influences include Fela Kuti And His African Beats, alongside Eric B And Rakim. The crew were one of the few bands to endure into the 90s from the early 80s' old-school hip-hop movement that emerged in Ladbroke Grove, London. NSO Force have been articulating their reality lyrics since 1984 and built a solid reputation at clubs and venues across London. In 1989 the NSO Force released their debut, 'Give It Up', for Vinyl Solution, which proved especially popular in dance venues. They followed the release through the Whole World Recording group in 1990, echoing Peter Tosh with '400 Years'. The song succeeded in gaining the band a hardcore following, while they were concurrently admired as prominent performers on the underground scene. In 1993 the band crossed over to the mainstream with their third release, 'Chains'/'In Too Deep'. The song featured on mainstream radio and held the number 1 position on the hip-hop chart for three weeks. The group followed the hit in 1995 with their fourth release, 'The Capital (Land Of The Lost)', a heavier track that led to their eventual signing with China Records. The NSO Force were not overtly militant, although they maintained that they could not be bought, divided or ruled - hence the band's initials, inspired by the Malcolm X stance: No Sell Out. In 1998 the band were asked to perform on Supercharger's 'Tick Like A Bomb', which featured the classic line, 'Like a time bomb tickin' -Yo - the plot thickens - A tale of two cities - but it ain't Charles Dickens'. The NSO Force also shared a French-only release with the Cash Crew, contributing a reference to their west London roots, 'Notting Ill'. Their association with China led to the release of 'Money', a self-production that introduced the vocals of an up-and-coming Malaysian soul vocalist, Blue, who performed a variation on 'Love Come Down', while the NSO Force demonstrated their hip-hop skills to full effect.

● ALBUMS: *Friends In Low Place* (Indochina 1998)★★★.

NU GROOVE RECORDS

Revered New York-based record label owned by Frank and Judy Russell but established in the public's mind and ears by house producers and twins Rheji and Ronnie Burrell, who had formerly recorded for Virgin subsidiary Ten as Burrell. It was originally created for them as 'an alternative outlet . . . because we had a lot of material that we were doing and we couldn't put it all out on Virgin', but went on to become their priority operation. The first record on the label was Tech Trax Inc's 'Feel The Luv' in August 1988, created by Rhji. Further early material arrived from Ronnie's Bas Noir project and Rheji's 'You Can't Run From My Love'. The original plan was to release a record by each brother every two weeks, and they have not fallen far short of that blistering schedule. Among their more successful vinyl expeditions have been 1989's 'It's Power House Brooklyn Style' - created by Powerhouse, aka Masters At Work, 1990's 'The Poem' and 'Rydims' (Bobby Konders) and Transphonic's 'Tune In Light Up' and 'Bug Out'. Most featured the keyboard talents of Peter Daou (formerly, and incredibly, a member of the Beirut Jazz Trio, where he grew up). Together with wife Vanessa he released 'Law Of Chants' and 'Part Two' (as Vandal). Rheji was also behind the *New York House N Authority* album (SBK 1990), a softer, more reflective affair. Another significant record from this time was 'Major Problem', an anti-drugs parody from Lennie Dee and Ralphie, which utilized samples from Yello and others. 1991 brought the *Metro* EP, a weighty, bass-driven house cut from Rheji, and Lost Entity's 'Bring That Back On'/'The Verge', which boasted the label's familiar deep soul feel. Other examples were Howie How and Little Carlos's 'Cause I Need You' (as the Divine Masters), the Vision's 'Laidback And Groovy', created by Eddie 'Satin' Maduro, and Transphonic ('Club Tools (Professional Use Only)'). 1992 brought Ize 2's 'House Trix' (an Isaac Santiago production). This was also the label that housed Joey Negro's Mr Maize scam, when his club hit 'Together' was licensed to the USA. When the single topped the dance charts journalists tried to hunt down the entirely fictional Mr Maize. Other notable appearances included Victor Simonelli (under the guise of Groove Committee) with 'Dirty Games', and the Houz Negroz 'How Do You Love A Black Woman', produced once more by the Burrell brothers. Tracing the Nu Groove discography remains an arduous but rewarding task for fans of high-class house music.

● COMPILATIONS: *Nu Groove - Here Comes That Sound Again* (Passion 1998)★★★★.

NWA

The initials stand for Niggers With Attitude, which was the perfect embodiment of this Los Angleles group's outlook. They comprised Dr. Dre (b. Andre Young), DJ Yella (b. Antoine Carraby), MC Ren (b. Lorenzo Patterson) and Eazy E (b. Eric Wright, 7 September 1973, Compton, California, USA, d. 26 March 1995, Los Angeles, California, USA). Founder-member Ice Cube (b. Oshea Jackson, c.1970, South Central, Los Angeles, California, USA), arguably the most inspiring of the rapping crew, departed for a solo career after financial differences with the band's manager (which would later be recorded in a highly provocative song that attacked him for, amongst other things, being Jewish). However, all the band's members had long CVs: Dr. Dre had DJed for World Class Wreckin' Crew, and had produced Ice Cube's first band, CIA. Both Eazy E and DJ Yella had recorded and produced several rap discs under their own names, the former funding his Ruthless Records label, allegedly, through illegal activities. Other early members of the posse included Arabian Prince and D.O.C. NWA's first single was 'Boyz N' The Hood', marking out their lyrical territory as guns, violence and 'bitches'. Though *N.W.A. And The Posse* was their debut album, they only performed four of the raps on it, and to all intents and purposes, *Straight Outta Compton* counts as their first major release. For those attracted to the gangsta rappers first time round, this was more of the same, only sharper and more succinct. A landmark release, in its aftermath rap became polarized into two distinct factions; traditional liberal (reflecting the ideas of Martin Luther King) and a black militancy redolent of Malcolm X, albeit much less focused and reasoned. In 1989 the FBI investigated *Straight Outta Compton*'s infamous 'Fuck Tha Police', after which Cube left the group. It set a precedent for numerous actions against NWA, including the first time anyone in the music industry had received a threatening letter from the FBI. *Efil4zaggin* (Niggaz4life spelt backwards) which made US number 1, also surpassed the outrage factor of its predecessor by addressing gang rape and paedophilia, in addition to the established agenda of oral sex, cop killing and prostitution. Musically, it contained furious blasts of raggamuffin and 70s funk, but that was somehow secondary. It did reveal some humour in the band, i.e., on 'Don't Drink That Wine' (which jokingly encourages drug abuse instead), or lines like, 'Why do I call meself a nigger, you ask me? Because my mouth is so muthafuckin' nasty, Bitch this bitch that nigger this nigger that, In the meanwhile my pockets are getting fat.' However, such wit was stretched paper-thin over a clutch of expletives and obscenities. The UK government used the Obscene Publications Act to seize copies but were forced to return them following legal action. Ultimately the BPI withdrew their support from Island Marketing's successful action. Counsel for the defence was Geoffrey Robertson QC, who had played a similar role in the infamous *Oz* trial of 1971. Expert testimony from Wendy K of Talkin' Loud Records, rap author David Toop and psychologist Guy Cumberbatch of Aston University swung the case. This prompted a variety of statements from British MPs outlining their intention to toughen up the law. However, even the anti-censorship lobby must concede that NWA's by turns ludicrous ('Find 'Em Fuck 'Em And Flee') and dangerous ('To Kill A Hooker') songs have blurred the generally positive influence of the rap movement. As the decade progressed it became obvious that the remaining members of NWA were spending more time on their solo projects, Dr. Dre, in particular, going on to enjoy huge success both as an influential artist and producer with Death Row Records, the phenomenally successful label he co-founded with Marion 'Suge' Knight. His acrimonious parting from Eazy-E over monies owed through Ruthless Records was celebrated in records by both artists. Yella has been quiet, co-production credits on Ruthlesss aside, while Ren released a disappointing solo ablum and EP.

● ALBUMS: *NWA And The Posse* (Ruthless 1987)★★★, *Straight Outta Compton* (Ruthless 1989)★★★★, *Efil4zaggin* (Ruthless 1991)★.

● COMPILATIONS: *Greatest Hits* (Virgin 1996)★★★.

O'NEAL, SHAQUILLE

b. c.1971, Newark, New Jersey, USA. O'Neal is the star of the previously obscure Orlando Magic basketball team ('Rookie Of The Year' in 1992). After the media picked up on his demonstrative play, notably his cult slam-dunk action, he emerged as a major multi-media star of the early 90s - so much so that a record contract was just around the corner, and the format was hip-hop. His generally sport-related raps such as '(I Know I Got) Skillz' and 'Shoot Pass Slam' kept the cash-tills rattling, the latter song being the soundtrack to the Reebok commercials of which he was the high-profile star. He did possess some history in the hip-hop idiom, having previously been a break-dancer in Newark until his size made the activity impossible/ludicrous. Later he moved to Germany where his father, Sgt Phillip Harrison, took a post. He relocated to San Francisco to attend high school, playing for 68-1, who won the state championship. From there he was picked up by Louisiana State University coach Dale Brown, from where he joined Orlando. Basketball and music are by no means his only interests. In February 1994 he appeared in his first film, *Blue Chips*, with Nick Nolte. Incredibly, he had already penned his own autobiography, at the age of 21. His recording career was recovering from critical reaction to his long-playing debut, which featured over-familiar Gap Band breakbeats funnelled through maestros like Erick Sermon (EPMD), Def Jef, Ali Shaheed (A Tribe Called Quest) and Fu-Schnickens. The final set was delivered for the approval of no lesser men than Scarface, Big Daddy Kane and Ice Cube.

● ALBUMS: *Shaq Diesel* (Jive 1993)★★★, *You Can't Stop The Reign* (MCA 1996)★★★.

OAKENFOLD, PAUL

Oakenfold was active in club promotions from the early 80s and became one of the most successful DJs and remixers of the 90s. Having trained as a chef, he decided to pursue a career in music after he had been introduced to the decks by his friend Trevor Fung in 1981. He later moved to New York, where he worked for a number of record companies and regularly visited the Paradise Garage. When he returned to the UK he worked for Champion Records, promoting Jazzy Jeff and Salt-N-Pepa, among others, and later Profile and Def Jam Records. He also DJed at the Project Club in Streatham, London, and wrote a hip-hop column in *Blues And Soul* magazine under the name Wotupski. In 1987, along with Danny Rampling and a few others, he visited Fung and Ian St. Paul (who later helped to set up TIP Records) in Ibiza, where he went to clubs such as Amnesia that were playing a mixture of Chicago house, pop and indie. On his return, Oakenfold recreated the Balearic feeling at a few after-hours parties at the Project Club and towards the end of the year, with St. Paul, he organized a similar club at the Sanctuary in London's West End; initially called Future, the club night became Spectrum when it moved to Heaven in 1988. Spectrum, along with Rampling's Shoom, helped to establish the underground acid house movement. Later, Oakenfold played at a number of the huge Sunrise and Biology parties, opened shows for the Stone Roses and the Happy Mondays, and toured the world with U2. In 1989 he set up the label Perfecto Records and remixed the Happy Mondays' 'Wrote For Luck' with his musical collaborator Steve Osborne. The pair have subsequently remixed for a variety of artists including Arrested Development, Massive Attack, M People, New Order, the Shamen, the Stone Roses and U2, and have recorded under a number of names including Grace, Virus, the Perfecto Allstarz and Wild Colour. Oakenfold has compiled a number of compilation albums for the Ministry Of Sound and in 1994 was employed by East West Records as an A&R consultant. During the 90s he helped to popularize the trance sound and has become one of the best-known DJs in the UK, graduating from house towards a melodic, commercial style of trance.

OAKTOWN'S 3-5-7

Half-hearted female rap troupe from the USA whose strings were pulled by an indulgent Hammer. Following the latter's defection from Capitol the group appear to have been washed up in the blood-letting. The group comprised local Oakland, Calfornia-rappers Sweet LD (b. Djuana Johnican), Terrible T (b. Tabatha King), Vicious C

and Sweat P. The latter was formerly a cheer-leader with the Oakland Raiders. By 1991 only Johnican and King remained.
● ALBUMS: *Wild And Loose* (Capitol 1989)★★★, *Fully Loaded* (Capitol 1991)★★★.

OL' DIRTY BASTARD

New York rapper Ol' Dirty Bastard is a member of the American rap band Wu Tang Clan. His first solo album, however, was disappointingly formulaic. The album was interesting only on those tracks ('Brooklyn Zoo', 'Cuttin' Heads' and 'Snakes') which featured the familiar beats of the Wu Tang producer, RZA. Other guests from Wu Tang Clan included Method Man, The Ghost, and U God. At the time of the album's release, Ol' Dirty Bastard was pursued by police into an apartment. It was not a burglary, he claimed, but an attempt to escape from an assassin. A week later the same assailant shot him twice in the back.
● ALBUMS: *Return To The 36 Chambers: The Dirty Version* (WEA 1995)★★★★.

OLIVE

Olive are a studio-bound project inaugurated in 1995 by Tim Kellet, Robin Taylor-Firth and singer Ruth-Ann Boyle (b. 1971, Sunderland, England). Kellet had formerly been a member of the horn group Rebop while at music college in Manchester, England. He subsequently joined Vini Reilly's Durutti Column, before 10 years spent as a sideman for Simply Red. He finally left that group after the hugely successful *Stars* tour, retreating to a purpose-built home studio he had financed in Derbyshire. The first result of his self-employment was a successful co-production venture with the Lighthouse Family. Taylor-Firth had previously worked in the Sheffield area with underground dance artists Nightmares On Wax, playing and co-writing their 1995 album. Via a mutual friend he made the acquaintance of Kellet, and the two agreed to work together on a collaborative project. The final piece of the jigsaw was completed by Ruth-Ann, a Sunderland native who had sung with many underground bands in that city and also contributed a sample of her voice to Vini Reilly's 1996 album. Kellet discovered her by accident, playing a keyboard sample while in Reilly's company, and enquiring as to the origin of the voice. One hastily convened meeting later, Ruth-Ann had become the third and final member of the trio. They made their debut with 'Miracle', the perfect showcase for Ruth-Ann's

haunting vibrato, released in July 1996 on RCA Records. The re-released 'You're Not Alone' brought the group a UK number 1 hit in May 1997.
● ALBUMS: *Extra Virgin* (BMG 1997)★★★, *Miracle* (BMG 1997)★★★.

OLYMPIC RECORDS

Record company formed in Liverpool by James Barton and Andy Carroll, named after their respected club night. Barton was a DJ who served his apprenticeship on the Northern club scene, going on to launch one of the best-known venues, Cream. He was then instrumental in setting up Olympic Records in 1992 with Carroll, who was also a DJ. The label earned its biggest success with Seven Grand Housing Authority's (Terrence Parker) 'The Question'. Barton also furnished K-Klass, who remixed the record, with management services, and introduced them to their, and his, future employers, DeConstruction. He joined the latter label in early 1994 to take a hand in their A&R operation, though he retained his interests in Olympic and Cream.

OM RECORDS

'The idea of Om is to cover the spectrum of house music and to do absolutely the best stuff that house can offer', explained DJ Nick Hook, who founded the UK label Om together with *New Musical Express* dance correspondent Sherman and Morgan King. The label was thus inaugurated with three double-pack EPs that displayed just that: a *pot pourri* of modern house, labelled *Absolute Om, 1 - 3*. Other bands on the label included mainstays Soundsource (essentially Morgan King, whose recordings, such as 'Take Me Up' and 'One High', also appear on Sweden's B-Tech imprint), ex-Guerilla act Euphoria, Bump and Marine Boy (who are one-time Ruts member Segz and engineer Steve Dub's deep house/ambient project, distinguished by releases of the calibre of 'Fluid'). 1994 releases included 108 Grand featuring Roy Galloway's 'Love U All Over'.

OMAR

b. Omar Lye Fook, 1969, Canterbury, England. Omar was born the son of a Chinese Jamaican father and an Indian Jamaican mother. A former principle percussionist of the Kent Youth Orchestra, he would later graduate from the Guildhall School Of Music. His debut singles were

'Mr Postman' and 'You And Me' (featuring backing vocals from Caron Wheeler), before his debut album was released, via Harlesden's Black Music Association's Kong Dance label, on a slender budget. Nevertheless, it reached the Top 60. In its wake, Omar's name suddenly began to crop up everywhere, be it as a singer, writer or producer. Following a high-profile Hammersmith Odeon concert in December 1990, Gilles Peterson of Talkin' Loud persuaded financial backers Phonogram to open their wallets. The debut album was slightly remixed and re-released, the title track having already earned its stripes as a club favourite. Although by definition a soul artist, Omar's use of reggae, ragga and particularly hip-hop has endeared him to a wide cross-section of the dance community. RCA won the scramble to sign Omar after departing from Talkin' Loud in January 1993. Since then, Omar has continued to collaborate with a number of premier R&B artists - songwriter Lamont Dozier, keyboard player David Frank (famed for his contribution to Chaka Khan's 'I Feel For You'), bass player Derek Bramble (ex-Heatwave), Leon Ware (arranger for Marvin Gaye) and no less than Stevie Wonder himself, who contacted Omar after hearing his 'Music' cut.
● ALBUMS: *There's Nothing Like This* (Kongo Dance 1990)★★★, *For Pleasure* (RCA 1994)★★★, *This Is Not A Love Song* (RCA 1997)★★★.

ON U SOUND SYSTEM
(see Clail, Gary, And The On U Sound System)

ONE DOVE
This trio from Glasgow, Scotland, caught the nation's imagination in 1993 with their mellow musical depths. The group comprises Ian Carmichael (b. 1 June 1960, Glasgow, Scotland), Jim McKinven (b. David James McKinven, c.1959, Glasgow, Scotland) and former chemical engineering student Dot Allison (b. Dorothy Elliot Allison, 17 August 1969, Edinburgh, Scotland). McKinven had been in an early incarnation of the Bluebells (rehearsal only), but was best known for his stint in Altered Images. Carmichael owns Toad Hall Studios, and has engineered or produced for many Glaswegian acts (Orchids, Bachelor Pad, etc.). The group made their first public appearance at the Rock Garden, Queens Street, Glasgow, in August 1991. The fact that Andy Weatherall became involved attracted some initial attention, but there was more to the group than merely

another of his side projects. They had already broken into the rave scene's élite with the single 'Fallen', prior to their collaboration. It was released on Soma, before the band had changed their name from their original selection, Dove. However, litigation followed from representatives of Supertramp (the band had inadvertently used a sample from an Italian house record that in turn had sampled the prog-rockers). They met Weatherall in Rimini in 1991. After he agreed to work with them there was some discussion in the press that One Dove's debut album would signal another landmark episode, à la Primal Scream's *Screamadelica*, but this was perhaps over-optimistic. It was at least a solid, musically enthralling collection conveying One Dove's biggest influence: King Tubby and Jamaican dub music.
● ALBUMS: *Morning Dove White* (London 1993)★★★.

100TH MONKEY
(see Guthrie, Andy)

ONE LITTLE INDIAN RECORDS
The roots of the UK One Little Indian record label lie in the anarcho-punk scene of the early 80s, particularly in one of its pioneering bands, Flux Of Pink Indians. The precursor to One Little Indian was Spiderleg, which released records by the System, Subhumans, and Amebix in addition to Flux's own material. Both labels were run by Derek Birkett (b. 18 February 1961, London, England), Flux's bass player, alongside friends and colleagues from the independent punk scene. Early releases included ones by Annie Anxiety, D&V and the Very Things. Reflecting on the mistakes made earlier, the label used expensive and tasteful cover art by Paul White's Me Company. When the Sugarcubes, a band Birkett previously knew when they were Kukl, broke through, financial security was assured. While One Little Indian retains its identity as the 'ethical indie', the operation is constructed on level-headed business practices: 'Our motives are artistic and business is reality'. Unlike many labels, the roster of bands does not have a uniform image or sound. Music on the label includes the bright and breezy pop of the Popinjays, Heart Throbs and the Sugarcubes, the dance sound of the Shamen and Finitribe, the delicate, crafted pop of Kitchens Of Distinction and the shattering volume of What? Noise. The label was also the temporary home for They

Might Be Giants, who released *Lincoln* and two singles. The recent mainstream success of the Shamen has consolidated their position in the independent charts. The massive success of Björk was long overdue and was financially very welcome, although other outfits, such as Daisy Chainsaw, failed to fulfil expectations. Recent signings include Compulsion, Credit To The Nation and the revitalized Chumbawamba. The label has released several 'Best Of' compilations which act as a good introduction.

● VIDEOS: *One Little Indian* (Virgin Vision 1990).

ONE RECORDS

Record label run by Eddie Colon (pronounced 'Cologne'), a former Kiss FM DJ, former proprietor of Renegade Records and a recording artist in his own right (achieving a US hit with 'Upfront') and the celebrated Roger Sanchez. They first met in 1991 when Colon was still a struggling DJ. The first One record was 'No Way' by Countdown, produced by Toddy Terry/Kenny 'Dope' Gonzalez. The release schedule continued apace with material by Murk's Oscar G, more Kenny 'Dope' Gonzalez ('Axis Project', etc.) and Victor Simonelli ('I Know A Place') - almost a who's who of US house producers. The label was invoked 'to bring quality records out of New York ... a soulful, house type of sound. We want to start developing artists. I'm an old song guy and I don't like this whole track thing'. One would sign Farley and Heller as their remix team, as well as UK singer J.B. Braithwaite ('Love Me Tonite'). In January 1994 the operation unveiled Sanchez's first ever long-playing release.

● ALBUMS: Roger Sanchez *Secret Weapons Vol. 1* (One 1994)★★★, various artists *The Sound Of One* (One 1994)★★★.

ONYX

Hardcore gangsta rappers from Queens, New York, USA, Onyx are led by Sticky Fingaz (b. Kirk Jones), with the rest of the group initially comprising Fredro Starr, Big DS and DJ Suavé Sonny Caesar. Their intense, gun-fixated image quickly became a popular receptacle for ill-conceived teenage fantasies in both the US and UK. They originally recorded a solitary single for Profile Records, 'Ahh, And We Do It Like This', before switching to Columbia Records. Boasting titles such as 'Blac Vagina Finda', a visual image of bald heads and bad attitudes, their debut album was co-produced by Jam Master Jay (Run DMC). It sold in huge quantities, arguably because the music itself, on tracks such as 'Throw Ya Gunz', was undeniably exciting as well as forceful. As if to live up to the group's image, Fingaz found himself in trouble for allegedly assaulting a passenger on a United Airlines flight to New York from Chicago O'Hare airport. Group member Fredro also appeared in Forrest Whitaker's film, *Strapped* in 1993, and (with Sticky) in Spike Lee's *Clockers*. By the advent of the group's second album in 1995 their ultra-violent image had been usurped by the arrival of Staten Island's Wu Tang Clan, but Onyx still offered ample evidence of their ability to hammer home their message in tracks such as 'Two Wrongs' ('Two wrongs don't make a right, But it sure do make us even'). *Shut Em Down* was a better attempt at recapturing the energy and attitude of their debut.

● ALBUMS: *Bacdafucup* (Columbia 1993)★★★, *All We Got Iz Us* (Def Jam 1995)★★, *Shut Em Down* (Def Jam 1998)★★★★.

OPUS III

UK vocalist Kirsty Hawkshaw (b. *c.*1969), attired with boots and mohican haircut coupled with dayglo beads, led this pop house outfit on their breakthrough single, 'It's A Fine Day'. An update of Jane & Barton's faint ballad, mixing poetry with sweet, haranguing vocals, it added a generic backbeat and little else. Hawkshaw had led a gypsy lifestyle since leaving school (her father composes theme music for television programmes, including *News At Ten*, *Grange Hill* and *Countdown*). As a child she recorded cover versions of the hits of the day for cheap compilation albums, before travelling around the free festival circuit selling home-made jewellery (and MCing for Spiral Tribe). She met the outfit's boiler room staff, Ian Dodds, Kevin Walters and Nigel Munro, at a rave. They form part of the Ashebrooke Allstars, and also recorded as A.S.K. ('Freedom We Cry' for MCA). The follow-up single was a cover of King Crimson's 'I Talk To The Wind'. Nurtured by her record company and band as a chanteuse straddling the pop/rave market, Hawkshaw failed to provide adequate substance to sustain her strong visual image. However, the band did eventually return in 1994 with 'When You Made The Mountain', and a new, 'spiritual' album.

● ALBUMS: *Mind Fruit* (PWL 1992)★★★, *Guru Mother* (PWL 1994)★★.

ORB

The Orb is really one man, Dr Alex Paterson (b. Duncan Robert Alex Paterson, hence the appropriation of the Dr title), whose specialist field is the creation of ambient house music. A former Killing Joke roadie, member of Bloodsport, and A&R man at EG Records, he formed the original Orb in 1988 with Jimmy Cauty of Brilliant fame (for whom he had also roadied). The name was taken from a line in Woody Allen's *Sleeper*. The band first appeared on WAU! Mr Modo's showcase set *Eternity Project One* (released via Gee Street Records), with the unrepresentative 'Tripping On Sunshine'. However, their first release proper came with 1989's *Kiss* EP, again on WAU! Mr Modo (which had been set up by Paterson with Orb manager Adam Morris). It was completely overshadowed by the success of the band's subsequent release, 'A Huge Ever-Growing Pulsating Brain Which Rules From The Centre Of The Ultraworld'. It was an extraordinary marriage of progressive rock trippiness and ambience, founded on a centrepoint sample of Minnie Riperton's 'Loving You' (at least on initial copies, later being voiced by a soundalike due to clearance worries). The group signed with Big Life, but Cauty departed in April 1990. He had wished to take Paterson and the Orb on board in his new KLF Communications set-up. There was no little acrimony at the time and Cauty re-recorded an album that was to have been the Orb's debut, deleting Paterson's contributions, and naming it *Space* (also the artist title). In the event the ethereal 'Little Fluffy Clouds', with cowriter Youth, was the next Orb release, though that too ran into difficulties when the sample of Rickie Lee Jones attracted the artist's displeasure. Paterson did at least meet future co-conspirator Thrash (b. Kristian Weston) during these sessions, who joined in late 1991 from a punk/metal background, hence his name (though he had also been a member of Fortran 5). Their debut album (and the remix set of similar title) was based on a journey to dimensions beyond known levels of consciousness, according to the participants. It soared, or perhaps sleepwalked, to the top of the UK album charts, and led to a plunge of remixes for other artists (including Front 242 and Primal Scream). The album was fully in tune with, and in many ways anticipative of, the blissed-out rave subculture of the early 90s, mingled with dashes of early 70s progressive rock (Pink Floyd were an obvious reference point). There was also an LP's worth of the band's recordings for John Peel's Radio 1 show. This included a 20-minute version of 'Huge Ever-Growing . . . ', which prompted fellow disc jockey Andy Kershaw to ring the BBC to complain, mockingly, about the return of hippie indulgence on a gross scale polluting the nation's airwaves. The Orb signed to Island Records in 1993 following a departure from Big Life that took seven months (and eventually the high court) to settle. The contract with Island allowed Paterson to continue to work on collaborative projects through their own label Inter-Modo, outside of the Orb name. Other projects included a remix album for Yellow Magic Orchestra, though a previous request by Jean Michel Jarre for them to do the same for his *Oxygene* opus was declined. They also took the opportunity to play live at unlikely venues such as the Danish island of Trekroner, and generally appeared to be making a hugely enjoyable time of their unlikely celebrity, Paterson even being made honorary president of Strathclyde University's Student Union. However, their first studio set for Island, *Pomme Fritz*, saw them witness the first signs of a critical backlash. This was seemingly unfounded as their musical growth could not be disputed; this progress continued with *Orblivion* in 1997.

● ALBUMS: *The Orbs Adventures Beyond The Ultraworld* (WAU! Mr Modo/Big Life 1991)★★★, *Peel Sessions* (Strange Fruit 1991)★★★, *Aubrey Mixes, The Ultraworld Excursion* (WAU! Mr Modo/Big Life 1992)★★★, *UFOrb* (WAU! Mr Modo/Big Life 1992)★★★, *Live 93* (Island 1993)★★, *Pomme Fritz* (Island 1994)★★★, *Orbvs Terrarvm* (Island 1995)★★★★, *Orblivion* (Island 1997)★★★.

ORBIT, WILLIAM

b. William Wainwright, England. In addition to heading the Bass-O-Matic group, Orbit has remixed for the likes of Prince, Madonna ('Justify Your Love', *Ray Of Light*), Belinda Carlisle, S'Express, Shamen, Seal, Les Negresses Vertes, the Cure ('Inbetween Days') and Shakespears Sister, though he gave up remixing in 1993 so it would not overshadow his own work. As a teenager Wainwright would make his own music by splicing tapes together to produce sound collages. He started cutting songs as part of Torch Song, and released two albums, *Wild Thing* in 1984 and *Exhibit A* in 1987, with Laurie Mayer. He then took the name Orbit and brought in vocalist

Peta Nikolich for his debut, having retained Mayer as his co-writer. This set included bizarre cover versions of the Psychedelic Furs' 'Love My Way' and Jackie Mittoo's 'Feel Like Jumping'. The club favourite 'Fire And Mercy' brought him to the attention of dance pundits. This was housed on *Strange Cargo*, a collection of soundscapes recorded between 1984 and 1987. *Strange Cargo II* also steered away from the electronic house music that had marked Orbit's work with Bass-O-Matic, and resembled instead the experimental pieces of Brian Eno or Holger Czukay. Eventually the Madonna remix brought him to the attention of Rob Dickins, chairman of Warner Music, and together they set up the N-Gram Recordings label in 1995. (Orbit had previously founded Guerrilla Records which released progressive house artists such as Spooky and D.O.P. and which folded in 1984.) The first release on N-Gram was a single by cellist Caroline Lavelle, whom Orbit discovered when she played on Massive Attack's 'Home And Away'. An album followed, as well as Orbit's first release for his new label, a continuation of the *Strange Cargo* series. N-Gram also gave him the opportunity to work with the Torch Song trio once more, while *Pieces In A Modern Style* was an interpretation of twentieth century classical music.

● ALBUMS: *Orbit* (MCA 1987)★★★★, *Strange Cargo* (MCA 1988)★★★★, *Strange Cargo II* (IRS 1990)★★★, *Strange Cargo III* (IRS 1993)★★★, *Strange Cargo IV* (N-Gram 1995)★★★, *Pieces In A Modern Style* (N-Gram 1995)★★.

ORBITAL

This UK ambient techno outfit have done much to deliver the possibilities of improvisation to live electronic music. Unlike many other groups, their stage performances do not depend on DAT or backing tapes. They also use more varied samples than is the norm, including sources as diverse as the Butthole Surfers on 'Satan' and Crass on 'Choice'. Comprising brothers Paul Hartnoll (b. 19 May 1968, Dartford, Kent, England) and Phillip Hartnoll (b. 9 January 1964, Dartford, Kent, England), the Orbital name was first suggested by their friend Chris Daly of the Tufty Club. With several 'M25' dance parties happening so close to their homes in Dunton Green, they named themselves after the UK's least adored stretch of road. It also helped to convey the idea of tape loops, which are so central to their craft. Before the band began its active life in 1987, Paul had played with an outfit by the name of Noddy And The Satellites

as well as doing labouring odd jobs, while his brother had been a bricklayer and barman. They made their live debut in the summer of 1989 at the Grasshopper, Westerham, Kent, joining the ffrr Records imprint shortly afterwards. They opened their account for the label with the UK Top 20 single 'Chime' in March 1990, setting a pattern for a sequence of dramatic, one-word titles ('Omen', 'Satan', 'Choice', 'Mutations'). They moved to Internal Records for 'Raddiccio' in October 1992, while work continued apace on their remixing chores. These included work on releases by artists as diverse as the Shamen, Queen Latifah, Meat Beat Manifesto and EMF. Their first two albums, beginning with *Untitled* in 1991 (subsequently referred to as *Untitled 1*), showcased their ability to sustain a musical dynamic over a full-length album, a rare ability within their field, which saw them bracketed alongside artists such as Underworld and the Orb. In 1994 they appeared as headliners at the Glastonbury Festival and contributed to the *Shopping* film soundtrack. They also released *Snivilisation*, a largely instrumental political concept album which was successful on both a musical and thematic level. Meanwhile, their live work earned them an award for Best Live Show at the *New Musical Express*'s BRAT Awards as they made a triumphant return to Glastonbury in 1995. If previous albums had always hinted at a cinematic bent, 1996's 'The Box' was a fully fledged film soundtrack - comprising four distinct movements with vocal versions by lyricist Grant Fulton and Tricky singer Alison Goldfrapp. The film itself was Orbital's own exploration of science-fiction adventurism, ironically filmed in the highly terrestrial environs of Milton Keynes. It was followed by the release of Orbital's fourth studio album. The exquisitely dense rhythms on the six tracks that comprised *In Sides* emphasized the group's critically acclaimed accommodation of the experimental with the accessible. It included tracks such as 'The Girl With The Sun In Her Hair', recorded using solar power as a reaffirmation of the group's anarchist/environmental standing.

● ALBUMS: *Untitled 1* (ffrr 1991)★★, *Untitled 2* (Internal 1993)★★★, *Snivilisation* (Internal 1994)★★★★, *In Sides* (Internal 1996)★★★★, with Michael Kamen *Event Horizon* soundtrack (London 1997)★★.

ORGANIZED KONFUSION

Duo comprising Pharoahe Monch and Prince Poetry, whose music is distinguished by both a rare knack for samples/rhythm tracks and a smooth lyrical flow. Coming from Jamaica and New York, respectively, the band's members absorbed everything from jazz and reggae to gospel in their youth. They met at high school in 1986, signing to a small independent after honing their skills. No recordings emerged from the contract, and they switched instead to Disney-funded Hollywood Basic, scoring immediate success with the number 1 rap hit, 'Walk Into The Sun', and a well-received debut long player (which also included a second hit single in 'Open Your Eyes'). The title track, 'Stress', from their second album set out their stall with an attack on racist taxi drivers, and music industry incompetents. Joined by Q-Tip (A Tribe Called Quest) on 'Let's Funk', these were just two of the best tracks on another excellent album, with Prince Po indeed the '...exec with the intellectual concepts that elevate you like steps' ('Let's Organize').
● ALBUMS: *Organized Konfusion* (Hollywood Basic 1991)★★, *Stress: The Extinction Agenda* (Hollywood Basic 1994)★★★, *The Equinox* (Priority 1997)★★★.

ORIGINAL CONCEPT

Long Island, New York, four-piece who made an early impression on hip-hop's underground scene with their 1986 single, 'Knowledge Me'/'Can You Feel It', following it with the mighty 'Pump That Bass'. The former was mainly notable for being the first of several rap tracks to sample the Art Of Noise's 'Close To The Edit'. On album Original Concept concentrated squarely on entertainment, using comedic raps over dance-orientated grooves. Mainman Dr Dre (not the Dre of NWA/solo fame) went on to DJ for the Beastie Boys and co-host *Yo! MTV Raps* with Ed Lover.
● ALBUMS: *Straight From The Basement Of Kooley High* (Def Jam 1988)★★★.

ORIGINAL ROCKERS

Midlands, UK-based dance outfit, led by DJ Dick (b. Richard Whittingham) and musician Glynn Bush, who have been compared to the On-U Sound troupe via their ambient dub/deep trance techniques. They made their debut in February 1992 with a single, 'Breathless', dedicated to DJ Dick's club of the same name. Their 1993 single

'Rockers To Rockers' was originally issued a year earlier as the b-side to limited edition promos of 'Push Push', (previously titled 'Come Again'). As is usual, it was based on deep dub grooves, with adventurous drum and bass patterns. Other singles include the self-descriptive 'Stoned', recorded in collaboration with fellow-Birmingham outfit Groove Corporation.
● ALBUMS: *Rockers To Rockers* (Different Drummer 1993)★★★.

OSBY, GREG

b. 1961, St Louis, Missouri, USA. New York-based saxophonist who has attached jazz's cool to a militant hip-hop beat. Following his work with the M-Base project (including Steve Coleman and Cassandra Wilson), Osby decided he wanted to record a more free-ranging, one-off hip-hop record: 'The purpose for this record was to function as an 'either/or', meaning that it could rest solely as a hardcore hip-hop record without any jazz or musicians at all, and that it also would be a strong musical statement without breakbeats or anything. I wanted it to bridge the gap'. Alongside jazz musicians including Geri Allen and Darrell Grant, he enlisted the aid of hip-hop producers Ali Shaheed Muhammed (A Tribe Called Quest) and Street Element, and a variety of rappers. Osby had actually begun life as an R&B musician, only discovering jazz when he attended college in 1978. Though setting up M-Base as a streetwise jazz/hip-hop enclave, he had little time for the work of Gang Starr or Digable Planets, who sample from jazz but do not, generally, work with live musicians. That did not stop him from being bracketed alongside those artists, however.
● ALBUMS: *Greg Osby And Sound Theatre* (Watt 1987)★★★, *Mind Games* (JMT 1989)★★★, *Season Of Renewal* (JMT 1990)★★, *Man Talk For Moderns Vol X* (Blue Note 1991)★★, *3-D Lifestyles* (Blue Note 1993)★★, *Black Book* (Blue Note 1995)★★★, *Art Forum* (Blue Note 1996)★★★.

OTHER RECORDS

Other Records, originally the recording outlet for acclaimed house artists A Man Called Adam, has expanded since its formation in 1993 to become one of the UK's premier deep house record labels. The idea for the label came when Sally Rodgers and Steve Jones of A Man Called Adam broke away from their previous home at Big Life Records. Rather than look for a new deal, the duo elected to set up their own label. Eschewing the prevailing trend for progressive house and trance records, Other was envisaged as a home for the type of deeply melodic material A Man Called Adam had patented. They were inspired to pursue their own path by like-minded friends such as Roberto Mello (of Sensory Productions) and DJ D, both of whom would later work with Other. The label's first release was A Man Called Adam's 'I Am The Way'. That, and subsequent records such as Beachflea's self-titled EP and Diane Mathis's 'Never Give Up', fell somewhere between the dominant dance strains in the UK of the time - hard house and garage. The duo began to work with Mike Ward of the About Time soul label, bartering their production services for the right to release house mixes of vocal tracks by former Prince backing singer Rosie Gaines and the aforementioned Diane Mathis. As well as further A Man Called Adam material such as 'Love Come Down' and 'Easter Song', other artists on the label included Reel Houze (a collaboration between Mello and DJ D), Jose Padilla and Maria Naylor. By 1996, and riding on a crest of acclaim, Other Records had become financially viable for the first time, proving once again that independent labels remain the touchstone for developments in the UK dance scene.

● ALBUMS: various artists *Other* (Other 1995)★★★.

OTHER TWO

The most purely dance-orientated project of the three major New Order spin-offs, the Other Two features arguably the least attention-seeking members of the Manchester quartet: Stephen Morris (b. 28 October 1957, Macclesfield, Cheshire, England) and Gillian Gilbert (b. 27 January 1961, Manchester, England). Recording at their own studio in rural Macclesfield, they debuted on the charts with the number 41-peaking 'Tasty Fish' in 1991. The follow-up, 'Selfish', came two years later, and featured fashionable remixes by both Moby and Farley And Heller. The Other Two also tampered with the work of other artists, as well as earning several credits for television and soundtrack motifs.

● ALBUMS: *The Other Two & You* (London 1993)★★★.

OUI 3

Oui 3 are Blair Booth (b. California, USA, vocals, programming), Phillip Erb (b. Switzerland, keyboards) and Trevor Miles (lyrics, rapping). In addition, their debut album featured the formidable rhythmic skills of Youth (Killing Joke, Brilliant, etc.), Jah Wobble, Galliano and the Brand New Heavies. It revealed an obvious debt to PM Dawn, with a flat, distinctively English rapping style. Booth was once a sidekick of Terry Hall of the Specials/Fun Boy 3 (as part of Terry, Blair and Anouschka), while Erb worked alongside Billy MacKenzie (ex-Associates). Together they met unknown rapper Miles, who shared their interest in George Clinton and Lee Scratch Perry. Their speciality was a witty mix of vocals and raps, with clever observations on a series of tightly wound scenarios. 'Break From The Old Routine', for example, depicted a collapsing relationship: 'We ain't gelling these days - we're congealing'. They returned to their reggae roots with the 45 'Arms Of Solitude', which featured of all things, an Augustus Pablo mix.

● ALBUMS: *Oui Love You* (MCA 1993)★★★.

OUR TRIBE

Our Tribe is essentially Rob Dougan and Rollo Armstrong. They first met when Armstrong travelled to Australia with his friend Will Mount (later to become Gloworm) after finishing university. He met Dougan, who was then training to be an actor in Australia, signing a deal together for the rooArt label (nothing was released). On his return to England Rollo became a successful producer in his own right, and when Dougan emigrated they teamed up again. Their debut release for ffrr, 'I Believe In You', became a number 1 in the dance lists in the early 90s. Mel Medalie of Champion Records soon came along with the offer of both recording opportunities and their own subsidiary label (Cheeky). It was this that housed the duo's 'Understand This Groove' (as Franke), Gloworm's 'I Lift My Cup' and the OT Quartet's 'Hold That Sucker Down', a Top 10 hit. Our Tribe went on to remix for U2 ('Numb'), Pet Shop Boys ('Can You Forgive Her', 'Absolutely Fabulous'), M People ('How Can I Love U More?'), Wonderstuff ('Full Of Life'), Shola ('Love, Respect & Happiness'), Raze ('Break 4 Love') and Gabrielle ('Dreams'). The duo were also behind the writing and production of Kristine W's 'Feel What You Want' and Our Tribe featuring Sabrina Johnston's 'What Hope Have I?'.

OUTCASTE RECORDS

This label was set up in May 1994 by Shabs Jobanputra to promote new Asian music in the UK. Among its releases are Nitin Sawhney's two albums *Migration* (1995) and *Displacing The Priest* (1996), Shri's *Drum The Bass* (1997) and Badmarsh And Shri's *Dancing Drums* (1998). Their first compilation, *Untouchable Outcaste Beats* (1997), included tracks by a number of these and other contemporary artists working in this area, as well as material by fusionists from the 60s and 70s such as Shankar, Wolfgang Dauner and the Dave Pyke Set. Outcaste have also run successful club nights in London at the End and Notting Hill Arts Club, which, as well as featuring DJs, present live music, rappers, traditional dancing, poetry and films. Although some of their music blends British dance styles with traditional Asian music in the same vein as much of the so-called Asian Underground, the label's artists, notably Nitin Sawhney and Shri, have a much broader scope that combines all kinds of sounds bound together by the Asian theme. In 1997 the label signed a distribution agreement with the American hip-hop label Tommy Boy Records.

OUTER RHYTHM RECORDS

A subsidiary of the UK label Rhythm King Records, Outer Rhythm was established in 1989 to license hot 'outside' products. Early releases on the label included Leftfield's single 'Not Forgotten' (1990), released before that band had become a duo. They also had success with material under licence from R&S Records, including Digital Excitation's 1992 trance hit, 'Pure Pleasure'. They imported heavily from Detroit, notably Random Noise Generation's 'Falling In Dub' in early 1992, which had originally been housed on 430 West Records and Germany's Hithouse stable. The label closed in June 1992 owing to 'changing forces in the market place'.

OUTHERE BROTHERS

This rap outfit from Chicago, Illinois, USA, consist of the singer and lyricist Malik and the producer Hula. Malik previously wrote the lyrics to Jazzy Jeff And The Fresh Prince's worldwide hit, 'Boom Boom Shake The Room'. He had also been a member of another group, Lidell Townsell And M.T.F., who had a Top 20 US hit with 'Nu Nu'. He agreed to work with Hula through a mutual Jazzy Jeff connection. Hula produced the rapper/DJ team's Grammy award-winning platinum single, 'Summertime'. They were originally joined by two other members, who promptly disappeared on their first trip to Europe. As the Outhere Brothers they enjoyed considerable success first with 'Pass

The Toilet Paper' then two UK number 1 singles, 'Don't Stop (Wiggle Wiggle)' and 'Boom Boom Boom'. The latter stayed at the top of the charts for several weeks in 1995, and featured a memorable video of the two Chicago Bulls fans playing basketball. Both singles were big sellers in Europe, despite a near absence of mainstream radio play due to their risqué lyrical contents. In April 1995 the duo were investigated by New Scotland Yard following a justified complaint from a Bradford mother that the album, purchased by her 10-year-old daughter, was obscene, with especially deliberately provocative titles such as 'I'll Lick Your Pussy' and 'Fuck U In The Ass'. At the same time further complaints were received about the lyrics of a bonus track on their number 1 hit, 'Don't Stop (Wiggle Wiggle)'. In September 1995 another single, 'La La La Hey Hey', appeared in the UK charts. The repetitive nature of their work indicates a short commercial life and thousands of parents will breathe a sigh of relief.
● ALBUMS: *1 Polish 2 Biscuits And A Fish Sandwich* (Eternal/WEA 1995)★★, *The Party Album* (WEA 1996)★★.

OUTKAST

Atlanta, Georgia duo comprising Andre 'Dre' Benjamin and Antoine 'Big Boi' Patton, who broke big with 'Player's Ball' - produced by TLC backroom gang Organized Noise. It comprised tales of the streets of their local East Point and Decateur neighbourhoods. Sadly songs like 'Get Up And Get Out' introduced wholly regrettable lines like 'I learned the difference between a bitch and a lady, but I treated them all like ho's'. They were signed to LA & Babyface's LaFace imprint. 'Elevators (Me & You)' became a major rap chart success in July 1996, as did the following album *ATLiens*.
● ALBUMS: *Southerplayalisticadillacmuzik* (LaFace 1994)★★★, *ATLiens*)LaFace 1996)★★★.

OUTLAW POSSE

UK duo of the early 90s comprising DJ K Gee and rapper Bello, originally titled Brothers Like Outlaw, who saw the potential of their debut album neutered by a long-delayed release schedule. Disillusioned, it was some small time before the release of their next record, the 'Party Time' 45, which included a sample of the Cookie Crew's 'Born This Way'. Here they worked with a singer (Alison Evelyn) and live percussion. Although some accused them of jumping the jazz-rap bandwagon, they had actually prefaced their interest in such things as long ago as their 1989 debut single, 'Original Dope', which sampled Donald Byrd. Bello rapped memorably on the KLF's 'What Time Is Love', and also produced tracks for Upfront, while Karl has remixed for numerous artists inlcuding Queen Latifah, Mica Paris, Young Disciples and Omar. The group enlisted a live crew entitled Push, and gigged widely through Europe and Scandanavia during the 90s, eventually shortening their name to simply Outlaw. The group split shortly thereafter, Bello going on to record solo as Mister Bello. He also inaugurated his own label, Krazy Fly, to which he signed Upfront Ruddies, a crew he also manages.

● ALBUMS: *My Afro's On Fire* (Gee St 1990)★★★★.

OUTSIDE

Namely one Matt Cooper (b. *c*.1973, England), who is widely recognized among club and genre cognoscenti as the most talented arrival on the jazz/funk scene in the last decade. Classically trained on the piano, he went on to a deal with Dorado Records that allowed him to install a new digital recording studio in his own north London residence. Their relationship began with the singles 'No Time For Change' and 'Big City', whose featured vocalists included Cleveland Watkiss, with a bass line from Gary Crosby, before collaborating with fellow Dorado interns D*Note and jazzmen like Steve Williamson and Ronnie Laws. A third single, 'Movin' On', was completed as a typically strong and energetic debut album was assembled in late 1993. Outside also comprise Patrice Blanchard (bass) and Byron Wallen (trumpet), plus various session musicians as the occasion demands.

● ALBUMS: *Almost In* (Dorado 1993)★★★, *Discoveries* (Dorado 1997)★★★.

OVERFLASH

Announcing his musical style as 'Cyberdeath', Overflash is the creation of Swedish-born 'musical deviant' Devo. Employing high-tech midi-computer technology in addition to his own screaming vocals, Overflash's musical output encompasses everything from baroque to techno and death metal. Calling on guitars, percussion instruments, strings, vocoder voice treatments and a wide variety of samples, his debut album was released on MNW Records in 1994 - though Overflash had originally been founded in 1986.

Despite its eclecticism, *Threshold To Reality* was criticized for the artist's over-employment of pulp cyberpunk imagery that lacked lyrical dexterity.

● ALBUMS: *Threshold To Reality* (MNW 1994)★★.

OVERLORD X

b. *c*.1968. Hackney, London, England. Overlord X is a Brit-rapper who first arrived on Music Of Life's *Hard As Hell* compilation. However, he made his name with the verve of two excellent albums for Island Records, which were particularly successful in Europe. Indeed, *X Versus The World* went platinum in France, making it the most popular hardcore hip-hop album in that territory. Although not immediately recognizable as hardcore in the musical sense, there remained a lyrical exactitude that defied compromise. The influence of Public Enemy and Chuck D, in particular, has always been self-evident, notably on cuts like 'Prologue 1990', which featured a sample of the former's 'Bring The Noise'. However, Overlord had little time for NWA's ghetto-romanticism: 'Trying to say we're niggers, who the fuck are you? Coming from this brother with an attitude' ('You Can't Do It In London'). An alliance with ragga stars Midrange and Kandy on *X Versus The World* proved his diversity. He also produced their recordings as part of the X-Posse, and began work on his own film and a documentary about Hackney. Perhaps Overlord X's influence in the medium of television has had the greatest impact, however. Terry Jarvis, a well-known BBC producer, directed the promo clip, '14 Days In May', through which Janet Street Porter commissioned him to provide continuity links between sections of *Def II*. He subsequently became producer for that show for 18 months, before providing the title-song and music for sitcom *The Real McCoy*. However, a 1992 record deal with Jarvis was less successful. His imprint, Down To Jam, was financed by Motown, but its life span was truncated by financial considerations. Overlord X, no longer employing that name, regrouped in 1994 as part of Benz.

● ALBUMS: *Weapon Is My Lyric* (Mango Street 1988)★★★, *X Versus The World* (Mango Street 1990)★★★★.

OWENS, ROBERT

A long-time collaborator with Mr. Fingers in Fingers Inc, Owens provided the vocal for early house classics such as 'Washing Machine' and 'Music Takes Me Up'. He also sang on classics

including Frankie Knuckles' 'Tears' and (uncredited) on the Bobby Konders production, Jus' Friends' 'As One'. Owens grew up, inspired by Stevie Wonder, Patti LaBelle and others, with a church choir background, going on to sing in several bands. As a youth he travelled between his Los Angeles-based mother and Chicago-stabled father, where he was first introduced to house music. Ironically his first experience of a warehouse party left him overpowered, and he left after 15 minutes. He would later watch the assembled masses through a window, and decided to begin DJing himself, combining deck skills with his own vocals. It was at this point that he was introduced to Larry Heard, aka Mr Fingers. Owens would select from the tunes presented to him by Fingers and choose the ones for which he wished to write lyrics. This paved the ground for Owens' breakthrough performance on Fingers Inc's 'Can You Feel It?'. When his songwriting partnership with Fingers broke up due to financial pressures, he recreated the method with Frankie Knuckles and David Morales (hardly a step down in quality) for his debut solo album. He was eventually dropped from his contract with Island in 1992 despite US success with 'I'll Be Your Friend' (which came out on Paul Oakenfold's Perfecto, and was remixed by Morales and Satoshi Tomiie) and the self-produced 'You Gotta Work'. Owens remains one of house music's great showmen, offering uplifting live sets with his Freetown posse (which was also the name of the label he helped to establish). Earlier he had been the star turn on the first house package tour to London, which arrived on English shores in February 1987. 1994 saw him defect to the Musical Directions imprint.
● ALBUMS: *Rhythms In Me* (4th & Broadway 1990)★★.

P

P.O.W.E.R.

Their initials standing for People Oppressed by the World's Empire Ruling elite, it would not take genre commentators long to predict a similarity in style and presentation to Consolidated. P.O.W.E.R. too deal in doses of polemic rap spliced with heavy rhythmic surges and undulations. The group comprises Krys Kills and Che 'Minister Of Defence' - a rapper and DJ, respectively, who met while studying law at college in Portland, Oregon. Their debut single, 'Racemixer', was released on Nettwerk/Play It Again Sam Records, as well as the follow-up album, which was crammed with message-lyrics like 'Guerilla Warfare' and 'Modern Day Slavery'.
● ALBUMS: *Dedicated To World Revolution* (Nettwerk 1994)★★★.

PAL JOEY

Pal Joey is merely the best known of New Yorker Joey Longo's (b. *c*.1964) innumerable aliases. He earned his spurs with early house recordings on pivotal New York deep house imprint Apexton, also playing out regularly in Manhattan. Like so many others he began life working in a record shop, Vinyl Mania, before becoming an apprentice at a local studio.
His more recent recordings, which have steadily built an audience in clubs, generally consist of loose, happy house textures, often released on his own label, Loop D' Loop. Examples include 'Flight 801' from 1991, or Espresso's 'Ping Pong' for Maxi Records from earlier the same year. Other names he hides behind include Earth People, Soho (not the UK outfit - scoring a big hit with 'Hot Music'), House Conductor, Espresso and Dream House. As Pal Joey his productions include 'Jump And Prance', arguably the first ska/house tune, for Republic. He has produced widely, notably for Boogie Down Productions (half of *Sex And Violence*, also appearing alongside KRS-1 on R.E.M.'s 'Radio Song'). Other clients include Deee-Lite (remixing their 'What Is Love' and 'ESP').

More recently he is often to be found working under the CFM Band moniker (Crazy French Man).

PANDORA

b. Amelia Pandora, Sweden. One of her country's many emergent techno/dance stars of the early 90s, Pandora made her debut in 1993 with 'Trust Me'. The single, which featured a rap section provided by friend and colleague K-Slim, immediately catapulted her to the top of domestic dance charts and also created a strong impression throughout mainland Europe. While many similar female dance singers have simply served as a focal point for backroom mixers, Pandora - whose resemblance to Marilyn Monroe has been continually remarked upon - proved herself very much a creative presence with the release of her accompanying debut album. *One Of A Kind* featured several noted Swedish producers, including Dr Maxx Family, Sir Martin and T:O:E:C.
● ALBUMS: *One Of A Kind* (Virgin 1993)★★★.

PAPA CHUK

b. Charles Roberts, c.1969. Hardcore hip-hop artist from Houston, Texas, where he moved in 1991 from his native Austin. As a child Papa Chuk, 'The Desolate One', practised rapping along to b-side instrumentals, and was obviously strongly influenced by Naughty By Nature's Treach in his delivery. His debut album saw him also introduce a Jamaican patois/dancehall style, notably on cuts like 'Make Way For The Rudeboy', though other tracks like 'Desert Dog' and 'Down And Dirty' needed more to distinguish them.
● ALBUMS: *Badlands* (Pendulum 1994)★★★.

PARAS, FABIO

London-based DJ renowned for his sets in the 90s at Boy's Own parties, and equally admired for his 'bongo mixes' and eclectic record collection (i.e., playing the Clash to bemused but still receptive punters). His remixes inlcude React 2 Rhythm's 'I Know You Like It', Aloof's 'On A Mission', Deja Vu's 'Never Knew The Devil' and Outrage's 'Drives Me Crazy' (which sampled the Fine Young Cannibals song) and 'Tall 'n' Handsome'. The last named cut was issued on his own label, Junk, which he set up to house percussion-based material. He has also released material for Cowboy as Charas.

PARIS

b. c.1968, San Francisco, California, USA. Paris is a hardcore black Muslim rapper, widely shunned by the mainstream for his militant views. Based in San Francisco, Paris recorded his first single, 'Scarface Groove', in 1989. However, his breakthrough came with 'Break The Grip Of Shame', a typically informed and effective rant against the degradation of black communities and the need for change. It was a sublime piece of West Coast hardcore, the first fruits of his deal with Tommy Boy, which saw him hailed on MTV. The video was a provocative cocktail of footage containing uniformed revolutionaries in Africa, and images of Malcolm X and the Black Panthers. This was a fitting introduction to Paris' craft, a self-made man who remains responsible for his own production and management, backed only by DJ Mad Mike. He graduated from the University of California in 1990 with an economics degree. Public Enemy took him on tour and they could have found fewer more suitable warm-up acts. Despite being accused in some quarters of being dour and worthy, Paris nevertheless injected a focused, reasoning intelligence where discussions of evil reached beyond the lure of the bedroom or the villainy of the local law enforcement agency. However, tracks like 'Bush Killer' were openly inflammatory, even if they were also fun - a good example of his willingness to bookend cerebral discussion with revenge fantasies. He runs his own record label, Scarface, set up in 1987, which at one point looked likely to sign up Ice-T following his split with Warners. He did, however, produce several acts from the Bay Area, and also cut an album with Conscious Daughters, though his excellent *Sleeping With The Enemy* set did not have a UK release. He was accused of assaulting Chris Joyce, an executive for the company which originally distributed Scarface Records, in 1994.
● ALBUMS: *The Devil Made Me Do It* (Scarface/Tommy Boy 1990)★★★, *Sleeping With The Enemy* (Scarface/Tommy Boy 1992)★★★★, *Guerilla Funk* (Priority 1994)★★★.

PARK, GRAEME

b. c.1963. Classically trained saxophonist and clarinetist turned DJ, famed for his sets at such venues as Manchester's Haçienda and London's Ministry Of Sound. He began his career in the music industry by working behind the counter (buying in second-hand stock) at Nottingham's

Selectadisc Records. His boss, Brian Selby, purchased a reggae club entitled Ad-Lib, but on opening night did not have a DJ and hence asked his first lieutenant Park to take the job. Park carried on DJing there for several years, but as his listening tastes broadened (especially with the advent of hip-hop and electro) he eventually began to incorporate more adventurous music into his sets. He went on to play at Sheffield's Leadmill, Nottingham's Kool Kat and the Haçienda, alongside Mike Pickering (M People). His style could be categorized as deep house and garage, although, as he prefers to state, 'If you look at my playlists over the past eight years, you'll find a common thread - songs'. His most famous remix was probably for New Order and the England World Cup Squad's 'World In Motion'. Other remix credits include D-Influence's 'Good Lover' and work with Temper Temper and Eddie 'Flashin'' Fowlkes. He was voted *Mixmag* DJ of the year in 1992, but he remains a good-humoured and approachable representative of his craft: 'It's nice to be important, but it's more important to be nice'.

PARKER, TERRENCE

USA-born Parker burst into the UK public's imagination when 'The Question', by his *nom de plume* Seven Grand Housing Authority, was played by Tony Humphries at Cream in Liverpool. The track was taken from the *Soul Beats* EP, built over a sample of Kenny Gonzales' 'Axis Project'. Among those who were astonished by the track were James Barton of Olympic Records (who subsequently joined DeConstruction), and he and others walked over to inspect the record's label. The track was soon licensed from Detroit's Simply Soul label to Olympic, arriving with a K-Klass remix. Parker had been making house music since 1988, at which point he joined Mark Kinchen to become Separate Minds for the techno soul track, 'We Need Somebody'. He also remixed and produced in Detroit under the aliases Express, Trancefusion, Transsonic and Simply Soul. His earlier releases included 'Call My Name', recorded for Detroit label 430 West. He was additionally responsible for running Intangible Records - at all stages defying the musical bent of his geographical home by remaining faithful to his love of Chicago house rather than techno. In confirmation of this, 1994 saw the release of the *Disco Disciple* EP.

PARTY POSSE

Afflicted with poverty at their inception, this band of Harlem, New York-rappers originally practiced in the most un-party-like space of their local graveyard. The trio of DJ Alphonse Constant and rappers Randall Barber and Tedd Lewis were undettered. In actual fact that piece of hallowed ground has achieved something approaching notoriety since, being used for a Doug E. Fresh video. They formed in Harlem in the late 80s, passing by unobserved until Kool Moe Dee visited their school. Inspired by him, they eventually won themselves a contract through his manager, who organised an audition for Moe Dee's home label, Jive. Moe Dee would also make an appearance on their debut album ('Just Look At Us'), which was characterised by old school positivity ('Strivin'') and locker room humour ('Steppin' In Doo Doo')
● ALBUMS: *It's Party Time* (Jive 1989)★★★.

PEACE, LOVE AND PITBULLS

Comprising Joakim Thaström (music, lyrics, vocals), Niklas 'Hell' Hellberg (programming), Peter Puders (guitar) and Rikard Sporrong (guitar), the imaginatively named Swedish group Peace, Love And Pitbulls operate in musical territory somewhere between heavy metal and hardcore techno - Nine Inch Nails are an obvious influence. They formed around the central figure of Thaström. Previously a member of Ebba Grön - widely celebrated as Sweden's closest approximation of the Sex Pistols - in the 80s he concentrated on a solo career with mixed results. A two-year period of recuperation in Amsterdam preceded his return to Sweden to form Peace, Love And Pitbulls in 1992. The results were accurately portrayed to the press as 'a kind of vitriol reality'. Notably, the group's debut album was the first time Thaström had written lyrics in English. 'I needed to change languages because I wanted to be able to shout "Yeh, Baby!" in a song without sounding ridiculous', he told the press. Songs such as 'Do The Monkey', 'Hitch-Hike To Mars' and 'Reverberation Nation' confirmed that he lost none of his powers of outrage in translation.
● ALBUMS: *Peace, Love And Pitbulls* (MNW 1993)★★★.

PENISTON, CE CE

b. Cecelia Peniston, 6 September 1969, Phoenix, Arizona, USA. Peniston started acting at school when in her early teens. She went on to appear in numerous talent contests and also won the beauty pageants Miss Black Arizona and Miss Galaxy. She worked as a backing singer and while still at school wrote 'Finally', which would become her first solo single. Fresh out of college, and with only the faintest hopes of a music career, she nevertheless sprang into the Top 10 lists of both the UK and USA on the back of a speculative demo. The music that backed 'Finally' bore more than a passing resemblance to the Ce Ce Rogers underground hit, 'Someday'. A singer and dancer slightly reminiscent of late 70s soul, most of her compositions are piano-based with strong similarities to Aretha Franklin and Whitney Houston. While her modelling career has been put on the backburner, her attitude to singing remains refreshingly uncomplicated: 'What I know best is singing my lil' old heart out'. 'We Got A Love Thang' became a second hit early in 1992, as did the re-released 'Finally', before the release of her debut album, which was somewhat disjointed. She has also sung backing vocals on Kym Sims' 'Too Blind To See'. Her second album included contributions from house gurus David Morales and Steve 'Silk' Hurley, but was generally more urban R&B-focused. This trend continued with *Movin' On*.

● ALBUMS: *Finally* (A&M 1992)★★, *Thought Ya Knew* (A&M 1994)★★★, *Movin' On* (A&M 1996)★★★.
● COMPILATIONS: *Best Of . . .* (A&M 1998)★★★.

PERFECTO RECORDS

Having released a few one-off tracks, including Izit's 'Stories' (via London Records), the well-known DJ Paul Oakenfold set up the eclectic Perfecto Records in 1989. He began with tracks by Gary Clail, Carl Cox, Robert Owens and Jimmy Polo, but as Oakenfold was involved with various other projects in the early 90s, the label was put on hold for a few years. Perfecto Allstarz's 'Reach Up' relaunched the company in 1994, followed by tracks from BT ('Embracing The Sunshine' and 'Loving You More'), Grace ('Not Over Yet' and 'Skin On Skin') and others. As well as these mainstream acts, Oakenfold has promoted artists such as Man With No Name, Johann and Virus on the offshoot Perfecto Fluoro, which aimed to capitalize on the popularity of the 'Goa' trance sound. Perfecto subsequently released albums by BT and Grace as well as a number of compilations,

notably *Perfection* and Oakenfold's trance collection *Fluoro*. Perfecto Red was set up in 1997 and has since released material by Little Louie [Vega] And Marc Anthony, Mystica and Family Stand, among others.

PETTIBONE, SHEP

Famed for his remix and production work in the late 80s and early 90s for Bros, Madonna and other such pop acts, Pettibone's early origins lie in hip-hop. Together with Arthur Baker, he was behind the Jazzy 5's groundbreaking 'Jazzy Sensation'. At the same time as hip-hop DJs were developing new techniques, Pettibone pioneered the 'mastermixes' of Kiss FM Radio by segueing records together to build 'sequences', almost like movements in classical music. Later he moved into an area loosely described as disco, reviving the sounds of Loleatta Holloway to great success, ensuring his status as an in-demand mixer for large-budget studio sessions.

PHARCYDE

Spaced-out rappers who first hit big with 'Ya Mama', a series of ridiculous and escalating insults (also referred to as 'Snaps' or 'Playing The Dozens') traded between the vocalists, on the Delicious Vinyl label. It was typical fare from this free-flowing West Coast crew, though somewhat derivative of A Tribe Called Quest and Dream Warriors. However, their observations remained genuinely funny, housed in swinging, almost harmonised rap couplets, jazz breaks and quirky narratives: 'We're all jigaboos - might as well take the money' was a half-stinging, half self-mocking assertion. The single, 'Passing Me By', even contained a definition of old school stylings. They contributed one of the most effective cuts on the Brand New Heavies' *Heavy Rhyme Experience* collection, and returned the favour by remixing the latter's 'Soul Flower'. Based in Los Angeles, their goofy, fast talking style defied the early 90s rash of gangsta vinyl from that area with a dogma-deflating blend of cool, loopy rhythms and cultural lyrics. The group comprise Romye, Tre, Imani, Fat Lip, DJ Mark Luv and J-Swift.
● ALBUMS: *Bizarre Ride II The Pharcyde* (Delicious Vinyl 1992)★★★, *Labcabincalifornia* (Go-Beat 1996)★★★.

PHOTEK

b. Rupert Parkes, 1972, St. Albans, Hertfordshire, England. Parkes became interested in hip-hop while at school and later developed a taste for jazz and funk and learnt to play the saxophone. In 1989 he was turned on to dance music, in particular, the Detroit techno sound of such artists as Derrick May, after a visit to the hardcore night 'Telepathy' in north-east London. After moving to Ipswich in the early 90s, Parkes began working at a record shop owned by Rob Solomon, with whom he also began to record original material. An early result was the 1992 jazz-inflected hardcore track 'Sensation', recorded as Origination, which was picked up by Ray Keith, a friend of Solomon's who was involved with Soho's Black Market Records and was influential in the rave scene at the time. The following year Parkes and Solomon released 'Make You Do Right'/'Out Of This World' under the same name, and as Studio Pressure recorded 'Jump Mk2' for Certificate 18 Records. In 1994 Parkes launched Photek Records and with it a series of singles, 'Photek 1-6', which began towards the end of that year. By this point he was established as an important name in the underground drum 'n' bass scene and was receiving the support of such DJs as Kemistry, Peshay, Storm and LTJ Bukem, who had been a regular visitor to Solomon's shop. As a result Parkes recorded a number of tracks for Bukem's labels as Aquarius over the next few years, including 'Drift To The Centre'/'Waveforms' (Looking Good 1995) and 'Dolphin Tune'/'Aquatic' (Good Looking 1996). With his growing popularity he attracted attention from a wider audience and was invited to remix artists such as Attica Blues, Therapy?, Dr. Octagon and later Björk; at the same time the major labels became interested and in 1995 Photek signed to Virgin subsidiary Science Records. His first release was the *Hidden Camera* EP (1996), followed by 'Ni-Ten-Ichi-Ryn' (1997) and the album *Modus Operandi*. In 1998 a new track, 'Yendi', accompanied the release of the album's title track as a single. As he was emerging, Parkes' subtle style led the media inadequately to proclaim him as the leader of a new 'intelligent' drum 'n' bass sound, after the raw energy of early jungle. By the time of his work on Science he had distilled his approach into a unique, personalized style quite unlike anything else around. Despite its variety and diverse influences *Modus Operandi* is coherent throughout, as, with his thrifty instru-mentation, the attention is mostly focused on Parkes' incredibly detailed drum programming. Many tracks such as 'The Hidden Camera' and 'KJZ' have a jazz feel, employing cyclic double bass and impressionistic chordal effects, as Parkes' taut drum sounds fidget underneath. At the same time, others such as 'Aleph 1' and 'Minator' illustrate the techno influence in their choice of sounds, while 'Smoke Rings' and 'The Fifth Column' are virtually all drums accompanied by abstract associative sounds. With his economical, static approach and a high level of abstraction, Parkes has summed up the direction of the most creative dance music of the 90s in the most eloquent form.
● ALBUMS: *Modus Operandi* (Science 1997)★★★★.

PIGEON PIE RECORDS

London record label headed by Joe Borgia which in its first few years of operation has earned itself a healthy reputation with its first dozen or so releases. The catalogue began with two La Comoora records, 'Oki-Dokey' and 'Te Quiero'/'What Is Love'. Subsequent releases included Rhythm Eclipse ('Feel It In The Air'/'Thru The Night'), Marco Polo ('Zuazuzua'), Cecer ('Skyline', 'I Need Your Love'), Delphine ('Baby Don't You Go'), Mind The Gap ('Mind The Gap'), FOD ('All It Takes'), Jupiter ('Destiny') and Love To Infinity ('Somethin' Outta Nothin''). The latter, a garage cut from brothers Andrew and Peter Lee, was typically well received by the dance music press.

PLANET 4

Stockport, Lancashire record label who moved to their own offices and studio in Manchester in 1993. Their roster of releases includes Coventry DJs Parkes and Wilson (ex-Limbo recording artists) with 'American Slide', under the name the Ritmo Rivals. Others include Ultracynic (formerly famous for 1992's 'Nothing Lasts Forever'), who recruited a new singer to record 'Got To Have It', plus one-time Evolution vocalist Yvonne Shelton ('I Chose') and Paramist ('Release Me'). The Ritmo Rivals followed up in 1994 with 'Believe In Me'. The label is distributed through Network.

PLANET DOG RECORDS

This subsidiary of Ultimate Records was formed in London in 1993 by Michael and Bob Dog. The original idea was to release material by some of the bands that had been performing at their renowned Megadog parties in the early 90s, following the successful sales of cassette compilations of such groups. Rather than the familiar collections of insubstantial club anthems, these tapes had contained more listenable electronic music, an approach that was adopted at Planet Dog. Their first releases came from Banco De Gaia and Eat Static in 1993, since which time they have brought out albums and singles by these and other artists, including Children Of The Bong, Future Loop Foundation and Timeshard. At the same time they have put together a number of compilations, including the *Feed Your Head* series. Believing that most established artists save their best work for their own releases, these have generally featured material from unsigned acts in an effort to ensure quality. In this way, and with their choice of unique groups, Planet Dog have successfully managed to steer clear of many of the transient fashions of the dance music scene and established their own identity, methods and sounds that mirror the eclectic and broad-minded feel of their associated parties.

PLUS 8

Plus 8, the record label based in Windsor, Ontario, run by Richie Hawtin and John Acquaviva (b. *c.*1963, London, Canada), has become one of the most influential outlets for new techno and acid. The idea began when Hawtin attended club nights in Detroit at the Shelter and the Music Institute, witnessing the DJing of Derrick May, Juan Atkins and Kevin Saunderson. In this club scene, he met partner Acquaviva and fellow Canadian Dan Bell. The latter helped them to translate their ambitions of making music from theory into practice. Plus 8 was set up in May 1990, taking their name from the familiar Detroit practice of spinning records pitched up to 'plus 8' percent. Their breakthrough release was Cybersonic's 'Technarchy', which featured Bell alongside Hawtin and Acquaviva, quickly followed by Kenny Larkin's excellent *Metropolis* EP, which created a recognizable Plus 8 sound: hard, analog, and distorted. One of the first European countries to embrace Plus 8's harder sound was the Netherlands, and a significant signing for the label was Dutchman Speedy J. In 1991 they launched the sister label Probe, which introduced itself with F.U.S.E.'s *F.U.* Probe, now no longer releasing records, was the more steadfast hard techno label, allowing Plus 8 to develop more sur-

real, ambient forms of dance music. Plus 8 also hooked up with Novamute, the dance offspring of Mute Records, to license Probe releases and Plastikman (another Hawtin pseudonym) material in the UK, with Hawtin and Acquaviva continuing to oversee quality control, from inception to finished artwork. Design was apparently a priority, the Concept series of releases in 1996 being a case in point - a collection of 12 records/24 tracks of minimal funk, produced by Hawtin, released over 12 months, and forming a beautifully packaged box set. Other merchandise has included a comic book, Plus 8 condoms, mugs, T-shirts, mouse-mats and artwork by Hawtin's brother, Matthew. Meanwhile, Plus 8 continues to release high-quality electronic music.

● ALBUMS: Various: *From Our Minds To Yours* (Plus 8 1991)★★★.

PM DAWN

One of the few rap acts able to sing in a more conventional fashion, PM Dawn comprised brothers Prince Be (Attrell Cordes) and DJ Minute Mix (Jarrett Cordes). Hailing from New Jersey (their step-father was a member of Kool And The Gang), the brothers' backgrounds were shrouded in tragedy. Their real father died of pneumonia when they were children, and their brother Duncan drowned when he was two years old. They came from a highly musical family - 10 of their aunts and uncles were rappers and DJs in the genre's early days in the 70s, when Prince Be started rapping as a youngster at family parties. They were equally influenced by 60s pop and duly incorporated harmonies in their work - hence the later tag, Daisy Age Soul. They cut demos in 1989, including their first song, 'Check The Logic', at a Long Island studio. After signing to the Gee St label, they took the name PM Dawn, indicating 'the transition from dark to light'. A debut single, 'Ode To A Forgetful Mind', was released in January 1991. Its follow-up, 'A Watcher's Point Of View', broke the UK charts, introducing their melodic hip-hop to a larger audience. The debut album saw them turned away by representatives of the Beatles in their attempts to sample 'Let It Be'. However they were more successful in negotiations with Spandau Ballet, who allowed them to build the song 'Set Adrift On Memory Bliss' out of 'True'. PM Dawn went as far as to promote the release with an old 'new romantic' picture of Hadley and co, confirming their mischievous humour. It hit number 3 in the

UK charts. When the album emerged in September 1991, it saw them grow out of the De La Soul comparisons that had previously plagued them, as one of the most concise, creative forces in rap/dance. All seemed to be running smoothly for PM Dawn in 1991, until an unfortunate experience at the end of the year. While Prince Be took part in the live filming of a gig at New York's The Sound Factory, Boogie Down Productions main man KRS-1 became angered at what he considered disrespectful remarks made by Prince Be during a *Details* magazine interview, and forcefully evicted him from the stage, smashing a record on Minute Mix's turntable in the process. In 1992 the duo achieved two minor UK hits, 'Reality Used To Be A Friend Of Mine' and 'I'd Die Without You', which featured on the soundtrack to Eddie Murphy's *Boomerang* film. With Prince Be also appearing in a Nike trainers' commercial, the latter 45 climbed to US number 3. Following the release of 'Looking Through Patient Eyes', which heavily sampled George Michael's 'Father Figure', PM Dawn released a long-awaited second album in April 1993. While writing tracks for *The Bliss* album, Prince Be had Boy George in mind, and the former Culture Club singer duetted on 'More Than Likely', which also became a single. 'Fly Me To The Moon', meanwhile, sampled U2's 'The Fly'. However, critics still considered it to be a lesser album than their stunning debut. Minute Mix, meanwhile, had changed his name to J.C. The Eternal, and Prince Be had become The Nocturnal. PM Dawn also contributed to the AIDS benefit *Red Hot And Dance*, as well as remixing for Simply Red, and several benefit shows (Earth Day, LIFEbeat's CounterAid, etc). *Jesus Wept* was a disappointing collection that favoured bland R&B stylings over the hip-hop samples.

● ALBUMS: *Of The Heart, Of The Soul, Of The Cross, The Utopian Experience* (Gee Street 1991)★★★★, *The Bliss Album ...? (Vibrations Of Love & Anger & The Ponderance Of Life & Existence)* (Gee Street/Island 1993)★★★, *Jesus Wept* (Gee Street/Island 1995)★★.

POLO, JIMMY

b. *c.*1966, Alabama, but raised in Chicago, Illinois. Polo sang in gospel choirs as a boy, before becoming a musician in his teens around the local circuit. His first recorded outing was 'Libra Libra' in 1985 on Chicago Collection. His breakthrough hit, 'Shake Your Body', also emerged on that label, but the artist later complained bitterly that no royalties were forthcoming. Consequently Polo moved to the UK to join Champion, but this led to the break-up of Polo's original Libra Libra group. 1989 brought another genre classic in 'Free Yourself'/'Better Days', released on Urban Records in the UK, and played keyboards for Soul II Soul. He also immersed himself in the UK's nascent acid/rave scene, alongside flatmate Adamski, who dedicated his 1990 hit album to Polo (they also recorded together on the 1992 single, 'Never Goin' Down'). The same year he signed to Perfecto for the soul-influenced 'Express Yourself' single, and released his first album.

● ALBUMS: *Moods* (Perfecto 1992)★★★.

POLYGON WINDOW

(see Aphex Twin)

POOR RIGHTEOUS TEACHERS

Trenton, New Jersey-based trio comprising the gregariously named Wise Intelligent, Culture Freedom and Father Shaheed, all advocates of the Five Percent Islam creed. Their debut album included the hot 'Rock Dis Funky Joint' 45, and sold over 400,000 copies, crossing over into the pop market. Their second album included the groundbreaking pro-women single cut, 'Shakiyla (JHR)', but failed to match the sales of its predecessor. *Black Business* was a celebration of the progress made by their black brothers and sisters in commerce and business, and was produced by Shaheed with the aid of Tony D. It included the single 'Nobody Move', which was inspired by albino reggae toaster, Yellowman. Indeed, PRT's most distinctive attribute is Wise Intelligent's highly effective blending of the reggae DJ's intonation with his partners' hip-hop skills.

● ALBUMS: *Holy Intellect* (Profile 1990)★★★★, *Pure Poverty* (Profile 1991)★★★, *Black Business* (Profile 1993)★★★★, *The New World Order* (Profile 1996)★★★.

POP ART

Hip-hop record label, based in Philadelphia, USA, controlled by Lawrence Goodman, the cousin of Steady B. The latter issued an impressive answer record to LL Cool J's big hit, 'I Can't Live Without My Radio', which established the imprint. Its other high profile releases included another artist well versed in the tradition of answer records, Roxanne Shanté. Goodman is now the manager of Da Youngsta's.

PORCUPINE TREE

Colin Balch (b. 2 July 1970, Melbourne, Australia; bass), Richard Barbieri (b. 30 November 1957, London, England; keyboards, ex-Japan), Steve Wilson (b. 3 November 1967, Kingston-Upon-Thames, England; guitar, vocals, programming) and Chris Maitland (b. 13 May 1964, Cambridge, England; drums) have been widely ascribed with bringing progressive rock back into vogue in the 90s. Wilson is the guiding light behind Porcupine Tree, which allows him to indulge his interests in ambient dance music and left-field, psychedelic rock. He began recording solo in 1992 with the release of *On The Sunday Of Life*, before eventually recruiting a full complement of band members to help live performances from the summer of 1995 onwards. Critics reviewing the group's material, particularly the *Moonloop* EP in 1994 and *The Sky Moves Sideways* album the following year, immediately pigeonholed the group as a contemporary Pink Floyd. Wilson was somewhat perturbed by this: 'We've always had the Pink Floyd comparison and, yes, there's a certain spaciousness, a grandeur to what they do that has set some precedent. But there are modern influences, for instance sampling or the use of trance rhythms, that I don't hear in their music.' *Signify* did indeed have some Gilmour shades, but ultimately they sound like themselves, and on that album they demonstrate that they have originality, great harmonies and intergalactic travel potential. Tracks such as 'Waiting Phase One' and 'Waiting Phase Two' hypnotically rumble and build into a glorious peak.

● ALBUMS: *On The Sunday Of Life* (Delerium 1992)★★★, *Up The Downstair* (Delerium 1993)★★★, *Yellow Hedgerow Dreamscape* limited edition (Magic Gnome 1994)★★★, *The Sky Moves Sideways* (Delerium 1995)★★★, *Staircase Infinities* mini-album (Blueprint 1995)★★★, *Signify* (Delerium 1996)★★★★.

PORKY'S PRODUCTIONS

'Hull's only record label' - which sprang to prominence when they unveiled Opik (Murray, Dean Dawson, Rob Everall and Chris Devril) and their 'Feel Yourself' monster, which DeConstruction went on to licence. By the time Opik became successful in the early 90s the Yorkshire, England-based label had already established itself with cuts such as Fila Brazilia's 'Mermaids' and Heights Of Abraham's *Tides* EP. Heights Of Abraham comprised ex-Chakk members Jake Harries and Sim Lister, the latter co-writer of Cath Carroll's England Made Me album), plus Ashley & Jackson guitarist Steve Cobby.

PORTISHEAD

Portishead were named after the sleepy port on the south-west coast of England where Geoff Barrow (b. c.1971) spent his teens. His intentions in forming the band were simple: 'I just wanted to make interesting music, proper songs with a proper life span and a decent place in people's record collections.' Barrow started out as a tape operator, working in a minor capacity with Massive Attack and Neneh Cherry, and also wrote songs for Cherry ('Somedays' was included on *Home Brew*). With the aid of an Enterprise Allowance grant he recruited jazz guitarist and musical director Adrian Utley (b. c.1957), drummer/programmer Dave and vocalist Beth Gibbons (b. c.1965), whom he encountered on a job creation scheme while she was singing Janis Joplin cover versions in a pub. Together they recorded a soundtrack and film, *To Kill A Dead Man*, with themselves as actors because 'we couldn't find anyone else to do the parts'. At this point they came to the attention of A&R man Ferdy Unger-Hamilton at the Go! Discs subsidiary Go! Beat, who encouraged Barrow to remix Gabrielle's 'Dreams'. He was sufficiently impressed with the results to sign the band immediately, despite several other interested parties. The singles 'Numb' and 'Sour Times' emerged to good press reaction, although the debut album slipped in and out of the charts with little fanfare. There was some problem with marketing the band - both Barrow and Gibbons were reluctant to do interviews, and had no initial interest in playing live. Instead the press campaign saw painted mannequin dummies distributed in strategic locations throughout London, ensuring press coverage outside of the expected media. Word of mouth continued to push the band's profile and, with virtually no radio support, the group's third single, 'Glory Box', entered the UK charts at number 13 in January 1995. Aided by a distinctive, gender-swapping video (visuals are central to the band's approach), its arrival came on the back of several 'album of the year' awards for *Dummy* from magazines as diverse as *Mixmag*, *ID*, *The Face* and *Melody Maker*. Mixing torch songs with blues, jazz and hip-hop, their sound became known as 'trip hop'. The interest also translated to America, where the album sold over 150,000 copies without the band even setting foot there. They were then awarded the Mercury Music Prize for best album of 1995. Following their success, the band were invited to contribute to several soundtracks, including two low-budget art films and *Tank Girl*. The long-awaited follow-up to *Dummy* was severely delayed when Barrow, a self-confessed perfectionist, reached a creative impasse that almost destroyed the band. His perseverance paid off, however, when *Portishead* was released in September 1997 to excellent critical reviews. Although first single 'All Mine' had suggested some variation to the Portishead sound, the album covered essentially the same ground as their debut, albeit in an impressively stylish manner.

● ALBUMS: *Dummy* (Go! Beat 1994)★★★★, *Portishead* (Go! Beat 1997)★★★.

POSITIVA RECORDS

Nick Hawkes set up Positiva in January 1993 as the dance subsidiary of EMI. He had previously worked for XL Records with such acts as the Prodigy, SL2 and House Of Pain. He was joined by the journalist and DJ Dave Lambert, who helped with club-orientated A&R. Their first release was Exoterix's 'Void', but it was the Disco Evangelists' 'De Niro' that brought the label its first real success. It was followed in the summer of 1993 by a number of club hits, notably Wall Of Sound's 'Critical', Hyper Go-Go's 'Never Let Go' and D-Tek's 'Drop The Rock'. In July the label released its first album, *The Positiva Ambient Collection*, which featured tracks by some of the best-known artists in this area, including Aphex Twin, Black Dog Productions, Irresistible Force, Moby, the Orb and Orbital. Later that year, Judy Cheeks, in collaboration with Frankie Foncett, gave Positiva its first Top 30 hit with 'So In Love'. Mainstream success continued during 1994 with new artists Barbara Tucker ('Beautiful People' and 'I Get Lifted') and Reel 2 Real ('I Like To Move It', 'Go On Move' and 'Raise Your Hands'), as well as Hyper Go-Go ('Raise' and 'Its Alright') and Judy Cheeks ('Reach'). At the same time, releases such Pan Position's 'Elephant Paw' and the Disco Evangelist's 'A New Dawn' maintained a connection to the club scene. Some of the label's mainstream and more underground hits were collected on the album *Phase 2*, which was released towards the end of 1994. Over the next few years Positiva continued to achieve similar success with estab-

lished artists, as well as new faces including Amos ('Let Love Shine'), BBE ('Seven Days And One Week'), Jeremy Healy ('Stamp' recorded with Amos), Ruffneck ('Everybody Be Somebody'), 2 In A Room ('Ahora Es'), Umboza ('Cry India' and 'Sunshine') and X-Static ('I'm Standing'). In 1996 Kevin Robinson joined the A&R team and Positiva launched Additive Records to foster more experimental projects. In the same year they released Mixmaster Morris's mix album *The Morning After* and the charity compilation *Earthtrance* (which was compiled by Andy Guthrie and 21-3 Productions' Jaki Kenley). *Earthdance* included material by Eat Static, Hallucinogen, Koxbox, Man With No Name, Medicine Drum, Sven Vath and System 7, among others, and raised over £40,000 for the Earth Love Fund. Around this time the label started a monthly residency at the Ministry Of Sound. In 1997 Adam F became Positiva's most successful artist, notably with the single 'Circles' and the album *Colours*, while Amos and Healy, Brainbug, PF Project, Qattara, DJ Quicksilver and others enjoyed Top 40 hits. Positiva have also released a number of compilations on behalf of Mark Allen's psy-trance club Return To The Source, notably *Sacred Sites* in 1997.

● ALBUMS: Various: *The Positiva Ambient Collection* (Positiva 1993)★★★★, *Phase One* (Positiva 1994)★★★.

POSITIVE BLACK SOUL

Doug-e-tee (b. Amadou Berri, 29 May 1971, Dakar, Senegal; vocals/rapper) and DJ (b. 11 August 1969, Dakar, Senegal; rapper). This Senegalese hip-hop duo began working together in 1988, having previously been fierce rivals within Dakar's tiny but vibrant rap scene. Having honed their style performing at numerous parties and nightclubs, the duo supported MC Solaar when he played in Senegal in 1992; Solaar was highly impressed and brought them to France to support him there in the same year. Also in 1992, they contributed a track to a compilation of modern Senegalese music given away with a French art magazine. This track, 'Bagn Bagn Beug', was subsequently given a limited release on cassette for the Senegalese market. In 1993 the duo recorded *Boule Fale*, their debut cassette album. Released the following year only in Senegal, it went on to sell 10,000 copies. While performing at a nightclub, they met Baaba Maal and subsequently contributed a rap to 'Swing Yela', a track on Maal's internationally acclaimed album *Firin' In Fouta*.

They were discovered by Mango Records at the recording session and recorded *Salaam*, their debut for the label, in Paris and London using a mix of programmed beats and live musicians (including members of the bands of Maal and Youssou N'Dour). The album presented the duo's positive and political lyrics over a varied musical backdrop of hip-hop, reggae, funk, jazz and traditional West African sounds.

● ALBUMS: *Salaam* (Mango 1995)★★★.

POSITIVE-K

From Queens, New York, Positive-K (b. *c.*1967, Bronx, New York, USA) is yet another of rap's mouthpieces to augment his B-boy/breakbeat hip-hop with messages from the Nation Of Islam. After being inspired by his view of a Grandmaster Flash show in Echo Park from his grandmother's window, he immersed himself in hip-hop culture as a child. He was 18 years old when he made his first appearance on vinyl with the *Fast Money* compilation, subsequently hooking up with First Priority. A second various artists' credit came with the label's 1988 compilation *Basement Flavor*. His releases for the label would include 'Quarter Gram Pam', 'Step Up Front' and 'I'm Not Havin' It', at the same time as he duetted with Grand Puba on Brand Nubian's debut set. He moved over to his own Creative Control Records for the release of 'Night Shift', which was subsequently picked up by Island/4th & Broadway. It was produced by Big Daddy Kane, who also guest rapped. Positive had met him some years previously when enjoying a bus ride rap battle between New York and Philadelphia. More successful still, however, was 'I Got A Man', which established him both in his native country and the US. Somewhat less cerebral than previous efforts, it was still great fun, with lines boasting that 'I'm a big daddy longstroke, your man's Pee Wee Herman'. In the afterglow of its success his Creative Control empire flourished, signing artists like Raggedyman.

● ALBUMS: *Da Skills Dat Pay Da Bills* (Island 1992)★★★.

POV

New Jersey four-piece comprising Marc Sherman (b. *c.*1974, aka The Rapper Extraordinaire), Ewarner 'E' Mills (b. *c.*1974), Hakim 'HB' Bell (b. *c.*1975) and Lincoln 'Link' DeVulgt (b. Virgin Islands) whose sound encompasses reggae and R&B, with the uniting structure of hip-hop rhythms. Their initials stand for Point Of View. Within their line-up stands not only a conventional rapper, but also one (Link) who takes a reggae/dancehall DJ approach. They made their debut with 'Anutha Luv', under the tutelage of Hakim Abdulsamad (the Boys etc.). But it was Michael Bennet who decided to take the group to Jamaica, recording the sweet 'Summer Nights' single at his Kingston studio. They boast of distinguished parentage too; bandleader Hakim 'HB' Bell is the son of Robert 'Kool' Bell, of Kool And The Gang fame, who served as co-executive producer on their debut album. This comprised two quite distinct sides. The first, the 'Beat U Up' side, was formulated by uptempo dance and swing material, while the second, 'Beat U Down', offered Link's dancehall chants and Sherman's hip-hop verses set to the impressive soulful harmonising of the whole group. It included their duet with Jade, 'All Thru The Nite'. Their backgrounds (Sherman's father is an import/export director) have disabused them of any naivety about the music business, and each member owns their own separate publishing company. Hakim is also responsible for HB Productions, which handled (in tandem with Robert Bell) backroom duties on the band's debut album.

● ALBUMS: *Handing' Out Beatdowns* (Giant/RCA 1993)★★★.

POWER, BOB

b. USA. Bob Power is a self-effacing yet prolific producer who has worked with the best east-coast R&B/hip-hop acts from the 80s onwards. Self-described as a 'soul music producer/engineer', Power began his musical career while at Webster College in St. Louis. Inspired by the great blues guitarists of the era (Buddy Guy, Otis Rush and Albert King), he switched courses to study music theory. He also studied composition and conducting, playing his own contemporary classical music as well as appearing on the St. Louis 'chitlin' circuit as the lone white boy in black bands covering Marvin Gaye and Temptations songs. He subsequently attained a master's degree in jazz from Lone Mountain College in San Francisco. He stayed in California between 1975 and 1982, working on the television series *Over Easy*. He also began writing jingles, and eventually scored adverts for clients including Coca-Cola and Mercedes Benz. Power then moved to New York to work in the Calliope Studios on 37th Street. Asked to sit in as engineer on a hip-hop session, he found himself overseeing the break-through sessions for Stetsasonic. He continued his liaison with rap groups thereafter, linking with A Tribe Called Quest, the Jungle Brothers, De La Soul and Black Sheep. By the mid-90s he was given charge of a production suite at Sony Music Studios in New York. His profile as a producer continued to grow through work with Me'Shell N'degéocello, D'Angelo and Erykah Badu. The latter gave Power his first number 1 R&B single, 'On & On', while N'degéocello's *Peace Beyond Passion* received a Grammy nomination for best engineered album.

PRAGA KHAN

Comprising Jade 4U (b. Nikki Danlierop, Belgium) and Maurice Engelen (b. *c*.1974, Belgium), the latter an 80s DJ and 'New Beat' pio-neer, by 1993 Praga Khan had sold over half a mil-lion records together under various guises, such as Lords Of Acid, Channel X, Digital Orgasm and Jade 4U solo. Danlierop was certainly a vivacious character; she had apparently been 'sacked' from the band at one stage for 'biting' her partner on stage, due to overexcitement. As Praga Khan they had enjoyed a 1991 rave hit with 'Injected With A Poison', which cased a furore when it entered the Top 20 due to perceived drug connotations. It went to number 1 in Japan. In the USA they were signed to Rick Rubin's Def Jam on a five-album contract, where Rubin hoped to market them as his 'next big thing'. On the commercial break-through of their music they commented: 'We have to see techno/rave for what it is, as the rock 'n' roll of the 90s'.
● ALBUMS: as Digital Orgasm *Come Dancin'* (Dead Dead Good 1992)★★★, *Spoon Full Of Miracle* (Profile 1993)★★★.

PRANA

This psychedelic trance group was formed in London in 1993 by Tsuyoshi Suzuki and Nick Taylor (Snake Thing), who had met in Tokyo in the early 90s and recorded there as Blissed. In 1994 they released material on the Inter 1 Records (*Genesis* and *Indigo* EP) and Dragonfly Records compilation, *Order Odonata Vol. 1*, before signing with Suzuki's new label, Matsuri Productions. The following year Prana produced a number of EPs for that label, including *Scarab* and *Future Space Travellers* (a collaboration between Suzuki and the Swedish group Athena), as well as appearing on various compilations. Their debut

album *Cyclone* arrived early in 1996, by which time Taylor had moved to Australia and Suzuki had begun working with Andy Guthrie. During the next year they wrote and recorded a number of tunes which, together with five remixes of tracks from *Cyclone* by Snake Thing (Taylor), Tristan And Process, the Green Nuns Of The Revolution, Chakra and Total Eclipse, formed Prana's second album, *Geomantik*. Owing to other commitments, the pair did not release any new material until 'Kollage' on the Matsuri compila-tion *Forever Psychedelic* in 1998. One of the most imaginative psychedelic trance groups around, Prana create exciting, spacious textures from unimaginable rips, squeaks and creaks, blended with subtle riffs over a varied foundation of solid, funky grooves; notable examples are 'Boundless' (1997) and the remix of 'Alien Pets' on Matsuri's *Let It Rip* compilation (1997).
● ALBUMS: *Cyclone* (1996)★★★, *Geomantik* (1997)★★★★.

PRESSURE DROP

Originally Justin Langlands (percussion), Mike Puxley (keyboards) and Gareth Tasker (guitar), Pressure Drop made their debut with 'Feeling Good - Touch 1 2 3' for Big World in March 1990. The group met at the Heavy Duty Club where Langlands was DJing. It was he who obtained the bank loan in order to set up an eight-track studio in his front room. However, afterwards the group would re-emerge as a duo of Langlands and Dave Henley (a hairdresser at London's Kensington Market, and Langland's partner in Blood Brothers, who had remixed Pressure Drop's first record) whose four-track *Sampler EP* in 1991 made waves. This featured live Hammond organ, Joanna Law, Galliano and Mark Cornell and included Indian tabla and African drums. The most notable track was 'You're Mine', an adaptation of 'Transfusion', by the group's alter-ego, the Blood Brothers. However, despite selling over 30,000 copies on a German independent label, their debut album did not receive a UK release, a fate shared by its follow-up. In 1997 they secured a deal with the Higher Ground label (a Sony joint venture). The title of their 1998 release was an accurate reflec-tion of their commercial fortunes to date.
● ALBUMS: *Upset* (IDE/Logic 1990)★★★, *Front Row* (1991)★★★, *Elusive* (Higher Ground/Hard Hands 1998)★★★.

PRESSURE OF SPEECH

Taking their name from a condition of manic depressives, a stage at which victims are unable to express the multitude of ideas and words engulfing their minds, it should come as no surprise that Mickie Mann was once a psychiatric nurse in Aberdeen, Scotland. After a spell in the army he joined Orbital, the Shamen, Meat Beat Manifesto and Ultramarine, among others, as live sound engineer. Pressure Of Speech were formed with lighting expert Luke Losey and DJ Stika, formerly of Fun-Da-Mental and Spiral Tribe. They made their debut with the track 'Surveillance' on Planet Dog's *Feed Your Head* compilation, before stepping out on their own with 'X-Beats' on the North South label. Their debut album was one of the most specific and obvious assaults on the UK's Conservative government within the previously largely apolitical techno/dance movement. They also proved keen to take their music out to a live audience, touring as part of a Megadog-styled collective.
● ALBUMS: *Art Of The State* (North South 1994)★★★.

PRIME MINISTER PETE NICE AND DADDY RICH

After the break-up of US rappers 3rd Bass, of the three former members MC Serch was the first to release a solo album, *Return of The Product*. The remaining two, DJ Daddy Rich and Pete Nice (b. Peter Nash), spent a year cutting their debut set. 3rd Bass were always going to be a tough act to follow, and the fact that Nice was still self-consciously rapping about being white in a black market did not help. However, there was much to like in the sustained intelligence of his rhymes, and Rich's convoluted rhythmic strutures. Nice also set up his own record label, Hoppoh, signing talented Latino newcomer Kurious.
● ALBUMS: *Dust To Dust* (1993)★★★.

PRINCE PAUL

b. Paul E. Huston, 2 April 1967, Amityville, Long Island, New York, USA. Alongside Daddy-O, Prince Paul is the second of Stetsasonic's founding members to enjoy notable extra-curricular activities. Similarly his production credits take pride of place in his list of achievements. Probably his proudest moment came in helming De La Soul's *3 Feet High And Rising*, though other credits included the Fine Young Cannibals. His other notable productions included the anti-crack 'You Still Smoking That Shit?', and 'Don't Let Your Mouth Write A Check That Your Ass Can't Cash'. He set up his own Doo Dew label in the 90s, with signings including Resident Alien. However, by 1994 the contract with the label's sponsors had turned sour and he embarked instead on a collaboration with old-Stetsasonic hand Fruitkwan as part of the rap super group Gravediggaz.

PRINCIPLE, JAMIE

Famed for his breathy, Smokey Robinson-styled delivery, USA-born Principle's classic early house recordings were 'Waiting On My Angel' and 'Baby Wants To Ride'. The latter gave this Chicago house master and innovator a hit after a long time in the shadows (although a more or less identical version appeared at the same time from Frankie Knuckles). Following 'Rebels' there was a long absence from the nation's dancefloors punctuated only by US tracks 'Cold World' (during a brief liaison with Atlantic Records) and 'Date With The Rain' on a Steve 'Silk' Hurley compilation. He re-emerged with a US smash in 1991 with 'You're All I've Waited 4', self-written and co-produced with Hurley again.

PRIORITY RECORDS

A record company that was established in 1985, originally to piece together compilation records, Priority has established itself in the intervening period as one of America's most pre-eminent rap stables. Former Capitol employee Bryan Turner (b. Canada), the label's president, acknowledges the hit-and-miss nature of their business plan: We didn't sit down and decide to have a rap label, it just sort of happened. Rap was exciting - it was music that kids really wanted'. However, the label has never been strictly a one-genre affair. They still package compilations, and alongside their high-profile hip-hop acts, who have included NWA, Ice-T (following his departure from Warners) and Ice Cube, their most recent signings include Carole King. However, they lost their deal with Eazy-E's Ruthless nest when their contract expired in 1993, allowing the latter to move to Relativity Records.
● ALBUMS: NWA: *Straight Outta Compton* (Ruthless/Priority 1988)★★★★. Ice Cube: *Amerikkka's Most Wanted* (Priority 1989)★★★★.

PRO-JECT X

Very much in the vein of the Lifers Group in the USA, Pro-Ject X was started in England in 1994 to allow a musical platform for the inmates of Strangeways prison, Manchester. A soul/hip-hop/reggae collective, the idea was formulated by Headley Aylock, an MA student in pop/jazz and the proprietor of Summit Records, alongside Phil Ellis, who has also worked in prisons in East Anglia. In 1994 he organized the first Pro-Ject X gig alongside the BBC Philharmonic Orchestra. The rest of the group were all prisoners and included Andy Miller and Mark Beckett (both serving six years on separate armed robbery offences), Harvey Black (two years for robbery and blackmail) and the two middle-aged front men - Prince Hammer and Prince Marley. Hammer claimed to have preached as a street poet in the Bronx and Jamaica, while Hammer prided himself on being the father of 27 children. With members drawn from tough Manchester areas such as Withenshawe and Moss Side, the group conveyed their concerns to the outside world with a 1995 single, 'The Summit', recorded with A Guy Called Gerald and Justin Robertson, two highly prominent dance artists with strong personal sympathies for the inmates. The future of the project was limited, however, by the impending release dates for several members.

PRODIGY

This Essex-based band, which consists of Liam Howlett, Keith Flint, Leeroy Thornhill and MC Maxim Reality, is one of the first dance acts to achieve the same level of success and media coverage as rock groups. During the 80s Howlett was a breakdancer and DJ with the hip-hop group Cut To Kill, but, inspired by the sounds of such artists as Meat Beat Manifesto and Joey Beltram, he began to write his own hard, edgy dance music. The Prodigy signed to XL Records in 1990 and in February the following year released their first single, 'What Evil Lurks', which proved popular in the underground rave scene.

Their next record, 'Charly' (which used samples of the famous public information advertisement), was equally popular, but on its commercial release it reached number 3 in the UK charts and brought the group to the attention of a wider audience. Its success spawned a number of similar 'toytown techno' releases from other bands, including tracks based on *Roobarb And Custard*

and *Sesame Street*. The band had already made a name for themselves performing at parties around the country, but differed from many anonymous dance acts by presenting a frenetic live show, with Flint and Thornhill dancing and Maxim on vocals. Their mainstream success continued with a series of hits, including 'Everybody In the Place', 'Fire', 'Out Of Space' and 'Wind It Up', which were included on their debut album, released in 1992. *Experience*, perhaps the most consistent set of hardcore tunes, was a frantic blend of hard fidgeting breakbeats, rumbling basslines, rigid, angular melodic ideas and fragments of vocals, interspersed with the occasional breakdown. Howlett mostly employed harsh, metallic, edgy synth sounds, which were frequently offset by pianos and trivial sounds, serving to relieve the tense industrial feeling. Their next single, 'One Love' (which had been released earlier that year as an anonymous white label entitled 'Earthbound'), hinted at a change of direction in 1993, confirmed a year later by 'No Good (Start the Dance)' and the album *Music For The Jilted Generation*, which entered the charts at number 1.

Two more singles, 'Voodoo People' and 'Poison', continued the band's success. While they retained some elements of the hardcore sound (notably the breakbeats), the group broadened their sound with 'radio-friendly' vocals ('No Good'), heavy rock guitar ('Their Law' and 'Voodoo'), environmental sounds ('Break & Enter' and 'Speedway'), flute ('Poison' and '3 Kilos') and live drums. At the same time they dropped the angular, hardcore-style melodies and created an individual sound more influenced by techno-style repetition and abstraction, but still distinctively Prodigy. The band's reputation as a live act was further enhanced in the summer of 1995 by successful performances at Glastonbury and various other festivals, an area traditionally dominated by rock. Over the next 12 months they continued to tour around Europe, Australia and America. In March 1996 the Prodigy had their first UK number 1 single with 'Firestarter'. Combining clattering breakbeats, dirty sub-bass and whining guitar with Flint's punk-influenced vocals, the single appealed to a wide audience and brought the band to the attention of the rock press. In performances on that year's festival circuit, the band were joined by the guitarist Gizz Butt.

Towards the end of the year, 'Breathe' became the Prodigy's second UK number 1 and confirmed their popularity with a mainstream audience both at home and abroad. In June 1997 *Fat Of The Land* entered the charts at number 1. As with *Music For The Jilted Generation*, the album continued to explore new combinations of sound. By now they had completely abandoned the hardcore touches and, if anything, *Fat Of The Land* moved towards a punk and thrash style, blending techno and breakbeat sounds with guitar, live drums and vocals to create a distinctive, futuristic hybrid of rock and dance.

● ALBUMS: *Experience* (XL 1992)★★★, *Music For The Jilted Generation* (XL 1994)★★★★, *Fat Of The Land* (XL 1997)★★★★.

● VIDEOS: *Electronic Punks* (XL Recordings 1995), *Evolution* (Visual 1997).

● FURTHER READING: *Electronic Punks: The Official Story*, Martin Roach. *Prodigy: Exit The Underground*, Lisa Verrico. *Prodigy: The Fat Of The Land*, no author listed. *Adventures With The Voodoo Crew*, Martin James. *Prodigy - An Illustrated Biography*, Stuart Coles.

PRODUCTION HOUSE

London record label set up in 1987 by Phil Fearon, formerly of Brit-funk act Galaxy, with help from Laurie Jago. Primarily orientated towards hardcore and rave music, the self-distributed imprint rose to prominence in 1992 via the success of Acen ('Trip II The Moon') and Baby D ('Let Me Be Your Fanstasy'), both of which reached the top of the national dance charts and also broke the mainstream listings. Solo artist Acen (b. *c.*1972, Tottenham, London, England) had been unlucky not to do so previously with 'Close Your Eyes', which sold 25,000 copies without ever entering the charts. In the event 'Trip II To The Moon', Production House's 42nd release, would be the one to bring them their first hit. Other notable signings include the House Crew ('Keep The Fire Burning' and 'We Are Hardcore'), Nino ('Future Of Latin', from Terry 'The Chocolate Prince' Jones), Brothers Grimm's ('Field Of Dreams' and 'Exodus' - which sampled Mike Oldfield's 'Tubular Bells') and X Static ('Ready To Go'). A subsidiary outlet, Special Reserve, was also founded to house swingbeat and soul, beginning with MC Juice's 'Freak In Me'.

PROFESSOR GRIFF

Brought up in Long Island New York along with 13 brothers and sisters, Griff (b. Richard Griffin, Long Island, New York, USA) formed The Universal Revolutionary Freedom Fighters Society (TUFFS) in his youth, providing study groups and martial arts training for young people. It was while he was offering a security service that he first met Chuck D of Public Enemy. Griff's CV subsequently included a residency as part of Public Enemy's 'Security Of The First World' team, before, in the best traditions of hip-hop, he managed to stoke huge controversy before he ever performed his first rap. As Public Enemy's 'Minister Of Information', Griff went on record to state that the Jewish people were responsible for the majority of the world's wickedness, including the selling of his own race into slavery. The quote's explosive value had little to do with the fact that Griff's historical vision so obviously lacked substance, but it served instead to bring rap right into the mainstream of racial debate, highlighting the danger of allowing a platform to those neither gifted nor educated enough to use it (it is worth noting, however, that Griff insists he was misquoted). His role as Public Enemy's diplomat ended when he was unceremoniously ejected, but Griff persevered with a solo career that has produced music of some note. Fuelled by what many commentators have ascribed as paranoia theory, his second album, after signing with Luther Campbell's record label, revealed tight, harsh funk backing to his incendiary polemic, backed by his own band, the Asiatic Disciples.

● ALBUMS: *Pawns In The Game* (Skywalker 1990)★★★, *Kao's II Wiz *7* Dome* (Luke 1991)★★★★, *Disturb N Tha Peace* (Luke 1992)★★★.

PROFILE RECORDS

One of the earliest hip-hop labels, formed in 1981 in New York by Steve Plotnicki and Cory Robbins with a loan from their parents of $70,000. The catalogue began with a single by Grace Kennedy, before their second release, and first rap record, 'Young Ladies' by Lonnie Love. They were down to the last $2,000 of their parents' investment when they scored their first hit, with 'Genius Rap' by Dr. Jeckyll and Mr. Hyde (namely Andre Harrell, now president of Uptown Enterpises, and Alonzo Brown, who was also 'Lonnie Love', respectively). Another significant benchmark was Run DMC's 'Sucker MCs' 1983 cut, a ruffhouse hit which helped to establish the 'new school' tradition, as well as enlarging rap's vocabulary. Run DMC continued to provide the label with their greatest successes throughout the decade. In

January 1994 Plotnicki bought out Robbins to take sole ownership of the label.

● ALBUMS: for ratings see individual entries of the artists. Run DMC: *Raising Hell* (Profile 1986). Special Ed: *Youngest In Charge* (Profile 1989). Poor Righteous Teachers: *Holy Intellect* (Profile 1990). Various: *Diggin' In The Crates Volume One* (Profile 1994).

PROPELLERHEADS

Alex Gifford played piano for Van Morrison, saxophone for the Stranglers and was a member of the Grid before he met Will White when the latter was drumming for Junkwaffle at a gig in Bath. In 1996 Wall Of Sound released their first recording, the EP *Dive*, which later that year was given worldwide coverage as the theme to an Adidas advert. In November the Propellerheads brought the big beat sound to the Top 40 with 'Take California' and early the next year, 'Spybreak' fared even better. On the strength of the latter the group were invited by David Arnold to participate in his album of *James Bond* theme remakes, and their contribution, 'On Her Majesty's Secret Service', became their first Top 10 hit. As a result, they recorded some of the incidental music for the film *Tomorrow Never Dies*. 'OHMSS' was successfully followed by 'History Repeating' (featuring Shirley Bassey) and the album *Decksandrumsandrockandroll*. Since its release they have been involved in projects with the Jungle Brothers and De La Soul. The main components of their characteristic blend of hip-hop, grungey rock and 60s kitsch can be heard in such tracks as 'Spybreak', which features chunky riffs and prominent drumbeats with various effects, corny Hammond melodies and *Mission Impossible*-style bongos. 'Bang On!' and 'Better?' offer slightly different versions of the same idea. While the band claim that their music is not complex and is primarily dance-orientated, after a few listens the album sounds rather one-dimensional and seems to rely on tired hip-hop and acid jazz clichés.

● ALBUMS: *Decksandrumsandrockandroll* (Wall Of Sound 1997)★★★.

PROPHETS OF THE CITY

The most prominent early group involved in the South African rap scene, Prophets Of The City (Ready D aka DJ Explode, rapper Shaheen, dancer Ramone, dancer Jazmo, graffiti artist Googa, breakdancer Mark and reggae rapper Ishmael) formed in Soweto in 1984 and witnessed at first hand the censorship prevalent in their home country as it lurched towards democracy. Many of the tracks on their first domestic album were censored by the MFP, who handle South Africa's record distribution. The group, who were influenced as much by UK rap groups such as Hijack as much as their American counterparts, first came to wordwide attention with 'Understand Where I'm Coming From', which was placed on the Tommy Boy Records sampler *Planet Rap*. Back in South Africa the video, including a satire on a former president, was again banned, despite progress towards a more egalitarian state. By 1995 the group had relocated to England, attracting a large audience with their energetic live shows and television appearances. Their debut UK single, 'Never Again', returned to the subject of apartheid with the caustic opening line: 'Excellent! A Black President!'. It was followed by *Universal Souljaz*, their fourth studio album, but the first to be released internationally.

● ALBUMS: *Universal Souljaz* (Nation 1995)★★★.

PSYCHICK WARRIORS OV GAIA

Ethnic trance team from the low countries, often featuring 'organic' live percussion, whose main member is Bobby Reiner. Their debut single, 'Exit 23', appeared in 1991, followed by 'Maenad', both on Belgian record label KK. Their most widely renowned release, however, was 'Obsidian'. They also joined the throngs in the Midi Circus tour. As for the collective's musical ethos, Reiner would note: 'One of our main ideas about making dance music is the deconstruction of old values, deconstruction of what music is about and re-establishing ritual and trance states'. Former member Robert Heyman later went on to form Exquisite Corpse.

● ALBUMS: *Ov Biospheres And Sacred Grooves (A Document Ov New Edge Folk Classics)* (90s)★★★, *Record Of Breaks* (KK 1995)★★★.

PUBLIC ENEMY

Hugely influential and controversial New York rap act, frequently referred to as 'The Black Sex Pistols'. Public Enemy were initially viewed either as a radical and positive avenging force, or a disturbing manifestation of the guns 'n' violence-obsessed, homophobic, misogynist, anti-Semitic attitudes of a section of the black American ghetto underclass. The group's origins can be traced to 1982 and the Adelphi University, Long Island, New York. There college radio DJ Chuck D (b.

Carlton Douglas Ridenhour, 1 August 1960, Roosevelt, Long Island, New York City, USA) and Hank Shocklee were given the chance to mix tracks for the college station, WBAU, by Bill Stephney. Together they produced a collection of aggressive rap/hip-hop cuts under the title *Super Special Mix Show* in January 1983. They were eventually joined by Flavor Flav (b. William Drayton, 16 March 1959, Roosevelt, Long Island, New York City, USA), who had previously worked alongside Chuck D and his father in their V-Haul company in Long Island, and rang the station incessantly until he too became a host of their show.

In 1984 Shocklee and Chuck D began mixing their own basement hip-hop tapes, primarily for broadcast on WBAU, which included 'Public Enemy Number 1', from which they took their name. By 1987 they had signed to Rick Rubin's Def Jam label (he had first approached them two years earlier) and increased the line-up of the group for musical and visual purposes - Professor Griff 'Minister Of Information' (b. Richard Griffin), DJ Terminator X (b. Norman Rogers) and a four-piece words/dance/martial arts back-up section (Security Of The First World). Shocklee and Chuck D were also to be found running a mobile DJ service, and managed Long Island's first rap venue, the Entourage. The sound of Public Enemy's debut, *Yo! Bum Rush The Show*, was characteristically hard and knuckle bare, its title track a revision of the original 'Public Enemy Number 1' cut. With funk samples splicing Terminator X's turntable sequences, a guitar solo by Living Colour's Vernon Reid (on 'Sophisticated Bitch'), and potent raps from Chuck D assisted by Flav's grim, comic asides, it was a breathtaking arrival. That Public Enemy were not only able to follow up, but also improve on that debut set with *It Takes A Nation Of Millions To Hold Us Back*, signified a clear division between them and the gangsta rappers. Their nearest competitors, NWA, peaked with *Straight Outta Compton*, their idea of progress seemingly to become more simplisticly hateful with each subsequent release. Public Enemy, on the other hand, were beginning to ask questions. And if America's white mainstream audience chose to fear rap, the invective expressed within 'Black Steel In The Hour Of Chaos', 'Prophets Of Rage' and 'Bring The Noise' gave them excellent cause. That anxiety was cleverly exploited in the title of the band's third set, *Fear Of A Black Planet*. Despite their perceived

antagonistic stance, they proved responsive to some criticism, evident in the necessary ousting of Professor Griff in 1989 for an outrageous anti-Semitic statement made in the US press. He would subsequently be replaced by James Norman, then part-time member Sister Souljah. *Fear Of A Black Planet*, their first record without Griff's services, nevertheless made use of samples of the news conferences and controversy surrounding his statements, enhancing the bunker mentality atmosphere which pervaded the project. The 45, '911 Is A Joke', an attack on emergency service response times in ghetto areas, became the subject of a barely credible Duran Duran cover version, strangely confirming Public Enemy's mainstream standing. *Apocalypse 91* was almost as effective, the band hardly missing a beat musically or lyrically with black pride cuts like 'I Don't Wanna Be Called Yo Nigga' and 'Bring The Noise', performed with thrash metal outfit Anthrax. In September 1990 it was revealed that they actually appeared in an FBI report to Congress examining 'Rap Music And Its Effects On National Security'. Despite their popularity and influence, or perhaps because of it, there remained a large reservoir of antipathy directed towards the band within sections of the music industry (though more thoughtful enclaves welcomed them; Chuck D would guest on Sonic Youth's 1990 album, *Goo*, one of several collaborative projects). Either way, their productions in the late 80s and early 90s were hugely exciting - both for the torrents of words and the fury of the rhythm tracks, and in the process they have helped to write rap's lexicon. 'Don't Believe The Hype' (1988) became as powerful a slogan in the late 80s/early 90s as 'Power To The People' was almost 20 years earlier. Similarly, the use of 'Fight The Power' in Spike Lee's 1989 film *Do The Right Thing* perfectly expressed suppressed anger at the Eurocentric nature of American culture and history. In the 90s several members of the band embarked on solo careers, while Hank Shocklee and his brother Keith established Shocklee Entertainment in 1993, a production firm and record label. They released their first album in three years in 1994 with *Muse Sick-N-Hour Mess Age*, though touring arrangments were delayed when Terminator X broke both his legs in a motorcycle accident. The album was released on 4 July - American Independence Day. Again it proved practically peerless, with cuts like 'So Watcha Gone Do Now' putting the new breed of gangsta rappers firmly in their place. Following its release, Flav was charged with possession of cocaine and a firearm in November 1995, while Chuck D. became a noted media pundit. In 1998 the original line-up regrouped for a new album, which also served as the soundtrack for Spike Lee's *He Got Game*.

Public Enemy's legacy extends beyond rap, and has attained a massive cultural significance within black communities. The effect on the consciousness (and consciences) of white people is almost as considerable.

● ALBUMS: *Yo! Bum Rush The Show* (Def Jam 1987)★★★★, *It Takes A Nation Of Millions To Hold Us Back* (Def Jam 1988)★★★★, *Fear Of A Black Planet* (Def Jam 1990)★★★★, *Apocalypse '91 The Enemy Strikes Black* (Def Jam 1991)★★★, *Muse Sick-N-Hour Mess Age* (Def Jam 1994)★★★, *He Got Game* soundtrack (Def Jam 1998)★★★.

● COMPILATIONS: *Greatest Misses* features six 'new' tracks (Def Jam 1992)★★★★, *Twelve Inch Mixes* (Def Jam 1993)★★★.

● FURTHER READING: *Fight The Power - Rap, Race And Reality*, Chuck D. with Yusuf Jah.

PUDGEE THE PHAT BASTARD

Having already written part of MC Fatal's verse on the Main Source track 'Live At The BBQ', and providing material for both Roxanne Shanté and the Ghetto Girls, Pudgee came to his solo career with something of a reputation. Insisting on a formulaic blend of sexual boasting, the predictability of his rhymes, though occasionally amusing, were tempered effectively by the funky backing of Trickmasterz. His debut album boasted a head to head clash with Kool G Rap, with whom Pudgee's voice has often been compared.

● ALBUMS: *Give 'Em The Finger* (Giant 1993)★★★.

PUFF DADDY

(see Combs, Sean 'Puffy')

PULSE 8 RECORDS

Pulse 8 is, by accident or design, the British home of the female vocalist, with label personnel seemingly unable to resist signing or licensing a belting diva performance on garage or house discs. As A&R director Steve Long pointed out: 'We are quite keen to sign male vocalists. But there don't seem to be many about'. Managed by Frank Sansom, the duo behind the label had originally promoted artists including New Kids On The

Block, Foster & Allen and even Max Bygraves. They moved to dance because they believed 'the real artists, the future artists, album artists, are going to come from the dance area'. The label's most prominent artist was arguably Rozalla, whose 1991 cut 'Faith (In The Power Of Love)' brought them chart success. Other releases included 4T Thieves' 'Etnotechno' in 1991, licensed from Italy's Calypso imprint and Friends Of Matthew's 'The Calling' from the same year, a follow-up to 'Out There'. Other pivotal artists were Sue Chaloner ('Answer My Prayer' and 'I Wanna Thank You'), Rave Nation ('Stand Up') and Clubland (introducing Zemya Hamilton) ('Hold On (Tighter To Love)'), both from 1991. Their major hits of 1992 included Reckless ('Reckless Karnage'), Debbie Malone ('Rescue Me (Crazy About Your Love)'), and Rozalla ('Are You Ready To Fly?'). Rage (Pierson Grange, Angela Lupino, Tony Jackson, Jeffrey Sayadian and Toby Sadler) would take them into the Top 10 with, of all things, a Bryan Adams song - 'Run To You'. It was produced by Barry Lang and Duncan Hannant. Lang had previously overseen Amii Stewart's 'Light My Fire', Hannant having worked with Bomb The Bass and Betty Boo. However, the lynchpin producers behind the label's output are Band Of Gypsies. They recorded cuts such as 'Take Me Higher' in their own right, as well as providing Australian singer Juliette Jaimes with hits in 'Stand Up' and 'Summer Breeze' (and working with Chaloner and Rozalla). Other material arrived from Lee Rogers (ex-Temper and her own group, Suspect, and also a Hollywood actor, with 'Love Is The Most'). The label fell out with Rozalla when she attempted to release her debut album, recorded at Pulse 8's expense, on Epic. Pulse 8 won the subsequent court case in February 1992, despite Rozalla having at no time signed a contract. Their quest for a talented male vocalist alighted on Keith Nunnally, who, fronting Intuition, provided 'Greed (When Will The World Be Free)', a revision of the same artist's DJ International oldie. Pulse 8 is also the mother label to the Faze 2 subsidiary, famed for its contribution to the world of toytown techno with Urban Hype (Bobby D and Mark Lewis) and 'A Trip To Trumpton'. That group had previously scored with the more sober 'Teknologi'.

PWL

Hardly the coolest record label on the dance scene, owned as it is by the Stock, Aitken & Waterman triad, PWL has nevertheless made a massive contribution to the subculture by licensing mainstream successes (on PWL Continental) from Europe, including DJ Professor, 2 Unlimited, Capella and RAF, while PWL International has offered the Toxic Two ('Rave Generator'), Opus III ('It's A Fine Day'), Vision Masters ('Keep On Pumpin' It') and Undercover ('Never Let Her Slip Away', 'Baker Street', etc.). In addition there was a rave off-shoot/promo label Black Diamond which origi-nally housed tunes including 'Rave Generator' and 2 Unlimited's 'Workaholic', until they crossed over. However, Black Diamond disappeared in 1992 to be replaced by 380, headed by John Barratt, and named after its address at a con-verted church on Manchester's Deansgate. Its career began with Family Foundation's 'Xpress Yourself', then Ultracynic's 'Nothing Is Forever'.

QDIII

b. Quincy Jones III. British-born, Los Angeles, California, USA-based early 90s hip-hop producer. The son of Quincy Jones, QD got the rap bug as a breakdancer for Nike, before attending jams and street parties. There he was introduced to the work of the new rap kings, which built on his abiding love of soul legends like Stevie Wonder. However, it was the production work of Mantronik (Mantronix) that really caught his attention, especially a track entitled 'Cold Getting Dumb' by Just Ice. Among his earliest commis-sions as a producer/remixer was a cut for T La Rock, 'Nitro', while he was still living in New York. He next approached Warner Brothers, who suggested he put together a compilation album to showcase new talent. The resultant *Soundlab* eventually led to Justin Warfield being signed - whose expansive debut album was helmed by QDIII. It also spurred QD on to further produc-tion work, most notably with LL Cool J and Ice Cube. These two heavyweights anchored his rep-utation via the highly successful *14 Shots To The Dome* (three tracks) and *Lethal Injection* (four tracks), respectively. He has gone on to produce and remix for a myriad of other talents, including Tairrie B, Naughty By Nature, Da Lench Mob, Yo Yo (the latter two both out of Ice Cube's stable), En Vogue, Special K, Queen Latifah and the Whooliganz. He continues to run his own com-pany, Soundlab productions, titled after the com-pilation album that made his reputation.

QUEEN LATIFAH

b. Dana Owens, 18 March 1970, East Orange, New Jersey, USA. Rap's first lady, Queen Latifah, broke through in the late 80s with a style that picked selectively from jazz and soul traditions. The former Burger King employee maintained her early commitment to answer the misogynist armoury of her male counterparts, and at the same time impart musical good times to all genders. After working as the human beatbox along-side female rapping crew Ladies Fresh, she was just 18 years old when she released her debut single, 'Wrath Of My Madness', in 1988. A year later her debut long-player enjoyed fevered reviews: an old, wise head was evident on the top of her young shoulders. Production expertise from Daddy-O, KRS-1, DJ Mark The 45 King and members of De La Soul doubtlessly helped as well. By the time of her third album she had moved from Tommy Boy Records to a new home, Motown Records, and revealed a shift from the soul and ragga tones of *Nature Of A Sista* to sophis-ticated, sassy hip-hop. She subsequently embarked on a career as an actor, notably in the hit streetwise black comedy, *Living Single*, where she played magazine boss Khadijah James. Her film credits already include *Juice*, *Jungle Fever* and *House Party 2*. As if that were not enough, she additionally set up her own Flavor Unit record label and management company in 1993, as an outlet for new rap acts as well as her own record-ings. The first release on it, 'Roll Wit Tha Flava', featured an all-star cast including Naughty By Nature's Treach, Fu-Schnickens' Chip-Fu, Black Sheep's Dres and D-Nice. She also guested on the Shabba Ranks single, 'Watcha Gonna Do'. Previous collaborations had included those with De La Soul ('Mama Gave Birth To The Soul Children', in that band's infancy) and Monie Love (the agenda-set-ting 'Ladies First'). Queen Latifah represents an intelligent cross-section of hip-hop influences. Though she is a forthright advocate of her race's struggle, she is also the daughter of and brother to policemen. *Black Reign*, in fact, is dedicated to the death of that same brother: 'I see both sides. I've seen the abuse and I've been the victim of police who abuse their authority. On the other side you've got cops getting shot all the time, you got people who don't respect them at all'. While a little too strident to live up to the Arabic meaning of her name (Latifah equates to delicate and sen-sitive), Queen Latifah remains one of the most positive role models for young black women (and men) in hip-hop culture: 'Aspire to be a doctor or a lawyer, but not a gangster'. As one of the singles lifted from *Black Reign* advocated: 'UNITY (Who You Calling A Bitch?)'. Following a lengthy hiatus owing to acting commitments, Latifah returned to recording with 1998's *Order In The Court*.

● ALBUMS: *All Hail The Queen* (Tommy Boy 1989)★★★★, *Nature Of A Sista* (Tommy Boy 1991)★★★, *Black Reign* (Motown 1993)★★★,

Order In The Court (Flavor Unit 1998)★★★.

QUEST, J.

b. c.1967, New York, USA. J. Quest began singing in public at the age of 10 when he toured the USA as soloist with the New York Boys' Choir. As a child he had sung along to his heroes Marvin Gaye, Whitney Houston and Luther Vandross. In 1993, he met Lisa Lisa while in the studio with his manager and through her he was introduced to the producer Junior Vasquez, who asked Quest to sing on several tracks on which he was working, two of which later appeared on his debut album ('Brand New Luv' and 'Behind The Scenes'). On *The Quest Is On* Quest also sang with hip-hoppers Pudgee The Phat Bastard (the first US single, 'Anything') and Ill Al Skratch ('Up And Down'). The latter was a remix of a song that had origi-nally appeared on the soundtrack to the film *Jason's Lyric*. The music combined urban hip-hop with R&B in a manner most readily reminiscent of R. Kelly, doubtlessly aiming for a similar target audience.

● ALBUMS: *The Quest Is On* (Mercury 1995)★★★.

QUIRK

Mark Allen and Tim Healey met while they were both DJing at Return To The Source in London. Healey had previously worked for Sony Records and began writing and co-producing trance after a visit to a Pagan party in the early 90s. He subse-quently released material under a number of names, notably the Unconscious Collective and his solo projects Squid and Sephalopod, for such labels as Aquatec, Blue Room, Flying Rhino and Phantasm. As DJ Squid, Healey began to play in the chill-out at Return To The Source in the mid-90s. Quirk's first release was 'Cognitive Dissidents/Dimension Disco' for Krembo Records in 1996, followed by the track 'Robotised', written for the Matsuri compilation *Truth Of Communication* in the same year. Rather than con-tinuing to release singles, Allen and Healey con-centrated on writing enough material for an album, *Machina Electra & Fornax Chemica*, which arrived at the beginning of 1998 along with the EP *Dance With The Devil*. Conscious of the formulaic nature of much trance of the time, Allen and Healey aimed to challenge listeners' preconcep-tions, commenting that they wanted 'to keep people dancing and keep them guessing - the quirkier the better'. To promote the album the

pair embarked on a tour of Japan, Australia, New Zealand and South Africa, presenting highly imaginative, improvised performances of their material in which Allen DJed pre-recorded material from CDs while Healey controlled samples and synthesizers. On stage Quirk are joined by Marcus Conrad, who accompanies the music with visual sequences made from black-and-white pictures that he manipulates with various analogue and digital effects to create colours and patterns. Later the same year they released the *Dark Matter* EP. Healey continues to DJ with Return To The Source and a variety of other parties and to collaborate with others on projects, including Mr Resister (for Aquatec) and Filthy Beasts (Phantasm). Much of Quirk's music is highly abstract in a melodic sense, with only one or two riffs ever present at one time as Allen and Healey have instead concentrated on original, often pitchless sound sources. Each track is characterized by Quirk's detailed production and eccentric samples, which include operatic singing ('Lo-Fi Sci-Fi'), a table tennis match ('Ping') and telephone conversations ('Spy vs Spy'). While 'Ping', 'Spy vs Spy' and 'Lo-Fi Sci-Fi' present familiar four-on-the-floor beats, 'Institute' follows no recognized stylistic patterns and instead creates a challenging, fragmented piece of abstract sounds. Although Quirk should be whole-heartedly praised for their original experimentation, their music is sometimes overwhelmed by random sounds, and at times, it tends to lack any real groove or feeling.
● ALBUMS: *Machina Electra & Fornax Chemica* (Matsuri 1998)★★★★.

R&S RECORDS

Ghent Belgium techno label/talent pool founded by Renaat Vanderpapeliere and Sabine Maes in the early 80s. R&S's high profile has been earned on the back of some of the dance scene's most innovative artists: Kevin Saunderson, Derrick May, Dave Angel ('Planet Function', 'Stairway To Heaven'), Joey Beltram ('Vol 1-2', etc.), C.J. Bolland ('Ravesignal 1-3'), Jam & Spoon ('Stella') and the Aphex Twin ('Didgeridoo') - a who's who of techno in itself, have all seen their vinyl bedecked by the familiar R&S emblem of a reering steed. In 1987 Code 61 provided the label with 'Drop The Deal', which became an early balearic hit and established R&S's credentials. From their roots in the much-maligned 'Belgian new beat' scene, the label picked up the Detroit sound and nurtured it into a hard house style best recalled on tracks like Spectrum's 'Brazil'. Subsequent records like Human Resource's 'Dominator' and Beltram's 'Mentasm' proved hugely important to the UK's rave generation. However, it is far more than a one horse stable, as can be discerned by its subsidiary operations. These include Apollo (ambient), Global Cuts (uplifting club house), Outrage (experimental) and Diatomyc (acid). Notable also have been two series of compilations, *TZ* (Test Zone) and *In Order To Dance*. The latter gathers highlights from the R&S roster at more or less regular intervals, providing DJs and clubbers with the most important cuts. The label set up a UK outlet at the beginning of 1993, which co-ordinates releases and promotion in tandem with the six-person team in Ghent, while former employee Marcus Graham left to form ITP with DJ Eddie Love Chocolate. Among the label's most satisfying current projects have been Jaydee ('Plastic Dreams'), Biosphere ('Microgravity'), C.J. Bolland ('The 4th Sign'), Source ('Organized Noise') and Locust, whose album project for Apollo was produced in association with a documentary. R&S planned to delve further into multimedia projects with a

MTV tie-up party and the inclusion of a computer game, film and subliminal artwork as part of *In Order To Dance 5*. Plans for a 'helicopter shuttle service' for staff members between Ghent and London were probably an exaggeration, but it would be unwise to rule anything out bearing in mind R&S's formidable former achievements and appetite for dance music.

● ALBUMS: Various: *In Order To Dance Volumes 1-5* (R&S 1990-94)★★★.

RACIC, ROBERT

b. *c.*1958, Australia, d. 25 October 1996, Sydney, Australia. A DJ, producer and remixer, Robert Racic first began to work as a DJ in Sydney in the early 80s. He was one of the first Australians to import New York garage and Chicago house records and as such became widely regarded as 'benevolent godfather' to the nebulous Australian dance scene. He was fundamental in sponsoring the development and success of indigenous dance-influenced groups such as the Rockmelons and Machinations, as an alternative to conventional rock music. Racic began producing for the experimental duo Severed Heads, whose single 'Greater Reward' (1988) became the bestselling import in the USA that year and reached number 19 in *Billboard*'s Club Play chart. After further success with Severed Heads for Canadian label Nettwerk Records, Racic produced three further chart singles with Brisbane dance group Boxcar (for Pulse 8 Records). His biggest chart success came in 1994 when Severed Heads' 'Dead Eyes Opened' reached number 12 in the Australian charts. Racic died in 1996 as a result of a brain virus.

RAHEEM

From the Geto Boys' Houston, Texas stable, Raheem embraces that group's familiar offensiveness, but has no little musical dexterity to offer. His debut album spanned reggae ('Punks Give Me Respect') and rock ('Shotgun'), but some of the words on the follow-up were so nasty that he was elevated to the level of 'the new Scarface'. A dubious honour but one which Raheem would doubtless relish.

● ALBUMS: *The Vigilante* (Rap-A-Lot 1988)★★, *The Invincible* (Rap-A-Lot 1992)★★, *Tight 4 Life* (Tight 2 Def 1998)★★★.

RAKE

b. Keith Rose, USA. As the Rake this obscure old school rapper released 'Street Justice' on Profile Records in the early 80s, a revenge narrative which concerned itself with the lack of justice visited on two criminals who raped the protagonist's wife. It was written by Blatt and Gottlieb, two professional songwriters better known for their work with the Four Tops. However, though it caused headlines because of its violent nature, the single's follow-ups failed to attract similar attention.

● ALBUMS: *The Art Ensemble Of Rake/The Tell-Tale Moog* (WHF 1996)★★★.

RAKIM

b. William Griffin Jnr., Long Island, New York, USA. Between 1987 and 1992, Rakim released four influential albums in partnership with Eric B that have accorded him the status of one of rap's greatest figureheads. His complex, cross-referencing lyrics and relaxed delivery style inspired a new generation of hip-hop artists in the 90s, including the hugely successful Wu-Tang Clan, Nas and Dr. Dre. Following the duo's split in 1992, Rakim worked on the soundtrack to *Gunmen* before disappearing into seclusion for five years. He returned in 1997 with the long-awaited *The 18th Letter*, a smooth soulful album that earned praise for Rakim's imaginative and intelligent rhyming on tracks such as 'The 18th Letter' ('Nobody's been this long-awaited since Jesus/I heard the word on the street is/I'm still one of the deepest on the mike since Adidas') and 'The Mystery (Who Is God)'. The album also came with a greatest hits bonus CD, *The Book Of Life*, a compelling selection of the music which made Rakim the legendary figure he is today.

● ALBUMS: *The 18th Letter/The Book Of Life* (Universal 1997)★★★★.

RAMMELZEE

b. Jean Michel Basquiet, France. The single 'Beat Bop', credited to Rammelzee V. K-Rob, was first released as a limited edition on the Tartown Records label in the early 80s. It featured a live band backing track and a 'space funk' rap. Profile Records would be the first to realize its commercial potential, re-releasing it for the US market in 1983. Up until that point Rammelzee, whose pseudonym is made up of three segments, Ramm, Elevation and Z, the latter indicating two-way energy, was better known as a graffiti artist. An exciting record, the pseudo-mystical lyrics and liberties taken with the English language rendered it practically indecipherable to many listeners. Nevertheless, 'Beat Bop' became a staple of the early hip-hop electro movement, and was later included on Profile's *Diggin' In The Crates* compilation of old school rap. Mo' Wax Records founder James Lavelle later cited it as 'one of the most inspirational rap records of the 80s', while Ministry Of Sound disc jockey DJ Harvey called it 'one of the classic pieces of old skool hip-hop'.

RAMPLING, DANNY

b. 15 July 1961, London, England. Former bank manager Rampling is a staple of the Manchester DeConstruction label, a member of the Kiss FM team, and a hugely popular DJ the world over. DJing since the age of 18, he was pre-eminent in the balearic movement in the late 80s, and has successfully negotiated dozens of shifts in dance music's climate since. He was pivotal in importing the acid sound, after playing legendary sets at Ibiza clubs such as Koo and Pacha. His nights at south London's legendary Shoom Club, which he opened with his wife Jenny in 1988, are now legendary. Shoom introduced many of the 'Phuture' tracks imported from Chicago, though Rampling also mixed this up with other dance sounds, he himself having come from a soul background. He waited some time before releasing his first record, Sound Of Shoom's 'I Hate Hate' in 1990, a cover of an obscure soul cut from Razzy Bailey sung by Steven Eusebe. In the meantime he had remixed for the B-52's, Beloved, Erasure and James Taylor Quartet, among many others. He went on to form the Millionaire Hippies, who have released strong singles like 'I Am The Music, Hear Me!', featuring the vocals of Das Strachen and Gwen Dupree, with remixes from Farley And Heller.

● ALBUMS: *Love Groove Dance Party Vols. 1-2* (Metropole 1996)★★★.

RAP

Rap is a term adopted from the jazz tradition, where it indicates 'speaking' or 'talking'. Musically, too, the development of rap into a billion dollar industry in the 80s and 90s can be traced to 'jazz poets' such as Gil Scott-Heron and the Last Poets. In its modern form, rap began with the 1979 single 'Rapper's Delight', released by the Sugarhill Gang on Sylvia Robinson's Sugarhill Records. The first line of this song; 'A hip-hop, the hi-be, To the hi-be, The hip-hip-hop, You don't stop rockin', also coined the term with denotes rap's parent movement - hip-hop (which embraces graffiti art, music, breakdancing and ghetto culture). Rap music generally relies on two components - the MC or rapper, and the DJ, responsible for constructing musical accompaniment, often with the aid of 'samples' from other records. Originally rap was an entirely street-linked phenomenon, as rival troupes competed at street parties and warehouses in a manner similar to that of the reggae sound systems. There are other similarities between the two musics - one of the first to pioneer hip-hop was Jamaican Kool Herc, and the rap MC has similarities to reggae's DJ or toaster. Other 'old school' artists including Afrika Bambaataa and Grandmaster Flash subsequently took rap into the political arena, Flash's 'The Message' being a particularly evocative record in the early 80s. By the mid-80s the dominant force in rap became 'B-Boy' culture, epitomised by Run DMC of Def Jam Records and LL Cool J. Other originators such as KRS-1 of Boogie Down Productions continued to produce quality recordings. By the late 80s NWA and Public Enemy had taken the music to, in hip-hop parlance, 'the next level'. As the deeply politicized voice of dispossessed black youth culture, both groups were viewed with suspicion by the white music industry and traded on the fact (Public Enemy memorably titling one of their albums *Fear Of A Black Planet*, NWA sponsoring the development of gangsta rap). Though NWA's vitriol soon became artistically sterile, Public Enemy have persevered to become rap's single most important commentators. A former member of NWA, Ice Cube, became a potent commercial force in the 90s, alongside his near-namesake, Ice-T. Both were dogged by accusations of misogyny and the glorification of violence. However, at their best, each had something valuable to say about the society in which they lived and its representation in the media - unlike a slew of egomaniacal exhibitionists such as the Geto Boys. Gang Starr successfully reiterated the link between jazz and rap with a series of lauded experiments throughout the 90s, while Cypress Hill built an entire career on discussing the benefits of marijuana consumption. More commercial acts, including Vanilla Ice and MC Hammer, brought rap to MTV cameras and a wider public, but they were consistently denigrated by purists.

Of the white rappers, the only act to appeal across the racial board remained the consistently innovative Beastie Boys. By the mid-90s Dr Dre and his protégé Snoop Doggy Dogg had relocated rap's epicentre to Los Angeles, framing the G-Funk sound which became the dominant urban mantra of the period. The west coast's ascendancy has subsequently been challenged by the dynamic creative forces within the Wu-Tang Clan, as well as Nas and Fat Joe Da Gangsta. Rap has developed at an astonishing pace since its inception, retaining its position as the preferred outlet for those in America's depressed inner cities and articulating views which would otherwise remain unheard. That it thrives on a diet of adverse publicity and notoriety should come as no surprise to those familiar with the conditions that have bred it.

RAP-A-LOT RECORDS

Houston, Texas-based rap label run by James Smith (b. c.1964), who has seen considerable financial reward for his efforts in promoting ultra-hardcore rappers like the Geto Boys and sundry spin-off projects. One of several items of real estate to his name is a 30 acre ranch where he hosted Source Magazine's debate about gangsta rap. His opinion: 'This rap shit is the biggest challenge to this government in a long-ass time. It's bigger than Martin Luther King and all them'. His empire has expanded to include new talent like 5th Ward Boys and Raheem, though they hardly provide stylistic diversity.
● ALBUMS: Geto Boys: We Can't Be Stopped (Rap-A-Lot 1991)★★★. Scarface: The World Is Yours (Rap-A-Lot 1993)★★★.

RAPINO BROTHERS

Italian producers, remixers and writers, the Rapino Brothers are Marco Sabiu and Charlie Mallozzi. Sabiu is a keyboard player and programmer, who admits to being classically trained ('though trying to forget it'). Former drummer Mallozzi, meanwhile, provides the musical knowledge behind the group, and most of its strategy. After working initially in their native Bologna, Italy, the duo moved to London in May 1992. Their career since then has boomed, and they have become fixtures on the club remix circuit via work with Vegas ('She'), Freaky Realistic ('Something New'), Heaven 17 ('Fascist Groove Thing'), Candyland ('Rainbow'), Dayeene ('Around The World'), London Boys ('Baby Come

Back') and Milan ('Affectionately Mine'), among others. As artists they also employ their own act, Rapination, which features assorted vocalists, and they quickly scored a UK Top 40 success in January 1993 with the aid of Kym Mazelle's vocals on 'Love Me The Right Way'.

RAPPIN' IS FUNDAMENTAL

Among the forerunners of one of rap's many clashes with different genres, in this case doo-wop. The trio consists of Easy Mo Bee (b. Osten Harvey, brother of producer 'LG' Harvey), JR and AB Money, all Brooklyn neighbours, raised under the paternal wing of their local church. JR (b. Darron Strand) decided to put on hold his career in Wall Street for the music business in 1987. There is little to dislike about Rappin' Is Fundamental and their mix of funky beats with breezy a cappella breaks and doo wop harmonies, with the possible exception of their rather laborious name. Influenced by vocal harmony groups like the Flamingos, they were certainly among the more sophisticated members of New York's hip-hop culture. They were keen to differentiate themselves from anything so one-dimensional: 'We don't want to be looked on as just rappers. We're born singers, we're bona fide dancers and natural rappers. We're all round entertainers.' However, they were dropped by A&M, after their debut album stiffed, but were still active in 1994, independently releasing 'Helluva Guy'.
● ALBUMS: The Doo Hop Legacy (A&M 1991)★★★.

RAVE

Specifically a one-off gathering for late-night consumption of pre-recorded dance music in the late 80s early 90s, a musical definition of rave is more problematic. Descending from the acid house sound and ethos, the main fare tends to be fast techno and hardcore records, pitched between 125 and 140 bpm and often released on tiny independent labels with little background information. Some of rave's established anthems include Toxic Two's 'Rave Generator' and Human Resource's 'Dominator'. Like other forms of dance music, rave has its favoured DJs and remixers. However, arguably the most recognizable and popular of the 'rave' acts are Liam Howlett's Prodigy. Other acts venerated include Altern 8, Bizarre Inc, Bassheads and early K Klass material.

RAW BREED

Alongside Onyx, with whom Raw Breed are all too frequently compared, this Bronx, New York troupe encapsulate the 'Nastee nigga' term which has been coined to address their sound. After a brief sojourn with Jam Master Jay of Run DMC, Raw Breed hooked up with Ice-T's Rhyme Syndicate to launch their career. The band comprise Mark Rippin (cousin of Ultramagnetic MCs' Kool Keith) and four others, and kicked off their career with the 'Rabbit Stew' 45, which dissed 'all the wack MCs, and wack groups that came out in '93'.

● ALBUMS: *Loon Tunz* (1993)★★★, *Killa Instinct* (Warners 1996)★★★.

RAW FUSION

Comprising Digital Underground members DJ Fuze and Money B, who opened their account with 'Throw Your Hands In The Air'. Instead of following the P-Funk fixation of their erstwhile employers, as Raw Fusion the duo concentrated instead on a more mellow, reggae tinged delivery. Despite the presence on their debut of old sparring partners Shock G. and Shmoovy Shomoov, along with Tupac Shakur, the resulting album was no classic. A second set introduced filthy rhymes from Money B, dubbed up by Fuze, on 'Freaky Note', but again failed to capture the magic of Digital Underground at their best.

● ALBUMS: *Live From The Styletron* (Hollywood Basic 1992)★★, *Hoochiefied Funk* (Hollywood Basic 1994)★★.

RAW STYLUS

Signed to Acid Jazz Records on the basis of 1992's 'Pushin' Against The Flow', Raw Stylus have undergone a comparatively long incubation. Their early career was as a covers band on the north London circuit. Then the singer Jules Brookes, a former *Boxing Weekly* journalist, and Ron Aslan, his songwriting partner and production wizard, began to write their own material. Inspired not only by Marvin Gaye and Curtis Mayfield, they also looked to the clean-cut production of Steely Dan for a lead. Their first release was the white label 12-inch, 'Bright Lights Big City', in 1989, before 'Pushin'' announced their arrival properly. Paul Weller was so impressed he offered to play guitar on the song. On the back of hugely successful gigs at the Brixton Fridge in London they signed to James Lavelle's Mo' Wax Records label. However, after the club hit 'Many Ways', problems arose, and they switched to Acid Jazz instead. They began their career there with a Bill Withers cover, 'Use Me'. By this time female vocalist Donna Gadye had become a semi-permanent fixture, replacing Marcella (aka Debbie French). However, soon after they changed labels again, this time to Wired, an offshoot of Michael Levy's M&G Records. The studio chosen for the band's debut album, River Sound in New York, was owned by producer Gary Katz, who produced the early Steely Dan albums so admired by the band.

● ALBUMS: *Pushing Against The Flow* (Wired 1995)★★★.

RAZE

This US house group from Washington, DC, was essentially Vaughn Mason, aided by the singer Keith Thompson (b. Bronx, New York, USA). Raze perfected the house formula with club classics 'Jack The Groove', which was originally released in 1986 but broke the UK Top 20 in January the following year. 'Let The Music Move U', and particularly 'Break 4 Luv' (a US dance number 1) also became house standards. Controversy followed 'Break 4 Luv' when Thompson alleged that Mason had wrongly appropriated all the writing and publishing credits. They eventually reached a settlement, after which Thompson started a solo project and founded his own label, Level 10. Mason persevered as Raze, notably with 'Bass Power' (on Champion Records 1991), which featured the singer Pamela Frazier and the rapper Doug Lazy.

REACT RECORDS

UK label established by former Rhythm King director James Horrocks with new partner Thomas Foley. After Rhythm King had gone overground in a big way, Horrocks bailed out, and kicked around for a couple of years before taking up an A&R job for Really Useful's short-lived dance label (also called React). Afterwards he moved on to his own project, initially packaging compilations such as *Deep Heat*, *Thin Ice* and *Megabass*. The first single proper came about via ex-bootlegger John Truelove, who, as the Source featuring Candi Station, recorded 'You Got The Love'. It would sell over 200,000 copies in the UK. It was at this point that Horrocks made the acquaintence of Foley, who introduced him to the house scene (establishing the React-backed Garage night at Heaven). He has gone on to be the prime mover behind the label's highly successful *Reactivate* compilation series. On the single front React maintains an enviable reputation. Their biggest releases include Age Of Love's classy 'Age Of Love', arguably the perfect example of trance house, remixed by Jam And Spoon. In 1991 React were joined by scene stalwarts Fierce Ruling Diva, a duo of Amsterdam DJs Jeroen Flamman and Jeffrey 'DJ Abraxas' Porter (famous for hosting the Planet E club in Amsterdam and an after-hours barge club, Subtopia). In 1991 they released 'Rubb It In' for the label, then 'You Gotta Believe' a year later. The label also signed Italian producer Alex Lee, releasing his 'Take It' in June. The latter artist was drafted for national service in Italy for two years just as his career was beginning to take off. They also provided a home to GTO (who recorded two of the earliest singles on the React catalogue in 'Listen To The Rhythm Flow' and 'Elevation'), Ether Real ('Zap'), Elevator ('Shinny') and MASH ('U Don't Have To Say U Love Me').

REAL McCOY

Formed in the late 80s by O-Jay (b. Olaf Jeglitza, Germany), Real McCoy are among Germany's most successful dance acts. Under the name MC Sar And The Real McCoy, his debut record, the anthemic 'It's On You' (1991), became a number 1 hit in 12 countries and was followed by a number of international Top 20 hits including 'Pump Up The Jam Rap', 'Don't Stop' and 'Make A Move'. Emerging as a trio featuring 'Patsy' Patricia Petersen (b. New Jersey, USA) and Vanessa Mason, in 1994 Real McCoy had a US Top 5 single with 'Another Night'. Their American success paved the way for work with such songwriters as Billy Steinberg (Bangles, Madonna, Whitney Houston) and the producer Shep Pettibone (Madonna, Janet Jackson, Pet Shop Boys). The Real McCoy also collaborated with the Ace Of Base production team Ekman and Adebratt. The input of such noted figures resulted in the release of the album *Another Night*, a US Top 20 success that sold over one million copies and topped charts throughout Europe and Asia.
● ALBUMS: *On The Move* (Hansa 1991)★★, *Space Invaders* (Hansa 1994)★★★, released in the USA as *Another Night* (Hansa/Arista 1995)★★★, *One More Time* (Arista 1997)★★★.

REAL ROXANNE

b. Adelaida Martinez. One of a strange flurry of rapping namesakes to emerge in the late 80s, after the release of U.T.F.O.'s 'Roxanne Roxanne'. This Puerto Rican female MC, based in New York, was arguably the most talented, releasing a powerful debut album aided by the production genius of Jam Master Jay (Run DMC), Howie Tee and Full Force, who were behind U.T.F.O.'s original 'Roxanne Roxanne', and discovered Martinez when she was waitressing in Brooklyn. Sadly, when the 'Roxanne' fracas finally died down, she was left without a bandwagon to hitch her career to.
● ALBUMS: *The Real Roxanne* (Select 1988)★★★★, *Go Down (But Don't Bite It)* (Select 1992)★★.

REBEL MC

After leaving his Double Trouble partners (Michael Menson and Leigh Guest), famed for the bubblegum ska hit 'Street Tuff', London based former electronics student Rebel MC (b. Michael Alec Anthony West, 27 August 1965, Tottenham, London, England) has earned greater plaudits as a solo artist. Double Trouble would go on to score minor hits with 'Love Don't Live Here Anymore' and 'Rub-A-Dub', without their former leader. Originally considered the UK's Hammer, the Rebel's more recent work is characterised by ragga beats, fast rhymes and roots harmonics. It was heartfelt music with a solid Rastafarian mes-sage. It was learned, no doubt, from his earlier stints on the live reggae circuit, having set up the Beat Freak sound system with jungle innovator DJ Ron. The single 'Rich An' Getting Richer' was an excellent social commentary rant with dub synchronized, orchestral mixes. On *Black Meaning Good* he was joined by Tenor Fly, Barrington Levy, P.P. Arnold, and Dennis Brown, the more political agenda emphasized by its sleeve dedica-tion to: 'scapegoats of the British judicial system'. 'Rebel Music', meanwhile, was remixed by Pasemaster Mase of De La Soul. The son of a semi-pro cricketer, West helped start the 'People Against Poverty And Oppression Movement', and joined with 'Musicians Against The War' in the days of the Gulf conflict. More lastingly, he helped establish his own Tribal Bass label, working with homegrown UK rap talent including the Demon Boyz and others.
● ALBUMS: *Black Meaning Good* (Desire 1991)★★★, *Word, Sound And Prayer* (Desire 1992)★★★, with Double Trouble *21 Mixes* (Desire 1990)★★.

RECYCLE OR DIE

German record label associated with the Harthouse Records/Eye Q group, whose managing director is Heinz Roth. They had the sum total of their product, six albums, released in the UK for the first time in 1994. Each CD arrived in a cover painted by a cult German arist, packaged in recyclable cardboard. The albums were: *Straylight* (Dominic Woosey), *Looking Beyond* (Ralf Hildenbeutel), *Constellation* (Oliver Lieb), *Baked Beans* (Helmut Zerlett), *Archaic Modulation* (Stevie Be Zet) and *Rhythm & Irrelevance* (#9 Dream). Roth: 'It's very much like a community project . . . Recycle Or Die is not an ambient label. It's more experimental. It's not like putting together a couple of sounds and smoking a joint'. Recycle Or Die took a stage in the 1994 Montreaux Jazz Festival, where Ralf Hildenbeutel, Sven Vath's engineer, played.

RED BANDIT

This US rapper first came to prominence with the release of 'I'm Back' in 1990, an answer song to Lisa Stansfield's 'All Around The World'. Featuring a strong hook sung by the song's producer, Dr Freeze, alongside samples of Stansfield's hit, it became a cult item on British and USA radio. When an album emerged it offered two sides to Red Bandit's craft, the sensitive lover mode embodied by the title track, and a 'dance' side, the former featuring additional accompaniment from Bell Biv DeVoe's Ricky Bell. The dance side was less artistically successful, typically utilising the over-familiar strains of Freeze's 'Poison' drum motif in an approximation of Euro 'hip-house'. However, by 1992 Red Bandit had left Motown Records, moving instead to Creative Control (through London Records). He also embarked on a career in broadcasting as the hip-hop disc jockey on WNWK and WNYE in New York.
● ALBUMS: *Cool Lover Boy* (Bandit 1990)★★★.

RED FOX

b. *c*.1970, St. Catherine, Jamaica, West Indies. An artist who un-self-consciously mixes hip-hop and reggae, Red Fox was initially compared to Yellowman when he appeared at sound systems in his native country, due to his light complexion. However, it wasn't until he moved to New York (still at the tender age of 16) that his musical career found its feet. Following stage shows alongside dancehall stars like Shabba Ranks and Buju

Banton, he hooked up with producer Peter McKenzie to record 'Come Boogie Down' on FM Records. It quickly became a cult item both in his adopted home of Brooklyn and back in Jamaica. In 1992 he teamed with Brand Nubian to duet on the memorable 'Black Star Liner' cut. That outfit returned the compliment to Red Fox on 'Hey Mr. Rude Boy', from his debut album, *As A Matter Of Fox*. It was preceded by the roughneck 'Dem A Murderer' 45, which, like the album, entwined dancehall and rap into a presentable cocktail. Further singles 'Born Again Black Man', a straight reggae song, and 'Ghetto Gospel', sandwiched an appearance at Jamaica's annual Sting festival.
● ALBUMS: *As A Matter Of Fox* (Elektra 1993)★★★.

RED NINJA

These underground British rappers recorded the memorable singles 'War Bytes' and 'Ninja Dawn: Day Of Dread' for Zoom Records in 1989. Two subsequent releases, 'Danger Zone' and 'Hellz A Place I Know' emerged on their own label, after which half of the original line-up broke away from the group. No further sightings ensued until 1993, when, fully regrouped and energies restored, they announced the release of their debut album via a promotional single 'Down With Hop'. They also took a hand in releasing a record by one of their protégés, MC Lethal's 'Portrait Of The Young Man As An Artist'.
● ALBUMS: *Red Ninja* (Zoom 1994)★★★.

RED SNAPPER

Red Snapper are one of a number of bands who, in the mid-90s, began creating instrumental music from textures and beats after the rise of ambient, dance music and hip-hop. The American David Ayers (guitar), Ali Friend (double bass) and Richard Thair (drums) formed the group in London in 1993 after a varied musical background that included working in a number of jazz and rock groups in the 80s. The three have on occasion been joined by the saxophonists Allan Riding and Ollie Moore and the singer Beth Orton. Friend and Thair played with Dean Thatcher in the Aloof, before Thair and Thatcher formed the Flaw record label in 1993 and produced a series of breakbeat tracks. Red Snapper's first release, the *Snapper* EP, was released on Flaw the next year and was followed by live performances, including an appearance at the Glastonbury Festival. After two more EPs the

group signed to Warp Records, who in 1995 collected the first three releases on *Reeled And Skinned*. 'Mooking' and 'Loopascoopa' accompanied their debut album, *Prince Blimey*, in 1996. Red Snapper have been involved in remix projects for such artists as Garbage and Ken Ishii and have themselves been remixed by DJ Food and Squarepusher. As is the way with imaginative, intelligent bands such as Red Snapper, numerous bizarre terms have been used to describe their music, particularly trip-hop and jazz. Their jazz flavour comes not from the their aesthetic of experimentation and improvisation in absolute music, creating sounds that do not necessarily adhere to any formulae, following the tradition of such innovators as Charles Mingus and Miles Davis. Hip-hop and jungle rhythms, twangy 50s guitar and overblown saxophone can be heard in the music, yet they are merely flavours in Red Snapper's own abstract soundtracks. Where they meet with dance music is not so much in the sounds used, but in the concept of rhythmical, structureless textures that house and techno brought to the popular conscience.
● ALBUMS: *Prince Blimey* (Warp 1996)★★★★, *Making Bones* (Warp 1998)★★★.
● COMPILATIONS: *Reeled And Skinned* (Warp 1995)★★★.

REDHEAD KINGPIN AND FBI

b. David Guppy, *c*.1970, Englewood, New Jersey, New York State, USA, and nicknamed after his bright red hair. Guppy is a polite, dignified humourist whose raps mingle coy allusion without lapses into vulgar detail. After all, his mother is a serving member of the police force, and he refused to swear on his albums in case she hears the cussing. His career began when he hooked up with Gene Griffin's Sutra Records, via an introduction from his former camp counsellor. He determinedly set out his stall against B-boy culture, insisting instead on moral rectitude in all matters. If that seemed a little boring, then the message was rescued by his excellent breakthrough single, 'Do The Right Thing'. Although he has gone on to score several minor hits with songs like '3-2-1 Pump', he has yet to equal that moment of artistic and chart success. His backing band, the FBI (For Black Intelligence), consisted of DJ Wildstyle, Bo Roc, Lt. Squeak, Buzz and Poochie. The group later changed its name to Private Investigations.
● ALBUMS: *A Shade Of Red* (Virgin 1989)★★,

The Album With No Name (Virgin 1991)★★★, *React Like You Know* (Virgin 1993)★★★.

REDMAN

New Jersey-based rapper whose debut album broke the Top 50 of the US *Billboard* album charts, failing to get a UK release until much later in the year, after it had moved over 300,000 copies on home turf. Enshrining the new ethos of cannabis as the drug of choice ('How To Roll A Blunt'), there was also room for the traditional braggadacio ('Day Of Sooperman Lover', 'I'm A Bad'). As superb an album as it was, from the cover shot of the artist up to his elbows in blood onwards, many critics also noted it was a little close to EPMD. Not surprising considering that he was a member of their Hit Squad, alongside K-Solo and Das EFX, and that Erick Sermon had produced it. In fact Redman had spent two years living with the latter when both his parents chucked him out of their respective homes because he was 'selling drugs and shit'.
● ALBUMS: *Whut? Thee Album* (RAL 1992)★★★, *Dare Iz A Darkside* (Def Jam 1995)★★★, *Muddy Waters* (Def Jam 1996)★★★.

REECE, ALEX

b. London, England. One of the pioneers of drum 'n' bass and jungle, Reece's work has consistently demonstrated musical intelligence and dexterity in opposition to the common perception of the limitations of these genres. As a result he became one of the first jungle artists to be signed to a major label, Island Records subsidiary Blunted, in 1995. They faced considerable competition for his signature, a testament to the impact made by his early recordings for Goldie's Metalheadz label. His musical apprenticeship came as a sound engineer, and with savings of £2,000 from this work he set up his own home studio, using a sequencer and sampler in preference to computer-generated sounds. His first release, 'Basic Principles', sold 5,000 copies, and he contributed to several other projects by the Metalheadz collective. Probably his breakthrough release, however, was the scintillating 1995 track, 'Pulp Fiction'. His debut for Blunted, 'Feel The Sunshine', was released in November and reached number 67 in the UK charts. It was re-released early in 1996 with better distribution and reached number 26, selling 40,000 copies. Using clipped, sparse jazz rhythms in a warm, accessible manner, the single's success was attributed to Reece's ability to make drum 'n' bass music more accessible than the more frenetic work of Goldie or Photek, other artists working in similar territory. Another facet to set him apart from such peers was his preference for working in the studio rather than accepting lucrative disc jockeying commissions. His work as a remixer included commissions for Underworld's 'Ban Style' for Junior Boy's Own and Neneh Cherry's 'Woman' for Virgin Records. His second single for Blunted, 'Candles', was released in the summer of 1996 and brought further chart success.

● ALBUMS: *So Far* (Island 1996)★★★.

REEL 2 REAL

Featuring the antics of The Mad Stuntman (b. c.1969, Trinidad, West Indies), whose vocals towered over the house ragga breakthrough 'I Like To Move It'. A resident of Brooklyn, New York, since the age of nine, Stuntman took his name from the Lee Majors television series *The Fall Guy*. He met prolific producer Erick 'More' Morillo through a friend and the two combined on tracks for Strictly Rhythm which they never envisioned to be crossover material. They were proved emphatically wrong by the sustained sales of 'I Like To Move It', when it was licensed to Positiva in the UK. Its chart life was an erratic one, running a sequence of weekly positions which read 10, 12, 12, 10, 9, 7, 5, 8, 7, 7, boosted by a 40-date club tour - all this and the fact that at no stage was it playlisted by Radio 1 DJs. They followed up with 'Go On Move'.

● ALBUMS: *Move It* (Positiva 1994)★★★, *Reel 2 Remixed* (Postiva 1995)★★, *Are You Ready For Some More?* (Positiva 1996)★★.

REESE PROJECT

Along with Inner City, the Reese Project is the other regular home to Detroit techno guru Kevin Saunderson (b. Kevin Maurice Saunderson, 9 May 1964, Brooklyn, New York, the second syllable of his middle name provided the 'Reese'). He had relocated to Detroit at the age of 15, and was a proficient running back in college football until he became a DJ. His musical inspirations were his mother, a former member of the Marvelettes, and his brother, a road manager for rock bands. His first release would be 'Triangle Of Love' on Juan Atkins' Metroplex imprint, before breaking through with 'The Sound'. With techno in its infancy, Reese's 'Rock To The Beat' (1987) was a hugely influential, hypnotic marvel. His other

early releases came as either Reese or Reese Santonio (Saunderson with DJ Tone aka Antonio Eccles). The Reese Project was incorporated in 1991 to allow a venue for his more soul-inspired techno outings. It was specifically geared towards productions of around 120bpm (making it 'in tune' with the human heartbeat, and also, apparently, the abilities of his vocalists). However, as Saunderson recounts: 'The Reese Project is not about me, myself and I. It's not about indulging myself musically. It's my chance to take a back seat, and give the platform up to talented people who only need a break, but give back as much as they get'. The three main vocalists on the album - Raechel Kapp, LaTrece and Terence FM - who featured on the single 'I Believe' (Kapp taking the honours on 'Direct Me', LaTrece on 'So Deep'), are part of a family environment overseen by Saunderson's wife Ann, who also writes the words and melodies. They met after Saunderson recorded his first remix for Wee Girl Papa Rappers' 'Heat It Up' for Jive, where she formerly worked. 'I Believe' was one of two minor UK hits in 1992 (number 74), the other being 'The Colour Of Love' (with Kapp on vocals, number 52). A further single, 'Miracle Of Life', featured Kapp alongside Byron Stingily of Ten City. In furtherance of his ambitions to give Detroit musicians a chance, he also reactivated the KMS label to expose undiscovered talent. A new line-up of guest artists was recruited for the group's 1994 tour, though Kapp was retained after returning from having her child.

● ALBUMS: *Faith Hope And Clarity* (Network 1992)★★★, also issued as a double remix set in 1993).

REINFORCED RECORDS

This US hardcore label was begun in 1990 by Gus Lawrence, Mark, Dego, and Ian, who collectively record as 4 Hero. It was their debut, 'Mr Kirk's Nightmare', that opened the label's catalogue. After consistently innovative releases from Nebula II ('Seance'/'Atheama'), Manix ('Oblivion (Head In The Crowds)') and others from One II One and Basic Rhythm, the quartet were joined by a fifth member, former New York-based graffiti artist Goldie, who took on the A&R, Graphic Design and spokesperson roles. He had previously recorded as the Ajaz Project before his first outings on Reinforced as Rufige Cru. He is also behind the Metalheadz project. Other early releases on the label included material by Doc

Scott (as Nasty Habits - 'As Nasty As I Wanna Be'), Internal Affairs and Primary Sources. As with that other mainstay of hardcore music, Suburban Base, Reinforced recognize the contribution hip-hop and breakbeats have made to the foundation of the music. The label closely observed the shifts in techno during the 90s, being a staple source of 'darkside' hardcore in 1992. So too the arrival of ambient techno, or what they preferred to describe as 'a blues for the 90s kind of ambient', previewed on their continuing 'Enforcers' series of experimental EPs. These used newer signings AK47, Covert Operations, Peshay (Coventry's Neil Trix), Open Skies (Norwegian techno crew Bjorn Torske, Ole J Mjos and Rune Hindback) and Myserson, a Philadelphian import.

● ALBUMS: 4 Hero: *Parallel Universe* (Reinforced 1994)★★★, Various: *The Definition Of Hardcore* (Reinforced 1994)★★★.

RELATIVITY RECORDS

New York-based label which originally preached the word of rock guitar *à la* Joe Satriani and Steve Vai, initially as part of Important Record Distributors in 1979. Come the 80s and the label was licensing 'alternative' UK rock like the Cocteau Twins and Gene Loves Jezebel, while Sony purchased a 50% stake in the company in 1990. However, in 1991 the musical climate was changing, and president Barry Kobrin and his staff noted the commercial progress of rap and hip-hop records. Their first tentative signing was 2 Black 2 Strong, which never worked out. A&R chief Peter Kang was subsequently given a wider brief, and the company brought rap label Violator under their wing. The first successful release was Chi Ali's debut album in March 1992, which inspired confidence throughout the label with its 70,000 sales (in half the time it would have taken an established rock outfit to move that many copies). Together with its distribution company, Relativity Entertainment Distribution, the company then signed a deal in 1993 with Ruthless Records, and also established the new Lifestyle imprint. That effectively meant that under one company, HQ, there existed no less than three powerful hip-hop camps: Ruthless (Eazy E, Hoez With Attitude, Kokane, Blood Of Abraham, MC Ren), Violator (Fat Joe, Beatnuts, Chi Ali) and Lifestyle (Black Caesar). In addition, Relativity signed its first 'own brand' artist, Common Sense. Their biggest initial success came with Fat Joe's 'Flow Joe' single, a *Billboard* Rap number 1 hit.

RELOAD

UK band based in Yeovil, Somerset, featuring former DJ Mark Pritchard and one-time Aphex Twin collaborator Tony Middleton (the 'other' twin, who shares the same date of birth as Richard James). The duo also record under several different monikers including Global Communications, Link, E621 and Rebos. They have their own label, Evolution, though their debut album came via the Infonet imprint. Their work blends dark hardcore with ambient strains, augmented by multimedia presentations drawing in environmental sounds like the ticking of clocks. *A Collection Of Short Stories* arrived with a book of accompanying essays written by their friend Dominic Fripp. Some of the text was designed to be read in-sync with the music. Both Pritchard and Middleton actually draw on a strong musical devotion to the likes of Peter Gabriel, Jean-Michel Jarre and even the Smiths, as well as the more anticipated Detroit techno and Eurobeat. Their *Auto Reload* EP late in 1993 continued to cement their profile with the more demanding club-goers. In 1993 they signed with indie label Dedicated, for whom they had previously remixed the Cranes and Chapterhouse.

● ALBUMS: *A Collection Of Short Stories (Soundtracks Without Films)* (Infonet 1993)★★★. As Global Communications: *76:14* (Dedicated 1994)★★★.

RENEGADE SOUNDWAVE

London born and bred esoteric dance trio, whose recordings have been variously described as 'Dance-Noise-Terror' and 'Chas 'n' Dave with a beatbox'. The group originally consisted of three multi-faceted instrumentalists, Danny Briotett (ex-Mass), Carl Bonnie and Gary Asquith (ex-Rema Rema; Mass). 'We're a by-product of punk. It forged the way we think, though the sound is nothing to do with it.' Their first single, 'Kray Twins', emerged on Rhythm King Records, the sound of a television documentary set to a throbbing bass undertow. After the equally notorious 'Cocaine Sex' they switched to Mute Records because of the greater eclecticism of their catalogue. A series of dancefloor singles such as 'Biting My Nails' and 'Probably A Robbery' prefaced a debut album that included an unlikely cover version of the Beat's 'Can't Get Used To Losing You'. Their aggressive dancefloor attack was continued the same year with *In Dub*, on which 'Holgertron' made use of the theme music to BBC Television's *Doctor Who*. The group re-emerged in 1994 with another fine album, one of the tracks, 'Last Freedom Fighter', announcing that 'We've all been asleep for a very long time'. It was a welcome return, though Bonnie had long since left for a solo career. Briotett also worked alongside his wife, Linda X, as half of Planet X (who recorded the James Bond tribute 'I Won't Dance', and 'Once Upon A Dancefloor').

● ALBUMS: *Soundclash* (Mute 1990)★★, *In Dub* (Mute 1990)★★★, *HowYa Doin?* (Mute 1994)★★★, *The Next Chapter Of Dub* (Mute 1995)★★★.
● COMPILATIONS: *RSW 1987-1995* (Mute 1996)★★★.

REPHLEX RECORDS

Record label set up by the Aphex Twin and Grant Wilson-Claridge, a friend from school. The idea was to offer local Cornish DJs some new material to play, and the first releases were all the Aphex Twin under various guises; Caustic WIndow, Blue Calx etc. New signings, however, include the intriguing u-Ziq. Other artists signed for one-off or longer deals included Seefeel, Kosmic Kommando (eponymous debut EP) and Kinesthesia.

● ALBUMS: Various: *The Philosophy Of Sound And Machine* (Rephlex 1992)★★★★.

REPRAZENT

(see Size, Roni)

REPRESENT RECORDS

Collective rap troupe/record label formed in the early 90s, based in Nottingham, England. The group numbers four DJs and five rappers, who include label head and general spokesperson Parks. However, it was one of his fellow rapping crew, Mr 45, who first brought the label to the wider public's attention via his 'Radford (You Get Me)' cut on the *Ruffneck* EP. Also part of the operation is a soul band and a reggae artist, D-Link. The collective was set up on the back of an enterprise allowance grant, which allowed them to build their own DIY studio having previously recorded demo tapes on more primitive equipment. There is no connection between Represent and the well-regarded UK hip-hop fanzine of similar name.

REPUBLIC RECORDS

Record label founded by Ian 'Tommy' Tomlinson and David Lee (aka Joey Negro) in 1989, as a subsidiary of Rough Trade Records. Lee was in charge of A&R and released material by M-D-Emm, Blaze, Phaze II and Turntable Orchestra, some of which were actually Lee in disguise. As well as the occasional licensing agreement (notably Kym Mazelle), they pressed on with a catalogue of material distinguished by releases from the aforementioned M-D-Emm ('Can't Win For Losing') and Phaze II ('I Wanna Do It' and 'Burning To The Boogie').

RHYTHM INVENTION

Rhythm Invention are a UK duo of Nick Simpson and Richard Brown. Together they offered one of the better examples of the 'trance dance' formula, or deep house without the sexuality, or rave without the front running electronics. Their early singles 'Crunch' and 'I Can't Take It' caught the media's attention with their simple but irresistible percussion effects. Typically, their 1993 effort, 'Ad Infinitum', was fairly uneventful, but produced a tangible hypnotic effect.

● ALBUMS: *Inventures In Wonderland* (Warp 1993)★★.

RHYTHM KING RECORDS

One of the UK's largest and most successful mainstream dance labels, Rhythm King was an idea originally mooted in 1976 by two friends, Martin Heath and James Horrocks, who shared a love of Motown and soul music. An initial parent deal with a major was abandoned when that label refused to pay a minimal advance to licence an American track, 'Love Can't Turn Around'. They hooked up instead with Daniel Miller's highly successful independent label, Mute, who granted them the necessary artistic freedom and budget. One of their first signings was 3 Wise Men, arguably the first ever British rap group. Another notable early rapper, Schoolly D, was licensed from the US to their Flame subsidiary. Other signings included Chuck Brown and Gwen McCrae. The other subsidiary, Transglobal - was a disco-styled operation, which delivered a hit with Taffy's 'I Love My Radio'. It had been popular in clubs for several months before Transglobal gave it a stock release, their reward coming with a number 6 national chart success. 1987 was a quiet year for the label, though King Sun/D Moet's 'Hey

Love!' picked up lots of airplay (but few sales), and Shawnie G's 'Mission Impossible' and Denise Motto's 'Tell Jack', licensed from the *Chicago Jackbeat* compilations, kept things ticking over. It was 1988 before Rhythm King re-established itself with the Beatmasters' featuring the Cookie Crew's 'Rok Da House', which had ironically been a flop when released in its original version a year previously. It was at this point that Horrocks' growing dissatisfaction with the label's direction forced him to leave, going on to establish React Records. Undeterred, Adele Nozedar stepped in and new commercial heights were achieved with Bomb The Bass hitting number 5 in the charts, and S'Express (Mark Moore having originally brought Taffy, the Cookie Crew and Beatmasters to RK's attention) bringing them a first number 1 with 'Theme From S'Express' in the summer of 1988. This triumvirate of bands (S'Express, Bomb The Bass and the Beatmasters) continued their ascent throughout the year, both in albums and singles sales. The 1989 signings were a less viable crop, however. Rapper Merlin, who had originally appeared on Bomb The Bass's 'Megaton', proved a disappointment, as did Hotline, a house duo from Huddersfield. The saving grace was Baby Ford, who provided a run of hits, while the label expanded in opening the Outer Rhythm subsidiary, ostensibly to license tracks. Their major success of the 90s would prove to be D:Ream, though other artists included bhangra house duo Joi, industrial dance groups KMFDM and Sheep On Drugs, and indie pop outfit Sultans Of Ping.
● ALBUMS: Bomb The Bass: *Into The Dragon* (Rhythm King 1988)★★★★. S'Express: *Original Soundtrack* (Rhythm King 1989)★★★.
Beatmasters: *Anywayawanna* (Rhythm King 1989)★★★. Baby Ford: *Ooo The World Of Baby Ford* (Rhythm King 1990)★★★. D:Ream: *Dream On Vol. 1* (Rhythm King 1993)★★★.

RHYTHM SAINTS

The Rhythm Saints collective are the creation of Los Angeles, California, USA house producer/remixer Stephen Nixon. Though he is responsible for songwriting, the group also includes several singers, such as Shade, Mike Heath and J. Philip Gillespie. The Rhythm Saints' debut album, *Deep Sustained Booming Sounds*, was released in 1994, and was followed a year later by the critically acclaimed *Golden*. Both explored Chicago and New York house traditions in an energetic style, with lyrics written with much

greater dexterity than is the norm for dance records. Nixon and the Rhythm Saints' ability to sustain themselves over a full album also distinguished them from their more singles-orientated peers, causing *Billboard* writer Larry Flick to advise readers to 'lose yourself in some of the best dance music you will hear this season.'
● ALBUMS: *Deep Sustained Booming Sounds* (N'Soul/Velocity 1994)★★★, *Golden* (N'Soul/Velocity 1995)★★★★.

RHYTHMATIC

Based in Nottingham, England, this 'old school'-modelled house music group released their debut single, 'Nu-Groove', for Network Records in early 1992. It achieved a degree of notoriety by employing a sample taken from the film *The Angel Who Porned Her Harp*. Half of the act was Mark Gamble alongside Mark Ryder; Leroy Crawford was a further contributor. Another single, 'Energy On Vinyl', in 1992 (as Rhythmatic[2]), was followed by *Splat! What A Beautiful Noise*, which proved less popular than expected.
● ALBUMS: *Splat! What A Beautiful Noise* (Network 1992)★★.

RISING HIGH COLLECTIVE

Namely one Casper Pound (b. *c*.1970), of The Hypnotist fame, and also the man who formed Rising High Records, and vocalist Plavka (b. Los Angeles, California, USA). Pound's ancestry extends to spells in A Homeboy, A Hippie, And A Funki Dred, before he found Top 75 success no less than seven times in his own right, and also navigated three Top 40 remixes into the charts, including the Shamen's number 1, 'Progen'. Plavka came to fame via the former group, gracing their first Top 30 cut, 'Hyperreal'. She came to London in 1989, immersing herself in the rave scene and passing herself off as a journalist in order to make the acquaintance of the Shamen. After they broke through together she quit the group to concentrate on projects where she could have more input into the songwriting, in addition to her much-admired operatic soprano range. She met Pound in 1991, the duo releasing their first single, 'Fever Called Love', in December of that year, for R&S. It was a stunning cut, above and beyond the novelty value of hearing a genuine techno track with genuine vocals. It was not until the summer of 1993 and a Hardfloor remix that the song really took off, however. After slightly misfiring with 'Reach', which was nevertheless a minor hit, 'There's No Deeper Love' (whose lyrics quietly provided a text on astrology and the formation of the universe) proved another club hit, this time with the progressive house faction. They made an acclaimed appearance at the 1993 Reading Festival, as well as many PAs at venues like the Ministry Of Sound, Heaven and Camden Palace. 1994's *Liquid Thoughts* EP provided further well-received slices of deep trance. They additionally recorded together as Dominatrix (two EPs, *Possession* and *Discipline*) while Plavka released a solo single, 'Maximum Motion' (all on Rising High or their Ascension/Sappho subsidiaries), and guested for Jam And Spoon ('Right In The Middle').

RISING HIGH RECORDS

Record label founded in London, England, in February 1991 by Casper Pound, initially as an outlet for his own material, having recently disengaged from chart act A Homeboy, A Hippie And A Funki Dred. Having spent time living in Italy he returned to England bluffing his way into studio work with reggae producer Mad Professor and hi-NRG man Ian Levine. Soon he had learned enough to give his own operation a shot. Since its inception (the honour of first release going to Pound as The Hypnotist, with 'Rainbows In The Sky'), the label has grown to be much more than an inventive young man's hobby. Rising High has been at the forefront, if not beyond it, in all of the major developments of dance music in the 90s. Pound has developed a second sense in recognising or anticipating trends such as jungle/breakbeat, trance and finally ambient. Their early hardcore techno is best sampled on Aural Assault, Earth Leakage Trip and Project One releases. As Pound asserted, unrepentantly, at the time: 'I like nosebleed techno, the more nosebleedy the better'. A good example was Earth Leakage Trip's techno rave anthems on the *Neopolitan* EP, which featured the improbably bombastic 'The Ice Cream Van From Hell' - a furious rhythm track anchored by coy samples. A regular feature of the label has been the artistic growth of Mixmaster Morris (aka the Irresistable Force). After making his debut for the label with 'Space Is The Place' his recordings have continued to be a prominent fixture of Rising High's release schedule. As Rising High has grown it has spawned its own subsidiary imprints. Sappho (specialising in the harder, experimental end of the techno spectrum, set up in conjunction with RH A&R scout Pypee) and Ascension. They also brought the exciting sounds being developed in Germany at Harthouse/Eye Q via a link-up as Harthouse UK (earning significant kudos for giving the British public Hardfloor's 'Hardtrance Acperience'). Yet Rising High has also retained an endearing self-mockery and unfettered approach to dance music. Their slogans: 'You're going home in a fuckin' ambience', or Mixmaster Morris' 'I Think Therefore I Ambient' notwithstanding. Most of 1993/94's innovations were in the latter sector, flooding the market with a noble array of compilations such as *Chill Out Or Die* and *Definitive Ambient Collection* - the former specially packaged by Mixmaster Morris, the latter by German ambient meister Peter Namlock. That duo also recorded together for the label under the title Dreamfish.

● ALBUMS: Various: *Techno Anthems Vol. 1 & 2* (Rising High 1991)★★★★, *Chill Out Or Die 1 & 2* (Rising High 1993)★★★, *Secret Life Of Trance 1, 2 & 3* (Rising High 1994)★★★. The Hypnotist: *The Complete Hypnotist* (Rising High 1992)★★★. Peter Namlook & Mixmaster Morris: *Dreamfish* (Rising High 1993)★★★.

RME

The acronym standing for Rhymes Made Easy, the Birmingham, West Midlands, England trio RME comprise rappers Coolski and Scraggs alongside their DJ, DME. Of gastronomic as well as musical dexterity - they all met while chefs at a Cajun restaurant - the group unveiled their debut single in 1994. 'On A Jazz Tip', though well-received by critics, was only slightly representative of their more usual hardcore rap fare. It made an easy fit, however, with the vogueish discourse then prevalent between the rap and jazz communities.

ROB BASE AND DJ E-Z ROCK

Light-hearted, New York-based rap unit distinctive through its exploration of musical genres, and an aversion to speech-only raps. Samples and lifts from Motown, James Brown (paricularly on the latter's production of Lyn Collins' 'Think (About It)', which gave them a breakthrough hit in 1988 with 'It Takes Two') and others set the tone for the duo, while Base's lyrics, although tending to highlight his romantic prowess, do so in a way which doesn't reach the listener as egotistical. He got into trouble for sampling Maze's 'Joy And Pain',

however, when he neglected to credit its source. Base (b. Robert Ginyard, Harlem, New York) jettisoned DJ E-Z Rock (b. Rodney Bryce, Harlem, New York) in time for his second album, which this time round hoisted choruses from Marvin Gaye, Edwin Starr and even native American rock band, Redbone. The most effective slice of the action was a reworking of Starr's classic 'War' cut.
● ALBUMS: *It Takes Two* (Profile 1988)★★★. As Rob Base: *The Incredible Base* (Profile 1989)★★.

ROB'S RECORDS

This Manchester-based label was set up by Rob Gretton, the manager of New Order, in 1990. Their first release was the Beat Club's 'Security' in November of that year, which was followed by singles from A Certain Ratio, Anambi and Sub Sub. Their biggest success came when Sub Sub's second single, 'Ain't No Love, Ain't No Use' (which featured the singer Melanie Williams), reached number 2 in the UK charts in 1992. Since then they have continued to release material by these and other artists. The subsidiary label Pleasure was set up to concentrate on electronica, including artists such as Mr Scruff and Strangebrew, while Manchester Records focused on guitar bands.

ROBERTS, JOE

Roberts is a Manchester-based soul-dance vocalist, and an ex-mod who was brought up in a commune (when his parents moved from London to Karling in Norfolk, his father switching jobs from economist to carpenter). This background can be gauged in his lyrics, which come heavily laden with 'peace and love' metaphors, but also reflect the early influence of Sly Stone, Al Green and Marvin Gaye, who were introduced to him by later collaborator Eric Gooden. He had also learned the piano from the age of eight, and this was reflected in the musicianship of his club music. After moving to Manchester in 1981, he became a member of local covers band the Risk, who eventually used Roberts' own songs. He hit sprightly single form on cuts such as 'Love Is Energy' - recorded with the aforementioned Gooden, whom he had met at college, and is his current songwriting partner - and 'Back In My Life'.
● ALBUMS: *Looking For The Here And Now* (London 1994)★★★.

ROBERTS, JULIET

The term house diva does not fully cover the career or capabilities of Juliet Roberts, who is in addition a proficient singer-songwriter, and a veteran of the early days of British soul. Unlike many in the field, she did not learn her craft at the church choir, having instead been brought up in the more restrained Catholic faith. However, music was still in her blood. Her father was formerly a member of the calypso band the Nightingales, and took her to various concerts. Her first performances came as a member of reggae band Black Jade, before she signed solo to Bluebird Records in 1980, a label set up by her local record shop in Paddington, north London. Two tracks, a cover version of the Police's 'The Bed's Too Big Without You' and 'Fool For You', emerged, while she was still engaged in her day job as a sports tutor. They were enough to attract the attention of fellow Londoners the Funk Masters. She appeared as lead singer on their Top 10 hit 'It's Over', in 1983. After a year's sabbatical in the USA she embarked on her music career proper, and, within a week of returning to British shores, was enlisted as singer for Latin jazz band Working Week. When that group floundered (after several noble releases), she finally signed to Cooltempo as a solo artist.
● ALBUMS: *Natural Thing* (Cooltempo 1994)★★★.

ROBERTSON, JUSTIN

Robertson (b. 1968) is a UK songwriter, producer and remixer who has worked on tracks by the likes of Talk Talk ('Dum Dum Girl') Yargo ('Love Revolution') Finitribe ('Forevergreen'), Erasure ('Snappy'), React 2 Rhythm ('Intoxication'), Inspiral Carpets ('Caravan And Skidoo'), Shamen ('Boss Drum'), Coco Steel & Lovebomb ('Feel It'), Gary Clail ('These Things Are Worth Fighting For'), Sugarcubes ('Birthday' and 'Motorcrash'), Happy Mondays ('Sunshine And Love') and the rather less-celebrated Candy Flip ('Red Hills Road'). He was even asked to do his thing for the Fall. On his remixing ethos: 'With me its always a case of to butcher or not to butcher. Usually its the former'. His first remix was actually housed on Eastern Bloc's Creed operation (Mad Jacks' 'Feel The Hit'), and he is one of a number of famous people to have staffed that record shop's counters. He started DJing while at Manchester University, playing parties because, more or less, he had the best record collection. It was through his purchases at Eastern Bloc that he eventually landed a job there (establishing the Spice club with fellow internee, Greg Fenton). Robertson is now the motivating force behind hip Manchester outfit Lionrock, who specialise in warm, uplifting house. The group's singles include 'Packet Of Peace' (which cracked the charts and featured a rap from MC Buzz B) and 'Carnival' in 1993, which again collared numerous Single Of The Week awards. The band's full line-up has included Roger Lyons (keyboards/electronics), Paddy (bass), Mandy Whigby (keyboards) and Mark Stagg (keyboards). Robertson was also behind the label which housed Lionrock's first record, MERC. This was formed with Ross McKenzie, and stood for Most Excellent Record Company. Other releases included Life Eternal's 'Come Into The Light' and Dub Federation's 'Space Funk' and 'Love Inferno' releases, prior to that group splitting in 1994. Robertson later abdicated much of his responsibility for the imprint, signing to DeConstruction as a solo artist. In the mid-90s he toured with Primal Scream.

ROCK, PETE

One of rap's most respected producers, only Marley Marl is ahead of him on the quality/quantity thresholds. It was the latter that introduced Pete Rock to the world via his WBLS *Marley Marl In Control Show* in 1989. Rock has gone on to work with everyone from forerunners Heavy D (his cousin), Slick Rick, EPMD and Run DMC (including their first single, 'Down With The King') to new talents in the shape of Lords Of The Underground (actually offering vocals on their 'Flow On') Nas and K-Solo. Other projects include his soundtrack work on *Who's The Man* and *Menace II Society*. His remix roster is almost as impressive, with engagements with Brand Nubian, Public Enemy, House Of Pain, Das EFX, Father and non-rap artists like Shabba Ranks and Johnny Gill. Based in Mount Vernon, New York, he went on to join with C.L. Smooth for a release under his own name. The album housed the hit single (US 48) 'They Reminisce Over You (T.R.O.Y.)'. He also put together the Untouchables producer network/umbrella organisation for the activities of himself and co-conspirators Eddie F, Dave Hall and Nevelle Hodge.
● ALBUMS: With C.L. Smooth: *Mecca & The Soul Brother* (Elektra 1992)★★★. *The Main Ingredients* (Elektra 1994)★★★.

ROCKSTEADY CREW

These US-based breakdance/hip-hop pioneers of the 80s were led by the celebrated Crazy Legs (b. Richie Colon) - one of the earliest examples of Latin influence in the hip-hop genre - and Frosty Freeze (b. Wayne Frost). When B-boys first embraced 'The Freak' craze (inspired by Chic's song of the same title), the Rocksteady Crew stayed true to their origins and became the most successful and widely respected of the breakdancers. They dealt firmly in old school hip-hop culture which included grafitti, breakdancing, and tongue-twisting, call and response rhymes. They were as much acrobats as dancers, displaying their wares in Central Park alongside competing crews like the Incredible Breakers, Magnificent Force and U.T.F.O. As breakdancing evolved they threw new shapes, enlisting the developing cultures of dance, including moonwalking, bodypopping and robotics. Displaying a combination of the latter they were committed to celluloid history via a scene in the 1983 dance movie, *Flashdance*. They were also a huge influence on other crews, the Kaliphz being just one of the hip-hop groups formed after seeing them perform.
● ALBUMS: *Ready For Battle* (Charisma 1984)★★★.

RODNEY O AND JOE COOLEY

Street-orientated duo who, having lacked adequate repayment on their first three albums (each of which sold 200,000 copies), elected to go it alone on the fourth, *Fuck New York*. They had to sell their cars and possessions to get it done, but they were confident of a return having taken control of the means of production. On that album's provocative title, Rodney elaborates: 'The crux of the LP is about the people who are ripping off New York rap fans. It speaks about the reluctance of some New York people to break a West Coast artist because they feel that rap started in New York'. It was hardly the most diplomatic way to introduce themselves to East Coast hip-hop fans, however.
● ALBUMS: *Fuck New York* (Psychotic Records 1993)★★★.

ROGERS, CE CE

b. Kenny Rogers. The gentle giant from Cleveland, Ohio, Rogers is not actually a house artist *per se*, but certainly his records for Atlantic made him a hallowed name in those circles.

'Someday' sold over 100,000 copies on import before his record company finally had the good sense to release it in England as the b-side to 'Forever'. 'Someday' quickly became a house classic and was subsequently remixed and remodelled. It formed the basis for rave anthems like Liquid's 'Sweet Harmony' and Urban Shakedown's 'Some Justice', among others. Ironically, when Marshall Jefferson first brought him 'Someday' the artist himself had little faith in it. Rogers was born the son of a music teacher, alongside three brothers and sisters, and was raised on a diet of gospel and soul. It was certainly a musical family. His rapping brother Marcski signed to CBS, while his sister Sonia is a backing vocalist (for Intense among others). Before Rogers left school he toured with the Jazz Messengers, before meeting up with the likes of Branford Marsalis at Berkeley. From there he moved to New York, where Marshall Jefferson spotted him in a club leading Ce Ce And Company (who included subsequent solo artist Sybil). It was Jefferson who introduced him to Atlantic Records at the age of 25. Following 'Someday' his other great moment came with 'All Join Hands', again later re-released, this time on East West. It came with a David Morales remix, and was a second all-consuming, passionate, pure house affair.
● ALBUMS: *Ce Ce Rogers* (Atlantic 1989)★★.

ROLLO

One of the pre-eminent producers in UK house music, Rollo's work is distinguished by his eclectic sources. In 1991 he set up the label Cheeky Records and the following year released two singles on which he had worked, Gloworm's 'Lift My Cup' and Franke's 'Understand This Groove'. However, it was Felix's 'Don't You Want Me' (DeConstruction Records, 1992) that established his name at the forefront of the house scene, eventually selling 2,500,000 copies worldwide. The following year he began remixing for artists as diverse as the Pet Shop Boys, Gabrielle, M People, the Wonderstuff and the footballer Ian Wright, as well as producing singles by Our Tribe ('I Believe In You') and High On Love ('In My World'). In 1994 he was even more prolific, remixing for Raze and U2 among others, and producing for Kristine W., Gloworm and Our Tribe. Most significant of that year's activities was his work on two singles by the DJ Sister Bliss, 'Life's A Bitch' and 'Oh What A World', who subsequently joined Rollo as part of Faithless.

RON C

b. Ronald Pierre Carey, Oakland, California, USA. Rapper Carey moved to Dallas at the age of 17. However, by the spring of 1990 he anticipated gangsta's rap's flirtation with unlawfulness by being convicted of 'Possession of a controlled dangerous substance with intent', ensuring an unseemly hiatus in his recording career.
● ALBUMS: *'C' Ya* (Profile 1990)★★★, *Back On The Street* (Profile 1992)★★★.

RONIN RECORDS

Taking its name from an ancient term for a Samurai warrior who has elected to go 'solo', UK label/artist collective Ronin Records is made up of various members of the musical tribe which formerly travelled under the name 23 Skidoo. In the early 90s the line-up included the pseudonymous Alex Baby, Sketch, Johnny 2 Bad, Fritz C, Agzi and the DJing team of Force And K-Zee. The latter, as well as running their own clubs and recording music for adverts and jingles, are also well known for their contributions to the UK hip-hop culture (including the *X Amount* EP for Ronin). Based in London, Ronin have their own studio complex cum living quarters. The participants have produced an admirable body of work on their own imprint, which began with Ronin Inc's 'Soul Feels Free'. The same name was employed for 'On Tha Mix', while other affiliated artists include Paradox ('Jailbreak'), Bahal And Nal Street Gang ('Summer Breeze'), International Stussy Tribe Force ('Pure Power') and Normski ('Rockin' On The Dancefloor').

ROOTS

Philadephia-based rap crew comprising rapper Tariq Trotter (aka Black Thought), rapper Malik B, bass player Hob and drummer Ahmir Thompson. Specialising in old school freestyling, many comparisons to Digable Planets or Gang Starr's jazz-flavoured hip-hop followed the release of their debut mini-album. However, the Roots are more of a self-contained musical unit, relying on their own talents rather than samples or session musicians. The band was started in 1987 when Trotter and Ahmir were students at Philadelphia High School For The Performing Arts. They learned to earn a crust on the busking circuit, until their manager arranged a European tour for them. They were spotted by Geffen while playing in Germany, who signed the group (for the US,

Talkin' Loud taking responsibility for the UK). A second long playing set, *Do You Want More*, featured top jazz guests plus the Roots' own rap protégés, the Foreign Objects.

● ALBUMS: *From The Ground Up* mini album (Geffen 1994)★★★, *Do You Want More* (Geffen 1994)★★★★, *illadelph halflife* (DGC 1996)★★★.

Roxanne Shanté

b. Lolita Shanté Gooden, 9 November 1969, Queens, New York, USA. Shanté came to prominence at the tender age of 14 via her belated answer record to U.T.F.O.'s 1984 rap hit, 'Roxanne, Roxanne'. Gooden was walking outside a New York housing project when she overheard three men discussing U.T.F.O.'s cancellation of a show they were promoting. In turn Gooden offered them a reply record. The onlookers, DJ Mister Magic, Tyrone Williams and Marley Marl, took her up on the offer. Her version, 'Roxanne's Revenge', mixed sassy, indignant raps with a funky backbeat. It was a massive hit, which sold over a quarter of a million copies in the New York area alone, and spawned a flood of answerback records (well over a hundred at the final count), as rappers queued to take up the challenge. U.T.F.O. replied by suing her for using their b-side as the rhythm track. Shanté was still only 14 years old, and forced to stay away from school because of all the attention. Her arrival was cemented by further singles 'Have A Nice Day' and 'Go On Girl', produced by Marley Marl, with lyrics penned by Big Daddy Kane. Her debut album saw the conscious rhymes of songs like 'Independent Woman' (though it was written for her by a man) spliced by saucy narratives like 'Feelin' Kinda Horny'. By 1986, Shanté was being edged from the centre of the female rap stage by The Real Roxanne (Adelaida Martinez) and her turntable wizard Hitman Howie Tee. Perhaps her most infamous post-'Roxanne' moment came with the release of 'Big Mama', which would see her take out her frustrations by dissing other female rappers Queen Latifah, MC Lyte, Yo Yo and Monie Love.

● ALBUMS: *Roxanne's Revenge* (Pop Art 1987)★★★, *Bad Sister* (Cold Chillin' 1989)★★★, *The Bitch Is Back* (Livin' Large 1992)★★.

Roz

b. *c.*1972, Bronx, New York, USA. After a youth spent singing in school and church choirs, and a course in classical music at New York's Mannes College, Roz broke through in 1994 with what she

described as 'sassy hop'. She had originally come to prominence in hip-hop circles when D-Nice invited her to sing on 'Get In Touch With Me', from his *To The Rescue* album. After this D-Nice agreed to make his rapping skills available for Roz's debut single, 'A Yo Ah'lte (Hey Yo Alright)'. This track, originally based on another song, 'So What', was created in the studio with producer Carl Bourelly, after he invited the singer to introduce some chants - the resulting 'Aaa-Yo's' being so distinctive they gave the track its title. Roz subsequently wrote the rest of the song around that hookline. It was Bourelly who first discovered the young singer at a local nightclub, before launching her on the session-singing market. She had already recorded as backing vocalist for Dannii Minogue, the Hi-Five and Melissa Morgan, and toured with Monie Love, before she embarked on her solo career.

Rozalla

Zambian born rave queen, whose singles like 'Are You Ready To Fly?' were surefire dancefloor meteorites. She began life singing over records at fashion shows and nightclubs at age 13. She then performed with a band in Zimbabwe, going on to become that nation's most famous famale singer. At the age of 18 she appeared as an extra (a prostitute) in Richard Chamberlain's *King Solomon's Mines*. Despite parental misgivings, she subsequently launched a recording career in England. Singles like 'Everybody's Free To Feel Good' (created by 3 Man Island/Band Of Gypsies duo Nigel Swanston and Tim Cox) duly apeared on Pulse 8, who released her debut ablum. This came after something of a legal squabble, with Rozalla attempting to take the studio tapes to Epic. Pulse 8 objected and won their day in court.

● ALBUMS: *Everybody's Free* (Pulse 8 1992)★★★, *Look No Further* (Epic 1995)★★★.

RPM

This Brighton, Sussex, England-based 'trip-hop' trio comprise Stefan, AJ (aka Adjaye) and Joe. Signed to James Lavelle's Mo Wax Records in 1993, they played a large part in popularising both the label and what became known in the UK press as trip-hop or ambient hip-hop. They made their debut with the smooth single, '2,000', which utilised a vibraphone to add musical texture. Allied to their long-standing jazz influences (John Coltrane, Miles Davis), plus samples from the Apollo space flights and electronic loops, the finished product added up to an aurally arresting and unusual musical vision.

RUFFHOUSE

Columbia's rap subsidiary, home to Joe 'The Butcher', which enjoys a primarily hardcore roster, including Cypress Hill, Tim Dog and Nas, though the A&R policy did extend to offering contracts to artists with strong commercial potential like Kriss Kross and the Goats. In 1994 they picked up on the then-homeless Schoolly D.

RUMBLE

This Toronto, Canada-based rapper, signed to the UK label Gee Street Records, made his debut with 'Safe', a smooth blend of R&B and laid-back rhymes. His second effort, 'Tuff', was promoted with a highly regarded remix version by DJ Muggs (Cypress Hill). This time the rhythms and beats were more animated, in an effort to demonstrate the span of Rumble's abilities. His debut album was recorded in Kingston, Jamaica (at Junior Reid's One Blood Studios) and London, New York and Toronto, a geographic diversity which was reflected in the finished product. Sadly the self-titled debut failed to sell in significant quantities outside of the Canadian market.

● ALBUMS: *Rumble* (Gee Street 1994)★★★.

RUN DMC

New York rappers Joe Simmons (b. 24 November 1966, New York, USA; the brother of Russell Simmons, their Rush Management boss), Darryl 'DMC' McDaniels (b. 31 May 1964, New York, USA) and DJ 'Jam Master Jay' (b. Jason Mizell, 1965, New York, USA) originally came together as Orange Crush in the early 80s, becoming Run DMC in 1982 after graduating from St. Pascal's Catholic School. They had known each other as children in Hollis, New York, Mizell and McDaniels even attending the same kindergarten. After circulating demos the group signed to Profile Records for an advance of $2,500, immediately scoring a US underground hit with 'It's Like That'. However, it was the single's b-side, 'Sucker MCs', which created the stir. It single-handedly gave birth to one of rap's most prevalent terms, and almost became a genre in its own right. Many critics signpost the single as the birth of modern hip-hop, with its stripped down sound (no instruments apart from a drum machine and scratching from a turntable, plus the fashion image of the B-boy: street clothing, chiefly sportswear, and street

language). In the wake of the single's success their debut album went gold in 1984, the first time the honour had been bestowed upon a rap act. They cemented their position as hip-hop's men of the moment with furious touring, and appearances on the *Krush Groove* film, a fictionalised account of the life of Russell Simmons, who was now joint-head of Def Jam with Rick Rubin. They also took a hand at the prestigious King Holliday (a Martin Luther King tribute) and Sun City (Artists Against Apartheid) events. They broke further into the mainstream on both sides of the Atlantic in 1986 when, via Rubin's auspices, they released the heavy metal/rap collision 'Walk This Way' (featuring Steve Tyler and Joe Perry of Aerosmith). Its disinctive video caught the imagination of audiences on both sides of the Atlantic. The partnership had been predicted by earlier singles, 'Rock Box' and 'King Of Rock', both of which fused rap with rock. By 1987 *Raisin' Hell* had sold three million copies in the US, becoming the first rap album to hit the R&B number 1 mark, the first to enter the US Top 10, and the first to go platinum. Run DMC also became the first rap group to have a video screened by MTV, the first to feature on the cover of *Rolling Stone*, and the first non-athletes to endorse Adidas products (a sponsorship deal which followed rather than preceded their 'My Adidas' track). Sadly, a projected collaboration with Michael Jackson never took place, though they did duet with Joan Rivers on her television show, and held street seminars to discuss inter-gang violence. Subsequent efforts have been disappointing, although both *Tougher Than Leather* and *Back From Hell* contained a few tough-like-the-old-times tracks ('Beats To The Ryhme', 'Pause' etc.) among the fillers. The former album was tied to a disastrous film project of similar title. In the 90s Daniels and Simmons experienced religious conversion, after the former succumbed to alcoholism and the the the latter was falsely accused of rape in Cleveland. Singles continued to emerge sporadically, notably 'What's It All About', which even sampled the Stone Roses. Despite an obvious effort to make *Down With The King* their major comeback album, with production assistance offered by Pete Rock, EPMD, the Bomb Squad, Naughty By Nature, A Tribe Called Quest, even Rage Against The Machine, and guest appearances from KRS-1 and Neneh Cherry, it was hard to shake the view of Run DMC as a once potent, now spent force. Unsurprisingly, this was not their own outlook, as

Simmons was keen to point out: 'The Run DMC story is an exciting story. It's a true legend, its the sort of life you want to read about'. True to form, they enjoyed an unexpected UK chart topper in 1998 with a Jason Nevins remix of 'It's Like That', originally on their 1984 debut.

● ALBUMS: *Run DMC* (Profile 1984)★★★★, *King Of Rock* (Profile 1985)★★★★, *Raising Hell* (Profile 1986)★★★★, *Tougher Than Leather* (Profile 1988)★★★, *Back From Hell* (Profile 1990)★★★, *Down With The King* (Profile 1993)★★★.

● COMPILATIONS: *Together Forever: Greatest Hits 1983-1991* (Profile 1991)★★★★, *Together Forever: Greatest Hits 1983-1998* (Profile 1998)★★★★.

● FURTHER READING: *Run DMC*, B. Adler.

RUTHLESS RAP ASSASSINS

Manchester, England-based, and self-styled 'North Hulme' soundsculptors comprising Dangerous 'C' Carsonova (vocals, turntables), MC Kermit Le Freak (vocals) and Paul Roberts (guitar). Ruthless Rap Assassins formed in that district in the mid-80s, earning their reputation via local gigs. They were signed by EMI in 1987 after they had heard their debut single, 'We Don't Care'. Placed on the Syncopate subsidiary, the first result was the *Killer Album*, whose 'Go Wild' effectively sampled Steppenwolf's 'Born To Be Wild'. Even better was 'The Dream', which utilised the funked up groove of Cynade's 'The Message' to underpin this tale of West Indians moving to England in the 50s, and the subsequent dashing of their hopes and spirits. The militant aesthetics of *Killer Album* came as something of a shock to those who still considered such daunting music the preserve of inner-city Americans. The follow-up selection, however, cut much deeper. Tracks like 'Down And Dirty' proved an effective parody of rap's pre-occupation with matters sexual, while 'No Tale, No Twist' observed some clever jazz touches. The group remained inventive and militant, the single 'Justice (Just Us)', proving a particularly defiant swipe at the majority white populace. Though they split afterwards due to record label and public indifference, the Ruthless Rap Assassins' legacy as the first worthwhile UK hip-hop band remains.

● ALBUMS: *Killer Album* (Syncopate 1990)★★★★, *Think - It Ain't Illegal Yet* (Murdertone 1991)★★★.

RUTHLESS RECORDS

This record label, formed by Eazy E in 1987, was by legend founded on profits from its proprietor's illegal activities. Certainly its early output reflected Eazy E's underworld origins, with the accent firmly on hardcore hip-hop artists (although he also signed a number of R&B acts including prototype swingbeat singer Michel'le and JJ Fad). Ruthless subsequently became the first home to the 'gangsta rap' phenomenon - the controversial hip-hop form pioneered by Eazy E's own group, NWA, on their *Straight Outta Compton* debut. This multi-million-seller's volatile, anti-establishment lyrics established the blueprint for a whole generation of hardcore rappers. A hitch came when in-house producer Dr. Dre, so central to much of the label's success (which at the time included nine gold albums), left in bitter acrimony in the early 90s. The public slanging match between Eazy E and general manager Jerry Holler did not abate until Dre persuaded Jimmy Iovine at Interscope to let him set up his own label, Death Row Records. In 1993 Relativity Records stepped in to bring Ruthless, whose coterie of artists now included Hoez With Attitude, Kokane, Blood Of Abraham and MC Ren, under their wing, after the original contract with Priority Records had expired. Post-Dre, the label's fortunes dipped, and it was a non-hip-hop act, the R&B group Bone Thugs-N-Harmony, who delivered their major successes of the mid-90s. Following Eazy E's death in March 1995 his wife, Tomica Woods-Wright, took over the label. The roster now includes long-standing associates JJ Fad, Michel'le, Above The Law, MC Ren and D.O.C., plus newer artists such as Blulight and N/X (Nation Unknown). Woods-Wright, the subject of some controversy herself as heir to the disputed Ruthless throne, secured a new distribution agreement with Epic Records in 1997 Some key albums include; JJ Fad *Supersonic* (Ruthless 1988), Eazy E *Eazy-Duz-It* (Ruthless 1989), NWA *Straight Outta Compton* (Ruthless 1989), D.O.C. *No One Can Do It Better* (Ruthless 1989), NWA *Efil4zaggin* (Ruthless 1991), MC Ren *Kiss My Black Azz* (Ruthless 1992), Above The Law *V.S.O.P.* (Ruthless 1993) and Bone Thugs-N-Harmony *E. 1999 Eternal* (Ruthless 1995).

RZA

b. Bobby Steels, USA. Considered by many to be rap's most proficient producer since Dr Dre, by

1995 RZA was balancing a solo career alongside work with the Wu-Tang Clan and Gravediggaz (as Prince Rakeem). Unlike Dre, whose reliance on George Clinton samples prefigured a myriad of artists employing ritual 'G-Funk' backing, RZA's minimalist approach recalls the work of Public Enemy's Bomb Squad. While Public Enemy's work is more politicised, RZA and his colleagues prefer to draw on religious elements, martial arts and inter-gang rivalry. As manager as well as producer of the Wu-Tang Clan, RZA has effectively set this agenda, writing and recording at a furious pace from his own basement studio. As a producer he made a massive impact with his work on the Wu-Tang Clan's landmark *Enter The Wu-Tang Clan: 36 Chambers*, before producing several projects involving members of that band. The first was Method Man's *Tical*, then Raekwon The Chief featuring Tony Starks' 'Only Built For Cuban Linx..' single. He has also worked with Wu-Tang Clan affiliate Shyheim The Rugged Child and produced tracks for Tricky, Cypress Hill and Shaquille O'Neal, as well as remixes for Supercat and SWV. At the end of 1995 he combined with his cousin Genius for the jointly-credited *Liquid Swords*, which made its debut at number 9 in the *Billboard* album charts.

● ALBUMS: with Genius *Liquid Swords* (Geffen 1996)★★★★.

S'EXPRESS

Home to Mark Moore (b. 12 January 1966, London, England), who was arguably the best British interpreter of the late 80s Italo-house phenomenon. Moore is half-Korean, though his early claims that he had a twin brother in that nation's army were spurious. More factual were the revelations that he was put into care at the age of nine, when his mother had a breakdown. As a youth he ligged outside Siouxsie And The Banshees gigs begging 10-pence pieces to get in. After the punk explosion, he made his name on the domestic DJ circuit, notably the Mud Club. He broke through with a series of singles that combined Euro-pop stylings with a hard funk spine: 'Theme From S'Express', 'Superfly Guy', 'Hey Music Lover' and 'Mantra For A State Of Mind' among them. Afterwards, the chart action dissipated somewhat. 'Nothing To Lose', ironically one of his strongest singles, stalled at number 32, as dance music upped a gear and discovered hardcore. Moore set up the Splish label, through Rhythm King, in the early 90s, opening with Canadian-born singer Tiziana's 'Seduce Me' and Yolanda's 'Living For The Nite', licensed from Underground Resistance. Former S'Express vocalist Linda Love would go on to record with Word Of Mouth ('What It Is (Ain't Losing Control)'). A delayed second album, *Intercourse*, failed to revive S'Express's fortunes, despite the gifted vocal presence of Sonique. A sample of John Waters ('Bad taste is what entertainment is all about') preceded a demonstrably shabby, tongue-in-cheek rendition of 'Brazil' on the album's best track. Moore would continue to earn a crust as a remixer, however, notably on Malcolm McLaren's 'Something's Jumpin' In Your Shirt' (with William Orbit) and Saffron's 'Fluffy Toy' (with Peter Lorimer).

● ALBUMS: *Original Soundtrack* (Rhythm King 1989)★★★, *Intercourse* (Rhythm King 1992)★★.

S-1000

The moniker of Spencer Williams, who had previously remixed for the Sugarcubes and the Art Of Noise, and, alongside Paul Gotel, was half of Well Hung Parliament. 'I'm Not Gonna Do It' was a typical bouncing dub 45, while he scored further club hits with 'Flatliner' and 'Look Inside'. Williams also has the distinction of having been 'on the ground', literally, when the Los Angeles earthquake struck. He was actually in the middle of a set at the Sketch Pad in Hollywood when the earth started moving. S-1000 has now moved from Guerilla to Deep Distraxion.

SABRES OF PARADISE

Andy Weatherall's favoured dance emporium, whose releases include 'Smokebelch' - arguably the techno tune of the early 90s. In addition to Weatherall, Nina Walsh helms the ship, aided by Jagz Kooner and Gary Burns. Walsh was a regular at Weatherall's Shoom evenings during the heady days of 1988's acid scene. She in turn worked for the Boys Own stable. Before joining the Sabres she also worked with Youth's (ex-Killing Joke, Brilliant, etc.) WAU/Butterfly recordings. The duo set up their own label under the Sabres name, and released work from the likes of SYT, Blue, Secret Knowledge, Musical Science, Waxworth Industries, Jack O' Swords and the Corridor. The label operation eventually became known as Sabrettes. There was also a studio and club (based in a brick-dust cellar under London Bridge) both titled Sabresonic, as was the group's debut longplayer. This seamless collection of post-Orb, dreamscape dance, with a vaguely industrial edge, increased the avalanche of plaudits that usually accompany Weatherall's best work. Together with assistants Gary and Jagz, Weatherall has turned the Sabres into one of the UK's premier remix teams. Among their work are remixes of everyone worth noting in the dance scene, right through to hardcore rockers Therapy? Two other accomplices, Mick and Phil, help out with live work. The group have contributed one track, 'Sabres Them', to the film *Shopping*. Typically, despite the otherworldly grandeur of this music, the Sabres studio remains located above a Tandoori restaurant in West Hounslow.

● ALBUMS: *Sabresonic* (Sabrettes 1993)★★★, *Haunted Dancehall* (Warp 1994)★★★, *Sabresonic II* (Warp 1995)★★★.

SABRETTES

Originally titled Sabres Of Paradise, after Andy Weatherall and Nina Walsh's band of the same name, this emergent label has so far released Voodoo People's *Altitude* EP, the Cause's 'Through The Floor and Charged' (aka DJs Scott Braithwaite and Craig Walsh, Nina's brother), and two 12-inch techno opuses from Inky Blacknuss (DJ's Alex Knight and Andrea Parker). Future plans include a collaboration between Les from Holy Ghost and Anna Haigh (ex-Bocca Juniors). The label is stated to be based on Nina Walsh's personal taste. It gives her an outlet to escape the perennial 'DJ's girlfriend' tag with which she has found herself labelled, following her relationship with the much in-demand Weatherall.

● ALBUMS: Various: *Pink Me Up* (Sabrettes 1994)★★★.

SADAT X

b. Derrick Murphy, 29 December 1968, New Rochelle, New York, USA. Sadat X initially rose to prominence as a member of Brand Nubian, one of the most politicized and controversial rap acts of the 90s. Having worked on three high-impact albums with that group, *All For One*, *In God We Trust* and *Everything Is Everything*, he elected to turn solo in the mid-90s. His debut record for RCA Records, *Wild Cowboys*, was titled after the 'black cowboys', erased from the history books, who helped to establish cities such as Chicago in preindustrialized America. It extensively featured his younger protégé, rapper Shaun Black, and hit out at the lazy eulogies to gun culture of the west coast gangsta rappers. Instead, Sadat emphasized the need for young blacks to rise above the prejudice of an unjust system and their own expectations: 'A lot of black people don't want to help themselves. They don't want to study or educate themselves, which is something they gotta do, 'cos nobody else's gonna do it for them.' After promoting the album Sadat embarked on an extensive European tour and also discussed the possibility of a Brand Nubian reunion.

● ALBUMS: *Wild Cowboys* (Loud/RCA 1996)★★★.

SAGOO, BILLY

b. *c*.1965, Delhi, India. Billy Sagoo is one of the godfathers of British bhangra beat (a fusion of contemporary influences with bhangra, the traditional Indian musical form). A producer, mixer, songwriter and solo artist, Sagoo and his family moved to Birmingham, England, when he was six months old. As a teenager he turned his back on the legal career his parents had planned for him, and immersed himself in imported American soul records. Afterwards he acquired his first turntables and began basic scratch DJing in his bedroom. His fusion tapes were sold to his friends, until eventually he began to add his parents' bhangra music to the mix. Galvanized by the discovery, he started to assemble tapes for local radio, and was eventually offered a contract with the Indian music label Oriental Star Records. He became their in-house producer before teaming up with Nusrat Fateh Ali Khan, also a member of Oriental Star's roster. Their collaboration, *Magic Touch*, became one of Ali Khan's most successful records and launched Sagoo as a mainstream star. A follow-up collaboration arrived in 1997, by which time Sagoo was being acknowledged in periodicals such as Rolling Stone as one of the true innovators of 90s British dance music.

● ALBUMS: with Nusrat Fateh Ali Khan *Magic Touch* (Oriental Star 1991)★★★, *Rising From The East* (Telstar 1997)★★★, with Khan *Magic Touch II* (Telstar 1997)★★.

SAHKO RECORDINGS

Finnish purveyors of weird electronic music, whose releases are housed in silver sleeves drilled with tiny holes, or, in the case of CDs, cardboard envelopes. Headed by architect-cum-label-manager Tommi Gronlund, the two principal artists are techno animateur Mika Vainio (otherwise known as Ø) and ambient/easy listening vendor Jimi Tenor. The latter's *Sahkomies* was particularly well received in mainland Europe, while Vainio's *Metri* demonstrated a unique and incredibly sparse approach to techno. Indeed, it was Vainio's music that had inspired Gronlund to set up the label in the first place. While big names such as Richie Hawtin and Mixmaster Morris all spoke highly of their efforts, the label remained completely anonymous within their native Finland. Undeterred, they entertained audiences with an all-nighter at London's Quirky club and announced a new UK distribution arrangement in 1994.

SAINT ETIENNE

By far the most dextrous of those bands cursed with the 'indie-dance' label, and one of the few to maintain genuine support in both camps. Pete Wiggs (b. 15 May 1966, Reigate, Surrey, England) and music journalist Bob Stanley (b. 25 December 1964, Horsham, Sussex, England) grew up together in Croydon, Surrey, England. In the early 80s, the pair began to experiment with party tapes, but did not make any serious inroads into the music business until forming Saint Etienne in 1988, taking their name from the renowned French football team. Relocating to Camden in north London, the pair recruited Moira Lambert of Faith Over Reason for a dance/reggae cover version of Neil Young's 'Only Love Can Break Your Heart'. Issued in May 1990 on the aspiring Heavenly Records label, the single fared well in the nightclubs and surfaced on a magazine flexidisc remixed by labelmates Flowered Up (who appeared on the b-side) in July. Another cover version, indie guitar band the Field Mice's 'Kiss And Make Up', was given a similar dance pop overhaul for Saint Etienne's second single, fronted this time by New Zealand vocalist Donna Savage of Dead Famous People. Then came the infectious, northern soul-tinged 'Nothing Can Stop Us' in May 1991. Its strong European feel reflected both their name, which helped attract strong support in France, and their logo (based on the European flag). It also benefited from Sarah Cracknell's (b. 12 April 1967, Chelmsford, Essex, England) dreamy vocals, which would dominate Saint Etienne's debut, *Foxbase Alpha*, released in the autumn. Cracknell had formerly recorded with Prime Time. 'Only Love Can Break Your Heart' was reissued alongside the album, and provided them with a minor chart hit.

Throughout the 90s the only critical barb that seemed to stick to Saint Etienne with any justification or regularity was that they were simply 'too clever for their own good', a criticism that Stanley clearly could not abide: 'The image that the media has built up of us as manipulators really makes us laugh'. *So Tough* revealed a rich appreciation of the vital signs of British pop, paying homage to their forerunners without ever indulging in false flattery. *Tiger Bay*, toted as a folk album, transcended a variety of musical genres with the sense of ease and propriety that Saint Etienne had essentially patented. The medieval folk/trance ballad 'Western Wind', and the instrumental 'Urban Clearway', redolent of, but not traceable to, a dozen prime-time television themes, were just two of the bookends surrounding one of the greatest albums of that year. It was followed by a fan club-only release, *I Love To Paint* limited to 500 copies. In 1997 Sarah Cracknell released a solo album, having previously recorded a duet with Tim Burgess of the Charlatans, 'I Was Born On Christmas Day', released at the end of 1993 in a failed attempt to mug the Christmas singles market. The band recorded their comeback album, *Good Humor*, in Sweden.

● ALBUMS: *Foxbase Alpha* (Heavenly 1991)★★★, *So Tough* (Heavenly 1993)★★★, *Tiger Bay* (Heavenly 1994)★★★, *Casino Classics* (Heavenly 1996)★★★, *Good Humor* (Creation 1998)★★★.

● COMPILATIONS: *You Need A Mess Of Help To Stand Alone* (Heavenly 1993)★★★, *Too Young To Die - The Singles* (Heavenly 1995)★★★★, *Too Young To Die - The Remix Album* (Heavenly 1995)★★★.

● VIDEOS: *Too Young To Die* (Wienerworld 1995).

SALT TANK

Internal Records' signings who, under the 'intelligent techo' mantle, have broke several musical barriers, notably supporting Hawkwind on live dates. Their sequence of releases runs chronilogically *ST1*, *ST2* and *ST3*, the latter EP comprising seven different 'stereotypical' approaches to modern techno, all of which are carried off with aplomb. They are a duo comprising Malcolm Stanners, who had worked with Derrick May and Kevin Saunderson in the late 80s, and partner David. They made their debut with 'Ease The Pressure'/'Charged Up', which sold well in mainland Europe, then 1993's 'Sweli'/'Meltdown' - a record packaged to resemble a Djax-Up Beats disc, with David's telephone number on the label. The first person to 'phone was Andy Weatherall. *ST3* also featured samples of Simple Minds and David Byrne (Talking Heads).

● ALBUMS: *Science & Nature* (Internal 1996)★★★, *Wave Breaks* (ffrr 1997)★★★★.

SALT-N-PEPA

Cheryl 'Salt' James (b. 8 March 1964, Brooklyn, New York, USA) and Sandra 'Pepa' Denton (b. 9 November 1969, Kingston, Jamaica, West Indies) grew up in the Queens district of New York City. They became telephone sales girls and envisioned a career in nursing until fellow workmate and part-time producer Hurby 'Luv Bug' Azor stepped in. He asked them to rap for his group the Super Lovers (credited on record as Supernature) on the answer record to Doug E. Fresh's 'The Show'. They started recording as Salt 'N' Pepa (correctly printed as Salt-N-Pepa) which was adapted from the Super Nature recording 'Showstopper'. At that time they were under Azor's guidance, and released singles such as 'I'll Take Your Man', 'It's My Beat' and 'Tramp', the latter a clever revision of the old Otis Redding/Carla Thomas duet. They also used the female DJ Spinderella aka Dee Dee Roper (b. Deidre Roper, 3 August 1971, New York, USA), backing singers and male erotic dancers to complete their act.

Their big break came in 1988 when a reissue of an earlier single - 'Push It' - reached the UK number 2 spot and was also a hit on the US R&B chart. Later that year a remake of the Isley Brothers' 'Twist And Shout' also went into the Top 10. Between those two they released 'Shake Your Thang' (once again, a take on an Isley Brothers track, 'It's Your Thing'), which featured the instrumental group EU. Nominated for the first ever Rap Grammy in 1989, they refused to attend the ceremony when it was discovered that the presentation of that particular bauble would not be televised - withdrawing to show solidarity with hip-hop's growing status. Their most confrontational release was the 1991 'Let's Talk About Sex' manifesto, something of a change of approach after the overtly erotic 'Push It'. 'Do You Want Me' was similarly successful, encouraging the record company to put out *A Blitz Of Salt 'N' Pepa Hits*, a collection of remixes, in their absence. Both Salt and Pepa were otherwise engaged having babies (Pepa in 1990, Salt in 1991; DJ Spinderella would make it a hat-trick of single mothers in the group a short time later). In the interim they could content themselves with being the most commercially successful female rap troupe of all time, and the first to go gold. They subsequently enjoyed an invitation to appear at President Clinton's inauguration party. They returned to the charts in 1994 with their highly successful collaboration with En Vogue, 'Whatta Man'. It was a return to their 'naughty but nice' personas, typically suggestive and salacious. After a lengthy absence they returned with *Brand New*, which saw them struggling to assert themselves against the brasher style of the new rap queens Foxy Brown and Lil' Kim.

● ALBUMS: *Hot Cool & Vicious* (Next Plateau 1987)★★★, *A Salt With A Deadly Pepa* (Next Plateau 1988)★★★, *Blacks' Magic* (Next Plateau 1990)★★, *Rapped In Remixes* (Next Plateau 1992)★★★, *Very Necessary* (Next

Plateau/London 1993)★★★★, *Brand New* (London/Red Ant 1997)★★★.
● COMPILATIONS: *A Blitz Of Salt 'N' Pepa Hits* (Next Plateau 1991)★★, *The Greatest Hits* (London 1991)★★★★.

SAMPLING

The art of sampling was first introduced to an international audience in 1979 when the Sugarhill Gang used a reconstructed Chic track, 'Good Times', as backing for their 'Rapper's Delight' success. Others followed, notably Grandmaster Flash' 'Adventures Of Grandmaster Flash On The Wheels Of Steel', which featured cut-and-paste segments from Chic, Queen, Blondie and other rap artists including Spoonie Gee and the Sugarhill Gang. Similarly Afrika Bambaataa's 'Planet Rock', which many cite as the first real hip-hop record, utilized the work of others, in this case Kraftwerk's 'Trans-Europe Express' and 'Numbers'. While hip-hop and rap remained underground there was little interest taken by anyone in the format. However, as soon as corporations sniffed out profits, half a dozen lawsuits were brought against those who had indulged in 'copyright violation'. Among the most notable sufferers were England's Shut Up And Dance. Long considered an act of plagiarism at best, it is only in recent years that sampling the work of older artists has been seen to be beneficial to both parties. Many artists, from James Brown to Spandau Ballet, have seen their work reassessed and reappraised in the wake of major hip-hop artists sampling their work. By allowing Us3 to ransack the Blue Note vaults, the same label experienced a doubling in their US sales when *Hand On The Torch* broke big. In many ways it has become the stamp of approval to an artist's longevity: certainly all the major rock acts, from the Beatles (2 Live Crew and others) to Jimi Hendrix (the Pharcyde), have experienced their wares being rehabilitated. Among the most-sampled catalogues are the works of James Brown (hugely influential in the initial development of rap) and George Clinton and P-Funk/Parliament (specifically in the west coast traditions of Ice Cube and Too Short). Also popular have been more conventional rock sources such as Grand Funk Railroad (KRS-1 and De La Soul) and Aerosmith (Run DMC), reggae (Bob Marley in particular) and jazz. Like everything else, sampling cuts both ways; in September 1991 Chuck D of Public Enemy sued the marketing company promoting St. Ides Malt liquor for using his voice without permission. Public Enemy also took legal action against Madonna for using their rhythm to underscore her 'Justify My Love' single.

SANCHEZ, ROGER

Widely regarded as one of the hottest US remixers, New York-based Sanchez made his name with a series of devastating releases for Strictly Rhythm, such as Logic's 'One Step Beyond'. He finally made his solo long-playing bow with an album in January 1994. As might have been expected from the man who provided Juliet Roberts with hits like 'Free Love' and 'Caught In The Middle', it preferred a blend of sweet soul and house. It was released under the name, Roger S, already familiar through his remixes for Michael Jackson and others. Graced by the deep house vocals of Jay Williams, it reinstated his integrity in the underground dance scene at a time when he was handling more and more major-league clients. It was released on One Records, which he jointly owns with Eddie Colon. He also set up a management company with UK partner Marts Andrups (who also represents Benji Candelario and Danny Tenaglia in Europe) titled Indeep, signing artists such as vocalist Melodie Washington. Sanchez was also partly behind the Sound Of One hit, 'As I Am', for Cooltempo, and Logic's 'One Step Beyond'. He recently produced an album for Kathy Sledge, among sundry other projects.
● ALBUMS: *Secret Weapons Vol. 1* (One Records 1994)★★★, *Secret Weapons Vol. 2* (Narcotic 1995)★★.

SANDALS

Nouveau hippies the Sandals consist of Derek Delves (vocals; ex-Espresso 7, A Man Called Adam), John Harris (flute, vocals), Ian 'Easy' Simmonds and Wild Cat Will (ex-Batniks; drums). Signed to Acid Jazz, they confessed to being conceptual recording artists rather than musicians, specializing in a Latin-tinged trance-funk, and operating in the manner of a 60s collective. They came together initially in a seedy Soho bar in the summer of 1987, organizing a 60s-style 'happening' night (named Violets), with poetry readings, party games and jazz spots. Since then they have opened a shop, Rich And Strange, which sells their art and second-hand fashion. After which they also started their own club night, Tongue Kung Fu, which was exported to Los

Angeles, Tokyo and Istanbul. They run their own label too, the appropriately titled Open Toe stable. Their debut performance as the Sandals came at the 1990 Soho Jazz Festival, while their first single, 'Profound Gas', was remixed by old friends Leftfield (Derek having been a one-time member of A Man Called Adam with Leftfield's Paul Daley). Their second effort, 'Nothing', was premiered on the opening of a new series of youth television programmes, *The Word*. 1993 also brought excessive gigging across several festivals and continents, before sessions on their debut album began in earnest. Before this they released their third single, 'We Wanna Live', which was produced as a 'live remix' by the Disco Evangelists and Sabres Of Paradise - with all three parties performing on the studio take.

● ALBUMS: *Rite To Silence* (Open Toe 1994)★★★.

SASHA

b. 4 September 1969, Bangor, Wales. Manchester-based 'Top DJ pin-up' whose regular nights include Renaissance (Manchester) and La Cotta (Birmingham). A former fish-farm worker and grade 8 pianist, after pioneering Italian house in 1989 and 1990 he made his name with a jazzy, garage style as a remixer on projects such as Mr Fingers' 'Closer' and Urban Soul's 'He's Always' and 'Alright'. Sasha moved to DeConstruction in 1993 in a three-album contract. Most had expected him to sign with Virgin following the success of his BM:Ex (Barry Manilow Experience) cut, 'Appolonia', a double-pack 12-inch with a running time of over an hour, on their Union City Recordings subsidiary. 'Appolonia' originally emerged as an obscure Italian white label promo, and was a record Sasha played regularly at the end of his sets at Shelley's in Stoke without ever being able to discover the identity of its originators. As nobody could find out any further details he decided to re-record it himself. The first result of the liaison with DeConstruction was 'Higher Ground', recorded with production partner Tom Frederikse and vocalist Sam Mollison. He also provided a single, 'Quat', for Cowboy, who were originally set to release 'Feel The Drop', which ended up as the b-side to 'Appolonia'. Sasha was also signed up to PolyGram Music in 1993 for publishing, indicating that at last dance songwriters were beginning to be taken seriously by the music industry, rather than as short-term recording artists. As Sasha himself expounded: 'I've plans for bigger things. I don't want to be restricted by

the dancefloor. That's where my inspiration is, but I want to do something with a little more longevity than the latest number 1 on the Buzz chart'. He has thus far, however, turned down interview opportunities with the *Daily Mirror* and *Sun*. Among his many other remix/production clients have been Ce Ce Rogers, Unique 3 ('No More') and soundtrack composer Barrington Pheloung.

SAUNDERSON, KEVIN
(see Inner City, Reese Project)

SAWHNEY, NITIN

b. 1964, England. One of a new wave of Asian acts achieving mainstream acceptance in the UK music industry - following the pioneering work of Apache Indian, Kaliphz (now Kaleef) and Babylon Zoo - Nitin Sawhney has developed an eclectic mix of Indian music elements with the innovations and techniques of British jazz, dance and rock styles. A Hindu Punjabi, Sawhney was born in England just a year after his parents relocated there from Delhi. As well as listening to traditional Indian music at home, he quickly adopted to a number of instruments, including piano and flamenco guitar. He then formed his first jazz group, the Jazztones, before graduating to playing guitar with the James Taylor Quartet in 1988. Afterwards he returned to traditional music by forming the Tihai Trio with percussionist Talvin Singh (later a collaborator with Björk and Massive Attack). By the early 90s he was spending much of his time recording music for film, television and theatre, and also released his debut solo album, *Spirit Dance*. This was recorded for World Circuit Records with the aid of an Arts Council grant following an extensive search for music industry backing. As was the case with the follow-up collection, *Migration*, the album combined Western instruments such as flamenco and jazz guitar with drum and bass loops, electronica and classically inspired Indian singing. As he told the press, 'The whole thing I'm trying to do is show there are no barriers, it's just about checking other cultures and finding where they meet up.' For his second outing he moved to Outcaste Records, a division of PR agency Media Village. The album was then given widespread radio exposure by the patronage of Gilles Peterson on Kiss and Jazz FM. One of its tracks, 'Ranjha', was subsequently included on the high-profile *Rebirth Of Cool* compilation album. 1996's *Displacing The*

Priest was promoted by the successful club single, 'Into The Mind', and confirmed the growing audience for Sawhney's evocative Anglo-Indian hybrid.

● ALBUMS: *Spirit Dance* (World Circuit 1991)★★★, *Migration* (Outcaste 1994)★★★, *Displacing The Priest* (Outcaste 1996)★★★.

SCANNER

Named after the hand-held device that can intercept telephone and radio calls, Scanner comprises the UK-based duo of Robin Rimbaud (b. *c*.1964) and Steve Williams - who are regularly on patrol to pick up conversations on mobile phones, replaying them alongside their own studio sounds. In turn their recordings were adorned with some of the more memorable/bizarre findings into which they had tuned with their own scanner, from aural pornography to static and more everyday conversation. These delights had graced two albums for Ash International by 1994. The equipment was originally purchased from a group of fellow hunt sabateurs who were using it to monitor police movements. Rimbaud also runs the Electronic Lounge, a monthly 'event' in the ICA bar, and lectured on the art of 'scanning' at London University. The duo have also remixed for Autechre and Reload.

● ALBUMS: *Spore* (New Electronica 1995)★★★, *Delivery* (Earache 1997)★★★, with Signs Ov Chaos *Michael Jackson* (Earache 1997)★★.

SCARFACE

b. Brad Jordan, USA. Formerly a member of Houston's nastiest, the Geto Boys, Scarface's 'official' solo debut (an album of sorts had prefigured *Mr Scarface Is Back*) was a familiar roll-call of sex and street violence, with the titles reading like a litany of horror movies ('Body Snatchers', 'Born Killer', Diary Of A Madman'). The follow-up repeated the formula to an ever greater degree of success, eventually going platinum. Though there was much skullduggery and blatant misogny apparent again, there was at least light to lift the shade. The hardcore rapper was not too hardcore to include tracks such as 'Now I Feel Ya', which spoke openly of his relationship with his son and parents. In real life he suffers from depression, which was also documented on bloodcurdling tracks like 'The Wall'. His suicide attempt, triggered by his girlfriend announcing she was leaving him, had been depicted on the sleeve of a previous Geto Boys album. The first single from a projected fourth album was 'Hand Of The Dead Body', a duet with Ice Cube that defended rap against various charges laid at its door in the 90s. The key to Scarface's craft can be located in the fact that he boasts of first seeing the film *The Warriors* at age eight. Sadly, he has never quite grown out of it.

● ALBUMS: *Mr. Scarface Is Back* (Rap-A-Lot 1991)★★★, *The World Is Yours* (Rap-A-Lot 1993)★★, *The Diary* (Virgin 1995)★★★, *The Untouchable* (Virgin 1997)★★★, *My Homes* (Rap-A-Lot 1998)★★★.

SCATMAN JOHN

b. John Larkin, *c*.1942, USA. One of the more unlikely success stories of the mid-90s, Scatman John is a side-project for jazz singer and pianist John Larkin. Based in Los Angeles, California, USA, he performed widely at festivals and at piano bars throughout the world. Despite his prolific work in jazz, however, it was within the house music tradition that he eventually became a star. He was discovered by Manfred Zähringer, owner of Danish label Iceberg Records, in Frankfurt, Germany, in 1994. Larkin passed him some tapes of his 'bebop poetry' renditions, which impressed the label owner greatly. However, no record label he approached would take seriously the prospect of a 50-year-old jazz pianist improvising scat vocals over a pop dance rhythm. Eventually he found a sympathetic home at BMG Ariola Hamburg and Axel Alexander. He paired Larkin with producers Tony Catania and Ingo Kays, with whom he recorded a single, 'Scatman'. Though sales were slow initially, the single earned repeated plays on mainstream radio and eventually became a massive Europe-wide hit. A remix version was produced by disc jockey Alex Christensen to ensure that the record also appealed to dance club audiences. 'Scatman' eventually sold over 600,000 copies in Germany alone, reaching number 2 in the national charts. It also topped charts in Scandinavia, Austria, Switzerland, France, Belgium, The Netherlands, Italy, Spain and Turkey. It peaked at number 3 in the UK charts. A second single, 'Scatman's World', also sold heavily in Europe and preceded the release of a debut album of the same title, by which time the attraction was wearing a little thin for some.

● ALBUMS: *Scatman's World* (BMG 1995)★★★★.

SCHOOLLY D

b. Jesse B. Weaver Jnr., Baltimore, Philadelphia, USA. Posturing street rapper who, together with his DJ Code Money (b. Lance Allen, USA), was an early pioneer in 'gun rap', a format that featured an abundance of violence and vendettas, and the glorification of the MC's personal armoury. Allied to the usual sexual declamation, it was a limited worldview but a partially effective one. Following 1984 singles 'Maniac' and 'Gangster Boogie', Schoolly D released an independent, eponymous album that was notable for the track 'PSK - What Does It Mean'. PSK transpired to be an acronym for Park Side Killers, a gang of Schoolly's aquaintance in Philadelphia. Though this breakthrough album will ensure Schoolly D's name remains hallowed in the annals of gangsta rap, he has done little since that would otherwise justify his inclusion. Still rapping over the basic, unadventurous scratching of Money, Schoolly D has not been seen to move on; whereas greater intellects have explored gang violence as a means of illustrating the big picture, Schoolly D has proved happy merely to indulge in, often horrific reportage. Song titles such as 'Mr Big Dick' and 'Where's My Bitches' speak volumes about the lyrical insight displayed on the vast majority of his output. The first light at the end of the tunnel came with *Am I Black Enough For You?*, which at least incorporated a few more socio-political concerns, with cuts such as 'Black Jesus' opening up new, potentially much more interesting, avenues of provocation. The title track, too, was more insightful than previous fare had led us to expect: 'All I need is my blackness, Some others seem to lack this'. By the time of his 'comeback' album of 1994, Schoolly had progressed further still. Renouncing the basic samples that had underscored most of his career, he now employed a full live band, including Urge Overkill's Chuck Treece, Joe 'The Butcher' Nicolo and co-producer Mike Tyler. Recently he has made telling contributions to the soundtracks of *The King Of New York* and *The Blackout*.
● ALBUMS: *Schoolly D* (Schoolly-D 1986)★★★, *Saturday Night - The Album* (Schoolly-D 1987)★★, *Smoke Some Kill* (Jive 1988)★★, *Am I Black Enough For You?* (Jive 1989)★★★★, *How A Black Man Feels* (Capitol 1991)★★★★, *Welcome To America* (Ruffhouse/Columbia 1994)★★★★.
● COMPILATIONS: *The Adventures Of Schoolly D* (Rykodisc 1987)★★★.

SCHUTZE, PAUL

b. Australia. With a background in industrial/*avant garde* music, notably the Melbourne jazz artists Laughing Hands and film scores, Schutze was quick to see the possibilities in the artistic marketplace opened up by techno. Although *More Beautiful Human Life* was his first recording for R&S subsidiary Apollo, it was in fact his sixth album in total. This was a collage of sounds and noises melded into a cinematic narrative, underpinned by his studies of Indian percussion and tabla music. Schutze has also undertaken remixing chores for guitar bands like Main and Bark Psychosis, in an attempt to broaden both his and their musical palates.
● ALBUMS: *New Maps Of Hell* (Extreme 1994)★★★, as Uzect Plaush *More Beautiful Human Life* (Apollo 1994)★★, *Abysmal Evenings* (Virgin 1996)★★★, *Site Anubis* (Big Cat 1996)★★.

SCIENTISTS OF SOUND

Boasting four different birth locations (Nigeria, Mauritius, St Lucia, Jamaica), the Scientists Of Sound are based in England, and comprise J-Blast 'The Weak Rhyme Wrecker' (ex-J-Blast And The 100% Proof), DJ Aybee 'The Underground Nigga', Kool Sett and Cherokee 'Mr Mibian'. A colourful press release claimed they were originally one person, travelling through the universe, when they were split into four component parts and spread around the globe. After adapting the personas of indigenous creatures, they reunited in England as a result of influencing their parents to travel to the UK. This unwieldy ethos was continued in their live shows (a choeorographed approach often compared to Leaders Of The New School) and embraced in the way each member as regarded as a different anatomical appendage of the central being: J-Blast the mouthpiece, Kool Sett the heart, etc. Signed to the Underdog's Bite It! label after debuting with a 1992 EP, their first release for their new employer was 1994's 'Bad Boy Swing'.

SECRET CINEMA

Secret Cinema is essentially techno artist Jeroen Verheij, from Amsterdam, Netherlands, and his 'Timeless Attitude' was one of the biggest club singles of 1994. Verheij's career had begun in a noticeably harder style (the European derivative of techno known as 'gabba') with his debut single, the relentless 'Solar System', issued on Meng Syndicate Records. His follow-up, 'No Violence', was released on Paul Elstak's Rotterdam label, and was credited to Stomach Basher. Afterwards Verheij entered a transitory period. 'I just didn't know what to do. I was like, "Shall I go into the hard stuff or shall I go for something totally different." In the end, I decided to keep experimenting. I bought some gear and nobody ever knew what had happened to Jeroen Verheij.'

He re-emerged by teaming up with his friend Michel and starting the EC and Brave New World labels. After Secret Cinema's debut with 'Timeless Attitude' he released 'Point Blank', credited to Meng Syndicate. Both singles saw him maintain an allegiance to the hard beats and minimalism of gabba, but these tenets were now combined with a more eclectic approach and a less feverish tempo. The next Secret Cinema single, 'Straight Forward', continued to explore new dimensions to his sound, and included the distinctive sound of the digeridoo which had been such a prominent instrument in early 90s techno.

SECRET KNOWLEDGE

Dance collective featuring the writing skills of singer Wonder (b. West Virginia, USA) and Kris Needs, a man with a long and shady history. His chequered past includes stints in pub rockers the Vice Creems, and a part-time position as John Otway's bongo player. He began writing for *ZigZag* magazine in 1975, going on to take over the editorship in 1977. In the 80s and 90s he concentrated on writing dance reviews for *Echoes* and other magazines. Wonder, meanwhile, had formerly fronted a Munich, Germany-based jazz/blues band titled Strange Fruit. Unlike many of the predominantly soul-based female vocalists who regularly add their voices to house/trance cuts, Wonder is responsible for writing lyrics as well as the occasional melody (including 'Sugar Daddy'). The duo met together in the late 80s in New York, recording a one-off rap single together, 'Rap Too Tight'. Once they had returned to the UK, and Needs had discovered the burgeoning Acid House movement, they cut their first track under the Secret Knowledge flag: 'Your Worst Nightmare'. Influenced by the deep house of New York's Strictly Rhythm label, they followed their debut with 'Ooh Baby', one of the first releases on Andy Weatherall's Sabres Of Paradise label. Next up came one of the biggest club hits of 1993, 'Sugar Daddy'. In its wake Secret Knowledge were elevated to the status of hot producers/remixers. Among their other collaborative monikers are Delta Lady (reflecting a more urbane, funk-based side to their nature), Four Boy One Girl Action (whose 'Hawaiian Death Stomp' combined Needs with David Holmes and members of the Sabres enclave), the Rabettes (featuring Weatherall's girlfriend Nina's assorted rabbits and guinea pigs), Hutchbern, The Pecking Order (featuring various impersonations of chickens) and Codpeace (with Alex Paterson of the Orb). Needs has also stepped out as a remix artist, converting artists from many fields incuding the Boo Radleys. They clashed with the compilers of the excellent *Trance Europe Express 2* in mid-1994 over their contribution, 'Afterworld'. The lyrics addressed Wonder's cousin, an AIDS sufferer, but the track was deemed to be out of context on an otherwise instrumental set. While compromises were still being discussed, a vocal-less version was 'inadvertently' included instead, as Needs discovered after returning from touring with Primal Scream. They issued the 'correct' version on Kris' Stolen Karots label instead.

● ALBUMS: *So Hard* (deConstruction 1996)★★★.

SECRET LIFE

Secret Life initially consisted of Charton Antenbring (disc jockey and reporter for UK magazine *The Big Issue*), Andy Throup (classically trained pianist and studio owner) and Paul Bryant (vocals). Secret Life was officially an umbrella organisation with a number of producers and musicians (notably Throup's studio co-owner, Jim Di Salvo) also contributing. They made headlines with 1992's 'As Always' cut for Cowboy Records (whose Charlie Chester manages the band), which was among that label's biggest successes. It was based on Stevie Wonder's 'Songs In The Key Of Life' (which had previously been issued in a 'house' version by Chicago-based Ricky Dillard of Nightwriters' fame). However, after Masters At Work remixed 1994's 'Borrowed Time', which was on the first demo the band passed to Chester, their manager realised their potential might extend beyond the dance frontier and into the pop market. As a result Chester moved them over to Pulse 8 Records in an eight-album deal that year, with the group reduced to a core duo of Bryant and Throup. A radio-friendly single, 'Love So Strong', and an album followed in 1995.

● ALBUMS: *Sole Purpose* (Pulse 8 1995)★★★.

SEEFEEL

An intriguing combination of introspective ambient textures (though they abhor the term) and propulsive guitars has distinguished Seefeel's career. Guitarist and songwriter Mark Clifford answered an advert that Justin Fletcher (drums) had placed on a noticeboard at Goldsmith's College, London. They added Darren 'Delores Throb' Seymour (bass) and set about auditioning over 70 hopefuls for the singer's job. In the end Clifford responded to another ad: 'Wanting to join or form band into My Bloody Valentine and Sonic Youth', and called ex-animation student Sarah Peacock, who had placed it. As her tastes reflected Seefeel's personal creed, a distillation of MBV's guitar abuse with ambient's drone, she was immediately taken on board. They made their recording debut with the *More Like Space* EP - which confused BBC Radio 1 disc jockey John Peel as to whether to play it at 33rpm or 45rpm. Two EPs and an album for Too Pure Records quickly followed, with 'Pure, Impure' featuring a spectral Aphex Twin remix. They also collaborated and toured with heroes the Cocteau Twins (the question Clifford asked Peacock when he telephoned her was whether or not she liked them). Another EP in 1994, *Starethrough*, was their first for Warp Records, and again provoked interest, coinciding with and reflecting a move from indie to dance coverage in the UK music weeklies. *Succour* was another bold and well-received album, but coincided with Clifford starting work on a solo project, while the other members reconvened as Siren.
● ALBUMS: *Quique* (Too Pure 1993)★★★, *Succour* (Warp 1995)★★★.

SHABAZZ, LAKIM

At the forefront of the Nation Of Islam movement, Shabazz entered the stage with *Pure Righteousness*, an early production by DJ Mark the 45 King, which submitted a powerful blow for the Afrocentricity movement. Shabazz began his rapping whilst still at school, his interest initially awakened through an appetite for poetry. He took part in a succession of low-key, competitive MC clashes, until meeting the 45 King, who had recently relocated from New Jersey to New York. After losing contact for a while, he heard Mark mentioned on the radio, and called him up. Together they put together a handful of tracks, and Shabazz was subsequently signed to Tuff City

via label boss, Aaron Fuchs. The second of his albums for the latter featured a more oppressively pro-Muslim stance, especially the unequivocal 'When You See A Devil Smash Him'.
● ALBUMS: *Pure Righteousness* (Tuff City 1988)★★★, *The Lost Tribe Of Shabazz* (Tuff City 1990)★★.

SHADZ OF LINGO

Hailing from Atlanta, Georgia, rappers Lingo and Kolorado alongside DJ Rocco won plaudits for their furious mix of hip-hop, dancehall reggae and jazz styles, only occasionally lapsing into the cool groove of geographical neighbours like Arrested Development. Their background as jingle writers partially explained this eclecticism. Having met at high school in Virginia, the trio decided to make a career in music, after several abortive attempts at rapping, by forming their own production company in 1988. When they launched Shadz Of Lingo they hit on an effective old school style, inviting producers of note such as Erick Sermon (EPMD), Diamond D. and Solid Productions in to help them. Live, the band are noted for their freestyle approach, with Kolorado claiming never to write lyrics down, tailoring them instead for each individual occason.
● ALBUMS: *A View To A Kill* (ERG 1993)★★★.

SHAKTA

(see Digitalis)

SHAKUR, TUPAC

b. Tupac Amaru Shakur, 16 June 1971, New York City, New York, USA, d. 13 September 1996, Las Vegas, Nevada, USA. The controversy-laced gangsta rapper '2Pac' was the son of two Black Panther members, and his mother was actually pregnant with her son while being held in a New York prison. As a teenager Shakur studied at the Baltimore School Of Arts, before he moved to Marin City, California with his family and began hustling on the streets. His first appearance on the hip-hop scene came with a brief spell as part of Digital Underground, but it was with his debut *2Pacalypse Now* that he announced himself as one of rap's newest talents, while gaining censure from various quarters for the album's explicit lyrical content. He gained his first crossover success in July 1993 with 'I Get Around'. The platinum-selling album which housed it, *Strictly 4 My N.I.G.G.A.Z.* offered a rare degree of insight, with glints of wisdom like 'Last Wordz' - 'United we stand, divided we fall, they can shoot one nigga, but they can't shoot us all'. To further his views he ran the Underground Railroad network for troubled teenagers in his native Oakland, California. His acting career was also burgeoning, following a memorable performance as Bishop in Ernest Dickerson's *Juice*. After appearing in director John Singleton's film *Poetic Justice*, alongside Janet Jackson, he was dropped from the same director's *Higher Learning*. Shakur took things into his own hands when he was also removed from the set of Allen Hughes' *Menace II Society* when he attacked the director, for which he received a 15 day jail sentence in February 1994. He did, however, make it on to the final cut of the basketball movie *Above The Rim*. Shakur's run-ins with the police had escalated in line with his profile as a prominent black artist. He was arrested in 1992 when a fight he was involved in resulted in the accidental death of a six-year-old boy, although the charges were later dismissed. He was accused in October 1993 of involvement in the shooting of two plain clothes policemen (later dismissed), and one count of forceful sodomy of a female fan. He was already on bail for an outstanding battery charge for allegedly striking a woman who asked for his autograph, and had also been arrested in Los Angeles for carrying a concealed weapon and assaulting a driver. Further controversy followed when a tape of *2Pacalypse Now* was found in the possession of a man arrested for murder. Shakur was found guilty of the sexual assault in November 1994, but the following day (30 November) was shot and robbed in the lobby of Quad Studios in New York's Times Square. Shakur later accused Biggie Smalls (Notorious B.I.G.), Andre Harrell and Sean 'Puff Daddy' Combs of involvement in the shooting, directly leading to the east coast/west coast feud that would eventually result in the deaths of both Notorious B.I.G. and Shakur himself. Following the shooting incident, Shakur was sentenced to four and a half years in jail on February 7 1995. The epic *Me Against The World* was released while he was serving his sentence, but still debuted at number one in the US charts. Meanwhile, Marion 'Suge' Knight, president of hip-hop's most successful label Death Row Records, had arranged parole for Shakur, who eventually served only eight months of his sentence. Newly signed to Death Row, Shakur released the sprawling double set *All Eyez On Me*, which entered the main Billboard US chart at number 1. The reviews were both supportive

and outstandingly good, and the album sold over 6 million in its first year, and generated a huge hit single with the Dr. Dre duet 'California Love'. During 1996 Shakur began concentrating on his acting career again, appearing in *Bullet* and *Gridlocked* (opposite Tim Roth). Further drama came when he was gunned down in Las Vegas on 8 September after watching the Mike Tyson-Bruce Seldon fight at the MGM Grand, and died five days later. Various explanations were given, including the theory that Notorious B.I.G. arranged the shooting after Shakur had bragged about sleeping with his wife, Faith Evans. The east coast/west coast rivalry continued after his death, leading to Notorious B.I.G.'s murder in similar circumstances six months later. In a further twist, Orlando Anderson, the chief suspect in Shakur's murder, was shot dead on 29 May 1998. Since his death Shakur's recorded legacy has generated several posthumous releases, amid ugly squabblings over his estate. *R U Still Down?* (released on his mother's new Amaru label) collects unreleased material from 1992-94.

● ALBUMS: *2Pacalypse Now* (TNT/Interscope 1992)★★★, *Strictly 4 My N.I.G.G.A.Z.* (TNT/Interscope 1993)★★★, *Me Against The World* (Out Da Gutta/Interscope 1994)★★★★, *All Eyez On Me* (Death Row/Interscope 1996)★★★, as Makaveli *Don Killuminati: The Seven Day Theory* (Death Row 1996)★★.

● COMPILATIONS: *R U Still Down? (Remember Me)* (Amaru 1997)★★★.

● VIDEOS: *Thug Immortal - The Tupac Shakur Story* (Xenon Entertainment 1998).

● FURTHER READING: *Tupac Shakur*, editors of Vibe. *Rebel For The Hell Of It: The Life Of Tupac Shakur*, Armond White.

● FILMS: *Bullet, Gridlocked, Gang Related* (1998).

SHAMEN

From the ashes of the moderately successful Alone Again Or in 1986, the Shamen had a profound effect upon contemporary pop music over the next half decade. Formed in Aberdeen by Colin Angus (b. 24 August 1961, Aberdeen, Scotland; bass), Peter Stephenson (b. 1 March 1962, Ayrshire, Scotland), Keith McKenzie (b. 30 August 1961, Aberdeen, Scotland) and Derek McKenzie (b. 27 February 1964, Aberdeen, Scotland; guitar), the Shamen's formative stage relied heavily on crushing, psychedelic rock played by a relatively orthodox line-up. Their debut album, *Drop*, captured a sense of their colourful live shows and sealed the first chapter of the band's career. Soon after, Colin Angus became fascinated by the nascent underground hip-hop movement. Derek McKenzie was rather less enamoured with the hardcore dance explosion and departed, allowing Will Sinnott (b. William Sinnott, 23 December 1960, Glasgow, Scotland, d. 23 May 1991; bass) to join the ranks and further encourage the Shamen's move towards the dancefloor. In 1988, their hard-edged blend of rhythms, guitars, samples, sexually explicit slideshows and furious rhetoric drew anger from feminists, politicians and - after the scathing 'Jesus Loves Amerika' single - religious groups. That same year the band relocated to London, slimmed down to the duo of Angus and Sinnott who concentrated on exploring the areas of altered states with mind-expanding psychedelics. By 1990 the Shamen's influence - albeit unwitting - was vividly realized as the much-touted indie-dance crossover saw bands fuse musical cultures, with the likes of Jesus Jones openly admitting the Shamen's groundbreaking lead. By this time the Shamen themselves had taken to touring with the 'Synergy' show, a unique four-hour extravaganza featuring rappers and designed to take the band even further away from their rock roots. After four years of such imaginative adventures into sound, 1991 promised a huge breakthrough for the Shamen and their fluctuating creative entourage. Unfortunately, just as the group inexorably toppled towards commercial riches, Will Sinnott drowned off the coast of Gomera, one of the Canary Islands, on the 23 May 1991. With the support of Sinnott's family, the Shamen persevered with a remix of 'Move Any Mountain (Pro Gen '91)' which climbed into the Top 10 of the UK chart, a fitting farewell to the loss of such a creative force. Mr C (b. Richard West), a cockney rapper, DJ and head of the Plink Plonk record label, had joined the band for a section of 'Move Any Mountain (Pro Gen '91)'. Although many found his patois ill-fitting, his rhymes founded the springboard for UK chart success 'LSI', followed by the number 1 'Ebeneezer Goode' - which was accused in many quarters for extolling the virtues of the Ecstasy drug ('E's Are Good, E's Are Good, E's Are Ebeneezer Goode'). The Shamen denied all, and moved on with the release of Boss Drum. Its title track provided a deeply affecting dance single, complete with lyrics returning the band to their original, shamanic ethos of universal rhythms.

Placed next to the teen-pop of 'LSI' and 'Ebeneezer Goode', such innovative work reinforced the Shamen's position as the wild cards of the UK dance scene, although recent recordings have been lacking in fresh ideas or further hit records.

● ALBUMS: *Drop* (Moshka 1987)★★★, *In Gorbachev We Trust* (Demon 1989)★★★, *Phorward* (Moshka 1989)★★★, *En-Tact* (One Little Indian 1990)★★★, *En-Tek* (One Little Indian 1990)★★★, *Progeny* (One Little Indian 1991)★★★, *Boss Drum* (One Little Indian 1992)★★★★, *Different Drum* (One Little Indian 1992)★★★, *The Shamen On Air* (Band Of Joy 1993)★★, *Axis Mutatis* (One Little Indian 1995)★★, *Hempton Manor* (One Little Indian 1996)★★.

● COMPILATIONS: *Collection* (One Little Indian 1997)★★★, *The Remix Collection (Stars On 45)* (One Little Indian 1997)★★★.

SHARP, JONAH

Ambient artist located in San Francisco who records as Space Time Continuum on his own Reflective Records. In 1993 he undertook an album with Peter Namlock for Fax, and a second collection with Californian hippie mystic Terrence McKenna for Caroline. Originally a jazz and session drummer in the UK, he played at several London parties as a DJ before relocating to the USA. He has since set up a new studio in San Francisco. As well as his own *Flourescence* EP, other Reflective releases have included a Namlock remix CD and a techno-flavoured 12-inch by emiT ecapS.

SHE

Female MC who debuted with 'Miss DJ (Rap It Up!)', on the Clappers Record label, produced by Dennis Weedon. However, she would go on to record under sundry other titles, including Ms DJ and her own name, Sheila Spencer. Before her break in the music world she had sung in Brooklyn choirs from the age of five, and trained as an actress. Her resumé is undoubtedly a varied one. She would later become a national figure via her role as Thomasina in NBC's soap, *Another World*. She also previously sung backing vocals for Kurtis Blow's debut album, and was Muhammed Ali's cheerleader.

SHE ROCKERS

Comprising schoolmates Donna McConnell and Antonia Jolly, who formerly worked with Alison Clarkson (later Betty Boo) before that artist broke solo. Originally intending to become a news journalist and tennis pro respectively, their discovery of rap, particularly the work of Run DMC, LL Cool J and other B-boys, turned them onto the hip-hop bug. They decided to form the band with Clarkson after seeing Salt 'N' Pepa play live at London's Astoria venue. They took their name from an extension of McConnell's stage name (She-Rock), and saw their debut recording, 'First Impressions', housed on the compilation *Known To Be Down*. Unlikely though they viewed it to be at the time, the track came to the attention of Chuck D. The result was a collaboration with Professor Griff called 'Give It A Rest', which also featured DJ Streets Ahead. However, on returning to England from the USA, Clarkson went solo leaving her former partners as a duo. Two singles, 'Jam It Jam' and 'Do Dat Dance', marked out their new territory - cultured hip-house. The latter was produced by Technotronic. Their roots in pop, dance and rap were given equal billing on the attendant album, which brought a blend of mellow, often humourous raps, with an undertow of house music and the disco strains of Chic. There were conscious raps among allusions to their love life, 'How Sweet It Is' pointing out how violence at hip-hop shows was overexposed compared to much greater outbreaks elsewhere. The set was neutered, they claimed, by pressure from their record company. They had wanted it to be a hardcore hip-hop set. A public disclaimer about the album being only half good, and not having had any say on the track listing, did not help its sales profile.
● ALBUMS: *Rockers From London* (Jive 1990)★★.

SHERWOOD, ADRIAN

b. *c*.1958. A pioneering force in UK reggae, Sherwood's first attempts to set up labels in the late 70s were disastrous, and cost him a great deal of money in the process. Despite such misadventures, he persevered, and set up the On-U-Sound label to house ex-Pop Group singer Mark Stewart's New Age Steppers project. Over a hundred albums and singles have subsequently been released, including music by Bim Sherman, Dub Syndicate and Mothmen (an embryonic Simply Red). Sherwood styled On-U-Sound after the reggae model of 'house bands' (Revolutionaries, Soul Syndicate, etc.). The label/organization also played out as a sound system, in a similar fashion to its Jamaican counterparts. Among the notable long-term protagonists at On-U-Sound have been Bonjo (African Head Charge), Bim Sherman and Skip McDonald, Doug Wimbush and Keith LeBlanc (Tackhead). However, Sherwood is equally renowned for his production skills, which he learned at first hand from Prince Far-I and Dr Pablo. The Fall, Depeche Mode and Ministry have been among his notable clients. On-U-Sound came to the attention of the public outside reggae circles when self-styled 'white toaster' Gary Clail entered the charts. However, neither this, nor any other individual release, can be described as representative of the rock-reggae-dance fusion that On-U-Sound have fostered. On-U-Sound's eclecticism remains rampant, but as Sherwood himself concedes: 'I'm first and foremost a passionate fan of reggae music'.
● COMPILATIONS: Various Artists: *On-U-Sound Present Pay It All Back Volume 4* (On-U-Sound 1993)★★★, *Reggae Archive Volumes 1 & 2* (On-U-Sound)★★★, *Various Discoplates Collection Part 1* (On-U-Sound 1998)★★★★.

SHOWBIZ AND AG

Bronx-based compatriots of Diamond D, Showbiz And AG were forced to make their mark in hip-hop by establishing their own independent label, Showbiz Records, to house their debut EP, *Soul Clap* (1991). It immediately created a buzz, leading them into a deal with London Records. AG had previously worked freestyle battles with Lord Finesse in high school, who introduced him to Showbiz. The partnership formed, they hustled through New York in a failed bid to get a contract. However, when their debut EP landed, particularly through the sucess of the 'Diggin' In The Crates' cut, they were hot news on the scene. Their profile was galvanised by Showbiz's highly successful remix of Arrested Development's 'Tenessee'. He has gone on to foster the careers of Big L and Deshawn.
● ALBUMS: *Represent* (London 1992)★★★.

SHRI

The multi-instrumentalist Shrikanth Sriram was brought up in Bombay where he trained as a classical tabla player from an early age. As a teenager he developed a taste for jazz, in particular the fusion styles of John McLaughlin, Jaco Pastorius and Joe Zawinul, and consequently developed a more groove-orientated approach to playing, learning the bass guitar. He later played percussion in Indus Creed, one of India's most successful rock groups, and bass in the jazz band Azure Hades, with which he recorded an album. On the strength of this, he was invited to the UK by Simon Dove of the Yorkshire Dance Centre to work with Talvin Singh, and he subsequently returned to work on a contemporary dance project. On the strength of his work in Nitin Sawhney's live band, Shri signed to Outcaste Records and released his debut album *Drum The Bass* in 1997. Here he blended his own particular approaches to percussion, bass, flute and other instruments with the sounds and techniques of UK dance music, to produce a collection of evocative, atmospheric tracks. In 1998 he released a second album, *Dancing Drums*, a collaboration with the DJ and producer Badmarsh that tended towards a drum 'n' bass and breakbeat sound. The title track from this album and Shri's own 'Meditation' were included on Outcaste's excellent compilation, *Untouchable Outcaste Beats*, in 1997.

● ALBUMS: *Drum The Bass* (Outcaste 1997)★★★★, with Badmarsh *Dancing Drums* (Outcaste 1998)★★★★.

SHUT UP AND DANCE

Hip-hop/house artists PJ and Smiley (both b. c.1969) comprise this duo, who are also producers and owners of the Shut Up And Dance Record label (run from a bedroom in Stoke Newington). The group formed in Spring 1988, the record label coming a year later. This saw releases by the Ragga Twins ('Spliffhead'), Nicolette and Rum & Black. Shut Up And Dance all began with the intoxicating club cut '5678', which eventually moved over 14,000 copies. This helped fund Shut Up And Dance as a full-scale label enterprise, with a penchant for the absurd, their own '£10 To Get In' and 'Derek Went Mad' being good examples. One 12-inch, 'Lamborghini', stitched together Prince and Annie Lennox (Eurythmics), and though it made the UK Top 60, radio stations refused to play it fearing punitive writs. The duo had originally recorded a novelty single under the name Private Party which featured various characters from the *Thunderbirds* and *Muppets* television programmes. Their anonymity was enhanced by the lack of detail that usually accompanied their releases, helping them become leaders in the UK's underground dance scene.

Musically they spliced their recordings with samples drawn from a myriad of sources; predictable dub reggae through to techno beats. However, it was the number 2 chart smash 'Ravin' I'm Ravin'' (sung by Peter Bouncer) which brought them real commercial attention, more than they either envisaged or welcomed. It also sent copyright lawyers into apoplectic overdrive. They spent almost two years struggling in court following action taken by the MCPS on behalf of six major record companies for uncleared use of samples. Although they returned with an EP in 1994, the appropriately titled *Phuck The Biz*, their legal problems were far from over, their business having long since been declared bankrupt. It would be a shame if their brushes with the law overshadowed classic records like 1992's 'Autobiography Of A Crack Head'.

● ALBUMS: *Dance Before The Police Come* (Shut Up And Dance 1990)★★★, *Death Is Not The End* (Shut Up And Dance 1992)★★★, *Black Men United* (Pulse-8 1995)★★.

SHYHEIM

b. Shyheim Franklin, c.1979, Staten Island, New York, USA. Child prodigy who does not take kindly to comparisons to Kriss Kross et al, whose debut album emerged when he was only 14. He had first come to hip-hop via the sounds of LL Cool J and Run DMC, and as a child learnt to rap along with them before graduating to verses of his own. His break came when producer RNS heard him rapping on the street in front of his block in Stapleton Projects, a dwelling he also shared with the young Shyheim. Together they worked on demos in RNS' studio, before attracting the interest of Virgin Records. More talented than most, Shyheim's depiction of inner ghetto violence did strike a chord, and was not related in the tedious 'my gun's bigger than your gun' mantra of too many artists. His 'On And On' single, for example, contained the somehow touching line: 'Ain't never had a good Christmas, So who's Santa Claus?'. Compared by many to a young Rakim (Eric B And Rakim), Shyheim's posse of homeboys (Do Lil's, Rubberbandz, KD, the Down Low Wrecker) were all present on his debut album, as were his 'brother artists', the Wu Tang Clan (Prince Rakeem of that crew being his next-door neighbour).

● ALBUMS: *Aka The Rugged Child* (Virgin 1994)★★★, *The Lost Generation* (Virgin 1996)★★★.

SILENT MAJORITY

A hip-hop group from Lausanne, Switzerland, Silent Majority are among the cream of the Euro-rap generation challenging French and UK domination of the genre. Comprising DJ Goo, and MCs Nya and R Test, they deal in various languages (English, French, Spanish and even Swahili). The variety of linguistic styles is matched by DJ Goo's supple rhythmic layers, which rarely lapse into the straight imitation of west and east coast American styles that so often afflicts European rap producers. Their 1994 debut album, *La Jamorite Silencieuse*, duly received glowing reviews in several European hip-hop magazines.
● ALBUMS: *La Jamorite Silencieuse* (Unik/Big Cheese 1994)★★★.

SILENT RECORDS

San Francisco label headed by managing director Kim Cascone, who had previously been in charge of sound on two David Lynch movies, *Twin Peaks* and *Wild At Heart*. Formed in 1989 (the first release being PGR's 'Silent', which gave the label a name), the company is the ultimate ambient/subsconscious operation, based on a desire to experiment with the dynamics and properties of sound. Cascone's own Heavenly Music Corporation is but one of the names on the catalogue, whose discography included over 50 records by 1994. Others include Cosmic Trigger, Michael Mantra, Spice Barons and Thessolonians. The label is best sampled on the popular compilation series, *From Here To Eternity*. 'What we're about is open systems, an inclusive kind of nurturing of ideas, and of using people who have some kind of a different spin on the genre'.

SIMMONS, RUSSELL

b. *c*.1958, Hollis, Queens, New York, USA. Simmons' artistic and business sense has seen him become the ultimate B-Boy millionaire, bullet-proof Rolls Royce notwithstanding. His entrepreneurial interests began by promoting disco parties while he was studying sociology at City College Of New York. Rush management was formed in 1979, and quickly escalated following the success of Kurtis Blow and Fearless Four. His first writing credit came with Blow's 'Christmas Rap'. However, no one can accuse Simmons of having fortune fall in his lap. He was part of the Rush team who picketed MTV in order to get them to play black videos (Run DMC's 'Rock Box',

although Michael Jackson was the first to be played), and has maintained his commitment to black development. Throughout the 80s Def Jam, the label, would be the dominant force in the music, via the work of Run DMC and Public Enemy. Though he would eventually split from Rick Rubin, Simmons' stature in the eyes of the hip-hop audience has hardly decreased. In 1993 Rush Management was valued at $34 million, with seven record labels, management, fashion (the Phat line) and broadcasting interests. The president of the company is Carmen Ashurst-Watson, but Simmons remains responsible for the company ethos: 'My only real purpose is managing and directing. I sacrifice all the time for my artists. It's my job to make sure they have rich black babies'.

SIMONELLI, VICTOR

b. *c*.1967, USA. Brooklyn-based producer of the early 90s who learnt his craft at the knee of Arthur Baker, working in his Shakedown Studio. After editing work on tracks by Al Jarreau and David Bowie, he joined Lenny Dee to establish Brooklyn Street Essentials, a remix team. He has worked widely in this territory ever since. His own *noms de plume* included Groove Committee (cutting 'Dirty Games' for Nu Groove), Solution, Ebony Soul and the Street Players. Throughout he has maintained his belief in working with fully fledged songs rather than simply strong rhythmic tracks. He has recently recorded with Tommy Musto as part of Colourblind.

SIMPLÉ E

Talented female rapper who broke through in 1994 with her debut single 'Play My Funk', a Top 20 US R&B chart success. Taken from the *Sugar Hill* motion picture soundtrack, and produced by Dwayne Wiggins of Tony Toni Tone!, it revealed her to be able to switch from sung passages to gripping raps without missing a beat. Her debut album was aided by the production of Terry T and S.I.D. Reynolds.
● ALBUMS: *The Colourz Of Sound* (Beacon 1994)★★.

SINDECUT

North London rap collective Sindecut spent their early days performing at the Swiss Cottage Community Centre, before releasing an eponymous debut single in 1986. Other members congregated around the nucleus of rapper Crazy

Noddy and DJ Fingers, including Lyne Lyn (rapper), DJ Don't Ramp (producer), Mix Man G, Mad P and, later, Spike Tee and Louise Francis. Various members travelled to America in 1987/88 to get a deal with B-Boy Records, but lost out on the chance of a deal when label boss Bill Kamarra was sent to prison. They elected to set up their own label, Jgunglelist, instead (an interesting use of the term before it was hijacked by the 'jungle' club movement). The Sindecut made their name with the infectious rhythms of 'Posse'. It was an imposing stew of ragga vocals and hip-hop breaks. Their first club hit, though, was 'Sindecut Kickin' Yeah', on another independent label, Baad. They grew up with the similarly formulated Soul II Soul, merging soul and reggae with rap: 'Its just our influences really. Americans have a lot of influences but they tend to make one type of music. We want to make music that we are influenced by and put it together into a new sound'. Their debut album showcased raps backed by orchestrated strings and frantic live drums - an almost 'new age' hip-hop affair.
● ALBUMS: *Changing The Scenery* (Virgin 1990)★★★.

SINGH, TALVIN

b. 1970, London, England. Talvin Singh is one of the first artists to help bring traditional Indian tabla music to the mainstream, combining it with the rhythmic surges of drum 'n' bass. By 1997, he was able to speak in an assured fashion about the historic place and function of traditional Indian music: 'This has been happening for 15 years. But there's a different agenda for us now than saying, "Let's cash in on the Asian sound for the Western scene." It's about bringing music to people's attention which they've probably never heard before.' Head of the Omni Records label, based in south London, Singh is a virtuoso tabla player and an accomplished composer and arranger. As a child he travelled to India's Punjab region to study percussion with his uncle and grandfather. By his early 20s he was already a veteran of recording sessions with Björk, Sun Ra and Future Sound Of London. Through projects such as the compilation album *Anokha: Soundz Of The Asian Underground*, he has also helped establish other Asian artists, including Osmani Soundz, Amar and Milky Bar Kid. Anokha, also the name of the weekly club night Singh hosts at the Blue Note club in London, translates as 'unique' from Urdu. Both the club and his recording projects reflect an

interest in the sounds and styles of Britain as well as affection for the Indian musical tradition. As he told Rolling Stone magazine: 'I love Indian culture, and I love my music, but we now live on a planet which is very small. It's a mixed culture, mixed vibes. You just have to study and respect certain traditions, then bring your character across in what you do.' Before launching his solo career in 1997, Singh found time to produce a percussion-based album, *One World, One Drum*, and appeared on Björk's world tour.
● ALBUMS: *Talvin Singh Presents Anokha: Soundz Of The Asian Underground* (Mango 1997)★★★.

SIR MIX-A-LOT

Seattle based DJ/MC and producer (b. Anthony Ray) who broke with 'Posse On Broadway', a statement of intent released on his own label in 1986, which would go on to sell over a million copies. Further crossover success arrived with rap's second great rock/rap coalition: a cover of Black Sabbath's 'Iron Man', performed in conjunction with Seattle thrash outfit Metal Church. By the time of his second album Sir Mix-A-Lot was sampling Prince's 'Batdance', and maintaining his sharp, political edge - though he is too light-hearted and deft of touch to be considered truly gangsta. His Rhyme Cartel is signed to Def American records, and he can boast a platinum and gold album for *Swass* and *Seminar*, respectively. Sir-Mix-A-Lot's use of unlikely sources, the synthesized pop of Devo and Kraftwerk measured against the conscious lyrics of rappers like Public Enemy, was a unique combination. However, there were some crude sexual japes on tracks like 'Mack Daddy', and he was hardly shown in the best light by the pro-gun swagger of 'No Rods Barred'. He did enjoy another huge hit in 'Baby Got Back', however.
● ALBUMS: *Swass* (Nastymix 1988)★★★★, *Seminar* (Nastymix 1989)★★★, *Mack Daddy* (Def American 1992)★★, *Chief Boot Knocka* (American Recordings 1994)★★★, *Return Of The Bumpasaurus* (American Recordings 1996)★★.

SISTER SOULJAH

b. Lisa Williamson, USA. Rapper who became something of a *cause celebre* when President-elect Bill Clinton verbally attacked her during his campaign. On June 13 1992 he declared that Souljah had made 'racist remarks' and 'advocated violence against whites' in an interview with *Rolling Stone* magazine. As if having such political heavyweights on her case were not enough, she also found herself being sued by former producer Michael Shinn, after she listed him as a 'two-faced backstabber' on the sleevenotes to her 1992 Epic album. The source of their inital disagreement was not disclosed, but she was dropped from the label after its release in any case. The album is still worth investigating however, notably on cuts like 'State Of Accomodation: Why Aren't You Angry?' and 'Killing Me Softly: Deadly Code Of Silence', which featured guest shots from Chuck D and Ice Cube respectively. She also worked with Public Enemy, joining the band in late 1990 after accompanying them on their US lecture tour. However, her contribution (rapping on 'By The Time I Get To Arizona' from *The Enemy Strikes Black*) was disappointing and her tenure with the band was a brief one. She had already appeared on Terminator X's single, 'Wanna Be Dancin' (Buck Whylin')', and would also guest on his debut solo album.

● ALBUMS: *360 Degrees Of Power* (Epic 1992)★★★.

SIZE, RONI

Reprazent, a Bristol, England drum 'n' bass collective, came to national prominence in 1997 when its founder and leader, Roni Size (b. *c*.1968, England), was awarded that year's Mercury Prize. Much of the acclaim centred around Size's melding of the new with the old - the propulsive jungle beats accompanied by live drums and double bass. The group - Size (compositions, programming), DJ Krust, Onallee (vocals), MC Dynamite and rapper Bahmadia (a former protégé of Gang Starr) - came together on Bristol's highly fertile and disparate club scene. As a result, Reprazent's sleek, highly musical take on drum 'n' bass is equally informed by hip-hop, funk, soul and house. Size was expelled from school at the age of 16, and starting attending house parties run by Bristol mavericks the Wild Bunch (later Massive Attack). His future partner, Krust, enjoyed a brief dalliance with fame as part of the Fresh 4, whose 'Wishing On A Star' reached the UK Top 10. Reprazent's debut album, *New Forms*, was released on Full Cycle Records, which Size runs in partnership with DJ Krust. Size was keen to describe the mélange of influences as intuitive: 'If Krust walks into the studio and his head is nodding, that's enough. I know I've got a result there. He doesn't need to touch a button or tell us what he thinks, 'cos we already know what

he's thinking.' In consolidation of their mainstream breakthrough (the most significant for jungle since Goldie's debut), Reprazent set out to become the summer sound of 1997 with a series of festival appearances (including Tribal Gathering).

● ALBUMS: *New Forms* (Full Cycle/Talkin' Loud 1997)★★★★.

SKINNY BOYS

Comprising brothers MC Shockin' Shaun (b. Shaun Harrison, Bridgeport, Connecticut, USA) and DJ Super Jay (b. James Harrison, Bridgeport, Connecticut, USA), plus their cousin Jock Box (b. Jacque Harrison, Bridgeport, Connecticut, USA). After first being drawn to the funk of James Brown and George Clinton, these young men were invigorated by the East Coast rap phenomenon. Super Jay grew particularly enamoured of Grandmaster Flash, and ditched his previous instruments (accordion and organ) to concentrate on DJing with a local partner. He was subsequently joined first by his brother, then cousin Jock Box, whose 'human beatbox' style resembled that of the Fat Boys' Darren Robinson. Indeed, the Skinny Boys moniker was a tongue-in-cheek reference to the latter band. Playing local skating rinks, they eventually came to the attention of Mark and Rhonda Bush. The former would offer the trio production, while the latter managed them and wrote their raps ('based on our ideas', the Skinny Boys claimed). In 1985, their first 12-inch single emerged, 'We're Skinny Boys'/'Awesome', on their manager's Bush label. A second single, 'Feed Us The Beat'/'Jock Box' saw them switch to Warlock, which also released their debut album. On the back of this exposure the trio were eventually signed to the Jive imprint. They would tour with the likes of Jazzy Jeff And The Fresh Prince, Kool Moe Dee, Salt 'N' Pepa and, suitably, the Fat Boys, building a strong local following. Their second album, once again helmed by the Bushes, included 'I Wanna Be Like', which namechecked Prince, Michael Jackson and Bill Cosby as suitable role models. Despite the good intentions and strong start, the title of their final album for Jive in 1988 proved sadly ironic.

● ALBUMS: *Weightless* (Warlock 1986)★★★, *Skinny & Proud* (Jive 1987)★★★, *Skinny, They Can't Get Enough* (Jive 1988)★★.

SKINT RECORDS

This label was set up as a subsidiary of Loaded Records in 1995 by Damian Harris (aka Midfield General) and played an important role in the development of the sound known as big beat. Skint emerged from a scene in Brighton based around the 'Big Beat Boutique', from which the movement took its name, where Fatboy Slim was a resident DJ. Their first release was Fatboy Slim's 'Santa Cruz' in 1995, which was followed by a series of singles including Hip Optimist's 'Anafey' and Midfield General's 'Worlds/Bung'. The next year their compilation album, *Brassic Beats Volume One* (1996), featured tracks by these artists and others, notably Bentley Rhythm Ace, Cut Le Roc, Leuroj and Req. The label has since achieved widespread success and recognition, notably through Fatboy Slim's single 'Everybody Needs A 303' and the album *Better Living Through Chemistry* (1996), and Bentley Rhythm Ace's debut album *Bentley Rhythm Ace* (1997), as well as the second and third volumes of the *Brassic Beats* series (released in 1997 and 1998, respectively). Subsequent album releases include the Lo-Fidelity Allstars' *How To Operate With A Blown Mind* (1998) and Req's *One* (1997) and *Frequency Jams* (1998). Although there is a notable difference between many of their acts, much of Skint's music is characterized by funky breakbeats and catchy riffs, and blends rock instrumentation with the sounds and approach of dance music. At the same time it often has a rough edge and purveys a sense of kitsch, reflecting the label's light-hearted attitude and willingness not to take themselves too seriously. In January 1998, after approaches from a number of major labels, Harris signed a contract with Sony Records that allowed to him to remain in control of Skint's output.

SL2

SL2 consist of two Essex-based DJs, Slipmatt (b. Matthew Nelson, *c.*1967) and Lime (b. John Fernandez, *c.*1968), who were joined by video 'stars' Jo and Kelly for live appearances. Already well established as DJs on the rave circuit, they introduced themselves to a wider audience with the acid-influenced debut single, 'Do That Dance', and its follow-up, 'The Noise'. Their next single, 'DJ's Take Control', sold out of its original 1,000 pressing on Awesome within two hours and was picked up by XL Records. The song was built around a keyboard line from the Nightwriter's

1987 underground house cut, 'Let The Music Use You'. The b-side, 'Way In My Brain', employed the reggae bass line of 'Under Me Sleng Ten' and pre-saged the style of their next release. A UK Top 10 hit, 'On A Ragga Tip' was their most successful record and brought the jungle style into the charts for the first time; it was in part based on Jah Screechie's 'Walk And Skank'.

SLAM

Like so many groups operating in the techno field, Glasgow, Scotland-based Slam are a duo, comprising Orde Meikle and Stuart McMillan. They also embody the genre's tradition of not limiting themselves to one activity. They perform regularly as DJs at the Arches and Sub Sub clubs in Glasgow, and are also responsible for running the pre-eminent Soma Records label, as well as remixing for A Man Called Adam, Sunscreem ('Love You More'), Perception, Mark Bell, Botany 5, DSK ('What Could We Do'), Joey Negro and Kym Sims ('Too Blind To See'). Slam took clubland by storm in 1992 with 'Eterna', repeating the feat in 1994 via their earthy revision of Jean-Michel Jarre's 'Chronologie 6'. After attending outdoor raves in Berlin, Holland, and Belgium, Jarre confessed he rather liked what they had done to his opus. Slam were less charitable: 'I read an interview with Jarre which gave me the impression that he's very excited about the European dance scene, but doesn't quite understand it and doesn't have the right contacts. So we had no qualms about ripping his track to pieces.' The release of 'Snapshots' in 1995 confirmed Slam's continued artistic growth. It was followed in the early months of 1996 by 'Dark Forces', and the duo's long-awaited debut album, *Head States* This revealed a cumulative debt to cinema soundtracks, hinted at by 'Dark Forces' sweeping time signatures and repetitive invention. Shortly before its release the duo travelled to Belgrade to become one of the first acts to perform in the former Yugoslavia since the 1995 peace accord.
● ALBUMS: *Head States* (Soma 1996)★★★.

SLATER, LUKE

b. *c.*1968, St. Albans, Hertfordshire, England. Turned on to music via early experiments with sounds and noises on his father's old reel-to-reel, rather than by any affinity to a particular musical subculture, Slater set about defining his vision during 1989 on the fledgling label Jelly Jam, an offshoot of the Brighton record shop of the same name where he was working at the time. A batch of Detroit-influenced tracks were spat out at an alarming rate, and a contract with D-Jax Records soon followed that saw Slater adopting the guise of Clementine. However, it was not until his link-up with Peacefrog Records in 1993, and another change of name to Planetary Assault Systems, that Slater's name became widely known and praised. He became heralded as the UK torch-bearer for the Detroit sound, managing to capture the essence of that city's musical qualities, whether recording pounding, abrasive sounds as Planetary Assault Systems for Peacefrog, or alluding instead to classical textures as the 7th Plain for GPR. However, Slater's furious output during 1993/4 soon started to take its toll: 'I began to realise you can't do everything, I was beginning to lose focus on what I originally intended to do in the first place.' Taking time out from a hectic studio and DJing schedule, Slater returned in 1997, with *Freek Funk*, recorded in his home studio in Crawley, Sussex. With *Freek Funk*, Slater has achieved what so many aspire to - a highly accomplished and highly variable album, unique and accessible, that pushes musical boundaries more than most. With plans to further his trans-formative powers into song structures and a muted plan to take out a full live band, Slater is not content merely to stay ahead of the incessant marching beat of the dance rhythm.

● ALBUMS: *X-Tront - Volume 1* (Peacefrog 1993)★★★, *X-Tront - Volume 2* (Peacefrog 1993)★★★, as Morganistic *Fluids Amniotic* (Input Neuron Musique 1994)★★★★, as 7th Plain *Four Cornered Room* (GPR 1994)★★★★, as 7th Plain *My Yellow Wise Rug* (GPR 1994)★★★, *Freek Funk* (Novamute 1997)★★★★.

● COMPILATIONS: Planetary Assault Systems *Archives* (Peacefrog 1996)★★★★.

SLEEPING BAG RECORDS

New York City based rap label who first brought the world Mantronix and Todd Terry. The label was inaugurated by Willie Socolov and Arthur Russell when they released the latter's 'Go Bang' as Dinosaur L. The second single was 'Weekend' by Class Action. While that 45 was being plugged by Juggy Gayles, Socolov met with Gayles' son, Ron Resnick. Resnick would become vice-presi-dent of the company, as they went on to establish a rap platform which boasted EPMD before they defected to Def American. Other acts included Joyce Sims and Cash Money And Marvellous.

Socolov and Russell were no musical purists, and were happy to describe themselves as: 'Two white, middle-class, Jewish hucksters'. Incidentally, Sleeping Bag was named after Socolov's ultimate bachelor behaviour - having a sleeping bag over his mattress to save making the bed. They opened a UK office through Rough Trade in 1990, but afterwards their influence waned.

● ALBUMS: Mantronix: *Mantronix* (Sleeping Bag 1985)★★★. Cash Money And Marvellous: *Where's The Party At* (Sleeping Bag 1988)★★★. T La Rock: *On A Warpath* (Sleeping Bag 1990)★★.

SLICK RICK

b. Richard Walters, South Wimbledon, London, England. Of Jamaican parentage, Walters moved to the USA at the age of 14, going on to attend New York's High School of Music & Art. By the time his solo career started, Slick had already enjoyed his five minutes of rap fame (as MC Ricky D) by backing Doug E. Fresh on his mas-terpiece, 'The Show'. Not the most enlightened of hip-hop's rappers, as 'Treat Her Like A Prostitute' on his debut album confirmed, Slick Rick does, however, live up to his name on his more impres-sive numbers. These included his standard, 'The Ruler'. It was also impossible to argue with the superb production by Rich himself alongside Jam Master Jay (Run DMC) and Hank Shocklee and Eric Sadler (the Bomb Squad). His second album was recorded in just three weeks while he was out of jail on bail, and facing up to ten years for attempted murder (shooting his cousin and his friend, then undergoing a high speed car chase which ended in both him and his girlfriend breaking legs). It continued the jazzy rhythms of his debut, which would attain platinum status in his adopted US homeland. Rick's confident, effi-cient half-sung delivery also proved a powerful influence on subsequent rappers, including Snoop Doggy Dogg.

● ALBUMS: *The Great Adventures Of Slick Rick* (Def Jam 1988)★★★, *The Ruler's Back* (Def Jam 1991)★★, *Behind Bars* (Island 1995)★★★.

SLINKY WIZARD

As with many such groups, the history of this trance outfit goes back to the parties in Goa of the early 90s. Dominic Lamb began DJing at acid house clubs in London in 1988. Two years later he was travelling in India and met Adam Boyd in Goa, where they developed an interest in the techno-trance sound being played there. Lamb then DJed in Goa and around the world before returning to the UK in 1992, when he and Boyd wrote their first track together. Joining up with George Barker and 'Ronnie' Biggs (who had both been organizing 'Goa'-style parties in Britain), Slinky Wizard recorded *The Wizard* EP in February 1994 with Simon Posford (Hallucinogen) at Butterfly Studios; it became the first release on Flying Rhino the following December. However, the band tragically lost Boyd in an accident that summer. After collaborating with a number of different producers over the next 18 months, including Technossomy's Matt Evans ('Shivari Thing' and 'The Wandering Prophet') and the Green Nuns Of The Revolution's Dick Trevor ('Shitty Stick'), in 1996 the band worked with Gus Till of Butterfly Studios, who had previously worked for INXS and Dogs In Space and quickly became a permanent member. 'Funkus Munkus' was released on Flying Rhino's *First Flight* compilation, and 'Licenced To Slink', a psy-trance take on the *James Bond* theme, was featured on the same label's *Air Born*. In 1997 Slinky Wizard's contributions to the *Black Rhino* and *White Rhino* collections signalled a change of tack as they moved from the standard 'Goa'-style riffs and melodies of 'Funkus Munkus' to the stripped-down, abstract sound of 'Sacred Fist' and 'People Like Us'. The following year the band released *The Monkey Comes Cheap* EP and were also planning their first album. In the meantime, Lamb has continued to DJ at trance parties and festivals around the UK, Europe, Asia, North America and Australasia.

SLIP 'N' SLIDE RECORDS

Slip 'N' Slide was launched in the UK as a subsidiary of Kickin' Records for less hardcore tastes in 1993. The first record to cause a major ripple was Adonte's house track 'Dreams', mixed by Pete Lorimer. In the year of their inception they continued to plough a bold furrow with hits by Diggers ('Soweto', produced by Lyndsay Edwards of Disco Evangelists fame), the trance house of H.A.L.F. ('I Don't Need You Any More') and Soundscape ('Amoxa'), while club hits were provided by Boomshanka ('Gonna Make You Move', though the duo also record for their own Can Can imprint as Avarice) and Rock & Kato ('Jungle Kisses'). The label also licensed a compilation from German imprint Suck Me Plasma! (*Dance 2 Trance*, Norman etc.), and scored with Vivian Lee's 'Music Is So Wonderful' (remixed by Fire Island). Other artists include 3 Man Jury ('Digital Autopsy'), Decoy ('Open Your Mind'), John Bullock (whose 'Hendrix' sampled one of the great man's riffs), Men Of Faith ('Dance') and more.

● ALBUMS: *Dance & Trance* (Slip 'N' Slide 1993)★★★.

SMIF N WESSUN

Brooklyn, New York, USA-based outfit, named after the famous gun-making duo, Smif N Wessun arrived as the second act on Nervous Records' subsidiary, Wreck, in 1993. Rappers Tek and Steele first broke vinyl cover with two tracks, 'Black Smif n Wessun' and 'U Da Man', housed on Black Moon's *Enta Da Stage* album. The association with the latter began when they used dancer Tracy Allan, who turned out to be Buckshot's sister, on stage in their early days. They went on to support their mentors on their national tour with Das EFX. The production team responsible for *Enta Da Stage*, DJ Evid Dee and his brother Mr. Walt (aka Da Beatminerz), were also present for Smif N Wessun's debut single, 'Bucktown'. It sold over 75,000 units in its first three weeks of release.

● ALBUMS: *The Shining* (Wreck 1994)★★★.

SMITH AND MIGHTY

Duo from Bristol, Avon, England, comprising Rob Smith and Ray Mighty who broke through in 1988 with two memorable cover versions of Burt Bacharach/Hal David songs, 'Anyone' and 'Walk On By'. Both were effortless, breezy interpretations of the originals, tuned up via dub house and hip-hop stylings, garnished with the sensitive addition of female vocals. London Records were first off the mark in signing them up, having previously worked on their own Three Stripe imprint (which also issued records like Tru Funk's '4AM (The Lucid Phase)'. However, the momentum was lost when the debut LP for Bristolian artist Carlton bombed. Smith and Mighty's reputation for the Midas touch was lost with that album, and in the fast-changing world of dance music they became yesterday's men. However, they persevered in relative silence (as well as fathering six children between them), re-emerging in 1994 with a new album and single, a cover of Diana Ross's 'Remember Me', featuring their new vocal discovery, Marilyn. Their highly individual breakbeat style, which remained with them over the years, was sampled on the U2 cover, 'Drowning Man', while elsewhere the album contained denser material akin to the 'jungle' movement. Underpinning it all, however, was the seismic bass that had characterized their early recordings, their philosophy on low frequency incorporated into the album's title.

● ALBUMS: *Bass Is Maternal - When It's Loud, I Feel Safer* (More Rockers 1995)★★★.

SMITH, LARRY

b. Hollis, Queens, New York, USA. Smith formed Orange Crush (which also featured Davey DMX - or Davey D - and Trevor Gale), in his first foray into hip-hop. After this he went on to become one of rap music's most important producers. His credits included work with Jimmy Spicer and early Kurtis Blow, before he oversaw the first two Run DMC albums. In the process he helped to create the spare, minimalist rhythm tracks and sound that would define the 'new school'. His influence waned as the 80s progressed, though he did helm three albums by Whodini.

SMITH, WILL

b. 25 September 1968, Philadelphia, Pennsylvania, USA. Rap music's most successful crossover artist, Smith started his career as one half of DJ Jazzy Jeff And The Fresh Prince. Although it was lightweight in comparison with the threatening 'street' style of Public Enemy and NWA, the duo's inoffensive, bubblegum rap made them a crossover success, with 1988's *He's The DJ, I'm The Rapper* going double-platinum and 'Parent's Just Don't Understand' winning the duo a Grammy. Smith's inventive and charming rapping style brought him to the attention of NBC, who cast him in the starring role of *The Fresh Prince Of Bel-Air*. Smith shone as the streetwise tough suffering culture shock in affluent Beverley Hills, and the sitcom went on to become one of the station's most successful series, running until 1996. Film stardom beckoned, with Smith making his debut in 1992's *Where The Day Takes You*. He gained further acclaim for his role in 1993's *Six Degrees Of Separation*. The same year he released his final album with DJ Jazzy Jeff, topping the UK charts with 'Boom! Shake The Room'. A string of film roles followed which pushed Smith into the superstar league, beginning with 1995's *Bad Boys* and culminating in *Independence Day* (1996) and *Men In Black* (1997), two of the most successful movies ever made. Smith also recorded under his own name for the first time, topping the US and UK charts with the infectious theme tune from *Men In Black*. He also found the time to release his solo debut, *Big Willie Style*, a smooth pop-rap production which featured 'Gettin' Jiggy Wit It', another ridiculously catchy hit single.

● ALBUMS: *Big Willie Style* (Columbia 1997)★★★.

● FILMS: *Where The Day Takes You* (1992), *Six Degrees Of Separation* (1993), *Bad Boys* (1995), *Independence Day* (1996), *Men In Black* (1997).

SMOOTH, JOE

b. Joseph Welbon, USA. One of early house music's most distinctive vocalists, recording material like 'Time To Jack' and working with Fingers Inc. He actually started out as a DJ in 1983 at the Smart Bar in Chicago. There the staff were so impressed by his mixing that they dubbed him Joe Smooth for the first time. A genuine musician, he insisted on bringing his keyboards and drum machine on stage with him for his live shows. He went on to produce two house classics in 'You Can't Hide' (with Frankie Knuckles) and 'Promised Land' (later covered by the Style Council). His debut album featured guest vocals rather than his own as he concentrated on his musicianship. The singers included Anthony Thomas, former backing vocalist to the Ohio Players. The set included both 'Promised Land' and an unlikely cover of 'Purple Haze'.

SMOOTHE THE HUSTLER

Smoothe The Hustler brings the requisite social history to the US's west coast rap genre, having begun his first prison sentence at the age of 18 for illegal gun possession. At that time he claims to have earned his living as a drug pusher, but his stay in the local penitentiary convinced him of the need to secure alternative employment. He found it as a rapper, pressing up his initial 12-inch record ('My Everyday Lifestyle Ain't Nothing But A Hustle') and distributing copies directly to record shop outlets and radio stations. It brought him a contract with Profile Records who released his debut album, *Once Upon A Time In America*, in 1996. The critical reception was immediate, and Smoothe found himself catapulted to the forefront of mid-90s solo rappers dealing in what he loudly proclaimed to be 'the reality experience'.

● ALBUMS: *Once Upon A Time In America* (Profile 1996)★★★.

SNAKE THING

Nick Taylor is one of the best-known trance artists in Australia, where he lives in Byron Bay. In 1991 he began working in Tokyo with Tsuyoshi Suzuki as Blissed, and recorded an EP (*Blissed*) and an album (*Rite Of Passage*) that were released on POD Communications two years later. The pair consequently became Prana when they moved to London in 1993. Taylor worked on the first Prana album, *Cyclone* (1996), before returning to Australia where he began recording under the names Snake Thing (for TIP Records) and Reflector. After contributing a remix of 'Scarab' to Prana's second album, *Geomantik*, in September 1997, he released the EP *Scorch*, which signalled a move towards a psychedelic breakbeat sound. During the same year he also mixed the compilation *Feel The Noize* for Matsuri.

SNAP!

Durron Butler (b. Maurice Durron Butler, 30 April 1967, Pittsburgh, Pennsylvania, USA) was initially a drummer with a heavy metal band in his hometown. Later he joined the army and was posted to Germany where he became a bomb disposal expert. Whilst there he teamed up with Rico Sparx and Moses P. for several musical projects. After his discharge he returned to the States but went back to Germany to tour with the Fat Boys. German based producers Benito Benites (b. Michael Munzing) and John Garrett Virgo III (b. Luca Anzilotti), operating under pseudonyms, had put together a project they would call Snap!, after a function on a sequencing programme. Previously the producers had recorded widely in their Frankfurt studio, for their own label, Logic Records. They also ran their own club, Omen. Notable successes prior to Snap! included the 16-Bit Project ('Where Are You' and 'High Score') and Off's 'Electric Salsa', which featured Sven Vath as singer. They then recorded a song called 'The Power' which was built from samples of New York rapper Chill Rob G (Robert Frazier)'s 'Let The Rhythm Flow'. They added the powerful female backing vocals of Penny Ford, who had previously worked with George Clinton, Chaka Khan and Mica Paris, amongst others. Jackie Harris (b. Jaqueline Arlissa Harris, Pittsburgh, USA) was also credited for providing 'guide' vocals, and appeared in press interviews. The record was first released on the Wild Pitch label in America with the credit 'Snap featuring Chill Rob G'. However,

after the first 30,000 sales problems with Chill began to manifest themselves and they sought a replacement. They chose Butler, who was now renamed Turbo G. He had already recorded for Logic as back-up rapper for Moses P. Chill was allowed to release his own version of 'The Power' in America. Around the rest of the world a new version, featuring Turbo G, topped the charts. To promote the record he and Ford toured widely, before the latter embarked on a solo career. She was replaced by Thea Austin. Throughout Benites and Garrett utilised Turbo G as the public face of Snap!, remaining shadowy figures back in their Frankfurt studio, which was now a hugely impressive complex. Though they continued to score colossal hits with 'Oops Upside Your Head' and 'Mary Had A Little Boy', dissent had set in. Turbo wanted more artistic input, and hated 'Rhythm Is A Dancer' the projected lead-off single for the band's second album. When a substitute, 'The Colour Of Love', crashed, the duo went ahead without his agreement. Their judgement was proved correct when 'Rhythm Is A Dancer' became another international smash (the biggest selling UK single of the year). But by now the rift between the parties was irreconcilable. Turbo G had signed up for a solo career (debuting with 'I'm Not Dead' on Polydor Records) while the Snap! single was still climbing in several territories. Austin too found herself a solo contract. The producers proved that they could survive without a front man when 'Exterminate!', the first record not to feature Turbo G, became another million-seller. Austin was replaced by Niki Harris, formerly backing singer to Madonna, on 'Exterminate!' and 'Do You See The Light (Looking For)', but by the advent of 1994's *Welcome To Tomorrow* Snap!'s new singer was 'Summer'. A former dancer on the *Fame* television series, she had also worked as an actor in Spike Lee's *School Daze* and the Arnold Schwarzenegger vehicle *The Running Man*. Her singing background included sessions with Janet Jackson, Patti LaBelle and Snoop Doggy Dogg. Her vocals presided over further Snap! hits with 'Welcome To Tomorrow' (the group's ninth successive UK Top 10 hit) and 'The First, The Last Eternity'. Subsequent singles in 1996, featuring Rukmani and Einstein, failed to break into the UK Top 40.

● ALBUMS: *World Power* (Arista 1990)★★★, *The Madman's Return* (Arista 1992)★★★, *Welcome To Tomorrow* (Arista 1994)★★★.

● VIDEOS: *World Power* (BMG Video 1990).

SNEAKER PIMPS

One of the most unusual and potentially exciting groups to emerge out of the alternative rock milieu of the mid-90s, the Sneaker Pimps were immediately signed up by One Little Indian Records in the UK, a contract with Virgin Records in the USA being brokered shortly thereafter. The group's elegant fusion of dance, indie and electronic sounds is dependent on the collaborative work of keyboard player Liam Howe, famed for regularly displaying his first ever purchase, a £20 Casio synthesizer, at the group's live shows, and guitarist Chris Corner. The pair had grown up together in Hartlepool, England, before relocating to London. Prior to Sneaker Pimps, both had spent several years working on the fringes of the electronic and experimental dance scenes as FRISK and then Line Of Flight. Anglo-Indonesian vocalist Kelly Dayton (b. 1975), formerly of London indie group the Lumieres, was brought in for their new project, broadening the horizons of the previously studio-bound Howe and Corner, as the trio began playing low-profile gigs with a live rhythm section. The group made its debut in April 1996 with 'Tesko Suicide', which incorporated elements of folk among the trip-hop beats and attracted strong critical praise. Much of *Becoming X*, the group's debut album released in August that year, was informed by a budget-mentality, the recording taking place at Howe's father's house in his tiny bedroom. Dayton reportedly sang the album's vocals while sitting in a nearby cupboard due to the lack of space. Despite this, the Sneaker Pimps fermented a sound that encouraged very different perceptions of the environment in which it was created - the instrumentalists' lightness of touch combined with an aura of rhythmic space to offset the claustrophobia evident in the vocals. '6 Underground', was included on the soundtrack to *The Saint*. The group appeared regularly on evening radio and charmed critics with their fresh, unsullied approach both to music-making and the media. Howe subsequently began working on remix projects, including a new version of the Shamen's 'Move Any Mountain'.
● ALBUMS: *Becoming X* (One Little Indian 1996)★★★.

SNOMAN

b. LeBaron Frost, Alexandria, Virginia. An alternative to the rural langour of fellow Atlanta-based rappers Arrested Development or Gumbo, Snoman's ruse is to retreat to the East Side old school artistry of the pioneering hip-hop artists and B-Boys. He began writing his first poetry at the age of nine, and was subsequently inspired by the imported sounds of Run DMC. Following an appearance on the *Conquest Of A Nation* compilation he made his personal bow with the single, 'Money'. Backed by DJ Nabs, Snoman created a smooth, flowing blend of hip-hop with intelligent, often introspective rhymes: 'It's very important to me that I write good, strong lyrics especially since I found it hard to express myself when I was growing up'.
● ALBUMS: *The Exceptional One* (Conquest/Ichiban 1993)★★★.

SNOOP DOGGY DOGG

b. Calvin Broadus, 1971, Long Beach, California, USA. Snoop Doggy Dogg's commercial rise in 1993 was acutely timed, riding a surge in hardcore rap's popularity, and smashing previous records in any genre. *Doggy Style* was the most eagerly anticipated album in rap history, and the first debut album to enter the *Billboard* chart at number 1. With advance orders of over one and a half million, media speculators were predicting its importance long before a release date. As is *de rigeur* for gangsta rappers such as Snoop, his criminal past casts a long, somewhat romanticized shadow over his current achievements. He was busted for drugs after leaving high school in Long Beach, and spent three years in and out of jail. He first appeared in 1990 when helping out Dr. Dre on a track called 'Deep Cover', from the film of the same title. Dogg was also ubiquitous on Dr. Dre's breakthrough album, *The Chronic*, particularly on the hit single 'Nuthin' But A 'G' Thang', which he wrote and on which he co-rapped. After presenting a gong to En Vogue in September 1993 at the MTV video awards, Dogg surrendered himself to police custody after the show, on murder charges. This was over his alleged involvement in a driveby shooting. Inevitably, as news spread of Dogg's involvement, interest in his vinyl product accelerated, and this played no small part in the eventual sales of his debut album. Critics noted how closely this was styled on George Clinton's *Atomic Dog* project. Many also attacked the abusive imagery of women Dogg employed, particularly lurid on 'Ain't No Fun'. His justification: 'I'm not prejudiced in my rap, I just kick the rhymes'. If the US press were hostile to him they were no match for the sensationalism of the English tabloids. During touring commitments to support the album and single, 'Gin And Juice', he made the front page of the *Daily Star* with the headline: 'Kick This Evil Bastard Out!'. It was vaguely reminiscent of the spleen vented at the Sex Pistols in their heyday, and doubtless a good sign. He was asked to leave his hotel in Milestone, Kensington on arrival. A more serious impediment to Snoop's career was the trial on charges of accessory to the murder of Phillip Woldermariam, shot by his bodyguard McKinley Lee. The trial was underway in November 1995 and attracted a great deal of media attention, due in part to Dogg's defence attorney being Johnnie Cochran, O.J. Simpson's successful defender. During the trial Snoop's bail was set at $1 million. The verdict on 20 February 1996 acquitted Dogg and McKinley Lee of both murder charges and the manslaughter cases were dropped in April. The trial had not overtly damaged his record sales; his debut has now topped seven million copies worldwide, and the follow-up *Tha Doggfather* entered the US album chart at number 1. A subsequent falling out with the ailing DeathRow Records saw Dogg transferring to the No Limit Recordings label.

● ALBUMS: *Doggy Style* (Death Row 1993)★★★★, *Tha Doggfather* (Death Row 1996)★★★.
● VIDEOS: *Murder Was The Case* (Warners 1994).

SOHO

Identical twin sisters Jackie (Jacquie Juanita Cuff) and Pauline (Pauline Osberga Cuff) were both born on 25 November 1962 in Wolverhampton, England. Together with guitarist Tim London (b. Timothy Brinkhurst, 20 November 1960) they comprised the briefly successful dance band Soho. They started singing in the early 80s as student nurses in St Albans. After meeting London they became Tim London's Orgasm, and Tim London and the Soho sisters before settling on Soho. Another early member was Nigel Dukey 'D' who left in 1989. They signed to Virgin Records for early singles 'You Won't Hold Me Down' (1988), and 'Message From My Baby' (1989). These and their first LP proved flops. Despite garnering lots of press, their brand of dance was a little less frenetic than the burgeoning Acid House scene and they were dropped in 1989. They spent the next year singing covers in an Italian disco, before signing a new deal with Savage Tam Records. Their breakthrough came

with their second single for the label, 'Hippychick', which sampled Johnny Marr's guitar effervescence from the Smiths 'How Soon Is Now'. Lyrically, it challenged the prevailing new age ethos of blissful hegemony ('Got no flowers for your gun'). However, Soho proved unable to capitalise on the success of the single. Tim and Jacqueline had a daughter in 1993, Charlie, and they were finally encouraged back into the studio for a new album to celebrate his arrival. The band re-emerged, as Oosh, in 1994, with a single and album entitled 'The View'.

● ALBUMS: *Noise* (Virgin 1989)★★, *Goddess* (Savage 1991)★★, as Oosh *The View* (Magnet 1994)★★.

SOMA RECORDS

Scottish record label based in Otago Street, Glasgow, opened in July 1991 and championed by Orde Meikle and Stuart McMillan, better known as the duo behind Slam. Other members of the team are Dave Clark, Nigel Hurst, Jim Muotone and Glen Gibbons. The latter two are Slam's studio engineers, played the major role in starting the Soma imprint, and also record for the label as Rejuvenation (*Work In Progress* 1992, 'Requiem' 1993, 'Sychophantasy' 1994). Slam had originally been an all-night party convention which evolved into an umbrella remix-production team. A record label was the obvious next step: 'Soma was set up to fill a void in Scottish music', noted Meikle. 'No one was paying attention to dance music here, so the label is a medium or catalyst for some of these people who are very talented, but don't have the confidence to approach a major record company down south'. Early signings included Rejuvenation, Dove and G7. Dove released 'Fallen' for them, before becoming One Dove and moving to Boy's Own Records. Amongst other triumphs, the label housed Otaku's 'Percussion Obsession', the first vinyl outing for Back To Basic's Ralph Lawson, Sharkimaxx's 'Clashback' (aka Felix Da Housecat) and Piece & Jammin's *One For The Road* EP.

SON OF BAZERK

Flavor Flav protégé rapper backed by a six-piece No Self Control troupe whose employment of the Bomb Squad on their long playing debut drew favourable comparisons to the masters, Public Enemy, themselves. Likewise hailing from Long Island, New York, he is best known for the single, 'Change The Style'. Chuck D went so far as to describe him as the 'hardest rapper' he had ever heard. The band's second single was 'Bang (Get Down, Get Down)', housed on Bill Stephney and Hank Shocklee's SOUL label.

● ALBUMS: *Bazerk Bazerk Bazerk* (MCA 1991)★★★.

SON OF NOISE

This UK rap group recorded their first single for their own Little Rascool Records before moving to the cult London, England label, Kold Sweat. The derivative but well-executed 1992 single, 'Crazy Mad Flow', was their most impressive recording prior to the release of their debut album, *The Mighty Son Of Noise*. Stylistically similar to Naughty By Nature, Son Of Noise lost their identity in an attempt to imitate the hardcore stance of their USA brethren such as Ice Cube and Slick Rick (including all too frequent references to guns and drug deals). The lapse was forgivable, though their endorsement of Buju Banton's violent homophobic statements, noted by several critics, was not. By 1995 and their second album, Son Of Noise had been forced to secure finance from German label Tribal House, though they still used their own label. The theme of *Access Denied: Bullshit & Politics Pt. 1* was the apathy of the UK music industry towards domestic rappers.

● ALBUMS: *The Mighty Son Of Noise* (Kold Sweat 1992)★★, *Access Denied: Bullshit & Politics Pt. 1* (Little Rascool 1995)★★★.

SOUL II SOUL

This highly successful UK rap, soul and R&B group originally consisted of Jazzie B (b. Beresford Romeo, 26 January 1963, London, England; rapper), Nellee Hooper (musical arranger) and Philip 'Daddae' Harvey (multi-instrumentalist). The early definition of the group was uncomplicated: 'It's a sound system, an organisation (which) came together to build upon making careers for people who had been less fortunate within the musical and artistic realms.' The name Soul II Soul was first used to describe Jazzie B and Harvey's company supplying disc jockeys and PA systems to dance acts. They also held a number of warehouse raves, particularly at Paddington Dome, near Kings Cross, London, before setting up their own venue. There they met Hooper, formerly of the Wild Bunch and subsequently a member of Massive Attack. Joining forces, they took up a residency at Covent Garden's African Centre before signing to Virgin

Records' subsidiary Ten Records. Following the release of two singles, 'Fairplay' and 'Feel Free', the band's profile grew with the aid of fashion T-shirts, two shops and Jazzie B's slot on the then pirate Kiss-FM radio station. However, their next release would break not only them but vocalist Caron Wheeler, when 'Keep On Movin'' reached number 5 in the UK charts. The follow-up, 'Back To Life (However Do You Want Me)', once more featured Wheeler, and was taken from their debut *Club Classics Volume One*. The ranks of the Soul II Soul collective had swelled to incorporate a myriad of musicians, whose input was evident in the variety of styles employed. Wheeler soon left to pursue a solo career, but the band's momentum was kept intact by 'Keep On Movin'' penetrating the US clubs and the album scaling the top of the UK charts. 'Get A Life' was a further expansion on the influential, much copied stuttering rhythms that the band had employed on previous singles, but Jazzie B and Hooper's arrangement of Sinead O'Connor's UK number 1, 'Nothing Compares To You', was a poignant contrast. Other artists who sought their services included Fine Young Cannibals and Neneh Cherry. The early part of 1990 was spent in what amounted to business expansion, with a film company, a talent agency and an embryonic record label. The band's second album duly arrived halfway through the year, including Courtney Pine and Kym Mazelle in its star-studded cast. However, despite entering the charts at number 1 it was given a frosty reception by some critics who saw it as comparatively conservative. Mazelle would also feature on the single 'Missing You', as Jazzie B unveiled his (ill-fated) new label Funki Dred, backed by Motown Records. Although *Volume III, Just Right* made its debut at number 3 in the UK album charts, it proffered no substantial singles successes, with both 'Move Me No Mountain' and 'Just Right' stalling outside the Top 30. Jazzie B would spend the early months of 1993 co-producing James Brown's first album of the 90s, *Universal James*, and Virgin issued a stop-gap singles compilation at the end of the year. The group's fourth studio album was not available until July 1995, as Caron Wheeler returned to the fold. However, the accompanying hit single, 'Love Enuff', was sung by ex-Snap! singer Penny Ford. The group were dropped by Virgin in April 1996, but signed up to Island Records for the release of *Time For Change*.

● ALBUMS: *Club Classics Volume I* (Ten 1989)★★★★, *Volume II: 1990 A New Decade* (Ten

1990)★★★, *Volume III, Just Right* (Ten 1992)★★★, *Volume V - Believe* (Virgin 1995)★★★, *Time For Change* (Island 1997)★★★.
● COMPILATIONS: *Volume IV - The Classic Singles 88-93* (Virgin 1993)★★★★.

SOUL SONIC FORCE

With Cosmic Force, the Soul Sonics were part of Afrika Bambaataa's ever-expanding Zulu Nation enclave. Alongside scratch DJ Jazzy Jay, Pow Wow and G.L.O.B.E., they featured rapper Mr Biggs, who had been working with Bambaataa as far back as 1974. Pow Wow, in turn, had a hand in producing 'Planet Rock', while G.L.O.B.E. was responsible for patenting the 'MC popping' technique, a desription he preferred to rapping, which saw him dropping in and out of rhymes at short notice, producing an effect not unlike a faulty microphone. He was also responsible for may of the group's lyrics. He had met Bambaataa while he was attending Bronx River High School, and was already friends with Pow Wow, who had perfected his rapping skills in nearby parks. Soul Sonic Force began as a nine-piece affair, which MC's gradually dropping out, including Lisa Lee who would remain with Bambaataa as part of Cosmic Force. In tandem with their mentor they would appear on four hugely influential singles, 'Zulu Nation Throwdown Part 2', 'Planet Rock', 'Looking For The Perfect Beat' and 'Renegades Of Funk'. Their impetus was interrupted in 1983 when both Mr Biggs and Pow Wow were convicted for armed robbery. When Bambaataa resurrected the name again in 1991 for *Return To Planet Rock*, it was merely a disguise for the Jungle Brothers.
● ALBUMS: with Afrika Bambaataa *Planet Rock - The Album* (Tommy Boy 1986)★★★★.

SOULS OF MISCHIEF

Part of Del Tha Funkee Homosapien's Oakland-based Heiroglyphics enclave, Souls Of Mischief debuted with some panache on their 1993 album. With samples drawn from a selction of artists as diverse as Grover Washington, Curtis Mayfield and Main Source, it demonstrated their ability to blend mellow beats without the jive pimp talk so readily available in their neck of the woods from Too Short. The group comprises Tajal (b. *c.*1977), A-Plus (b. *c.*1976), Opio (b. *c.*1976) and Phesto (b. *c.*1977). Their recording career began when Del's cousin, Ice Cube, sorted him out with a recording contract, he in turn suggesting the Souls Of Mischief should be next up. They recorded a song

with Del entitled 'Burnt' (featured on the b-side to 'Mistadobalina'), from whence they were spotted. Tajal and A-Plus were kickin' lyrics alongside label-mate Spice-I while still in eighth grade, and their vocal dexterity was a standout feature on their debut album, with combatitive rhymes overlaying the production work of A-Plus, Del, and Heiroglyphics production guru, Domino. This group certainly operate well together, hardly suprising since: 'We all went to the same elementary school, junior high, and most of us went into the same high school'.
● ALBUMS: *'93 Till Infinity* (Jive 1993)★★★, *No Man's Land* (Jive 1995)★★★.

SOULSONICS

Seen as a west coast answer to the Brand New Heavies, Soulsonics were one of the first native American flowerings of what that continent terms 'urban alternative' (more specifically Acid Jazz in UK parlance). The group were formed by Willie McNeil (b. Kansas, Misouri, USA; drums, ex-Animal Dance, formerly a cohort of Joe Strummer) and Jez Colin (b. England; bass). Primarily a live attraction, the band were inaugurated after Colin had returned home to London and caught the energy of the Talkin' Loud movement at Dingwalls nightclub. Determined to export that culture to Los Angeles, he formed the King King club with McNeil. The Soulsonics grew out of the club, initially as a quartet, with regular jamming sessions slowly extending the band's roster. Rather than a direct copy of UK groups like Galliano, Soulsonics tempered their fusion with a more specifically Latin flavour of Jazz, a style that has always been popular within California.
● ALBUMS: *Jazz In The Present Tense* (Chrysalis 1993)★★★.

SOUND FACTORY

A top quality Euro dance duo, the Sound Factory are Emil Hellman (songwriting/instrumentation/production) and St James (vocals). They were formed in Sweden in 1992 after Hellman had established his name as a DJ and remixer. Their debut of that year, 'Understand This Groove', proved an immediate success. As well as selling well in Europe it sold over 140,000 copies in the USA. Two further successful singles, 'To The Rhythm' and 'Bad Times', preceded the release of their debut album the following year.
● ALBUMS: *Sound Factory* (Cheiron 1994)★★★★.

SOURCE

Essentially UK born John Truelove, whose 'You Got The Love' (React), featuring Candi Station, was a classic summer of love piece, though it originally came out in 1991 on his own label. It was built on Frankie Knuckles' house classic, 'Your Love', and did more than any other record to catapult the coda 'Throw your hands in the air' into the nation's lexicon, hitting number 4 in the UK charts. The Source label was relaunched in 1993 as well as a new techno offshoot, Truelove Electronic Coalition. Source's other big number was 'Sanctuary Of Love', which led to him breaking from his original agreement with Food Records after its success.

SOUTH CENTRAL CARTEL

Fronted by MC Havoc Da Mouthpiece, whose father was a member of the Chi-Lites, the ranks of South Central Cartel are also inhabited by rappers Prodeje, Havikk Da Rymesman, LV Da Voice (the group's 'singer') and DJ's Kaos #1 and Gripp. Formed in 1986, the group which evolved into SCC had originally titled themselves Mafia Style and New Authority. The group hail from Los Angeles, as made explicit in the choice of their title, and released material on their own GWK (Gangstas With Knowledge) label. Like Compton's Most Wanted before them, they peddled hard street narratives, best displayed on singles like the self-explanatory 'Gang Stories'. They managed to sell over 200,000 copies of their debut album on GWK, before flirting with a contract to the Quality emporium. Eventually Havoc contacted Russel Simmons, whom he had met while at a Black Music convention, which led to the band joining Sony's RAL/Def Jam stable for 'N' Gatz We Trust. As with previous work this boasted live musician backing, the advantages of which were tempered by the fact that they largely stuck to recreations of generic George Clinton riffs. However, in the wake of South Central Cartel's success Prodeje, who helmed the production, has gone on become a successful mixer and producer, working with Public Enemy, LL Cool J and Spice I. SCC themselves also scripted and starred in a public service film encouraging young people to use their vote.
● ALBUMS: *South Central Messages* (GWK 1992)★★★, *'N Gatz We Trust* (RAL/Def Jam 1994)★★, *All Day Everyday* (Def Jam 1997)★★★.

SPECIAL ED

b. Edward Archer, c.1973, Brooklyn, New York, USA. Special Ed debuted with a superb, precise album, produced with numbing ferocity by Hitman Howie Tee. Archer had previously practised his lyrics in junior high school, perfecting his rhymes until he hooked up with Tee who agreed to produce some tracks for him. These were promptly delivered to Profile Records who immediately expressed an interest and sanctioned Special Ed's debut album. Though he was only 16 when this was released, the rhymes were mature and supremely confident. Over half a million sales confirmed his arrival. There was a more romantic discourse evident on the follow-up, which while less abrasive, was still an examplory introduction. Still largely with Tee, he produced four of the tracks himself. He also introduced a number of his friends, including his brother Drew Archer and homeboys 40-Love, Little Shawn and DJ Akshan. There was, however, a three year hiatus between *Legal* and his third album, proposed for 1993 release. The time was spent: 'Working with groups and putting together a studio and office in Brooklyn'. He also produced a track for Tupac Shakur's *Strictly For My Niggaz*. He was reported to be working with Gang Starr's DJ Premier, Large Professor and A Tribe Called Quest's Q-Tip on sessions for the new album, while further collaborations placed him alongside Master Ace and Buckshot (Black Moon) in the highly successful Crooklyn Dodgers project ('Crooklyn').
● ALBUMS: *Youngest In Charge* (Profile 1989)★★★, *Legal* (Profile 1990)★★, *Revelations* (Profile 1995)★★★.

SPEECH

b. Todd Thomas, 1968, Milwaukee, Wisconsin, USA. Rapper Speech was exposed to the benefits of education early in life - his parents published the Milwaukee Community Journal and he himself writes a regular column for the *20th Century African* newspaper. He also regularly addresses race issues on university lecture tours. His first band, the Disciples Of Lyrical Rebellion, were formed at the Art Institute Of Atlanta during his studies there. The Disciples evolved into Secret Society, who subsequently changed name to Arrested Development. Developing a coherent and persuasive Afrocentric philosophy, the multi-member Arrested Development moved into the same house and released a ground-breaking debut album, *3 Years, 5 Months, And 2 Days In The Life Of...*, cited by many critics as the most significant breakthrough album of 1992. It brought them two Grammy Awards as Best New Artist and Best Rap Duo Or Group. A second and final studio album, *Zingalamaduni*, Swahili for 'beehive of culture', emerged in 1994. Speech's debut album followed in 1996 and paired him with collaborators such as Laurnea Wilkerson and Pappa Jon. Self-produced, it relied on a blend of soul, jazz, rap and funk similar to that propagated by Arrested Development, but placed greater emphasis on his own lyrics and ideas. Central to these was 'Like Marvin Gaye Said (What's Going On?)', an update of Marvin Gaye's anxieties about the future of the ghettos, updated to reflect developments in the 90s.

● ALBUMS: *Speech* (Chrysalis 1996)★★★.

SPEEDY J

b. Jochem Paap, c.1969, Rotterdam, Netherlands. Speedy J is a successful solo artist who started DJing in the early 80s and earned his nickname through his fast mixing and scratching technique. After picking up the house bug from America, he began to record his own hard house material; his first efforts, 'Lift Off' and 'Take Me There', came out on a 12-inch compilation on Hithouse Records. He then became the first European act to sign to Ritchie Hawtin's label Plus 8, which released two EPs including *Intercontinental*. At the same time he also produced work for the labels Evolution, Stealth and R&S Records (as Tune). A track on the Plus 8 compilation *From Our Minds To Yours Volume 1* (1991), 'Pull Over', might have proved just another footnote had it not been picked up by the rave scene and released by Music Man Records, and it subsequently became his best-known record. His third EP for Plus 8, *Rise*, featured another big club hit, 'Something For Your Mind'. However, Paap was beginning to become stereotyped as a conventional house operator where his vision was originally broader. As a result, he developed the Public Energy pseudonym for such material and began recording more divergent, experimental work as Speedy J. After remixes for the Shamen and Björk, the album *Ginger* was released on Warp Records in 1993 as part of their *Artificial Intelligence* series. The single 'Pepper' also proved to be a success when it came out on Warp in the UK, Paap's own Beam Me Up! label in Europe and Plus 8 in the USA and Canada. At the time of its release he

described his next album, *G-Spot*, as 'more dynamic and soulful', and less produced than the first. With his smooth production he moved further away from accepted dancefloor tactics, producing a more elegant complex collection whose highlights include 'The Oil Zone' and 'Fill 17'. He also records as Country And Western, the name he used for the first 'Positive Energy' release, which was originally a dancefloor hit for Speedy J on Plus 8. It was remixed under this title with the aid of Effective's Simon Hannon and Lawrence Nelson. Paap has also remixed tracks by artists such as Killing Joke, Sven Vath and Secret Cinema.

● ALBUMS: *Ginger* (Warp 1993)★★★, *G-Spot* (Warp 1995)★★★, *Live* (Harthouse 1995)★★★, *Public Energy No. 1* (Novamute 1997)★★★★.

SPENCER, J.

A 90s hip-hop/jazz fusion saxophone player, Spencer (b. c.1971, Oakland, California, USA) originally emerged via Motown Records's MoJazz subsidiary imprint as a talented harbinger of a 'new age in jazz and rap'. The result was 'A little bit of hip-hop/A little bit of jazz', as one track on his debut album, *Chimera Vol. 1*, suggested. Writing credits included several for his friend, Elijah Baker (Tony! Toni! Tone!), alongside his own compositions. He was joined on sessions for the project by Derrick Hall (bass), John 'Jubu' Smith (guitar) and Tommy Bradford (drums). The additional rapping personnel included Mike D, P. Funk and Vitamin C, all fellow natives of Oakland, plus the 'Flat Lip Horns' brass section. The follow-up collection, *Blue Moon*, was released at the end of 1995 and peaked at number 49 in the *Billboard* R&B charts.

● ALBUMS: *Chimera Vol. 1* (MoJazz 1993)★★★, *Blue Moon* (MoJazz 1995)★★★.

SPICE I

b. Byron, Texas, USA. Part of the new wave of Oakland rappers., Spice I was discovered by his neighbourhood's most imposing figure, Too Short. Though he was born in Texas, he was raised in Hayward, before spending the final years of his adolesence in Oakland. A second album, *187 He Wrote*, contained plenty of the funky beats for which that area is renowned. This was gangsta rap in its most primal form, including cuts like 'I'm The Fuckin' Murderer', and the single, 'Dumpin' 'Em In Ditches'. Despite its simplistic formula, the album proved a runaway success. going from number 97 to number 1 in *Billboard*'s R&B chart in one week.

● ALBUMS: *Spice I* (Jive 1992)★★★, *187 He Wrote* (Jive 1993)★★★★, *The Black Bossalini (A.K.A. Dr. Bomb From Da Bay)* (Jive 1997)★★★.

SPIRAL TRIBE

At the forefront of alternative culture and its attempts to embrace the new sounds of the 90s, Spiral Tribe will probably never leave their crusty-techno reputation far behind. Not that it would seem to unduly worry them. As part of the free festival movement, members have personal injunctions against them in most parts of England. Indeed, they headed to Europe in mid-1993 where legislation against travelling musicians is much more relaxed. They see music as a fluid, evolving medium, going to the extent of sampling the sound of their parties and feeding it back into the mix - thereby giving the audience an active role in proceedings. They came to the attention of the populace at large, *Sun* readers notwithstanding, by staging two huge outdoor raves: the first at Castlemorton, the second at Canary Wharf. Their first single, 'Breach Of The Peace', arrived in August 1992, followed by 'Forward The Revolution' in November. They were helped in no small part by the financial assistance of Jazz Summers, former manager of Wham! and Yazz. A debut album, *Tecno Terra*, was recorded during commital proceedings at Malvern Magistrates Court concerning the Castlemorton affair - one of the most notorious live music events of recent years, and one which saw any number of media reports bearing false witness to what really happened. Via draconian legal rulings Spiral Tribe were forced to stay within 10 miles of the court, and managed to squat a deserted farmhouse where they could record. The resulting album was perhaps a less worthy cause than the plight of travelling sound systems themselves, especially where it embodied the cod-mysticism of 'chaos theory' (ie references to the number 23). Elsewhere Spiral Tribe's philosophy is well worth investigating: 'If industrialisation had to happen in order for us to get Technics desks and Akai samplers, so be it - in the same way that the blues grew out of the pain and suffering of the slaves that built the American railways'. Their membership is fluid, numbering about fifteen DJ's and musicians at any given time.

● ALBUMS: *Tecno-Terra* (1993)★★★.

SPOOKY

This London, England-based progressive/ambient dance duo comprise Charlie May (b. 7 March 1969, Gillingham, Kent, England) and Duncan Forbes (b. 29 January 1969, Yeovil, Somerset, England). They signed to Guerrilla Records for their first release, 'Don't Panic', in May 1992. The name came about as a 'last minute decision, which just seemed to fit in with the sound of our music'. May had previously worked as a sound engineer and caffeine research analyst, seeing service in groups such as Psi'Jamma and as keyboard player for Ultramarine. His partner Forbes had played in a variety of indie bands, including Red Ten, and enjoyed temporary positions as a school chef, van driver and bar tender. Influenced by sounds as diverse as the Cocteau Twins, Derrick May, Underworld and others, Spooky won fans as much for their remixing talents as their own product (which included the well received singles 'Land Of Oz', 'Schmoo' and 'Little Bullet'). Their remix clients include Ultramarine, William Orbit, Sven Vath and Billie Ray Martin (ex-Electribe 101). As with work recorded under their own name, these remixes offer a textured, tranquil shimmer to proceedings. However, their steady progress was interrupted in 1994 after their debut album had achieved excellent reviews when a phone call informed them that Guerrilla had closed down. They continued to play live despite being deprived of recording outlets, until re-emerging in 1995 with a new label, Generic Records funded by A&M Records. They made their return with the *Stereo* EP, which moved further away from conventional dance music and into the sphere of ambient composers such as Michael Nyman.

● ALBUMS: *Gargantuan* (Guerrilla 1993)★★★, *Found Sound* (Generic 1996)★★.

SPOONIE GEE

b. Gabe Jackson, Harlem, New York, USA. Spoonie-Gee was so-called because he only ever ate with that utensil when he was a child. As a youngster he proved adept at poetry, and was often to be found hanging out at the Rooftop Club, where early DJs like DJ Hollywood and Brucie B held sway. His recording career began at Enjoy Records, whose owner, Bobby Robinson, was his uncle. His most notable records included 'New Rap Language' with the Treacherous 3, backed by his own standard, 'Love Rap', on the flip. It featured his brother, Pooche Costello, on congos. They had grown up together in the same house as Bobby Robinson, his wife acting as surrogate mother when her sister died when Spoonie was just 12. Later he cut the family ties to join the growing band of deserters housed on the competing Sugarhill imprint. His hits for the label included 'Spoonie's Back' and 'Monster Jam', plus a reissue of his debut for Peter Brown's Sound Of New York USA label, 'Spoonin' Rap'. His career slowed in the mid-80s, and in 1984 he was to be found working in a rehabilitation centre for the mentally disabled. Three years later he once again found success, this time on Aaron Fuchs' Tuff City label, with the Marley Marl/Teddy Riley-produced *The Godfather*.

● ALBUMS: *The Godfather* (Tuff City 1987)★★★.

SQUAREPUSHER

In the mid-90s Tom Jenkinson was one of a number of artists who attempted to create more integrated music in the midst of a splintering scene. He began playing the bass guitar and drums as a teenager, inspired by his father's collection of dub records; from there he became interested in 70s jazz fusion artists such as Stanley Clarke, Weather Report and Chick Corea, and later, the music of Miles Davis, Charlie Parker and Dizzy Gillespie. When he was 15 he switched on to electronic music having heard LFO's 'LFO' (1990) and the music of Carl Craig. As the Duke Of Harringay he released a number of tracks on the Zoom Records spin-off Spymania, including the *Conumber* EP and 'Alroy Road Tracks'. The latter set the tone for Squarepusher's style, which blended virtuosic bass guitar, electronic sounds and complex jungle, jazz and funk drum grooves, often structured with chord sequences. A remix of DJ Food's 'Scratch Yer Head' (1996) was followed by interest from such labels as Ninja Tune Records, Warp and R&S Records; however, as a result of his friendship with Richard James, his first album, *Feed Me Wierd Things*, was released on Rephlex. He signed to Warp in 1996 and released the *Port Rhombus* EP in July, followed the next year by the album *Hard Normal Daddy* and two further EPs, *Vic Acid* and *Big Loada*. The *Burning'n Tree* collection (1997) featured his pre-Warp material gathered together. He has had an enthusiastic, if occasionally somewhat hysterical, response from the press. Squarepusher is best when he successfully integrates his diverse influences with his musical skill; 'Papalon', from *Hard Normal Daddy*,

presents various understated jazz and jungle rhythms, with a number of subtle textures created from bubbling bass guitar and bass clarinet, as well as floating, oscillating chords, while the remix of DJ Food's 'Scratch Yer Head', after an onslaught of coarse drums, settles into a relaxed chord sequence that frames Jenkinson's tasteful melodic basslines. However, there is sometimes a tendency to become boring when his drum programming becomes over-intricate and fidgety, and he develops an Aphex Twin-style nastiness-for-the-sake-of-it attitude. There is also a feeling on *Hard Normal Daddy* that he has created a number of interesting pastiches – 'Cooper's World' (70s television cop theme), 'Papalon' (Miles Davis's *Bitches Brew*), 'E8 Boogie' (an indulgent jazz-rock trio), 'Fat Controller' (funky big beat) – mingled with mediocre electronic and jungle tunes, rather than producing a coherent whole.

● ALBUMS: *Feed Me Wierd Things* (Rephlex 1996)★★★, *Hard Normal Daddy* (Warp 1997)★★★, *Burning'n Tree* (Warp 1997)★★★.

STAKKA BO

This Swedish dance/pop/rap group won admiring glances from the likes of Mike Pickering (M People, etc.) in the early 90s for their highly rhythmic pop dance workouts, which closely resembled the output of the Stereo MC's. The use of English by Johan Renck and Oscar, the group's rappers, lacked authenticity, however, and several UK critics were dismissive. In their view, singles such as 'Here We Go' (UK number 13, September 1993) and 'Down The Drain' (UK number 64, December 1993) followed the Stereo MCs' formula (deep bass, 'cool' raps augmented by female vocal intermissions) too closely. The resultant debut album, released early in 1994, failed to live up to expectations and their international contract with Polydor Records was not renewed.

● ALBUMS: *Supermarket* (Polydor 1994)★★.

STEADY B

b. Warren McGlone, c.1970, Philadelphia, USA. Steady B boasts distinguished lineage, he is the cousin of Lawrence Goodman, owner of the Pop Art label. Perhaps Steady B's lack of headline reviews has more to do with his decision to stay in his native Philadelphia rather than any lack of talent or forbearance. Originally inspired by old school rappers Run DMC and Whodini, his debut release was in fact a direct answer record to another big influence, LL Cool J., 'I'll Take Your

Radio' being a challenge to the originator of 'I Can't Live Without My Radio'. He was just 15 years old, and a steady stream of hits would follow: 'Fly Shante', 'Just Call Us Def' and 'Do Tha Filla'. On the back of these cult items he won himself a contract with Jive, which has seen the release of five albums in as many years. Although none have brought great commercial reward, each has seen workmanlike performances straddling both the pop-rap and hardcore markets. He has now launched a new group, C.B.E.

● ALBUMS: *Bring The Beat Back* (Jive 1987)★★★, *What's My Name?* (Jive 1987)★★, *Let The Hustlers Play* (Jive 1988)★★★, *Going Steady* (Jive 1990)★★★, *Steady B V* (Jive 1991)★★.

STEPHAN, TOM

b. 1970, New York, USA. A well-respected house disc jockey from New York, Stephan made a major impact in 1995 with the release of 'Filthy Hetero', credited on to Tracy And Sharon. This immediately acquired classic status in gay and 'handbag house' clubs throughout the UK and USA. Building on that impetus, in February 1996 he compiled the 70-minute compilation, *Drag Addict* - advertised in the press as 'Guaranteed more bitch per minute'. This mix tape featured staples of the New York gay house scene such as Ride Committee ('Accident'), Morel's Grooves Part 8 ('Officer, Where's Your Brother?') and UK artists including Love And Sex ('I Just Want Your Boyfriend') and Candy Girls ('Wham Bam'). The album also included a second outing for Tracy And Sharon, 'Get To Know Me'.

● ALBUMS: *Drag Addict* (Hut 1996)★★.

STEREO MC'S

This UK rap/dance outfit's commercial breakthrough was the result of both sustained hard work and an original talent. The band comprise three women and three men; Rob Birch (b. Robert Charles Birch, 11 June 1961, Ruddington, Nottinghamshire, England; vocals), Nick 'The Head' Hallam (b. 11 June 1962, Nottingham, England; synthesizers, computers, scratching), and Owen If (b. Ian Frederick Rossiter, 20 March 1959, Newport, Wales; percussion, ex-Bourbonese Qualk), plus Cath Coffey (b. Catherine Muthomi Coffey, c.1965, Kenya - 'I can't tell you my real age because I act and tell different casting directions various different ages), Andrea Bedassie (b. 7 November 1957, London, England), and Verona Davis (b. 18 February 1952, London, England) on backing vocals. Hallam and Birch had been friends in Nottingham since the age of six. There they formed a rock duo titled Dogman And Head, before moving to London in 1985 when they were 17 years old. Together they started recording rap music, though keeping intact their original love of soul, and set up their own label Gee Street Records with John Baker and DJ Richie Rich, from their base in Clapham. They were given a cash windfall when they were each handed £7,000 by a property developer to move out of their adjacent flats. This allowed them to establish the Gee St studio in a basement on the London street of the same name. The Stereo MC's first recording was 'Move It', released before the duo recruited Italian-British DJ Cesare, and formed their alter-ego remix team, Ultimatum. In the meantime, Island Records signed up Gee St for distribution, re-releasing 'Move It' in March 1988. Their first remix as Ultimatum arrived shortly afterwards (Jungle Brothers' 'Black Is Black'). Cesare left after a tour supporting Jesus Jones, stating that he was unhappy with the band's direction and financial arrangements. He would go on to produce in his own right. Hallam and Birch pressed on, recording a debut album, *Supernatural*, with Baby Bam of the Jungle Brothers. They also recruited Owen If, originally for live percussion, who had previously been employed at Pinewood Studios as a special effects trainee, working on films like *Batman* and *Full Metal Jacket*. A support tour with Living Colour turned out to be a disaster, however. 1991 brought their first crossover hit with 'Lost In Music', based on the Ultimatum remix of the Jungle Brothers' 'Doin' Your Own Dang'. Their remixes have since encompassed artists like Aswad ('Warrior Re-Charge'), Definition Of Sound ('Wear Your Love Like Heaven'), Disposable Heroes Of Hiphoprisy ('Television - The Drug Of The Nation', 'Language Of Violence'), Dream Warriors ('Follow Me Not'), Electronic ('Idiot Country Two'), Mica Paris ('Stand Up', 'Contribution'), Monie Love ('It's A Shame', 'Monie In The Middle'), PM Dawn ('Reality Used To Be A Friend Of Mine'), Queen Latifah ('Dance 4 Me') and U2 ('Mysterious Ways'). Coffey was added to the line-up for 'Elevate My Mind', her two female compatriots joining shortly after. She enjoys a concurrent career as an actor and dancer, mainly in black theatre productions. She was even in the famed Broadway flop version of *Carrie*. 'Elevate Your Mind' actually gave the group a Top 40 hit in the

US - a first for UK hip-hop. Bedassie arrived as a qualified fashion designer, while Davis had formerly worked in a hip-hop act with Owen If, titled Giant. The powerful *Connected* was released in September 1992 to mounting acclaim; previous albums had all been well received, but this was comfortably their most rounded and spirited effort. However, it was not until the title-track and the exquisite rhythms of 'Step It Up' hit the UK charts that it was brought to the wider audience it richly deserved. In its wake the Stereo MC's collared the Best Group category at the 1994 BRIT Awards ceremony, part of a growing volume of evidence that locates the band within the commercial dance field rather than their roots in hip-hop.
● ALBUMS: *33, 45,78* (4th & Broadway 1989)★★★, *Supernatural* (4th & Broadway 1990)★★★, *Connected* (4th & Broadway 1992)★★★★.
● VIDEOS: *Connected* (1993).

STETSASONIC

Among rap's elder statesmen with origins in 1981, Brooklyn's Stetsasonic were hugely influential on a number of fronts. They were one of the few bands of their generation to promote the use of live instruments, and there was simply no hip-hop comparison to their onstage power. Via their 'A.F.R.I.C.A.' 45 (1985) they helped usher in a new wave of black consciousness and ethnocentricity/positivity, which both De La Soul and the Jungle Brothers would further streamline. Proceeds from the song were handed over to the Africa Fund for humanitarian relief projects. Alongside Run DMC, Stetsasonic were instrumental in promoting the rock/rap crossover, yet maintained an articulate rap narrative, best sampled on their classic second album, *In Full Gear*. 'This Is A Hip-hop Band' they announced on its cover - it was, but not like any hip-hop band had sounded before. They were joined by the Force MD's on an exemplory version of the Floaters' 'Float On', and also tackled the contextual rap history lesson of 'Talkin' All That Jazz', which would pre-date the jazz/rap phenomenon by at least three years. Their third album included direct political point-making exercises like 'Free South Africa'. Fittingly, it was Stetsasonic who were chosen to represent rap at the Nelson Mandela concert in London. DJ Prince Paul (b. Paul Huston) and lead rapper Daddy-O (b. *c.*1961, Brooklyn, New York, USA) were the lynchpins

behind the group, who also included Delite, Fruitkwan (aka Fuquan) and DBC. The split came in 1990 when Daddy-O decided that Statsasonic were beginning to exhaust their possibilities. Both Prince Paul and Daddy-O subsequently become in-demand producers and remixers. The former has produced Fine Young Cannibals, in addition to underscoring De La Soul's *3 Feet High And Rising*, while Boo-Yaa Tribe adopted his hard funk drum effect. Daddy-O remixed for Mary J. Blige, also working with artists as diverse as Queen Latifah, Big Daddy Kane (notably *It's A Big Daddy Thing*) and the Red Hot Chili Peppers. DBC recorded a handful of tracks for independent labels. Any bad blood which may have existed at the time of their dissolvement would appear to have been forgotten when the news broke that the original line up recorded together again in 1993. Prince Paul also collaborated with Fruitkwan as part of the Gravediggaz.
● ALBUMS: *On Fire* (Tommy Boy 1986)★★★, *In Full Gear* (Tommy Boy 1988)★★, *Blood Sweat And No Tears* (Tommy Boy 1991)★★★.

STOP THE VIOLENCE MOVEMENT

Set up by prominent members of the New York hip-hop community in 1989, the Stop The Violence Movement was just that - a lobby to bring about a ceasefire in the endless gang warfare in the black ghettos. Numbering amongst its contributors Kool Moe Dee, Public Enemy, Stetsasonic, Boogie Down Productions and many others, a single was released on the Jive imprint, 'Self Destruction', in 1989. It would become the movement's anthem.

STRESS RECORDS

A UK-based division of DMC Ltd, who are also responsible for the early 90s magazines *Mixmag* and *Mixmag Update*, and artist management. DMC was originally set up as a DJ club, providing exclusive megamix albums in the 80s for DJs. It was an operation that evolved into releasing remix albums every month. In the process DMC gave a lot of young producers a break as these reached the ears of A&R staff. They thus discovered the likes of Sasha, who like many artists made his first recordings on DMC. Stress grew out of a younger element, like David Seaman (half of Brothers In Rhythm), getting involved in DMC. After entering the DMC chamionships he was invited over to New York to play at the New Music Seminar and was offered a job in the late 80s. Rather than merely 'passing on' their trained-up production discoveries to the major labels and talent scouts, Stress was inaugurated to provide them with an in-house outlet, should they prefer it. Nick Gordon Brown and Seaman remain the prime movers behind Stress, which exists as a separate, independent entity within the DMC umbrella, having the final say on A&R decisions. Records like Rusty (David Syon and Andrea Gemelotto)'s 'Everything's Gonna Change', Hustlers Convention's *Groovers Delight* EP and Last Rhythm's 'Last Rhythm (Sure Is Pure '92 remix) established the label. Some of their bigger hits over the 1993/1994 period included Chris & James' 'Club For Life', Reefa's 'Inner Fantasy', Bubbleman's 'Theme' and Brothers In Rhythm's 'Forever And A Day'. The same duo also remixed Voices Of 6th Avenue's 'Call Him Up' for the label. In 1994 Reefa! contributed 'Inner Fantasy'/'Get Up Stand Up', while other releases included Masi's 'Apache', Mindwarp's 'Too' (the Boston, USA-based crew's follow-up to 'One') and Coyote's 'Jekyll & Hyde'.

STRICTLY RHYTHM RECORDS

Manhattan, New York, house stable which, whilst still remaining a cult taste in their native country, has become the most popular of all foreign labels in the UK. The Strictly Rhythm boss is one Mark Finkelstein, who established the company in 1989. An unlikely source of cult idolatory, the be-suited Finkelstein has an MSC in Aeronautics and an MBA from Harvard in finance. 'Everybody's heard of the label but few can name three acts on it. If you ask me if I'm happy with that then I'd have to say yes, because at the end of it the philosophy and vision are mine. But I'd be equally happy if one act came along and blew that away'. He also insists on a blanket ban on sampling, pointing out that 'it's just theft of somebody else's idea, when we should be creating our own'. Finkelstein originally entered the music business by taking over Spring Records for three years (home to various earlier dance artists like Isis - or Todd Terry in disguise. He recruited Gladys Pizarro from the latter as his A&R right hand. The label went on to score enormous cult success with their weekly releases (accelerating to two a week in 1993), with each pressed on superior quality Europadisc vinyl. Records like Logic's 'The Warning', Underground Solution's 'Luv Dancing', Slam Jam's 'Tech Nine' (Todd Terry), the Untouchables' debut EP (Kenny 'Dope' Gonzalez)

and others set the tone. Pizarro left in 1991, joining Nervous, her role taken by DJ Pierre and George Morel (ex-2 In A Room). However, when Pierre elected to return to his own recording projects, Pizarro swtiched back. The change did little to interrupt the flow of hits, with Photon Inc's 'Generate Power', Simone's 'My Family Depends On Me' and New Jersey duo William Jennings and Eddie Lee Lewis' Aly-Us project (whose 'Follow Me' became a massive club staple). It is important not to underestimate the role DJ Pierre played in Strictly Rhythm's development. As an artist and musician Pierre offerred 'Annihilating Rhythm' by Darkman, the aforementioned 'Generate Power' by Photon Inc. (with Roy Davis Jnr), 'Love And Happiness' by Joint Venture alongside Morel, and dozens more. Gonzalez continued his ascendency by providing material like Total Ka-Os' 'My Love'. Erick 'More' Morillo, too, was just as prolific - claiming to have released over 25 records on Strictly Rhythm during 1993 alone (the best of which included the Smooth Touch sequence). Morillo was also behind 'I Like To Move It' (Reel 2 Real), which, like Barbara Tucker's 'Beautiful People', was licensed to Positiva in the UK. 1993 saw the label set up a rap/hip-hop subsidiary, Phat Wax. Widely revered, and often imitated, Strictly Rhythm has enjoyed a longevity in musical fashion which defies the short shelf-life usually afforded house styles. One of the few UK-based acts on the stable was Caucasian Boy ('Northern Lights'), but generally it was a one-way import deal for British dance fans. In 1994 Hardheads' 'New York Express' broke big for the label, with its escalating BPM count once again sucking in the dance fraternity. Others from more recent times include 2 Direct (Anthony Acid and 'Brutal' Bill Marquez)'s 'Get Down'/'Free' and Morel's Grooves Part 5, with 'I Feel It' (Morel with vocalist Zhana Saunders). But this is merely the tip of the iceberg. It would be possible to spend an entire encyclopedia merely documenting the Strictly Rhythm discography. They remain the connoisseur's house label, with their name as close to a guarantee of quality as the music comes.

STRICTLY UNDERGROUND

Record label based in Romford, Essex, England, and run by Mark Ryder, who records on the imprint as Fantasy UFO. Under the latter title his first single was 'Fantasy' for XL, which just missed the Top 40. The second, 'Mind Body And Soul', with a hip house rap from Jay Groove (b. London), and vocals from Stella Mac, was licensed to East West via Strictly Underground. Ryder liaised with DJ Hype for 1991's Sound Clash record, 'The Burial'. Their other major artists include/included M-D-Emm, Warrior, Tigers In Space and Sonic Experience.

STRUCTURE RECORDS

Structure is an umbrella organisation based in Germany for a series of labels which includes Monotone, Trance Atlantic and Digitrax Int. After an initial flurry of acid tracks in 1988, Trance Atlantic was the first of these associated labels to make a name for itself in 1991, by reinstating the 303 sound. In the process mainman J. Burger became one of the first to predict the re-emergence of that musical format. The most notable examples were to be found in Bionaut's 'Science Wonder' and Mike Inc's 'Trance Atlantic Express', an 11-minute epic. Structure was formed in early 1992, releasing just over a dozen releases in its first two years with pressings limited to 2,500 copies. Artists included the aforementioned Bionaut and Mike Inc, alongside Air Liquide (Ingmar Koch and Jammin' Unit) and Walker. The labels in the group are organised to represent differing musical approaches: Structure (acid), Blue (ambient), Digitrax (ambient/techno) and Monotone (hardcore).

SUB SUB

Pop dance crew from Manchester, England who have been together since 1989, originally comprising Melanie Williams (vocals), Jimi Goodwin, Jezz Williams and Andy Williams. Their earliest releases were based more in the DIY-bedroom techno mode than that which would bring them to *Top Of The Pops* and the Top 10. 'Space Face' was a white-label release hawked via the boot of their cars, followed by the instrumental *Coast* EP. This was the only result of a deal they inked with Virgin Records, before transferring to New Order manager Rob Gretton's Robsrecords, who reissued it in August 1992.

Their breakthrough hit arrived with the stirring 'Ain't No Love (Ain't No Use)', with a particularly virulent mix from DJ Graeme Park. In its wake they were invited to produce remixes for a range of artists (including Take That and, insult of insults, Sinitta). They have thus far kept their credits to more credible productions. Their 1994 album was preceded by a single, 'Respect', which introduced their new vocalist, Nina Henchion.

● ALBUMS: *Full Fathom Five* (Robsrecords 1994)★★★.

SUBSONIC 2

Include Me Out was widely praised as one of the most impressive debuts of 1991, a legitimate compliment to one of UK rap's most inriguing new formations. DJ Docta D and MC Steel provide the hands on the steering wheel, which veers wildly from R&B to funk and Motown, taking in breakbeats and some of the smarter rhymes heard in the parish. The pair met after Steel addressed a demo, recorded on his own portable studio, to Heatwave Radio. This pirate station, helmed by Docta D, took to the tape in a big way, with continued requests urging him to seek out the cassette's creator. Afterwards they spent three years working together on new material, with cuts like 'Dedicated To The City', with its captivating jazz saxophone, boosted by the literacy of English and Russian graduate Steel. While the title recalled many hardcore rappers concerns about authenticating themselves with tales of urban mayhem, 'Dedicated' is merely a delightful nod to the lyricist's direct environment, a celebration of its vibrancy and variety. Or 'Unsung Heroes Of Hip-Hop', which cleverly mocks the sheepish competition between hardcore crews which too often merely produces imitation: 'Well, do you really wanna base a career, On an '84 Run DMC idea?'.

● ALBUMS: *Include Me Out* (Columbia 1991)★★★.

SUBTERFUGE

An alias for Thomas Barnett (b. *c*.1967), who once held down a day job alongside Chez Damier, a friend of Juan Atkins and Derrick May, who had recorded for the former's KMS label. Through these connections Barnett met May and recorded 'Nude Photo' with him for Transmat (as Rhythim Is Rhythim). The duo fell out when Barnett received no monies for the track and his name disappeared from the credits. After dropping out and working in his own home-studio he re-emerged on Infonet with the *Liquid Poetry* EP. He also worked for the Dutch label Prime, putting out a set of 'Nude Photo' remixes. A series of EPs, then the *Synthetic Dream* album followed, a set overshadowed by the poverty he was experiencing while recording it, which is evident throughout its tough, remorseless grooves.

● ALBUMS: *Synthetic Dream* (Prime 1993)★★★.

SUBURBAN BASE

This label is the home of hardcore techno and breakbeats, and was established by Dan Donnelly in Romford, Essex, England, in 1990 as an offshoot of his record shop, Boogie Times (which is also called Suburban Base). Good examples of the Suburban Base sound are Sonz Of A Loop Da Loop Era's 'Far Out', which transferred from the Boogie Times label, or Aston And DJ Rap, who also worked on a production basis under the alias Rhythm for Perfecto records. They released the 'Vertigo' single in May 1993. Earlier worthy samples of the label's product came with Q Bass's 'Hardcore Will Never Die'. Danny Breaks (with the rave anthem 'Far Out'), Timebase (aka DJ Krome and Mr Time), M&M, Austin Reynolds (an in-house studio operative who recorded 'I Got High' under his own name and as the Phuture Assasins with the *Future Sound* EP) filled out the artist roster. The homegrown talent also included E Type (studio engineer Mike James) and Run Tings (shop worker Winston Meikle). Rachel Wallace (once a star of a *South Bank Show* talent contest), who featured on the remix of M&M's 'I Feel This Way', was given full billing on her own single, 'Tell Me Why'. However, their biggest hit came with the 'kiddie techno' novelty, 'Sesame's Treet', by the Smarte's (Chris Powell, Tom Orton and Nick Arnold). Suburban Base set up an offshoot, Fruit Tree, for house productions, hiring Luke Coke as its A&R man. This was because they were so pleased with his work on their material through his job at Phuture Trax Promotions. That imprint's life began with Vibe Tribe's 'Rock It', which again was Austin Reynolds, who also remixed for Andronicus and East 17. A further subsidiary was launched as an outlet for compilations, Breakdown Records. This does not involve exclusively Suburban Base tracks, but also scans the shelves for important hardcore tunes which may have escaped the net. In 1992 the label had signed a US deal with Atlantic worth a reported $500,000.

● ALBUMS: Various: *Base For Your Face* (Suburban Base 1992)★★★, *Drum & Bass* (Breakdown 1994)★★★.

SUGARHILL GANG

Englewood, New Jersey troupe, whose 'Rapper's Delight' was hip-hop's breakthrough single. They gave the music an identity and a calling card in the first line of the song: 'A hip-hop, The hi-be, To the hi-be, The hip-hip-hop, You don't stop rockin'. Master Gee (b. Guy O'Brien, 1963), Wonder Mike (b. Michael Wright, 1958) and Big Bank Hank (b. Henry Jackson, 1958) saw massive international success in 1979 with 'Rappers Delight', based on the subsequently widely borrowed rhythm track from Chic's 'Good Times', over which the trio offered a series of sly boasts which were chatted rather than sung. Considered at the time to be something of a novelty item, 'Rapper's Delight' was significantly more than that. Sylvia and Joe Robinson had recruited the three rappers on an *ad hoc* basis. Hank was a former bouncer and pizza waiter, and brought fresh rhymes from his friend Granmaster Caz (see Cold Crush Brothers). The backing was offered by Positive Force, a group from Pennsylvania who enjoyed their own hit with 'We Got The Funk', but became part of the Sugarhill phenomenon when 'Rapper's Delight' struck. They would go on to tour on the Gang's early live shows, before the Sugarhill house band took over. Smaller hits followed with 'The Love In You' (1979) and 'Kick It Live From 9 To 5' (1982), before the group faded and fell apart in the early 80s. The Sugarhill Gang were already assured of their place in hip-hop's history, even if reports that Big Bank Hank was working as a Englewood garbage man in the 90s are correct.

● ALBUMS: *Rappers Delight* (Sugarhill 1980)★★★, *8th Wonder* (Sugarhill 1982)★★.

SUGARHILL RECORDS

Joe Robinson Jnr. and Sylvia Robinson were behind this label, named after the comparatively affluent locale in Harlem, though they themselves had moved to Englewood in New Jersey. It was not necessarily the first rap label, but by far the biggest and most important. The inspiration came from their teenage children's enthusiasm for the hip-hop movement and its celebrity MCs, particularly the 'live jam' tapes. Sylvia already had a music legacy. It is widely recalled that she had scored a Top 20 hit in 1973 with 'Pillow Talk'. However, she had also scored as Little Sylvia for Savoy, and duetted with her guitar tutor Houston 'Mickey' Baker', at which time she also met Joe, on the duet 'Love Is Strange'. Joe's background, conversely, was in real estate, but he gained an introduction to music via his wife. Together they opened a club entitled the Blue Morocco in the Bronx, and by the end of the 60s had started the All Platinum label. This housed soul and funk records by George Kerr, Linda Jones, the

Universal Messengers and others. Joe also owned the rights to the Chess back-catalogue. They convinced Morris Levy to assist them in a new venture and, in 1979, Sugarhill's rap agenda was launched with 'Rapper's Delight'. By sampling the huge Chic hit 'Good Times', it effectively gave birth to the debate over artistic authorship which has dominated rap since. It did, however, have precedents, one of which Sylvia Robinson was only too aware of: 'Strange Love' had also been subject to disputes over plagiarism. Their reputation as financially irrascible operators is enshrined in rap legend, though so is their contribution to the development of the music. Employing the Sugarhill house band (Keith LeBlanc, Skip McDonald, Doug Wimbush - who had met as part of Wood Brass & Steel, a funk outfit who had also performed regular duties for the Robinsons' former label All Platinum - later to move to the UK and become Tackhead), a steady stream of rap classics followed. These included Four Plus One's 'That's The Joint', and 'The Message' and 'White Lines' by Grandmaster Flash and Grandmaster Melle Mel respectively. The success was rapid, but led to complications over finance. Specifically, they were accused of not paying their artists' royalties, a charge they defend vehemently. Despite the acrimony over the Grandmaster Flash And The Furious Five infighting debacle, Joe Robinson Jnr., for one, does not countenance their widely read press statements: 'Who gives a fuck what those fuckin' bums think? Them guys was drug addicts using crack when it first came out. Flash never wrote a song, never did a rap - son of a bitch was never in the studio when a record was made out of here. It's all in the court records'. He was referring to the 1983 case, which, although they won, forced Sugarhill into financial difficulties. They linked up with MCA but to no avail. Sugarhill would eventually go under in the mid-80s following problems with distributors. They had been left behind by new technology - their policy of never hiring outside producers severely damaging them when sequencers and samplers were introduced, as no-one in the company knew how to use them. They eventually sold their ownership of Chess, but the Robinsons remain in the music business, and currently run publishing and licensing companies in New York (Sylvia had made a brief return to recording with 'Good To Be The Queen', an answer record to Mel Brooks' 'Good To Be The King' rap). As for the late lamented Sugarhill, it is nice to see at least one label with as colourful a history as the music it played such a major role in advancing.

● COMPILATIONS: *Rapped Uptight Vol. 1* (Sugarhill 1981)★★★, *Rapped Uptight Vol. 2* (Sugarhill 1982)★★★, *Old School Rap: The Sugarhill Story* (Sequel 1992)★★★, *The Sugarhill 12-inch Mixes* (Castle 1994)★★★, *The Sugarhill Records Story* (Rhino 1997)★★★★.

SUNS OF ARQA

Exceedingly pleasant, sitar-soaked, cross-cultural house music, often to be caught live at Planet Dog events. The main man behind Suns Of Arqa is Lancashire-based Mick Ward, whose fusion of flute, violin, keyboards and sitar in highly original in the dance music sphere. Previous to their celebrity in the dance scene, Suns Of Arqa had already recorded a set for ROIR in association with Prince Far I. In 1994 they had 'Govinda's Dream' remixed by A Guy Called Gerald.

● ALBUMS: *Cradle* (Earthsounds 1992)★★★, *Kokoromochi* (Arka 1993)★★★★, *Juggernaut Whirling Dub* (Arka 1995)★★★★, *Shabda* (Arka 1995)★★★.

SUNSCREEM

Lucia Holmes, from Maidstone, Kent, England, of half-Swedish parentage, is the vocalist and programmer with this band, who developed an affinity for the nether regions of the UK pop charts in the 90s. They have their own Essex-based studio, and were touted as the first live band playing rave music, scoring with singles such as 'Luv U More' and 'Perfect Motion' (which went Top 20). Their version of Marianne Faithfull's 'Broken English', performed live on television show *The Word*, also won them admirers. The other main mover behind the band is technical guru Paul Carnell, along with Darren Woodford, Rob Fricker and Sean Wright. However, the aforementioned studio (in the building of which Carnell had played a major role) brought them grief in 1993 when they left some of their friends in charge while they went on holiday, returning to discover that they had made use of their time by recording an album, *Panarama*, for the Big Fish label.

● ALBUMS: *03* (Sony 1993)★★★, *Change Or Die* (Sony 1996)★★★.

SUPEREAL

A London-based duo of Peter Morris and Paul Freegard who branched out to cult dancefloor status following their origins in Meat Beat Manifesto. Their music incorporated the more forboding elements which were always associated with their former employers, as well as rich breakbeats and informed treatments of house styles. Tracks such as 'Terminal High RIP' seem to have been provoked by a restless, playful spirit, which was somewhat lacking in MBM. Their career had begun in 1990 with 'Body Medusa', before 'United State Of Love' for Guerilla in 1992. The first of these was remixed by Leftfield, the second by Slam.

● ALBUMS: *Elixir* (Guerilla 1992)★★★.

SURE IS PURE

Remix team probably best known for their work with the Doobie Brothers, an unlikely teaming which saw the soft rockers back in the charts after several years absence. Based in Stoke On Trent, Staffordshire, England, Sure Is Pure are built around lynchpin DJ Kelvin Andrews, and they have also undertaken remixing chores for INXS, Yothu Yindi ('Treaty') and other major league outfits. They have recorded in their own right, including the 1991 EP *Proper Tunes* for their own imprint Gem. The same label would also be the first home to their 'Is This Love Really Real?' single, featuring vocalist Aphrique, before it transferred to Union City in 1992. Again for Gem they picked up and remixed Unique featuring Kim Cooper's 'Danube Dance'. In 1994 Andrews formed an indie rock band called Camp Carnival, who recorded a version of Sure Is Pure's 'Grind Zone Blues' (from the *Out To Lunch* EP), and signed to Vinyl Solution.

SUZUKI, TSUYOSHI

b. 26 November 1967, Tokyo, Japan. One of the most influential figures in the psychedelic trance movement of the 90s, Suzuki works as a DJ and recording artist and is responsible for A&R and creative development at Matsuri Productions, which he co-founded with John Perloff in 1994. He began playing the drums when he was 12, studied film and media at university and later learned to DJ with the help of a friend. He formed various experimental rock bands inspired by the Yello Magic Orchestra, Kraftwerk and David Sylvian, and in 1991 began working with Nick Taylor (Snake Thing) as Blissed. The pair recorded an EP (*Blissed*) and an album (*Rite Of Passage*) that were released on the German label POD communications in 1993. A spell in Goa inspired a change in direction and in July 1993 Suzuki moved to London where he and Taylor formed Prana. The following year Suzuki began DJing at the Return To The Source parties with which he has continued to perform. He has since became one of the best-known and most well-travelled psychedelic trance DJs and has played virtually everywhere in the world that has a psy-trance scene, while producing two albums and a number of tracks with Prana and developing Matsuri. In 1997 he released 'Re-Cycle Frequency'/'Ama No Kawa' as Joujouka (a Japanese-based project with Takeshi Isogai) with plans for an album the following year that will also be used as the soundtrack for a Sony Playstation game. Unlike many more established 'names' in dance music, he has refused to compromise his values and with his DJing, various productions and record label continues to create, encourage and promote new experimental music from around the world, helping to maintain the original spirit of the Goa scene in the face of much commercialization.

SWEET TEE

b. Toi Jackson, Queens, New York, USA. Female MC, re-discovered by Salt 'N' Pepa's producer Hurby Lovebug, whose breakthrough single was 'I Got Da Feelin''. She had originally recorded for Paul Winley, ('It's Like That Y'All') and Champion Records ('Its My Beat' with Jazzy Joyce). 'Vicious Rap', produced by her mother, carried a false arrest narrative, and was one of the prototype conscious rap singles. However, there was little to be heard from her following a singular album for Profile in 1989, and two singles, 'On The Smooth Tip' and 'Let's Dance'. In 1995 Sweet Tee contributed a track for the *Show* soundtrack 'What's Up Star' under the name of Suga.

● ALBUMS: *It's Tee Time* (Profile 1989)★★★.

SWEMIX RECORDS

This Swedish dance label was formed in 1989 by a number of DJs, led by Jackmaster Fax (Rene Hedemyr) and JJ (Johan Jarpsten), who recorded for the label as Dynamic Duo. Once described as the Scandinavian equivalent of the UK's DMC enclave, each month Swemix released a Remixed Records double-album package of the 'hottest club hits'. The label was founded in the belief that they could remix better and more suitable cuts than those issued by the major record companies. Thus, their roster grew to accommodate Milli Vanilli, Neneh Cherry, Pasadenas and Gloria Estefan and others. Working in this area, they revolutionized the Swedish, and to some extent, mainland European, dance music scene. Among their higher-profile signings were Da Yeene and Dr. Alban, who set up the Alphabet Street club in Gothenburg, a frequent haunt of many of the Swemix principals. It was this artist more than any other who established both the label and a new style of euro-dance in the 90s, signing to Arista via Logic Records. Other staples of the Swemix catalogue included the Stonebridge remix team who recorded as Mr Magic; artists such as Frankie LaMotte and Terry Leigh were signed to the subsidiary Basement Division. Two other spin-off labels, B-Tech and Energy, released Clubland's 'Hold On' and Paradise Orchestra's 'Colour Me', which was later licensed to Pulse 8. Swemix has subsequently became Cheiron and no longer deals exclusively in dance.

SYSTEM 7

Ambient dance duo featuring Miquette Giraudy (b. 9 February 1953, Nice, France; synthesizers, samples) and the more celebrated Steve Hillage (b. Stephen Simpson Hillage, 2 August 1951, Walthamstow, London, England; guitars, samplers, synthesizers). Giraudy is a former filmmaker from the south of France, where she met up with Hillage's band, the cult synth prog rockers Gong. Her films had included *More* and *La Vallee*, both of which featured Pink Floyd on their soundtracks. Fascinated by synthesisers, she became a self-taught musician and in the current format writes most of the material before Hillage adds a layer of guitar work. Hillage enjoys his own cult following through his work with Kevin Ayers, Gong and the Steve Hillage Group, and had become enveloped in the ambient house explosion via the work of Spooky, the Drum Club, Orbital, Black Dog and Fluke, before collaborating with another listening favourite, the Orb. In turn System 7 have been joined on vinyl by a host of rock, pop and dance stars; Alex Paterson (Orb), Youth (Killing Joke/Brilliant), Mick McNeil (Simple Minds) Paul Oakenfold and Derrick May. Their recording career started in August 1991 with 'Miracle' on Ten Records, after which they moved to Big Life but sought their own Weird &

Unconventional imprint. Singles of the quality of 'Freedom Fighters' and 'Sinbad' have helped them garner a considerable reputation among both their peers and late-night ravers searching for the perfect chill-out tune. An opportunity for old prog-hippies to meet with ambient dance youth.
● ALBUMS: *System 7* (Ten 1991)★★★, *777* (Weird And Unconventional/Big Life 1993)★★★★, *Power Of Seven* (Butterfly 1996)★★, *Golden Section* (Butterfly 1997)★★★.
● COMPILATIONS: *System Express* (Butterfly 1996)★★★.

SYZYGY

Syzygy are London, England-based duo Dominic Glynn and Justin McKay, who first met at the end of the 80s, when Glynn was working part-time providing BBC Television's *Doctor Who* series with incidental music. Mutually inspired by Detroit techno (Derrick May, Juan Atkins, etc.), their first recordings emerged on the Infonet record label, before they adopted the names Mind Control and Zendik for two further 12-inch releases. They subsequently signed more permanently to Rising High Records as Syzygy. Two EPs, *Discovery* and *Can I Dream*, began to push their profile in the 'intelligent techno' club scene. A debut double album, meanwhile, drew its title from 'the collective consciousness of the planet, a phenomenon for which there is no easy explanation'. An extended concept album, it took as its theme a musical fable of the earth's development.
● ALBUMS: *The Morphic Resonance* (Rising High 1994)★★★.

T

T-EMPO

One of the major proponents of what has been fetchingly described as 'handbag house' is Tim Lennox (b. *c*.1966, Birmingham, Midlands, England). Lennox, like many before him, has stepped out from behind the decks to switch from being DJ to producer. He had been DJing for ten years, starting at a gay club called Heroes, in Manchester, before helping set up the notorious Flesh events at the Hacienda in 1991, settling on current home Paradise Factory shortly afterwards. His first recorded effort, featuring a typically striking vocal from Sharon D. Clark and help from producer Aron Friedman and Damon Rochefort (of Nomad fame), was a cover of Cuba Gooding's 'Happiness', released under the title Serious Rope. A second cover, this time of Barbara Mason's 'Another Man', also sustained critical approval. This diarama of a Brooklyn housewife dumped by her man for another lover, also male, had the camp, heightened sense of drama intrinsic to the 'handbag house' style. This was released as Shy One, after which he switched to the T-Empo name in order to engender a more structured approach to making music. Hence his band evolved, featuring Adam Clough, session singer Loretta and engineer Simon Bradshaw. After the huge success of 'Another Man' several record companies were fighting to sign Lennox, and he eventually opted for ffrr, based on their good record with gay/hi-NRG/house acts. However, a third release, 'Saturday Night Sunday Morning', the first to use the pseudonym T-Empo, arrived jointly with the exclusive gay record label Out On Vinyl, on which Lennox holds a director's chair. His remixing skills also rose in popularity, and, again under the name T-Empo, included the Brand New Heavies ('Dream On Dreamer'), RuPaul ('House Of Love'), Grace Jones ('Slave To The Rhythm'), Joe Roberts ('Lover') and K Klass ('Rhythm Is A Mystery'). The Joe Roberts mix was a particular triumph, when ffrr promoted it to a-side status over a version from Lennox's hero, David Morales.

T-POWER

b. Mark Royal, *c*.1968, England. Jungle artist Mark Royal began making hip-hop with a number of MCs, before working with the hardcore trio Bass Selective, who enjoyed success with singles such as 'Blow Out Part II' in the late 80s. He then developed an interest in ambient music and drum 'n' bass, and, working with the engineer Cris Stevens, found a sympathetic home at SOUR Records. The first T-Power single, 'Lipsing Jam Ring', was released in 1994 and soon became a staple of the 'hardstep' scene. It was followed in 1995 by the acclaimed 'Mutant Jazz', a collaboration with MC Ultra that merged jungle rhythms with elements of jazz. Royal himself was wary of the jungle tag, describing his sound as 'electronic, ambient jazz', and adding 'I knock about on the fringes because my stuff isn't geared towards the jungle scene. You've got the underground scene and then I'm left of that.' Other releases included 'Natural Born Killers' and 'Step Into Lite' and the albums *The Self-Evident Truth Of An Intuitive Mind* and *Waveform*. Confirming his eclectic tastes, the latter included a variety of ideas, including the grooveless 'Life In The Freezer' and the hard techno of 'Postcards From Pluto'. During this time, Royal also recorded as Atomic Dog and Deep Thought Ltd. After the dark sounds associated with the T-Power work, Royal and Stevens went on to produce more light-hearted, funky material as Chocolate Weasel with Ninja Tune Records.
● ALBUMS: *The Self-Evident Truth Of An Intuitive Mind* (SOUR 1995)★★★, *Waveform* (Anti-Static 1996)★★★.

T. LA ROCK

b. *c*.1961, Bronx, New York, USA. Although he continued to be prominent in the 90s, old school rapper T. La Rock can boast quite a heritage in the 80s. His brother, Special K, was signed to the original Sugarhill label. He had also met Rick Rubin of Def Jam, before the latter had seriously established his label. Together the duo recorded 'It's Yours' on Party Time records. La Rock fell out with Rubin when he discovered that he was also fostering the career of LL Cool J, who would inherit his king of the B-boys title. He cut one album, produced by himself, DJ Doc and DJ Mark The 45 King in 1987 for Virgin subsidiary Ten. When he resurfaced in the 90s with *On The Warpath* Todd Terry was in the producer's chair. The original version of the record, which had

taken four months to record, was scrapped in favour of a new Terry production. He had initially come to the Sleeping Bag offices to offer La Rock the chance to rap over one of his productions. The resulting album, which was originally to have included on stage banter and was vaunted to the press as *On Tour*, contained a much less hardcore, more commerical slant than expected. As a concession to his long-term supporters it also included 'Its Yours', which had previously been a much sought after and unobtainable old school classic. Alongside this were excursions into swingbeat, and a return to old B-boy stylings in 'Warpath'.
● ALBUMS: *Lyrical King* (Ten 1987)★★★, *On A Warpath* (Sleeping Bag 1990)★★★.

T99

This group, whose roots were in Belgian new beat, produced one of 1991's biggest rave tunes with 'Anasthasia', after which they moved from XL to Columbia. The followed it up with 'Nocturne', sung by Perla Den Boer with a rap from Zenon Zevenbergen. Their debut album saw them add another, more speedy rapper for several of the cuts, but they were still some way short of the artistic mark set by the Detroit stalwarts, which they were desperately trying to emulate. However, the resonant 'Anasthasia' was later sampled by both 2 Unlimited and even Kylie Minogue. T99 is a duo of Patrick De Meyer and Oliver Abeloos.
● ALBUMS: *Children Of Chaos* (Columbia 1992)★★★.

TACKHEAD

A UK dub/hip-hop/dance outfit who formed in 1987 and released a remarkable first single, 'The Game', with a Brian Moore (football commentator) sample and backbeat that comprised metal guitar and electro 'Hi-NRG' attack, together with football chants. The band comprised Keith LeBlanc (previously behind the groundbreaking 'Malcolm X' single; percussion, keyboards), plus Doug Wimbush (bass) and Skip McDonald (guitar). Together they had previously operated as the Sugarhill Gang house band, in their home town of Bristol, Connecticut, USA, performing on the likes of 'Rapper's Delight', 'The Message' and 'White Lines'. Before which they had also been major contributors, as Wood Brass & Steel, to many of the recordings which emerged from another Sylvia Robinson label, All Platinum.

Migrating to London in 1984, they became a central component in Adrian Sherwood's On U Sound label. Sherwood became the mixmaster who would take the trio's basic tracks and add a little club magic. Although they all appeared on LeBlanc's solo work, their first recording as Tackhead came with Gary Clail as vocalist in 1987 - *Tackhead Tape Time* - which was jointly credited. They subsequently recruited Bernard Fowler, who appeared on their best album, *Friendly As A Hand Grenade*. Its follow-up set, *Strange Things*, was an unfortunate shot at crossover success, following the band's relocation to the US. Guest contributions from Melle Mel, Lisa Fancher and even Mick Jagger on harmonica did little to elevate a dour reading of dance-rock. In 1991 Leblanc joined with Tim Simenon (Bomb The Bass) in a new project titled Interference.
● ALBUMS: As Gary Clail's Tackhead Sound System: *Tackhead Tape Time* (Nettwerk/Capitol 1987)★★★. As Tackhead: *Friendly As A Hand Grenade* (TVT 1989)★★★★, *Strange Things* (SBK 1990)★★.

TAIRRIE B

b. Los Angeles, California, USA. Tairrie (pronounced Terry) was one of executive producer Eazy-E's less successful protégés. Heralded as 'the rap Madonna', she failed to achieve significant sales with the release of her debut album, *The Power Of A Woman*. Despite incorporating two tracks produced by Schoolly D and the eloquence of songs such as 'Ruthless Bitch', it failed to inspire a long-term career. Some critics suggested that the delivery, although tidy and competent, lacked power. The singer soon changed tack to front the hard rock-orientated Manhole (now called Tura Satana). Reflecting on her experiences in the male-dominated world of hip-hop, she was somewhat resentful of her treatment: 'Eventually, instead of me feeling comfortable in the scene I grew up in and the culture I love, I became really alienated. And I lost a lot of respect for the whole scene. You have people like Dr Dre who beats women, you have rapists and murderers, all these people in the music involved in crimes against women. It wasn't fun anymore, and there wasn't any reason to be involved in it anymore.' One carryover to her new career in Manhole was this feminist perspective, made explicit by that group's rape-berating debut release, the *Victim* EP.
● ALBUMS: *The Power Of A Woman* (Comptown 1990)★★.

TALKIN' LOUD RECORDS

Gilles Peterson's extension of the original Acid Jazz empire, which has, if anything, gone on to outshine that UK imprint. Peterson originally ran a jazz funk pirate station from his own garden shed. He subsequently gained his own show on the leading Invicta pirate in exchange for lending them his transmitter. Taking a residency as the jazz room of the Electric Ballroom in Camden, North London, he was invigorated by the legendary atmosphere and freeform dancing that occurred there. The formula was relocated to Soho's Wag Club, then Camden's legendary Dingwalls Club . The first Talkin' Loud nights began at the Fridge. He had returned to piracy after his Mad On Jazz show had been axed after encouraging people to join the anti-Gulf War marches, and he eventually settled at Kiss-FM. In the meantime he was also working alongside Eddie Piller at Acid Jazz, before splitting to form his own label, named after his Talkin' Loud nights, when the finance was put forward by Phonogram. Signings included Galliano, Young Disciples, Omar (before he departed for RCA), Urban Species and others. Talkin' Loud's greatest moments so far have included the trilogy of Galliano releases that culminated in 1994's *The Plot Thickens*, which at last saw the band doing the business for the label, the Young Disciples' 'Apparently Nothin' 45 with Carleen Anderson's unmistakable vocal, and Omar's 'There's Nothing Like This' cut. The Urban Species debut album was also widely applauded. New signings include hip-hop/jazz fusioners the Roots, from Philadelphia, as Talkin' Loud continued to explore a number of new musical horizons. Peterson also started a new club, The Way It Is, with James Lavelle of Mo Wax. In 1997 another new signing, Roni Size/Reprazent, won that year's Mercury Music Prize for their *New Forms* album. Acts like Nu Yorican Soul also helped raise the label's profile to a level to match its earlier peak.

TANGLED FEET

UK act Tangled Feet are the brainchild of Jason Relf, who is responsible for guitars, keyboards, bass and programming as well as vocals. Relf began his career at the age of 16, writing, arranging and playing bass in a 12-piece funk band, Zoock, which kindled his interest in production after he oversaw their three studio sessions. Beginning to use sequencers for the first time in mid-1989, he released his first single under the name of Solar Plexus which had some strong reviews from the dance music press and which received support from top DJs such as Sasha. He then moved on to Astralasia, and played keyboards on their first single, 'Celestial Ocean', and co-wrote and performed on their second single and album, 'Politics Of Ecstasy'. While still a member of the band he began to collaborate with Scott James, DJ at the well-known 'Shave Yer Tongue' club. Together they released two singles under the name S.Y.T., 'Cairo Eclipse', on the Sabres Of Paradise label, and 'Blooma', on Leftfield's Hard Hands imprint. Relf was joined in Tangled Feet by his friend and associate Paul Douglas (vocals, guitar, programming) in late 1993. Their first release together was 'Messiah', which also featured the Rays, a band Relf was producing at the same time. It was remixed by the Pylon King (who gained excellent reviews for releases such as 'The Voices Of Khwan' and 'Zexos Empire'). Strangely, Tangled Feet found themselves signed to heavy metal label Music For Nations' subsidiary, Devotion.

TASSILLI PLAYERS

Tassilli Players worked on an open-house philosophy, with a floating pool of musicians centred around ex-Cosmics and Harare Dread member Dave Hake. Hake came from Coventry, England, where his contemporaries included the 2-Tone ska bands the Specials and Selecter. He later relocated to Manchester where he discovered Coxsone Dodd's Studio One label, which became a major influence on the performer's aspirations. He embarked on a period of self-discovery, including a spell in a Kibbutz, a sojourn with a Bedouin in the Sinai Desert, a hasty retreat from war-torn Israel and a tranquil period of rejuvenation in Ireland. It was the latter visit that inspired the concept of the Tassilli Players. In London he became involved with Zion Train, who produced his series of experimental dub albums. The play ers also featured on a series of dub compilations, including *Dubhead* and *Lead With The Bass*. In addition to his own Tassilli Players projects, Hake forged a strong relationship with Zion Train and joined Chris 'Forkebeard' Hetter as part of the band's distinctive brass section. The duo were recognized for their contribution to the archetypal *Homegrown Fantasy*, which demonstrated their talents on 'Dance Of Life' and a version of the Gladiators' 'Get Ready'. By 1996 the duo continued to pursue Tassilli projects alongside a continuous touring schedule. The Players were also recruited to provide the captivating horn riff on Morcheeba's reggae-styled 'Friction', featured on the acclaimed *Big Calm*.

● ALBUMS: with Zion Train *Great Sporting Moments In Dub* (Universal Egg/Zion 1994)★★★, *The Wonderful World Of Weed In Dub* (Universal Egg 1997)★★★, *In Outer Space* (Universal Egg 1997)★★★, *At The Cow Shed* (Universal Egg 1997)★★.

TECHNO

An easy definition of techno would be percussion-based electronic dance music, characterized by stripped down drum beats and basslines. However, the real roots of techno can be traced back to the experimental musicologists like Karl Heinz Stockhausen. In terms of equipment there was no greater precedent than that set by Dr Robert Moog, who invented the synthesizer in California, and provoked the first fears of the 'death of real music' that have shadowed electronic recordings ever since. If Chicory Tip's 'Son Of My Father' was the first to employ the Moog in 1972, then Kraftwerk were certainly the first to harness and harvest the possibilities of the synthesizer and other electronic instruments. Kraftwerk served as godfathers to UK electro pop outfits like the Human League (in their early experimental phase) and Depeche Mode. It is hard to imagine now but groups like these and even Gary Numan proved a huge influence on the US hip-hop scene and the development of New York 'electro' in the early 80s (particularly Afrika Bambaataa's 'Planet Rock'). Nevertheless, techno as we now know it descended from the Detroit region, which specialized in a stripped-down, abrasive sound, maintaining some of the soulful elements of the Motown Records palette, over the innovations that hip-hop's electro period had engendered. Techno also reflected the city's decline, as well as the advent of technology, and this tension was crucial to the dynamics of the sound. As Kevin Saunderson recounts: 'When we first started doing this music we were ahead. But Detroit is still a very behind city when it comes to anything cultural'. Techno as an umbrella term for this sound was first invoked by an article in *The Face* in May 1988, when it was used to describe the work of Saunderson (particularly 'Big Fun'), Derrick May (who recorded techno's greatest anthem, 'Strings Of Life') and Juan Atkins ('No

UFO's'). The Detroit labels of note included May's Transmat, Juan Atkins' Metroplex, Saunderson's KMS, Underground Resistance, Planet E, Red Planet, Submerge and Accelerate. Much like house, the audience for techno proved to be a predominantly British/European one. Labels like Rising High and Warp in the UK, and R&S in Belgium helped build on the innovations of May, Atkins and Carl Craig. UK artists like the Prodigy and LFO took the sound to a new, less artful but more direct level. According to Saunderson, the difference between most Detroit techno and its English re-interpreters was that it lacked the 'spirituality' of the original. Had he wished to produce more controversy, he might have substituted 'blackness' - nearly all of the main Detroit pioneers were black. Most UK techno, conversely, at least until the advent of the jungle genre, were white. Most techno utilizes the establishment of a groove or movement by repetition, building a framework that does not translate easily into more conventional musical terms. Some obviously find this adjustment difficult, but the variations in texture and tempo are at least as subtle as those in rock music - often more so, due to the absence of a lyrical focus.

TECHNOTRONIC

Belgian commercial techno/house outfit created by producer Jo 'Thomas DeQuincey' Bogaert. He was looking for a female rapper to sing over a backing track he had produced, before stumbling upon Ya Kid K (b. Manuella Kamosi) in the Antwerp rap group, Fresh Beat. Kamosi had moved to Belgium from her native Zaire at 11, and later spent some time in Chicago, where she was introduced to rap and deep house. With Bogaert she recorded 'Pump Up The Jam', which eventually reached number 2 in the UK charts in 1989. The single was actually credited to Technotronic featuring Felly (a model who appeared on the cover). However, when the first album *Pump Up The Jam* was released, they were rebilled as Technotronic Featuring Ya Kid K. The album also featured MC Eric, whose most notable contribution was the chant sequence on 'This Beat Is Technotronik'. Follow-ups included 'Get Up (Before The Night Is Over)' with Ya Kid K, 'This Beat Is Technotronik', 'Rockin' Over The Beat', 'Megamix' (Bogaert on his own) and 'Turn It Up' (Technotronic Featuring Melissa And Einstein). Ya Kid K went on to perform on Hi Tek's 'Spin That Wheel' in 1990 (a version of which was included on Technotronic's *Trip On This* remix album) and later pursued a solo career. She was replaced by Reggie Magloire (who had previously worked with Indeep) for the album *Body To Body*. Bogaert later recorded a solo album, *Different Voices*, for Guerilla Records.

● ALBUMS: *Pump Up The Jam* (Epic 1990)★★★, *Trip On This* (Epic 1990)★★★★, *Body To Body* (Epic 1991)★★★.

● VIDEOS: *Pump Up The Hits* (1990).

TECHNOVA

David Harrow was previously a London musician best known for his work with the On-U-Sound team on material by Gary Clail, Lee Perry, Bim Sherman and, under his own auspices, for Jah Wobble's *Without Judgement* album. As Pulse 8 (not the record label) he also issued 'Radio Morocco', the first ever single on Nation Records in October 1989. His first UK release as Technova was 'Tantra', a 25-minute trance/ambient affair with a strong reggae undertow, released on the Sabres Of Paradise imprint. He had impressed the latter's Andy Weatherall with an appearance at the Sabres Christmas party, accompanied by naked (except for luminous paint) tattooed and pierced dancers. The single was actually taken from an album released in Australia on the Shock label in 1993, though Weatherfield quickly announced plans to re-release it on the Sabres imprint. 'The basic idea of the album is to simulate a long journey. It's totally seamless and it took a lot of prepartion to get it to flow the way that I wanted'. The project made plentiful use of DAT-recorded environmental sounds picked up on Harrow's own journey through Australasia.

● ALBUMS: *Trantic Shadows* (Shock 1993)★★★, *Transcience* (Emissions Audio Output 1995)★★.

TEN CITY

Consistent, sometimes spectacular Chicago house group, with Byron Stingily's falsetto always the focus. The other members were Byron Burke and Herb Lawson. They met in a rehearsal studio in Chicago in 1985, Herb being drawn from R&B band Rise, while Stingily was then fronting B Rude Inc. The trio recorded two singles as Ragtyme, 'I Can't Stay Away' and 'Fix It Man'. In 1986 they signed to Atlantic and made the name change. The debut single, 'Devotion', was an instant hit (it would later be revamped by Nomad for their '(I Wanna Give You) Devotion' hit). Their production was helmed by Marshall Jefferson,

who was responsible for shaping much of their early character and sound. The band began making steady progress in the late 80s, going chartbound in the UK the following year with 'That's The Way Love Is'. Ten City, aside from the Jefferson connections (their union ended by the advent of Ten City's third album), are good writers in their own right, having provided for Adeva and Ultra Nate among others. Their sound is also distinguished by the live musicianship. If plagiarism amounts to tribute, then their basslines, rhythms and melodies have reappeared often enough to suggest a lasting influence on dance music.

● ALBUMS: *Foundation* (East West 1988)★★★, *State Of Mind* (East West 1990)★★★★, *No House Big Enough* (East West 1992)★★★★, *Love In A Day* (Columbia 1994)★★★, *That Was Then, This Is Now* (Columbia 1994)★★★.

TENAGLIA, DANNY

Italian-American Tenaglia has, together with keyboard player Peter Dauo, played host to an impressive slew of garage/house cuts emanating from New York in the 90s. He first turned to dance music when hearing a mix tape for the first time, subsequently selling them for the artist concerned. He was a keen enthusiast in the early disco boom, and played his first gig at a local club in Bayside, Queens, New York, when he was still 14. From there he picked up on musical trends as they occurred, being particularly influenced by the early innovations of David Morales and Kevin Saunderson. His productions of cuts like 'Glammer Girl' by the Look (a Jon Waters tribute), and the techno-jazz innovations of his partner Dauo, built an enviable reputation, as his profile grew alongside that of fellow New Yorkers DJ Duke and Junior Vasquez. Naturally this helped bring in the remix projects, including Right Said Fred and Yothu Yindi. Despite his obvious musical merits Tenaglia has yet to crack the US scene, which contrasts alarmingly with his popularity in Europe and even the Orient. In the UK his reputation has been franked by performances at the musically sympathetic Ministry Of Sound club nights.

● ALBUMS: *Hard And Soul* (Tribal UK 1995)★★★.

TERMINATOR X

b. Norman Rodgers. One of the last of the Public Enemy fold to release a solo record, Terminator X's efforts reflect his work with his principal employers, minus the intrusion of Chuck D or

Flavor Flav. Aimed squarely at the dance end of the hip-hop market, *Valley Of The Jeep Beets* was primarily a collection of deep, bass-driven hip-hop chops, and confirmed him as one of the finest DJs in the business. It saw vocal contributions from Andrew 13 and Sister Souljah, on a combination of hard funk and scratchy raps. As Public Enemy prepared to tour in support of their 1994 album he was unfortunately involved in a serious motorbike accident, breaking both his legs. However, this setback did not deter the release of his second solo outing. The highlight of this set was 'G'Damn Datt DJ Made My Day', on which he duelled on the turntable alongside Grandmaster Flash. Other old school legends including the Cold Crush Brothers and Kool Herc popped up elsewhere.
● ALBUMS: *Terminator X And The Valley Of The Jeep Beets* (CBS/Columbia 1991)★★★★. With The Godfathers Of Threatt: *Super Bad* (RAL 1994)★★★.

TERRY, TODD

Terry is a US house production innovator and expert with a reputation second to none (in fact, some journalists from specialist magazines took to nicknaming him 'God' for easy reference). An established producer and DJ, he learned his trade playing early house and hip-hop at parties in New York. 'Bongo (To The Batmobile)', a major signpost in the development of acid house, and further singles like 'Can You Party?' and 'A Day In The Life Of A Black Riot' were credited to the Todd Terry Project alias. In addition to an album and singles on Champion (including the mighty 'Put Your Hands Together'), he also cut records for Strictly Rhythm, Nervous and Freeze (SAX's 'This Will Be Mine'). His distinctive use of samples underpins all his production and remix work: 'What I try to do is to make an art out of the samples'. This often involves multi-layers of creative theft without allowing a given example to offer its 'signature' to the listener. His remix clients have included Bizarre Inc ('I'm Gonna Get You') and Snap!, and he also collaborated with old friend Tony Humphries to remix Alison Limerick's 'Make It On My Own'. 'Whenever I do a remix I strip the vocal right down and use just a little bit. That's why I don't do many remixes, they are a long way from the original'. A good example was the magic he worked on PM Dawn's 'From A Watcher's Point Of View' and Everything But The Girl's 'Missing', the latter resurrecting the indie

duo's career and re-establishing Terry's name as a leading remixer. He owns his own home-studio, the Loudhouse, in his native Brooklyn, and released a new album in 1997.
● ALBUMS: *This Is The New Todd Terry Project Album* (Champion 1992)★★★, *Ready For A New Day* (Manifesto 1997)★★★.

THA BRIGADE

A 90s Swedish hip-hop collective, Tha Brigade comprise Siege, Uppercut, Cymebeline-Scratchcliffer and Capo Boia, who were all born in their native Gothenburg at the turn of the 70s. They actually formed before leaving school, adopting the traditional hip-hop culture of break-dancing and graffiti from as early as 1985. They recorded their debut EP, *First Blood - The Evolutionary Promo*, on a bedroom-based porta-studio in 1993. Although issued in limited quantities, it did attract the attention of the UK-based rapper Blade, who helped them to secure more widespread distribution. Unlike other Swedish rappers (such as Leila K. and Deep Fried), Tha Brigade offer a hardcore variant of Scandinavian hip-hop, inspired by the west coast gangsta rap of Ice Cube or Cypress Hill.

THA DOGG POUND

The release of Tha Dogg Pound's debut album in 1995 came at a time when their mentor and the best-known member of the Death Row Records/Dr Dre enclave, Snoop Doggy Dogg, had just gone on trial charged with murder. The duo of Delmar Arnaud (Dat Nigga Daz) and Ricardo Brown (Kurupt Tha Kingpin), both from Los Angeles, California, USA, were largely responsible for 1994's *Murder Was The Case* film soundtrack, introducing a sound that used Dre's patented G-Funk formula as a launching pad, but they largely steered clear of gangsta rhetoric in their lyrics. With guests including Snoop Doggy Dogg himself, Nate Dogg, Rage and Michel'le, the album was bound to attract interest from hardcore rap fans, but *Dogg Food* also revealed a comparative deftness of touch and a penchant for self-parody largely lacking in their more esteemed colleagues. However, the sexually explicit content was rumoured to be still strong enough to end Warner Brothers Records' alliance with Interscope Records, Death Row's distributors, even though the album sold a million copies in the USA alone.
● ALBUMS: *Dogg Food* (Death Row/Interscope/Island 1995)★★★.

THAT KID CHRIS
b. Chris Straropoli, Queens, New York, USA. That Kid Chris has widely been cited as America's answer to Joey Negro. Certainly he is at least as prolific, having released dozens of disco-influenced house singles in the early 90s including 'Feel The Vibe' (Digital Dungeon Records), 'Power Of The Darkside' (Strictly Rhythm Records) and 'Get Down With The Genie' (Floorwax Records). Straropoli began his career in the hip-hop-dominated music scene of Queens, New York, where he began work as a DJ playing electro jams. His earliest influence was Jellybean's sets at The Funhouse. Straropoli became a rap DJ proper at the Limelight club before switching to hard house on the east coast rave scene. However, his recorded output relies continually on samples of 70s disco and soul culled from his father's record collection. He made his breakthrough with the release of 'Big Time', a track heavily influenced by Al Pacino's performance in the movie *Carlito's Way*. That and subsequent 12-inches saw him find a sympathetic audience in the UK where he was widely celebrated alongside Josh Wink as the 'new face' of melodic American dance music in the mid-90s.

THOMAS, KENNY
b. *c*.1969, London, England. Thomas was one of the most popular UK soul dance vocalists. His biggest UK hit came in 1991 with 'Thinking About Your Love' (number 4), while his debut album sold more than 600,000 copies in the UK alone. Other hit singles spawned by that debut included 'Outstanding', 'The Best Of You' and 'Tender Love', and also resulted in a Brit Award nomination for Best British Male Vocalist and Best British Newcomer. The warm, relaxed dance grooves of that debut were replicated on a second album that continued Thomas's massive commercial success. Guest musicians this time round included the Young Disciples, Nu Colours and the Reggae Philharmonic Orchestra. This time some of the bonhomie of the original set was more restrained, with a slightly more mature lyrical vision reflecting more real-life experiences.
● ALBUMS: *Voices* (1991)★★★★, *Wait For Me* (1993)★★★.

THREE BEAT RECORDS
Liverpool, England, dance label, headed by joint partner Hywel Williams, a local rave organiser, alongside Dave Nicoll, Jonathan Barlow and Phillip Southall. Three Beat is also responsible for running a series of club nights in and around Merseyside. They signed a licensing deal with London/ffrr in 1994, having built their reputation with records like New Atlantic's 'Take Off Some Time'. Although Three Beat reamined indepedent ffrr were to be given first choice over licensing any of their product. The first release under the new arrangement was 2 Cowboy's 'Everybody's Gonfi-Gon', a huge hit. Their mid-90s roster included Cordial, Neuro Project, Jeaney Tracey, Bong Devils, Supernature, Bandito and Vicki Shepherd, in addition to the aforementioned New Atlantic.

THREE MAN POSSE
Also known in abbreviated form as 3MP, this Bristol, Avon, England rap trio comprise DJ Lynx and MCs Kriss and Kelz. MC Kriss was an aficionado of hip-hop during the period when the Wild Bunch/Massive Attack held sway in Bristol. He joined with his two partners in time to feature on Smith And Mighty's underground dance hits, 'Anyone' and 'Walk On'. However, a prolonged hiatus (strangely similar to the fortunes of Smith And Mighty) intervened before the release of the aptly titled 'Better Late Than Never' single for Terra Ferma Records in 1994. Encouraging reviews confirmed their return to form, buoyed by UK support slots to Ice-T and Greg Osby, as well as their own weekly show on Bristol's Galaxy Radio.

3PHASE
Signed to Novamute, 3Phase is essentially Sven Roehrig (b. Berlin, Germany) plus his various associates and technological aides. He in turn is part of the Berlin-based Tresor club and label, which has achieved lots of good press (not least via the patronage of the Orb's Alex Paterson). His debut album (*Schlangenfarm* translates as 'Snake Farm') revealed Roehrig's debt to his industrial music past - he had formerly been a member of Justice League, Tox Movement and Boom Factory, and his earliest major influence was Throbbing Gristle. The 3Phase banner had first been invoked as his interests in techno grew, and also reflected the post-Wall Berlin spirit which gave birth to a regenerated club scene. In 1992 he collaborated with DJ Dr. Mottke for 'Der Klang Der Familie', which became the theme song to Berlin's third annual Techno festival - the Love Parade. It also

provided the title of Tresor's first compilation album, and became a massive European-wide hit in its own right.

● ALBUMS: *Schlangenfarm* (Novamute 1993)★★★, *Rota* (Novamute 1993)★★★.

THREE TREE POSSE

Eco-conscious rappers with origins in the Far East as well as central Europe, Three Tree Posse are a trio of rappers based in Switzerland. Though their beats and rhythms have admirably combined influences drawn from the jazz and funk traditions, their initial attempts to grapple with the English language only served to emphasise that it was not their mother tongue. Nevertheless, there was enough quality on their 70-minute 1993 debut album to recommend it as Switzerland's first convincing musical statement in the hip-hop idiom.

● ALBUMS: *The Fascinating Story About The Quest Of 3 Trees* (Tree 1993)★★★.

TIME RECORDS

Nottingham, England, label run by Dave Thompson and Chris Allen, based around the Squaredance Recording Studio and Venus club nights. Via a monthly mail-order release schedule they built up an admirable catalogue, pushing out double pack EP's which matched established acts like Moodswings and Deja Vu with new, up and coming outfits. A good example was April 1993's *Back In Time* EP, wherein four 'classics' (DIY's 'Excommunicate', Association's 'Ciao', Mad's 'India Kinda' and IDG's 'Family') were remixed by the God Squad, Back To Basics, Sure Is Pure and Huggy. This process threw up a series of techno and house gems, some of which were licensed to R&S and Flying. In 1993 they launched the Emit imprint for collections of ambient music. 'Ambient music is taking what house was supposed to be about quite a bit further. Its more of an international language'. The company is not to be confused with the Brescia based Italian dance label (famed for work with Carol Bailey, Deadly Sins, Usura and Silvia Coleman).

● ALBUMS: Various: *EMIT 0094* (emiT/Time 1994)★★★.

TIMELORDS

Conceived by the mischievous Bill Drummond and Jimmy Cauty, this fictitious group registered a surprise UK number 1 with the novelty 'Doctorin' The Tardis' in the summer of 1988. Inspired by the television series *Dr Who*, the insis-tent tune incorporated the glam rock thud of Gary Glitter, who even joined the duo when they performed the song. The spoof was continued in *The Manual*, a book credited to the Timelords, in which Drummond espoused his theories of how to create a number 1 hit. The front cover of the tome enthused 'The Justified Ancients Of Mu Mu Reveal Their Zenarchistic Method Used In Making The Unthinkable Happen'. The Drummond/Cauty partnership soon enjoyed even greater success with the dance-orientated pranksters KLF, whose title also served as the Timelords' record label.

● FURTHER READING: *The Manual*, The Timelords.

TIN TIN OUT

UK dance group Tin Tin Out consist of Darren Stokes and Lyndsey Edwards. The group was formed in 1993 when Stokes, also a renowned DJ, was A&R Director for Pulse 8 Records (responsible for signing, among others, Gloworm's 'I Lift My Cup' and Urban Cookie Collective's 'The Key'). He met Edwards, an acclaimed keyboardist and musical technician, on a session for the label. Adopting the name Tin Tin Out they undertook a burgeoning repertoire of remixes, including Jon Pleased Wimmin ('Passion'), Lisa Moorish ('That's The Way It Is') and Michelle Gayle ('Freedom'). In their own right they reached the UK charts with 'The Feeling', which featured rapper Sweet Tee, and with a memorable version of 'Always Something There To Remind Me' featuring Espiritu singer Vanessa Quinones (the song was later used on UK television's football programme *Endsleigh League Extra*). In 1995 they were signed to VC Recordings. They enjoyed a huge UK chart hit in 1998 with a version of the Sundays' 'Here's Where The Story Ends', featuring the vocals of Shelley Nelson.

TIP RECORDS

After five years of organizing parties and making music, Raja Ram and Graham Wood (of The Infinity Project, hence the label's name) formed TIP in 1994 to promote psychedelic trance. Ian St. Paul (who had organized the legendary Future and Spectrum parties in 1987/8) managed the label until Rich Bloor took over the ropes in March 1996. The first release was The Infinity Project's 'Stimuli'/'Uforica') and over the next few years TIP released full-on trance by some of the top artists in the area, including Astral Projection

('Enlightened Evolution'), Doof ('Lets Turn On'), Green Nuns Of The Revolution ('Conflict'/'Cor'), Hallucinogen ('Angelic Particles'/'Soothsayer') and Laughing Buddha ('Infinite Depth'/'Andromeda'). At the same time they produced a series of different-coloured compilations whose covers featured 'Goa'-style images. Artists' albums followed, including monumental works by Astral Projection (*Trust In Trance*) and Doof (*Let's Turn On*). The *Infinite Excursions* compilations have displayed a more relaxed side to TIP with their dubby, softer psychedelic flavour, while the *TIP Singles* series aimed to make available deleted classics and forthcoming releases. In 1998 they launched a new label, 10 Kilo, which accommodated more 'downbeat and eclectic styles' touching on the electro/breakbeat sound in collaborations with Adam Freeland. At the same time they continued to organize parties around the world and were developing new artists such as Growling Mad Scientists, Orichalcum, Psychopod, Snake Thing and Synchro, encouraging them to experiment rather than adhere to any particular styles.

TJ RHEMI

Before he signed to Nation Records in 1996 Rhemi had already worked as a musician in a number of capacities. He played jazz with Andy Hamilton and his own fusion band, Saaz, studied with the composer John Hamilton at the Birmingham Conservatoire, produced a number of bhangra bands, and played guitar with a variety of groups. Accordingly, he brings a broad range of influences to his music, 'from be-bop to jazz-funk, folk to classical Indian, Bach to hip-hop to drum and bass'. His first release for Nation was the track 'Is It Legal' on the compilation *Fuse 3: Global Choas* (1996), which was followed by his debut single, 'The Fusionist', in 1997. During that year he worked on remixes for several artists, including Natasha Atlas, Alibi and Tony Di Bart, while 'Mind Filter' was featured on the compilation *Outcaste Untouchable Beats* (Outcaste 1997). The following year he released *The Skrutinizer* EP, the title track of which appeared on the album *Mind Filter*. Here he presents a set of tracks that display all his influences, tied together by his skill and musicality. Hip-hop and drum 'n' bass grooves sit beside samples of traditional music from various cultures, interspersed with dub basslines, funky riffs and snippets of melodies, all blended with various live instruments including guitar, flute,

tabla and dholki to create an eclectic yet integrated album. Other work has included DJing at nights such as Sitar Funk (at 333, in London) and Swaraj (Blue Note, London).

● ALBUMS: *Mindfilter* (Nation 1988)★★★★.

TOBIN, AMON

b. Rio de Janeiro, Brazil. Tobin visited Europe as a child and returned to the UK in his teens when he developed a passion for hip-hop, blues and jazz, including the music of Grandmaster Flash, Lightnin' Hopkins, Eddie Palmieri and Thelonius Monk. When he was 17 he began experimenting with his own sounds with a sequencer and a 'horrible little Casio sampling keyboard'. After spending two years making music in Portugal and Madeira he settled in Brighton and made a number of recordings for Ninebar Records as Cujo. His first EP, *Curfew*, came out in June 1995 and was followed by the *Salivate*, *Breakcharmer* and *Adventures In Foam* EPs in 1996. Cujo also featured on Ninebar's compilation *Joint Ventures* (1996). Later that year he signed to Ninja Tune Records to record a number of tracks and consequently released the *Creatures* EP in November. In 1997 he produced two singles ('Chomp Samba' and 'Mission'/'Tubukula Beach Resort') that were taken from his first album, *Bricolage*. After the *Pirahna Breaks* EP towards the end of 1997, he did not release any new material until 'Like Regular Chickens' in May 1998, which was the opening track from *Permutation*. Here, Tobin drew on a wide variety of musical sources, including drum 'n' bass, jazz, hip-hop and samba as well as the lesser-known South American-style batucada. 'People Like Frank' begins with a lazy, double bass-led hip-hop groove, supporting ethereal string textures and a noodling trumpet, before an onslaught of frantic, Latin-influenced drums reminiscent of jungle. 'Nightlife', meanwhile, blends jittery drum 'n' bass with exotic orchestral textures. Tobin's tendency is towards abstract, listenable 'soundtracks' that develop through various textures and ideas, rather than big, danceable numbers.

● ALBUMS: *Bricolage* (Ninja Tune 1997)★★★, *Permutation* (Ninja Tune 1998)★★★★.

TOBY, GLENN 'SWEET G'

b. New York, USA. A man of many guises and a minor house music legend Toby started off his music career as part of Cultural Vibe, who were heartily welcomed for their 1986 house epic, 'Ma

Foom Bey', and other singles such as 'Power'. He was subsequently brought in as producer with Stephanie Mills, Jay Williams and even Run DMC. By the early 90s he had linked with Victor Simonelli in two ways. He recorded 'I Want To Hold You' as part of Groove Committee, before using Simonelli as guest producer on his latest project, Nu-Civilisation. Their career began promisingly with the double a-sided 12-inch, 'When Will We Be Free?'/'Destiny'.

TODDY TEE

b. c.1965, Compton, Los Angeles, California, USA. One of the Los Angeles old school, Toddy Tee is as signifcant to the development of West Coast rap as Afrika Bambaataa is to the New York scene, though he rarely receives the credit. This probably has a great deal to do with the lack of musical archive his career has produced. One important such document was the *Batteram* tape, a live outing circulated in similar fashion to the Zulu Nation's 'throwdowns'. It was later revisited in Ice-T's 'Six', and documented the LAPD's new weapon in the war against crack houses, an armoured car that they could drive straight into suspect's houses. The tape was one of a sequence traded between Toddy Tee and fellow rhymer Mixmaster Spade, but proved much more popular than anything which had gone before. In the wake of its success it was eventually released as a single on Evejim in 1986, which would add 'Just Say No' to Tee's discography two years later. However, this provides scant testimony to the man's influence.

TOMATO RECORDS

Dance record label established by Ross Nedderman and Tim Reeves (formerly of Virgin) in Lillie Road, London, England. Reeves had previously been best known for dropping an 'E' in the middle of a seminar at Manchester's In The City conference. Tomato's first release was Pascal's 'Bongo Massive' - a first taste of the percussive conga sound which rapidly became fashionable for a few months thereafter. It led to descriptions in some quarters as 'the bongo label', which was something of a simplification. Nedderman and Reeves pressed on regardless, releasing the *2 Clouds Above 9* album, sponsored by the computer game company Sega, which gave new producers and musicians the opportunity to record for the first time. They themselves also recorded, as Two Shiny Heads, a track for Guerilla ('Dub House Disco'). Other releases such as Infinite Wheel's

'Lake Of Dreams' (which used everything from kettle drums to xylophone in execution of its percussion) and Nature Boy's eponymous EP and 'Ruff Disco' 12-inch maintained their credentials in the world of underground dance, and the boys intend to keep things 'red, round and light-hearted' for the forseeable future.
● ALBUMS: Various: *Cream Of Tomato* (Tomato 1993)★★★.

TOMMY BOY RECORDS

A record label hugely important to the development of hip-hop and rap, Tommy Boy was the tiny entity that brought the world Afrika Bambaataa, Keith LeBlanc ('Malcolm X'), and the songwriting/production genius of Michael Jonzun and Arthur Baker. The label was formed by Tom Silverman in his living room on East 85th Street in New York. He had previously been running a magazine entitled *Dance Music Report*, in the process of which he became captivated by the electro funk movement in Europe. Early Tommy Boy releases included projects by Bambaataa's MCs, recording under the name Cotton Candy. The breakthrough release was 'Jazzy Sensation', built on Gwen McRae's 'Funky Sensation' and concocted by Bambaataa, and producers Baker and Shep Pettibone. It was a precursor to 'Planet Rock', a hugely successful collision between Kraftwerk's 'Trans Europe Express' and Alan Shacklock's Ennio Morricone-inspired 'The Mexican', which lit the 'electro' fuse. Tommy Boy was instrumental in developing the sound, which dominated rap in the mid-80s. Afterwards, they explored rap's fallout with high-quality signings like Queen Latifah and Digital Underground. Their second great innovation arrived with the introduction of De La Soul and 'Daisy Age Soul'. In its wake the label was signed up to Warners, and Big Life also picked up several of their artists for UK distribution, though there were plans to open a UK office in 1994. Their biggest ever hit, however, came with Naughty By Nature's 1990 single, 'OPP'. More recently they have seen worldwide chart returns for Latin hip-hoppers K7 and the more thuggish House Of Pain.

TONE LOC

Tongue-in-cheek Los Angeles artist (b. Anthony Smith - his stage name derived from his Spanish nickname, Antonio Loco), Tone Loc's hoarse raps boast of incredible personal sexual allure, allied to a background of smooth jazz, soul and bluebeat.

His debut album featured the two worldwide 1990 hits, Wild Thing' and 'Funky Cold Medina', both built on sparse rock samples. The songs were written by Marvin Young, aka Young MC, 'Wild Thing' going on to become America's second biggest-selling single of all time. It also created one of the strangest moral panic scares of its era, when certain pundits suggested it gave rise to the 'Wilding' craze, where young black men prowled the streets in order to rob, rape and kill. This was simple paranoia, and clearly had nothing to do with the career of Smith, whose alarmingly deep, husky vocals always enabled a sense of humour and self-deprecation to permeate through his recordings. *Loc'ed After Dark* made the US number 1 spot, only the second rap album to do so. 'All Through The Night', the first single from his follow-up LP, featured the Brand New Heavies in support. However, its failure to crack the Top 20 indicated a small reversal in his fortunes. He has also contributed dialogue to the animated film *Bebe's Kids*, and starred in *Posse*.
● ALBUMS: *Loc'ed After Dark* (Delicious Vinyl 1989)★★★, *Cool Hand Loc* (Delicious Vinyl 1991)★★★.

TOO MUCH JOY

From Westchester County in New York, USA, an affluent neighbourhood devoid of the ghetto culture celebrated in much rap parlance, Too Much Joy still managed to attract controversy in 1990. By performing cover versions of 2 Live Crew songs at a concert in Miami, Florida, they became the subjects of an obscenity case (later dismissed by jury). In the process they became rap's least likely victims of censorship. Their debut album, 1988's uninspiring *Son Of Sam I Am*, included a version of LL Cool J's 'That's A Lie'. However, by the advent of *Cereal Killers* they had performed what some critics termed 'a Beastie Boys in reverse' - moving from their hardcore hip-hop roots into the hardcore punk of early Hüsker Dü.
● ALBUMS: *Son Of Sam I Am* (Alias 1988)★★★, *Cereal Killers* (Alias 1991)★★★.

TOO SHORT

b. Todd Shaw, 28 April 1966, South Central, Los Angeles, California, USA. Diminutive rapper from Oakland, California, where he moved at age 14. His first introductions to rap, not a familiar form on the west coast at this time, came after hearing the Sugarhill Gang and Melle Mel. On the back of three years hustling, Too Short eventually signed to indepedent label 75 Girls. His first two albums, though musically valid, suffered from an over-reliance on hackneyed tales of pimping and gun fights. After three albums he set up his own Dangerous Music company in 1986, co-founded with manager Randy Austin. *Born To Mack* whistled up sales of over 200,000, from the trunk of the artist's car, and Jive records became intrigued by this parochial phenomenon. They re-packaged *Born To Mack* which went on to go gold. Lyrical matters had, however, only improved marginally on the arrival of his first Jive album proper, *Life Is...Too Short*, which went platinum and stayed in the US pop charts for 78 weeks. The artist has never offered much in the way of justification: 'No one can lay any guilt trips on me and tell me that I'm corrupting the youth of America or that I'm disrespecting all females. It's just a money thing'. Despite such myopia, the album was at least a more considered effort than the following collection, *Short Dog's In The House*, where titles like 'Bitch Killa' illustrated the sort of material on offer. Its saving grace was a double take with Ice Cube on his anti-censorship hymn, 'Ain't Nothing But A Word To Me'. The largely unappetising lyrical fare rode roughshod over an otherwise acceptable melange of funk and breakbeats. Musically, Too Short had always based his career on a limited diet of samples drawn from Sly Stone, Graham Central Station, Kool And The Gang etc. Although *Short Dog's In The House* gave him his second platinum album, 90% of those sales were exclusively in Oakland and its neighbouring districts. Something of a departure, especially for an artist as one-dimensional as Too Short, arrived with *Shorty The Pimp*. This exaggerated his hustling image, inspired by *Superfly* and other blaxploitation films, and extolled the adventures of his semi-autobiographical alter-ego Shorty the Pimp. It saw the introduction of permanent collaborators Art Banks and Shorty B. *Get In Where You Fit In*, meanwhile, quickly retraced his steps to earlier material, rapping over crude sexual anecdotes, and sent him straight to number 1 in the US R&B charts. However, there was evidence that by 1994 Too Short was growing a little jaded with his one-track career, and its effect on his private life: 'I'm not in control of my bad boy image anymore. It's grown legs and run away with itself. People believe Too Short the raper's Too Short the man'.
● ALBUMS: *Born To Mack* (Dangerous 1986)★★★★, *Life Is...Too Short* (Dangerous 1988)★★★, *Short Dog's In The House* (Jive

1990)★★★, *Shorty The Pimp* (Jive 1992)★★★, *Get In Where You Fit In* (Jive 1993)★★★★, *Gettin' It* (Dangerous 1996)★★★.

TOOP, DAVID, AND MAX EASTLEY

Ambient sculptors based in north London, England, whose albums have brought many admiring glances via their organic use of animal and wildlife sounds, interfacing with experimental technology. Contrary to what might have been expected of the dance scene in the 90s, Toop is a well-known author and writer for *The Times* and *The Face*, as well as being one of hip-hop's most powerful advocates and chroniclers. He first performed with Eastley as far back as 1971, after meeting at Alexandra Palace Art College in the mid-60s. They have been working on atmosphere-music ever since - Toop releasing several solo albums for Brian Eno's label, as well as taking a role in experimental pop band the Flying Lizards.
● ALBUMS: *Buried Dreams* (1994)★★★. Solo: David Toop *Screen Ceremonies* (Wire Editions 1995)★★★★, *Pink Noir* (Virgin 1996)★★★, *Spirit World* (Virgin 1997)★★★.

TORTOISE

Formed in Chicago, Illinois, USA, in 1990, Tortoise are an instrumental group founded by Douglas McCombs (of Eleventh Dream Day) and Johnny Herndon (of Precious Wax Drippings and The Sea And The Cake) as an experiment. By 1994 they had recruited John McEntire (drums) and Dan Bitney (percussion) and set about work on their self-titled debut album. A richly formulated collection of atmospheric collages, combining dub reggae bass, electronic, jazz, ambient and classical movements, it saw them become the toast of a number of US and UK magazines. *Rhythms, Revolutions And Clusters*, a remix project drawing principally on the debut, was released the following year with the aid of newly installed fifth member, Dave Pajo (of the Palace Brothers). A second album, *Millions Now Living Will Never Die*, followed early in 1996. All their albums are licensed to City Slang in the UK from the USA independent Thrill Jockey. The group were also celebrated in novel form in *Low Fidelity*, author Timothy White vividly narrating his protagonist's trip to London to find every record by Tortoise he could. *TNT* was less experimental, concentrating on meandering jazz-fusion complete with suitably pretentious song titles including 'In Sarah, Menchen, Christ And Beethoven There Were

Women And Men' and 'I Set My Face To The Hillside'.
● ALBUMS: *Tortoise* (Thrill Jockey 1994)★★★, *Rhythms, Revolutions And Clusters* (Thrill Jockey 1995)★★★, *Millions Now Living Will Never Die* (Thrill Jockey 1996)★★★★, *TNT* (Thrill Jockey 1998)★★★.

TOTAL DEVASTATION

Three-piece rap crew from California, composed of lead rapper Rasta Red Eye (b. Puerto Rica), lyricist Soopa Dupa (b. Cuba) and DJ Tuf Cut Tim The Fat Beat Maker (b. Mexico). Their home turf is nicknamed 'The Mission', a tightly knit Hispanic community within San Francisco. Although they all grew up in the neighbourhood, it was not until a New Year's Eve Party in 1988 that they discovered they shared the same musical tastes. Together they created Hogstatus, a fully blown production company, in anticipation of their forthcoming career. Eventually PGA Records picked up on their demos, releasing their debut single, 'Many Clouds Of Smoke', in 1993. Selling over 60,000 copies in California alone, its pro-marijuana lyric did not dissuade major label Arista from taking an interest.
● ALBUMS: *Total Devastation* (Arista 1993)★★★.

TOURNESOL

Techno duo comprising Danish pair Tommy Dee and Thomas 'Tutor' Lange. Their first recording bout came via a track on *Secrets*, a 1991 compilation album prepared by the Danish government to showcase new artists. They went on to work alongside Kenneth Baker, before a remix of Cut N Move's 'Give It Up', which sold especially well in Germany and mainland Europe. Their debut album, *Kokotsu*, was named after the Japanese term 'trance', while their own name is derived from the professor of Herge's comic stories.
● ALBUMS: *Kokotsu* (Apollo 1994)★★★.

TOYTOWN TECHNO

A sub-subgenre of dance music, 'Toytown Techno' was the term invoked to describe the strange phenomenon of records that emerged from 1991 to 1993 which were essentially themed on children's television and other signature tunes. A precedent had been set with the KLF alter egos Justified Ancients Of Mu Mu's 'Doctorin' The Tardis', but in reality it all started off with the Prodigy's 'Charly'. This used the infamous UK children's information film dialogue. It broke the Top 10 but was quickly considered an embarassment by Liam Howlett, as accusations of 'cheapening', even 'killing', rave music followed. However, so did a legion of impersonators. The Smarte's 'Sesame's Treet' (Suburban Base) was probably the best known and most successful, despite the fact that it came from a stable previously known as the antithesis of commerical music. There was soon no let-up in the avalanche. Urban Hype provided 'A Trip To Trumpton' (Faze 2), Mike Summer the *Magic Roundabout* tribute 'Summer Magic', Shaft offered 'Roobarb And Custard' (ffrr), while the *Blue Peter* theme was mugged for Monster Rush's 'The Hypnotizer' (G-Spot). Horsepower trotted up with the *Black Beauty*-themed 'Bolt', while DJ Excell's 'Just When You Thought It Was Safe' brought in the film world by sampling the famous bass-line from *Jaws*. The various shady individuals behind this surfeit soon realised the resonance of computer signature tunes, paving the way for Ambassadors Of Funk's 'Super Mario Land' and Power Pill's 'Pac Man'. Toytown Techno was an early example of post-rave, multi-media entertainment in its most insidious form. Hardly any of these tunes are worthy of more than a single play, but each managed to raise a smile on first hearing - at least among non-puritans.

TRANCE INDUCTION

Holland trance/ambient outfit led by one Tjeerd Verbeek, who broke through with the amazing 'New Age Heartcore'. This looped guitar distortion over a melange of techno to quite startling effect. An eclectic debut album saw him fuse Detroit rhythms with all manner of musical subcultures, from house to bhangra.
● ALBUMS: *Electrickery* (Guerilla 1994)★★★.

TRANSCENDENTAL LOVE MACHINE

This UK team from south London made their debut with 'Unity', followed by *The Silver Atomic EP*, on which they shifted towards trance/dub aesthetics. Following *The Dragonflymania* EP came *The Love Machine Remixes*, part of which was shortlisted by the BBC Television as the theme to their Winter Olympics coverage. Following a further EP, *Machine Mania*, the group unveiled a debut album for Hydrogen Dukebox records, which had also housed the earlier releases.
● ALBUMS: *Orgasmatronic* (Hydrogen Dukebox 1994)★★★, *I've Got The Battery* (Duke 1996)★★★.

TRANSCRIPTION CARRIERS

Based in Kingswood, Bristol, Avon, England, rap group the Transcription Carriers were initially inspired by early UK rap artists such as Derek B and Overlord X. Led by MCs Mister Deed, Kant Control and Reborn, alongside DJ Beanz, the group convened as part of the time-honoured hip-hop tradition of collective breakdancing and graffiti activities. In 1990 they decided to launch a rap group, taking the name Transcription Carriers after one member's former occupation. Their first recording was issued in 1992, a 12-inch white label released via the auspices of the T-Cut Bristol sound system and BRC (the Bristol Rhyme Coalition). It was not until 1994, however, that they began to earn significant coverage for their *The Haemorrhoid Fry-Up* EP.

TRANSEAU

b. Brian Transeau, Washington, DC, USA. Brian 'BT' Transeau made an immediate impact on the UK experimental house music scene in 1995 with the release of *Ima* for Perfecto Records. A largely instrumental collection, it won admirers from within the dance music community as well as the alternative music press. As the artist told *Billboard* magazine in 1997, 'I think people are starting to gravitate toward music like this because so-called alternative bands have become this generation's equivalent to 80s hair bands. There's nothing atypical or alternative about them.' He then began work on remixing the Tori Amos tracks 'Talula' and 'Putting The Damage On'. Amos was so impressed with the results that she agreed to collaborate on a duet with Transeau, 'Blue Skies', based on 'Divinity', an instrumental track from the album. This was added to the delayed US release of Transeau's debut (on Kinetic/Reprise Records) and quickly became a huge alternative dancefloor hit when released as a single.
● ALBUMS: *Ima* (Perfecto 1995)★★★.

TRANSGLOBAL UNDERGROUND

Formed in west London, England in 1991 as a loose collective of DJs and musicians around the nucleus of Alex Kasiel (b, Tim Whelen, 15 September 1958, London, England; keyboards, programming), and Hamid Mantu (b. Hamilton Lee, 7 May 1958, London, England; drums, programming), Transglobal Underground released 'Templehead', their debut single, in June of that year. Its mix of pounding house rhythms with sampled Tibetan chants introduced a dance/world fusion explored in greater depth two years later on their debut album, *Dream Of 100 Nations*, which added the extraordinary silk and spice vocals of Natasha Atlas (b. 20 March 1964, Brussels, Belgium), various rappers and a diverse assortment of sampled Eastern, African and Caribbean voices and instruments to the cross-culture stew. Now regulars on the festival circuit and godparents to a growing global dance music subculture of bands, DJs and record labels, the group released *International Times* in October 1994. Whilst offering no radical departures from the 'ethno techno' sound of its predecessor, the album featured fewer samples, relying more on live musicians including Egyptian violinist Essam Rachad, tabla player Satin Singh and free jazz guitarist Billy Jenkins. Following an album of remixes and *Diaspora*, a justifiably well received solo album from Natasha Atlas, the band's third album proper, *Psychic Karaoke*, featured a string section, slower tempos and an atmosphere of experimentation. A genuinely mature piece of work, it used regular band collaborators such as bassist Count Dubulah and clarinettist and keyboard player Larry Whelen to remodel the basic sound of previous albums into something darker and more hypnotic. There were echoes of dub reggae, film scores and even European art rockers such as Can in places. In the summer of 1996 advertising companies suddenly seemed to recognise the potential for the band's music as a soundtrack. 'Templehead' was used in a worldwide Coca Cola campaign, whilst the title track of *International Times* featured in a North American campaign for Levi jeans. Atlas's second solo album released on the Mantra label in 1997, *Halim*, featured more acoustic, traditional-sounding elements alongside the modern dance material. In 1998 *Rejoice Rejoice* featured Transglobal Underground's broadest musical mix yet, with Hungarian gypsy bands and an Indian drum troupe guesting on different tracks.

● ALBUMS: *Dream Of 100 Nations* (Nation 1993)★★★★, *International Times* (Nation 1994)★★★, *Interplanetary Meltdown* (Nation 1995)★★★, *Psychic Karaoke* (Nation 1996)★★★, *Rejoice Rejoice* (Nation 1998)★★★.

TRANSIENT RECORDS

This trance label was set up in 1994 by Russel Coultart, Lawrence Cooke and Simon Moxon. In February the following year, Disco Volante's 'El Metro' became Transient's first release and was followed by the compilation *Transient: Nu Energy And Trance*. Since then they have released singles by Astral Projection (notably 1996's 'Mahadevah'), Cosmosis, Elements Of Nature, Laughing Buddha, Lords Of Choas, Psychaos, Slide and Syb Unity Network, among others, as well as albums from Astral Projection (*Astral Files* and *Dancing Galaxy*) and Cosmosis (*Cosmology* and *Synergy*). Their compilations, which include the *Transient* series, Otherworld's *Dance Trance And Magic Plants* and the more chilled-out *Transient Dawn*, have featured tracks by these groups and others including Doof, Earth Nation, Electric Universe, Koxbox, MFG and X-Dream. In 1998 they released the charity album *Earthdance*, which followed on from the party of the same name the previous year. Transient have two subsidiary labels, Automatic and West Ten Records.

TRANSMAT RECORDS

US dance label run by Derrick May, releasing most of that artist's best work as Rhythim Is Rhythim in the late 80s, i.e. 'The Dance', 'Strings Of Life' and 'It Is What It Is'. Other artists included X-Ray ('Let's Go'), Psyche ('Elements'), K. Alexi Shelby ('All For Lee Sah') and Suburban Knight ('The Art Of Stalking'). It is impossible to overestimate the importance these records had on the evolution of techno. The label was reactivated in 1992 with Dark Comedy's *War Of The Worlds* EP.

TRAX RECORDS

Legendary Chicago record label, the home to much of the early Chicago house sound, headed by Larry Sherman. Among the hugely influential artist roster were Mr Fingers' seminal 3-track single, 'Beyond The Clouds' (which housed 'Washing Machine') and Mr Lee, with 'Pump Up Chicago'. Less celebrated but just as successful artists included Grant & Dezz's 'You're Too Good' and Virgo Four's 'Do You Know Who You Are?' from 1989.

TREACHEROUS 3

One of the forerunning creative forces within rap music, comprising original members Kool Moe Dee, L.A. Sunshine, Special K and DJ Easylee. The group was formed in 1978, releasing their debut single a year later, 'New Rap Language', on Enjoy Records. From its title to its dialogue, it predicted the new age of black rap music. It was followed by hip-hop standards 'Body Rock' and

'Feel The Heartbeat', before the group moved to Sugarhill for 'At The Party', 'Action' and 'Yes We Can Can'. In 1986 Kool Moe Dee left to record his debut solo set, *Go See The Doctor*. The other members also pursued their own projects in the interim. However, in March 1994 the original line-up reunited to perform on *Old School Flava*. Recorded in Atlanta and New York, the album featured a roll call of old and new school rap heroes in its credits: Grandmaster Flash, Doug E Fresh, Big Daddy Kane, Chuck D (Public Enemy), KRS-1, Melle Mel, Rakim (Eric B And Rakim), Heavy D, Raheem (Furious Five) and Tito (Furious Four). As Easylee commented at the project's announcement: 'The new school of rap seems to be looking for identity and roots. This is the right time for us to reunite, because the new rap family is opening their arms to the old school, paying respect to those who got the ball rolling'.

● ALBUMS: *Old School Flava* (WRAP 1994)★★★.

TRICKY

b. *c*.1964, Knowle West, Bristol, England. A laid-back hip-hopper, formerly of Bristol group Massive Attack, Tricky rapped on 'Daydreaming' and 'Five Man Army' from the latter's *Blue Lines* debut, and also wrote and produced one track, 'Karma Coma', for the follow-up. In late 1993 he released his first solo single, the trippy 'Aftermath', which came after informal sessions with Mark Stewart (ex-Pop Group; Mark Stewart And The Mafia; On-U-Sound System, etc.) on a four-track mobile. He employed the services of 18-year-old local girl Martina (though the song was recorded when she was only 15) on vocals, releasing it on his own Naive label. Despite its strong critical reception, Tricky was, in the best traditions of Massive Attack, reticent about his abilities: 'I don't really consider myself to be a rapper. I'm more of a lyricist really'. *Maxinquaye* was one of the critical successes of 1995, an atmospheric and unsettling record exploring the darker recesses of its creator's mind, particularly on 'Hell Is Around The Corner' and 'Feed Me'. Stylistically, the album ranged from the dramatic hard rock cover version of Public Enemy's 'Black Steel In The Hour Of Chaos' to the mock soul of 'Abbaon Fat Tracks', alongside the expected trip-hop rhythms. The *Nearly God* release was a compelling side-project that saw Tricky collaborating with guest vocalists including Bjork, Neneh Cherry and Terry Hall. *Pre-Millennium Tension* made for even more uneasy listening, with tracks

such as 'Tricky Kid' and 'Fury' being both threatening and paranoid in turn. By 1998's *Angels With Dirty Faces*, however, Tricky had begun to sound like a pastiche of himself as song after song stooped further into dark isolation against a relentlessly droning musical backdrop.

● ALBUMS: *Maxinquaye* (4th & Broadway 1995)★★★★, as Nearly God *Nearly God* (Durban Poison 1996)★★★, *Pre-Millennium Tension* (Island 1996)★★★, *Angels With Dirty Faces* (Island 1998)★★.

TRISTAN

Another of the Leamington Spa-based trance artists that emerged in the 90s, Tristan was a drummer, influenced by jazz, psychedelic rock and dub, before he caught the dance bug and began DJing in 1988. He started to record in 1993 while DJing in the UK and around Europe at well-known trance parties organized by TIP, Return To The Source and Escape From Samsara, as well as smaller underground events. Since then he has released a number of records as a solo artist and also in collaboration with others. One of his first releases, the *Desert Music* EP (Matsuri Productions 1995), was recorded with 100th Monkey (Andy Guthrie). He has also worked with Manmademan on 'William' (21-3 Productions 1996), Process on 'KV23'/'Random Factor' (Flying Rhino 1997) and Orange Peel on 'Sensory Deception'/'Citrus' (21-3 1997). Other labels for whom he has recorded include Aquatec, Phantasm and TIP.

TROUBLE FUNK

At the forefront of Washington's early 80s go-go music scene, Trouble Funk's call and response vocals, and Mack Carey's mighty percussion, predicted the emergence of rap, notably on the single 'Drop The Bomb'. Trouble Funk's first album of similar title was released on the Sugarhill imprint, hip-hop's first home. In truth they were more accurately a development of the physical funk tradition (Parliament etc.). Go-go was developed by Chuck Brown from drum breakdowns he would use in clubs to link Top 40 covers. Trouble Funk are still active, and ever popular in their native home of Washington.

● ALBUMS: *Drop The Bomb* (Sugarhill 1982)★★★, *In Times Of Trouble* (DETT 1983)★★★, *Saturday Night Live From Washington, D.C.* (Island 1985)★★, *Trouble Over Here/Trouble Over There* (Island 1987)★★★.

TRUE LIFE MATHEMATICS

True Life Mathematics was a one-off collaboration between Public Enemy producer Hank Shocklee, Carl Ryder and K. Houston, featuring the vocals of Eric Sadler. However, a veil of secrecy overshadowed the roles of the participants, whose identities were never formally confirmed. Their single album contained several party-related quips and typically buoyant beats but it remains something of an 80s rap obscurity.

● ALBUMS: *Greatest Hits* (Select 1988)★★★.

TTF

Also known as The Time Frequency, this trio was formed in Glasgow in early 1991, led by principal songwriter and artistic director Jon Campbell. Their debut EP, *Futurama*, was released as a white label in October 1990 and sold 4,000 copies in Scotland. Mary Kiani featured as a guest vocalist on the group's second EP, *Real Love*, and subsequently became a permanent member. They were eventually signed to Jive Records as their popularity grew throughout Scotland, and consequently enjoyed three number 1 singles there. However, they were denounced by some as 'downmarket' and 'accessible' and criticized for their 'hands in the air' approach. Significantly, they were one of the few dance groups of the time to perform live and one of a similarly limited number who refused to mime. Subsequent hits included 'The Ultimate High', 'New Emotion' and 'Real Love', the latter ensuring an appearance on the UK television chart show *Top Of The Pops*. After the group's debut album, which included a cover version of Cerrone's disco classic 'Supernature', Kiani left the band to pursue a solo career.

● ALBUMS: *Dominator* (Jive 1994)★★.

TUCKER, BARBARA

Tucker's induction into the world of music came in the early 90s at the hands of Tommy Musto and Victor Simonelli, who used her vocals on a range of their products. Her delivery and visual presence soon established her as an icon of New York's gay/Hi-NRG scene. In the UK it was the soul/house cut, 'Beautiful People', which utilised the 'Deep Deep Inside' hook from Hardrive's track of the same name, remixed by C.J. Mackintosh, which gave her an audience. The song was produced by Lil' Louie Vega, with whom Tucker runs the Underground Network Club in New York. The cast of backing singers reflected the esteem she is held in within that community, numbering Michael Watford, India and Ten City's Byron Stingily within their ranks.

21-3 PRODUCTIONS

Jaki Kenley and Si Wild set up 21-3 in October 1996 in Leamington Spa when they felt the 'Goa' trance sound was becoming stagnant. At the time, many labels were cashing in on what the media termed the 'new acid house' by releasing compilations of mediocre tunes; although their roots were in the trance scene (Kenley put together the charity compilation *Earthtrance* for Positiva Records in 1996), 21-3 wanted to move away from the formulaic four-on-the-floor, Indian scale sound and encouraged acts who used more breakbeats, making 'funkier and sexier' music with a psychedelic flavour. Their first release, Manmademan's 'William/Delerium' (1996), proved a success and was followed up by a series of singles by artists including Funkopath, Tristan and DJ Orange Peel, Pan and Digitalis. The excellent compilation *All Boundaries Are Illusion* (1997) included a number of those artists as well as Eat Static, Deviant Electronics and Medicine Drum. *Elastic*, released the following year to an enthusiastic response, featured further investigations of the psychedelic sound, notably the big beat-style breaks of the Germinating Seeds Of Doda's 'Upside Down', the drum 'n' bass feel of Digitalis's 'Not Human', and the crazy noises in Manmademan's 'Know Tomorrow' and the Funkopath remix of Bentley Rhythm Ace's 'Space Hopper'.

TWIN HYPE

This gimmicky duo of real life 'hip-hop twins' Glennis 'Sly' and Lennis 'Slick' Brown began to rap in New York City, New York, USA, in the late 80s. Signed to Profile Records, their debut self-titled album, released in 1989, graced the *Billboard* Top 200, ostensibly owing to the novelty value of the project. Its success was not repeated and the twins subsequently disappeared from view - though another pair of twins - named simply Twinz - repeated the formula to greater commercial effect in the 90s.

● ALBUMS: *Twin Hype* (Profile 1989)★★.

2 LIVE CREW

US rap headline-makers from Miami, Florida (via California), formed in 1985 around central figure Luther Campbell. 2 Live Crew became unlikely figures in a media censorship debate when, in June 1990, *As Nasty As They Wanna Be* was passed sentence on by a judge in Broward County, Florida. In the process it became the first record in America to be deemed legally obscene (a federal appeal court overturned the decision in 1993). Their right to free speech saw them defended by sources as diverse as Sinead O'Connor, Bruce Springsteen and Mötley Crüe, but the overbearing impression remained that 2 Live Crew were a third-rate rap outfit earning first division kudos by little more than circumstance. Their debut set, recorded before Campbell became an actual member, marked out the band's territory. To this end, 2 Live Crew have several times expressed themselves to be an adult comedy troupe, 'The Eddie Murphys of Rap', in the best traditions of crude party records by Blowfly and others. Hence, 'We Want Some Pussy' and other, inconsequential, mildly offensive tracks. Campbell was the founder of the band's record label, Luke Skyywalker Records (shortened to Luke Records when film-maker George Lucas, who created the Luke Skywalker character in the film *Star Wars*, filed suit), while Campbell's compatriots in 2 Live Crew numbered Trinidad-born Chris Wong Won, New Yorker Mark Ross and California DJ David Hobbs (under the psuedonyms Brother Marquis and Fresh Kid Ice on the 'clean' version of *Move Somethin'*). Their music was underpinned by the familiar 'Miami Bass' sound of synthesized, deep backbeats. *As Nasty As We Wanna Be*, replete with 87 references to oral sex alone, included the notorious 'Me So Horny', built around a sample from *Full Metal Jacket*. It is an unquestionably offensive lyric, but no more so than those by the Geto Boys or others. There are probably worse examples within the 2 Live Crew's own songbook - 'The Fuck Shop', which samples Guns N'Roses guitar lines, or 'Head Booty And Cock' which became almost a battle-cry, notably when repeated by chanting fans on the Phoenix, Arizona-recorded live album. Advocates of record stickering such as the Parents Music Resource Center (PMRC) and Florida attorney/evangelist Jack Thompson, argued strongly that the group's records should not be available for sale to minors. A retail record store owner arrested for selling a copy of their *Move Somethin'* - albeit to an adult - was later acquitted. The group itself was then arrested for performing music from the *Nasty* album in an adults-only club, sparking charges by anti-censorship groups that the law enforcement officials were becoming over-zealous. There is not much doubt that this was true - Miami has one of the biggest pornography industries in the country, and it was obvious the moguls behind it were not being pursued with equal vigour, if they were being pursued at all - not that the band were going out of their way to help improve their public image (while doubtless realizing the commercial advantages of such notoriety). Luther Campbell claimed on CBS network TV show *A Current Affair* during 1992 that he had had oral sex on stage with female fans in Japan. Campbell had been acquitted a year previously for giving an obscene performance in his home state of Florida. In 1993 they became legal ground-breakers again, this time over their 1989 parody of Roy Orbison's 'Pretty Woman'. For the first time, Acuff Rose Music Inc were suing an artist on the grounds that their version tarnished the image of the original. On top of all the heat Campbell released a solo album, *Banned In The USA*. The scandal abated somewhat, and as 2 Live Crew's otherwise unremarkable career progressed, there was even an AIDS awareness ditty on *Nasty Weekend* - 'Who's Fuckin' Who'. They also promoted safe sex with their own brand of Homeboy Condoms, one of their more acceptable acts of misogynist titillation.

● ALBUMS: *The 2 Live Crew Is What We Are* (Luke Skyywalker 1986)★★★, *Move Somethin'* (Luke Skyywalker 1988)★★, *As Nasty As They Wanna Be* (Luke Skyywalker 1989)★★, *As Clean As They Wanna Be* (Luke Skyywalker 1989)★, *Live In Concert* (Effect 1990)★★, *Sports Weekend (As Nasty As They Wanna Be Part II)* (Luke 1991)★★★, *Sports Weekend (As Clean As They Wanna Be Part II)* (Luke 1991)★★, *Shake A Lil' Somethin'* (Lil' Joe 1996)★★, *The Real One* (Lil' Joe 1998)★★.

● COMPILATIONS: *Best Of* (Luke 1992)★★★, as The New 2 Live Crew *Back At Your Ass For The Nine-4* (Luke 1994)★★.

● VIDEOS: *Banned In The USA* (1990).

2 LIVE JEWS

A crude spin-off from the ranks of 2 Live Crew, this was Miami-based MCs 'Moisha' Lambert and Joe 'Easy Irving' Stone's idea of a good joke. The song titles gave the game away very quickly: 'Oui! It's So Humid', 'Accountant Suckers' and 'Beggin' For A Bargain'.

● ALBUMS: *As Kosher As They Wanna Be* (Kosher 1990)★★.

2PAC

(see Shakur, Tupac)

2 TOO MANY

West Philadelphia act sponsored by local boys made good DJ Jazzy Jeff And The Fresh Prince. 2 Too Many's debut single, 'Where's The Party', was hugely reminiscent of their better-known colleagues' style, with a penchant for fun over gangsta or socio-political concerns. The duo comprise Jazz (b. Armique Shartez Wyche, *c*.1972), L'il Troy (b. Troy Carter, *c*.1973) and Ant Live (b. Anthony Fontenot, *c*.1974). They had been rapping together since the late 80s, before Jazz and Troy linked up in the 9th Grade, bringing aboard cousin Ant to finalize the band's line-up. They took their name from their high-school poverty; whenever they would attempt to embark on an evening's entertainment or activity, they always found enough to pay for one, and thus became: 2 Too Many. However, fortunes changed when they met Will Smith (aka the Fresh Prince) when he was recording next door to their rehearsal room. They introduced themselves and invited him to see them play. The result was a contract with his own Willjam Productions through Jive Records. He teamed them up with Hula and Fingers, the production duo behind his huge 1991 success, 'Summertime'. They envisaged long careers on the strength of this, spending many hours researching the music business in libraries to make sure they would not fall prey to unscrupulous business dealings, and acquainting themselves with management and production disciplines.

● ALBUMS: *Chillin' Like A Smut Villain* (Jive 1992)★★★.

2 UNLIMITED

Cod-house act from Holland who enjoyed two weeks at the top of the UK charts with 'No Limits', featuring Anita Dels' diva vocals and Ray Slijngaard's hilarity-inducing chorus of 'Techno! Techno! Techno! Techno!'. It was magnificently parodied in an episode of television series *Spitting Image*, where the puppet Anita recited 'No lyrics, no no no no, no no there's no lyrics'. An album of the same name contained further variations on the formula, though arguably of an even lower quality threshold. Slijngaard rejoices in the distinction of having previously been a chef at Amsterdam airport - affording snide journalists the opportunity of comparing 2 Unlimited's brand of Euro-pop with greasy fast-food. Dels previously worked as a secretary, singing part-time with the Trouble Girls. The men behind the group are Jean-Paul De Coster and Phil Wilde, of Byte Records (who previously tasted success with Bizz Nizz's 'Don't Miss The Party Line'). Their philosophy is redolent of the Euro-techno axis, but anathema to traditional British views of artistic imput: '2 Unlimited is trendy music that appeals to the youths, it's not aggressive so the kids kids can enjoy it. There's also a strong melody that stays in the head, and the visuals are good too'. They readily admit to creating music to satiate a market rather than attempting to build a fan base around any creative vision. The statistics, whilst not exonerating them, did prove them to be entirely correct in their suppostion - in 1993 2 Unlimited sold over a million singles in Britain alone. 'No Limits' was also the biggest-selling European record of the year, while their second album sold nearly three million copies. Earlier success had included the arguably more interesting 'Workaholic'.

● ALBUMS: *Get Ready* (PWL 1992)★★★, *No Limits* (PWL 1992)★★★, *Real Things* (PWL 1994)★★.

● VIDEOS: *No Limits* (1993).

TYREE

b. Tyree Cooper. Cooper first got involved with music at the age of 15, gatecrashing parties led by Farley Jackmaster Funk and Jesse Saunders. Together with friend Mike Dunn he hung out with the likes of Saunders and eventually met Marshall Jefferson, borrowing his 808 to record his first demos. His first release was 'I Fear The Night', sung by his sister 'Chic', then 'Acid Video Crash', 'Acid Over' and 'Turn Up The Bass' (with Kool Rock Steady). His debut album, meanwhile, included the anti-Todd Terry message, 'T's Revenge'. Tyree also worked with Martin 'Boogieman' Luna as Cool House ('Rock This Party Right') and other members of the DJ International inner sanctum.

● ALBUMS: *Tyree's Got A Brand New House* (DJ International 1989)★★★.

TYRREL CORPORATION

Named after the economic monolith depicted in cult sci-fi film *Blade Runner*, this Redcar, England-based pop house duo's *North East Of Eden* set was one of the genre's most striking pieces in 1992. Joe Watson's smooth tones helped create a unique hybrid of house and Philly soul, with accessible lyrics tackling the personal and the political (as in 'Ballad Of British Justice'). The other pricipal of the band is lyricist and synthesizer player Tony Barry (though Watson also provides keyboard expertise). He had left Redcar for London in 1984, ending up as a pub manager. Watson, after working as a bingo caller, followed him down from the North East six years later, and stayed on his couch. They embarked on their musical adventures, with various day jobs enlisted to fund night recordings. Tyrrel Corporation made their debut in 1990 with the release of '6 O'Clock' on tiny independent About Time Two Records. Straightaway it showcased their strengths. While the song was undoubtedly in tune with the modern house sound, they imposed their song-writing skills rather than simply working a groove. 'A lot of the stuff around at the moment, you could never sit down and play it in a bar, but everything we do is a song and can be played that way' attested Watson. Signing to Cooltempo (originally through Charlie Chester's Volante subsidiary) follow-up singles 'The Bottle' and 'Going Home' were equally effective, with critics drooling at what one described as the lyricism of the Smiths combined with the funk of Mr Fingers. While '6 O'Clock' took British licensing laws to task, the time in question being the legal opening hour, 'The Bottle' continued their drink associations with the mighty hookline 'the bottle is mightier than the pen'. The subject matter of 'Going Home' was much more downbeat, reflecting the sharp decline of the industrial North East and the death of its culture. This was a theme more fully explored in their debut album.
- ALBUMS: *North East Of Eden* (Cooltempo 1992)★★★★, *Play For Today* (Cooltempo 1995)★★★.

U-KREW

First formed, as the Untouchable Krew, as far back as October 1984, the U-Krew are a rap five-piece from Portland, Oregon, USA, led by drum programmer Larry Bell and lead rapper Kevin Morse. They scored quick hits with 'If U Were Mine' (US number 24) and 'Let Me Be Your Lover' (number 68), but faded afterwards.
- ALBUMS: *The U-Krew* (Enigma 1990)★★★.

U.T.F.O.

Their initials standing for UnTouchable Force Organization, East Wimbush, Brooklyn-based U.T.F.O. comprised the talents of Doctor Ice, Kangol Kid (both concurrently breakdancers for Whodini) and The Educated Rapper, later joined by Mix-Master Ice. Their second single, 'Roxanne, Roxanne', set the New York City rap kids alight as they complained of an unobliging female, over a rhythm track built from Billy Squier's 'The Big Beat', and produced by Full Force. It would see an answer record from Roxanne Shanté that outsold their own version, and a whole industry that grew up around the phenomenon (the Real Roxanne, the Original Roxanne, and Sparky D). The trio turned to rock/rap crossover for *Lethal*, before reggae and swingbeat took over on their most recent work. Nothing, however, has managed to replicate the success of their landmark single. *Bag It And Bone It* looked to crude sexual rhymes for sales but even that missed that boat.
- ALBUMS: *U.T.F.O.* (Select 1985)★★, *Skeezer Pleezer* (Select 1986)★★★, *Lethal* (Select 1987)★★★, *Doin' It* (Select 1989)★★, *Bag It And Bone It* (Jive 1990)★★.

U96

aka Hamburg, Germany DJ Alex Christensen (b. c.1967, Hamburg, Germany), whose single, 'Das Boot', reached the Top 20 in 1992. A revision of a 10-year-old Klaus Doldinger film/televison theme, this might have been unexpected had it not been for the fact that it had spent nearly three months on top of the German charts. In the UK it was originally released on Dave Dorrell's Love label in January, before being remixed by Mickey Finn and licensed to the M&G label in August. The album that followed was full of techno stompers and commercial electronica.

● ALBUMS: *Das Boot* (M&G 1992)★★★.

UBIK

North London-based duo of Dave Campbell and Viv Beeton who formed to release their own material after offering remix and production work for Michael Rose and Kym Mazelle. They debuted with 'Techno Prisoners', a Detroit-derived mantra that featured the hook from Rochelle Fleming's 'Love Itch'. It cost just £70 to record (the hire of the DAT machine), but introduced them and their local Zoom label to many new admirers.

● ALBUMS: *Just Add People* (Zoom 1992)★★★★.

ULTRA NATÉ

b. 1968, Baltimore, Maryland, USA. Soul/disco/garage diva, who first rose to fame via the club hit, 'It's Over Now'. Ultra Naté (which is her real name) is a former trainee psychotherapist. She was originally spotted by the Basement Boys in 1989, going on to sing backing vocals on Monie Love's debut album. The Basement Boys then persuaded her to step into the spotlight: 'Every now and then I'd go in the studio and do some stuff. We just wrote 'It's Over Now' one night, by chance. They started circulating the demo and it created a really big buzz and they gave it to Cynthia Cherry who'd worked for WEA years ago. She originally started at Jump Street Records and signed the Basement Boys as artists. She brought my tape to Peter Edge at WEA, they signed me and the rest is history'. Reminiscent of a souped up Philly soul singer, or Donna Summer, Ultra Naté has all the correct stylings down to a tee, measuring jazz, funk and gospel within her compass. All are made distinctive by her slightly unconventional, and highly arresting, vocal phrasing. And for once, a garage vocalist with lyrics which, taken in isolation, aren't an embarassment. Her second, wildly diffuse, album for WEA, *One Woman's Insanity*, broke her internationally, and included duets with Boy George (who wrote the song, 'I Specialize In Loneliness' for her), as well as D-Influence, Nellee Hooper, Ten City and Basement Boys. She enjoyed a massive international hit with club hit 'Free'.

● ALBUMS: *Blue Notes In The Basement* (WEA 1991)★★★, *One Woman's Insanity* (WEA 1993)★★★★, *Situation Critical* (AM:PM 1998)★★★.

ULTRAMAGNETIC MC'S

This Bronx, New York-based four-piece rap troupe incorporated the best traditions of jazz and funk in their polished, rhythmic style. Having worked with Boogie Down Productions' KRS-1 among many others, the Ultramagnetic MC's earned their reputation at the forefront of rap, pioneering the use of the sampler in hip-hop. The band comprised: Maurice Smith (aka PJ Mo Love; DJ), Keith Thornton (aka Kool Keith; lead MC), Trevor Randolph (aka TR Love; rapper and co-producer) and Cedric Miller (aka Ced Gee; MC and co-producer). The group emerged from posses such as The People's Choice Crew and New York City Breakers just as Kool Herc and Afrika Bambaataa's work saw hip-hop break cover. Their own backgrounds could be traced to underground basement clubs like the Audobon Ballroom, Sparkle and the Back Door. Their first album served as a direct influence on the 'Daisy Age' rap of subsequent acts such as De La Soul and PM Dawn, although those bands subsequently left Ultramagnetic MCs trailing in their commercial wake. Singles such as 'Give The Drummer Some' (from which, nine years later, English techno pioneers Prodigy would sample their controversial 'smack my bitch up' lyric) showed them in their best light: call-and-response raps demonstrating individual members' self-espoused talent in the best traditions of the old school. They were not always so dextrous, however. While *Funk Your Head Up* included, 'Poppa Large', it also housed the appalling 'Porno Star'. On *The Four Horsemen*, and its attendant singles, 'Two Brothers With Checks' and 'Raise It Up', the group unveiled an 'intergalactic hip-hop' concept, and a new methodology (notably Kool Keith rhyming in double-speak on 'One Two, One Two'. More down to earth was 'Saga Of Dandy, The Devil & Day', an account of the negro baseball league co-written with historian James Reilly. Following the group's split Ced Gee and TR Love offered their production skills to several artists including Boogie Down Productions' landmark *Criminal Minded* set, as well as Tim Dog's infamous 'Fuck Compton'. Keith collaborated with the Prodigy and set up his own Funky Ass label. In 1998 the original members re-formed to record an album.

● ALBUMS: *Critical Beatdown* (Next Plateau

1988)★★★★, *Funk Your Head Up* (Mercury 1992)★★★, *The Four Horsemen* (Wild Pitch 1993)★★★.
● COMPILATIONS: *The Basement Tapes 1984-1990* (Tuff City 1994)★★.

ULTRAMARINE

Ultramarine are a London, England-based progressive dance duo comprising Paul John Hammond (b. 12 December 1965, Chelmsford, Essex, England; bass, keyboards) and Ian Harvey Cooper (b. 15 August 1966, Derby, England; programming, guitars). They took their name from an album by A Primary Industry, who in turn had first seen it used for a Mexican brand of Mescal. Both members of Ultramarine were veterans of the latter band, Hammond having also played with God And The Rest. Previously, both had worked in a variety of professions, Paul as an orchard worker and in publishing, Ian as a furniture salesman and insurance clerk. Influenced by the Canterbury Scene (Kevin Ayers, Robert Wyatt, etc.) and modern dance music (Massive Attack, Orbital, Spooky, Digable Planets), Ultramarine made their recording debut in 1989 with 'Wyndham Lewis', on Belgian label Les Disques Du Crepescule. After a further single, 'Folk', in 1990, Ultramarine moved on to Brainiak, then Rough Trade Records, before their current home, Blanco Y Negro. Their debut album, *Every Man And Woman Is A Star*, was based on an imaginary canoe journey across America. Song structures were embossed by a dub-heavy backbeat and strong, resonant melodies. By the time of its follow-up, *United Kingdoms*, their Canterbury influences were beginning to show, and Robert Wyatt was invited to join them in a rendition of a 100-year-old weaver's folk song, 'Kingdom', and 'Happy Land'. Wyatt's old sparring partner Ayers also wrote Ultramarine's double EP, *Hymn*. Bel Air took as its theme paranoias and anxieties about the approaching millennium, though this time the musical terrain encompassed Latin jazz and ethnic pop without ever being grand or pompous. Song titles such as 'Schmaltz' revealed that the band had not lost their self-deprecating sense of humour.
● ALBUMS: *Every Man And Woman Is A Star* (Rough Trade 1992)★★★, *Every Man And Woman Is A Star - Expanded* (Rough Trade 1992)★★★★, *United Kingdoms* (Blanco Y Negro 1993)★★★, *Bel Air* (Blanco Y Negro 1995)★★★, *A User's Guide* (New Electronica 1997)★★★.

UMC's

A popular underground hip-hop concern from Staten Island who broke big when 'Blue Cheese' dropped. Hass G and Kool Kim (both b.c.1971) were initially noted for the wild, funk-fuelled rhythm motifs, and freestyle rhymes that dominate their recordings. The group, together with producer RNS, were originally titled the Universal MC's, but when they signed to Wild Pitch (via their friends Gang Starr), they decided it sounded too old school. They first met while catching the ferry home from the Statue Of Liberty, where they both had summer jobs. They had actually made their debut in 1989 on the tiny New York independent Rough Justice, on a compilation album that included their 'Invaders Of My Fruit Basket' and 'Party Stylin''. 'Blue Cheese' and 'One To Grow', the latter featured on Island's *The Rebirh Of Cool* set, gave them immediate hits with Wild Pitch. However, by the advent of their second album they had 'toughened up': 'Our new direction comes from what we went through after having two number 1 singles'. After this, record company complications intervened. When they came back with a more hardcore attitude, as demonstrated by the second album's 'Time To Set It Straight' and 'Hit The Track', they still maintained the positivity evident on their earlier recordings. 'I remember a time when if a brother pulled out a gun on somebody he was a punk. Or if you jumped somebody you was a pussy'. Some critics lamented the loss of their more playful personas; nevertheless, they were undoubtedly masters of both approaches.
● ALBUMS: *Fruits Of Nature* (1992)★★★, *Unleashed* (Wild Pitch 1994)★★★.

UMMM

Italian record label distinguished by tracks such as Gayland's 'Get By', which like many of their releases was among the most authentic garage anthems outside of the American heartland. Ummm has become closely associated with a camp/gay stylistic bent, as evidenced by tunes such as Olga's 'I'm A Bitch', a banging Hi-NRG affair with a vocal sample repeating simply that line, DJ Ivan's 'All Night' and Alex Party's 'Read My Lips' (licensed to Cleveland City). 1993 saw the release of CYB's 'Snakebite', while the following year brought Long Leg's 'See On'.

UNANIMOUS DECISION

Formed in south London, England, in 1990, Unanimous Decision's debut recording was the *Rap Sings The Blues* EP, released on Kold Sweat Records in 1992. The EP included the throwaway 'Simply Wack' track, which sampled the *Benny Hill* and *Muppet Show* television themes in an effort to parody the 'only style of rap that gets played on the radio'. Ironically, 'Simply Wack' was picked out by radio programmers in exactly the manner that the lyrics decried, and their more earnest material was totally ignored. The group, producer Paul T, rappers Bravo, Eveready, Chich and DJ Rob G, were left even more cynical about the plight of British hip-hop. Eveready was formerly a member of the DJ team Vice Versa, and had also won a rap competition on Kiss FM disc jockey Dave Pearce's show, leading to an aborted contract with the now defunct Reachin' Records. A second Unanimous Decision EP, the six-track *It Ain't Clever*, followed in July 1993.

UNCANNY ALLIANCE

This dance duo comprised Yvette and Brinsley from Queens, New York, who enjoyed a club hit with their debut single 'I Got My Education' in 1992. Both were long-term friends, regularly attending the Paradise Garage club, where New York's garage style was first perfected. Together they formed Deep Inc. in 1990, transfiguring into Uncanny Alliance shortly afterwards. Despite the pervading liberal tolerance vibe of dance music, 'I Got My Education' was actually an attack on fake beggars - chastizing them for feigning injuries. Although it was extremely immediate and funny, the pair have failed to ignite commercially since then.

UNDERCOVER

One of Stock, Aitken And Waterman's less blessed creations, Undercover seemed to have been unveiled for the sole and ignominious purpose of releasing cover versions of golden oldies revamped for the 90s - their idea of revamping being to insert a sickly backbeat underneath. Most notable was the breezy chart smash 'Baker Street', which was symptomatic of their cod house efforts. It was pieced together in just half an hour so that the participants could catch the FA Cup Final kick-off that afternooon. 'I can't understand why some bands take so long to produce records', was a deeply incriminating statement in the circumstances. The guilty trio comprised John Matthews, John Jules and producer Steve 'Mac' McCutcheon (who had previously co-written and produced Nomad's 'Devotion', 1991's biggest-selling dance single, and also helmed Linda Layton's '(I'll Be A) Freak For You'). The two Johns had previously been club and pirate radio DJs together, working for a month as part of WLR Radio's failed franchise trial. Their 1992 album consisted entirely of cover versions written to the same irritating formula, albeit with the occasional sprinkling of Italian piano. Their nomination for a BRIT award was one of the most singularly revealing indictments of the state of the UK music industry.

● ALBUMS: *Check Out The Groove* (PWL 1992)★★.

UNDERDOG

aka Trevor Jackson. One of UK hip-hop's most prominent remixers and production experts, Jackson also oversees the succesful Bite It! label and design company. His love of rap was developed during a childhood spent listening to Grandmaster Flash and his old school companions on import, and he even tried to become a self-taught scratcher. Eventually he turned to sampling instead, inspired by the Art Of Noise's cut-up technique. Bite It! was originally formed for the design of record sleeves, notably Stereo MC's' *33, 45, 78*, but began releasing hip-hop product in the 90s. Among these artists were Scientists Of Sound and the Brotherhood, though his first remix commission was for the-then unheard ragga artist C.J. Lewis. However, Jackson's hip-hop remixing abilities were what brought him to the public's attention, notably House Of Pain's 'Top Of The Mornin' To Ya' - which made the UK Top 10. After a further House Of Pain production, 'Who's The Man', he also undertook remixing duties for the Pharcyde's 'Soul Flower', the Young Black Teenagers' 'Tap The Bottle' and New Kingdom's 'Good Times' - three deeply satisfying and impressively diverse hip-hop readings. There was also work for house divas Shara Nelson ('Down That Road', 'One Goodbye In Ten') and Carleen Anderson ('Nervous Breakdown') as well as U2 ('Stay'). More tongue-in-cheek was a remixed version of the Sabres Of Paradise staple, 'Theme', in which Jackson appeared to attack the cult of personality surrounding Andy Weatherall. He mixed the acclaimed 1996 debut album from UK rappers the Brotherhood and released an excellent remix of

Lisa Germano's 'Love Sick' on his Output label in 1997.

UNDERGROUND RESISTANCE

Perhaps one of the most influential and certainly the most secretive of Detroit's techno labels/acts, Underground Resistance (UR) was founded in November 1990, under the supervision of Mike Banks. Initially working alongside Juan Atkins, Jeff Mills and Rob Hood, Banks and UR promoted the techno sound through the release of innovative sounds. Early releases were either classic house tracks, such as the uplifting 'Living For The Night' featuring Yolanda, or hard-edged, insistent salvos, such as the *Sonic* EP and 'Waveform'. Blake Baxter, the 'Prince of Techno', was one of the few to be welcomed as an outside producer in the label's early stages, releasing the minimalist classic 'When A Thought Becomes U'. Via such releases UR and Mad Mike did much to revitalize a flagging techno scene, particularly in Europe, where clubbers appreciated the harder sounds largely ignored in UR's native territory. UR toured widely, playing live sets, which were captured on the album *Revolution For Change*, alongside stunning DJ sets from Mills. Throughout the 90s UR continued to release a combination hard-techno (with the Mills-influenced 'X-101' and 'X-102' releases standing out) and warm, electro-inspired jazz-funk (perhaps the label's finest moment coming with the release of the sublime *Galaxy To Galaxy* double pack). Following the departure of Mills, allegedly for political reasons, when Mills and Hood went on to establish Axis Records, Banks and Atkins continued to record as UR, using new DJs, Alan Oldham, and later, DJ Rolando and James Pennington - recording on UR as the Aztec Mystic and the Surburban Night, respectively. Recent releases, such as the impressive 'Electronic Warfare', demonstrate UR's continuing ability to stretch across sonic frontiers.

UNDERWORLD

This Romford, Essex-based group was formed in the early 90s by Karl Hyde and Rick Smith, who were joined by the DJ Darren Emerson. Hyde had previously worked with Deborah Harry and at Paisley Park Studios, and Smith had recorded with Bob Geldof; together they had a band called Freur in the late 80s. Their first release was 'Big Mouth' as Lemon Interupt for Junior Boy's Own Records, which was followed by 'Dirty' under the same name. They had their first success as Underworld in early 1993 with 'Mmm Skyscraper ... I Love You', and later that year with 'Rez', both of which became popular with the dance fraternity. While the latter was a straightforward dance track that arranged a few analogue riffs and regular four-on-the-floor drums, as well as busier tribal-sounding percussion, into various build-ups and breakdowns, 'Mmm Skyscraper ...' was a more varied and carefully structured track that introduced Hyde's vocals into a rich, psychedelic techno sound. During this time the band gained respect in wider circles by performing live at various events, including Megadog and the MIDI Circus and achieved further recognition and popularity in 1994 when they released the album *Dubnobasswithmyheadman*. Building on the same kind of diversity as 'Mmm Skyscraper ...' the album featured a broad-ranging techno style that was at times deep and psychedelic, and at other moments, melodic and almost pop-like, and was always characterized by Hyde's fragmented lyrics. Mixing elements of what were apparently unreconcilable styles, including ambient, house, techno and dub, with pop sensibilities, it appealed to a broad audience and was hailed by sections of the rock press as the most important dance album of the time, while purists had reservations about the group diluting their techno sound. Much of the sound from this innovative album continued to have resonances in music produced into the late 90s. In June 1995 they received an enthusiastic response when they played a number of dates in America with the Chemical Brothers, the Orb and Orbital. In the same year they released a single, 'Born Slippy', which gained mass exposure in the soundtrack to the film *Trainspotting*; it was subsequently reissued in 1996 and became a huge chart hit. The group's second album, *Second Toughest In The Infants* (1996), which introduced breakbeats and elements of drum 'n' bass into the sound, was even more successful than its predecessor, despite being a darker and, at times, more claustrophobic set. That year the group also headlined a number of dance and rock festivals, including Reading and Tribal Gathering's Big Love. Emerson has remixed a number of artists including Björk and Orbital, and continues to DJ around the UK. At the same time, Hyde and Smith have been involved with the art and design collective Tomato, which has experimented with various innovative multimedia projects, as well as various commercial projects including advertising and promo videos. In 1998 Underworld and Tomato

combined in a series of performances aimed at blurring the lines between bands and visual artists.
● ALBUMS: *Dubnobasswithmyheadman* (Junior Boy's Own 1994)★★★★, *Second Toughest In The Infants* (Junior Boy's Own 1996)★★★.

UNION CITY RECORDINGS

UCR was launched as a subsidiary of Virgin's Circa label by Rob Manley, Circa's A&R manager, and Simon Gavin in the early weeks of 1992, 'to take advantage of the one-off, 12-inch market that's so vibrant in Britain'. The label was operated as a 'part-time' concern, with both principal movers staying on Virgin's payroll. Union City Recordings licensed brightly during the 90s, picking up Mark Kinchen's 'Burnin'', and TC1992's Top 40 hit 'Funky Guitar'. More home-grown product included the gospel-tinged 4 Love song, 'Hold Your Head Up High'. 'We wanted to build a faster response little number that always covered its costs. The majors are guilty of saying that there are no faces in dance music, thus pres-surising people into giving them faces, so you get two keyboards and a couple of girl dancers miming to a DAT. Why try to maufacture an image that doesn't exist?' They were also represented by the ethnic dance of Mombassa and the techno of Metropolis and Earthbeat (two of Future Sound Of London's many guises). They signed M.A.N.I.C. (Lee Hudson and Keiron Jolliffe, who met on a YTS scheme) in 1992, after the success of their 'I'm Comin' Hardcore' white label, which they re-released. A second Mark Kinchen tune, 'Always', followed, as did Sasha's first solo record (as BM:Ex). By 1994 UCR was Virgin's last dance/club offshoot, having jettisoned both More Protein and Ronin.
● ALBUMS: Various: *Colours: A Compilation* (UCR 1993)★★★.

UNIQUE 3

Dance and rap chart crossover act, of not-incon-siderable ability, and a wide range of talents. Their debut album kicked off with 'Music Melody', which dented the UK charts, a sharp, witty rap, before continuing with the techno-flavoured 'Gicicality', the Detroit house of 'Theme III' and the ragga tinges of 'Reality'. Sadly, their acquaintance with the charts seems to have been a passing one.
● ALBUMS: *Jus' Unique* (Ten 1990)★★.

UNITED FUTURE ORGANIZATION

A trio of former DJs, numbering French-born Raphael Sebbag and Japanese personnel Tadashi Yabe and Toshio Matsuura, based in Japan, whose mix of dance-jazz, Latin and club sounds has endeared them to a British audience. Talkin' Loud boss Gilles Peterson heard their singles 'I Love My Baby' and 'Loud Minority' and chose the band (aka UFO) to launch a new label, Brownswood. The idea was to contrast natural elements in urban settings, though the label was actually named after his 'local'. There is a warm, breezy feel to their material, and a genuine conflagration of styles. Their debut album featured contribu-tions from Galliano and MC Solaar, plus jazz lumi-naries Jon Hendricks and Japanese talent like singer Monday Michiru. As part of their Brownswood/Phonogram contract, they were invited to supervise a Japanese jazz compilation.
● ALBUMS: *United Future Organization* (Brownswood 1993)★★★, *3rd Perspective* (Talkin' Loud 1997)★★★.

UNITED STATES OF SOUND

Comprising Ken Sharman and Lars, the Glaswegian-based U.S.S. first came to prominence in 1993 with the hugely popular progressive cut, 'Oscillator'. The track stood out readily from the mass of 12-inches, a fact the band attributed to the care they exercise in the studio, even down to pro-gramming their own software for editing sounds. To this end they have their own high-tech estab-lishment within earshot of the Parkhead football ground, where record company executives flocked flashing chequebooks following the record's impact. Resolutely, the duo decided to link with local independent Bomba instead, ensuring they retained full artistic control. Lars was initially influenced by the work of Derrick May, going on to work as a DJ himself, and believes his perspective as a regular on the turnta-bles is valuable in assessing what it is that audi-ences want.

UPTOWN RECORDS

Uptown was launched in Manhattan, New York, in 1986, as a specialist black label, concentrating primarily on R&B-styled rap. The label was set up by Andre Harrell (b. *c*.1959), formerly part of Dr. Jeckyll And Mr Hyde, who scored a major hit in 1981 with 'Genius Rap'. After leaving the duo he went to college to study communication and business, before joining Russell Simmons at Rush Management. It has been said that Harrell left Def Jam when he failed to persuade Simmons that they could market Heavy D as 'sexy'. Nevertheless, it was via that act that the label was established, and the 'big guy' also introduced Harrell to one of his most significant early signings, the proto-New Jill Swing act Gyrlz (Uptown having already provided the platform for Guy). Other acts on the label would include Jodeci and Mary J. Blige, becoming one of the pre-eminent dance/hip-hop labels of its age. Harrell, who also produced the movie *Strictly Business*, described his tastes as those of 'a lifestyle entertainment entrepreneur'.

URBAN COOKIE COLLECTIVE

Urban Cookie Collective achieved a major breakthrough in 1993 with 'The Key: The Secret', one of the most riveting dance tracks of the season. The band comprises Rohan Heath (keyboards), Diane Charlemagne (ex-Nomad Soul; vocals), Marty (MC) and DJ Pete (DJ). The project is masterminded by Heath, who had formerly worked with Yargo and A Guy Called Gerald. He had learned classical piano as a child, going electric in time to perform with the latter two outfits. He had decided on music after abandoning a PhD at Vermont University. After a tour of Japan supporting the Happy Mondays, he left A Guy Called Gerald to release 'Hardcore Uproar' as Together, which made number 12 in the UK charts in August 1990. After a brief stint with Eek A Mouse, he elected to concentrate on solo work, and inaugurated Urban Cookie Collective. 'The Key: The Secret' was originally a track written at home by Heath, in a soul/hip-hop vein, produced by Chapter And The Verse on the tiny Unheard Records imprint. However, after a remix provoked a massive club response it was picked up by Pulse 8, who also issued a double album the same year.
● ALBUMS: *High On A Happy Vibe* (Pulse 8 1993)★★★.

URBAN DANCE SQUAD

A group who deliberately blur the boundaries between rock, rap and dance music, Amsterdam, Netherlands' Urban Dance Squad originally comprised Rude Boy (b. Patrick Remington; rapper, singer) plus the pseudonymous Magic Stick (drums), DJ DNA (programming), Silly Sil (bass) and Tres Manos (b. Rene van Barneveld; guitar). Their 1989 debut album for Arista Records, *Mental*

Floss For The Globe, included the hit single 'Deeper Shade Of Soul', which peaked at number 21 in the US charts, and was a Top 40 entry in several other countries. Their debut album, with its combination of riveting guitar lines, samples and rapping, was an obvious precursor to 90s crossover acts such as Rage Against The Machine. Their impact on the charts looked to be a fleeting one, however, until they re-emerged in 1994 with an accomplished collection for the Virgin Records-backed Hut imprint. For this the group eschewed the sample-heavy style of old, having slimmed down to a quartet with the departure of DNA. By the advent of 1996's *Planet Ultra*, the group had moved towards writing in a more traditional vein, with Rude Boy preferring to sing rather than rap. Many of the contents were written during jams while the group toured the USA to promote *Persona Non Grata*. The keyboards on *Planet Ultra* were provided by Belgium's Wizards Of Ooze, and production by Phil Nicolo of the Butcher Brothers.
● ALBUMS: *Mental Floss For The Globe* (Arista 1989)★★★★, *Persona Non Grata* (Hut 1994)★★★, *Planet Ultra* (Virgin 1996)★★★.

URBAN SPECIES

From their formation in Tottenham, London, England, in the late 80s, Urban Species were widely tipped as the next potential breakthrough in UK hip-hop. They originally comprised lead rapper Mint (b. Peter Akinrinola) and DJ Renegade (b. Winston Small), whose partnership principally involved messing about in their north London bedrooms, since when added the services of toaster Slim (b. Rodney Green). The trio started to produce small runs of white labels, distributing them under the names of either Mint or Renegade. This earned them a reputation among both the pirate radio stations and clubs, where they would be invited to appear. Even the hip New York stations Kiss and WBLS picked up on one of their tracks, 'It's My Thing', but the group were hamstrung by finances and unable to capitalize. Their next cut, 'Got To Have It', was the one that brought them to the attention of Talkin' Loud boss Gilles Peterson. By 1991 he had their signatures. Their eclectic blend of ragga, dub, and even acoustic folk rumblings has seen them placed in several musical categories, from soul to rap and jazz fusion, and comparisons to Arrested Development continued to flourish. Their second single as Urban Species, 'Listen', shared its title with their first LP, and featured 'fourth' member Lynette Bracewaite, alongside live guest musicians such as Galliano and Incognito. Guest vocalists have also included MC Solaar (a fellow-traveller on the Talkin' Loud roster) and Maysa Leak, and Urban Species have built their reputation as much on the back of impressive live appearances as much as their studio touch.

● ALBUMS: *Listen* (Talkin' Loud 1993)★★★.

Us3

One of 1993's most intriguing musical experiments, UK-based Us3 comprise Geoff Wilkinson and Mel Simpson. Wilkinson was best known for his Jazz DJ work, and met Simpson at his own Flame studio, where they discovered mutually inclusive tastes. Together they struck upon the idea of sampling some of their favourite old jazz tunes and mixing them in with their own material. The resultant 'And The Band Played Boogie' was released on Coldcut's Ninja Tune imprint, featuring the rapping of Born 2B, and created a critical buzz. By hook or by crook the record came to the attention of executives at jazz label Blue Note, who quickly deduced that most of the samples were lifted directly from their own catalogue. The miscreants were summoned, but then Capitol took the wholly laudable and progressive step of working out a deal whereby the duo could enjoy unlimited access to the Blue Note label archives. The result was an album of richly textured jazz and hip-hop, with guests including rappers Tukka Yoot (b. Jamaica), Kobie Powell and Rahsaan (all three of whom would secure deals with Capitol in the wake of the album's success), and jazzmen Gerald Presencer, Dennis Rollins, Tony Remy and Steve Williamson. The album, which was preceded by the singles, 'Cantaloop' and 'Riddim', proved a worldwide hit, selling particularly strongly in the USA. The foresight of the copyright holders at Blue Note has been amply rewarded too: since the release of *Hand On The Torch* interest in Blue Note back-catalogue has escalated and sales have doubled. Even Herbie Hancock, on whose 'Cantalope Island' the single 'Cantaloop' was loosely based, expressed his appreciation for their efforts. It would be used on the soundtrack to the *Super Mario Bros* film, and Barry Levinson's *Jimmy Hollywood*. They were also enlisted for Stephen Spielberg's *The Flintstones*. In the wake of their success, especially in the US and Europe, Wilkinson was asked by Toshiba/EMI to A&R a compilation of new

London jazz musicians. In 1994 Us3 released a remix album, and embarked on collaborative material with the Ragga Twins (famed for their contributions to Shut Up And Dance).

● ALBUMS: *Hand On The Torch* (Blue Note 1993)★★★★, *Us3 The Jazz Mixes* (Blue Note 1994)★★★, *Broadway & 52nd* (Blue Note 1997)★★★.

UTAH SAINTS

Formed in Leeds, Yorkshire, England, Utah Saints are a duo of Jez Willis (b. 14 August 1963, Brampton, Cumbria, England; ex-Surfin' Dove, Cassandra Complex) and Tim Garbutt (b. 6 January 1969, London, England; also a DJ at the Bliss club in Leeds). Both were formerly members of MDMA, who practised an unlikely and unappetizing hybrid of electro-gothic dance. They released five 12-inch singles on their own Ecstatic Product label, the band name taken from the chemical description for the 'Ecstasy' drug, though they initially claimed never to have actually used it. However, both were more than familiar with developments in the club scene. After MDMA Willis drifted into DJing, specializing in 70s disco evenings (Garbutt had already performed widely in such a role from the late 80s onwards). Together they established their name at their own Mile High Club nights at the Gallery in Leeds; these were such a success that corresponding events also transferred to York and then London. They then returned to recording, taking the Utah Saints name from the Nicolas Cage film, *Raising Arizona* (it had previously been employed on a MDMA b-side). The duo's move to house music, using samples and a driving backbeat, proved much more successful than the efforts of their former incarnation. After acclimatizing to the charts with 'What Can You Do For Me' (featuring a Eurythmics sample), they produced 'Something Good'. This was built around a Kate Bush sample (the line 'I just know that something good is going to happen') from 'Cloudbursting', but it had other strengths too. As Willis elaborated: 'We're trying to get a bit of rock 'n' roll into rave.' They later backed Neneh Cherry on a version of the Rolling Stones' 'Gimme Shelter' for the *Putting Our House In Order* campaign for the homeless in 1993, one of several acts to release the song. Their own follow-up was 'Believe In Me', this time featuring a sample of Philip Oakey of the Human League singing 'Love Action'. Other steals, meanwhile, are less obvious, and include heavy metal satanists Slayer and industrial funk band Front 242. *Utah Saints* sold over a quarter of a million copies in the USA in addition to its UK success. This was compounded by international touring with a wide range of bands. In just two weeks in 1993 they supported East 17, Take That and U2 at Wembley Stadium, then joined Moby and the Prodigy in Europe before returning to Leeds to support the Mission and Sisters Of Mercy. In contrast to their debut (recorded in six weeks) their second album was the result of a year in the studio, aided by co-producer Mark 'Spike' Kent (previously mixer to Depeche Mode and KLF). Their first release in over a year, 'Ohio', arrived in August 1995. This utilized a Jocelyn Brown sample (her 1984 hit 'Somebody Else's Guy'), but was atypical of the album as a whole where the sampling was now downplayed. Despite this, their playful instincts continue to offer an accessible bridge between rock audiences and the house/techno movement.

● ALBUMS: *Utah Saints* (ffrr 1993)★★★.

V., STEVIE

b. Steve Vincent, *c.*1964, Hertfordshire, England. Vincent became a minor pop star of the early 90s via his summer hit, 'Dirty Cash', which spent two months in the UK Top 10, under his then operating title, The Adventures Of Stevie V. 'Dirty Cash', with its insistent, cluttered arrangement, may not have pleased dance music purists, but its anti-materialism ethos did provide prototype commercial hip-house with one of its most notable crossover hits. Melody Washington, who featured prominently as the female vocalist on the hit, also duetted with Vincent on several of the tracks on his debut album. Vincent had begun playing the piano at five, subsequently learning bass and guitar. He formed a group at school, including one combo that included two of his teachers, called the Generation Gap. He then went to college, emerging with an electronics degree, becoming a freelance engineer afterwards. His first record release came in 1983, 'Ease Your Mind', produced by Arthur Baker. It sold well in the USA but did not become a domestic hit. Now a resident of Biggleswade, he recorded his debut album in 1990, with guest appearances from Mantronix, Monie Love and the Jungle Brothers. Reviewers decided that the artist had not revealed sufficient diversity and the presence of two separate versions of 'Dirty Cash' helped illustrate their arguments. Subsequent singles, such as 1991's 'Jealousy', were unable to repeat the success of his solitary major hit.

● ALBUMS: *Adventures Of Stevie V.* (Mercury 1990)★★★.

VAN HELDEN, ARMAND

b. Netherlands. Based in Times Square in New York, USA, Van Helden had, by the mid-90s, supplanted Masters At Work as the most in-demand remixer in the music industry. However, Van Helden himself was troubled by this reputation. As he told the *New Musical Express*: 'The perception in the UK is that I'm rolling in cash, but I could make a lot more money if I was a real entrepreneur and said yes to every remix I got offered.' As a testament to this, he claimed to have turned down offers to work with Mick Jagger and Janet Jackson in the same week in 1997. His childhood consisted of several foreign postings (his father was in the service of the US armed forces), though he eventually settled in Boston, losing much of his youth to cocaine addiction. Although he was a high-profile DJ on the American and continental European circuit for several years thereafter, his breakthrough in Britain came in 1996 with his house remix of Tori Amos's 'Professional Widow', which reached number 2 in the UK charts. Previously he had recorded 'Witchdocktor', an underground club favourite that regularly accompanied Alexander McQueen's fashion shows. Though a veteran of several different styles of house - including the techno, trance and tribal variations - his solo debut album was rooted in hip-hop (vocal samples included the Wu-Tang Clan and KRS-1).

● ALBUMS: *Sampleslaya ... Enter The Meat Market* (1997)★★★★.

VANILLA ICE

b. Robert Van Winkle, 31 October 1968, Miami Lakes, Florida, USA. Controversial white rapper who borrowed liberally from Hammer's blueprint for commercial success, and scored a UK/US number 1 with 'Ice Ice Baby' (15 million worldwide sales). Just as Hammer utilized easily reconisable rock/pop classics to underpin his rhymes, Ice used the same technique in reshaping 'Under Pressure', 'Satisfaction' and 'Play That Funky Music' for his repertoire. Winkle was raised by his mother in a poor area of Miami, and never knew his father. He spent his teenage years hanging out on the street. However, the later claims to the press about being stabbed five times were erroneous - in fact he had been slashed across his bottom on a singular occasion. Contrary to his new image he actually sang in church choir until he was 15 and had a stepfather who owned a Chevrolet dealership, before he was first discovered playing the City Lights in Dallas, Texas. His debut album covered all bases, the ballad-rap 'I Love You' sitting alongside the gangsta-inclined 'Go Ill' and dance pop of 'Dancin''. While rap aficionados held up their hands in horror at what they loudly decried as a phoney, Vanilla Ice responded by telling his detractors they could 'Kiss My White Ass' at an MTV Awards ceremony.

An obvious reference to contentions that rap was an intrinsically black music, his comments did little to pacify angry factions in the genre. Ironically, Public Enemy had originally encouraged their producer, Hank Shocklee, to sign him to their label, based on his good looks and snappy dance routines. However, following his huge success he fell foul of a management that wished to pigeonhole him within the teen-market. It would take several years before he fully extricated himself from the deal. Whether this, adverse press or a lack of genuine talent called a halt to Vanilla Ice's meteoric rise is a worthy debate. He certainly did little to bring the jury to a favourable verdict with his comeback album. In a desperate attempt to catch up with the gangsta set, *Mindblowing* made frequent references to 'blunts', while the music sampled James Brown and, predictably, George Clinton. It was a blueprint hardcore rap album, but one with fewer convictions, in both senses, than Ice-T or Snoop Doggy Dogg.

● ALBUMS: *To The Extreme* (SBK 1990)★★★, *Extremely Live* (SBK 1991)★★, *Mindblowin* (SBK 1994)★★.

VAPOURSPACE

(see Gage, Mark)

VASQUEZ, JUNIOR

Junior Vasquez (not his real name, he is in fact a German-American from Philadelphia, but declines to provide further details) found his induction into the world of dance music as a (reluctant) dancer at Larry Levan's Paradise Garage. He soon decided the life of a DJ was for him. He applied himself to his apprenticeship, working his way up the ladder via shops (working at Downstairs Records in the early 80s where he first met friends such as Shep Pettibone), clubs and house parties (notably the Kiss-FM bashes), until he had built his own following. This allowed him to put together his own clubs - starting with the Hearthrob nights at the Funhouse, then the Basline club, and finally the Sound Factory (owned by Christian Visca). One of New York's premier nights, it quickly saw Vasquez's reputation as a fiercely hot turntable operator soar. Innovating live by playing backwards and forwards, alternating rhythms and throwing in live samples, he offered a total aural experience. There was a visual dimension too; with Vasquez stepping out from behind the desks to present his adoring public with flowers. His reputation spread to the point at which Madonna was spotted at the Sound Factory on several occasions (he also DJed at her party to celebrate the launch of *Sex*). As a recording artist Vasquez provides Tribal Records with the majority of his labours, including cuts like 'X', 'Get Your Hands Off My Man' and 'Nervaas'. He has also written for artists including Lisa Lisa and Cindi Lauper and remixed for many others, ranging from Eat Static ('Gulf Breeze') to Ce Ce Peniston ('I'm In The Mood'). Vasquez's technique is described by the man himself thus: 'I seem my style rooted in house/club music. I like a harder modern sound'.

● ALBUMS: *Junior Vasquez Live Vol. 1* (Pagoda 1997)★★★.

VATH, SVEN

Frankfurt, Germany-based Vath (pronounced to rhyme with Fate) first DJed at his father's bar, the Queens Pub, playing old disco and Barry White records. He started his recording career as frontman for the Off, whose 'Electric Salsa' was a big European hit and one of the first for Michael Munzing and Luca Anzilotti, the duo behind Snap!. Vath grew up listening to various kinds of electronica – Tangerine Dream, Ryûichi Sakamoto, Holger Czukay and Jean-Michel Jarre – and was further inspired by the house explosion of the 80s. During the early 90s he became involved with trance, founding the pioneering labels Harthouse, Eye Q and the environmentally pleasing Recyle Or Die Records (whose CD-only issues use bio-degradable cardboard packaging). Following a spell in India Vath wrote *Accident In Paradise*, recognized as a masterpiece in the techno world and an important part of the early trance sound. However, the follow-up, the rather indulgent concept album *The Harlequin, The Robot And The Ballet Dancer*, did not fare so well; one commentator described it as 'overblown . . . self important . . . Wagner meets Tangerine Dream over a 909 beat'. In the mid-90s, after various other projects had not gone his way, Vath left the ailing Eye-Q and Harthouse which soon went bankrupt. However, with 1998's *Fusion*, Vath ditched the techno sound and produced a more melodic, funky, eclectic album that presented impressionistic washes over a mixture of textures, including samba rhythms ('Fusion') and relaxed breakbeats ('Sensual Enjoyments' and 'Trippy Moonshine'), sometimes touching on funky house ('Face It') and dark techno ('Schubduse').

● ALBUMS: *Accident In Paradise* (Eye Q 1993)★★★★★, *The Harlequin, The Robot And The Ballet Dancer* (Eye Q 1994)★★, *Fusion* (Virgin 1998)★★★.

VOLUME 10

With production credits for local hip-hop artists such as Torcha Chamba and the Baka Boys, Los Angeles, California, US rapper Volume 10's first album was more musically accomplished than most debutants. By the time it emerged he had already stirred up controversy with the release of a single, 'Pistol Grip Pump', a hardcore rap narrative on the law of the gun, and gun laws. Like many other rappers (notably Sir Mix-A-Lot), Volume 10 saw the ability to possess and carry personal weaponry as a major tenet of his constitutional rights. *Hip Hopera*, the album that followed in 1994, concerned itself with other conventional west coast rapper pursuits, which were summarized by one reviewer as 'getting paid, getting laid'.

● ALBUMS: *Hip Hopera* (Indie 1994)★★.

W

W., KRISTINE

b. Pasco, Washington, USA. A veteran of the European house/dance music scene, Kristine W. first came to prominence in 1994 when Mel Medalie, the head of UK label Champion Records, saw her perform in Las Vegas as a lounge act while attending a Lennox Lewis boxing match. He invited her to the UK to work alongside the producer Rollo, which partnership resulted in such songs as 'Feel What You Want' and 'One More Try'. When released as white label 12-inches, both were immensely popular, leading to a bidding war among US labels. Eventually she signed with East West Records, who brokered a production/distribution deal with Champion. Although 'Feel What You Want' was a major US club hit, the impetus of her career was hampered when East West and Champion severed their agreement in 1995 and the projected US release of 'One More Try' fell victim to these machinations. Eventually, she signed a new contract with RCA Records, for whom she recorded the album *Land Of The Living*, which included both singles.
● ALBUMS: *Land Of The Living* (RCA 1996)★★★.

WAGON CHRIST

Wagon Christ is Falmouth, Cornwall, England-based Luke Vibert, a star of the Rising High roster. Like his friend the Aphex Twin, with whom Vibert is a near-neighbour, this is another artist interested in pushing the possibilities of electronica, despite his musical origins as a drummer in a punk band.
● ALBUMS: *Phat Lab Nightmare* (Rising High 1994)★★★★, *Throbbing Pouch* (Rising High 1995)★★★.

WARFIELD, JUSTIN

Los Angeles, US-based rapper, yet a world away from that region's more typical hip-hop fare. Warfield (b. *c*.1973) dwells over raps which share a common line of descent with the narratives of the beat writers, alongside laid-back beats which borrow heavily from the psychedelic and acid rock traditions (Soft Machine, Moby Grape). There are liberal samples from everything from jazz to Led Zeppelin to keep the grooves fresh. Warfield grew up in the wealthy Laurel Canyon area. Brought up by hippy parents, he can justify lines like: 'Black as a pepper and a lyrical Jew' by his Jewish-Cherokee-Afro-American heritage. Warfield was making demos at the age of 14 and had his first deal three years later, subsequently forming his own band for live work, and coming to prominence via an appearance on QDIII's *Soundlab* compilation.
● ALBUMS: *My Field Trip To Planet Nine* (Quest 1993)★★★.

WARP 9

Among the most interesting of the electro hip-hop groups, New York, USA's Warp 9 were a project helmed by producers Lotti Golden and Richard Scher. They featured a full-scale band in Boe Brown (ex-the Strikers) and Chuck Wansley (ex-Charades), as joint vocalist/percussionists, plus Ada Dwyer (vocals) and DJ John 'Jellybean' Benitez. Scher, who came from a jazz background, handled keyboards, while Golden provided lyrics and further vocals. Golden had formerly recorded an early 'rap' single, 'Motorcycle', for Atlantic Records in 1969, and written 'Dance To The Rhythm Of Love', later recorded by Patti LaBelle. The duo started their partnership by producing Sharon Brown's 'I Specialise In Love' for Profile Records, before going on to work with groups such as Chilltown ('Rock The Beat') and Ladies' Choice ('Girls Night Out'). Warp 9 made their debut with 'Nunk', a tune highly typical of the period which was underpinned by a perfunctory Casio keyboard. They followed it with 'Light Years Away', which again indulged in electro's familiar science-fiction fantasies. Vocalist Dyer later took a major role in the theatrical production of *The Wiz*. Warp 9's two singles were regularly appended to a number of electro compilations in the late 80s and early 90s as the central personnel moved on to other production projects.

WARP RECORDS

Since its foundation in Sheffield, England, in 1989 by Rob Mitchell and Steve Beckett, as an offshoot from their record shop, Warp has played an important role in the development of dance music in the UK. Mitchell and Beckett had played together in an indie band, but on opening Warp they found themselves inadvertently cast into the flourishing acid house and techno scene of the late 80s. Their first release was the Forgemasters' 'Track With No Name' (pressed with the help of an Enterprise Allowance grant), which heralded the emergence of a Chicago- and Detroit-inspired minimal techno sound dubbed 'bleep'. This was followed by Nightmares On Wax's 'Dextrous' and early the following year, Sweet Exorcist's bleep anthem 'Test One'. Such was the response to this new sound that in the summer of 1990, both LFO and Tricky Disco's eponymous debuts reached the Top 20. As the rave scene developed, Warp changed their ethos and began to promote more listenable, experimental electronic music, 'to re-educate people who bought dance records to sit down and pay attention'. This approach was crystallized by the first *Artificial Intelligence* compilation, which included tracks by the Diceman (Aphex Twin), Autechre and Alex Paterson (of the Orb), and had a more reflective, cerebral feeling, with links to artists such as Brian Eno, Kraftwerk and even Pink Floyd. The series was extended and Warp released individual albums by several of the participants, including Polygon Window (Aphex Twin), Black Dog Productions, B12, FUSE (Ritchie Hawtin) and Speedy J. This so-called 'ambient techno' has resonances in some drum 'n' bass that appeared later in the decade, particularly the sound of Black Dog and Speedy J. It attracted substantial interest among the public and the media, such that Aphex Twin was one of the most talked-about artists in 1993. While continuing to release pure electronic material, Warp have begun to sign artists with more diverse styles, notably Sabres Of Paradise, Squarepusher, Red Snapper and Jimi Tenor. The *Blech* compilation (1996) confirmed this change of tack, where electronic sounds were blended with hip-hop beats, jazzy textures, drum 'n' bass grooves and snatches of dialogue, creating a fragmented electric style, similar in concept to that of Ninja Tune Records. Although the sounds have moved on, it seems that the idea of listenable dance music is still very much at the heart of Warp.

● COMPILATIONS: *Pioneers Of The Hypnotic Groove* (1991)★★★★, *Evolution Of The Groove* (1992)★★★★, *Artificial Intelligence* (1992)★★★★★, *Tequila Slammers And The Jump Jump Groove Generation* (1993)★★★, *Artificial Intelligence II* (1994)★★★, *Blech* (1996)★★★★.

WAS (NOT WAS)

An unlikely recording and production duo, childhood friends David Weiss (saxophone, flute, keyboards, vocals) and Don Fagenson (bass, keyboards, guitar) have used a variety of singers to front their records, including Sweet Pea Atkinson, Leonard Cohen, Harry Bowens and Donny Ray Mitchell. Their debut album sought to imbue dance music with an intellectual credibility which it had previously lacked. While musicians were plucked from sources as varied as P-Funk and MC5, 'Tell Me That I'm Dreaming' incorporated a mutilated sample of a Ronald Reagan speech. 1983's *Born To Laugh At Tornadoes* included, bizarrely, Ozzy Osbourne rapping, and a snatch of Frank Sinatra. Geffen rewarded their eclecticism by dropping them. They moved on to Phonogram, managing to focus much more clearly on their prospective dance market in the process. Their biggest hit was the anthemic 'Walk The Dinosaur', which topped the US singles chart for six weeks, while 'Spy In The House Of Love' had similar crossover appeal. However, the music industry knows them better for their numerous production credits. These include the B-52's, Iggy Pop, Bonnie Raitt and Bob Dylan. The latter fulfilled an ambition for Weiss, who had long held Dylan as his personal idol. *Are You Okay?* was critically lauded, and they remain an enigmatic attraction on the periphery of the dance scene. They reconvened in 1998.

● ALBUMS: *Was (Not Was)* (Ze-Island 1981)★★★, *Born To Laugh At Tornadoes* (Ze-Island 1983)★★★, *What's Up, Dog?* (Chrysalis 1988)★★★, *Are You Okay?* (Chrysalis 1990)★★★.

WATERS, CRYSTAL

Waters enjoys one of the more colourful backgrounds among dance music's modern female exponents. Born in South New Jersey, she majored in Computer Science at Howard University. Her father was jazz musician Jnr. Waters, and her great-aunt Ethel Waters. Indeed everyone in her family played an instrument, though some of her own initial forays were as the youngest member of the American Poets Society. Her entry into the music scene could hardly have been more dramatic. 'Gypsy Woman' was the song that did it for her, propelled by an unforgetable 'La Dee Dee, La Dee Da' refrain, and the production know-how of the Basement Boys, it became the summer anthem of 1991 in many clubs throughout Britain and Europe. At the time she was still employed as a computer technician issuing the FBI with warrants at the Washington DC parole board. The song eventually rose to number 3 in the UK charts, and brought her success over in America too, though her first album received mixed reviews. She returned in 1994 with '100% Pure Love', her first recording in over three years, and a second album. This time her songwriting was significantly stronger, representing a more satisfying, less rushed collection.

● ALBUMS: *Surprise* (Mercury 1991)★★, *Storyteller* (A&M 1994)★★★.

WATFORD, MICHAEL

A classy garage artist from New Jersey, New York, although he was born and raised in Virginia, Watford's distinctive, soulful baritone has graced a number of successful records since his debut, Holdin' On', for East West. He grew up performing song and dance routines for his parents with his brothers and sisters, before joining gosepl group The Disciples Of Truth at the age of five. From there he joined Smack Music (Michael and Debbie Cameron), the New Jersey production team from whom Adeva has also benefitted, in 1987. It took some time for Watford to progress to centrestage but this is typical of his retiring, almost reticent nature. It was 'Holdin' On' that provided the push. Originally housed on a 1992 Atlantic Records compilation (*Underground Dance Volume 1*), it was soon picked out by club DJs. The Smack team also worked on his debut long playing set, assisted by producer John Robinson. This housed successful singles 'Luv 4-2' and 'So Into You' which authenticated his appeal to club audiences and soul fans alike, though he maintains his deep religious beliefs.

● ALBUMS: *Michael Watford* (East West 1993)★★★.

WAU! MR MODO RECORDS

Headed by Adam Morris and Youth, but popularly conceived to be 'the Orb's record company' (Dr Paterson part-owning the company), after housing their debut single, 'A Huge Ever-Growing Pulsating Brain That Rules From The Centre Of The Ultraworld'. It cost only £20 to record, but led the label to a licensing deal with Big Life. WAU! Mr Modo is an acronym for What About Us!, the Mr Modo part referring to Orb manager Adam Morris's pseudonym. Future Orb member Thrash (aka Kristian Weston) engineered much of the

label's product, including Jam On The Mutha's 'Hotel California'. Outside of Orb activities the label also picked up releases like German import Maurizio's 'Play' at the end of 1992. The latter release added a 'Battersea Was An Island Of Mud' Orb remix, as well as another by Underground Resistance. Other releases included Shola's 'Hold On (Goa Mixes)' in 1991, Shola Phillips being the vocalist on the Orb's 'Perpetual Dawn'. The same year saw Zoe's 'Sunshine On A Rainy Day', a reissue of the September 1990 club 'grower', backed by remixes from the Orb, and produced by Youth. The latter split from WAU! Mr Modo in 1992 to establish Butterfly Records. while his former label continued with releases like Suzuki's 'Satelliete Serenade'. However, WAU! Mr Modo could do little to escape their Orb connections when the band terminated their contract with Big Life, with that record company serving an injunction on the label to prevent it releasing any records just in case they were by the Orb under a pseudonym.

● ALBUMS: Various: *Dancebusters* (WAU! Mr Modo 1990)★★★.

WAY OUT WEST

This eclectic dance-based duo was formed in Bristol by Jody Wisternoff and Nick Warren. The latter was a veteran DJ of the well-known Liverpool club Cream and had also previously collaborated with Massive Attack and Smith And Mighty. The duo originally released two independent singles as Echo in the early 90s and as Way Out West continued to record independently, releasing a brace of singles for Peace Of The Action. In 1994 they were signed by James Barton (the organizer of Cream) to DeConstruction Records and achieved immediate success with 'Ajare', released at the end of 1994. Following the success in the clubs of the single 'Domination' they achieved more widespread success when their atmospheric single 'The Gift' reached the UK Top 20 in the summer of 1996. Rather than issue a quick follow-up, Wisternoff and Warren became involved with remix and production work with Dubstar, Fluke and the Orb. With the proceeds from this work they were able to overhaul and upgrade their existing studio. Their self-titled debut album was branded by some sections of the dance community as the 'sunrise sound', reflecting the warm, dreamlike qualities of such songs as 'Blue', the album's first single. Way Out West have remixed a number of other artists

including Saint Etienne and Reprazent.
● ALBUMS: *Way Out West* (DeConstruction 1997)★★★.

WEATHERALL, ANDY

b. 6 April 1963. Dance magnate Weatherall began the 80s working on building sites and film sets before picking up DJ work. His career proper began with residencies at the Shoom and Spectrum clubs in the acid house boom of 1988. Afterwards he founded the Boys Own fanzine with Terry Farley and Steve Mayes, which concentrated on club music, fashion and football. When Boy's Own became a record label, he also appeared, as a guest vocalist, on a Bocca Juniors track. He made his name, however, by remixing Primal Scream's 'Loaded'. The likes of James, Happy Mondays, That Petrol Emotion, Saint Etienne, Grid, Meat Beat Manifesto, Big Hard Excellent Fish, S'Express, Orb, Finitribe, A Man Called Adam, Jah Wobble, Future Sound Of London, Moody Boyz, One Dove, Throbbing Gristle, Galliano, Flowered Up, Björk, Espiritu, Yello, Stereo MC's and New Order followed. His landmark achievement, however, remains his supervising role on old friends' Primal Scream's *Screamadelica* - the album that effectively forged a new musical genre. He also enjoyed a stint as DJ on Kiss-FM, before his eclectic, anarchic tastes proved too much for programmers. 'My background is rock 'n' roll. The Clash are still the best band in the world'. His recording methodology has been compared to that of Joe Meek, sampling strange sounds such as answerphones and dustbin lids for percussion - or 'Techno's Phil Spector's quoth *Q Magazine*. He has subsequently set up a further label, recording and remix operation under the title Sabres Of Paradise, which has also proved hugely successful. Weatherall continued to play out regularly at Sabresonic club nights, and in 1993 signed a major publishing deal with MCA Music.

WEE PAPA GIRL RAPPERS

This commercial UK female rap duo's lyrics floated on lively hip-hop and house tracks. The two components were sisters TV Tim (b. Timmie Lawrence, London, England) and Total S (b. Sandra Lawrence, London, England). They had been introduced to the world of US hip-hop by their club DJ friend 'Junior G'. Finding this new music infectious, they abandoned their previous loves of soul and hard rock to establish them-

selves as a rap act, taking their name from their father's habit of muttering 'Wee Papa' to himself when he got over-excited. The 'girl rappers' was a natural extension. Snapped up by Jive Records, they debuted with a rap version of George Michael's 'Faith', which just dented the UK Top 60. It was followed by 'Heat It Up', recorded with Cox and Steele (as Two Men And A Drum Machine) of Fine Young Cannibals fame. Reaching number 21 in the charts, it prefaced their most successful single, 'Wee Rule'. Nodding to reggae (and remixed by Aswad), it peaked at number 6 in the UK charts, while the accompanying debut album achieved massive sales in Europe. When they returned after a year and a half away with a second album, it saw them pursue a more commercial-dance direction, with the introduction of producers of the calibre of Cliville and Cole (C+C Music Factory), Coldcut and Danny D (D-Mob). However, their last significant chart position came with 'Blow The House Down'. Innocuous and obvious at best, they amicably dissolved in early 1991. Their most enduring legacy, perhaps, was a revamped theme for UK television's *Jim'll Fix It*.
● ALBUMS: *The Beat, The Rhyme, The Noise* (Jive 1988)★★★, *Be Aware* (Jive 1990)★★.

WELL HUNG PARLIAMENT

Essentially record promoter turned remixer Paul Gotel and Spencer Williams, of S-1000 fame. Their recording career began with 'We Can Be' for Cowboy Records, but they also functioned highly productively as a remix team - earning commissions for Nu Colour's 'The Power', Erire's 'I Just Can't Give You Up (Faze 2)', the Shamen's 'LSI', Synergy's 'One Way Only', Chosen Few's 'Positivity', Madness' 'Night Boat To Cairo' and Conrad's 'Doesn't Time Fly'.

WEST BAM

b. Germany. Judged by many to be the king of the 'Balearic beat', West Bam (who does not willingly surrender his full name) was a prime mover in the early days of acid house. DJing since 1983, he had indulged in industrial/experimental music before he was led to Detroit techno via house (he had, in fact, organised Berlin's first 'House Party'). He established his own Low Spirit record label in the late 80s (having released his first record in 1985), titled after his club night. This imprint housed songs such as Grace Darling's 'Dreams'. His own genre classics include 'Alarm Clock',

later sampled by Andy Weatherall for his remix of My Bloody Valentine's 'Glider', and 'Monkey Say, Monkey Do' from 1989. By 1994 he claimed to have over 100 productions to his name. The West Bam remix schedule was equally hectic, and included Deskee's 'Let There Be House' and Flower Ltd's 'Swinging Thing', before more of his own material such as 'The Roof Is On Fire' (for Swanyard Records in 1990). His 1994 single, 'Celebration Generation' (which included a Justin Robertson remix) saw him return to pure techno. It was followed by the similarly emphatic 'Bam Bam Bam' (remixed by Moby and jungle artist Jack Frost). West Bam's philosophy on the importance of dance music is crystal clear: 'Nothing reflects our time so exactly as electronic dance music. It's the first real international music.' He is currently signed, via Low Spirit, to Polydor Records.
● ALBUMS: *Bam Bam Bam* (Low Spirit/Polydor 1994)★★★★.

WEST COAST RAP ALL-STARS

A coalition of prominent west coast hip-hop stars who came together to preach the word of unity, and raise funds for inner-city youth projects. Some of the participants included Hammer, Eazy-E, Above The Law, Def Jef, Digital Underground, Young MC, Tone Loc, NWA, Michel'le, Oaktown's 3-5-7, Ice-T and King Tee. The album's title, which also reached number 35 in the *Billboard* charts as a single, referred heavily to the gang warfare in areas like South Central and Compton. A touch ironic, perhaps, when so many of the contributors were perceived by 'outsiders' as having exacerbated these problems with their gangsta rap mythology.
● ALBUMS: *We're All In The Same Gang* (Warners 1990)★★.

WEST STREET MOB

West Street Mob, formed in New York, USA, in the late 70s, were one of the less celebrated of Sugarhill Records' acts, despite the fact that Sugarhill owners Joe and Sylvia Robinson's son, Joey Jnr., was once a member. Their most significant release was the electro classic 'Breakin Dancin' - Electric Boogie', a version of the Incredible Bongo Band's interpretation of the Shadows' 'Apache'. This 'break' had long been a staple of the scratch mix DJs within the hip-hop community, and its familiarity was an important factor in its local popularity.

WESTSIDE CONNECTION

A three-way collaboration between rappers Ice Cube, Mack 10 and WC, Westside Connection was started as a riposte to what the participants saw as 'dissing' by their east coast colleagues. The tone of *Bow Down* was one of outright hostility, particularly on tracks such as 'King Of The Hill', Ice Cube's vindictive attack on the main protagonists in Cypress Hill. 'Sen-Dog you can't rap from the guts/And B-Real sounding like he got baby nuts/Comin' with voice high-pitched/The B in B-Real must stand for bitch'. More discerning hip-hop commentators reacted with dismay at one of the most vicious albums in gangsta-rap's already controversial history. In truth, the album was also a musical disappointment, displaying an over-reliance on repetitive, stripped-down funk to underpin its bleak lyrical narratives.
● ALBUMS: *Bow Down* (Virgin 1996)★★.

WHEELER, CARON

b. *c.*1962, England. Wheeler was raised in Jamaica; her father was a bass player, and her mother a singer with a Jamaican drama company. Wheeler's interest in music began at the age of 12, singing lovers rock with female reggae trio Brown Sugar, who had four number 1 singles in the specialist charts by the time she was 16. She moved on to form backing trio Afrodiziak, whose vocals were utlized live or on sessions with artists such as the Jam. Other backing duties for Elvis Costello, Phil Collins, Neneh Cherry and Aswad followed, and she earned a gold record for her liaison with Erasure in 1988. However, she became frustrated with the record business and effectively retired that year, taking a job in a library. The break refuelled her creative instincts, and when she returned as part of Soul II Soul in 1990 it was to her greatest success so far. Though never part of the group proper, she won a Grammy for Best Vocal Performance on 'Back To Life', one of the two platinum singles on which she sang (the other being 'Keep On Movin''). She subsequently embarked on her solo career by signing with Orange Tree Productions, eventually securing a contract with RCA. Her distinctive voice was soon utilized not only for the blend of pop, soul and hip-hop that had characterized the music of her former employers, but also for blasting the white domination of the UK record industry. Her alienation was revealed in the title track of her debut album: 'Many moons ago, We were told the streets were paved with gold, So our people came by air and sea, To earn a money they could keep, Then fly back home, Sadly this never came to be, When we learned that we had just been invited, To clean up after the war'. Afterwards, her frustration with Britain saw her move to the USA for a second collection. This diverse set included a collaboration with Jam and Lewis on 'I Adore You', the production of former Soul II Soul man Jazzie B on 'Wonder', and a cover version of Jimi Hendrix's 'And The Wind Cries Mary'.

● ALBUMS: *UK Blak* (RCA 1990)★★★, *Blue (Is The Colour Of Pain)* (RCA 1991)★★★, *Beach Of The War Goddess* (1993)★★★.

WHIGFIELD

b. Sannie Charlotte Carlson, Denmark. Whigfield, her stage-name derived from the surname of a former music teacher, made her debut in 1994 with 'Saturday Night', a repetitive example of Euro dance/pop which became a huge international seller on release in September of that year, reaching the top of the UK charts and selling over 750,000 copies in its first week of release. It was the Barcelona-based former model's debut single, though it had originally been released in Italy in 1992. Though purists saw it as the antithesis of art, Whigfield herself merely lapped up the attention: 'The greatest satisfaction was hearing cameramen and technicians on *Top Of The Pops* saying that they hated it, then afterwards hearing them all humming it.' She appeared widely on television with her distinctive braided hair to support the single, but several commentators questioned the authenticity of the product. They pointed instead to the involvement of producer Larry Pignagnoli (formerly behind Italian Euro star Spagna) and writer David River. The follow-up single, 'Another Day', adopted a similar approach to reduced effect. Before Whigfield Carlson had spent several years playing in a jazz-based duo, the Whigfield Project, with her brother in Denmark (her brother publicly disowned her after the success of 'Saturday Night'). A third single, 'Think Of You', accompanied the release of her debut album. In 1995 Whigfield presented an edition of *Top Of The Pops*, and drew a series of complaints for the revealing costume she wore.

● ALBUMS: *Whigfield* (Systematic 1995)★★.

WHITE TOWN

Jyoti Mishra (b. 30 July 1966, Rourkela, India) appears to embody a number of peculiar trends in 90s pop: the bedroom one-man band; the self-sufficient indie scene; the unexpected marriage of wildly different musical styles and traditions; and, so far at least, the 'unknown' act that leaps to number 1, apparently from nowhere, then disappears from sight. His family moved to Derby, England in 1969 and Jyoti's first brush with fame was playing keyboards with local band Daryl And The Chaperones. He then began touring the clubs as a solo synthesiser act, performing covers of Buzzcocks songs, before, under the influence of the Wedding Present and the Pixies, he formed White Town as a guitar band. He began releasing singles on his own Satya Records, at the same time producing other bands and DJing in indie clubs. Five more limited edition singles followed before the debut album came together, by which time the other band members had fallen away and White Town was, effectively, Mishra. A portly Asian on a scene that favours skinny white kids, he was something of a local character in the Midlands but it was not until Radio 1 disc jockey Mark Radcliffe began to play 'Your Woman', a bizarre fusion of dance-beats and sampled 30s jazz trumpet, cobbled together on Mishra's 8-track home studio, that White Town finally went overground. Re-released by Chrysalis Records, it went straight to the top of the UK charts in early 1997, despite Mishra's refusal to make a video or appear on *Top Of The Pops*. He went down well with music journalists, revealing a delightfully anorak knowledge of acts as diverse as the Rah Band, Michael Nesmith, Landscape and the Merseys but his first album on a major label was not really strong enough to justify the original promise.

● ALBUMS: *Socialism, Sexism and Sexuality* (Parasol 1994)★★★, *Women In Technology* (Chrysalis 1997)★★.

WHODINI

Brooklyn, New York-based trio of rappers who, from their formation in 1982, pioneered the commercial rap/rock crossover, while many also cite their earliest recordings as precuorsors to the New Jack Swing movement. Whodini are rappers Jalil Hutchins and Ecstasy (b. John Fletcher, *c.*1964), backed by talented old school DJ, Grandmaster Dee (b. Drew Carter; once described as 'the turntable's Jimi Hendrix). The latter won his reputation for being able to scratch with almost every conceivable part of his anatomy. Prominent in hip-hop circles since the earliest days of the movement, he had formerly worked the decks behind The Devastating Two Emcees (a female duo) and the Jazzy Four. More recently he became a convert to Louis Farakhan's Nation Of Islam movement. Generally Whodini's subject matter never wavered too greatly from reasonably gentlemanly references to the opposite sex. Their debut release, 'Magic's Wand' (a tribute to the DJ of the same name on WBLS New York, who gave them a start), was also the first rap single on the Jive imprint, and the first single in hip-hop history to have a promotional video filmed. Strangely, it was co-produced by Thomas Dolby, on a rare voyage outside of British techno pop. Following a second single, 'The Haunted House Of Rock', they established their name and popularity through the 'Friends' 45, which also crossed over to the soul audience. Other popular tunes included the 'The Freaks Come Out At Night', 'One Love', and 'Be Yourself', on which they collaborated with soul diva Millie Jackson - having always maintained an R&B flavour to their recordings. They were widely renowned for their innovative stage act, and were the first rap group to perform with their own dancers, Dr. Ice and U.T.F.O.'s Kangol Kid, undertaking two world tours in 1983 and 1984. Later they joined Run DMC, Kurtis Blow, the Fat Boys and Newcleus on a thirty venue 'New York City Fresh Fest' tour, which was so successful it was repeated in 1985. In the autumn of 1986 they released 'Growing Up', an anti-drug video financed by the New York State Division Of Substance Abuse. Although they would again tour in 1987, this time with LL Cool J, the late 80s saw band members sidetracked through marriage and having children, and record company and managerial problems did not help. They made their first comeback in 1990 with an album for MCA, but neither party really understood each other, and the reunion dissolved. They reformed again in 1991 for *Bag A Trix* (which included ballad funk courtesy of Midnight Star) and in 1993 for Terminator X's *The Godfathers Of Threatt* compilation, which included them alongside other old schoolers Kool Herc, Cold Crush Brothers and more. They kicked that set off with 'It All Comes Down To Money', which they were happy to put on record: 'People have a lot of nice things to say about us. They look at us as pioneers and all this but now I want our business to reflect that. We love doing what we do. But we like being taken care of too. And also everybody has kids and this is for them now'. Whatever, it was a welcome return for their langorous narratives, unaffected by the shifts in rap.

● ALBUMS: *Whodini* (Jive 1983)★★, *Escape* (Jive 1984)★★★, *Back In Black* (Jive 1986)★★★, *Open Sesame* (Jive 1987)★★★★, *Bag-A-Trix* (MCA 1991)★★★, *Six* (Columbia 1996)★★★.
● COMPILATIONS: *The Collection* (Jive 1990)★★★★.

WHOOLIGANZ

Mad Skillz (b. Scott Caan, *c*.1975; the son of actor James Caan) and Mudfoot (Alan Maman, *c*.1977) are two white rappers from Beverly Hills (zip code 90210 no less) who have been endorsed by one of the hottest names in rap, B-Real (Cypress Hill). This fortunate state of affairs came about when the duo were recording with QDIII in Los Angeles in the early 90s, where B-Real heard their demo. The first results of this match were aired on their 'Put Your Handz Up', which featured Everlast on its b-side cut, 'Hit The Deck'. They moved on to use the production skills of T Ray, the Baka Boys and Lethal (House Of Pain) for the follow-up album, fighting shy of too many comparisons to Cypress Hill or the Soul Assassins enclave.

● ALBUMS: *Make Way For The W* (Tommy Boy 1994)★★★.

WHYCLIFFE

b. Donovan Whycliffe, England. Born into a music-loving family of 12, his parents encouraged him to sing in the Pentecostal choirs in his youth. Whycliffe's name was first mooted when he handed over a demo tape to Tim Andrews of Nottingham's Submission Records. The ensuing buzz ensured that the A&R men flocked to his door, and he eventually signed to MCA Records. He scored a hit in 1991 with 'Roughside', backed by an album. He returned in 1993 with the single, 'Heaven', and a new long playing set the following year. Remix guidance was offered by Tim Simenon (Bomb The Bass) and C.J. Mackintosh. The producers on his second album, *Journeys Of The Mind*, were Chris Porter (famed for his work with George Michael) and Simenon.

● ALBUMS: *Roughside* (MCA 1991)★★★, *Journeys Of The Mind* (MCA 1994)★★★.

WIKMAN, ERIC

b. New Jersey, USA. Wikman was formerly a rock fanatic until his friend's dance mix tapes caught his attention. He was a quick and enthusiastic convert, particularly to the compilations of Mathias Hoffman (Mosaic and Harthouse Records). Wikman soon became involved in the creative process, remixing techno cuts in the early 90s for San Francisco's Megatone label with DJ Mark Lewis. On his own terms he cut 'Body Baby' on Champion Records, under the mantle Global Groove. The follow-up was 'Cry Of Freedom', before he began remix work for D:Ream and Michael Watford.

WILD PITCH RECORDS

New York rap label founded by Stu Fine, which was eventually distributed in England through EMI in 1994. Some of their biggest hits included Gang Starr's 'Manifest', Main Source's 'Fakin' The Funk' and Jamose's 'The Rhythmologist'. Their longstanding artists include Ultramagnetic MCs, while new signings offer Broken English, N-Tyce and The Coup. Their A&R Vice-President is MC Serch (ex-3rd Bass).

WILDCHILD

b. Roger McKenzie, 1971, Southampton, Hampshire, England, d. 25 November 1995, Southampton, Hampshire, England. Signed to Polydor Records' Hi-Life subsidiary, Wildchild enjoyed a major hit in November 1995 with 'Renegade Master', a UK number 11 hit. Previously he had worked prolifically on more underground dance projects, including several productions for Brighton label Loaded Records. He also ran his own label, Dark & Black. Wildchild moved to New York with his partner and manager Donna Snell, but returned to England to appear on *Top Of The Pops* with the success of 'Renegade Master'. He collapsed and died from an undiagnosed heart condition just one month later. His record label established a Wildchild Music Foundation in his memory.

WINK, JOSH

b. c.1970, Philadelphia, USA. The techno artist Josh Wink combines a number of influences, from deep house to acid jazz and more experimental electronic music. His musical taste came from his family's record collection that included Philip Glass, Stevie Wonder, Kraftwerk, Steely Dan and James Brown. He began DJing in 1987 in underground Philadelphia clubs. In 1990 he released 'Tribal Confusion', on Strictly Rhythm Records, an acclaimed single produced with King Britt and credited to E-Culture that was later sampled by Future Sound Of London. The reaction enabled Britt and Wink to establish their own production company, WinKing Productions, in Philadelphia. Over the next five years they remixed over 20 tracks, including Rozalla's 'Are You Ready To Fly?', Digital Orgasm's 'Running Out Of Time' and Book Of Love's 'Boy Pop'. In 1993 when King went on tour as the Digable Planets' DJ, so Wink continued as a solo artist, using a variety of names, including Wink, Winx, Winc, Winks and the Crusher. The records were released on a variety of dance labels such as Vinyl Solution, Strictly Rhythm, Nervous, Limbo and R&S Records. He also recorded 30-second musical compositions for television advertisements, as well as launching his own underground dance label, Ovum Recordings, in October 1994. In the mid-90s he was signed to Virgin Records in the USA and Mercury Records in Britain, releasing 'Higher State Of Consciousness' in 1995.

WINLEY, PAUL

USA-born Winley was a veteran R&B producer and songwriter, running the Paul Winley Jazzland Ballroom on Harlem's 125th Street, before setting up Winley Records in the same location. His musical interests began when his brother was a member of the Clovers in his native Washington, for whom Paul wrote songs. He went on to compose for Ruth Brown and Joe Turner. Together with Dave 'Baby' Cortez he formed a partnership recording doo wop groups like the Duponts, Paragons, Collegians and Jesters. His introduction to rap music came at the behest of his daughters, Tanya and Paulette, the former recorded 'Vicious Rap'. He became famed for a series of compilations entitled *Disco Brakes*, produced by DJ Jolly Roger, which won him his first admirers, combining as it did some of the most popular 'breaks' over which the park rappers would improvise routines. Popular cuts included Dennis Coffey's 'Scorpio' and New Birth's 'Gotta Get Knutt'. *Super Disco Brakes* would add standards like James Brown's 'Funky Drummer' (the so-named pecussionist, Clyde Stubblefield, would later be immortalised on Subsonic 2's 'Unsung Heroes Of Hip-hop') and Incredible Bongo Band's 'Apache' (versions of which would appear on Sugarhill - the first by the Sugarhill Gang and the second by West Street Mob - who featured the Robinson's son, Joey Jnr.), as well as the Meters and Creative Source. Yet until the aforementioned Sugarhill started he never took the opportunity to record anything by the rappers who were buying this product. When 'Rapper's Delight' hit he finally realised its potential, releasing records by, among others, his daughters, who rapped together on 'Rhymin' And Rappin'. Other outstanding releases included Afrika Bambaataa's *Zulu Nation Throwdown Parts 1 And 2*. However, Bambaataa became hugely aggrieved at Winley's business practices, notably the release of one of his live sets as the 'Death Mix', which was of substandard quality and essentially a bootleg. Indeed, Winley would later be arrested for bootlegging activities and copyright infringement.

WORLD FAMOUS SUPREME TEAM SHOW

One of Malcolm McLaren's many innovative experiments in modern music, this project saw 'Talcy' pull together a team of rappers, singers and DJs from New York and Los Angeles. In their early days the group had hosted their own show on New Jersey station WHBI, alongside the legendary Mr Magic, before the latter shifted to WBLS. The idea of their partnership with McLaren was to make a modern rap record themed on Shakespearean and Opera models, as demonstrated by the promotional single, 'Opera House'. Main vocalist Mona Lisa Young was saddled, however, by some uninspiring material, co-written between McLaren and MC Hamlet (b. Jason Van Sugars). The album includes a return to the happier times of 'Buffalo Girls'. Indeed, McLaren had formerly employed the Supreme Team on his *Duck Rock* album, where they rapped over T-Ski Valley's 'Catch The Beat'.
● ALBUMS: *The World Famous Supreme Team* (Charisma 1986)★★★, *Round The Outside! Round The Outside!* (Virgin 1992)★★.

WU-TANG CLAN

This chess-playing hip-hop posse, whose ranks total eight pseudonymous rappers - Shallah Raekwon, Method Man, Rebel INS, Ol' Dirty Bastard, U-God, Ghostface Killah, The Genius (GZA) and Prince Rakeem (RZA) - based themselves in Staten Island, New York, USA. Each of the team boasted keen martial arts prowess. Indeed their debut album was divided into two sides, Shaolin and Wu-Tang Sword, to symbolise the combat-like disciplines applied to their rapping. Both Rakeem and The Genius had also released solo records prior to their present duties, for Cold Chillin' and Tommy Boy, which sank without trace. And when the Clan as a whole signed with BMG, provision for each member to work as solo artists was enshrined in the contract. The Genius joined his third record company, Geffen, Method Man linked with Def Jam and Ol' Dirty Bastard with Elektra Records. Their producer/DJ, RZA, also worked alongside Prince Paul and Fruitkwan (ex-Stetsasonic) as part of the Gravediggaz. Affiliated group members include Shyheim The Rugged Prince, Killah Priest and Cappadonna. Wu-Tang Clan's musical armoury centres around old school rhyming and trickery, which with eight contributors offers ample opportunity for quickfire wise-cracking and playing off each other. The musical backing is one of stripped down beats, with samples culled from kung-fu movies. Such appropriation of martial culture is a theme which has occupied rap music from the days of Grandmaster Flash onwards. Their debut album quickly and deservedly notched gold status, setting the underground hip-hop scene alight in the process. It was recorded in their own studio, its '36 Chambers' suffix alluding to the number of critical points on the body as disclosed by Shaolin theology. However, all was not well with the Clan in 1994. U-God's two-year-old, Dante Hawkins, was hit in a gun battle crossfire as he played outside his babysitter's house on 13 March. The bullet destroyed one of his kidneys and damaged his hand. Just a day later a member of the band's inner circle of friends was killed in a separate incident. The Clan regrouped for 1997's *Forever*, a long sprawling record that rarely matched their debut or GZA's exceptional solo collection *Liquid Swords*. The most recent releases from the Wu-Tang stable have been Killah Priest's excellent *Heavy Mental* set, and Cappadonna's best-selling *The Pillage*.
● ALBUMS: *Enter The Wu Tang (36 Chambers)* (Loud/RCA 1993)★★★★, *Wu-Tang Forever* (Loud/RCA 1997)★★★★.
Solo: Cappadonna *The Pillage* (Razor Sharp/Epic 1998)★★★★. Ghostface Killah *Ironman* (Razor Sharp/Epic 1996)★★★. Killah Priest *Heavy Mental* (Geffen 1998)★★★★. Method Man *Tical* (Def Jam 1994)★★★. Raekwon *Only Built 4 Cuban Linx* (Loud/RCA 1995)★★★.
● VIDEOS: *Da Mystery Of Kung-Fu* (MIA 1998).

WYCLEF

b. Wyclef Jean, Haiti. Despite his parent group the Fugees having sold 11 million copies of their most recent album, in the process becoming the biggest rap crossover success of the 90s, lead rapper Wyclef Jean still found time to release a solo album in 1997. Long regarded as the mastermind behind the Fugees' intoxicating blend of rap, soul and Haitian music, Wyclef Jean is also active as a remixer and producer to the R&B/dance community (including the number 1 single 'No No No' by Destiny's Child). Guests on his debut solo effort included Lauryn Hill and Prakazrel Michel (his fellow Fugees), the Neville Brothers, the I-Threes, the New York Philharmonic Orchestra and Cuban superstar Celia Cruz. Tracks such as 'Sang Fezi' and 'Jaspora' exploited his own musical ancestry while adding modern production methods to produce an intoxicating and seamlessly rhythmic collection. The album was promoted by the release of 'We Trying To Stay Alive', a more contemporary-sounding effort that sampled the refrain from the Bee Gees' 'Stayin' Alive', and 'Gone Till November'.

● ALBUMS: *Wyclef Jean Presents The Carnival Featuring The Refugee Allstars* (Columbia 1997)★★★.

X CLAN

X Clan openly admitted that their recording activities were merely a front to promote the 'Blackwatch' ethos. They held a controversial Cultural Convention at London's Africa Centre in 1989 where they were heckled for their apparent endorsement of separatism and chauvinism. Blackwatch, or that part of it that the group felt able to relate to ousiders, is a movement created by black people, for black people, which invokes a larger brotherhood (specifically between different generations and strata of black society) in order to fight and defeat white oppression, through a variety of means: 'By any means necessary is one of the chief principles we have'. Membership of the rap outlet included rappers/spokesmen Professor X (b. Lumumba Carson; the son of black activist Sonny Carson and former manager of Positive-K), Brother J and DJ Sugar Shaft, plus associate member Lin Que/Isis. On record, as might be expected, they are utterly militant and uncompromising in their advocacy of their chosen lifestyle.

● ALBUMS: *To The East, Blackwards* (4th And Broadway 1990)★★★, *X Odus* (Polydor 1992)★★★.

X PRESS 2

Agressive UK acid house revisionists Rocky, Diesel and Daddy Ash (Ashley Beadle, of Disco Evangelists/Black Sunshine fame), who have run up an impressive sequence of club cuts ('Muzik Express', 'London X-Press', 'Say What', 'Rock 2 House' - remixed by Richie Hawtin and Felix Da Housecat) on Junior Boys Own. In addition to becoming one of that popular label's most talked-about acts, Rocky and Diesel are also well-known DJs in their own right, as is Beadle.

X-DREAM

This trance label was set up in 1994 by Russel Coultart, Lawrence Cooke and Simon Moxon. In February the following year, Disco Volante's 'El

Metro' became Transient's first release and was followed by the compilation *Transient: Nu Energy And Trance*. Since then they have released singles by Astral Projection (notably 1996's 'Mahadevah'), Cosmosis, Elements Of Nature, Laughing Buddha, Lords Of Choas, Psychaos, Slide and Syb Unity Network, among others, as well as albums from Astral Projection (*Astral Files* and *Dancing Galaxy*) and Cosmosis (*Cosmology* and *Synergy*). Their compilations, which include the *Transient* series, *Otherworld*'s *Dance Trance And Magic Plants* and the more chilled-out *Transient Dawn*, have featured tracks by these groups and others including Doof, Earth Nation, Electric Universe, Koxbox, MFG and X-Dream. In 1998 they released the charity album *Earthdance*, which followed on from the party of the same name the previous year. Transient have two subsidiary labels, Automatic and West Ten Records.

● ALBUMS: *Radio* (Blue Room 1998)★★★★.

XL RECORDS

The brainchild of Tim Palmer, managing director of Citybeat, who installed Nick Halkes (b. *c.*1967, Portishead, Bristol, England) as A&R chief. Halkes' background spanned various labels while he DJed his way through college at Goldsmiths University in London. It was while working for Citybeat that he picked up Starlight's 'Numero Uno' as his second signing, giving the label an instant Top 10 hit. On the strength of this, he was offered his own subsidiary imprint for 'underground' dance records. XL was born, and Halkes' Midas-touch with it. XL's most notable hits included the Prodigy's rich vein of form (beginning with 'Charly'), SL2 ('On A Ragga Trip', etc.), Liquid ('Sweet Harmony'), Moby (*UHF* EP), T99 ('Anasthasia') and House Of Pain ('Jump Around'). The latter was released on Ruffness, a further subsidiary founded by Halkes' friend Richard Russell. It also housed the mellow groove of Louie Rankin ('Typewriter'), licensed from the Blue Moon studios in Los Angeles. Other artists on XL included Nu-Matic (*Hard Times* EP), Cubic 22 (Peter Ramson and DJ Danny Van Wauwe - 'Night In Motion'), who also recorded under the guise of Set Up System ('Fairy Dust'). Halkes recorded alongside then-partner Russell as Kicks Like A Mule ('The Bouncer'). He defected to EMI in early 1993 to set up his new Positiva subsidiary, after being headhunted by the majors. Russell took over his A&R position.

YA KID K

b. Manuella Komosi, Zaire. This pop-dance rapper was originally introduced to UK audiences through her work with Technotronic. She had moved to Belgium when she was 11 years old, then Chicago, Illinois, USA, where she was introduced to rap and deep house music. On her return to Belgium she teamed up with Jo Bogaert of Technotronic. Together they performed on the international hit single, 'Pump Up The Jam', though her contribution was uncredited. She then appeared alongside professional and personal partner MC Eric on the breakthrough hit, 'This Beat Is Technotronic', which is considered by many to be the first 'hip house' record. They teamed up again with Technotronic for 'Get Up (Before The Night Is Over)', which was another major international hit. Afterwards Komosi appeared on Hi Tek's 'Spin That Wheel' in 1990, and contributed a song, 'Awesome', to the *Teenage Mutant Ninja Turtles II* film soundtrack. The birth of a child then interrupted her plans. Her projected solo career seems to have petered out since that time.

YAGGFU FRONT

Despite the unfriendly acronym (Y'All Gonna Get Fucked Up [if you] Front), and their grisly personal tags: D'Ranged & Damaged, Jingle Bel and Spin 4th, this Norfolk, Virginia trio have much to offer. They came together at university, with an educative platform that has provided them with more effective ammunition than the average gun-toting gangsta rappers. There they worked as DJs on North Carolina college radio before uniting as a trio. Using live instruments, including horns and piano, they have perfected a stimulating blend of sharply observed lyrics and clever samples. Their first release was the excellent 'Looking For A Contract', which detailed the lives of starving rap aspirants. Comparisons to A Tribe Called Quest notwithstanding, their debut album was also a splendid, intelligent affair. There were

comedic moments too, not least 'My Dick Is So Large', a thinly veiled parody of stupido ego-rappers. Nevertheless, their style was generally expressive: 'Basically the Yaggfu sound is emotional. We want to capture the way someone feels'.
● ALBUMS: *Action Packed Adventure* (Phonogram/Mercury 1994)★★★.

YAZZ

b. Yasmin Evans, 19 May 1963, Shepherd's Bush, London, England. Pop house singer who began her career in the music business as part of a quickly forgotten act, the Biz. After becoming a catwalk model and working as George Michael's stylist, she laid plans for a return to recording work. When she did so, she found rewards immediately, joining with Coldcut on 'Doctorin' The House'. In its wake 'The Only Way Is Up' soared to the number 1 spot in 1988, followed shortly after by 'Stand Up For Your Love Rights'. Both of the latter were credited to Yazz And The Plastic Population. After a couple of further hits and tours she took time out to have her first baby. She returned alongside Aswad in 1993 for 'How Long', but this failed to break the Top 30. A new solo single, 'Have Mercy', was the first evidence of her attempts to re-establish herself via a contract with Polydor.
● ALBUMS: *Wanted* (Big Life 1988)★★★, *The Wanted Remixes* (Big Life 1989)★★, *One On One* (Polydor 1994)★★★.
● VIDEOS: *The Compilation* (1989)★★★, *Live At The Hammersmith Odeon* (1989)★.

YELLO

A Swiss dance duo led by Dieter Meier, a millionaire business man, professional gambler, and member of the Switzerland national golf team. Meier provides the concepts whilst his partner Boris Blank writes the music. Previously Meier had released two solo singles and been a member of Periphery Perfume band Fresh Colour. Their first recording contract was with Ralph Records in San Francisco, a label supported by the enigmatic Residents. They opened their accounts there with 'Bimbo' and the album *Solid Pleasure*. In the UK they signed to the Do It label, launching their career with 'Bostisch', previously their second single for Ralph. They quickly proved popular with the Futurist and New Romantic crowds. Chart success in the UK began after a move to Stiff Records in 1983 where they released two singles and an EP. A brief sojourn with Elektra pre-

ceded a move to Mercury Records where they saw major success with 'The Race'. Accompanied by a stunning video - Meier saw visual entertainment as crucial to their work - 'The Race' easily transgressed the pop and dance markets in the wake of the Acid House phenomenon. On *One Second*, they worked closely with Shirley Bassey and Billy McKenzie (Associates), and have recently become more and more embroiled in cinema. Soundtracks include *Nuns On The Run*, and the Polish-filmed *Snowball*, a fairytale whose creative impetus is entirely down to Yello. Meier and Blank also run Solid Pleasure, the innovative Swiss dance label. In 1995 a 'tribute' album, *Hands On Yello*, was released by Polydor, with Yello's music played by various artists including Grid, Carl Craig, Orb and Moby.
● ALBUMS: *Solid Pleasure* (Ralph 1980)★★★, *Claro Que Si* (Ralph 1981)★★★, *You Gotta Say Yes To Another Excess* (Elektra 1983)★★★★, *Stella* (Elektra 1985)★★★, *1980-1985 The New Mix In One Go* (Mercury 1986)★★★, *One Second* (Mercury 1987)★★, *Flag* (Mercury 1988)★★★, *Baby* (Mercury 1991)★★, *Zebra* (4th & Broadway 1994)★★★, *Pocket Universe* (Mercury 1997)★★★.
● COMPILATIONS: *Essential* (Smash 1992)★★, *Hands On Yello* various artists remix album (Polydor 1995)★★★.
● VIDEOS: *Video Race* (1988), *Live At The Roxy* (1991).

YO YO

b. Yolanda Whitaker, 4 August 1971, South Central Los Angeles, USA. A protégé of Ice Cube, Yo Yo is one of the female rappers who likes to play it as rough and dirty as her male gangsta brethren. Her long-playing debut introduced her combative attitude, with frequent interjections from Ice Cube's Lench Mob posse. However, amid the assertive, abrasive lyrics lurked a sophistication that might not have been envisaged by the casual buyer. That album's torch song was 'Sisterland', a rallying call for her fellow female MCs. Titles on her third album included 'The Girl's Got A Gun', and her duet with Ice Cube, 'The Bonnie & Clyde Theme'. Better still, she managed to invert the usual gangsta trappings by acting as a female pimp on 'Macktress'. Yo Yo had previously contributed to Ice's debut, *AmeriKKKa's Most Wanted*, duetting on 'It's A Man's World'. This insight was confirmed by her leading role in the formation of the Intelligent Black Women Coalition.
● ALBUMS: *Make Way For The Motherlode*

(Atlantic 1991)★★★, *Black Pearl* (East West 1992)★★★★, *You Better Ask Somebody* (East West 1993)★★★, *Total Control* (East West 1996)★★★.

YOTHU YINDI

This, the most internationally recognizable aboriginal group, is led by spokesman and local headmaster Mandaway Yunipingu. The group is based in the remote, crocodile-infested region of Arnhem Land in the Northern Territories, Australia. Their name translating as 'mother and child', they became a force in both Australia and the rest of the world via their serene, indigenous sounds, with singing in their native Gumadj language. Their debut album was released in 1988, amid Australia's centenary jamboree, which became the focus of their cynicism. 'Treaty', from 1992, which decried Australian Prime Minister Bob Hawke's broken promise to draw up a treaty on Aboriginal rights, also crossed over to the UK dance charts. 'Our sole purpose as a band is that we're trying to develop and create an impact for our culture. And music has a universal language that can convey that.' Licensed from the Australian Mushroom label to Hollywood Records, it appeared in a remix from Melbourne DJ's Gavin Campbell and Paul Main and programmer/musician Robert Goodge. Resplendent in digeridoo, clap sticks and tribal chants, it quickly became a major club hit. However, this is only part of the group's appeal, which has also stretched to America, where *Billboard* magazine described them as the 'Flagship of Australian music.' It also saw Yunipingu recognized in his own land as Australian Band Of The Year in 1992.
● ALBUMS: *Homeland Movement* (Mushroom 1988)★★★, *Tribal Voice* (Mushroom 1991)★★★, *Freedom* (Mushroom 1994)★★★.

YOUNG BLACK TEENAGERS

Toasted as the first to release a single on Hank Shocklee and Bill Stephney's Sound Of Urban Listeners label, YBT are in fact three white teenagers, and one Puerto Rican (ATA) from Brooklyn, New York. Their provocative moniker was chosen, they declare, to pay tribute to hip-hop's true originators, to accept that it is primarily an Afro-American format, but that outsiders too are welcome. The group, formed in 1987, comprise ATA, Kameron, Firstborn and DJ Skribble, and their debut release, 'Nobody Knows Kelli', was a tribute to cult American anti-sitcom, *Married With Children*. Although the sleeve of their debut album was a cunning take on the *Beatles For Sale* tableau, the production was haphazard, despite the presence of the Bomb Squad. They switched from SOUL to MCA for the single, 'Tap The Bootle', which featured a guest appearance from Public Enemy's DJ Terminator X. Ultimately, however, they would fall out with Chuck D and Hank Shocklee, with whom Kamron had previously DJed in Roosevelt, Long Island. However, this was not before they had recorded 'To My Donna', an attack on Madonna for using Public Enemy's 'Security Of The First World' beat. Following the wit of their previous releases, YBT fell down heavily on political correctness. When challenged about the predominance of the word 'bitch' in their vernacular, ATA could only muster: 'When I say a girl is a bitch, I'm not saying she's a female dog. We're past that. Let's not take things at face value. Women just tend to be bitches, they tend to be moody...' Elsewhere they were more dextrous. Instead of merely sampling on *Dead End Kidz*, they reinterpreted, to excellent comic effect and with live instruments, ancient nuggets by Diana Ross, the Rolling Stones and even Rush. They are currently managed and produced by Bomb Squad worker Gary G-Wiz.
● ALBUMS: *Young Black Teenagers* (SOUL 1993)★★, *Dead End Kidz Doin' Lifetime Bidz* (MCA 1994)★★★.

YOUNG DISCIPLES

Although their roots were in the rave scene, the 90s UK band Young Disciples' debut single, 'Get Yourself Together', combined hip-hop with jazz inflections, and featured the voice of Carleen Anderson and MC Mell 'O' on either side. The group, who comprised the duo of Mark 'O' and Femi, would win much of their notoriety through Anderson's vocal attributes. It was she who wrote and sang on many of their best recordings, including 'Apparently Nothin''. Her final release with the Young Disciples was *Dusky Sappho*, a limited edition EP, after which she concentrated on her solo career. Femi and Mark continued to use the Young Disciples banner, though the former would also undertake remix work for Xscape ('Just Kickin'') and others.
● ALBUMS: *Road To Freedom* (Talkin' Loud 1991)★★★.

YOUNG MC

b. Marvin Young, 10 May 1967, England, but raised in Queens, New York City. Young went to college in California, earning a degree in economics from the University Of South California, where he also wrote material for Tone Loc (including co-writing credits on his big hits 'Wild Thing' and 'Funky Cold Medina'). His solo work was similarly within the framework of mainstream rap, a highlight being the Top 10 hit, 'Bust A Move' - winner of the Grammy for Best Rap Record. In its wake he started to appear on television advertising Pepsi soft drinks. He cited 'musical and ethical differences' as the reason for his move from Delicious Vinyl in the 90s, though he remained with 4th & Broadway/Island in the UK. By the time he became employed by Capitol, many critics pointed out that his material was becoming both overwrought and overproduced. Unlike many rappers, Young MC brought a post-AIDS conscience to his sexual boasts, as demonstrated on the second album's 'Keep It In Your Trousers'. He re-emerged in 1993 with the club hit 'Know How', a distillation of the 'Shaft' theme, produced by the Dust Brothers - aka his old friends from Delicious.
● ALBUMS: *Stone Cold Rhymin'* (Delicious Vinyl 1989)★★★, *Brainstorm* (Capitol 1991)★★★.
● VIDEOS: *Bustin' Moves* (1991).

YOUNG, CLAUDE

DJ and founder of Utensil Records, Claude Young is a rarity in the Detroit dance scene in that his releases do not fit neatly under the 'techno' banner. Attempting to escape the bitter urban desolation and drugs culture of the city, Young invested his time in music, but of a more soulful hue than his neighbours. Working first at radio station WHYT, Young eventually ran his own two-hour show, before putting together his first musical ideas. The record to launch him was the *One Complete Revolution* EP. Proving popular in the UK, this afforded him invitations to London clubs like Rotary and Quirky, before co-opted releases on D-Jax Up Beats and Christian Vogel's Mosquito label. In 1994 Claude Young announced plans to set up a further, UK-based label, Frictional.

YZ

New Jersey rapper most famous for his 'Thinkin' Of A Masterplan' cut. Bedecked in paisley shirts and dreads, YZ seemed to offer a neat distillation of Native Tongues philosophy with more street-orientated themes. Despite the good impression this made, it would be four years before a follow-up would be offered, by which time his DJ Tony D had been replaced by the Trackmasterz and God Squad, among others. As a member of the Five Per Cent Nation, a less disciplined than usual Muslim order, he produces a number of 'conscious' rhymes, but his main targets remain opposing MCs, holding Naughty By Nature in particular contempt.
● ALBUMS: *Sons Of The Father* (Tuff City 1989)★★★, *The Ghetto's Been Good To Me* (Livin' Large 1993)★★★.

ZION TRAIN

UK's Zion Train formed in 1990 and have proved to be innovators in the revolutionary new wave of dub. While many other groups preferred a revivalist stance, the north London-based co-operative have established an enviable reputation. The cross-cultural line-up consists of Molora (vocals, percussion), Neil (DJ, beats, bass), Colin C (melodica), Dave Hake (trumpet, also part of the Tassilli Players) and Chris Hetter (trombone). Influenced by Jah Shaka, Lee Perry and other dub masters, the group's dub/roots dance equation was first unveiled on the sequential singles 'Power One' and 'Power Two'. As well as recording dub sounds, the collective also ran the Bass Odyssey club and their own sound system, produced their own magazine, *The Wobbler*, and released the first promotional dub video, *Get Ready*, and a CD-ROM to accompany *Homegrown Fantasy*, their debut release for China Records. One of their most effective and highly regarded works was the 'Follow Like Wolves' single, a fertile cross between dub and house music, with samples drawn from the Specials' back-catalogue. In a departure from usual reggae practice, they subsequently instigated the (no copyright) Soundpool, allowing free sampling, and thus dispensing with the need for acquisitive lawyers. They have also worked with Junior Reid, Maxi Priest, Studio One veteran Devon Russell and the Dub Syndicate, as well as Indian tabla players and Brazilian drummers. In 1996 the group ventured into the ambient/house/acid dub territory and performed with artists including the Shamen, New Model Army and Gary Clail, and instigated the re-formation of Ruts DC for a collaboration on a live session for BBC Radio. The release of *Grow Together* featured Dave Ruffy, the Ruts' drummer, and an acid revival of the group's 1979 hit 'Babylon's Burning'. That single was followed by 'Rise', with which they achieved their first exposure on national daytime radio. Extensive touring and major festival appearances have secured the band

international popularity. They later released 'Stand Up And Fight', featuring Kate Cameron on lead vocals and a 19-minute soulful reggae remix.

● ALBUMS: *Passage To Indica* (Zion 1994)★★★★, *Great Sporting Moments In Dub* (Zion 1994)★★★, *Natural Wonders Of The World* (Universal Egg 1994)★★★, *Siren* (Universal Egg 1995)★★★, *Homegrown Fantasy* (China 1995)★★★, *Grow Together* (China 1996)★★★★, *Single Minded And Alive* (China 1997)★★★.

● COMPILATIONS: *Forward Roots* cassette only (Zion 1993).

ZOOM RECORDS

Camden, north London operation run by popular DJ Billy Nasty and Dave Wesson, whose clients include Delorme and 3:6 Philly. The label came to prominence in 1989 with the release of two singles by Brit hip-hoppers Red Ninja. Later their attention turned to the dance scene, releasing a particularly harsh techno album by Ubik in 1992. Later Nasty's reputation as a DJ was franked by being the first to appear on the Music Unites' *Journeys By DJ* series, with a set composed of modern house standards (Havanna, Leftfield, Gypsy). He also recorded alongside Morgan King as VFN Experience. Wesson similarly colluded with Leftfield to record 'The Hunter (The Returns)' (as Herbal Infusion). The duo have also remixed for Acorn Arts, Saint Etienne and Nush. Other members of the Zoom staff include the Sensory Productions team of three DJ's - Robert R. Mellow, Zaki Dee and Adam Holden, who released the double a-side 'Keep It Open'/'Jumping' for the label in 1992. Mello works behind the counter at the Zoom shop, while Dee provided a similar service at the Black Market emporium.

ZTT RECORDS

Formed in 1983 by producer Trevor Horn, a former member of the Buggles and Yes, and his wife Jill Sinclair, ZTT was one of the most innovative UK labels of the early 80s. Horn employed the sharp marketing skills of former *New Musical Express* journalist Paul Morley, whose obtuse style and interest in unearthing obscure talent was allied to a love of ephemeral pop. ZTT was an abbreviation of Zang Tumb Tuum, a phrase used by the Italian futurist Russulo to describe the sound of machine-gun fire. The artistic notions of the label were emphasized through elaborate artwork and a release policy that encouraged the use of multi-format pressings. The label was distributed by Island Records until 1986, after which it pursued the independent route. Among the early signings to the label were the Art Of Noise and Propaganda, both of whom enjoyed chart success and enhanced the label's *avant garde* reputation. The key act, however, was undoubtedly Frankie Goes To Hollywood, who conjured up a trilogy of spectacular UK number 1 hits in 1984 with 'Relax', 'Two Tribes' and 'The Power Of Love'. The release of fourteen different mixes of 'Relax' also established ZTT and Horn as pioneering forces in the remix market. Frankie's double album *Welcome To The Pleasure Dome* was quintessential ZTT, with arresting artwork, political slogans, and mock merchandising ideas included on the sleeve. The Frankie flame burned brightly until the second album, *Liverpool*, which proved expensive and time-consuming and sold far fewer copies than expected. The label continued its search for original talent, but all too often signed notably obscure acts who failed to find success in the mainstream. Among the artists who joined ZTT were Act, Anne Pigalle, Insignificance, Nasty Rox Inc. and Das Psych-Oh Rangers. Roy Orbison was also signed for a brief period and Grace Jones provided a formidable hit with 'Slave To The Rhythm'. ZTT suffered its most serious setback at the hands of former Frankie Goes To Hollywood singer Holly Johnson, who successfully took the label to the High Court in 1988 and won substantial damages after the group's contract was declared void, unenforceable and an unreasonable restraint of trade. The label then operated a joint venture with Warner Brothers for ten years, enjoying major success with Seal among others, before separating from the conglomerate in 1998.

ZYX RECORDS

Widely venerated as 'the Balearic label', ZYX is a German distributor and dance specialist that set up a UK operation in 1990, attempting to profit through 'cheaper imports and exclusive foreign product'. Their 1991 releases included De Melero featuring Monica Green's 'Night Moves' - a house standby brought up to date by Spanish brothers Cesar and Chito de Melero, DJs at Ibiza's Ku and Barcelona's The Club, respectively. 1992 brought Renee Thomas's 'I'm So In Love With You', from Fred Jorio and Sean Tucker. However, much of the label and A&R manager Alex Gold's notoriety during the 90s revolved around its public bust-ups with Network Records. ZYX overtures to obtain the license for Double You?'s version of KC And The Sunshine Band's 'Please Don't Go' were rejected. Network got KWS to record a version instead, earning a five-week number 1 in the process. The same thing happened with a second KC cover, 'Rock Your Body'. Originally a number 1 hit for Gwen McRae in 1974, once again it jumped in front of a proposed ZYX label release - who were at that time trying to license Baby Roots' mistitled 'Rock You Baby'. When Double You?'s manager Roberton Zanetti collapsed of nervous exhaustion it could have taken few people by surprise. ZYX did at least enjoy success by licensing two contrasting Euro hits in 1992, the hard German techno of Misteria's 'Who Killed JFK?', and the clean Italian house of Jennifer Lucass' 'Take On Higher'. Other notable hits included Interactive's 'Who Killed Elvis?', LA Style's 'James Brown Is Dead' and Area 51's 'Let It Move You', a piano-rave classic. Gold went on to establish a new record label in 1994, Escapade.

INDEX